Sojourners, Sultans, and Slaves

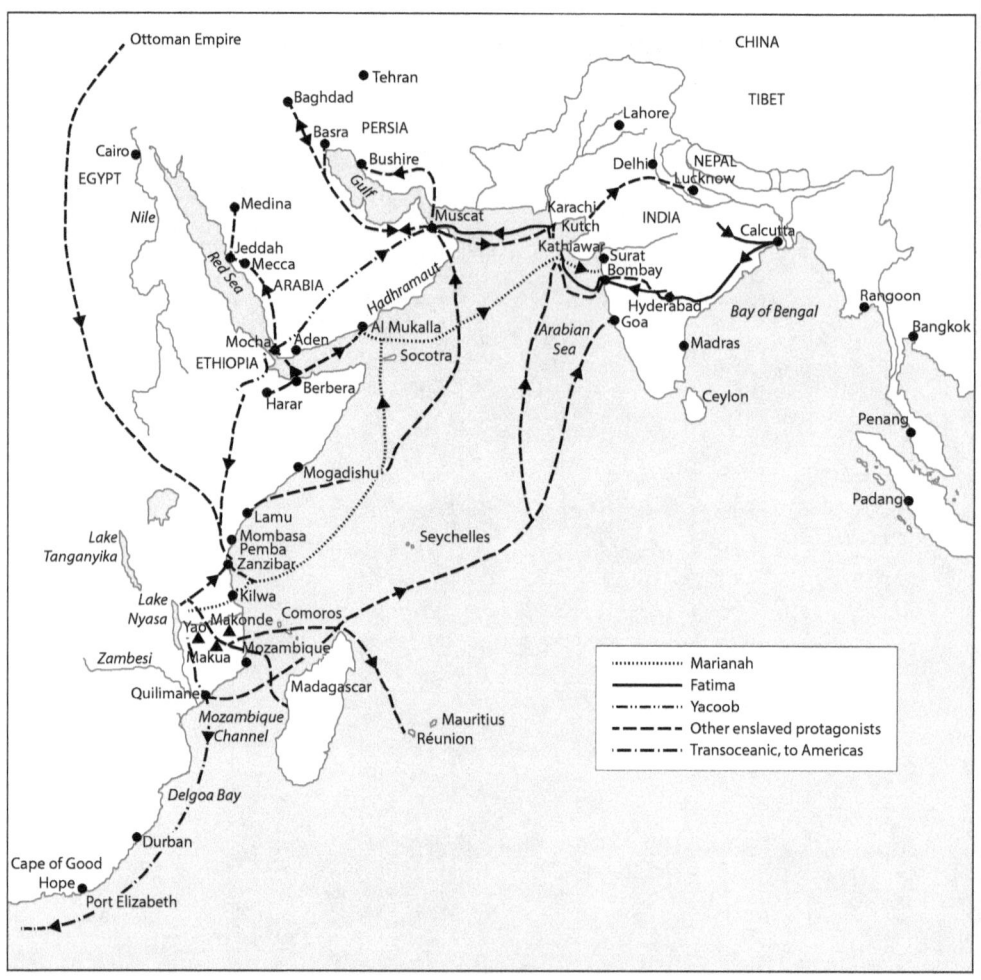

MAP 1. Western Indian Ocean world passages: Marianah, Fatima, Yacoob.

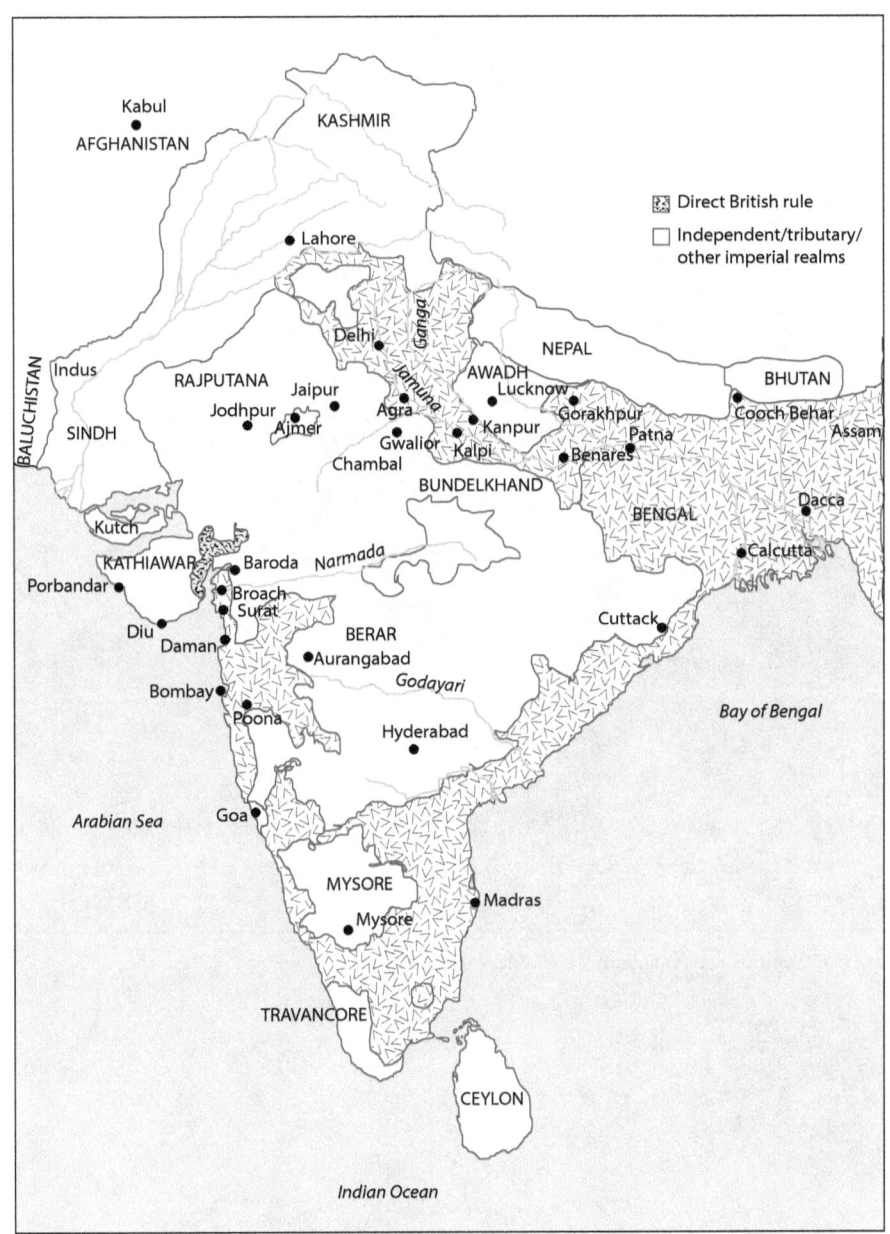

MAP 2. South Asia, 1837, showing some places associated with "free" cotton experiments and IOW slave trades (adapted from *Imperial Gazetteer Atlas of India*).

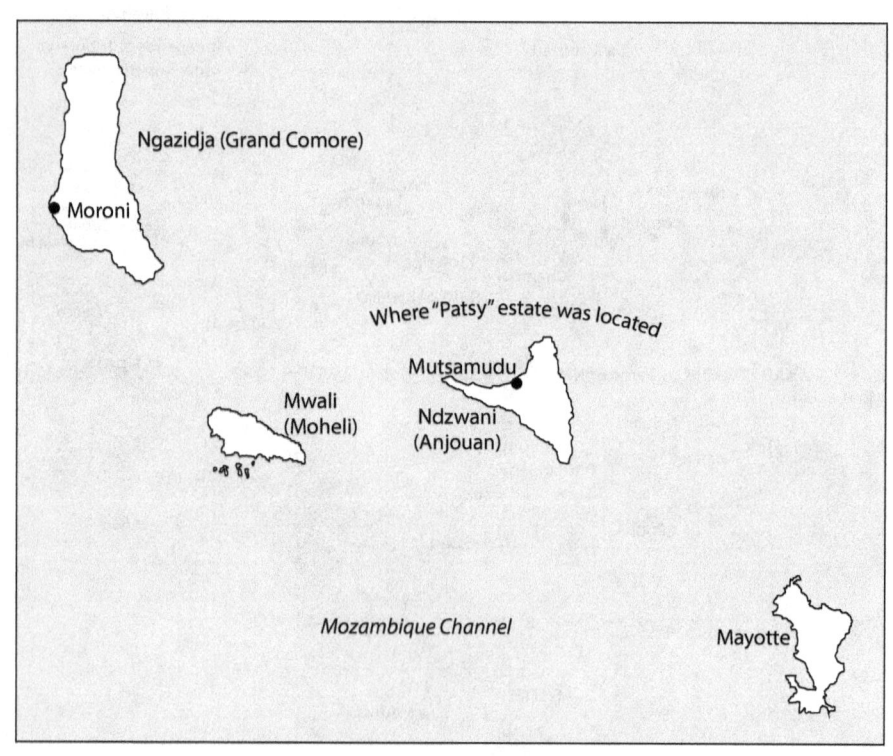

MAP 3. Comoros: an American slaveholder's island home.

Sojourners, Sultans, and Slaves

America and the Indian Ocean in the age of Abolition and Empire

Gunja SenGupta and
Awam Amkpa

UNIVERSITY OF CALIFORNIA PRESS

The publisher and the University of California Press Foundation gratefully acknowledge the generous support of the Peter Booth Wiley Endowment Fund in History.

University of California Press
Oakland, California

© 2023 by Gunja SenGupta and Awam Amkpa
All rights reserved. First Paperback Printing 2025

Library of Congress Cataloging-in-Publication Data

Names: SenGupta, Gunja, author. | Amkpa, Awam, 1959- author.
Title: Sojourners, Sultans, and Slaves: America and the Indian Ocean in the age of abolition and empire / Gunja SenGupta and Awam Amkpa.
Description: Oakland, California : University of California Press, [2022] | Includes bibliographical references and index.
Identifiers: LCCN 2022020000 (print) | LCCN 2022020001 (ebook) | ISBN 9780520389137 (cloth) | ISBN 9780520389151 (ebook)
Subjects: LCSH: Slavery—America—19th century. | Slavery—Indian Ocean—19th century. | Slave trade—America—19th century. | Slave trade—Indian Ocean—19th century. | Antislavery movements—America—19th century. | Antislavery movements—Indian Ocean—19th century.
Classification: LCC HT1048 .S46 2022 (print) | LCC HT1048 (ebook) | DDC 306.3/62097—dc23/eng/20220606
LC record available at https://lccn.loc.gov/2022020000
LC ebook record available at https://lccn.loc.gov/2022020001

ISBN 978-0-520-38913-7 (cloth : alk. paper)
ISBN 978-0-520-38915-1 (ebook)
ISBN 978-0-520-42477-2 (pbk: alk. paper)
Manufactured in the United States of America

32 31 30 29 28 27 26 25
10 9 8 7 6 5 4 3 2 1

GPSR Authorized Representative: Easy Access System Europe, Mustamäe tee 50, 10621 Tallinn, Estonia, gaps.requests@easproject.com

For Ruku and Ratan SenGupta

CONTENTS

List of Illustrations   *xi*
Acknowledgments   *xiii*

Introduction   1

PART ONE. BETWEEN EMPIRES: A NEW WAY OF TALKING
ABOUT SLAVERY, EAST AND WEST   25

1. Empire, Religious Law, and Slavery by "Free Will"   27
2. Human Rights from Calcutta through London to Boston   52

PART TWO. ANTISLAVERY EMPIRE VERSUS REPUBLIC OF
SLAVEHOLDERS?   85

3. Reverberations: American Overseers, Slavery, and "Free"
Cotton Experiments in India   87
4. The Slave Mistress and the Courtesan: Poverty, Patriarchy,
and "Proslavery Maternalism"   120

PART THREE. HOW MIGRATIONS MADE MEANING: IMPERIAL
ABOLITION, SLAVE TRADING, AND SUBALTERN SUBJECTS   149

5. "Domestic" Slavery and Colonial Belonging   151
6. Rulers, Rebels, and Refugees in Transnational Transit   172

7. Subaltern Prisms and Meanings of Freedom   202

PART FOUR. AMERICANS IN SULTANATES   225

8. Business, Sovereignty, and Fugitive Slaves   227

9. A Yankee Slaveholder, "Black Sultan," and European Imperialists in the Indian Ocean, 1870–1906   251

Epilogue. Crossing Slavery's Interoceanic Boundaries: Reflections   287

Notes   295
Index   345

ILLUSTRATIONS

MAPS

1. Western Indian Ocean world passages: Marianah, Fatima, Yacoob   *ii*
2. South Asia, 1837, showing some places associated with "free" cotton experiments and IOW slave trades   *iii*
3. Comoros: an American slaveholder's island home   *iv*

FIGURES

1. Rembrandt Peale, *Raja Rammohun Roy*, 1833   55
2. Louisa McCord (1810–1879)   122
3. Indian courtesan, c. 1830–50   122
4. Mary Ann Shadd Cary (1823–1893)   159
5. *Provincial Freeman*, 19 August 1854   160
6. Malik Ambar, c. 1605–10   178
7. John Frederick Lewis, *The Harem*, 1876   211
8. Emily Ruete (Sayyida Salme), c. 1856–80   212

TABLES

1. Principal Places of Purchase by Slaving Ships Sailing under the US Flag in the Western Indian Ocean, 1800–1869   229
2. Principal Places of Disembarkation of Western Indian Ocean Captives Traveling on US Ships, 1800–1869   230

ACKNOWLEDGMENTS

Ages ago, a conversation and visit to the West Bengal State Archives with our uncle, the late Barun De, mentor to generations of Indian historians, sparked our interest in comparative histories of servitude. Then, a lecture by Indrani Chatterjee at Fordham University offered intriguing glimpses of the new vistas that South Asian perspectives might open up for scholars of Atlantic slavery. For years afterward, however, such vistas remained unexplored as we both focused on other projects.

Fortunately, a series of fellowships and conferences resuscitated our proposal to challenge slavery's hemispheric boundaries. Fellowships from Brooklyn College's Ethyle R. Wolfe Institute for the Humanities, the Whiting Foundation, a Claire and Leonard Tow professorship, and Tow travel grants enabled preliminary research on the topic. Subsequently, New York University's Abu Dhabi Institute under Reindert Falkenburg funded our conference, *How Migration Makes Meaning*. Gila Waels and Nora Yousif worked magic to bring the event to fruition, while Martin Klimke, then history chair at NYUAD, offered expert stewardship. The historian Sugata Bose and the novelist (and our dear friend) Caryl Phillips headlined a keynote discussion on oceans in literary imagination and historical consciousness, while an interdisciplinary cohort of scholars and artists enthralled us by building bridges between the Atlantic and Indian Ocean worlds. They included Claire Anderson, Amir al Islam, Nezar Andary, Herman Bennett, Gwyn Campbell, Jose Dias, Alessandra di Maio, Henry Drewal, Cheryl Finley, Marisa Fuentes, Michael Gomez, Bayo Holsey, Dale Hudson, David Ludden, Sheetal Majitha, Elizabeth McMahon, Maaza Mengiste, Lauren Minsky, Jose Moya, Sam Pollard, Maurice Pomerantz, Edward Rugemer, Rima Saban, Donald M. Scott, Ella Shohat, Robert Stam, Bryan Waterman, Deborah Willis, and Robert J. C. Young.

Awam joined Deb Willis and Manthia Diawara—artists, friends, and mentors to countless cohorts of scholars—as they spearheaded the *Black Portraitures* conferences. Deb also launched the *Women and Migration* series, in collaboration with our friend, the visionary and dynamic Ellyn Toscano, ably assisted by Niki Kekos. At these venues, we sounded out themes included in this book, from Abu Dhabi and Johannesburg to Florence and Palermo, benefiting from exchanges with incredible scholars, whether as panelists or audience members, especially Fawzia Afzal-Khan, May Al-Dabbagh, Anna Arabindan Kesson, Kalia Brooks, Gayatri Gopinath, Sharon Harley, Cheryl Hicks, Sarah Khan, Pamela Newkirk, Sana Odeh, Anupama Rao, Arvind Rajagopal, and Fran Wilson. Some material covered in chapter 5 appeared in an anthology that emerged from these collaborations: *Women and Migration: Responses in Art and History*, edited by Deb, Ellyn, and Kalia (Open Book Publishers, 2019).

Meetings of the American Historical Association, a symposium on the urban Atlantic and the "Global Asia" initiative at NYU, Barnard College's Forum on Migration, a workshop organized in connection with *The Pursuit of Freedom* exhibition jointly by the Brooklyn Historical Society and the Weeksville Heritage Center, Franklin Day events at Brooklyn College, and a New York–based Women and Gender History Writing Group offered other opportunities to discuss local and transnational slavery histories. In these diverse contexts, we are especially grateful for the comments of Edward Alpers, Ana Lucia Araujo, Ricardo Cardoso, Kristen Celello, Amy Chazkel, Isabel Hofmeyr, David Ludden, Vanessa May, José Moya, Lara Vapnek, Barbara Winslow, and Peter Wood. On some of these occasions, Gunja learned much from presentations by John W. Franklin, Graham Hodges, Prithi Kanakamedala, Jennifer Scott, Manisha Sinha, Shane White, and Craig Steven Wilder. Meanwhile, a Mellon fellowship-in-residence at the Graduate Center of the City University of New York armed her with the discerning critiques of other interdisciplinary Mellon fellows, especially Alessandra Benedicty, Jessie Daniels, Grace Davie, Joseph Entin, Wendy Luttrell, and Jeff Maskovsky.

At Brooklyn College, Lorraine Greenfield is the light of the history department, and successive chairs have offered unfailing support and camaraderie: David Troyansky, Christopher Ebert, and Philip Napoli. During the long years that it took to write this book, K. C. Johnson supplied a valuable reading of a key chapter's early incarnation; Swapna Banerjee made gigantic contributions to our understanding of South Asian history; Brigid O'Keeffe's reflections on "Russia's races" greatly advanced the project to think about difference in transnational ways; Karen Stern and Lauren Mancia presented models of innovative scholarship to wring meaning out of sparse sources; Louis Fishman's vignettes about the Middle East seeped into our sense of the Indian Ocean world; and special friends Bonnie Anderson and Jocelyn Wills offered wisdom and encouragement that helped to nudge this book across the finish line. As chair herself, Gunja appreciated the scholarship of other history colleagues: Ben Carp, Andy Meyer, Mike Rawson, Steve Remy, and Chris Warren. She particularly valued the wit and solidarity of English department chair Ellen Tremper, as well as the courage of fellow chairs Naomi Braine and Alan Aja. Colleagues in women's and gender studies, especially Namita Manohar, Huma Ghosh, Pramila Nadasen, Mobina Hashmi, Irva Adams, Prudence Cumberbatch, Lynda Day, and Paisley Currah offered food for thought on intersectional identity formation. Shahrina Chowdhury, Nancy Berke and Fred Wasser, and above all, the students who took her courses on comparative slavery and freedom, made CUNY a special place to think and write. Recently, CUNY capped its contributions to this work with another Mellon-funded grant under its Black, Race, and Ethnic Studies Initiative (BRESI).

Over the years, numerous reference librarians at the British Library, the National Archives of India, West Bengal and Maharashtra State Archives, the New York Public Library, and libraries at NYU and CUNY offered indispensable help. More recently, Carlos Cruz of Brooklyn College, Mark Procknik of the New Bedford Whaling Museum, and Bowdoin Van Riper of Martha's Vineyard Museum deserve special mention. Iris Hanney and Robert Lester of Accessible Archives, Susan Inge of the Peabody Essex Museum, and Laura Seitter of the Walters Art Museum generously provided access to images used in this book.

We are deeply grateful to Niels Hooper of the University of California Press—a wonderfully supportive and intellectually rigorous editor—for his encouragement and advice on this project. Naja Pulliam Collins has kept us on track with efficiency and understanding. We thank the entire production team at UC Press. To our talented and painstaking anonymous readers, we are forever in your debt for making this a much better book than it was to begin with. Gunja's mentor, Clarence Mohr, passed away before this book was finished, but she will always remember his admonition that historians must tell stories about the past as truthfully and clearly as possible. Awam is fortunate enough to have his mentor, Wole Soyinka, around for advice and inspiration.

What can be said about Patricia Antoniello and Irene Sosa? That they are friends of a lifetime. That they have injected new meaning into the words, "Wednesday evenings," marking these as a schedule to love, listen, affirm, and question. Without them, this book would surely not have happened. Ella Shohat and Bob Stam have given us many things to treasure: their friendship, Iraqi food, and brilliant insights into "race in translation." In New York, Shahana Sen Mitul Foster, Alex Tuzhilin, Sankar Sen and Bob Albert, Indrani Chatterjee and Sumantra Sen, all sustained us with cuisine and conversation, and Gina Guerrieri listened patiently to talk about history and writers' blocks. Support networks of old friends around the world balanced work with life as we wrote: Nandini Sinha is Gunja's emotional rock; Sadhana Deshmukh and Azka Ayer, dear friends since Bombay; Christopher Vaz, Salim Darbar, Teesta Ghosh, Anjna Kirpalani, and Peter Vaz are our surrogate family in

Washington, DC; and Sabita Manian, Sunita Manian, and Arna Seal, inalienable parts of our lives. We thank Monji, Anand, Sanjay, Rahul, and Priya for being there for us, always. Abraham, Kader, and Nicole have rendered both filial support and astute advice on the book's artwork. As for Gunja's parents, they are really glad that we are finally publishing something with India in it. It is to them that we dedicate this book.

Gunja SenGupta
Awam Amkpa

Introduction

On 1 July 1865, as the curtains were coming down on a still young American nation's fratricidal blood bath to resolve its original sin of slavery, there appeared in the columns of the *Christian Recorder,* an organ of the Philadelphia-based African Methodist Episcopal Church that circulated among Black regiments in the Civil War South, an item entitled "An Interesting Relic." Positioned beside an account of emancipation in Maryland, the piece described the discovery by a German ditchdigger of a copper medal gilded with gold, at a depth of two feet under the ground in Gloucester County, New Jersey. One side of the artifact was said to depict an "exquisitely modeled" uniformed bust of "Charles, Marquis Cornwallis, a most active general," whose surrender to American and French armies at Yorktown in 1781 had marked the end of military hostilities during the American Revolution.[1]

The coin's reverse, however, featured a symbol of the British Empire's formal rise in the Indian Ocean world (IOW), even as it waned in continental North America. Commemorating the defeat of Tipu Sultan of Mysore in 1792, this face of the medal represented, in fine relief, the British General's acceptance of the vanquished Indian ruler's two young sons—eight and ten years of age—accompanied by an entourage of attendants. The *Christian Recorder* report speculated that the medal may have migrated to America in the possession of some "old soldier of the Marquis" who had "lost it while hunting in the neighborhood." And in that ground the memento lay for over half a century before turning up at the end of a ditchdigger's shovel. A British Museum catalog entry for a replica in bronze translates the inscription on the medal's reverse as "Let it be right to spare an enemy."[2]

As the art historian Sean Wilcock has noted, the ostensibly "paternalistic reception" by Cornwallis of the Indian princes, as well as their captivity in British custody for two years to guarantee their father's compliance with the terms of his surrender, captured the imagination of artists in Britain and India during the 1790s. The occasion was said to represent the "moral legitimacy" of a supposedly generous imperialism. Its imagery appeared in various media of arts and artisanry, including commemorative coins and medals.[3] It is thus entirely possible for a copper facsimile of the medal cataloged by the British Museum to have landed in the hands of a New Jersey resident who either traveled across the ocean or knew someone who did.

We might think of the 1790s British medal commemorating Cornwallis and the sultan's sons, excavated in 1860s New Jersey, as a multitemporal relic of imperialism serving as a metaphor for the times of transition and tissues of connection between disparate societies across two oceans. For as politics and destiny would have it, forty-seven years after the Anglo-Mysore war, a son of Tipu Sultan joined an interracial, intercontinental audience of abolitionists and imperial reformers in London's Freemasons' Hall. The group had gathered to inaugurate the British India Society (BIS), established to link the cause of the enslaved in North America with justice for the colonized in British India. There, the guest with Mysore roots would have heard one of the Society's architects, the fiery British abolitionist speaker George Thompson, declare that the path to striking the "manacles" off the "limbs of twenty-five hundred thousand of the colored children of the United States" lay through India: "When we prefer the Sugar of Bengal, and the Rice of Patna, and the Cotton of Bombay, to the produce of the despot-cursed regions of Carolina, and Louisiana, and ... Texas! Then, my Lord, we shall have Cotton without Slavery, Sugar without Slavery."[4]

For key BIS pioneers, however, mining the promise of a free market for labor in India had to go hand in hand with colonial reform and the extension of the antislavery project to that subcontinent. Founding members who shared this thinking included William Adam, a Scottish Unitarian minister who had lived in India for decades before assuming a professorship in Oriental Literature at Harvard University. Adam was networked, together with his friend, the Indian social reformer and liberal constitutionalist Raja Rammohun Roy, into transoceanic abolitionist circuits of travel and correspondence unpinned by new technologies of communication. Adam's scathing critique of the colonial edifice of bondage in India, published the year after BIS was launched, would help fuel overlapping controversies from Calcutta through London to Boston and Charleston over what slavery and freedom really meant in different parts of the world.[5]

For as the nineteenth century dawned, global systems of capitalism and empire knit the Atlantic and Indian Ocean worlds into international networks of trade and travel, and conquest and colonization, of labor and capital, and politics and ideology. The debates over slavery, colonialism, and meanings of freedom that resulted from this integration offer US scholars a common "material and meaningful framework" for "cross-fertilizing" national histories, historiographies, and epistemologies with the burgeoning scholarship on the Indian Ocean. Slavery and capitalism, locked in tight embrace, wove an Anglo-Atlantic exchange grid with distant lands, including those stretching from the Swahili coast of East Africa through the Persian/Arabian Gulf and the Red Sea, to the Indian subcontinent. At the same time, the shared legacies of British imperial influence and its protean politics of abolition splintered this international landscape along political and ideological lines. The tensions they produced played out within the diverse mosaics of hierarchy, patronage, and dependence that defined Indian Ocean societies, making them particularly rich laboratories for transnational comparison and connection. As such, they become theaters to problematize the meanings of slavery and freedom in different settings, as both historians and their nineteenth-century subjects experienced, codified, imagined, narrated, or contested the language and institutions defining those terms—whether as lived subaltern experiences,[6] work and family regimes, legal and administrative categories (often gendered), or political rhetoric. Moreover, it becomes possible to begin tracing the interoceanic transmission of these meanings, and to relate them to the various material structures and identity constructs they supported. In this context, our sprawling narrative mines multinational archives to shift the gaze of US slavery and abolition histories beyond the Atlantic world during the long nineteenth century. It fleshes out, on a granular level, the interface among the personal, domestic, and international politics of bondage and freedom, by tracking the circulation of people, the echo of ideas, and the resonance of policy among nodes of commercial exchange, imperial power rivalries, and reform activism extending from Anglo-America to the western Indian Ocean.[7]

Indian Ocean perspectives help to place notions of US historical exceptionalism within global contexts. They illuminate the fragile foundations and Atlantic reverberations of US mercantile projects, "free labor" experiments, and slaveholding in Afro-Asia, and illustrate the transoceanic reach of human rights campaigns. They show how discourses of poverty, kinship, and care could be adapted to defend servitude in different parts of the world, and reveal the tenuous boundaries that such discourses shared with liberal contractual definitions of freedom. Moreover, vistas trained on the western Indian Ocean enlarge our analytical canvas for reflecting on concepts that lie at the heart of the "Black Atlantic," such as diaspora and difference. From the vantage point of IOW historiographies, our intercontinental cast of past lives—of empire builders and émigrés, slavers and reformers, a "cotton queen" and courtesans, and fugitive slaves and concubines—offers windows to competing knowledge production and practices regarding "slavery in the East," and prompts reflections on the comparative workings of subaltern agency.

* * *

The opening pages of this book set the stage for recounting how the Atlantic and Indian Ocean worlds "hemorrhaged" into each other in a moment of transition.[8]

The sun had set on British colonialism in continental North America's thirteen colonies even as it began a sharp ascent over Britain's expansion in Afro-Asia. This shift produced a common discursive context, bound by empire, for wrestling with the leading issue of political economy, international relations, and human rights in the nineteenth century, namely slavery. However we may define "human rights" movements and periodize their origins, many nineteenth-century Anglo-Atlantic abolitionists traced something akin to that concept to Protestant and Enlightenment impulses to endow "human nature with . . . new capacity for reason, benevolence, . . . moral choice, and . . . inherent rights."[9] But what happened to these Atlantic perspectives when Anglophone bureaucrats and diplomats, reformers and missionaries, and merchants and aspiring planters traversing the IOW encountered an immense variety of types of bondage divorced in some cases from formal ideas about race, and defying binary constructs of slave and free, market and family?

As scholars of Afro-Asia have shown, the antislavery professions of the British Empire collided with imperial investment in local forms of bondage—and the construction of new ones—motivated variously by colonial revenue priorities, deference to indigenous elites, and aversion to public relief. Administrators in South Asia, for instance, sought to resolve these tensions by devising a new way of talking about slavery's differences, East and West. Anglo-Atlantic traditions of legal pluralism placed slavery in the category of "domestic" law (and in India, religious freedom) ostensibly outside the purview of parliamentary regulation. Such conventions had established precedents for leaving colonial slaveries alone, although strictly within the limits of expediency as judged by the East India Company (EIC),—the mercantile monopoly that launched British colonization of South Asia. Perceived threats to Asian forms of servitude posed by the British Parliament's prohibition of the international slave trade in 1807 galvanized an imperial discourse of slavery's distinctiveness "in the East." Such discourse homogenized the diversity of Indian forms of servitude into the singular "Orientalist" construct of an organic and "mild" system of social insurance sanctioned since times immemorial by tradition and religious law. Here, we are using the term "Orientalist" to signify colonial knowledge production about the supposedly eternal and "inherent" nature of Indian "institutions," in this case, slavery. At the same time, imperial bureaucrats proposed to reconcile British Asia's ostensibly familial relations of slavery and its function as a "poor law" with liberal ideals by codifying informal practices of self-sale or destitute parents' sale of children during famines, into the "free will" to make formal contracts.[10] Thus, imperial abolition forged new forms of service that in certain instances elided distinctions between coercion and free will.

Back in the Atlantic world, American slaveholders and failed India-returned free labor entrepreneurs on the one hand, and transnational abolitionists and imperial reformers on the other equally condemned colonial arguments that slavery in the "East" was different from slavery in the "West." But they did so from opposite ends of the political spectrum on human rights, within a riven global public sphere.

In the course of the century, Britain's campaign against foreign slave trading in the Indian Ocean embroiled American merchants and consuls in controversies over sovereignty and nationality involving their slave-trading Indian business partners in East Africa and African fugitives attempting to flee slavery in Indian Ocean islands on American merchant vessels. Aspiring American slaveholders who settled in the region following the US Civil War sought to acculturate to local norms of land tenure and labor control, adopting shifting approaches to such institutions as private property, contractual obligation, coercion, and patronage. The volatile landscapes of domestic and international politics—from local wars of succession and servile insurrections to great power rivalries and an officially antislavery US government—placed these would-be masters' fortunes on a roller coaster of uncertainty.

Recentering our vantage point on Indian Ocean slave trading "from below," we ask, In what ways did the captives, rebels, and refugees who crossed the Atlantic operators' paths—frequently women and children of African, South Asian, or Middle Eastern descent—use the institutions of colonial antislavery to assert their own claims to work, community, mobility, and security from poverty and violence? Subaltern interaction with structures of state and imperial abolition are worth comparing and contrasting from one oceanic world to another. For instance, in the resistance circles of North America, a feminist African American émigré to Canada such as Mary Ann Shadd Cary wielded the tool of diplomacy strategically to articulate a diasporic politics of freedom that inscribed Black women across the Atlantic as citizens, workers, wives, and mothers into an ostensibly color-blind, antislavery British empire ruled by a female sovereign. In the IOW, however, Britain's campaign against slavery served at least partly as a tool for buttressing the moral and material foundations of empire by integrating the emancipated as subjects and workers into the colonial state, often under duress. Moreover, some varieties of slavery in Afro-Asian societies assumed the form of patron-client relationships or served as strategies for kin incorporation, offering paths to social inclusion to certain categories of "dependents." There, while some subaltern rebels seized the language and structures of imperial abolition to support their claims to what the British defined as individual "rights," they could just as easily reject the option of colonial belonging in ways that interrupted linear and universalist narratives of liberty's progress under the British flag. They lead us to wonder, How might we theorize concepts at the heart of African American studies—such as agency, diaspora, and difference—against the broader horizons that materialize when we cross slavery's interoceanic boundaries?

* * *

The themes of this book emerge from the perspectives of historical figures positioned variously within the power structures and ideological spectrums of societies with servile populations across two oceanic worlds. There are the South Carolina slave mistress and cohorts of "daughter-purchasing" guilds of Indian courtesans and dancing girls, embedded from opposite ends of the Anglophone world in a tangled web of Anglo-Atlantic defenses of bondage as private poor relief. Within the framework of larger arguments over the merits of paternalism versus liberalism in free societies, such defenses touched on the braided discourses of poverty and matriarchy, family and the market, race and caste, and slavery's differences in East and West, illuminating the global contexts of local proslavery polemics. We will meet overseers from the American South, whose experiments with the cultivation of "free cotton" in India illustrate how configurations of political economy, state power, social hierarchies, and cultural traditions thwarted the transplantation of American-style settler colonialism in British India. The landholding dreams of these white men from the margins of antebellum slave society ran headlong into the complex matrices of imperial governance and local structures that mediated control over land and labor.[11] The accounts of these disappointed aspiring entrepreneurs helped forge a narrative back home in Mississippi and its sister states, of the "true slavery" and stasis of the British empire, and the invincibility of a benevolent slave republic founded on King Cotton.

The Slave South's transnational antagonists, reviled as antinational cosmopolites and pro-British conspirators, cut a broad swath across the field of human rights activism, taking on causes ranging from slavery and *sati* (the practice of immolating upper-caste Hindu widows on their husbands' funeral pyres) to land reform and free trade. Their geographical range extended from North America through Europe to Indian Ocean societies. They critiqued systems of legal pluralism that established an imperial tradition of accommodating "local" slavery arrangements everywhere the empire struck root. They took the colonial state to task for reading Hindu and Muslim laws in a proslavery light. They objected to impoverishing the colonized in ways that fostered slavery as a mode of subsistence and then institutionalizing informal arrangements of dependence into contractual relations of servitude, while creating new Atlantic-style forms of chattel bondage to mete out discipline and punishment. They mounted "free produce" movements to connect the enslaved's cause with that of the colonized. These critics' withering exposés of a mighty antislavery world sovereign's feet of clay would offer warring Americans a framework for forging conflicting narratives of comparative slavery and empire from opposite ends of their own ideological spectrum on slavery.

Such contesting accounts drew on information circulating through the medium of social networks and material infrastructure that molded an interoceanic public domain. This emerging global square connected the principal cities of the Atlantic world with the "second cities" and rural hinterlands of three continents. A submarine cable across the Atlantic, inaugurated in 1866, launched the wiring of the world. By the 1860s, revolutions in transport and communications had already begun to reconfigure territorial spaces of politics and international voluntarism. Steamships in the 1830s, and canals—the Erie in the 1820s, the Suez and Panama decades later—propelled maritime commerce and information sharing, even as railroads and tunnels that penetrated mountains promoted land-based exchanges. As Simone M. Müller has noted, the "shipping lines of Cunard, White Star, and Hapag-Lloyd" stimulated the global mobility of people, products, and we might add, news, while telegraph, postal, and parcel postal services disseminated word of goings-on in far-flung lands to distant corners of nation-states. Worldwide, information technologies that served as instruments of imperialism could also shape alternative geographies and ideologies of reform.[12]

The Civil War produced no consensus on slavery among Americans as they set out to seek their fortunes in the wider world. We track the travails of a Union surgeon from New Bedford, Massachusetts, transplanted as a wealthy slaveholder in the Comoros under the patronage of a business-minded sultan during Reconstruction. The commercial success of this New England planter later collided with the fallout from local wars of succession, enslaved soldiers and rebels, and colonial power rivalries, British anti-slave-trade patrols, and the wary indifference of an officially antislavery post–Civil War US government. Mediators make their appearance, such as US consuls and merchants who reported on Indian Ocean slavery through the prism of their interactions with the sprawling multiracial household of the Sultan of Zanzibar. That household, reproduced largely by enslaved mothers from Circassia to Ethiopia, was layered with complex hierarchies of rights and responsibilities attached to the varieties of kin statuses of both bonded and free members. Throughout the century, creditors, sailors, shippers, bureaucrats and missionaries played their parts, charting complex, contentious channels of exchange across oceans.

Above all, subaltern stories demonstrated how context—shaped by particular configurations of the nature of slavery and the workings of imperial abolition—shaped a diversity of relationships with the colonial state. Our marginalized rebels jostled with rulers as they sought to set the terms of their own lives, turning "freedom" into a hegemonic field of struggle over many meanings—of work, belonging, culture, mobility, and security against violence. The borders of difference over abolition and empire that emerged in the Atlantic and Indian Ocean worlds in the nineteenth century, offer tantalizing prospects for unearthing elusive enslaved experiences. As slave trade scholars have shown, it is when subordinate groups cross realms of contention over slavery—whether legal, jurisdictional, or ideological—that their voices enter the official archives that influence history writing.[13] Within these zones, where ideas and identities are disputed, disrupted, and sometimes remade in transit, the invisible "objects" of history appear to speak. To be sure, their perspectives are heavily mediated by the language and institutions of imperial abolition with which they interact, and which set the conditions of their presence in the archives: colonial police stations, law courts, reconnoitering cruisers, depositions, rhetoric, and policy. Still, however imperfect and fragmented, their interventions leaven and complicate the "truths" of slavery told by squabbling power brokers—whether local, national, or imperial—in different locales. The subalterns who populate the pages of this work include an international cast of women and children on the margins, enslaved and free, who appeared to seek reinvention through flight or emigration across borderlands erected by colonial campaigns against slavery. Other vignettes offer glimpses of elite *zenanas*, of East African fugitives making their way to the United States on American whalers, Africans landed in India on Arab vessels, and Indian concubines in the Gulf. The disparate circumstances of these historical figures, and the array of choices they appeared to make, raise the question whether fissures over slavery between different powers offered subordinate groups and individuals maneuvering space to assert their claims to citizenship or personhood, and community and mobility, while defying impressions about the neat polarities of "Oriental despotism" and English freedom.

* * *

This work builds on, but departs from, the voluminous and splendid body of transnational and comparative histories of US slavery and abolition that focuses primarily on the Atlantic world. The genealogy of historical geography that integrated the United States and its pre–nation-state incarnations into the Atlantic Ocean as a meaningful unit of study may be traced at least as far back to such early twentieth-century scholars of slavery and the African diaspora as W. E. B. DuBois, C. L. R. James, Melville J. Herskovits, and Eric Williams. Meanwhile, Frank Tannenbaum's *Slave and Citizen* (1946) would spur a series of debates among comparative historiographers of North and Latin America over the impact of formal institutions like church, state, law, and political economy, as well as demography on the enslaved's psychology, material conditions, opportunities for building family lives and community, and access to freedom and citizenship.[14] A few decades later, following the publication of Paul Gilroy's now canonical *The Black Atlantic: Modernity and Double Consciousness* (1993), an interdisciplinary cohort of scholars revised Gilroy's New World focus by charting the flow of people and politics, commodities and currency, technology and culture, and diseases and dogmas, among all four of the Atlantic ocean's surrounding landmasses and the islands in between.[15] This research has illuminated the reverberations of these exchanges in societies flung far from the Atlantic littoral. We have learned that new systems of power and knowledge reconfigured the identities of people involved in these transactions around race, gender, and other tropes of difference, through structures of political economy, productions of culture, and technologies of representation. Some have conceptualized the relationships among space, place, and nation in new ways, framing for instance, Anglo-American slave societies as a Spanish "periphery."[16]

As Isabel Hofmeyr has written, since the 1980s, the dynamics of international politics in East Africa, as well as the rise of China and India (among other factors), have spurred the emergence of the Indian Ocean world as a significant regional paradigm of transnational analysis. Organized around chronological and thematic principles different from those of Atlantic studies, IOW slavery scholarship has stressed the antiquity of trading systems "uncoupled from a militarized state"; the meshing of overlapping diasporas like the Yemeni *Hadrami* with European imperial interests; and perhaps most important, the coexistence of infinite incarnations of bondage, multiracial enslaved populations, and the absence of polar opposites of slave and free, chattel and kin, and market and family within many of these forms. Driven by the constraints of documentary sources, this work, compared with its Atlantic counterpart, focuses less on individual voices of the marginalized than on macrolevel analyses of the origins, nature, structure, and function of bondage, of demography and population flows, and gender roles, manumission, and resistance. Still, notable exceptions exist, with subaltern writers reading the archives both along and against the grain to flesh out histories "from below." Moreover, IOW anthologies have assembled interdisciplinary scholars who transcend traditional "Area Studies" approaches to mine multilingual sources within and across continents—from Afro-Asia through Europe and the Middle East.[17]

While it is important, as IOW scholars have reiterated, that we study forms of subordination that Atlantic world contemporaries described as slavery in the Indian Ocean on their own terms, the compartmentalization of slavery histories into diverse oceanic frames of reference tends to obscure the many ways in which these worlds intermingled. The integration of these regions into international economic and imperial systems in the nineteenth century produced correlations and connections in their slavery histories, and broadened the spatial and chronological canvas within which cosmopolitan historical actors experienced or engaged with meanings of bondage, abolition, and freedom.

Consider, for example, the nature of the antebellum South's interaction with the international politics of slavery, the extent of which a rich corpus of literature has established for the western hemisphere in recent years. Historians have traced the Caribbean roots of the American Civil War to conflicting visions of emancipation's outcome in the British West Indies; tracked the long shadow of the Haitian Revolution in fomenting sectional discord over slavery; shown that the Slave South's conviction in cotton's global clout powered the politics of free trade and secession; and documented slaveholders' endeavor to secure the future of slave property in the Americas—Cuba, Brazil, and the republic of Texas—by deploying the tools of foreign policy and military strategy. As Michael Woods observed, the planter elites have emerged from these accounts as "forward-looking businessmen who espoused free-trade liberalism in defense of their economic interests." What is clear from recent histories of proslavery internationalism is that in the 1830s and 1840s, slaveholding interests identified their primary adversaries as British imperial abolitionists bent on dominating the global economy by supplanting slave-grown staples in the Americas with produce cultivated in their Asian and African colonies.[18]

A perspective that ranges beyond the Americas, however, will also find surprising links between defenses of bondage in British Asia and the American South. Such connections were rooted in parallels between colonial contexts of legal pluralism that accommodated local usages related to "property," domestic relations, and religious practice. Moreover, the similar rhetoric of proslavery apologetics in the diverse settings of our narrative was forged in the transoceanic circulation of arguments that "domestic slavery" functioned as a form of social insurance within the organic framework of patriarchal households structured around supposedly "natural" hierarchies of race/caste/occupation and gender. Where British Orientalist discourses of South Asian servitude differed from American proslavery polemics was in their insistence that "domestic slavery in the East" was an essentially different species of dependence than chattel bondage in the Americas. Southerners vigorously denied this contention by claiming that in fact their own republic of resident slaveholders bore a closer resemblance to "Oriental"[19] arrangements of friendly master-slave relations than it did to the absentee slave societies of Britain's West Indian colonies, that it offered a paternalistic antidote to the perils of "pauperism" and revolution that plagued liberal free societies. In this context, this book illustrates the ways in which similar discourses of poverty and the idiom of family could be customized to support very different structures of subordination—from chattel bondage to patron-client relationships—across the globe from each other.

Moreover, there is a twist to this story that further scrambles the construct of neat polarities in the Atlantic World of British abolition versus American (South) proslavery, while illuminating the transoceanic circuits, adaptations, mutations, and manipulation of information about slavery on distant shores. An international cohort of human rights activists disputed British colonial generalizations about different slaveries in the East and West. They publicly pressured the East India Company to dismantle structures of servitude forged in their dominions through imperial acts of omission and commission. On the one hand, reformist critiques suggest how Atlantic frames of reference about plantation society and Whig-Republican definitions of freedom as individual rights and a free market for labor could mediate knowledge production about "slavery in the East." At the same time, the circulation of these critiques illuminates the ways in which transatlantic abolitionists could provide American defenders of slavery with grist to eviscerate British abolitionist imperialism while arguing simultaneously that the South's so-called "peculiar institution" compared favorably with both European imperialism and slave systems around the world. Thus, for instance, when the proslavery legal lion Thomas R. R. Cobb wrote a historical sketch of global slavery as a preface to his famous treatise of slave law in the American South, he drew selectively (and erroneously) on interpretations of Hindu law compiled by Orientalists like Henry Thomas Colebrooke that were contained in the abolitionist and BIS founding member William Adam's book *The Law and Custom of Slavery in India*. The difference was that while Adam was *arguing against* Orientalist proslavery readings of Indian religious law, Cobb was citing it as authoritative evidence of the universal nature of slavery.[20]

Other angles that illustrate synergies and disparities between the United States and the Indian Ocean world in shaping international discourses of slavery include the experiences of aspiring American settler colonialists, slaveholders, free labor agents, merchants, and State Department operatives in South Asia and various islands off the east coast of Africa. We are more familiar with the exploits of nineteenth-century Atlantic sojourners, whether it is William Walker, whose filibuster expedition in Nicaragua may have augured the advent of "US liberal imperialism," or Confederate exiles in Brazil and Cuba, who were integrated into hemispheric networks of kin and capital, grappling with Pan-American contests over race and labor.[21] Indian Ocean prisms unveil new facets of the historical experiences of globe-trotting would-be masters from the United States. Our narrative profiles three categories of these actors from our shared global pasts: slave-state overseers turned "free cotton" operatives in 1840s British India; a Massachusetts doctor who became a slave-owning sugar baron in the Comoros even as the Union he had fought to preserve launched and then abandoned an experiment in racial democracy in the 1870s; and New England mercantile diplomats, whose accommodation of slavery in the western Indian Ocean often positioned them against the more abolitionist British consuls in the region from the 1840s through the 1890s. The lenses we train on these figures straddle sectional divides in US slavery histories, expand the temporal perimeters of such accounts, and help parse the shifting relationship between the US state and its citizens abroad in the age of abolition.

At the same time, true stories of aspiring US settler colonialism and engagements with IOW bondage discourses offer the promise of broadening interoceanic angles on the historiography of slavery in the western Indian Ocean. Such interface perspectives have hitherto focused heavily on mercantile exchanges of enslaved peoples and goods between continents, fueled in the last quarter of the eighteenth century by, among other things, the prosperity of French sugar economies in the Mascarene Islands (including Mauritius and Réunion), and Saint Domingue. One body of work has tracked the flow of captives from southeastern Africa to the Americas via the Cape of Good Hope. This traffic peaked in the decades following the ebb of the Atlantic slave trade, when an Anglo-Portuguese treaty confined the transoceanic traffic to the South Atlantic. By the early nineteenth century, Mozambique had overtaken the Malagasy ports to emerge as a cosmopolitan hub of the international commerce in human chattel. Propelled by the business dealings of Portuguese and Arab merchants, Gujarati financiers, South American silver and African suppliers and consumers, this interoceanic trade fed the ravenous plantation economies and mines of Brazil, Cuba, and the western Indian Ocean. North American ships, capital, enterprise, and labor constituted a key link in these exchange webs, both within and outside the law, depending on the time and place of their operations.[22]

A second corpus of literature linking North America with the western IOW has explored the experiences of New England merchants who forged business coalitions with Swahili, Arab, and Indian traders, creditors, and consumers in Madagascar and Zanzibar, bartering slave-grown American cotton textiles, muskets, and silver for jerked beef, ivory, hides, and gum opal to service plantations and factories in Brazil, Cuba, and New England. Recent works have traced the legacies of these transactions to developments as varied as the move from mercantilism to industrialism in Salem, their impact on the local environment for textile manufacturing in East Africa, and the ecological costs they exacted on a continental scale. A common thread that emerges in some of this work is the vulnerability of foreign firms in East Africa to the caprices of local consumer demand, production and transportation patterns, and the business practices of regional magnates.[23] Our book pivots from an exclusive focus on American merchants who expected to leave the western Indian Ocean region soon to would-be settler-colonialist planters and entrepreneurs who expected to stay. It seeks to deepen our understanding of the tenuous and contingent position of sojourners negotiating unfamiliar cultural landscapes and patronage networks, caught between local, national, and imperial regimes of politics and law. Moreover, it positions them within international debates over bondage, showing how their words and actions on faraway plains and islands—whether a model cotton farm in India or a sugar plantation in the Comoros—played back home, in an America steeped in the politics of slavery, sectionalism, and race.

Crossing slavery's Atlantic boundaries also admits multiracial western IOW subalterns—primarily African, South Asian, and Middle Eastern—into the analytical canvas where we seek to broaden our thinking about concepts that students of African American studies have long pondered: agency and diaspora. We define the term *subaltern* as groups or individuals whose subordination was relational rather than absolute, and who experienced and navigated the world at the intersection of different discourses of power, whether of race, gender and kin status, class, caste, religion, language, or nationality, and so on.[24] Expanding the horizons of comparative African diasporic history makes it possible for us to relate these different discourses of power to the variety of subaltern relationships with the rhetoric, symbols, and institutions of slavery debates.

Decades ago, the feminist postcolonial theorist Gayatri Spivak posed the question of whether the subaltern "can speak." Scholars of Atlantic slavery have rightly asked to what extent enslaved peoples constrained by commodification could exercise any sort of will, if that is how we characterize the idea of agency. Moreover, historians have shown how the power relations that produced slavery archives in the western hemisphere set the stage for "epistemic violence," distorting or extinguishing enslaved subjects in ways that for too long were reproduced in professional history writing. Recently, Marisa Fuentes in particular has mined archival fragments and silences for the insights that they—in conjunction with contextual information—have the potential to generate about what she has described as the "dispossessed lives" of Bridgetown, Barbados.[25] For the IOW, Clare Anderson has pointed out that subaltern mobility produced a fragmented archive, so that transnational engagement with colonial documents of "surveillance and restraint" along the grain might illuminate intersections between marginalized histories (say, those of convicts), and empire, connecting disparate places.[26] Imperial abolition, adopted in this work as a discursive framework for thinking through the recovery of subaltern subjectivities, defined itself as a counterpoint, of course, to the disciplinary regimes of slave societies in the Americas. It produced an infrastructure calculated to write marginalized peoples quite explicitly into the official documentary record as beneficiaries of a benevolent empire. Such official appearances, while more visible than the unspoken presence of the enslaved in many New World archives, are still heavily mediated, and often fleeting. Nevertheless, they make it possible for us to place the subaltern subject—from "autonomous" Black Atlantic abolitionist authors to women and children rescued from slave ships in the Indian Ocean—within comparative contexts; and to reflect on whether and how subordinated peoples were able to negotiate meanings of dependence and aspirations to "freedom," personhood, and/or community in different hierarchical societies.

The complex interoceanic landscapes across which our protagonists moved—settings fractured along lines of politics and nationality, as well as overlaid by pluralisms of culture, law, and jurisdiction—serve as ideal theaters for understanding past struggles in ways that transcend the limitations of what the historian Walter Johnson described as the "jargon" of agency supposedly exercised by subordinate populations. This "master trope" of a great deal of scholarship on slavery in the United States, Johnson wrote, framed as the enslaved's will to preserve their humanity, collapses a variety of actions into the undifferentiated category of resistance by autonomous individuals without paying attention to the intersectionality of subaltern identities, or the multidimensionality of subaltern experiences. The historical subject in this framing becomes, in his words, "an individual slave" rather than "a Christian" or "a mother" or "the Igbo."[27] Indeed, writers of comparative slavery such as Dylan C. Penningroth have shown that by placing national or continental historiographies in conversation with each other, such as those of Black America and West Africa, we can unsettle the assumption that the assertion of subaltern subjectivity equals the quest for autonomy by "embodied individuals." For instance, kinship served as a way of controlling both dependent people and property in the United States and Gold Coast, paving the way for freed people in Ghana to lay claim to both the lineages and property of their former masters following emancipation, while fueling intrafamily struggles in the American South. Penningroth's history telling challenges binary and unitary constructions of master and slave, white and Black, locked in liberal individualistic struggles over autonomy.[28]

Anglo-American encounters with hierarchical societies in the Indian Ocean are rich with subaltern stories of strategic engagement that similarly scramble linear narratives and liberal meanings of freedom. Societies with slaves in these realms differed from their Western counterparts in significant ways. Scholarship on Afro-Asian societies has broadened the conceptual boundaries of slavery as a historical subject beyond its New World–centric incarnation as a static institution anchored in the legal construct of chattel bondage, the sociological condition of "social death," and the economic identity of forced labor—frequently, plantation and reproductive labor. These histories reject monolithic portrayals of slavery as a stationary status—the antithesis of Atlantic Enlightenment ideas of freedom, defined as individualism and free will. Rather, they emphasize the complex, dynamic character of slavery's manifestations as *processes* by which "uprooted outsiders" or "impoverished insiders" (to use Richard Eaton's formulation), moved along a continuum between alienation from and assimilation (however imperfectly) to the host society. But these processes were accompanied, as Jonathan Glassman has pointed out, by pressures from marginalized groups for greater social inclusion. Scholars of non-Western societies have drawn attention to the function of some forms of slavery in incorporating and expanding kin groups—a circumstance that led to the predominance of women and children among enslaved populations in these societies. To cite one well-known example, Indrani Chatterjee has pursued this line of analysis in the context of noble families in colonial India, demonstrating that slaves broke through ostensibly impenetrable lines of caste and communal lineage. Enslaved concubines, secondary wives, or adopted sons acquired as a part of inheritance strategies by Islamic ruling families helped make pluralistic households layered with complex hierarchies of rights and responsibilities attached to different kin statuses. From an Atlantic perspective, these circumstances muddied the lines between market and family, and master and slave.[29]

The functional importance of slavery to kinship and communal strength assumed even greater significance in contexts in which state power was weak and decentralized. In these situations, dependence on an influential (even royal) patron could lock an enslaved male separated from his own society of origin into a position of loyalty to the master, and could earn him positions of great trust and authority in the military, the treasury, or other branches of the bureaucracy. Such a dependent, in turn, lent his master power, prestige, and prosperity, and a measure of security from pretenders to his perch, including rivals from within the master's own family.

Moreover, in the western IOW's Muslim polities, the laws of slavery, unlike the slave codes written by planter-dominated local assemblies in the United States, stemmed from the Quran. In theory, Islam forbade the enslavement of fellow Muslims, legitimizing, rather, the enslavement of non-Muslim captives of war. It obligated masters to incorporate people they purchased into the Islamic community through conversion, conferring on the new converts the right to both subsistence and marriage. An enslaved concubine enjoyed special rights in exchange for her master's appropriation and exploitation of her womb, for her performance of sexual and reproductive labor. These included insurance against sale and the prospect of freedom upon the master's death if she bore him children. Her offspring were born free and entitled to some of the same rights—including those of inheritance—as those of siblings born of non-enslaved mothers. Finally, IOW societies did not conflate slave status with color or official race constructs, although multihued populations in these societies with slaves were by no means free of color prejudice.[30]

Despite discrepancies between law and practice, these features propel into sharp relief the very different makings and workings in the IOW of "diaspora," central to scholarship on African American history. In the Atlantic world, historical memories of captivity, forced removal, and racial slavery fused different African groups into a new sense of belonging to a coherent diaspora, which, as Paul T. Zeleza has suggested, is both a complex community created by "real or imagined genealogies and geographies," as well as a process-cum-space for navigating multiple belongings.[31] Yet IOW scholars have noted that in the regions they study, very different circumstances of power, belonging, and notions of difference may have undermined the relationship between collective memories of trauma and diasporic identity formation among subaltern communities. Of course, as Chatterjee has noted, in India at least, the colonial state, by seeking to link inheritance rights and political roles to "legitimate" lineages, marginalized enslaved dependents who might in earlier eras have shared equally in those privileges. This book's narratives of the ways in which subordinate populations engaged discourses of British imperial abolition in different oceanic worlds offer a common comparative framework for thinking through notions of diaspora.[32]

This comparative approach to subaltern subjectivities against the backdrop of imperial abolition is related to the book's scholarly interventions in IOW slavery historiographies in another way. It fleshes out the inaugural phases of British slave trade regulation unfolding within an increasingly integrated international framework of commerce and population dispersal. Age-old webs linked the "dhow cultures"[33] of East Africa through the Middle East to port cities and kingdoms deep in the heart of South Asia—Calcutta, Bombay, Kutch, Hyderabad, Awadh—in multidirectional exchanges of peoples and goods. Not only was bondage part of these resilient precolonial networks, it assumed forms that blurred the lines between family and property, making it hard for imperial legal authorities to maintain distinctions between so-called domestic slavery and trafficking. In the 1830s, the British colonial state in South Asia sought to suppress the international slave trade—in Africans especially—through "indirect rule," forcing tributary states to assume the risks and costs of such action. Resultant strikes of retaliation against Indian shipping on the high seas and conundrums around sovereignty, national identity, international law, and transnational trade relations from Arabian Sea shores to the Atlantic Ocean divided the colonial establishment and helped shape a cautious approach to antislavery activism in the IOW in the first half of the nineteenth century. Such reluctance set the stage for inconsistencies in British campaigns against IOW slave trading that other scholars have documented for later periods. Finally, this work "globalizes" Indian Ocean histories of bondage by tying colonial knowledge production about "slavery in the East" to the Anglo-Atlantic world's politics of slavery and poverty, as well as its contests over sectionalism, abolitionism, and colonial reform.

* * *

The book's principal themes emerge in the course of nine chapters grouped into four sections, shifting between and combining comparative and transnational modes of analysis and storytelling.

The two chapters in part 1 historicize and contextualize the colonial rhetoric and practice of slavery in British Asia within interoceanic frames of reference, recounting the human rights critiques they evoked from transoceanic abolitionists and colonial reformers. In chapter 1, the curtain rises on a moment of transition and ostensible contrast in the Anglophone world. Britain emerged from the American War of Independence with a mission that fused its colonial project, gaining momentum in Afro-Asia, with the "moral capital" of antislavery policy.[34] Even as chattel slavery, fortified by capitalism, came roaring back in the American Southwest, Brazil, and Cuba,[35] Africans in the Americas could hope for strategic alliances with the English who "as a nation" appeared to be their friends.[36] As the nineteenth century opened, however, controversy over the ways in which the abolition of the international slave trade applied to British Asia tested the limits of Britain's antislavery commitment. Professions of good intention collided with the overriding imperial imperatives of political expansion, revenue collection, and reluctance to expend public resources for poor relief. Such tensions generated inconsistent and often arbitrary attitudes toward Indian forms of servitude, justified by an imperial discourse of difference between domestic slavery in the East and the violent chattel principle of the West. Antebellum Americans on opposite sides of slavery debates would engage with this discourse of difference in different ways.

This chapter sets the stage for unraveling the strands of that interoceanic engagement against the backdrop of parallel principles of legal pluralism in North America and British Asia. The legal framework of prerogative that accommodated local laws and practices of slavery in colonial North America had established precedents for recognizing Indian forms of servitude under the separate jurisdictions of Muslim and Hindu law, as the British understood those laws through the medium of pundits and imams. Intra-imperial debate over the global implications of international slave trade abolition prompted learned bureaucrats to interpret the laws and practices of slavery in India through Orientalist prisms. At the same time, some imperial administrators proposed to bridge the gap between British antislavery rhetoric and proslavery practice by institutionalizing informal relations of dependence into contractual relations of servitude, or slavery by "free will."

Chapter 2 explores the ways in which Anglo-American abolitionists read ancient Indian judicial authorities and their British interpreters to fuse critiques of slavery and imperialism on a global scale. We enter the nonconformist worlds they made, shaped by cosmopolitan cultures of travel, correspondence, and print journalism that extended across three continents. We highlight, among other figures, the celebrated Indian social reformer Raja Rammohun Roy, who collaborated with the Baptist-missionary-turned-Unitarian-abolitionist William Adam. Roy's progressive reading of ancient Sanskrit literature and his campaign for women's rights in India, especially his crusade against the practice of *sati*, turned him into a hero to transatlantic antislavery feminists and a symbol in the United States of the argument for racial equality. Although meningitis cut Roy's life short in 1833 on the eve of a visit to Boston, his friend Adam physically entered the American public sphere in 1838 through a professorship in Oriental literature at Harvard funded by New England business interests in India. Adam published a treatise on slavery in India for interracial audiences in Boston. His account of this subject departed in important ways from customary laws and practices of slavery on local levels, as we can tell from the work of historians of India working with vernacular sources. Nevertheless, by reading Hindu and Muslim laws of slavery in an antislavery light, he made a compelling case that the imperial policy of legal pluralism had, in fact, created and codified forms of servitude not recognized by the East India Company's Muslim predecessors. Moreover, as an architect of the British India Society, Adam combined his critique of the imperial law of slavery with free-produce activism. These causes tied the boycott of slave-grown commodities in the Atlantic to the advocacy of prosperity for the colonized in Indian Ocean worlds.

In part 2, we turn to the Slave South's engagements with the international politics of IOW slavery. Chapter 3 tracks the odyssey of American cotton plantation overseers, recruited by the EIC to experiment with the cultivation of that golden staple with "free" Indian labor. Diverse stakeholders envisioned these endeavors as securing the independence of British business interests from US suppliers, while posing an alternative to slave-grown cotton in European markets. This segment explores the many ways in which the politics and representation of experiences that unfolded in the rural enclaves of British India reverberated in the urban nodes, legislative hallways, and newspaper columns that sustained a North Atlantic exchange grid.[37]

The larger story of the Slave South's brush with Britain's South Asian empire is woven together in part with the voices of the young white men who journeyed from the margins of their own society to a differently racialized colonial world across two oceans, in pursuit of fortune and adventure. Preserved in letters and journals that found their way into the public sphere via official reports and newspaper articles, these voices functioned much like travel narratives, illuminating the trajectories of their authors' evolving politics and senses of national identity. They recorded clashes between expectations of American-style settler colonialism and the complex structures of hierarchy, dependence, and patronage that arbitrated control over land and labor in 1840s British India. As hope turned into failure, the sojourners from the American South joined their compatriots back home in asserting their manifest destiny to dominate cotton culture through slavery. They offered ammunition for the proslavery argument that a republic of slaveholders took better care of subordinate populations under its custody than did an oligarchy of abolitionist-imperialists—whether in the North Atlantic or British Asia.

Chapter 4 broadens our gaze on defenses of servitude circulating between the two oceanic worlds through the prisms of poverty and gender. It tracks the transnational career of a web of proslavery tropes from the halls of Parliament in the 1830s and 1840s, through the pen of a South Carolina cotton baroness in the 1850s, to the brothels and colonial offices of eastern India in the 1860s and 1870s. These tropes rationalized servitude as social insurance woven into the fabric of private, patriarchal households. We illustrate their protean character by entering the worlds of two utterly disparate female "masters" from distant corners of Anglophone realms. On the one hand, there was that ardent champion of the twin pillars of patriarchy and white supremacy anchoring the foundations of privilege in the Old South: the South Carolina essayist and slave mistress, Louisa S. McCord. McCord countered British women abolitionists' appeals to end slavery on grounds of "Christian sisterhood" by representing "free" Britain as a breeding ground for "pauperism," revolution, and colonial oppression. Erasing utterly the productive and reproductive labor of enslaved people that sustained her world, she refashioned the rhetoric of poverty, patriarchy, and the naturalness of hierarchy that circulated from the western reaches of the Indian Ocean into the halls of Parliament, into a proslavery polemic of intergenerational charity, maternal duty, and divinely ordained authority.

We follow echoes of this familial idiom in the defense of bondage back to South Asia in the 1860s and 1870s, through the medium of a bill of sale of a girl child to a dancer by "caste." Documented as part of a judicial investigation into child trafficking by sex workers, this record highlights the colonial construct of this particular species of transaction—as distinct from the private contracts negotiated by royal households—as the principal form of slavery liable for archiving and prosecution. It becomes our window onto subversive communities of courtesans and sex workers who purchased and often adopted young girls during famines or under other dire circumstances, in order, they said, to both save the children and incorporate matriarchal familial-professional guilds from the ranks of nominally free women: victims of famines or floods, abused wives and widows, and African concubines. Suspended in fluid religious and caste identities, these communities challenged established principles of both Victorian morality and emerging genteel Indian notions of domesticity. This chapter then moves between the worlds made by these women—separated by vast chasms of place, power, and culture—in North America and British Asia. It suggests that their association with a common well of ideas about family and dependence fashioned disparate models of what we call "proslavery maternalism"—justifications for fundamentally different power structures in their respective settings, and with diverse implications for intersectional gender hierarchies within systems of servitude.

The scenes of contest that unfold through part 2 were underwritten by the blood and toil of human chattel, bonded labor, enslaved concubines, dependent kin, eunuchs, pawned children, sailors, and other historical figures spanning a wide spectrum of subordination. The chapters in part 3 turn to their elusive histories "from below," at the point of their encounters with the cacophonous politics of international and domestic slave trade abolition. The spectrum of subaltern interactions with British abolition raises key questions about the dialectics of structure and agency in comparative slavery histories: How do they relate to slavery's diversity, and to constructs of difference from one oceanic world to another? How did imperial abolition function as a hegemonic field of negotiation or dissent, supplying political strategies and material tools (like diplomacy and depositions), and language and symbols, for the assertion of subaltern subjectivity in various contexts? What did freedom mean in these settings? How might we theorize concepts like diaspora within comparative frames of reference? Equally important, what were the limits of the imperial campaign against slavery and slave trades, from the perspective of the objects of colonial benevolence, and their present-day scholarly chroniclers?

Chapter 5 is crafted from the archival traces of an international cast of women on the margins, nominally free or in bondage, who sought to remake their lives by crossing borders erected by abolition. We juxtapose, for comparative purposes, a diverse cast of characters that narrated or engaged with the discourse of imperial abolition as it sojourned from the Atlantic to the Indian Ocean. Our account begins in African America's circles of civil rights activism. We profile the pioneering freeborn journalist and emigration champion Mary Ann Shadd Cary against the backdrop of the famous antebellum *Lemmon* case, involving enslaved Virginians who voted for freedom with their feet during a stopover in New York en route to Texas. These historical figures represented interclass Black migrations to present-day

Ontario amid rising sectional tensions. They highlighted what portions of abolitionist Atlantic publics would have perceived as contrasts between empires of slavery and freedom—an American Southwest shrouded in the mantle of human bondage, and the Canadian West, where fugitives fled hoping to breathe free under British suzerainty wielded by an empress. Shadd Cary strategically embraced the Whiggish discourse of imperial abolition—of the onward march of progress, and "freedom" defined as equal opportunity, self-sufficiency, and a free labor market for women (as much as men) of the Afro-Atlantic diaspora—to challenge proslavery allegations that free societies descended into "pauperism" and revolution.

This book's action then moves across oceans back in time to British Indian magistrates' *Kacceri*—colonial offices that served as a locus for the information gathering, writing, authentication, and archiving that proved crucial to the daily operation and consolidation of empire.[38] There, colonial bureaucrats mediated and inscribed into the archives the testimonies of enslaved concubines or domestic workers attempting "freedom flights" from elite households. These cases had radically different outcomes depending on the priorities of colonial policy and the dictates of expediency, ranging from emancipation in one instance and murder that went unpunished in another. These cases also highlight the distinctions maintained by British administrators between domestic slavery within their dominions and international slave trades. The former implied a patriarch's right to mastery over his own household without interference from the colonial state (as well as slaveries within the territorial limits of British India), while the latter became a subject of imperial negotiation and proscription.

Chapters 6 and 7 switch gears from domestic slavery to international slave trades, highlighting the difficulties in legislating and regulating the boundaries between the two in the Indian Ocean. We cross the jurisdictional boundaries of the EIC's dominions into princely states on the west coast of India bordering the Arabian Sea, in present-day Gujarat, where one British bureaucrat claimed to see Africa stamped on the physiognomy of a local ruler, the Rana of Porbandar.[39] Africans had indeed been traveling to Indian shores in many roles, among them as captives aboard slave-trading Arab vessels that were plying centuries-old paths of commerce connecting East Africa through the Gulf with South Asian cities and kingdoms. The march of abolition and empire balkanized and realigned this world along routes of political, philosophical, and jurisdictional struggles over slavery, forging a contentious backdrop for subaltern crossings. We reconstruct that backdrop from multiple perspectives: antislavery colonial bureaucrats and naval commanders in Afro-Asia contending with their more cautious overseers and lawgivers from Calcutta to London, South Asian tributary states forced to assume the risks and costs associated with imperial slave trade abolition, irate operatives on the Arabian peninsula avenging British action by wreaking havoc against Indian shipping, and East African sultans juggling the politics of empire against the commercial interests of their multinational subjects.

But even as some of these globe-trotters of standing were knitting diverse oceanic spheres into exchange networks of commodity, capital, labor, and kin, there emerged an alternative model of circulation. Subalterns of various descriptions assumed the roles of captive, rebel, refugee, or migrant as they navigated international waters and nodes of commerce where British patrols faced off against slavers in the western Indian Ocean. The specifically African segments of the international traffic in humans in the western Indian Ocean caught the eye of colonial officials in the wake of West Indian emancipation in the 1830s. The records they generated lead us through the slaving paths of East Africa and the Arabian Peninsula; the counting houses, plantations, and *zenanas* of Zanzibar; and the business alliances that connected North America with East Africa through mercantile houses in western India. We cross the ship decks of slavers and antislavers into safe houses and police stations of South Asian provincial towns and regional capitals, on the trail of mobile subalterns and their various captors and "keepers." Within these realms of contention, otherwise invisible captives become legible in official records maintained by governments.[40] Subaltern testimonies recounted in chapter 7 turn slave statistics into names and places, and objects of imperial "benevolence" into witnesses and mediators among powerful men: sultans, *vazirs,* merchants, missionaries, and imperial bureaucrats. Migration stories from the "bottom up" flesh out marginalized people's brushes with formal institutions and instruments of imperial abolition: the state, law, police, antitrafficking patrols, or depositions. They illustrate how the nature of slavery in different contexts determined subaltern attitudes toward colonial belonging while undermining freedom's conflation with liberal individualism realized under imperial auspices. This chapter's scenes of subaltern subjectivity show that context configured the interplay of "freedom" with work, wages, mobility, gender, and family variously across different oceanic worlds.

Part 4 disentangles the threads that bound American investments in slavery with the western Indian Ocean world. Chapter 8 explores US complicity in IOW slave trades by training our lens on American merchants and consuls operating in the region. These figures entered controversies over the nationality and sovereignty of their slave-trading business partners hailing from Gujarati-speaking mercantile communities of western India, who merchandized American textiles made from slave-grown cotton to East African consumers. We argue that the Civil War opened up a chasm between an officially antislavery US government and its representatives and citizens in the IOW, who feared that British measures against slave trafficking would hurt their business interests. At the same time, new rigor in British naval operations against the slave trade in the 1870s and local American ambivalence on IOW slavery opened cracks for the mediating voices of marginalized subjects caught in the crosscurrents of great power rivalries, empire building, and labor conflicts. This chapter concludes by recounting the saga that unfolded one December evening in 1878 aboard the US barque *Laconia* as it lay anchored in the port of Zanzibar.[41] There, the paths of three alleged East African slaves from a Comorian island crossed the feuding worlds of British imperial abolition, US diplomacy, and American planters and merchants in the Indian Ocean. The *Laconia* incident produced dueling narratives of the identities of three Africans aboard the American whaler. These clashing scenarios were mediated by the varied stories the Africans themselves apparently told before different audiences, conveyed by translators in two different African languages. The resolution of the case turned on the pivot of these testimonies. It placed the narrators, whoever they were—whether captives as the British maintained, or fugitives as the Americans told the tale—on a passage to Massachusetts, far away from the Indian Ocean slave societies where they began their sojourn to visibility in the archives of two nations. That passage ended badly, but its documentary legacy has left intriguing glimpses into the perspectives of three Africans taking center stage in a diplomatic incident between two officially antislavery Atlantic powers in the Indian Ocean.

The *Laconia* incident offers a perfect segue to the final episode in this transnational saga of the United States in IOW contexts of slavery, abolition, and empire. It recounts a tale of tenuous mastery, beholden to the caprices of local patronage structures and European imperialism, entwined with local wars of succession and a slave rebellion. Shifting from sea to shore, our gaze settles in chapter 9 upon an American slaveholding estate on the Comorian island of Ndzwani (known as Johanna to the British, Anjouan to the French), from which the African protagonists aboard the *Laconia* had taken flight. There, against the backdrop of an expanding plantation economy helmed by European, American, and Arab masters since the middle of the nineteenth century, the fugitives' more privileged brethren among the enslaved population would live out a different meaning and experience of slavery. They served as armed soldiers in struggles over land, labor, and politics between their master, Sultan Abdullah III, and his one-time physician, Dr. Benjamin Wilson of New Bedford, Massachusetts. Wilson, a former Union surgeon, initially built a lavish lifestyle of settler colonialism resting on the personal patronage of an entrepreneurial monarch anxious to promote an agribusiness in sugar within his dominions. As the American's estate flourished, this renter suspected the sultan of designs to wrest it for the benefit of his son Salim. Abdullah, for his part, accused Wilson of joining hands with a dissident royal to foment a rebellion against his reign. The doctor framed his frantic appeals for the dispatch of a US warship to the western Indian Ocean in terms of American nationalism and the sanctity of private property. Yet these pleas fell largely upon deaf ears, American indifference to the region being reinforced by the sultan's apparently deft maneuvering of antislavery politics with both US and British authorities. In the immediate aftermath of Reconstruction, dispatches from the State Department placed Wilson on the defensive by questioning his relationship to slavery, the slave trade, and his treatment of workers. The American's woes were destined to mount as Ndzwani became a French protectorate. Colonial authorities now turned European lip service to "free" labor, as well as local traditions of unwritten contracts and "corporate" land tenure, into potent weapons to disrupt the Comorian New Englander's world. Wilson's experience with Indian Ocean systems of slavery and empire yielded the lesson that mastery meant little without local political clout, diplomatic cover, or imperial backing.

Taken together, these snapshots of historical figures and ideas in motion seek to expand the horizons of US slavery and abolition histories to the distant shores of the Indian Ocean, whose historiographical riches US historians have mostly yet to tap. In the pages that follow, migration makes meaning. In transit, slavery and freedom assume hydra-headed shapes—as language and experiences, as institutions and processes. Interoceanic comparisons unveil the many ways in which the representations and realities of "slavery" and "freedom" translated on regional and local levels into lives that we might compare, contextualize, and represent in relation to one another.

PART ONE

Between Empires

A New Way of Talking about Slavery, East and West

1

Empire, Religious Law, and Slavery by "Free Will"

[Throughout India], the relation of master and slave appears to impose the duty of protection and cherishment on the master, as much as that of fidelity and obedience on the slave; and their mutual conduct ... is marked with gentleness and indulgence on the one side, and with zeal and loyalty on the other!

—SIR HENRY T. COLEBROOKE, "MINUTE," 1812

The tendency of slavery is to humanize rather than to brutalize ... The accounts of travellers in Oriental countries, give a very favorable representation of the kindly relations which exist between the master and slave; ... Generally, however, especially if they be English travellers ..., they think it necessary to enter the protest, that they shall not be taken to give any sanction to slavery as it exists in America. Yet human nature is the same in all countries. ... if the general tendency of the institution in those countries is to create friendly relations, can it be imagined that it should operate differently in this?

—WILLIAM HARPER, *MEMOIR ON SLAVERY*, 1838

In late 1823, a group of magistrates in the city of Calcutta (present-day Kolkata), then the capital of the British Empire in India, signed a letter addressed to the governor general, alerting his office to the publication of a piece in the *Calcutta Journal* under the title "Slave Trade in British India." The article wondered what the "humane and enlightened community of this magnificent capital of our Eastern possessions," with its "splendid palaces, colleges and societies to promote the propagation of knowledge," would say if they learned a dreadful truth. This "depot of the commerce and riches of the East" hosted a slave mart in which "the manacled African is sold like the beast of the field to the highest bidder." Arab ships had reportedly landed 150 eunuchs (castrated males) that season, possibly bartered in Arabia for women carried away from India. The newspaper had learned that "200 African boys [were] emasculated" at the Red Sea port city of Jeddah (in present-day Saudi Arabia), and that "only 10 survived the operation." Appealing to a sense of Christian idealism and British nationalism, it called upon "Christians and British subjects" to act against the "illicit practices of these followers of Mahomet [sic]."[1]

The newspaper in which this account appeared had been launched by James Silk Buckingham, a Cornish mariner-turned-journalist who collaborated while in India with the celebrated Indian social reformer Raja Rammohun Roy. Buckingham would later publish a scathing indictment of slavery in the American South based on his own observations during a tour to entertain audiences in the United States with graphic travel accounts of Egypt and the Holy Land. He would, under the auspices of the British India Society, unite his advocacy of abolition in the Atlantic world with a critique of colonial misgovernment in British Asia. These perspectives represented a transnational counternarrative of the British Empire as an enabler of slavery and a perpetuator of poverty in the "East." How did this version of slavery and empire materialize, in the very years that African Americans were embracing "the English" as their friends? For answers, let us turn to an era of transition in the early nineteenth century, when the abolition of the Atlantic slave trade reverberated across the oceans in debates over the nature of different slaveries, East and West.

The sun set on British colonialism in large parts of North America even as it began a sharp ascent over Britain's expansion in Asia. The dynamics of this shift shaped a common frame of reference tied by empire, for debating the nature and meaning of slavery and freedom on an intercontinental scale. It set the stage for an assortment of rulers, rebels, and refugees to enter these contests from diverse vantage points across oceans. Shared contexts for defining the import of free will emerged most conspicuously at the moment in which sprawling, centuries-old empires of slavery in the Anglo-Atlantic world began apparently to unravel. The American and Haitian Revolutions, as well as the impending doom of the Atlantic slave trade marked that moment. It is at this temporal point—coinciding with the acceleration of empire in Afro-Asia—that we begin to disentangle the strands of correlation, transmission, and exchange that unfold in the pages of this book.

REPUBLIC OF SLAVERY VERSUS EMPIRE OF FREEDOM?

For centuries after the colonization of the Americas, Atlantic slaveholders, merchants, bankers, insurance agents, and consumers had not thought very much about the labor or human costs associated with the sugar that enriched their coffers or sweetened their beverages. Apologists rationalized the slave trade as an essential condition to maintain the British Empire's competitive edge in power and prosperity vis-à-vis its international rivals.[2] Yet from the start rulers had to contend with dissenters, however marginalized. Recent scholarship has emphasized the continuity and interracial character of transatlantic abolitionism from the eras of conquest and colonization in the so-called New World through the Revolutionary and national periods in North America. Manisha Sinha, for instance, has traced resistance to slavery in Atlantic world contexts all the way back to maroon communities on the west coast of Africa, insurrections aboard slave ships on the Middle Passage to the Americas, and early Quaker qualms about slavery. Enslaved Africans played a central role in defying New World bondage through flight, freedom lawsuits, and rebellions. Black writers on both sides of the Atlantic used the power of the pen to challenge the racial logic of slavery. From the satire of Lucy Terry Prince, the narratives of Ignatius Sancho and Olaudah Equiano, and the poetry of Phyllis Wheatley, Atlantic Creoles of African descent used their command of literacy and claims to Christian identity to expose the absurdity and cruelty of a chattel principle rationalized by constructs of African racial inferiority.[3]

Meanwhile, a revolution in moral consciousness shaped partly by Protestant and Enlightenment notions of humanism fueled discomfort with slavery in the age of Atlantic revolutions.[4] Historian Christopher Brown has argued persuasively that the American Revolution galvanized existing sentiments against slavery in Anglo-Atlantic societies into abolitionist action by making such action politically viable. Patriots and loyalists held each other responsible for the perpetuation of the odious traffic in human flesh against the dictates of natural law and Christian morality. Anticolonial North Americans blamed the rise of the Atlantic slave trade on their British colonial masters, while articulating a language of natural rights upon which slavery's opponents could draw. Their British adversaries, on the other hand, invoked the practice of chattel bondage in the colonies to denounce the hypocrisy of patriot claims to the historical liberty of Englishmen. Various transatlantic constituencies turned antislavery into a vehicle for realizing a range of goals. Thus, religious groups like evangelical Anglicans and British Quakers saw an opportunity to strike a blow against "nominal Christianity," or to campaign for a "new role in public life."[5]

Meanwhile, Black people interacted with British activists, institutions, and policy in ways that fueled the image of the English in North America as friends of African Americans. The landmark 1772 decision *Somerset v. Stewart*, delivered by the King's Bench in London, may have set the tone for a hope of interracial solidarity with transnational resonance. This case, which the historian Van Gosse has characterized as "the common-law precedent for all subsequent emancipations in the northern states,"[6] involved an enslaved plaintiff from Virginia named James Somerset, who asked the court to prevent his master Charles Stewart from transporting him to the Caribbean. The case materialized in the contexts of an increasingly visible Black and Brown presence in London and a long tradition of resistance to slavery in the Black Atlantic world. London's populations of color drew from enslaved "Negroes" imported into Britain by West Indian masters and from what runaway ads described as "Indian Black" bonded servants accompanying East India merchants and bureaucrats returning home from British Asia. A ripple of court cases in 1760s England gave notice of the spreading "contagion of liberty" among sections of these communities.[7]

Those seeking to throw off the shackles of chattel slavery found an early advocate in the trail-blazing abolitionist Granville Sharp, forever locked in historical memory with the outcome of Somerset's plea. Sharp helped secure the Virginian's freedom through a writ of habeas corpus that Lord Chief Justice William Murray, Earl of Mansfield upheld. Scholars generally agree that Mansfield ruled on narrow grounds. While conceding that so "odious" an institution such as slavery could only be supported by a resort to positive law, which Parliament had not established, the *Somerset* decision did not commit common law to a rejection of slavery in the colonies. Nevertheless, Black Londoners celebrated, Atlantic slaveholders fretted, and rumors of runaways seeking a passage to Britain circulated.[8] When, six years later, a different lord chief justice declared free any slave who stepped on English soil, thousands of human chattel in the metropole deserted their masters, and American slaveholders balked at bringing their slaves to the "mother country." In the antebellum era, decisions by the King's Bench would set precedents for the enactment of personal liberty laws by free North American states.[9]

When Britain's North American colonies erupted in rebellion, African Americans voted with their feet to give Lord Dunmore, the royal governor of Virginia, the opportunity to reaffirm the apparent supremacy of the "royal, rather than the republican" path to freedom. Months after meeting with a delegation of enslaved Virginians, Dunmore inaugurated the military recruitment of slaves by offering to emancipate those who left patriot masters for British lines. The Royal Ethiopian Regiment established under the governor's auspices sported white sashes bearing the inscription "Liberty to Slaves."[10] There were Black patriots to be sure, of whom the legendary Crispus Attucks of Boston Massacre fame remains etched in our collective memory as a pioneer. Northern states recruited enslaved soldiers with the promise of emancipation, so that no less than five thousand colonists of color served in the Continental Army and Navy. In general, the Revolutionary War disrupted the stability of slavery as patriots and loyalists confiscated each other's property, forcing slaveholders in some areas to "refugee" their human chattel into safe havens distant from their homes and farms. Enslaved people seized the occasion to flee, fight whichever side promised to liberate them, and petition courts and legislatures for freedom in terms that invoked the revolutionary language of liberty and equality. Elsewhere, bondspeople subverted work routines and sought to mount rebellions.[11]

Still, Black loyalists outnumbered patriots by a large measure, with an estimated twenty thousand slaves fleeing to British lines. The British General Clinton offered to settle them on confiscated patriot land. In New York, Guy Carleton balked at returning slaves required by the provisions of the Treaty of Paris. Officers of lesser rank handed out blank certificates of free passage to Nova Scotia and other places, fueling an exodus of African-descended populations from the nascent republic. Despite well-documented instances of British betrayal of Black loyalists, several thousand others left with the retreating imperial forces and settled in far-flung parts of the British Empire—from Britain itself to Canada, West Africa, and Australia.[12]

Black soldiers and refugees from the US Revolutionary War figured prominently in an experiment to establish a free Black colony in Sierra Leone in the 1780s. This project appeared to offer practical alternatives to the African slave trade while lending imperial projects an aura of moral authority. Interracial Anglo-Atlantic opponents of the slave trade, including the veteran evangelical lawyer of Somerset fame Granville Sharp and the celebrated former slave narrator Olaudah Equiano, saw West Africa as a place to resettle loyalists, large numbers of whom were living in poverty in London. There, these return migrants from the Black Atlantic would practice "legitimate commerce" and self-government. Morality and the market would work hand in hand to realize the promise of liberty that defined Britain's national self-image.[13]

In 1787–88, a few short years after Britain surrendered a key portion of its American empire in the Battle of Yorktown, a campaign to abolish the transatlantic slave trade had gathered steam and popular support.[14] Some historians have attributed this shift in attitude toward the slave trade and later slavery to the rise of free market capitalism, with explanations including the decline of Caribbean slave economies, reformers' class interests, and market-generated changes in cognitive style that prompted the public to make causal connections and assume moral responsibility for the suffering of distant populations.[15] Others have suggested that American independence dealt imperial confidence a blow and fueled the rise of abolitionism partly as a strategy to resuscitate empire and shore up metropolitan authority.[16] Those who disagree maintain that on the contrary, opposition to the slave trade coincided with bright prospects for Britain's future—new markets for British manufactures across the world, promising sources of raw material, rising staple crop production in the West Indies, and expanding clout in international politics thanks to the turmoil of the French Revolution and the weakness of the American Confederacy in the immediate aftermath of revolution. Rather, these critics argue, moral revulsion against the traffic in human flesh grew out of the sense, in Seymour Drescher's words, that "the world's most secure, free, religious, just, prosperous and moral nation" could not continue to perpetuate "the world's most deadly, brutal, unjust and immoral" affront to humanity.[17]

While the relative merits of these arguments are beyond the scope of the present account to weigh, it seems clear that a flurry of popular mobilization from London to the provinces—through voluntary organizations, the circulation of antislavery literature, lectures and petition drives—carried the momentum of the campaign against the slave trade into the halls of Parliament, where William Wilberforce would become its most famous advocate. A select committee of the House of Commons heard witnesses and evidence on the subject. Activists distributed compelling images such as Josiah Wedgwood's medallion depicting a manacled slave, kneeling with his face turned toward the heavens, pleading "Am I Not a Man and a Brother?" Prints circulated of an engraving of the slave ship *The Brookes,* its decks jam-packed with 609 slaves, including 131 children. Afro-Atlantic figures like Ottobah Cugoano and Equiano offered testimonials that brought disfranchised voices into the public sphere. Women signed petitions by the legion and became ready recruits to the cause of "anti-saccharite" movements targeting slave-grown sugar.[18]

But events in the larger Atlantic world were about to stymie the campaign for reform. Within one of the most productive nodes of Europe's New World empire, the Haitian Revolution ushered in the highwater mark of revolutionary antislavery, bringing together "slave resistance, revolutionary republicanism, and abolitionism ... in a heady mix," as Sinha has written.[19] In the halls of power, it raised the specter of radical politics at home and race war abroad. Yet antislavery politics regained its stride somewhat when Napoleon sought to reenslave the French Islands in the Caribbean. The Napoleonic wars attached strategic significance to a British abolition campaign to thwart France's Caribbean designs. In Africa, when the French threatened Sierra Leone, it made sense for the British to turn Bristol and Liverpool's slave trading vessels into tools of defense instead.[20] Meanwhile, by 1806 the winds of change were blowing over Westminster. The balance of power within the British Parliament had shifted from Caribbean slaveholding interests to antislavery ministers. Amid settled public opinion against trading in human chattel, the Abolition of the Slave Trade became law on 25 March 1807. It prohibited British subjects everywhere from trading in or transporting human chattel from Africa or within the empire, or outfitting ships for slave voyages. It marked the emergence of Britain's reputation as the leading foe of international slave trafficking on the world stage.[21] Three weeks earlier, across the Atlantic, President Thomas Jefferson had signed off on a ban against the African Slave Trade. The abolition of the slave trade in the United States followed a different path from that of Britain. Both acts were written to come into effect in January 1808.

Neither was particularly effective in bringing the commerce in human chattel to a halt.[22] Nevertheless, the politics of international slave trade abolition reverberated on a global scale in ways that brought the Indian Ocean directly into a comparative framework of slavery debates in the Anglo-Atlantic world. Even as Great Britain was seeking to remake its reputation as a foe of the foreign slave trade in Atlantic waters, the nascent United States had, in a fit of all sorts of schizophrenia, emerged on the world stage "half slave and half free." From New England through the mid-Atlantic states, places where slavery did not form the bulwark of the labor system enacted manumission through court or legislative action. Vermont led the way to abolition by outlawing slavery in its 1777 constitution, while in Massachusetts, freedom suits like those of plaintiffs Quok Walker and Mumbet forced the state to live up to its revolutionary principles of "mankind's" natural right to liberty. Pennsylvania pioneered the legislative approach to gradual emancipation that New York—the largest slave colony-turned-state north of the Mason-Dixon line, adopted in stages well into the early republican period.

The model of gradual emancipation was one that some British administrators in South Asia would suggest in reforming South Asian forms of bondage, as we shall soon see. But manumission raised in the early American republic—as it would in British India—the specter of unwelcome public relief expenditures. In 1799, for instance, New York freed all children born into slavery after 4 July 1799 with the proviso that such children serve their mothers' masters until they reached the age of twenty-eight if they were men, and twenty-five if they were women. The overseers of the poor would assume the care of any child whose services a slaveholder relinquished within a year of their birth. This "abandonment law" proved too costly to sustain and was repealed in 1812. Five years later, New York placed slavery in the state on the course of extinction by decreeing the emancipation of all slaves born before 4 July 1799, on 4 July 1827.[23] Gradual emancipation and apprenticeship would serve as models for emancipation proposals floated in European imperial domains across the seas.

New York was, of course, part of a young American republic born in an uneasy consensus on compromise. While the US Constitution steered clear of using the word *slave*, it institutionalized the notorious three-fifths clause, apportioning taxation and representation on the basis of a bizarre calculation that counted an enslaved person as a fraction of a free person. The fathers of the nation's founding documents also postponed the abolition of the international slave trade for twenty years and imposed fugitive slave laws on free states.

These constitutional protections, buttressed by the political heft of slaveholders in the new state, would secure the future of an emergent "second slavery" for a few decades. Emancipation had failed in the southern colonies-turned-states of revolutionary North America. These slave societies were about to become part of an expanding continental empire of slavery. Slavery and capitalism, braided together, powered and connected this empire with the larger Atlantic world. As scholars like Dale Tomich and Sven Beckert have noted, following its reverses in Haiti and the Anglo-Atlantic abolition of the international slave trade, slavery came charging back in Brazil, Cuba and the southwestern US lands expropriated from Indian nations like the Choctaw and Creeks through war or treaty. Driven by the Industrial Revolution and fortified by the political clout of slaveholders in reorganized Atlantic states, human chattel produced new commodities on a vast new scale for mass consumer markets. New machinery, the genetic engineering of crops, the mobility of enslaved property, and innovations in transport and communications all improved efficiencies. The plantation became a laboratory for modern techniques of management, accounting, and finance. New regimes of torturous industrial labor discipline materialized. A battery of experts—"engineers, chemists, iron makers, architects,"—bound the Upper South with slave societies elsewhere. Moreover, the political economy of slavery made the chattel principle a *national*—and indeed, global—institution rather than merely a southern one. Mills in Old and New England turned slave-grown cotton into textiles marketed to plantations in the American South, and to consumers in India and Africa. Northern bankers and merchants, as well as shipping, insurance, and land companies, invested heavily in slavery and the domestic slave trade, while the cotton trade infused valuable specie into Anglo-Atlantic economies.[24]

It was against this expanding domain of slavery in the Atlantic world that Great Britain seemed poised to define itself as an empire of freedom as it spread its influence in the Indian Ocean. There was, of course, a good bit of irony involved in this imperial self-construction. As we know well, British investors, manufacturers, and consumers were deeply complicit in sustaining the roots and branches of the "second slavery." British bankers helped underwrite the spread of the cotton kingdom in the American West. North America's slave-grown cotton kept the textile mills of Lancashire humming, and these mills in turn helped clothe consumers from Europe to the Indian Ocean in cheap, machine-made manufactures, arguably dealing Indian artisans a blow. Still, as the nineteenth century dawned, Britain's role as the world's police force against the international commerce in human chattel had infused its colonial project with a moral purpose as well as mechanisms to assimilate rescued captives into structures of colonial labor and subjecthood that appeared to stand in contrast to US proslavery policies. And the Napoleonic wars had given that imperial project a boost. Half a world away, European conflicts had triggered the transformation of the larger Indian Ocean world into a "British Lake," as Edward Alpers, among others, has written. The Dutch cession of Cape Town in South Africa, Ceylon in South Asia, and Java and Malacca further east established British control over the sea routes linking the Atlantic Ocean with East Africa and Asia, while the French surrender of the Mascarene Islands of Bourbon (La Réunion) and île-de-France (Mauritius), gave London a toehold in the western Indian Ocean.[25]

But even as the British Empire marched into Afro-Asia, carrying aloft the flag of slave trade abolition, there materialized early signs of trouble reconciling the ideals and practice of antislavery with government under colonial auspices. The promise of self-determination in West Africa, for instance, was falling short of fulfillment. The imperial vision of redemption was devolving into a slide toward corruption and coerced labor, setting precedents for an ambiguous legacy of colonial "freedom" in the age of Atlantic revolutions. The contradictions of that legacy would emerge full blown in Britain's rising empire in South Asia, shaping an imperial discourse of difference between slavery in the East versus that in the West.

Serving among other things as a rationale for accommodating Indian Ocean forms of servitude, that discourse would face challenges on many fronts. In Indian Ocean societies, subaltern groups would confound its assumptions. In the antebellum Anglo-Atlantic world, it would bring together two unlikely constituencies—proslavery Americans, on the one hand, and a coalition of transatlantic abolitionists and champions of imperial reform, on the other—in a scathing indictment of abolitionist imperialism from opposite angles.

Let us begin to pry apart the strands of this intercontinental story by turning to the far-flung reverberations of the international slave trade's abolition in 1807–8.

THE MANY GUISES OF SLAVERY'S LEGAL PLURALISM

The year 1808 began by ushering in the official abolition of the foreign slave trade in much of the Anglophone Atlantic world, although the law's enforcement was another matter. The same year, several time zones away, in the north central district of Bundelkhand in British India (see map 2), a colonial magistrate proposed a manumission plan for bondspeople in the imperial headquarters of Bengal Presidency. His recommendation recalled gradual emancipation plans under way in the early republican United States. Responding to reports of abuse that seemed to reflect subaltern complaints, he argued for laws "prohibiting the purchase or sale of all slaves, legitimate or illegitimate, after a specified time," and to set free all children deemed to have been born into slavery after a certain date. Moreover, he offered a legislative and judicial strategy of manumission that consisted in upending a system of legal pluralism that had governed colonial sanction of Indian forms of servitude since the late eighteenth century.[26] The magistrate's proposal went nowhere. But it became part of a matrix of arguments that brought Indian Ocean societies into a framework of comparison with Atlantic slavery by contending factions of imperial bureaucrats, missionaries, abolitionists and proslavery interests from North America through East Africa, Arabia, and Asia.

As Britain's colonial archives tell the story, the debate among nineteenth-century players over the nature and function of different slaveries, East and West, began seriously in the wake of Parliament's proscription of the international slave trade. But for the present-day historian of comparative slavery in North America and the Indian Ocean, a good place to begin contextualizing that debate is the colonial practice of legal pluralism on different continents. The British in South Asia were heir to a colonial Atlantic legacy of treating slavery as a private matter subject to local governance. The legal scholar Jonathan A. Bush has argued that Britain's North American colonies, as dominions of the Crown, (from the British rather than indigenous American perspective, of course) were governed not by Parliament or common law, but rather by royal prerogative. The framework of prerogative accommodated "divergent local practices" that departed from "the common law's traditions of anti-slavery rhetoric."[27] American slavery developed in practice as a racialized, self-reproducing labor force and technology necessary to sustain a variety of economic activities—whether plantation agriculture, farming, artisanry, domestic service, dock work, or sea-faring from the tropical South through the mid-Atlantic states to New England. In the Chesapeake and later South Carolina, wealthy, office-holding planters took lessons from colonial Latin America and the British Caribbean and turned to African slavery partly at least because Africans may have had better command over skills needed to clear land, practice forest husbandry, and cultivate tropical staples like rice. When in 1698 the Royal African Company's monopoly over the West African slave trade ended, a surge in the supply of slaves to North America brought African labor within the financial reach of lesser planters, just as the supply of white indentured servants was dwindling. Moreover, as Edmund Morgan suggested decades ago, from the perspective of slaveholders in an evolving slave society like Virginia, freezing the status of Africans into eternal unfreedom may have offered the additional political advantage of dividing workers along the color line.[28]

In British North America, statutory support of violently coercive labor practices that became an all-encompassing "institution" of social relations, economic structures, and cultural norms materialized at least partly as reaction to pressures from below. Freedom suits by biracial persons sired by white men, for instance, might prompt a colonial legislature to clarify that slave status derived from the civic identity of an enslaved mother they classified as "Negro." Or the threat of slave rebellions might lead to the institution's recognition by "an extensive set of police measures." Thus a 1669 Virginia law asserted that since the "obstinacy" of many "Negroes" could only be suppressed by violent means, if a master chanced to kill a slave in the course of punishing him for resistance, the murder would not be considered a felony because "premeditated malice" could not be presumed in a man's destruction of "his own estate."[29] In early South Carolina, the propensity of an increasingly Africanized labor force to resist by running away to Spanish Florida or by mounting insurrections—notably the Stono Rebellion—prompted lawmakers to pass measures designed to acculturate the native-born enslaved to accept the status into which they had been born by exhorting masters to treat their human chattel more humanely than had hitherto been the practice. These measures also stripped the enslaved of all sorts of rights—to assemble, travel, dress above what the dominant society deemed their station, keep horses, engage in commerce, or acquire literacy.[30]

In other words, North American slave law was a new construct, contingent on and *reactive* to shifting circumstances on the ground. Unlike slave societies in Latin America, which drew upon Roman law, North American legislators borrowed from that legal tradition only the provision of *partus sequitur ventrem*, decreeing that children would inherit slave status through their mothers. Moreover, colonial slaveholders anchored the social legitimacy of slavery in "normative systems such as honor and religion," which left the master-slave relationship outside the purview of formal law. A rhetoric of paternalism framed slaveholders' representation of that relationship, emerging full blown in the antebellum era. As a formal institution, slave law in North America focused on suppressing insurrection and did not address matters of private law affecting daily life: "work, family, religion, wages and private property," all of which were "left to private ordering."[31] Meanwhile, since the seventeenth century the doctrine of colonial conquest had vested the Crown with direct authority over conquered territories like Jamaica and Ireland, with the power to subject them selectively to common law, leaving room for local institutions to survive or take root. In North America this translated into a sort of colonial autonomy that permitted a master class of settler colonialists to institute chattel bondage and treat the governance of their property interest in human beings as a private matter.[32]

The principle of prerogative thus allowed slaveholders in British North America to create their own institutional support systems for racial slavery, while claiming the "rights of Englishmen" for themselves under common law.[33] By the time of the US Civil War, the language of "domestic institution" evoked the slaveholder's assumption of "personal authority" to "control his property." It established households as "realms of private power," as Stephanie McCurry has written, and conferred on the heads of these realms the untrammeled right to "govern" their "dependents."[34]

The legacies of colonial governance in North America are particularly useful in thinking through British legal discourses of slavery in India. The principle of prerogative—with its selective imposition of common law and accommodation of local practices—meshed well with the imperial drive in Afro-Asia to exert some judicial control, while recognizing indigenous legal systems as a way of buttressing stability, authority, and profit. As Lauren Benton has written, the "agents of colonial expansion"—whether commercial enterprises or governments—found themselves entrusted with "judicial authority independent of the state."[35] Yet they were not always anxious to assume the expenditures and hassles of creating entire judicial systems from scratch. It was more convenient to command enough control to mold the law to their economic, political, or cultural purposes, while retaining and sometimes *creating* ostensibly "traditional" laws and the authorities to enforce them.[36]

What resulted was a "fluid legal pluralism" before the onset of "high colonialism" in Afro-Asia.[37] Shortly after the British East India Company secured from the Mughals the Diwani (tax collection rights) over agrarian land in the eastern provinces of Bengal, Bihar, and Orissa, they instituted judicial reforms as part of their mandate to administer justice in these areas. In 1772, Governor General Warren Hastings divided the power of legal jurisdiction in each district between a civil and criminal court. Moreover, colonial law established a distinction between state law and personal law, declaring that in "all suits regarding inheritance, succession, marriage, castes and other religious usages or institutions, the laws of the Koran with respect to the Mohammedans and those of the Shaster with respect to Gentoos [that is, the *Dharmashastras* and *Smritis* of the Hindu lawgivers Manu and Narada] shall invariably be adhered to." Civil courts would hear such cases, with a supreme court in the company headquarters of Calcutta. known as Sadr Diwani Adalat, exercising the right to hear appeals of such cases. District criminal courts topped by a supreme court known as the Sadr Nizamat Adalat in Calcutta would administer Muslim law uniformly.[38]

Although the deference to local religious law as written in 1772 did not explicitly cover slavery under its purview, the Sadr Diwani Adalat ruled subsequently that "the *spirit* of the rule for observing the Muhammadan and Hindu laws was applicable to cases of slavery." As we shall see, the permeable lines between family and the market in certain types of households in the IOW did in fact imbricate slavery in institutions of marriage or concubinage, succession, and inheritance. Still, what is notable is that by placing slavery in the category of personal rather than state law, the colonial establishment gave itself the latitude to ignore forms of bondage practiced by elite households when expediency demanded. At the same time, however, colonial revenue collectors presided over the civil courts in each district—an arrangement that vested authority over cases involving property and revenue in British hands.[39]

As scholars of slavery in South Asia have noted, the East India Company, interested primarily in amassing profits through trade, agrarian production and revenue collection, had always proved reluctant to act against what they rationalized as centuries-old South Asian traditions of bondage, especially if these interfered with the interests of the colonial state. Indeed, as transatlantic abolitionists later charged, some colonial administrators even created and codified new forms bondage. Imperial proslavery policies sprang from important commercial, fiscal, political, and diplomatic considerations. These included, among others, the imperative not to alienate local elites or friendly foreign governments, to maintain public order and colonial authority, to avoid disrupting the company's revenue arrangements, to steer clear of expenditures for public relief during seasons of scarcity, to mobilize labor for public works, and to punish particular constructs of disorderly conduct or criminal behavior.[40]

Initially, the EIC itself engaged in various forms of slavery and slave trading. It perpetuated precolonial practices of enslavement for tax arrears and forced labor for public works or in service to elites and political authorities. It dispatched alleged criminals to company settlements like Bencoolen in Sumatra or St. Helena in the South Atlantic. Until the late eighteenth century, it purchased captives in Southeast Asia for transshipment via Madras to other destinations in India. European traders supplied enslaved "dwarfs" to the court of Charles II. Households in the colonial cities of Bombay, Calcutta, and Madras—whether European or Indian—purchased and employed domestic slaves. The *India Gazette* carried advertisements for human chattel and runaways.[41]

In the last few decades of the eighteenth century, the EIC, perhaps driven by an interest in protecting peasant taxpayers, enacted measures to prohibit transactions in persons who were not already enslaved. It also sought to draw a line between domestic and foreign slave trades, adopting measures, as Richard B. Allen has shown, to prohibit the exportation of children to the Mascarenes.[42] The abolition of the foreign slave trade in the Atlantic world, however, threatened to disrupt colonial accommodation of slavery in South Asia by blurring the distinction between slave trading across the national boundaries, on the one hand, and existing practices of bondage within British-governed dominions, on the other. The statute of the 51st Geo III, chapter 23, enacted in May 1811 to enforce the ban on international trafficking in human chattel, brought parts of the IOW directly and explicitly into the orbit of debate over the meaning and enforcement of transoceanic slave trade abolition. This act prohibited subjects of the British Crown, residents of territories subject to its jurisdiction, and persons living under "under the Government of the United Company of Merchants trading to the East Indies" from transporting or importing slaves from Africa or "from any other country . . . either immediately, or by Transhipment at Sea. . . ." Such deeds were declared a felony, carrying the penalty of exile overseas for a term of up to fourteen years, or hard labor for between three and five years, at the discretion of the convicting court.[43] These provisions prompted a flurry of consultations among bureaucrats, judges, and naval officers commanding British cruisers. What, they wondered, were the implications of international slave trade prohibition for South Asia, the primary seat of British imperialism?

The sweeping nature of 51st Geo III placed company functionaries on the ground in a bit of a pickle, for it threatened to upend existing norms of colonial governance and their relationship with friendly neighboring states. The expanding boundaries of the company's spheres of influence raised the question: What did "foreign" countries mean? Did parliamentary proscriptions of the international slave trade apply to slaves imported from realms annexed to company dominions following the passage of these laws? Did the measure's terms cover captives transported into company territories by land as well as by sea? What of fugitive slaves who might seek refuge in company territories of their own volition? Did these proscriptions apply to enslaved persons brought into company dominions *not* for the "purpose of being sold, given away, or otherwise disposed of"?[44] In other words, did these laws threaten to muddy the paramount distinction between the international slave trade and "domestic slavery" in South Asia, as the British understood the practices covered by that term? It was a distinction that defined early nineteenth-century abolition legislation in the Anglo-Atlantic, but here in South Asia, were champions of the slave's cause in a distant metropolis proposing to go further than they were prepared to do in their own neighborhood, and dismantle age-old relations of dependence through the tool of slave trade abolition?[45]

The chief secretary to the Government of Bombay framed these questions—rather self-servingly—in terms of a defense not of the property rights of slaveholders, but of *the rights of presumably destitute Indians to their own selves, and their free will to make contracts of self-sale.* He also questioned the impact of parliamentary regulations on the system of legal pluralism that British India's colonial masters had created to uphold such "rights." He wondered whether slave trade abolition applied to domestic slaves, "and *the property of individuals in themselves,* [our italics] such slavery being known and legalized under the laws of both the Hindus and Moosalmans [sic], according to whose codes the courts are bound to administer justice." Judicial authorities opined that 51st Geo III Chap. 23 applied only to traffic conducted by sea and was intended to target a specific evil, namely the African slave trade. As far as British South Asia was concerned, that regulation then translated into the proscription of the *East African slave trade* to the company's dominions. Colonial bureaucrats on the ground in South Asia judged that if Parliament had intended to strike against "domestic slavery" of immemorial vintage, it would have had to repeal earlier acts of Parliament giving "natives" the right to be governed by their own laws.[46]

Instructions such as these helped shape a transoceanic colonial discourse of bondage that steadfastly distinguished between the slave trade and slavery in the Atlantic world and their counterparts in British Asia. Significant differences did indeed exist between Atlantic slavery and the infinite assortment of bonded statuses in the Indian Ocean world (as IOW scholars have established). At the same time, it is hard to ignore the generalizations, categorical nature, and ideological function of Orientalist justifications of Indian varieties of servitude, especially because those occupying the bottom rungs of South Asian power relations begged often enough to differ from the official story maintained by the EIC. Around Indian forms of bondage, company officials constructed a rhetoric of "domestic slavery" with overlapping meanings that signified both a patriarch's mastery over his household and the integrity of age-old local customs. Notably, this colonial discourse of British Asian slavery more or less ignored European masters in India, focusing instead on their colonized peers, classified neatly into two groups defined by religious identity: Hindu and Muslim. Legitimized by a system of legal pluralism that offered the illusion of paralleling the "hands off" British policy toward colonial slavery in North America, this language of deference to difference would echo powerfully in the American South's defense of its own domestic institution a few decades later.

PROSLAVERY ORIENTALISM THROUGH ATLANTIC PRISMS: HENRY THOMAS COLEBROOKE

In the Anglo-Atlantic world, rationales for Indian forms of servitude were broadcast most effectively via the commentaries of Henry Thomas Colebrooke. Colebrooke belonged to a group of English and German Indologists who introduced

Europeans—and Americans like Ralph Waldo Emerson—to Indian philology and a canon of Sanskrit classics, selected with the help of a cohort of (Brahman) pundits. We might thus consider him an Orientalist in the historical sense of one learned in the languages and literatures of Asia. As an imperial interpreter who represented the laws and practices of India through the lens of assumptions about the "inherent" nature of Indians and the timelessness of their ways, however, we might also think of him as an Orientalist in the sense in which Edward Said used the term—a producer of knowledge about slavery that was implicated in the preservation of colonial power.[47]

The son of a former proprietor of the East India Company who went bankrupt following the financial crisis of 1772, Colebrooke left for India in 1782 at the age of seventeen. He remained there for over three decades, ascending from lowly administrative positions to a judgeship on the Court of Appeal in Calcutta. He also held an honorary professorship in Sanskrit and Law at Fort William College, and the presidency of the Asiatic Society founded by the better-known Orientalist, Sir William Jones. In a letter he wrote in 1794, Colebrooke attributed his long absence from home to his judgment that Bengal was a "better country to reside" than an England in the throes of Europe's revolutionary wars, which he deemed no place for "a son of liberty to live in." He was certain that "no Calcutta jury would send a man to Botany Bay, for speaking what is demonstratively true." If he had to leave Bengal for health reasons, it was to America that he would emigrate. He had bought land there and intended to invest future savings in American funds, although according his son he later lost faith in the US government and withdrew whatever nest egg he had accumulated across the Atlantic.[48]

Colebrooke biographers Rosane Rocher and Ludo Rocher credit their subject with having created a "database" and setting "methodological standards for a western discipline of Indology on the verge of professionalization and academicization." Driven at least partly by the practical dictates of his civil service, he "went to school with the Brahmins," according to Thomas R. Trautmann, and "engaged with Indian philology as a living tradition." He was said to have translated a "copious digest of Hindu law," a project launched on "the model of Justinian's Pandects" by Judge William Jones of the Calcutta high court, who did not live to complete it.[49] We must remember, however, that Colebrooke's portrait of slavery in South Asia, while influenced by the textual expositions of local pundits and imams, took pragmatic account of company interests. These worked their way into his response to the pressures of Atlantic antislavery on British policy in India. The passage of slave trade abolition in the Atlantic coincided with Colebrooke's rise to the pinnacle of his career as a key member of the supreme council of Bengal. He had the ear of Governor-General Minto, who appointed him both chief judge of the superior court and president of the revenue board.[50] He was thus well positioned to articulate the EIC's official story about Indian slavery. It was one that antagonists in the

Atlantic world's slavery debates would use selectively to champion their respective causes.

In 1812, Colebrooke authored a "Minute" titled "On the Operation of the Act for Prohibiting the Slave Trade, in India, and the State of Slavery in That Country." This document did not enter the colonial government's official records until the revival of the slavery question in December 1826, but did appear in the *Analysis of the Laws and Regulations of the Fort William Government in Bengal* published between 1805 and 1817 by John H. Harington, chief judge of the Sadr Diwani Adalat.[51] This work, available in local libraries, introduced bureaucrats such as a revenue collector in Surat on the west coast and the Scottish-American abolitionist William Adam in Calcutta to Colebrooke's portrait of slavery in India. Adam, in turn, would publish Colebrooke's version of "Slavery in the East" in an appendix to his 1840 critique of British policy on Indian slavery, which, together with Harington's *Analysis,* would serve as crucial sources for accounts of comparative slavery by Americans on all sides of the political spectrum in the nineteenth century.[52]

Colebrooke's Minute began by taking the broad scope of the Abolition Act as a new context for reviewing not simply the laws of slavery in India but also the "manners and feelings of the people" on a subject utterly "blended with their domestic habits." The exposition all but contained a spoiler alert at the outset: Colebrooke was about to make a case for "slavery in the East" that justified his counsel that metropolitan authorities weigh local circumstances with "tenderness and delicacy" while legislating for the colonies in British Asia. The principle of legal pluralism, together with what we might recognize as Orientalist constructions of an Indian worldview immune to historical change, structured his portrayal of bondage there.

Colebrooke adopted an analytical framework based on Atlantic categories of information about slavery to make a point about British Asian exceptionalism. The topics of law, honor, master-slave relations, emancipation, and division of labor between the household and the fields structured his discussions of the theory and practice of slavery in India. His sketch contrasted slavery in South Asia with what antislavery critics considered the most odious features of Atlantic slavery: the chattel principle, the sale of the enslaved away from their homes and their families, and the primacy of the profit incentive that underlay these atrocities. The structures and abuses of Atlantic slavery became the standard against which Colebrooke drew his portrait of South Asian difference.

Colebrooke's project sought to depict Indian forms of bondage as organic rather than foreign to South Asian societies. It began by drawing a sharp (although implicit) distinction with slave law in the Anglo-Atlantic world. Unlike the secular slave codes established by positive law in North America and the Caribbean, British Indian slaveries ostensibly enjoyed the sanction of two age-old religious traditions: the Hindu and the Muslim. First, who was, or became, a slave? Anglo-Atlantic lawmakers may have left the question of modes of enslavement murky, defining slave status primarily by reference to an identity construct that fused race (signifying power relations rationalized by physiognomy) with matrilineal descent ("Negro," born of an enslaved woman). By contrast, Colebrooke laid out Hindu law's exposition of a variety of different paths to slavery that blurred the boundaries between coercion and free will: "capture in war; voluntary submission to slavery [for different reasons including maintenance during famine]; involuntary, for the discharge of debt, or by way of punishment of specific offences; birth, as offspring of a female slave; gift, sale or transfer by a former owner; and sale, or gift of their offspring by parents." Muslim law likewise recognized slavery leading from the capture of infidels in war, or birth to a female slave. That recent contingencies had highlighted certain categories of slaves became clear from Colebrooke's observation that "some authorities have added, sale of their offspring by parents, in a dearth or famine."[53]

Colebrooke allowed that provisions governing power relations between masters and slaves bore similarities to their Atlantic counterparts. He read South Asian religious laws as endorsing the chattel principle in theory, with Hindu texts classifying slaves with "cattle, under the contemptuous designation of 'bipeds and quadrupeds'" and subjecting the slave's right of property, "even of his own acquisition" to "the indulgence of his master." A slave by birth or purchase had few options for emancipation except through voluntary manumission by the master. A slave who saved his master's life, could however, claim emancipation and "the portion of a son," while an enslaved woman who bore her master a child was entitled to "freedom" for herself as well her child. Furthermore, "temporary" slaves could revert to "free" status when the conditions of their enslavement disappeared: the discharge of a debt, or a master's promise of subsistence. Muslims on the other hand "strongly recommended" manumission as a "pious act," and conferred special privileges such as the right not to be sold, upon an enslaved concubine who bore her master's children: her "issue is free, and ranks with other illegitimate but acknowledged offspring of her master.[54]

Whatever the laws of slavery, it was practice that set British India apart from slave societies in the Atlantic world, according to Colebrooke, practice about which he drew generalized conclusions based on his observations of Bengal alone. Adopting Atlantic paradigms for understanding divisions of enslaved labor, he sought to establish the primacy of "domestic" over agricultural slavery among South Asian forms of bondage. "More trusty than hired servants, slaves almost exclusively are employed in the interior of the house for attendance on the members of the family, and in all the most confidential services." Every "opulent" person expected to own such bonded dependents. Concubines came from this group. Colebrooke added that concubinage did not carry a stain of immorality for Indians, and bore a "near and almost necessary connexion" with polygamy. Nor did household slavery impede the enslaved's rights to either marriage or proper childrearing as in the Atlantic, because masters, "out a sense of propriety," he asserted, arranged matches for their bondspeople. Moreover, Colebrooke argued that the ties of affection within the master's household promised a child who inherited the condition of her enslaved mother an upbringing filled with "indulgence."[55]

The most singular difference from Atlantic slavery in Colebrooke's image of South Asian forms of bondage was the absence of the profit incentive in determining the worth of human chattel. There existed "no urgent demand" or "brisk traffic" in this species of property. Indeed the most significant form of sale into bondage—one that dominated the colonial discourse of slavery in Asia and served as its most important rationale—was the transfer of children by destitute parents during famines and other circumstances of extreme want to guardians better able to care for them. The sums that exchanged hands in these transactions were "nominal," and driven not by "avarice" or "want of affection" on the part of the parents: "The known character of the people, and proved disposition in all the domestic relations, must exempt them from the suspicion of such conduct. But the pressure of want alone compels the sale...." Colebrooke went on to point out that as long as the state made no provision for the relief of the "indigent," this system would have to function in effect as a survival strategy for the poor. He regarded only two groups of purchasers as objectionable in this regard: well-off Hindu religious orders that paid higher prices for recruits, incentivizing kidnappings; and courtesans who trained trafficked girls in the art of dancing. Both practices were geared toward community or kin incorporation and, in the British bureaucrat's judgment, hard to prohibit thanks to the importance of dancing to "their religious festivals and celebrations." Colebrooke contended that it was only in the upper provinces of Bengal Presidency—western Bihar and Benares—that "petty landholders" employed slaves as herdsmen and ploughmen to help them cultivate their land. More substantial landowners commanded "tenants" that the author represented as hereditary serfs who paid rents and other dues for the privilege of tilling the soil or grazing their cattle on pastures to which their masters held title. They were no different from other peasants, except for restrictions on their right to move.[56]

Colebrooke deemed the parliamentary act against the slave trade too harsh and sweeping in its application. Confining his analysis to Bengal, he underplayed the extent of any foreign trade in slaves. He estimated that only a hundred entered British Asia annually by sea from East Africa on Arab ships. Nepal was the chief source of slave imports by land, but here again, he blamed oppressive "Nepalese rulers" who drove people to sell themselves or their children into slavery. The once significant export of slaves from British territories to French Islands had dwindled. The judge gave voice to the consensus in the Bengal government on the reach of the slave trade abolition act enacted by Parliament: "we have considered its provisions to be limited to the trade by sea." He spoke for imperial officials who maintained that the law went further in Asia than it did in the Atlantic, for it made no exemption for the transfer of slaves from one part of the British Empire to another. By imposing penalties on any British subject, who might embark "at one port for another" within the subcontinent, a distant metropolitan power was in effect conflating the slave trade with practices of domestic slavery without warning or legislation to restrict these in the first place. Let local authorities regulate this traffic, he urged. For, "in this country, slaves are in general treated with gentleness. The slave is a favored and confidential servant, rather than an abject drudge, and is as often held superior to the hireling in his master's estimation and his own, as placed beneath him in the scale of employment and comforts. The mildness and equanimity of the Indian's temper (or his apathy and slowness, if this better describes the general disposition of the people) contribute to ensure good treatment of the slave." What he advocated instead was ameliorative reform under colonial auspices.[57]

In 1812, the same year that Colebrooke wrote his Minute, the Nizamat Adalat lent sanction to his "restrained" reading of the slave trade abolition law's scope. That judicial authority instructed the magistrate of the district of Agra, south of Delhi in northern India, that the import of slaves was illegal only if the intent of such action was sale or some other form of disposition. In other words, it upheld the practice of slavery itself, distinguishing it from human trafficking for profit. With the approval of the governor general in council, the court institutionalized this reading of the law in a circular order in October 1814, thus establishing the template for company policy through the 1820s.[58]

RELIGIOUS LAW, POVERTY, AND THE MARKET: SLAVERY BY "FREE WILL"

Colebrooke's rosy portrait of the slave's lot in India did not go unchallenged. The pressures of abolitionist challenges abroad powered the voices of dissenting bureaucrats in South Asia, persuaded at least in part by subaltern appeals to the police and colonial courts. We follow the story of those pressures from below in part 3 of this book. For now, suffice it to note that they spurred within company circles a discussion of proposals for gradual emancipation and ameliorative reform. Couched in the language of "personal freedom," suggestions for reform reflected the influence of Atlantic antislavery, and evoked contemporaneous developments in an early republican United States emerging from its revolution somewhat half free. Counterarguments against slavery in early nineteenth-century colonial India would also serve in the 1830s and 1840s as the basis for Anglo-American abolitionist critiques of Colebrooke's defense of slavery in British India.

As early as 1808–9, the Bundelkhand judge Richardson had proposed a plan of gradual emancipation that echoed similar enactments in the emerging free societies of North America. Moreover, he offered a legislative and judicial strategy to severely limit colonial sanction of Indian forms of bondage within the traditional framework of legal pluralism. It consisted in jettisoning Hindu laws of slavery on the grounds that these had long been "dormant" under Muslim rule. He proposed that all disputes concerning slavery be governed only by the "strict provisions of the Mahomedan law," as long as at least one side in such cases identified as Muslim, on the grounds that such law served already as the "established system enforced by our criminal courts." If adopted, the text of these laws—allowing mostly for the enslavement of "infidels" captured in war, would have nullified most master-slave relationships. Richardson invoked the language of "justice," "spreading the blessings of personal freedom," and "increasing the stock of human happiness" as the basis for his suggested regulations.[59]

The government took no action on Richardson's suggested reforms, until antislavery pressures combined with reports before the court forced the issue of slavery into the government's deliberations. These reports suggested that "frequent irregularities had been practiced in the acquisition of slaves" and that female slaves in particular suffered "cruel" and "immoral" treatment. Chief Judge Harington, who had formerly served as a Persian translator in the Revenue Department, now seized the moment to address Richardson's proposal in his own Minute, and to draft a set of regulations based on the advice of Hindu and Muslim law experts, for the guidance of courts deciding slavery cases. The themes of slavery's function as "poor law"—that is, a mode of subsistence granted to the poor—rather than a profit-oriented mode of commerce, and the ostensible "mildness" of Indian masters, would supply thematic refrains linking Colebrooke through Harington to commissioners appointed to compile a report on Indian slavery in the age of West Indian emancipation and Anglo-Atlantic poor law reform in the 1830s and early 1840s.[60]

Harington agreed that slavery cases ought to be decided by "the courts of circuit" because, like Richardson, he saw them primarily as involving the "right of personal freedom." Revealing that alleged slaves frequently defied their owners, he noted that civil suits against masters took too long to resolve, depriving such defendants of their dependents' services even as the masters incurred the costs of subsistence and legal challenges without the prospect of reimbursement. But the chief judge rejected Richardson's suggestion of annulling Hindu laws of slavery on the grounds of precedent and religious freedom: the 1772 regulation and a subsequent ruling by the Diwani Adaulat had placed slavery within the purview of dual Hindu and Muslim legal systems, and more recent parliamentary guarantees of the "free exercise of religion" in the colonies implied the religious freedom to hold slaves. He saw the actual existence of slaveholding by Hindus when the British arrived as contradicting the notion that Muslim rulers had abrogated Hindu laws of slavery.[61] The rhetoric of religious freedom to hold slaves, however, masked very practical considerations. Among them were deference to colonized elites and, perhaps even more important, the problem of poverty.

The age of emancipation coincided with shifts in Anglo-Atlantic thinking about poverty and poor relief within free societies in the throes of transformation wrought by market revolution and industrial capitalism. We will draw out the implications of these developments for the discourse of slavery as "poor law" in some detail in the next section. For now, we turn to colonial attempts to fit South Asian forms of bondage into the contractual frameworks that drove market societies in the Atlantic world. Interpreters of South Asian religious laws of slavery, local bureaucrats, and reporters from the field chronicled the widespread practice of distress sales by adults of themselves and their children during famines or other moments of material crisis, in return for subsistence. Amid discussions of gradual abolition and amelioration in 1817, Bengal's judicial authorities proposed allowing such sales to continue, as long as they limited terms of service to specified periods—long enough to "indemnify the purchase without subjecting their descendants to perpetual slavery."[62]

In his Minute recorded the following year, Judge Harington proposed to bridge the gap between slavery and free will by transforming the self-sale or the sale of children by destitute parents into the freedom to make contracts. He argued that "voluntary contracts of hire and service" forged by competent adults, "whether for a limited period or for life," and whether in exchange for "wages or maintenance," were compatible with Blackstone's laws of England. The institutionalization and regulation of distress sales would convert "the Hindu practice of voluntary subjection to slavery, in times of famine or scarcity," into "a condition more favorable to the servant and his family." Parents could reserve the right to contract for the "support and service" of minor children under the age of fifteen who might otherwise "perish," on condition that such children become free at the age of twenty-five. He recommended semantic changes to describe the statuses that would result: parents and children bound to service under such contracts would be designated "hired servants" rather than "slaves," and the children born to people who had signed themselves into servitude would not inherit their servile condition.[63]

A proposed Regulation for the guidance of courts ruling on slavery that accompanied Harington's Minute added a gradual emancipation provision for the children of female slaves, urging that those born after the promulgation of the regulation be set free at the age of twenty-five. Building on earlier proposals presented to the court, he recommended that magistrates maintain two separate registers, "one of ascertained slaves, the other of hirelings whose services may have been engaged, on a stipulation of wages or maintenance, either for life or for a limited period exceeding three years."[64] By conflating agreements for service in perpetuity with indentures that carried expiration dates, Harington was in effect blurring the boundaries between slavery and free markets for labor, all anchored in the exigencies of poverty. Informal structures of dependence would thus be codified into formal contractual relations of master and slave. As the judge saw it, such covenants would represent not a fate consigned to hereditary slavery but rather the outcome of rational, individual choice. Customary traditions of dependence would assume the capitalist cast of contractual obligation by both master and slave.

In this context, we may well ask: Did Harington's reluctance to abandon Hindu laws of slavery, as Richardson had suggested, stem at least partly from his understanding of that tradition's accommodation of "voluntary slavery" arising out of poverty or other circumstances, compared with its Islamic counterpart? In other words, did Hindu laws of slavery, as the British understood them, open up the possibility of reconciling slavery with the "freedom" to make contracts for self-sale in ways that strict interpretations of Muslim law did not?

Consider for instance, the fact that the high court's consultations with Muslim law officers yielded the conclusion that while parents were allowed to hire out their children, "this contract becomes null and void when the child arrives at the years of discretion, as the right of parentage then ceases." A free adult, however, had the right to sign on to lengthy terms of indenture like seventy years.[65]

By contrast, of the fifteen categories of slaves enumerated by Hindu experts drawing upon the lawgiver Narada, which became part of colonial knowledge production about slavery, several involved some measure of free will, including persons who sold or mortgaged themselves for stipulated periods in times of famine, in exchange for food or some other "price," in order to discharge a debt, or as "condition of marriage with a slave girl." Other classes of "voluntary" slaves included "a Brahmin relinquishing a state of religious mendicancy" and "an apostate mendicant."[66] This catalog appeared to lend colonial rationales for slavery as a form of poor law, the weight of not merely custom but religious law under the system of legal pluralism. It offered a basis for infusing ancient Hindu codes with a market-oriented spirit of consent and contract.

The aspect of dependent relations that these discussions about amelioration missed, however, was affect—their nonmonetary social functions highlighted by scholars of South Asian slavery like Indrani Chatterjee. Thus, Harington's proposed regulation addressed questions that gave slavery meaning from an Atlantic perspective, among them what kind of work did slaves do? Were there limits to the master's power? The answers to such questions, entered into the public record as a basis for judicial decision making, nonetheless offered some basis for subordinate groups to challenge the grounds and terms of their subjection. Thus, Muslim legal experts opined that slaves—whether male or female—owed their masters service only to the "extent of their power and ability" in the areas of personal service and household chores, farmwork, clerical and mercantile tasks, artisanry, and concubinage. Patron-client relationships, as well as public and military service, which had historically conferred great power on certain categories of human chattel in Islamic states, were conspicuous by their absence in the list reproduced by Harington. Rather, his informers focused on the right of masters to employ or hire out slaves to engage "in baking and cooking; in making, dyeing and washing clothes; as agents in mercantile transactions; in attending cattle, in tillage or cultivation; as carpenters, ironmongers and goldsmiths; in transcribing; as weavers, and in manufacturing woolen cloths; as shoemakers, boatmen, twisters of silk or water drawers; in shaving; in performing surgical operations, such as cupping; and as farriers, bricklayers and the like." Within the household, slaves might perform for their masters the intimate services of valet or concubine: "anointing his body with oil, rubbing his feet, in attending his person while dressing, and in guarding the door of his house; [the master] may also have connexion with his legal female slave, provided she has arrived at the years of maturity, and the master has not previously given her in marriage to another." The Hindu law interpreters upheld the right of masters to compel their slaves to perform "impure" work, "such as [plastering] and sweeping the house, rubbing his master's naked body with oil, and clothing him, removing fragments of victuals left at his master's table and eating them, removing urine and human ordure, rubbing his master's feet."[67]

The regulation accompanying Harington's Minute also included law experts' interpretations of checks and balances on the master's power. Colonial officials drew on these accounts to make a case for the "mildness" of South Asian slaveries, especially in the face of abolitionist challenges during the 1830s and 1840s. Indian Muslim legal experts were reported to have advised that God, acting through a ruling authority, restrained the master's sovereignty over his slave: "If a master oppress his slave by employing him in any duty beyond his power and ability, such as insisting on his carrying a load which he is incapable of bearing, or climbing a tree which he cannot, the hakim, or ruling power, may chastise him; it is also improper for a master to order his slave to do that which is forbidden by the law, such as putting an innocent person to death, setting fire to a house or tearing the clothes of another, or to prostitute himself by adultery and fornication, to steal or drink spirits, or to slander and abuse the chaste and virtuous; and if a master be guilty of such like oppressions, the hakim may inflict exemplary punishment (literally by the right of God ... on principles of public justice)." But even more than Muslim law, it was Hindu lawgivers' admonitions that EIC apologists would showcase during Anglo-American slavery debates, as an illustration of the ostensibly familial nature of slavery in the East. Thus, the lawgiver Manu was interpreted to have enjoined masters of disobedient slaves from doing no more than to "beat his slave with a thick stick, or to bind him with a rope." More severe punishment consisted in having the master "pull his hair, or expose him upon an ass; but if the master should exceed the extent of his authority, he is liable to pay a fine to the ... ruling power."[68]

Still, Harington, sensitive to the demands of keeping up the reputation of imperial abolition at home and abroad, also proposed to codify protections for South Asian slaves in ways not afforded by Hindu and Muslim law. He recommended that in cases of contest over the claims of a master to human property, that the master assume the burden of proving his alleged chattel's enslaved status, and that evidence of "cruel" or "immoral" treatment be deemed grounds for emancipation. His regulation anticipated some provisions of the future 1843 act to "delegalize" slavery in India, by recommending the abrogation of Muslim law's exemption from capital punishment of masters convicted of the "willful" murder of their slaves and by urging that crimes against slaves carry the same penalties as those against free persons.[69]

Harington's departure for Europe on account of health buried his regulation until 1823. That year, an antislavery chief judge, William Leycester, who had already established a reputation for defying decorum and challenging the corporation he served, recorded a Minute denouncing the march of slavery under the aegis of British colonialism. Deploying the language of Atlantic abolitionism structured around the principles of liberal individualism, the natural equality of men, and the moral polarities of slavery and freedom, as well as person and property, he leveled a scathing indictment that accused colonial administrators of expanding the geographical reach and institutional support of various forms of bondage. Why, he asked, did an ostensibly anti-slave-trade empire confine its objections to slave trafficking by sea? He maintained that the boundaries between the slave trade and slavery were meaningless because British "protection" had assumed the "peculiar property of branding nations with slavery, who were protected from it before." Successive cessions of native states spread the "taint" of a "detestable traffic" in human beings: "as Nepaul [sic] was conquered, and the Mahratta combination annihilated, each act of sovereignty carried with it a secret clause—'You may now, your wives and children, be removed into Bengal as slaves; and, at the caprice of a slave-master be separated through sale and removed to any remote corner of the province boasting the enjoyment of British protection.'" Leycester's damning portrait of slaves being "lotted and sold at outcry in Calcutta" recalled the horrors of the Atlantic auction block. His reference to slave sales by the colonial state to liquidate a "balance of revenue" or satisfy a judicial decree raised the specter of new forms of bondage under imperialism. Moreover, he undercut the rationale of legal pluralism for accommodating bondage in South Asia by noting that "there can hardly be a legal Mahomedan slave, unless the free spirit of an English Legislature legalize it." Nor did respect for Hindu religious ordinances require tolerating "the vices of their civil policy." Antiquity offered no justification for taking "two equal men" and degrading both by recognizing one as the slave of the other, turning master into a "brute," and "reducing the slave to the level of an instinctive animal."[70]

It was in this context of an internal challenge to the rhetoric of imperial abolition that counterreformists within the East India Company recovered Colebrooke's testimony and channeled the focus of the discussion upon domestic slavery. When Harington returned to India, he sought in 1826 to revive discussion of the regulation he had proposed in 1818 by authorizing circuit court magistrates and revenue collectors to ascertain the relative extent of "domestic" versus "husbandry"-oriented slavery and to seek the opinion of local elites on his draft reforms. But Governor General William Amherst suspended that exercise, preaching restraint in

Colebrooke's name: "it appears to me impossible to doubt that Mr. Colebrooke would have been adverse to any further proceeding on this subject."[71] Thus it was that Colebrooke's Minute, making a case for a distinctive Slavery in the East, entered the official EIC records and was submitted to their board in London. Through this channel it would, along with Harington's *Analysis,* travel across the Atlantic to supply fodder for opposing arguments in comparative slavery discourses.

A key forum for publicizing the colonial state's stance—from Colebrooke through Amherst—of caution against interfering with what they cast as India's distinctive domestic slavery was about to unfold in Parliament in 1833. That year, the East India Company applied for a renewal of its expiring charter, about the same time that British lawmakers were deliberating on a bill for West Indian emancipation. These developments thrust the problem of slavery in the East onto the agenda of legislative debate. Thomas Babington Macaulay, a Whig lawyer with antislavery connections recently elected to Parliament and a future member of the advisory Council of India, joined other speakers in arguing against hasty action on systems of bondage about which Europeans knew little.[72]

And so it happened that Atlantic developments meshed with imperial interests on the ground in British Asia to muddy the construct of an antislavery empire defined against America's new republic of slavery. Colonial administrators rationalized that slavery in the East was inherently and invariably different from the horrors of Atlantic-style chattel bondage. Colonial conventions of plural laws propped up domestic slavery as expediency demanded, even as administrators proposed to formalize customary relations of dependence into contractual obligations of service. Yet colonial constructs of proslavery Orientalism did not go unchallenged. Dissent within the ranks of the EIC offered material for fashioning devastating critiques of British imperial claims to the "moral capital" of antislavery by both internationalist abolitionists and defenders of American slavery in the Atlantic world. Let us turn the page to revisit one side of that controversy—a worldwide web of reform activists who championed an array of subaltern causes across the borders of nation and empire from South Asia through the British Isles to North America.

2

Human Rights from Calcutta through London to Boston

> *[The] very same objections which are urged ... here against meddling with the subject of slavery, are relied upon [in India] and are brought forward with the same gravity against doing anything for the relief of the oppressed—a circumstance which may serve to show that in both countries it is rather the will than the power, that is wanting.*
> —THE LIBERATOR, 7 AUGUST 1840, IN A REVIEW OF WILLIAM ADAM, THE LAW AND CUSTOM OF SLAVERY IN BRITISH INDIA

A heady celebration to mark Caribbean emancipation was under way in Northampton, Massachusetts, on 1 August 1843. The town was home to an interracial utopian community known as the Northampton Association that boasted among its members the celebrated Black abolitionists David Ruggles and Sojourner Truth. For one of the community's architects—a transoceanic abolitionist, Unitarian minister, former Harvard professor of Oriental literature, and one-time Calcutta resident named William Adam—the jubilee on Emancipation Day had to have carried a new layer of significance. Mere months before, the British Parliament had "delegalized" slavery in India—a watered-down version of the abolitionist object that Adam had campaigned hard to achieve, by lecturing, writing a book, and helping to found an intercontinental voluntary association known as the British India Society (BIS). The reformist strands that forged the BIS ran back to a transnational web of humanitarian activism targeting despotism from the plains of Bengal through Europe to the American South. The causes they inspired included the twin goals of ending imperial abuses in India through parliamentary reform and ending slavery in the American South by promoting free-grown export staples in British India. From the perspective of "subaltern" South Asia, the years following the 1843 Indian Slavery Act would see little more than the accomplishment of what the historian Indrani Chatterjee has called "abolition by denial."[1]

Before we trace the transoceanic paths of activism that culminated in a British Indian incarnation of slavery's abolition, let us linger for a moment on the spirit of optimism on display that early fall day in early 1840s Northampton. To those assembled, the worldwide march against slavery appeared to have gathered stride. Inside the capacious First Congregational meeting house, the event opened with what the American Antislavery Society founder, William Lloyd Garrison, described as "the members of the Industrial Community" attending "*en masse,* in true abolition style." The Black Underground Railroad operator from New York, David Ruggles, took the chair. The speakers' roster included Stephen Rush, "a fugitive from the land of chains, whips and bowie knives," who said that he had been inspired to seek his freedom by the story of George Latimer, whom Massachusetts had sheltered, but also "from hearing his master ... cursing the abolitionists, of whom he formed a high opinion from that circumstance." But before Rush spoke, William Adam took the stage to deliver "the leading features of the anti-slavery movement in England, and the glorious results of West India emancipation."[2]

Adam's address, reprinted widely in abolitionist outlets, framed the movement against slavery in terms of a global struggle for human rights that transcended the peculiar circumstances or interests of any one nation. The themes of Christian morality, the virtues of free labor and its corollary of inexorable progress, and the opportunity to transform slaves into loyal citizens—from likely enemies of nation and empire into their most vigilant defenders—structured Adam's case against slavery. His survey of freedom's "providential stride" represented Caribbean emancipation as but one act in an inevitable drama of moral advance unfolding across the world, proceeding from the Somerset case to British antislavery in India and Russian action against "serfage" [*sic*]. Even America was "at last, beginning to open her eyes to the fact that she is a world's wonder, not for her liberty, but for her *slavery.*" He urged that the trembling slaveholders of "Brazil ... Cuba, and ... the southern States of this Union, [who clung] with maniac grasp to the monster that [was] eating out their vitals," be treated with "uncompromising firmness, due to unreasonable patients." Turning to Caribbean emancipation, Adam listed its benefits: a rise in the "spirit of enterprise," social mobility, the cultivation of "a new staple" (silk) in Jamaica, and the advent of steam power in the colonies. Above all, in what we may read as simultaneous appeals to British colonial nationalism, the defense interests of North American free states, and a play on the specter of race war, he noted that abolition had transformed "eight hundred thousand slaves" into "free, loyal ... subjects ... of the crown of England, which has made them men, and willing, if necessary, to fight *a l'outrance* against all slaveholding republics." American compromise with slavery, by contrast, risked engulfing the land in "a universal and destructive conflagration."[3]

The following year, in line with the spirit of worldwide solidarity on freedom's behalf, the Unitarian minister Samuel May of Boston received from John Bishop Estlin of Bristol "relics" for sale at a Massachusetts Anti-Slavery fair. Originating two oceans away, these consisted of locks of hair belonging to William Adam's friend, that iconic symbol of "colonial modernity" in India, the Bengali Brahman reformer Raja Rammohun Roy, who had died during a visit to England over ten years ago.[4] An announcement of the fair in the Garrisonian abolitionist newspaper the *Liberator* classified this donation of Roy's locks as a "curiosity" along with other items like samples of the late Jeremy Bentham's hair, a Moorish musical instrument, and a "Japan sealing wax box."[5]

These artifacts represented the transoceanic networks of activism within which Adam had honed his global vision of slavery's abolition. Known in abolitionist circles from Dublin to Boston as a "fast friend of Garrison ... George Thompson, Wendell Phillips, and other worthies of that class,"[6] this one-time Baptist missionary-turned-Unitarian wove his reformist outlook from cultural and political threads that ran back to what Lynn Zastoupil has described as antiestablishment impulses to modernize Britain and its empire in the early nineteenth century. Associated particularly with the Unitarians, these tendencies inspired transnational movements to abolish slavery, advance the rights of women, and promote Catholic emancipation, among other causes.[7] In the 1820s and 1830s, reform circles that shaped these campaigns intersected with the architects of what the historian Christopher A. Bayly described as "an ideological challenge to the 'despotism' of the Court of Directors of the East India Company as the epitome of metropolitan Toryism and a classic form of the 'old corruption.'" Consisting of British radicals and western-educated Indians, many of whom communed in what Clare Midgley has characterized as the utopian –inflected "cosmotopia" of the Calcutta Unitarian Committee, these critics forged an international public sphere defined by devotion to constitutional liberalism and human rights.[8] Their ascendancy coincided with an era of what Richard Huzzey has described as "antislavery pluralism," when opposition to slavery was no longer channeled through just one national organization.[9]

At the hub of this reform complex in Calcutta stood the legendary Brahman renegade Raja Rammohun Roy, whose rejection of Hindu polytheism and Christian Trinitarianism, priestcraft, and the claims of revelation, performed—as Andrew Sartori has noted—an ideological function similar to that of British anticlerical liberalism's quest for freedom of conscience, and the individual pursuit of rational self-interest.[10] These strands of thinking were on display on the banks of the River Hooghly in Calcutta at an event in 1822, where guests from Lisbon and Brazil joined British journalists and Indian reformers to commemorate the proclamation of constitutional government in Portugal two years before. The gathering toasted liberal revolutions by Iberians, Greeks, and serfs against all manner of autocrats—"the Bourbons to the Ottomans and the Tsars"—along with the mercantile imperialists of the EIC. Through travel, correspondence and print culture, notions of constitutional liberalism would share collaborative space with parliamentary reform, regulation of the EIC's monopoly, Catholic and Jewish

FIGURE 1. Rembrandt Peale (American, 1778–1860), *Raja Rammohun Roy*, 1833, oil on canvas, 30 × 25 inches (76.2 × 63.5 cm). Museum purchase, 1999, 137982, courtesy of the Peabody Essex Museum, Salem, Massachusetts.

emancipation, and the institution of a free press everywhere from the metropole to the colonies in order to keep governments accountable to the governed.[11]

From these overlapping networks of antiestablishment activists, religious radicals, and constitutional liberals, strung together by technological advances like steam printing presses and the telegraph, would spring the reform impulses that in subsequent decades merged the slave's cause in North America with the plight of the colonized in British India. Over these impulses loomed the spirit of Roy, who collaborated with transatlantic critics of slavery and champions of women's rights—however fleetingly—before his premature death in 1833 on the eve of a visit to Boston. His friend Adam, who strode into the American public sphere through the academic halls of Harvard in 1838, would help inject debates over empire and enslavement directly into antebellum America's sectional arguments. It is time, then, to turn the clock back to the second decade of the nineteenth century, when the worlds of Roy and Adam converged.

WHEN RAMMOHUN ROY MET WILLIAM ADAM

The Scottish-born Adam chose professional paths that placed him on a collision course with the East India Company from the start. He launched the Indian phase of his career as a Baptist missionary in the Dutch settlement of Serampore.[12] It was a forbidding milieu, where EIC officials maltreated English dissenters and Christianity held little sway.[13] Still, when the Scotsman first arrived in 1818, hope glimmered on the horizon. The evangelicals had identified a prime target of conversion, described in the Baptist *Periodical Account* as "Rama-Mohuna-Raya, a ... rich ... Brahmun of Calcutta ... a respectable Sanskrit-scholar ... well-versed in Persian ...; he also writes English with correctness, and reads with ease English Mathematical and metaphysical works."[14]

Twenty-four years older than Adam, Roy had been born into a landholding Bengali Brahman family, served as a banker to Europeans, invested in real estate, associated with British free traders, and interacted with religious radicals who influenced his approach to social and religious reform. As Sartori and Bayly have illustrated, Roy fashioned a creed of liberal egalitarianism out of ideas contained in the *Advaita Vedanta*. His creed could be used to support a host of causes defining transoceanic "benevolent empires," from South Asia through Britain to the United States: from antislavery and women's rights, to freedom of conscience, a free press, and parliamentary reform. Indeed, Roy attracted attention on both sides of the Atlantic through his promotion of women's education and the abolition of *sati*. He grounded this advocacy in a challenge to the scriptural authorities that seemed to have established roots in British Indian–style legal pluralism and have influenced colonial bureaucrats' reluctance to legislate against the practice. The newspapers he started publicized these challenges and channeled them into Atlantic media of exchange.[15]

Roy's critique of orthodox practices within his own Bengali Hindu community persuaded the Serampore Baptists that he was amenable to conversion. To their disappointment, however, his reading of Judeo-Christian texts in Greek and Hebrew led him to reject the dogmas of original sin and atonement and the notion of Jesus's divinity. During a project to translate the Gospels into Bengali, Roy interpreted the Greek preposition *dia* that occurred in the fourth Gospel as "all things were made *through* [rather than *by*] him." The interfaith discussions that followed cemented Adam's own growing skepticism about Trinitarianism. The "heathen" had, alas, created a "heretic," whom evangelical colleagues would lament as "the second fallen Adam."[16]

Adam and Roy grew close. They collaborated to form the Calcutta Unitarian committee in 1821, which launched a press and library and sponsored worship services led by Adam.[17] Roy's religious writings attracted attention among Atlantic reformers. Boston-based Unitarians like Henry Ware and William Ellery Channing founded the Society for the Promotion of Christianity in India in 1825, with the Christian abolitionist merchant Lewis Tappan serving as its treasurer and Adam as their paid agent in India.[18] Meanwhile, in 1828 Roy established the Brahmo Samaj, grounded in reformist interpretations of his own cultural heritage, leading American Unitarians to think of him as a "Hindu Unitarian."[19]

CROSSING THE BORDERS OF ANTISLAVERY BY LAND AND WATER

Despite their divergence on the subject of conversion to Christianity, Adam and Roy continued to share a common commitment to liberal reform that drew them into the defining human rights movement of their era: the abolition of slavery. American Unitarians like the gradual emancipationist editor of the *Christian Register*, David Reed, publicized Roy's rejection of *sati* and polygamy and his support of widows' inheritance rights based on his progressive interpretation of Vedic texts and Hindu law.[20] A nascent print culture that was displacing older traditions of oral arguments and manuscript circulation integrated South Asia into a transnational public sphere within which Unitarian reformers, liberal journalists, and evangelical missionaries disseminated Roy's essays and pamphlets on the *Vedanta* and social reform. Anglo-Atlantic periodicals recycled these, magnifying their impact by publishing the reviews and commentaries the writings inspired. Such channels of circulation introduced slavery critics like Ralph Waldo Emerson and later Henry David Thoreau to Indian philosophy via Roy's writings, among other sources, including of course, Colebrooke.[21]

Lata Mani's account of the debate on *sati* in colonial India makes it clear that Protestant clergy saw in Roy's critiques of Brahmanical orthodoxy a perfect opportunity to advance their proselytizing purposes. Zaspoutil has argued that Roy's writings also struck a chord with early Atlantic feminists, who entered the public sphere as "fundraisers, missionaries, and petitioners," to lobby against *sati*. Roy's denunciation of the crushing burdens of domestic drudgery and lack of educational opportunities for Bengali women resonated with early Western feminists accustomed to using the metaphor of "slavery" to decry women's limited options outside marriage and their lack of access to learning or property rights.[22]

In 1829—the same year that Roy and his *Brahmo Samaj* marked a significant legislative victory with the abolition of *sati* in India—the Boston Black civil rights activist David Walker invoked the specter of a bloody revolution for freedom in North America with the publication of his *Appeal to the Colored Citizens of the World*. His pamphlet appeared in the American South's slave quarters, spirited there by sailors of African descent plying the subversive waters of the Atlantic. By now, the American Colonization Society's policy of gradual emancipation with compensation for slaveholders and deportation to Liberia of ex-slaves was in tatters. Even as aspiring strivers of the master class dreamed of continental expansion, and even discussed the reopening of the international slave trade, an ostensibly loyal Virginia slave named Nat Turner led his people in a war of vengeance against Southampton's plantation regime in August 1831. A few months later, across the water in the British colony of Jamaica, another Black (Baptist) preacher named Samuel Sharpe ushered in the Christmas season with a massive slave rebellion unparalleled in the history of the British Caribbean. Blood and fire unleashed by the enslaved, followed by brutal reprisals, helped provoke massive public demonstrations, private correspondence, and parliamentary testimonies in London. These developments steered Parliament in 1833 toward the enactment of British Caribbean emancipation, deferred by a period of apprenticeship and accompanied by the payment of a hefty compensation to slaveholders. Recall that the same Whig government that accomplished the end of slavery in the Anglophone West Indies postponed action on servitude in British India on the plea that precipitate action would unleash local retaliation against British rule by offending indigenous customs and law. Notwithstanding this prevarication, public debate over slavery in India had now entered the horizons of Anglo-Atlantic reformers.

Larger Atlantic contexts of Black protest—from the Haitian Revolution to civil rights activism in North America—shaped nineteenth-century Anglo-American abolition. The African American press, spearheaded by the publication of the New York–based *Freedom's Journal* and voluntary associations like the Boston-based General Colored Association, set precedents for the rise of interracial immediatism.[23] Meanwhile, a new generation of white Americans, born in states that had emerged free through court or legislative action during and after the American Revolution, trod the path blazed by African-descended rebels against the terror of enslavement. Following Caribbean emancipation, interracial abolitionists sought to build pressure against the only slave society remaining in the Anglophone western hemisphere: the American South. The activist space they fashioned would, in the course of the antebellum era, come to be woven with widely disparate threads of appeal against slavery. William Lloyd Garrison's American Anti-slavery Society denounced slavery on moral and humanitarian grounds; advocated the immediate, unconditional, uncompensated (to slaveholders), and universal abolition of slavery; and excoriated the deportation of freed slaves from the land of their birth and labor. Meanwhile, evangelical abolitionists—women and men— reared in the millennial tradition of the Second Great Awakening, rooted their opposition to human property in a theology that emphasized free will, perfectionism, and disinterested benevolence, making the second coming of Christ contingent on the removal of social sins—the worst of which was slavery. When, in due course, antislavery entered politics, Jacksonian Free-Soilers championed equal access to western lands against the imperial designs of a monopolistic Slave Power. On the other hand, "free labor" Republicans, who ultimately proved more successful at the ballot box, defined freedom more modestly, as an individual's right to own themselves, and to sell their services in a free market for labor.[24]

And throughout this period, from the 1830s through the eve of the Civil War, reformers linked the cause of antislavery with free speech. As Joanne Freeman has pointed out, pro-Southern interests tried to suppress the "dangerous words" of slavery's critics with violence, invoking common law doctrines that allegedly gave the state power to curb individual liberty for common welfare.[25] Abandoned by the Supreme Court, which in 1833 held that the Bill of Rights did not apply to state or local governments, abolitionist newspapers suffered the violence of mobs who represented these publications as a public nuisance because they would supposedly provoke slave revolts, threaten the Constitutional right to hold slave property, and disrupt commerce.[26] Historians have long known that northern "gentlemen of property and standing," with great stake in the political economy of slavery, often instigated such mob action.[27] As early as 1837, the abolitionist editor Elijah Lovejoy died defending his press from a proslavery mob in Alton, Illinois. The following year, antiabolitionist hordes torched Philadelphia's Pennsylvania Hall, where a daughter of South Carolina, the antislavery feminist Angelina Grimke, thundered against her own section's "domestic institution." Against judicial doctrine that provided cover for these acts of mob violence and underpinned state power to suppress challenges to slavery—whether through the tabling of antislavery petitions in Congress or censoring abolitionist mail in slave states—antislavery publics were advancing alternative popular understandings of civil liberties. They were depicting free speech as a national right upheld by the federal constitution not through the courts but via public channels: lecture halls, novels and newspapers, petitions to legislatures, and private conversations around their dining tables.[28] Moreover, these channels extended overseas, connecting interoceanic publics through advances in shipping, the telegraph, and print technology.

The nonconformist worlds of Adam and Roy served as overseas nodes in these networks of transnational exchange, promoting individual freedom and human rights through avenues outside formal institutions of state and courts. Fourteen years before Lovejoy achieved abolitionist martyrdom in Illinois, the causes of press freedom and slavery intersected in a pioneer newspaper project within the Calcutta reform circles in which Adam and Roy circulated. It involved a radical English-language newspaper that died early, and a Cornish journalist and Roy associate named James Silk Buckingham. As a member of Parliament following his exile from India, this sojourner would supply evidence for tying the causes of colonial reform in India with slavery abolition in America. Buckingham served with Rammohun Roy as a coproprietor of the *Calcutta Journal*, which exchanged news items with Roy's Bengali newspapers.[29]

The scion of a seafaring family, Buckingham had sailed the Atlantic and the Mediterranean before arriving in the Indian Ocean world. A prolific travel writer, he recorded, among other things, his revulsion at slavery wherever he encountered it, from the "dismal coasts" of Norfolk, Virginia, to a Nubian "slave train of emasculated boys and cast-encased virgins" in Egypt. While living in India later as an independent mariner, he resigned his command of the trading vessel, the *Humayoon Shah*, when its owner, the Sultan of Zanzibar, allegedly ordered him to lead a slaving voyage to East Africa.[30] Buckingham moved into journalism instead, joining Roy in criticizing in the pages of the *Calcutta Journal* the monopolies imposed by the EIC, and advocating free trade.[31]

But the periodical's allegation in 1823 of the company's accommodation of the African slave trade in the heart of British India—a report that opened our narrative in the last chapter—may have proved to be the last straw. Company magistrates in Calcutta warned of the "injurious tendency" of the *Journal* article.[32] Buckingham was deported from India the same year. It is plausible that the piece's claims about manacled Africans in Calcutta exacerbated its publisher's enmity with local authorities, fueled by other articles critical of the EIC. Buckingham's close association with the irreverent Roy may also have colored the imperial government's heavy-handed handling of the Cornish journalist. Roy's papers had not only followed with sympathy the emergence of the Irish leader of Catholic emancipation, Daniel O'Connell, but raised more money from Indian readers, for the victims of the Irish famine in the early 1820s than Europeans had contributed. Amid these provocations, the Tory-aligned British Indian government not only exiled Buckingham from India but also imposed press censorship in South Asia until 1835.[33]

Back in England, Buckingham was not about to slink away in silence about his brushes with despotism in British Asia. He circulated Roy's position that a free press helped spread knowledge, promoted social progress, and alerted the government to public opinion. Elected to a reformed Parliament from Sheffield, he coupled his futile advocacy of immediate, uncompensated emancipation in the West Indies with arguments for the alleviation of colonial poverty in the East. During debate over the renewal of the EIC's charter in 1833, he protested that English rule had "reduced the natives" to states of misery more abject than "Egyptian bondage." Corporate colonialism burdened peasants with a decline in agricultural productivity, taxation to support a wasteful government, and monopolies to fund emoluments. The opium trade allegedly yielded a profit of one thousand percent, even as roads suffered from want of repair, mail moved at a speed of three miles an hour, and education languished. The Cornish journalist held Tories and Whigs alike complicit in shoring up a despotic Court of the Directors that functioned as "a daily parliament" for a country six thousand miles away. An "unrepresented country," India had been "invaded, ravaged, and devastated—all for 'filthy lucre and unholy gain.'"[34]

It was critiques of colonialism as virtual enslavement such as these that defenders of American slavery would seize to impugn as hypocritical, British abolition, which they conflated with the East India Company and the British government more generally. But scathing appraisals such as Buckingham's also breathed life into a corollary movement among liberal reformers on both sides of the Atlantic to join their Indian allies in marrying the cause of colonial reform in Asia with emancipation in the North Atlantic. Indeed, Buckingham played a central role in bringing Rammohan Roy to the attention of Britain's prominent Whig and reform spheres.[35]

In 1831, the same year that American abolitionist Garrison turbocharged interracial immediatism with the publication of the first issue of the *Liberator*, Roy alighted across the Atlantic at Liverpool to an impressive reception by the British press and dignitaries, from prominent reformers and intellectuals to King William. Zaspoutil has sketched a vivid portrait of the celebrity and curiosity that Roy commanded in Britain by this time—an account that leaves the impression that the Indian evoked a colonial mystique wrapped up in constructs at once exotic, exhibitionist, and familiar. The local press covered his train ride to Manchester, where large crowds turned out to see him. Curious bystanders gathered outside his London lodgings. Carriages laden with visitors waited in queue for an audience with him. Soirees hosted by Whig notables like the Marquesse of Lansdowne feted him. He met Fanny Kemble, the actor and future abolitionist wife of a Georgia slaveholder, in the London home of a mutual friend, the British lawyer and philanthropist Basil Montagu.[36] The future slave mistress and author of *Journal of a Residence on a Georgian Plantation* was reported to have commented that Roy's "picturesque dress and colour" made him "a remarkable object in a London ballroom."[37] The Indian visitor conversed about religion and politics with the utopian socialist Robert Owen, legendary slavery foes William Wilberforce and Lord Brougham, and the utilitarian philosopher John Stuart Mill. He debated phrenology with J. G. Spurzheim and prompted speculation among some contemporary students of science that brain size rather than climate shaped intellectual prowess and that skin color might not indicate racial difference. On a visit to London in 1833, the Philadelphia artist

Rembrandt Peale painted a portrait of Roy that the Boston Athenaeum subsequently acquired.[38]

In January 1832, the *Liberator* announced that Roy, whom it described as "the converted Brahmin," was expected to visit Boston, the epicenter of American abolitionism, in "May or June next."[39] By this time, the sensation from Calcutta had already become something of a shifting signifier for various causes across the political spectrum of reform in the United States. The most compelling of these was the use of his example by interracial progressives to challenge racial slavery and color prejudice. In the wake of Nat Turner's insurrection, as white Virginians from all over the Commonwealth blanketed its general assembly with petitions demanding gradual emancipation together with the colonization of African Americans, the *Liberator* published a piece countering notions of both white supremacy and Black deportation while promoting immediatism and equal rights. Titled "An Address to Congress," the essay was authored by an anonymous abolitionist who signed off as follows: "In closing this address, allow me to assume the name of one of the most enlightened and benevolent of the human race now living, though not a white man. Rammohun Roy." Prophesying that "future ages" would count the nation's "mixed population" as a "blessing" rather than a "tremendous curse," the writer argued that the "Northern hordes" who "poured into England" began to ascend the scale of civilization only when they shifted from warring to mating with other migrants like the more advanced Gauls and Flemings. The author attributed the "present superiority of the whites" to the "amalgamation ... of these different nations...." Having debunked the theory of white supremacy as an eternal fact of the ages, the pseudonymous "Rammohun Roy" went on to offer an antislavery reading of the US Constitution based on its endorsement of the natural rights of all men and its republican character. He cautioned against the loss of Black labor through deportation and denounced the slave states as "international outlaws for seizing, imprisoning and selling into slavery, all visitors of color arriving in Southern ports in pursuit of their lawful callings ... simply on account of their complexion!" In closing, the "Address" counseled "*immediate universal emancipation*" in order to forestall the transformation of slaves and free Blacks from "industrious, docile and valuable hands" engaged in agricultural pursuits into murderous revolutionaries.[40]

Even as an outpouring of appeals forced the Virginia legislature to take up the issue of emancipation, the *Liberator* published another piece titled "Address to the members of the Legislature of Virginia," written by someone the paper called "our esteemed correspondent Rammohun Roy."[41] This time, the alias Rammohun Roy advanced a case against African American expulsion from the land of their birth on perfectly practical grounds. Southerners would lose workers accustomed to laboring under the unhealthy and fatigue-inducing environment of their native states, and with it, their lucrative export economy. Betraying perhaps an evangelical distaste for rum and "Romanism" as much as slavery, the author argued that

Irish immigrants—"turbulent" and "intemperate"—would never make as "effective hands" as free Blacks. The author of this address also sought to alleviate the specter of race war by pointing out that free Blacks had not been implicated in the Nat Turner insurrection. By contrast, deportation might provoke North American–born Blacks to make common cause with their race brethren in South America and the West Indies, and threaten the United States. Much better, "Rammohun Roy" argued, to grant them their inalienable rights.

The identity of the "esteemed reporter" who assumed the pen name of the Bengali reformer remains a mystery. Whatever their racial affiliation, what is significant about the argument they made was its association of abolition and Black civil rights with a celebration—rather than denunciation—of "amalgamation" as a measure of peace and overall progress. And it was done in the name of an internationally renowned human rights champion of color. The reporter's familiarity with the local political landscape and concern with race marked them as American. At the same time, their positioning of the subjects of slavery, abolition, race, and civil rights within larger Atlantic and imperial British Asian frames of reference underscored the transnational connections of their campaign for immediatism. In this context, Rammohun Roy became simultaneously a universalistic signifier of human dignity and a personification of the case against racial hierarchies.

Abolitionists were not the only Americans who borrowed the symbolism of Roy to make a case for their cause. Champions of women's education drew upon the feminist activism of the real-life Roy to connect the progress of a society with the condition of its women. Thus, *Godey's Lady's Book,* the women's magazine associated with the construction of an ideal of "true" Victorian womanhood defined by the qualities of piety, purity, domesticity, deference, and guardianship of virtue in republican society, reported that Roy had remarked that Britain and America owed their "glory" to the character of their women. For it "was the *Mother* who brought up the infant, and inspired in him the love of knowledge and truth—who tutored the youth and formed his habits ... as man. It was the influence ... of the *Wife* that influenced men through life." Moreover, it was female education, Roy was noted to have suggested, that raised women in the Anglo-Atlantic "to be [their husband's] equals as companions, and their superiors in virtue." It was the "great secret in political economy." The piece went on to compare India unfavorably with America and to attribute the difference between these societies to the "superior intelligence and virtue" of American women, owing chiefly to their superior access to education. At the same time, the article linked female learning with evangelization, praising what it represented as the pioneering role of American Baptist missionaries to combat "superstitious customs and tyrannical opinions" in India. Roy, no longer alive when the *Godey's Lady's Book* piece was published, had of course broken with the Baptists over Trinitarianism, so the theory that evangelicals would dispel superstition in South Asia or elsewhere would likely not have won his confidence, but that does not matter. The point is that his celebrity had rendered him a powerful and elastic symbol of reform, amenable to appropriation by champions of disparate (if overlapping) trans-Atlantic causes from interracial immediatism and racial equality to more conservative visions of women's uplift through education, evangelization, and republican motherhood.[42]

Rammohun Roy never made it to the United States. Afflicted with meningitis, he passed away near Bristol in 1833, the same year that Garrison followed the trail of Black abolitionists like Paul Cuffe and Nathaniel Paul to England, to campaign against colonization and raise money for an industrial school for African Americans.[43] The contacts that the American made across the Atlantic included the abolitionist George Thompson and Irish rights activist O'Connell, both of whom would throw themselves into movements of colonial reform in the years to come. As such, these reformers would come to work closely with Roy's friend and associate William Adam. So let us turn from Roy to trace the trajectory of these alliances through the medium of a voluntary association, the British India Society, which sought to doom American slavery through the redress of free labor conditions in colonial India.

WILLIAM ADAM, WENDELL PHILLIPS, AND THE BRITISH INDIA SOCIETY

The Fifth Annual Meeting of the Glasgow Emancipation Society was in progress. It was the aftermath of the end of apprenticeship in the Caribbean. Before an audience of Scottish cotton manufacturers, imperial reformers, and religious-humanitarian abolitionists, the Liverpool-born immediatist, George Thompson, read out a message from the celebrated Boston abolitionist Wendell Phillips that linked the fate of the "beautiful prairies" of the American West, where the nation was rapidly expanding, directly to the success of an experiment underway in the "sunny plains of Hindustan."[44]

Phillips and his wife had left the United States for a two-year sojourn in Europe in June 1839. Not able to attend the Glasgow meeting in person, Phillips conveyed his address through an appropriate intermediary, the electrifying abolitionist lecturer Thompson, whom proslavery fury had driven from US shores a few years earlier. The missive rejoiced that an ongoing campaign to unleash "the industry of the pagan" in India [through cotton cultivation with free labor] was about to ensure that the westward "march of civilization" would be charted not by the "progress of the manacled slave coffle" but rather by the "quiet step of families" carrying the "household gods" of "peace, intelligence, and liberty." For adversaries immune to the appeals of morality, the voice of India came "clothed with the omnipotence of self-interest." The Glasgow group learned that US Senator from Kentucky Henry Clay had "coolly calculated the value of sinews and muscles—of the bodies and souls of men—and then asked us whether we might reasonably expect the South to surrender 1,200,000,000 of dollars at the bidding of abstract principles!" If the "genius" of India's "fertile plains" were unlocked, it might turn those dollars, that property in human flesh, into "dust in the slaveholder's grasp," just like "the gold in India's fairy tales."[45]

Phillips' hopeful abolitionist metaphors about the power of "free" Indian industry to transform slaveholding wealth into a mirage grew out of his association with a recently established voluntary association that sought to simultaneously kill American slavery, Indian poverty, and colonial injustice by promoting cotton cultivation by free workers in South Asia. Their British travels had brought the Phillips in close association with the Quaker abolitionist Elizabeth Pease, whose father, Joseph, had served as a guiding spirit behind the conception of joining reform causes across continents. A Darlington wool manufacturer, Joseph Pease had served on the committee of a voluntary association known as the Aborigines Protection Society (APS), formed in 1837 by Quakers and evangelicals.[46] Pease had campaigned against the apprenticeship system in the Caribbean and denounced the deportation schemes of the American Colonization Society. He and his daughter Elizabeth now entered a conversation about company misrule in India via concerns about the enslaved-like workers in British Guiana and Mauritius.[47] Meanwhile, news of a horrific famine in Bengal evoked the specter of putrefying corpses—of men, women, and children—poisoning the waters of the Ganges and Jamuna Rivers, cast there to save the cost of disposal. Parliamentarian and philanthropist Charles Forbes, who had led a mercantile enterprise in Bombay, delivered a speech before the Court of Proprietors of East India stock, urging measures to relieve suffering in the company's territories.[48]

Forbes's speech galvanized Pease to seek out a meeting with the MP, who as a Tory in domestic politics, did not often see eye to eye with his comrades in antislavery circles on issues like Parliamentary reform. Forbes exhorted Pease to "wage a holy war [for India] as he had done for the slaves [of the West Indies], and to rally the Quakers round the new standard."[49] Subsequently, Forbes enlisted Montgomery Martin, an Irish statistician who had traveled to South Asia, to explain the "cruel extortion" of India's land tax to the Peases over breakfast at Guildhall Hotel. Daniel O'Connell listened in on the meeting. The assemblage decided to print and circulate a circular—a "famine paper"—among members of the public and Parliament, and to bring the issue before the APS.[50]

During an omnibus ride to a celebration in Birmingham to mark the end of apprenticeship in the Caribbean on 1 August 1838, the Peases spoke to a company of men including O'Connell and the Parliamentarians Stephen and Charles Lushington. They broached the topic of a new frontier for freedom struggles: India. O'Connell and Stephen Lushington both went on to address slavery in India in their Birmingham speeches. Reporting on O'Connell's speech, the *Liberator* classified "the slavery of two millions of human beings [in America]" with the state of "the hundred millions of human beings who now suffer the degrading slavery of having no title to their land ... because the maladministration of the British Government in India has left them beggars in their native land...."[51] Slavery in India would henceforth feature on the agenda of the British and Foreign Anti-Slavery Society, which evolved from the organizing at Birmingham. Pease also persuaded the APS to hire the abolitionist and anticolonization activist George Thompson as a speaker.[52]

It was at this juncture, when in the aftermath of Caribbean emancipation British abolitionists had turned their attention to India, that William Adam moved physically to this field of Anglo-Atlantic activism. Adam, who tried his hands at journalism in India in the 1820s, had earned official EIC disapproval through his critiques of colonial racism.[53] Following the failure of his journalistic ventures, the former missionary held administrative positions with the EIC, which introduced him to various forms of bondage under company rule. As secretary to the Committee on Road Convicts, for instance, he learned about the practice of convict labor sanctioned by the government. While compiling census records in Calcutta, he discovered enslaved Africans in Armenian homes. His most significant venture, however, was a commission conferred by Governor General William Bentinck to undertake an official survey of the state of vernacular education in Bengal and Bihar, which resulted in a report advocating community involvement and the use of vernacular languages as the medium of instruction to spread education.[54]

Meanwhile, in 1838 Boston merchants who traded with South Asia raised funds to endow Adam with a professorship in Oriental literature at Harvard. An announcement in the *Boston Daily Advertiser* described the appointee as having lived in India for twenty years and achieved fluency in "Hindoostani, Persian, and some other dialects" in common use there besides Sanskrit, "which is now well known to be so intimately connected with the Greek, Latin, and Northern European languages ... that a knowledge of it is indispensable to a philologist of the present day."[55] Adam would serve in this position for only a year. More fateful was a trip to Liverpool during which, in January 1839, he traveled to the Pease home in Darlington on his way to London. There he met George Thompson. Drawing on his extensive firsthand experiences in India, he helped convince his hosts and their guests that circumstances warranted the creation of a new society, "to act promptly and solely on behalf of the people of India."[56]

Even as Elizabeth Pease was writing leaflets on the land tax, famine, and forced labor in India, British abolitionists received the sad news from the United States of the editor Elijah Lovejoy's martyrdom in service to the linked causes of free speech and antislavery.[57] In a timely conjunction of diverse reform planks, the discourse of "justice for India" now broadened to encompass the enslaved's cause in the Atlantic. Joseph Pease wrote Thompson that their mutual friend, the Birmingham Quaker Joseph Sturge, among others, had pointed out that sugar and cotton could be grown more cheaply in India than in Atlantic slave societies: "Can the US, Cuba, or the Brazils, with their slave labor, which costs 2/- to 2/6 per day, compete in a fair market with sugar and cotton cultivated in India by labour costing 3d a day? Is there not in India a population starving for want of employment? That population is more than sufficient to cultivate the sugar and cotton not for England alone, but for the whole world.... If then we could compel the EIC to take off their restrictions on the produce of East India ... that one act would set thousands of slaves free, because their employers would cease to find the employment of slave labour profitable...."[58] There followed a flurry of correspondence with the Board of Trade to ascertain the costs of producing export staples with slave labor, accounting for the price paid for human chattel and the expenses associated with their subsistence and insurance against their death or other losses. News of these exchanges, centered in Darlington, generated great interest in the commercial centers of Manchester, Liverpool, Glasgow, Nottingham, and Leicester.[59]

The humanitarian impulses of transatlantic abolitionists and imperial reformers came to converge especially closely with the manufacturing interests of an emerging hub of "internationalist capitalism" and free trade: Manchester. That city's textile manufacturers had long sought to diversify their sources of raw cotton supplies beyond the plantations of the American South. India beckoned as a potential usurper of the Cotton Kingdom's dominance. Chapter 3 deals with this dimension of our story in greater detail. At this point, it is enough to note that this collaboration among merchants and reformers culminated in the inauguration of the British India Society "in the presence of a large audience" in London's Freemasons' Hall in July 1839. The former Lord Chancellor and advocate of West Indian emancipation, Lord Henry Brougham, presided over the event. Numerous Indian luminaries, including princes from Awadh and Mysore, and merchants from Bombay and Calcutta, sat on the platform. George Thompson, described in a profile published later in the (Calcutta) *India Review* as "a friend of the Negro race ... eloquent and unwearied opponent of the Corn Laws ... professed *Friend of India*," brought the audience to its feet by excoriating "republican slaveholders—the worst and vilest in the world." Debunking their democratic pretensions, he thundered: "when will the men who hoist the cap of liberty in one hand, and flourish the scourge with the other—who place one foot on the declaration of rights which they have signed, and another upon the neck of the colored man—when will these be turned from their evil ways? Not when treaties shall be signed ... and pathetic appeals shall be made to their consciences, but they shall be starved from their course, when the free labor of the 100,000,000 of India shall compete with the uncompensated labor of the 2,000,000 in the valley of the Mississippi and on the plains of the Carolinas—then it shall be done."[60] The meeting also endorsed greater representation of Indian subjects in Parliament, land tax reform, and the abolition of company monopolies in opium and salt.[61]

The society that Adam had helped found established auxiliaries in Manchester and Glasgow. It counted among its officers Cobden, O'Connell, the abolitionist Thomas Clarkson, and the Manchester cotton manufacturer Henry Ashworth.[62] Its most prominent Indian partner was a Bengali businessman, banker, Brahmo Samaj leader, and architect of the Landholder's Society, known in Anglo-Atlantic reform circles as Rammohun Roy's successor and later introduced to Lord Brougham as "the head of everything liberal in India." As Sartori has argued, Dwarkanath Tagore shared Roy's vision of a "liberal political economy" and a "cosmopolitan empire," which would accord Indians their place as "full subjects" of the British Crown.[63]

It was Tagore who would persuade Thompson to visit India for fifteen months, during which the reformer, to the consternation of Phillips and Pease, was reportedly "invested with gorgeous apparel, resplendent jewellery . . . and the office of the 'Envoy to the Emperor of Delhi' in the grand white marbled audience hall of the Mughal court."[64] Thompson helped to create the Bengal British India Society, which recruited members from the graduates of Hindu College, a cohort styled "Young Bengal" that embraced a more radical commitment to civic equality and freedom from institutional constraints than their seniors had done.[65]

WILLIAM ADAM AND THE LIBERAL CHALLENGE TO PROSLAVERY ORIENTALISM

The BIS's roster of transoceanic supporters revealed the motley crew of sentiments, impulses, and interests that converged under its banner of justice for colonized Indians and enslaved Americans. Within this configuration, Adam's major intervention—one that would ricochet through channels of sectional discord in North America—was British complicity in the perpetuation and elaboration in South Asia of slavery systems similar to their Atlantic counterparts. Adopting the overlapping prisms of Christian morality and liberal individualism, Adam positioned slave status in the East as no different from that in the New World—a polar opposite of the "natural" and universal condition of personal freedom to which every individual was entitled.

More interestingly, Adam appeared to have taken a cue from Rammohun Roy by reading Hindu lawgivers in ways that contradicted colonially sanctioned contemporary practices. His interpretation of ancient Indian texts undercut the argument that reform would violate the EIC's ostensible commitment to cultural tolerance and inflame local opinion. It was this approach that makes Adam much more compelling than evangelical missionaries in India. While, say, Baptists with little understanding of diverse Indian cultures folded their critiques of slavery into sensationalist (and predictable) propaganda campaigns to "save" India from religious "barbarism," Adam's relative learning in Sanskrit texts made it possible for him to show how India's colonial rulers might have interpreted those very texts to undermine, rather than buttress slavery. Moreover, he tailored his narrative of the practices of slavery sanctioned by the government of India to illustrate the departure of such practices from authentic prescriptions of both Hindu and Muslim law.

The World Antislavery Convention, which opened on 12 June 1840 at Freemasons' Hall, afforded this Scottish-American agitator the first major international public forum in which to unveil what abolitionists saw as sordid continuities among colonial legacies of bondage in Asia and the Americas. Adam sat in the gallery in solidarity with women (including the American feminist Elizabeth Cady Stanton) who had been denied seats on the floor. The same year, he published in Boston and London a book titled *The Law and Custom of Slavery in British India*. It took the form of a series of letters to Thomas Fowell Buxton, who had assumed the mantle of antislavery leadership in Parliament when Wilberforce retired, diverging from immediatists on key questions including apprenticeship and, subsequently, the need to focus on slavery in Asia. Adam's address on Indian slavery at the international slavery convention in 1840 earned his book wide coverage in the abolitionist press on both sides of the Atlantic, making it a source of information for American commentators on all sides of the slavery question.[66] Proslavery writers contextualizing the American South within comparative frames of reference often cited Adam as well as the colonial Judge Harington on slavery in India.

At the outset of his book, Adam acknowledged that his exhaustive critique of colonial slavery in Asia might provide American defenders of slavery with ammunition to attack England by "tending to lessen the force of her example in the West Indies." Nevertheless, he was convinced that in the long run the cause of justice and humanity would be served by his exposure of "facts." He framed his abolitionist appeal in the expansive, immediatist language of universal human rights, and his activist authority in terms of his identity as a citizen of the world. Boston, already known for its "enlightened and philanthropic character" seemed an appropriate setting to launch an appeal to the "public opinion of the civilized world against slavery in India."[67]

Adam's exposition opened with an irony: the people of England who had just won the emancipation of eight hundred thousand slaves in the British West Indies, at the cost of 20 million sterling, were about to realize that slavery was a hydra-headed monster, and that "one of the heads" of the same hideous creature held millions of British subjects in thralldom in the East. Adam's argument rested on several prongs. First, he leveled a sustained critique of the colonial system of legal pluralism that claimed to rest on the (un-Christian and non-Christian) religious laws of Hindus and Muslims, in the name of liberal governance. Adam maintained that the British not only chose to read proslavery meanings into these codes but to extend and institutionalize those meanings. Second, he indicted colonial executive and legislative policies that either directly or indirectly created new forms of slavery and exacerbated old ones. These included statutes that established positive laws of slavery. But they also encompassed the sort of misrule that had galvanized the formation of the British India Society—misgovernment that fueled famines and induced the sale of self or children into slavery. Finally, Adam sought to debunk British constructions of the mildness of Indian "domestic" slavery by juxtaposing them against portraits of practice—distressingly familiar to Atlantic audiences—of "forced labor" in the agricultural sector.

Adam endeavored to illustrate, first and foremost, that the EIC's approach to legal pluralism did not embody a liberal commitment to noninterference by the state in the existing customs and usages of the country. Rather, the EIC had, through the instruments of case law and statutory law, *created* a legal and practical infrastructure of slavery similar to its Atlantic counterpart, under the cover of respect for ostensibly ancient and immutable local practices. Drawing heavily upon official documents generated by the corporation itself, he showed that the quest for power and concern for the bottom line governed British policy on slavery on India. Probing the genealogy of that policy through intracompany controversies over the law and custom of slavery in India, he introduced debates between Orientalist apologists of Indian forms of servitude and their dissenters into the public sphere. Adam also used compendiums of Hindu and Muslim law that had been translated for the benefit of civil court judges, who were aided by the legal opinions and expositions of pundits and imams attached to these courts. In particular, he drew upon the Bengal civil service official William Hay Macnaghten, who in turn had relied on Colebrooke as the most authoritative source of Hindu law.[68] All in all, Adam's book became an important conduit through which the commentaries of Colebrooke and Harington would find their way into American proslavery apologetics as sources for narratives of comparative slavery.

Adam argued that the EIC's agency in shaping the architecture of proslavery law rested in part on the fact that the traditions it used to buttress slavery might have been employed equally effectively to weaken it. He based his description of the Hindu laws of slavery on Colebrooke but emphasized how Hindu law *limited* the "liability to slavery," first of all by the strictures of caste. Thus, Adam maintained that in theory Brahmans could not be enslaved, and members of the other three broad "classes" of the Hindu "race," as he put it—namely, the military, commercial and farming, and servile—could only be enslaved by those of superior status in the caste hierarchy. Moreover, outcastes deemed "untouchable" were, for that reason, exempted from enslavement. In this context, he assigned the notion of consent a central role in Hindu law: a captive of war was not an automatic subject of enslavement but rather chose that condition by claiming "quarter." Or a person might sell himself in exchange for "maintenance."[69]

Moreover, Adam highlighted the paths to emancipation set forth in the *Shastras* but not mentioned by Colebrooke. A master might perform a manumission ritual to establish his benevolence if he were to take "a vessel of water from his shoulder" (the usual way in which water is carried by a slave), "and instantly break it" (halting servile duties). "Sprinkling his head with water containing rice and flowers, and thrice calling him free ... let the master dismiss him with his face towards the east." Adam went on to note other grounds for emancipation: a slave who saved his master's life, or an enslaved woman who bore her master a son. Even one who had sold himself for subsistence could earn liberation by gifting his master "a pair of oxen." A man who became a slave by marrying a slave might regain his freedom simply by divorcing his wife, and a man might stopping being a debt slave by repaying his debt. In other words, slavery was not an irreversible situation. For Harington, this had offered a way to turn traditions of dependence into contracts. For Adams, it signaled that consent played a central role in determining modes of enslavement so that its absence could nullify conditions of servitude.[70]

Proceeding to a description of slavery under Islamic law, Adam noted that the letter of that law recognized only two categories of slaves: "first, infidels made captive during war; and secondly, their descendants." He went on to list a litany of disabilities suffered by the enslaved, but noted that these were routinely violated in practice; the enslaved could, under certain circumstances, enjoy great power under their masters' aegis.[71]

Adam then laid out the ways in which the colonial establishment, acting through the supreme court of civil and revenue jurisdiction, had written the human chattel principle into civil law by classifying it with marriage and inheritance under the purview of religious laws. By contrast, he defined slavery strictly as a problem of "personal freedom and bondage," as well as one of a *free market for labor* rather than familial forms of dependence. Interpreting freedom as the right of a person to "the fruit of his own labor," he maintained that the infusion of a proslavery "spirit" into the principle of legal pluralism amounted to a positive— and new—affirmation of a master's prerogative to abrogate that right.[72]

This free labor perspective, and the framework of liberal individualism that underpinned it, served together with the "civilizing" influence of Christian benevolence as Adam's principal prisms for appraising Indian forms of bondage. He lamented that an ostensibly "Christian government" had lent the "sanction of the British name" to "antiquated systems of slavery originating in the barbarous ... policy of the Hindu and Muhammadan governments."[73]

However, such sanction did not simply acquiesce in existing local law and custom but rather *extended* the legal and practical paraphernalia of slavery. Harking back to the official burial of Richardson's 1808 proposal for the virtual delegalization of slavery in South Asia, Adam argued that the advent of Muslim rule in India had, in accordance with Islamic laws of conquest, brought about the formal suspension of Hindu law, including its provisions related to slavery. It was the British government that resurrected what had been "in every legal sense, a dead letter" for several precolonial centuries. Following Macnaghten's *Principles and*

Procedures of Muhamadan Law, he maintained that if the British had enforced the letter of Muslim law on slavery, India's version of the chattel principle would have died a virtual death. For the only forms of slavery it permitted—namely the enslavement of infidel captives of war, or their descendants—were either "non-existent or unprovable," while customary forms of bondage, forged through debt, kidnapping, or import, were all illegal.[74]

Adam proceeded to draw upon examples of case law to show that the British had created codes and conditions of slavery where none need exist. In the pages of his book, a Hindu lawyer admonishes the British judge of Dhaka for admitting a case in which a would-be master claimed a person as a slave simply on the grounds that the inhabitants of his district "supposed" that he was a slave, when Hindu law made no allowance for enslavement on those grounds. Women featured prominently in these cases, their stories underscoring, for their "Christian abolitionist sisters" across the seas, the horrors of communal property in female chattel, institutionalized by British courts. There was the case of a woman owned by two men, one of whom married her off to a slave owned by a third party without the consent of his co-owner, whereupon the court ruled that the "dispossessed" co-owner still retained a right "not to half her person, but to half her labor...." American abolitionist-feminists might have interpreted this outcome as intensifying the workings of patriarchal servitude: marriage had transferred property in the bondswoman's person to her husband's owner, but did not cancel her obligation to labor for her own co-owner. Adam also cited the instance of a free woman who upon marrying a slave became the property of her husband's master, so that in this case, marriage quite literally brought enslavement under law. Moreover, courts sanctioned the enslavement of destitute children. An emancipated mother, desperate for subsistence, sold her children; a Chittagong court in 1819 formalized their loss of freedom for perpetuity.[75]

Adam's narrative illustrated the ways in which colonial policy supplemented court decisions to spawn new forms of slavery. Most outrageous of all were statutes devised by the notorious Governor General Warren Hastings. Hastings had proposed to sell convicted felons as slaves and transport them to Bencoolen, in the island of Sumatra, to work on nutmeg and clove plantations, thus saving the government prison costs. Moreover, the British were prepared to flout the Muslim penal code, which they had established as the basis of a uniform criminal justice system. Muslim law allowed the master of the family of a murdered victim to forgive the murderer. The British, by contrast, sought to punish dacoits who roamed highways and plundered villages not simply with death but also by turning their families into slaves of the state, "to be disposed ... according to the discretion of the government." Adam noted that "native judges" had proved "too just, humane, and independent" to enforce this draconian measure.[76]

But what lent Adam's book the greatest relevance to the debate over the merit of free societies from the American perspective was his discussion of the connection between slavery and poverty. This discussion indicted British rule in India directly and explicitly, suggesting that imperial misrule exacerbated the problem of famines, making the sale of free children by their parents a "prolific" source of slavery from Bengal to Madras. He bemoaned the fact that "in India, whence an enormous revenue is drawn ... there is no established fund or regulated system for the relief of the destitute." This negligence turned slavery into a positive "good," for it furnished the sole survival strategy of indigent parents during seasons of catastrophic want and came to constitute "in Mr. Colebrooke's opinion, at least under the Bengal presidency, the chief source of domestic slavery." Adam noted the perversity of a "system of government under which that which is evil in itself, the effect of evil, and the cause of evil, becomes by dire necessity a comparative good." He contended that the practice of debt bondage also flowed from colonial indifference to the well-being of the governed. The *Journal of the Asiatic Society of Bengal* had published in 1837 "a copy of a servitude-bond" of a common variety, "by which a native, for a loan of fifty-one rupees at twelve per cent interest" mortgaged "his own labor and that of his family to the lender at all times and in all forms, for an indefinite period, until the amount of the loan shall be repaid, principal and interest, in full." Such a contract committed children to bondage following the death of their father until the debt was paid off.[77]

Finally, Adam sought to debunk Colebrooke's representation of the intimate, "domestic" nature of slavery in India by sketching detailed portraits of "agrestic" or "predial" slaves. Indian labor historians have dealt with relations of production in the countryside in great detail, but for our purposes, the point is that transatlantic abolitionists used accounts such as Adam's to demolish the contention of different slaveries, East and West. Adam presented in an appendix Colebrooke's 1812 commentary, which had been reproduced in a section of Harington's *Analysis*.[78] Adam juxtaposed these observations, which underplayed the existence of slavery in the agricultural sector, against his own description of the brutal forms of bonded labor in farming districts invisible in Colebrooke's Minute. Whereas Colebrooke had based his assessment of Indian slavery on his understanding of Bengal, Adam ranged far from headquarters—down to South India, and up again in Awadh, where Mississippi overseers would later head to cultivate cotton with "free" labor. Adam's strategy of juxtaposition wrote Indian slavery into the same orbit as its Atlantic counterparts.

In this context, Adam's portrait of "agrestic slavery" in the Tamil country of Madras Presidency to the south, and its manifestations in Malabar and Canara provinces to the west, would have struck the most significant chord of horrified recognition in abolitionist circles from Boston to London and Manchester. In the southern districts of India, and along the western coast, "field slaves" labored in "every department of husbandry." From sunup to sundown, on irrigated rice farms, enslaved men plowed and irrigated the land and sowed seeds, while women transplanted rice plants and joined men in harvesting the crop. In addition, bands of these unfree workers grew "dry grain" on cultivated, unirrigated lands on their own account, but under the watchful eye of a village accountant. They built fences, raised livestock, and in the absence of carts or draft animals, hauled agricultural produce to the market on their bare backs. When the harvest season ended, there were trees to fell and houses to build. Few breaks punctuated their workdays, which stretched into nights when they took turns staying awake to stave off wild animals and "trespassing cattle" from guard posts consisting of "sheds erected on an open platform in the center of the paddy field, several feet under water, exposed to the inclemency of the weather..."[79]

Masters of the antebellum US South—who touted the supposed material well-being of the enslaved people on their own plantations—might have read with satisfaction about the physical deprivation of "slaves" in an Indian South under the suzerainty of an ostensibly antislavery empire. For Adam, the Tamil or Malabar slaves' physical appearance signaled, louder than any word on an official page ever could, the poor quality of their subsistence. You could tell them, he wrote, from their "degraded, diminutive, squalid appearance, their dropsical pot-bellies contrasting horribly with their skeleton arms and legs, half-starved, hardly clothed, and in a condition scarcely superior to the cattle they follow at the plough." In Canara, they lived on paltry daily food allowances of rice, salt, and betel-nut, and in the Malabar they wore waistcloths, loincloths, or bunches of wild plantain leaves. Their huts resembled "large baskets," erected at the distance from "the habitations of the free castes." In Malabar, "a slave must not approach any of the free castes nearer than a distance of ninety-six steps, and if he wishes to speak to any of them he must stand at that distance and cry aloud to them." Moreover, even though they were allowed to sow dry grains, cultivate yams, and raise a plantation tree here or a jack tree there adjoining their rude huts, their masters reportedly owned the rights to the soil and trees. They were also bound to perform compulsory unpaid labor as part of their civil service. In Tanjore, for instance, the government collector could requisition agrestic slaves—even those that had converted to Christianity—to perform "onerous" forms of Hindu communal service, such as "to drag the enormous cars of idols round the villas or temples" by thousands of "enormous cables" attached to these divine vehicles, occasionally perishing under their gigantic wheels.[80]

Colonial administrators, Adam complained, deferred to the "ancient laws of Malabar" and vested the master with absolute power to judge his slaves' offenses and punish them by "flogging, putting them in stocks... working them in chains," and even taking their lives. More egregiously, when those groaning under these burdens fled to the more hospitable states of Mysore and Coorg, a Madras revenue collector suggested that the colonial government force the native rulers of those states to compensate the owners.[81] It was no small irony, Adam purported to show, that while enslaved Americans celebrated the warm embrace of the British Empire in the Atlantic, enslaved Indians sought to flee its tentacles in South Asia.

Worst of all, the Scottish abolitionist charged, the colonial state did not simply sustain the legal prerogatives of masters over their slaves but rather wrote itself into the slaveholding class, compounding demands made on unfree laboring groups for unpaid work. It built its public works and revenue infrastructure quite literally on the backs of coerced labor—at least in part. Thus, an English collector or magistrate reserved the right to requisition unfree gang labor to construct irrigation works, repair roads, transport the baggage of public servants and "marching regiments," and to "carry treasure-remittances from the several subordinate stations for the collection of revenue to the collector's treasury at Calicut." They carted stolen property recovered from robbers—together with the culprits themselves—to police stations. Slaves also lugged the company's tobacco to distribution depots for sale under armed guard, to prevent them from "running away." Adam wrote that these oppressive practices had fomented a rebellion in the mountainous terrain of Wynad in 1812 but failed to bring meaningful reforms.[82]

Indeed, the author of *The Law and Custom of Slavery in British India* offered a scathing indictment of the political economy that he said the EIC had introduced in British Asia, consisting of some of the worst features of Atlantic slavery's capitalism. The imperial regime had overturned a somewhat redeeming Indian tradition against selling bondspeople away from the estates of their birth. The EIC had inaugurated the practice of seizing and selling slaves in order to cover revenue arrears, and forced masters who defaulted to sell their workers for cash, away from the estates of their birth. Only in 1819 did the Madras Board of Revenue finally abolish this horrible colonial innovation. Thus, observed Adam, colonial corporate capitalism not only extorted an "enormous" revenue from an "abjectly impoverished people" but did it by transplanting an Atlantic system that separated enslaved families through sale as in the Americas.[83] At the same time, the establishment of new forms of slavery through measures like the "liquidation" of slave property to force masters to pay their tax arrears led to one inescapable conclusion: all the East India Company cared about was money and power. Through a combination of levies on immemorially untaxed land, monopolies to control production, and assaults against "individual rights," the EIC had created conditions ripe for rebellion.[84]

Adam highlighted the hypocrisy of the imperial position, which held that the suppression of slavery in India was to be postponed to facilitate the "gradual diffusion" of the notion among "all ranks of the community that rational liberty is the condition most conducive to the happiness and interests of mankind." Placing the colonialists squarely on par with slaveholders, he wrote, "It would be just as reasonable to expect by the diffusion of knowledge to convince slave-holders of ... the advantage *to them* of liberating their slaves, as it would be to expect to convince the British government that India ought to be liberated from British control, because it was unjustly and fraudulently acquired and has been most cruelly misgoverned, and because 'rational liberty is the condition most conducive to the happiness and interests of mankind.'"[85]

Adam's critique, disseminated on both sides of the Atlantic, helped energize the campaign to merge the causes of the enslaved in America and the colonized in Asia. The *Dublin Weekly Herald,* for instance, rejoiced at the publication of his book, for India was "the land of promise to England." Not only would the encouragement of cotton cultivation there help dismantle "the accursed slave system of America," but her "one hundred millions of subjects" offered a potential market for British manufactures. Indian slavery represented a "hidden obstacle" hindering the "progress to prosperity."[86] Across the Atlantic, the *Liberator* highlighted the success with which Adam had managed to undermine Colebrooke's narrative of difference between East and West, calling for the death of slavery wherever it existed. The *National AntiSlavery Standard* meanwhile recommended Adam's book to its readers with the comment that it "abounds with valuable . . . facts, which will be new to a very large portion of its readers."[87]

While Adam was wielding the power of his pen to bridge the campaigns to bring justice to the enslaved dispersed across two oceans, a fellow traveler from his Calcutta days was touring the slave societies of the American South. Even as James Silk Buckingham entranced southern audiences in the late 1830s by taking them on dramatic virtual tours of exotic lands inspired by his own travels, he was documenting his firsthand experience with the brutality of his hosts' so-called "peculiar institution." The Cornish agitator-turned Parliamentarian's American sojourn would produce a two-volume work titled *The Slave States of America* two years after Adam published his account of Indian slavery. Addressed to Britain's royal consort, it would urge the empire to emancipate the oppressed everywhere. Buckingham's report contributed to the abolitionist pressures that nudged Parliament to "delegalize" slavery in India and lent moral authority to trans-Atlantic movements to serve the American enslaved's cause by producing free cotton in India. So let us pick up his trail at the point of its intersection with a North America on the eve of sectional discord over slavery.[88]

CLOSING THE TRANSOCEANIC CIRCLE OF REFORM: REENTERING BUCKINGHAM'S TRAVEL TRAIL IN THE SLAVE SOUTH

On 19 October 1837, the one-time mariner, radical journalist, and former politician James Silk Buckingham touched New York's shore accompanied by his wife and young son. The family had made it through a rough, forty-three-day Atlantic voyage on the packet boat *President*. We have hitherto tracked Buckingham's trajectory through Calcutta newspaper columns excoriating colonial indifference to the

African slave trade in India, and into Britain's public sphere. On his return to his homeland, Buckingham had championed immediate West Indian emancipation. He also indicted colonial misrule in British Asia, a theme to which he would return—together with free trade and free labor—under the auspices of the British India Society following his American sojourn. Indeed, William Adam's account of slavery in India, like the BIS's critique of the EIC, rang with echoes of many of Buckingham's arguments. Now we close our narrative of the transoceanic circle of reform discourses in the age of empires in transition by reentering the path of Buckingham's travels in the only slave society remaining in the Anglophone western hemisphere by the late 1830s: North America's Slave South.

Buckingham, who had contributed to the well of positions that shaped visions of universal freedom from the plantations of the Caribbean to the colonies of British Asia, hoped now to contribute a third crucial link to the chain of campaigns for emancipation in Anglophone worlds. In the early 1840s, even as wildly disparate accounts of experiments to cultivate "free cotton" in India with overseer expertise from Mississippi began to explode in the pages of American newspapers with fury or euphoria, he brought eyewitness accounts of the horrors and hypocrisy of southern slavery back to Britain. These sought to debunk portraits of planter paternalism and happy slaves in America just as surely as Adam had endeavored to destroy the myths of mildness that inflected the Orientalist gaze on servitude in India.[89]

Buckingham's stated purpose in visiting the United States was not to assail slavery, as Thompson had done. Rather, he went in the role of an entertainer, paid to bring distant shores—especially Egypt and the Holy Land—home to American audiences through lectures, graphic enactments, and costumes. Heralded as he landed in New York as one who "came bearing fresh knowledge of the classical and scriptural countries," he was soon regaling crowds in Clinton Hall with such success that the *Knickerbocker Magazine* credited him with having "taken that 'many headed beast, the town' completely by the horns." He addressed distinguished guests from all walks of life, from Yale faculty to former President John Quincy Adams and Senator Henry Clay. In early 1838 he made his way to Washington, Baltimore, and Philadelphia, before retracing his steps up the Hudson and into New England. Then he headed south to Charleston, and down the coast to Savannah, before turning inland to visit Augusta, Macon, and Montgomery. He then pivoted southwest to the Gulf Coast, making his way from Mobile to New Orleans. When a bout of sickness and a tornado foiled his plans to sail up the Mississippi by steamboat, he headed to the East Coast at leisurely pace through Alabama, Georgia, and the Carolinas, traversing "the Blue Ridge country of the Old Dominion" and the cities of Richmond and Norfolk on his way to the seacoast.[90]

Buckingham's biographer has noted that the British sojourner's free trade credentials and evocative travelogues enthralled audiences who appeared to know little about his abolitionist politics. His lecture on Egypt "began with the approach to

Alexandria, then took his hearers up the Nile, through the baths of Cairo, underground into the catacombs, and finally to an ascent of a pyramid." His account of Palestine, transporting his audience from Tyre to Jerusalem "step by step," was delivered in costume—that of "an Arabian sheik—white robe, crimson cloak and turban, and a purple sash." The Savannah *Georgian* exulted, "We imagined that we ... were treading on 'holy ground,'" while the rabidly proslavery *Charleston Courier* marveled that Buckingham had "made the Bible a living book."[91]

Even during his tour, however, Buckingham was recording detailed, copious information that he would craft on his return home into a firsthand narrative of the ordeal of slavery and the illogic of its defense. His weighed the myths of slave society against its realities as he observed them. In a thematic refrain that historians of our own time would recognize, he evaluated slaveholders' claims of their society's humane relations of dependence against the practical workings of the chattel principle that treated human beings as commodities, credit, and collateral. His pages bristled with the tensions and contradictions of slave society: masters complaining about rebellious slaves while asserting that slaves were happy, would-be paternalists trafficking in the buying and selling of family members away from each other, and enslaved workers yearning for education denied them by lawmakers fearful of servile insurrections by their ostensibly contented human chattel.

Contesting the picture of materially well-off slaves, Buckingham told how while traveling by stagecoach to Columbia, South Carolina, he had encountered at "the earliest dawn of day, soon after four o'clock," a crew of "field-negroes" on their way to work, clad in "tattered and ragged fragments of garments hanging in shreds around their bodies." When a sigh of commiseration escaped his wife and traveling companion, "three or four voices immediately and impatiently exclaimed, 'Ah ... Madam, they are among the happiest of human beings; for when their work is over, they have no cares, as everything they need is provided for them.'" Buckingham reflected that by the logic that relief from subsistence produced happiness, "all the convicts of our penal colonies," not to mention prison inmates "confined for life in the dungeons of Europe, or cells of America," would qualify as happy, "the only difference of [the enslaved]'s lot from that of the rest of mankind, being, that they have to work harder, to suffer the loss of their personal liberty, and to be liable to be whipped if they murmured ... and shot if they offered the least resistance!"[92]

The chronicler from Britain went on to note that ten minutes later, "the very same individual" who had made the claim about happy slaves exclaimed, "I think the very devil's got into the n___s [sic] of late; for I've heard of more running away, and seen more rewards offered for their apprehension, within the last month, than I ever remember to have seen in the same space of time." Buckingham was certain that if he had pointed out the inconsistency of these statements, his southern travel companions would have dismissed the charge with a comment he had heard all too often in that part of the country: "Oh! but you are English abolitionists, who have abolished slavery in the West Indies, for the sake of encouraging a negro revolt in the Southern States, and thus revenging yourselves on America." Fearing that any dissent would inflame "the combustible materials" that surrounded them, the Briton kept quiet. He judged those born and bred in the slave states "impervious to reason" on the subject of slavery.[93]

Farther north, Virginia offered ample proof of the anxieties lurking behind southerners' familiar narratives of contented slaves. In Richmond, Buckingham observed white fears that the education of slaves would lead to slave rebellions. A trip to Monticello introduced him to an enslaved coach driver who confided that he would have sacrificed most of the pay he earned by hiring out his time, if he could only get a few lessons in reading. Richmond masters hired out "right smart" slaves to cover the cost of their subsistence and make a profit from their labor, even as they raised their "progeny" as "so much stock, to be fed, raised, and prepared for a market...."[94]

No theme figured more prominently in Buckingham's project to debunk claims of planter benevolence than that of the chattel principle on display in the domestic slave trade and its barely covert connections with the prime object of public revulsion in Britain: the international commerce in human flesh. While in Norfolk, Virginia, he was struck by the specious distinction that locals made between their own domestic slavery and the outlawed international slave trade, for his southern hosts appeared to ignore the smuggling of Africans into their own territories from Havana through Texas. Moreover, they had shamelessly institutionalized domestic transactions that displaced people of African descent from "Maryland and Virginia" to "Georgia, Alabama, Mississippi, and Arkansas." Within sight of his Norfolk hotel sat a slave depot. "Shoutings and cries" emanating from those premises entered the visitor's ears. He had learned that "slave-dealers of the town" warehoused their human articles there, "with as little food and clothing as is compatible with bare existence...." Drivers on horseback, equipped with "large whips," accompanied these gangs of "negroes, men, women, and children" traveling on foot. Those suspected of rebellion were chained together, the weary forced to keep pace by the crack of the attendant's whip. Buckingham reminded his readers that as dealers created parcels for the southern market, they separated families "without the slightest compunction." Any hint of revolt or "endeavour to regain their liberty," invited a shooting death "on the spot... and yet, if white American prisoners, taken in war, were to break from an English prison, murder their jailors, and escape in safety to their liberty and friends, they would be honoured and applauded throughout the land...." Norfolk slaves were deprived of all sorts of other basic personal freedoms: they had to observe a curfew, returning to their homes by "eight in the winter and nine in the summer; and a warning bell is rung every night at those periods." Any person of color found wandering the streets after that hour was apprehended by the night watch, imprisoned, and whipped if it was a second-time offense.[95]

Pressing on with theme of America's continued complicity in the international slave trade, Buckingham wrote that prisons created a ready conduit to the auction block for suspected fugitives unredeemed by their masters: "Some of these are of pure African birth . . . imported . . . by the slave-ships trading to the island of Cuba, and brought by illicit importation into the United States." Newspaper notices that caught the writer's eye during his stay in South Carolina told the story: "Committed to the jail of Laurens District, a negro woman, named Peggy. . . . Peggy is an African woman, about middle size, speaks quick, and appears rather insane, and fifty or sixty years old." Another advertisement told of a forty-five-year-old African man, a runaway imprisoned in Lancaster District, "five feet three or four inches high, speaks very broken, and says that he was set free," which Buckingham translated to mean that the victim was a recent import into the Americas. And then there were estate sales, such as the one scheduled in July in Columbia Market House. The wares consisted of "eight valuable negroes, belonging to the estate of Mrs. Mary Clifton, deceased," They were available "on a credit of one, two, three, and four years, with interest from the sale, on the whole, payable annually. One is a carpenter, two are first-rate cooks, one a carriage-driver, one a smart waiting-boy, two girls were brought up as house-servants, and the other is a little boy. The purchaser will be required to give good personal security, and also a mortgage of the property."[96]

Buckingham proceeded to instruct his British readers in the ways in which the Slave South harnessed the resources of language and law in the project of transforming people into commodities. He noted that as "Negroes" passed "from hand to hand, like other 'cattle,' their marks of individual, human distinction—names, ages, sex, gender, faded before the racialized nomenclature of classes of "animate chattel," and parcels of forced labor and body parts: "The men are usually called 'boys,' whatever may be their age. . . . . The terms 'gang,' describing a number working in company; 'hands,' describing a smaller number; and 'force,' describing a whole body of slaves on an estate, are in frequent use. A female negro is called 'a wench,' or a 'woman'; and it is this, perhaps, which makes the term 'woman' so offensive to American ears, when applied to white females, who must all be called 'ladies.'" Legal institutions buttressed the transformation of people into exchange values. Newspaper reports of court cases in Charleston's court of appeal taught him how carefully the law of slavery guarded investments in human chattel. Contractors who hired slaves were liable to compensate owners for the loss of their human chattel through death or "exposure." He shared with readers one case in which the "defendant employed plaintiff's slaves to work on the railroad, and covenanted 'not to expose the slaves to rain or other bad weather, or dangers of any kind.'" One of these slaves suffered a fatal injury when he jumped out of a hand-car of the Railroad Company transporting him over a frozen pond to his encampment after work, to avoid an oncoming locomotive. A jury held the contractor's overseer liable for the slave's accident.[97]

Buckingham showed that even the stirrings of conscience among masters seeking to manumit their slaves on their deathbed failed to withstand the relentless pressures of the chattel norm in slave law. He recounted how aspiring emancipators sought to protect their freed people from deportation from the state as required by law by bequeathing them in trust to an executor standing in for the master, and allowing "nominal" slaves to work for themselves. Such slaves, however, were legally liable to be seized and reenslaved. For evidence, he offered the case of "Rebecca R/Lame v. James Ferguson and John Dangerfield," in which a judge ruled that a will bequeathing slaves in trust to an executor under the arrangement that the slaves labor on their own time and governance was no more than "an attempt to evade the law of the State against emancipation of slaves, and, if attempted to be carried into effect by the Ex'or, will subject the slaves to seizure and ownership by any one, under the act of 1800."[98] Time and time again, Buckingham interpreted slave law as specifically designed to crush whatever predilections for paternalism individual masters might harbor.

Finally, the Cornish reporter anticipated arguments that the free-state Republican Party would make about the virtues of a free market for labor in the decade before the US Civil War arrived. His account of an "agreeably" entertaining conversation with a Virginia gentleman aboard a stagecoach touched on the theme of the dynamism of free societies versus the stagnation of slave states. Buckingham's slave-state traveling mate had admitted as "most of the candid and well-informed Virginians readily do," that [Black slavery] impeded his section's improvement by degrading labor in the eyes of white men. Buckingham portrayed a master class at odds with the march of progress. Men who lived off the incomes generated by their plantations developed habits of "indolence, recklessness, and extravagance." They expended their time in travel, and "hunting, shooting, fishing, racing, and play of various kinds." They chewed tobacco and drank wine, cordials, juleps, and brandy to excess. They read books of "mere entertainment," if they read at all. They were "hot and irascible, though generous to a fault." Moreover, unaccustomed to prudence or long-term planning, they allowed themselves to sink recklessly into debt.[99] Nor were their social inferiors within the white population any more inclined to exhibit enterprise or industry. For Buckingham, the extent of poverty in slave society offered one indication of its backwardness. He turned the argument that slavery was an antidote to pauperism on its head. He observed that Virginia enjoyed the dubious distinction of harboring the largest number of paupers of any state in the Union and expended one hundred thousand dollars annually on poor relief. The source of this problem—presumably felt most acutely among poor whites, lay in their distaste for menial work, which they associated with slave labor.[100]

Buckingham's Whiggish depiction of the Slave South's master class as decadent feudal lords resided on the pages of his travelogue in tension with his account of the relentless pursuit of profit that structured the business of slavery, and that scholars have portrayed as the "Old South's Modern Worlds," the drivers of global capitalism.[101] But whatever these contradictions, they added up to a damning indictment of American slavery of the sort that invariably elicited irate charges of British abolitionist conspiracy against the South's prosperous slave-powered export economy. What was more, *The Slave States of America* was addressed to Prince Albert, consort of Queen Victoria, as an offering intended to strengthen the resolve of the British government to persist in its "noble effort" to "strike off the chains of the captive, and bid the oppressed go free."[102]

Buckingham's withering portrait of North America's empire of slavery landed in the Atlantic world just as another cause he had championed was reaching a formal resolution in Parliament. Abolitionists had turned their attention to British colonial support of servitude in India. Since the EIC had secured a renewal of its charter in 1833, the problem of slavery in its Asian dominions had languished in the doldrums of bureaucratic inertia and the lack of political will for reform. In 1841, however, a new law commission, which had compiled a report on slavery in India while conducting legal research aimed at devising a uniform penal code for the subcontinent, presented its findings to Parliament. The report hewed rather closely to Colebrooke's interpretation of the distinctive nature and function of slavery in India. Nevertheless, the British and Foreign Antislavery Society now launched a public campaign to reclaim Britain's moral capital by relieving the "oppressed children of the East." A new Tory government in London, together with the arrival in India of a governor general attuned to abolitionist pressure, Lord Ellenborough, paved the path to the passage of Act V of 1843, for the "delegalization" of slavery in India. The law's provisions prohibited public officers from selling persons for defaulting on tax or rent payments or in order to execute court decrees. Courts were forbidden to enforce slavery; no slave was to be deprived of legitimately acquired property; an act deemed a penal offense if "done to a free man" would be "equally an offence" if done to a slave. The 1843 Act was arguably a cop-out. It emancipated few people held in bondage, but it did free the British of any obligation to either return alleged fugitives to their owners or enforce measures likely to rub their elite Indian allies the wrong way.[103]

In the decades that followed, the Government of India adopted an official stance that, as Indrani Chatterjee has suggested, amounted to a denial of the existence of slavery in the face of clear evidence of its persistence in various forms. Indeed, historians have shown that the colonial state flattened and commodified nuances of patron-client relations (which might include, say, the tradition of privileged groups giving loans to subordinates for purposes ranging from subsistence to marriage expenses) into contractual relations of exchange. Gyan Prakash, for instance, has argued that Enlightenment ideas about individual freedom and the market shaped provisions that propelled the *Kamia* laborers of agrarian Bihar into a formal state of debt bondage. They ostensibly entered "freely" into these legally enforceable arrangements, premised upon the use of their labor and bodies as collateral for money advanced by their employers. Moreover, labor laws like the Workmen's Breach of Contract Act of 1859 skewed the playing field in favor of employers, giving them legal redress against workers alleged to have refused to work after receiving advances. Among other things, historians have pointed out that the colonial state simply renamed household slaves "servants," operating within the unregulated boundaries of the domestic realm. Moreover, as Huzzey has noted, the advent of contract labor under master-servant law facilitated the large-scale migration of Indian indentured labor to Mauritius and various plantation destinations in the British Caribbean.[104] Such practices recalled the conversations about institutionalizing slavery by "free will" in the early nineteenth century by legal minds like Harington.

While Britons were debating the delegalization of slavery in India, overseers from the American South were conducting experiments in growing cotton in various parts of the subcontinent with free labor. Apoplectic slaveholders back in North America greeted the progress of these enterprises with virulent denunciations of the hypocrisy of antislavery imperialism. Ironically enough, abolitionist champions of colonial reform like Adam and Buckingham supplied slavery's defenders in America with material to impugn Britain's claims to antislavery capital. At the same time, the works of Orientalist apologists like Colebrooke and Harington, to which Adam had called attention, offered language that could be deployed in a more universal defense of slavery. The next section follows the threads of that story from the plains of Mississippi and the parlors and public spheres of South Carolina back to India via the mercantile circles and reformist hubs of Manchester and London.

PART TWO

Antislavery Empire versus Republic of Slaveholders?

3

Reverberations

American Overseers, Slavery, and "Free" Cotton Experiments in India

[One] of our negroes will do more work than five of the natives. They are something like our Choctaw Indians ... only much inferior in strength, courage, and energy. There is no forest for them to roam in here, as the Choctaws have, and they are therefore compelled to make a living ... by labor, and the rent to the Government eats out the profits of all they do cultivate ... You may say they [Indian peasants] have no master to order them to their work as you do slaves, but they are nothing like as well provided for or as happy.
—OVERSEER T. J. TERRY, QUOTED IN THE *EDGEFIELD ADVERTISER*, OCTOBER 21, 1841

The planters here are a different class of men, uneducated, having little or no knowledge of the principles of agriculture, and doggedly attached to the routine of America, whether applicable or not to present circumstances. In America they were overseers of negroes, who understood and did the work, while they looked on ...
—MADRAS COTTON SUPERINTENDENT R. WRIGHT, MARCH 1842

The fall season of 1841 did not lift the agricultural depression parts of the Deep South had sunk into in recent years. But for many defenders of slavery, it did bring cheering news from a distant land about the impending failure of an enterprise that only a couple of years before had raised the alarming specter of trans-Atlantic "plots" to undermine the Cotton Kingdom. From "cotton cities" to rural counties in the so-called "white gold" cultivating states of Alabama, Mississippi, and South Carolina, newspapers circulated reports of faltering experiments to grow "free cotton" in British India under the tutelage of overseers, most of them sons of the South's own soil, on contract with the mercantile corporation that inaugurated British imperialism in India.

The Gulf Coast port city of Mobile, Alabama, tied by the export trade in cotton to the Atlantic economy and still reeling from the devastating effects of the Panic of 1837, served as one conduit for these accounts. Its presses relayed a letter from remote, rural India to the weekly *Edgefield Advertiser*, published in a Black-majority, planter-dominated cotton district on the Savannah River in South Carolina. The missive came from T.J. Terry, described as a "plain working native" of the South, now stationed in Kalpi, in the north central district of Bundelkhand, "about six hundred miles from Calcutta." The letter described the allegedly fatal deficiencies of free-labor prospects in Terry's new field of operation. The author judged the "natives" whom he likened to "Choctaw Indians," no match for America's enslaved workers. He claimed that the state owned the land, extracting exorbitant rents from the peasants for its use, thus discouraging them from doing more than make "a mere living, which is nothing but a little rice." Without the benefit of animal food, "you may judge what sort of creatures they are for labor, compared with our negroes at the South."[1]

Terry then went on to introduce a rhetoric of comparative slavery that pro-Southern interests would frequently invoke to indict and connect British abolitionism with imperialism, even as they touted the "positive good" of their own system of chattel bondage: the colonized in India were impoverished slaves without formal masters, "nothing like as well provided for or as happy" as human chattel in the writer's own land. He listed a litany of other challenges to successful staple crop agriculture in India: no timber or horses, and puny oxen for plowing. The Mississippi overseer forecast a disappointing yield for the year: "200 pounds of cotton to the acre, and three acres to the hand," and that, too, of inferior quality compared with Mississippi cotton. Only a year into his sojourn in India, the writer had decided to return to the United States when his "engagement" with the East Indian Company ended. Importantly, news reports on this native son's foreign adventures concluded with the observation that globe-trotting had awakened and fortified his sense of American identity and exceptionalism. The overseer's route to South Asia had taken him through London, Paris, Lyons, Malta, Alexandria, and down the Nile to Cairo, before he sailed the Red Sea to Bombay and overland to Calcutta in the east. The voyage "excited the wonder" of this Mississippi cotton grower but also his "disgust" at experiences that apparently assaulted "his eyes and other senses." South Carolina's *Edgefield Advertiser* noted that world travel "caused [this southerner] ... to declare himself more of an American than ever."[2]

Terry's fanciful construction of the complex world of rural India would leave many historians of South Asia bemused. For US historians, however, the overseers' sojourns in British India bring together three intersecting stories. One illuminates the diverse contexts of political economy, state power, social hierarchies, and cultural traditions that made it so hard to transplant American-style settler colonialism and cotton culture using so-called free labor in British India. A second concerns the Slave South's engagement with the international politics of abolition, empire, and race beyond the Atlantic. Such engagement segues to a third theme by revealing the workings of a polarized Atlantic public sphere that made, channeled, and lost meanings in translation between two very different agrarian hinterlands in diverse oceanic worlds.[3] The scenes that unfold in the pages of this chapter shift back and forth from (arguably) feudal northern river basins and central mountain regions of colonial India; through sites of manufacturing and abolitionist activism in Manchester, London, and Boston; to cotton cities and capitalistic plantation districts of the antebellum South. Information circulated among these sites along channels supported by human networks and material infrastructure that combined to form a global public square. Thus, an overseer's letter might be transported by a warship or private merchant vessel to London, where it might make its way into the merchant chambers or free produce circles of Manchester. After 1840, it might be conveyed by steamship to New York, to be printed by a private resident in a Mississippi cotton district. Let us then set foot on these pathways, to track the myriad ways in which the politics and representation of "free cotton" experiments reverberated in the nodes of commerce, culture, and activism that sustained a North Atlantic exchange grid.[4]

A RIVEN INTERNATIONAL PUBLIC SPHERE

Slavery and capitalism, locked in tight embrace, anchored an interoceanic commercial network.[5] If the political economy of slave-grown cotton integrated the Anglo-Atlantic world, growing political and ideological divisions over slavery threatened to splinter it.[6] In this context, the overseers' transnational encounters connected a species of travel writing with the protean politics of slavery and abolition across diverse sites of reform and reaction within the roots and branches of the Anglo-Atlantic world. The white overseers who went to India in the quest for independent landownership wrote letters and journals that entered the public sphere through the medium of company documents and newspaper reports. Refracted through plural prisms shaped by their authors' entrepreneurial aspirations, as well as by familiar European Orientalist assumptions about agelessly inert Indians, they recorded clashes between American-style capitalism and settler colonialism, on the one hand, and the feudal matrices of hierarchy, dependence, and patronage that mediated control over land and labor in 1840s British India, on the other.

Yet the Americans' accounts were discordant enough to register differently in various centers of cotton exchange, fueling furious debates on issues that wove the

United States into a pan-Atlantic political economy. These were debates over tariffs, continental empire building, meanings of slavery, and ideas about race, as well as nationalism, colonialism, and the "world" politics of humanitarianism. Eventually however, the overseers' failure in India propelled their narratives along different paths, toward a common defense of the Slave South. Starting out as individual strivers with no discernible political investment in either chattel slavery or American nationalism, some of them emerged from their Indian summers affirming not only the Slave South's supremacy in world cotton production, but also the idea that human chattel fared better in the slaveholders' republic than the colonized did within Britain's Asian empire. A gendered ethos of dynamism underpinned the representation of Southern benevolence. As the overseers and southern press accounts articulated it, the march of slavery and American cotton was inextricably linked with the virtues of a dynamic American masculinity, defined against both allegedly effete Europeans and passive Indians.

The nineteenth-century strands of trans-Atlantic history that brought a taste of Mississippi to India ran back to the commercial chambers of Manchester. The Industrial Revolution had made that city both a site of international trade and a "node of traffic" in trans-Atlantic news, linking it to the "first cities" of the Atlantic and Indian Ocean worlds. British policies of mercantilism and protectionism fueled Manchester's textile industry, fed by slave-produced cotton, and cemented by technological advances and factory labor. At the same time, the city developed an activist political identity, with its mercantile and industrial interests supporting free trade as well as radical reforms like voting rights for the working class, adding up to what Jerome I. Hodos calls "an internationalist and meliorist capitalism"[7] sympathetic to the goals of transatlantic abolitionists. In this context, the aspirations of Manchester's textile manufacturers for independence from US slave-grown cotton ebbed and flowed through the antebellum era, fueled by factors as varied as the threat of boll weevil invasions and the impending crisis of Union. By 1840, champions of the enslaved in North America had buttressed these economic arguments for alternatives to American cotton with a humanitarian case for abolition. They were joined by critics who connected imperial economic policies of mercantilism and land taxes with famines and enslavement, and saw the development of Indian cotton cultivated by free labor as a solution to the problem of poverty there.[8] These diverse ends coincided with the interests of the EIC Court of Directors in London to promote the "the cultivation of cotton, sugar and other articles of commerce, suited to the European market," to advance their own material interests, lift their colonial dependents out of poverty through "improvements" in scientific agriculture, and convince England's mercantile community that the company was doing its part to support British industry.[9]

The British India Society grew out of this union of interests between merchants and reformers, and networked heavily with abolitionists across the Atlantic.[10]

Transatlantic steamers brought letters and newspapers from British reformers. The American abolitionist press and African American newspapers published excerpts of private correspondence and recycled pieces that appeared in London and Manchester publications. *The Liberator* reported on George Thompson's Manchester appearance in 1840[11] and on Garrison's speech at the annual meeting of the BIS in London earlier that year. On that occasion, the American had invoked a vision of a humanitarian world without borders and was met with loud cheers. "He was the true patriot and Christian ... who looked on the whole world as his country, and all mankind as his countrymen." Garrison described the enslaved as "a man and a brother," expressing sympathy for "the ... crushed, oppressed Indians," and the "not less than a million of slaves in India...."[12] When the *Manchester Times* covered the African American activist Charles Redmond's UK lecture series on race prejudice—"that unhallowed spirit of *caste*" and the "horrors of Lynch-law legislation," the *Liberator* picked up the story.[13] When the American abolitionist Wendell Phillips wrote to Garrison about his meeting with Thompson in the London offices of the BIS, and their visit to the House of Commons to hear a distinguished roster of reformist speakers with ties to both the EIC and cotton manufacturers, the readers of the *Liberator* learned about it.[14] The proceedings of the World Antislavery Convention, at which the concerns of the free produce movements converged with advocates of colonial reform, received wide coverage in the American press.

BEFORE THE AMERICANS ARRIVED: DEBATE OVER FREE COTTON PROSPECTS IN BRITISH INDIA

British optimism about India's prospects as a serious competitor to US cotton producers rested upon both the region's history of textile artisanry and its natural features of soil and climate. The objectives of textile manufacturers and abolitionists in Britain existed, however, in tension with the overriding imperative of corporate imperialism in India, namely revenue. Following the failure of early cotton endeavors, a host of imperial stakeholders, from manufacturers, merchants, and company directors in England to bureaucrats, local horticulturists, and commercial interests in India, had advanced sometimes overlapping but more often conflicting strategies to satisfy "the immense manufactures of England." Manchester and Glasgow industrialists urged state action centering upon the rate and mode of taxing cotton lands and the award of grants to encourage investment and experimentation with foreign seeds.[15]

By contrast, some colonial bureaucrats shifted the responsibility for creating favorable market conditions for an export-oriented cotton economy in India to Britain's mercantile community. Indian farmers, they argued, were rational economic actors who adopted subsistence strategies of diversified farming in response to revenue demands and the challenges of credit and infrastructure. The farmers also responded to considerations like the reliability and weight of foreign cotton yield, whether it could withstand drought and disease, whether the value of its seed equaled that of native varieties, and whether it was suited for markets both abroad and at home, where much of it was consumed. One official suggested that the government give *ryots* (farmers) the opportunity to pay their taxes in good quality cotton rather than money, on the understanding that the Manchester "memorialists" contract "to purchase that produce, paying a surcharge above the prime cost, to cover expenses.[16]

Yet the colonial establishment balked at any reforms that might disrupt the state's existing revenue arrangements or entail expensive improvements. The proposal to introduce revenue in kind was rejected on the grounds that it would create tens of thousands of separate cotton accounts with no guaranteed outcomes. The idea of building quays in Gujerat elicited the objection that rivers and channels shifted their channels periodically.[17] It cost less to frame India's failure to compete with American cotton as a problem of knowledge and culture on the part of the agricultural population. But surely it also reflected the decision makers' own assumptions about race and expertise. The import of American know-how was expected to help colonial officials both learn techniques and produce a body of knowledge on the science of cotton production through experimentation, while vesting the management of the enterprise in Anglo-American hands.

Correspondence among colonial officials betrayed no abolitionist intent whatsoever. Instead, when the free cotton experiments in India got underway, E. A. Webster, the US vice consul in Bombay, would write Secretary of State Daniel Webster in Washington that these ventures were no more than an extension of the British colonial policy of mercantilism and extraction, "of improving the cultivation of India by the introduction of the Mauritius sugar cane, the Chinese mulberry, American cotton," all with the ultimate goal of inflating EIC profits. Webster was convinced that the British had no interest in protecting the "manufactures of India," for they derived their revenues from taxes on land, "in some cases amounting to three-fifths of its produce. The plan of the company is simply to make India the producing and England the manufacturing company." The vice consul went on to offer his judgment that competition from French and German products lent urgency to the drive for mercantilism in British India. As it was, Americans dominated the trade in "course cottons" in East Africa. He wrote that from "the Cape of Good Hope to the mouth of the Indus an English vessel cannot dispose of a piece of this description of goods if an American vessel is in port." More alarming for the British, he reported, was the fact that despite the steady rise of discriminatory tariffs on American goods, these were beginning to make inroads against British manufactures, even in Indian ports. For the American envoy, the cotton experiments were apiece with British imperialistic adventures and quests for commercial supremacy elsewhere in the Indian Ocean: "The command of the coffee trade was probably one great motive for the occupation of Aden, and the command of the trade on the Indus and in Afghanistan had probably as much to do with the late invasion of that country, as the fear of Russian influence ... on the company's northwest frontier."[18]

American slaveholders and their allies disagreed. From its inception, the cotton project's connections with the British India Society lent it an abolitionist cast that furious southerners would judge a conspiracy against not simply their so-called domestic institution but a strike against the Union itself.

CAPTAIN BAYLES IN THE UNITED STATES

The man who would experience the Cotton Kingdom's fury firsthand was Brevet-Captain Thomas Bayles, of the 52nd Madras Native Infantry. While in service in the southern Mahratta region, Bayles had experimented on the native cottons of India, persuading farmers to plant a "cart load" of Bourbon cottonseed. Ill health had forced him to leave for England without learning the outcome of his endeavors, but news of his initiative reached the ear of the anti–Corn Law Parliamentarian Joseph Hume.[19]

Hume initiated a chain of introductions that put Bayles aboard the *Great Western* from Bristol on an EIC mission to recruit American skill and technology for India. Bayles sailed on 23 March 1839, only a few months before the rebellion aboard the slave ship *Amistad*. Disembarking in New York, the envoy secured credit through the British minister in Washington and launched his southern sojourn in Charleston, South Carolina, on May 6. He visited Sea Island cotton and rice plantations before winding his way along the Georgia coast and then via New Orleans and Mobile, to Natchez, Mississippi, reportedly home to the "best and most intelligent" cotton cultivators. It was February 1840, and Bayles's delicate mission had already weathered formidable challenges: yellow fever, the threat of violent opposition from local planters and population, and mistrust harbored by potential recruits as to his true identity, accreditation, and mission. He sought to overcome these by drawing upon health remedies learned in that other "trying country," India, by networking furiously among British merchants and American planters that he could trust, securing letters of introduction at each stop, and cautiously and furtively working his contacts without divulging the full extent of his US mission. Meanwhile, he tapped into the restlessness, quest for adventure, independence, and fortune that evidently animated enough young overseers or potential overseers to supply him a steady stream of applicants for his impending expedition to India.[20]

Most promising was "an intelligent young man" the Captain encountered on a visit to a plantation in Jefferson County that belonged to a cotton baron who had befriended him. Named Thomas J. Finnie, this overseer had sole charge of two plantations, each owned by a local widow, with one of whom he shared a residence.

Bayles could not match the combined salary Finnie made from managing the widows' plantations. But "from a spirit of adventure, and a conviction of realizing in the East an independence for himself by the pursuit in question," he agreed to not only embark for India himself, but to persuade other Mississippians to do the same. True to his word, Finnie recruited the young overseer of a large cotton plantation in the neighborhood of Petty Gulf. They contracted for a free round trip to India, an annual salary of 300 pounds for five years starting from an appointment date of 1 March 1840, and an annual "gratuity" for the successful training of Indian farmers in American methods of cotton cultivation. But to Finnie and the other overseers, infinitely more important than any annual salary or bonus was the opportunity that a position with the EIC would offer them for setting up as planters in their own right. In order to "induce efficient men" to join his South Asian cotton mission, Bayles held out to the southerners the promise that upon the expiry of their terms of service, "the farms they had formed would be made over to them on easy terms."[21] In light of tightening avenues to social mobility in the American South, the chance to reinvent themselves as landowners must have carried some attraction for young white men of slender means, perfectly in keeping with the ethos of mobility and filibustering that marked that age of continental expansion.

These men came of age in what the historian Brian Schoen has portrayed as an entrepreneurial Cotton South, committed to free trade, regional infrastructure development, and the empowerment of local merchants as replacements for northern factors. Yet economic hard times in the late 1830s constricted opportunities for young men of the overseer class, presenting overseas migration as a bold opportunity to seek fortunes abroad. Westward expansion required capital. An Indian trip sponsored by the EIC did not. Moreover, the financial crisis of 1837 and the international depression that followed in the early 1840s dimmed prospects for local and foreign investment in the region. As cotton prices fell, Mississippi in particular defaulted on British-held bonds. The Mississippi men set out for British Asia, then, amid economic crises that had sent an earlier spirit of optimism crashing.[22]

As Bayles made his way through the Grand Gulf, Petty Gulf, and Vicksburg, interviewing prospective "planters," rejecting many who struck him as supine, vacillating, or dissolute, his negotiations challenged the "secrecy" and "reserve" that the Briton had so carefully cultivated around his presence in the South. All hell now broke loose: "the planters raised all manner of obstacles" to his recruitment efforts, attacked him in the press, and accused him of being an imposter, warning prospective recruits that he represented cotton speculators who would lure unsuspecting victims to India and leave them destitute there. This ferment forced the EIC agent to secure arms for protection. Nevertheless, he managed to escape and even procure cotton gins, cleaners, and a gin wright along the way to New York through New Orleans, Augusta, Charleston, and Baltimore. Bayles and a contingent of ten men and their machines sailed for Bristol and London in June. The

Americans' Indian adventures began with an exercise in public relations. They experimented with the cleaning of Indian cotton with American saw gins before an audience of EIC leaders along with manufacturers, brokers, spinners, and mechanics from Liverpool and Manchester. And then the Mississippians sailed for Bombay and Madras, leaving in their wake a raging controversy over the meaning of their enterprise on their native side of the Atlantic.[23]

SLAVERY'S REACTION TO THE BAYLES EXPEDITION: APPEALS TO NATIONALISM AND ANTI-ABOLITIONISM

News of the Bayles expedition spread like wildfire through the American South, fueled by reports of abolitionist euphoria traversing lecture halls and newspaper columns from London and Manchester through Boston. *The Liberator* and the New York *Journal of Commerce,* whose founders included the abolitionist Arthur Tappan, printed correspondence exulting in the EIC's engagement of "many first-rate overseers from South Carolina." In stark contrast to the assessment that British bureaucrats in India would later offer of these recruits, abolitionists described them as "gentlemen, of considerable intelligence ... who have been all their lives engaged upon cotton plantations in the United States."[24] Such chronicles galvanized lords of the loom and the lash to jointly raise the alarm against what a widely published column described as an "Extraordinary project of England against the United States." For a brief moment, the threat from the East entered domestic debates over tariffs, slavery, and the security of the free American worker, promising economic nationalism a new lease of life in the South. Many in the Cotton South had hitherto embraced both slavery and free trade in an Atlantic exchange network that harmonized the intersectional interests of northern shippers, free-state grain growers, and American consumers in a fortified Union. It had signaled the South's "resounding rejection of a nation-centered economy."[25]

Now, however, free cotton experiments in India could be used to buttress a sense of nationalism that married devotion to US republican institutions with protective tariffs. During 1840, across the length of the country, from the Atlantic seaboard through the Mississippi valley, there emerged an alternative public sphere forged in the columns of newspapers as sectionally and politically varied as the sensationalist penny press the *New York Weekly Herald;* the Ottawa-based Democratic weekly the *Illinois Free Trader,* which had embraced the motto, "*Our Country, her Commerce, and her Free Institutions*"; and the proslavery, Whig-nativist *Liberty Advocate,* published in Mississippi's cotton country on the Louisiana border.[26] Throughout their pages reverberated a claim that an unholy alliance of "the British government, the East India Company and the British Anti-Slavery Society," was seeking to "build up its own interests at the expense of all the great planting interests of the United States." These forces allegedly commanded "an immense extent of country." For labor, they would exploit "their slaves, whom they call "ryotts" [sic], but who are really slaves in a most miserable state" to cultivate abundant quantities of cotton and sugar. It was only the latest phase of a conspiracy, outraged southerners claimed, that started with the destruction of sugar planters in Jamaica through the instrument of the "Abolition Society," paving the way for the influx of "East India sugar into market with a profit, which they could not do before without a protecting duty." The masters of empire were now prepared to move to the next phase of their operation—the spread of "abolition doctrines" in the United States in order to disrupt the South's cotton economy. "They have sent agents here, and books, and money, and all sorts of inducements to the fanatics to break up the system of slavery." Besides climate and soil, India's competitive promise was advertised to lie in its cheap labor: 3 cents per capita per day versus the 25 cents that "negro labor" was thought to cost. Unionist, nationalist Whig defenders of slavery urged measures to foil British attempts to destabilize the United States, by encouraging "our domestic manufactures, and the home consumption of cotton. In this way alone can we be independent of Great Britain."[27]

Juxtaposing reports on East India cotton with accounts of the 1840 World Antislavery convention, which they called the "Foreign Convention for the Abolition of slavery in the United States, now in session in the city of London, England," the proslavery press invoked nationalism to urge opposition to abolition. "We have no question that the United States will be singled out in its proceedings for the largest share of curses and denunciations. Slavery as it exists in this country will be found comparatively more odious and detestable than in any other." Critics contrasted the "enterprise, energy," of republican America with the "degraded, ... disfranchised" peasantry of monarchical Europe to highlight the abolitionists' alleged hypocrisy. Rejecting "all attempts to define or control ... any of our internal institutions," they linked European "lust of conquest" with the virtual enslavement of the colonized. "Let [Britain] knock the chains off the enslaved Hindoos. Let her retrace her steps as regards her ... mediated conquests of China. Then conventions can meet to consider negro slavery. ..." The *Liberty Advocate* maintained that India cotton was on par with a series of actions sanctioned by a hostile foreign government—the British Parliament—to undermine the American nation, including West Indian emancipation, the impressment of "negroes taken in slave ships" into the British service, and the institution of "Black regiments for life."[28]

Thus, protectionism, anti-abolitionism, and anti-Black racism were all projected as patriotic gestures, and discussion of Indian cotton provided a context to articulate these connections. In a speech in support of Henry Clay's policies of economic nationalism, Senator Oliver Smith of Indiana invoked the British author Robert Montgomery Martin's optimistic vision of "the manifold blessings" that would accompany the march of empire in India. He noted that such "blessings" would bode ill for US economic interests across sectors: "*On the one hand,* we behold a small island in the Atlantic, admirably adapted for commerce, and possessing a hardy, industrious, and skillful manufacturing population; *on the other,* a vast territory, situated in a distant hemisphere, with a soil exuberantly fertile, a varied and not ungenial climate, abounding in all the tropical products which the wants or luxuries of the Hyperborean can require, and teeming with myriads... of industrious, patient, and emulative human beings, whose love of agriculture and trade is unsurpassed by any other economic nation. It would appear as if nature herself had linked together the northern isle and eastern continent under the one crown for the wisest of purposes, namely, that by the interchange of commodities indigenous to each, the peaceful influence of commerce might become the handmaid of civilization."[29] Smith argued that the British "East Indies" had the resources to fulfill this dream of commercial communion, and he offered figures to buttress his case: Indian exports to Britain had trebled in nine years starting in 1831. Moreover, steam navigation had reduced transport costs, knitting distant lands into one "neighborhood": "CALCUTTA and BOMBAY will be laid along side of LIVERPOOL and MANCHESTER, while the inhabitants of the INDUS and the GANGES will mingle daily with those of the THAMES and the MERSEY." Surely southerners understood the "prejudice" that such a shrunken globe spelled for America's staple in the markets of Great Britain?[30] In addition, Britain's tariff policies appeared to favor reciprocal relations between the imperial power and her colonies, at the expense of American cotton: "Can American cotton compete, in the market of Great Britain, with the India cotton, while the American pays 70 cents to the 100 pounds, and the Indian 8 cents?" Most alarmingly, the senator raised the specter of East India cotton supplanting American "in our own markets." Was it therefore, not in the American planter's interests to "secure the home market against India cotton, either in the raw or manufactured state?"[31] Moreover, since cotton comprised the lion's share of American exports (62.5% during 1836–40, Smith contended), any threat to the South's supremacy in foreign markets for cotton would tip the United States's overall balance of trade in unfavorable directions.[32]

AMERICAN OVERSEERS IN INDIA

By the early summer of 1842, however, this narrative had begun to fracture, as reports on the difficulties of transplanting Mississippi into India began to filter in. Let us now turn our gaze to *mofussils* (rural districts) of the Northwest Provinces in the north central regions of British India, where the Indian chapters of the American sojourners' stories began to unfold in earnest.

These accounts emerge through disparate perspectives. They materialize in the sometimes discordant words of British stakeholders, are implied in the actions of their Indian subjects, and documented in journals kept by the planters themselves.

The journals, ranging in depth and detail from Terry's terse observations to Finnie's extensive commentaries, were selectively excerpted in the southern press to make the case for the slaveholders' republic. They also offer a basis for illuminating the ways in which the overseers interpreted and failed to adapt to the very different circumstances of land, labor, social structure and politics in India. It was a case of expectations honed in a milieu of American-style slave capitalism, running up against the feudal vestiges of Mughal-era land tenure and labor arrangements.

The first thing that the Americans learned was that India was no American frontier, where, as Sven Beckert's argument about "war capitalism" suggests, the state cleared arable land of their native occupants through war and treaty.[33] In India, by contrast, successive states had, as David Ludden has written, historically "expanded into agrarian space," embedded in elaborate networks of kin, caste, patronage, and ritual that interacted with state power while evading its full grasp. In the 1840s, when the boundaries of empire were still fluid, the EIC exercised few of the direct, coercive, proprietary powers over key factors of production to which Americans were accustomed through state support of slavery in the United States. Rather, the company contracted with local agrarian patriarchs with roots in Mughal India to disburse entitlements in exchange for revenue.[34]

In this context, the Americans were to encounter two agrarian Indian archetypes whose titles signified both "roles in the revenue system" and "property rights in land"[35]: the *zamindar* and the *ryot*. By the end of the eighteenth century, the zamindar came to be understood as a landlord who collected revenue for the state from virtual tenants on his estate, in return for title to his land. The ryots, by contrast, invoked, for imperial critics of *zamindari,* independent peasants inhabiting "little republics" of family farms down the ages, and paying rent directly to successive states, free of intermediaries. This construct of the "republican" ryot thus represented a far cry from the imagery of slavery advertised in the southern press back in the United States. In Bundelkhand, where the best-documented Americans accompanying Bayles would launch their experiments with "free-grown" cotton, the zamindars hailed from lesser lineages of the local ruling Rajput clans under Mughal (later, British) suzerainty, and presided over "subordinate castes" in hierarchical village communities woven by bonds of "intermarriage, land-owning, and labor movements." Wage workers in the area might be drawn from tribal populations perhaps displaced by encroachments upon forest lands, and others not able to meet their subsistence needs on family farms or looking for work during off-peak seasons. It was also a world in which nature and astrology punctuated the seasonal calendar with festival and ritual, thus meshing economic activity with the social and the cultural in inalienable ways.[36]

How did the overseers fit into these mediated agrarian structures of land tenure, where command over labor was at least partly predicated upon stable social relations, and the stars and the gods joined memory and accumulated knowledge of farming ways to determine agricultural schedules?[37] For a start, the Mississippians lacked a free hand in selecting sites to locate their farms, sometimes having to settle for inferior forfeited lands. Four of the planters accompanied by Bayles wove their way from the town of Kanpur in March 1841 through hamlets on the banks of the Jamuna River, in search of suitable sites to experiment in cotton cultivation. Notwithstanding the warnings of local farmers against the scarcity of water, "even for their own cattle," they settled upon Kotra Muckrundpoor as Finnie's field of operations. Terry chose Chowuk, Mercer Rath, and Blount, Soomairpoor Khas. In accordance with the recommendations of the district's revenue board, the government furnished each farm with a bungalow for the planter, together with forty pairs of bullocks and barns to house them; godowns for cottonseed, grain, and stores; a gin house; and a supply of carts and plows. Each farm was allotted an allowance of 5,000 rupees (approximately US $2,500 at the time) annually, to cover the expenses of maintaining this infrastructure.[38] The remaining Americans scattered across other parts of the country, in districts under the jurisdiction of the Presidencies of Madras to the south and Bombay to the west.

FINNIE'S FANTASIES OF FEUDALISM AND THE ATLANTIC PUBLIC SPHERE

As in many other realms of administration, colonial authorities in India tapped into a Mughal era precedent of land tenure to inaugurate their experiments in cotton cultivation with free labor. In eighteenth-century Bengal, for example, the government made tax-free land grants to prominent men (styled *chaudhuris,* among other titles), who entered zamindari by clearing land. They financed cultivation through cash advances to peasants for crops and labor.[39] Now colonial players envisioned a "mixed" model of production, which combined a "model" farm run directly by the planters, with the help of hired labor, with farming out cotton production to local zamindars and ryots.[40]

This context—refracted through the prism of Bayles's promises of land and Finnie's aspirations to plantation ownership—shaped the Mississippian's rather fantastical representation of himself as a zamindar to neighbors back in Natchez toward the beginning of his Indian sojourn. An account dated January 1842, published in the Whig *Mississippi Creole* via the *Natchez Courier,* laid out Finnie's feudal imaginings: "The land here is laid out in a manner similar to our townships, each containing some 5000 acres. I am now constituted a "Zemendar" [*sic*] or landlord, and have control [over a] ... village of 200 inhabitants, and although this number of people derive subsistence from my tract, yet not more than one-third of [the land] is cultivated." He reported that he had successfully trained his six "native" overseers "in my way of doing business." He had had one thousand acres "ploughed and cross-ploughed" in four or five days at a cost of 12.5 cents per day for each of two hundred plows; a "laboring man" commanded but a little over $1.62 per month, while "furnishing his own subsistence." Moreover, in the beginning at least, these workers seemed capable of improvement: "after we have ... learned the people how to use our implements [the American plow], they handle them with ... dexterity." He went on to share the "thrilling sensations" that surged as he beheld his "Arab steed ... bounding to and fro among 200 ploughs." This country suited a "poor but industrious man," who could here "start a business with what two or three negroes would cost in Mississippi and in ten years be better off than nine-tenths of the planters there"—an observation shot through with a sense of consciousness of the precarious turns of fortune in his native land.[41]

Pressing on with the theme of his rising status in the world, Finnie described the "large, comfortable home" the government had provided him. He commuted in lordly fashion from the colonial capital of Calcutta borne aloft on a palanquin by "twelve to sixteen men" who took turns carrying him for ten miles, in batches, as he reclined in his cushioned seat: "it is of course expensive." At home, when hot winds blew, there were servants to keep him cool: a water carrier continually wettened the lattice at the western door through which hot air entered, to condition the air. Then there were *pankers* (fans) suspended across the ceilings of each room and attached by rope to the wall outside the house, which attendants could pull through the night to keep the fans in motion. Indeed, Finnie was so delighted with the country and the climate, that he announced his intention to bring his brother to India once the young man finished his "collegiate studies" in Georgia.[42]

Optimism such as Finnie displayed was widely reported in the abolitionist press, connecting global cities with reform hubs. The *National Anti-Slavery Standard*, founded by Lydia Maria Child, an organ of the Garrisonian American Antislavery Society published "concurrently" in New York and Philadelphia,[43] cited letters from Finnie's location as a source for the judgment that "India is one of the best countries for the growth of cotton in the world."[44] It also echoed the *London Atlas*'s judgment that the planters "on the Bengal side, (with Captain Bayles as superintendent) are ... energetic in the prosecution of their plans."[45] The US vice consul in Bombay did his part to publicize Finnie's enthusiasm by enclosing with his official dispatches to Washington a piece published in the *Bombay Times* that featured the Mississippian's focus on the ostensibly Anglo-American personal qualities that, in combination with soil, climate, cheap labor, and slave-state expertise, were expected to transform the Indian countryside into a vast treasure trove of cheap, good-quality cotton: "constant application, decision, industry, and perseverance."[46] On the other side of the country, three Americans who had landed in Bombay and settled in Broach near the mouth of the Narmada River in the present-day western state of Gujerat began their assignment on a similarly high note.[47] By October 1841, they relayed to the US emissary in Bombay that they had planted three hundred acres of cotton, which "were looking as well as any they ever saw in America."[48]

Such confidence proved misplaced. The *Gazeteer of the Bombay Presidency* later recounted that the Americans, having secured 125 acres of "light soil" and 50 acres of the "best and most productive black soil" had tried unsuccessfully to plow before the rain fell. They then adopted "the native way of cleaning and preparing the land" before sowing their fields with New Orleans seed. At first, "an irrigated plot of Sea Island cotton" showed promise, but insects destroyed the plants before they could be harvested. When the planters experimented with growing local cotton "in American fashion on high and broad ridges thrown up by the plough," they produced outcomes no different from "cotton grown in the ordinary Broach way."[49]

At the end of the year, the three Americans departed Broach. Their perspectives on the failure of their free cotton experiments diverged sharply from those of their British employers. Early on, they had privately expressed skepticism that "the natives of this country" would ever succeed in the cotton enterprise, not for lack of ability, skill, or will on their part, but rather, because of "the discouragements of over taxation and their want of capital and implements for cultivating and cleaning the crop...." Nor were the Americans in Broach pleased with the terms of their own employment. They complained to the US Consulate that their "renumeration" [*sic*] was low compared with that of "most Europeans" in India, and warned that if the EIC did not improve their pay, they might not even serve out their agreed upon terms of five years. Initially, the American Consulate in Bombay and planters in Broach believed that those located near the headquarters of the government—in Bengal—might have better facilities at their disposal.[50]

As it turned out, Americans in closer physical proximity to the Bengal government were faring little better. Further east, Finnie's euphoria was fading as well, although this planter interpreted the sources of his failure differently than his Broach compatriots did. Finnie's troubles were owing not only to the vagaries of the weather and the depredation of insects but also to failed attempts to enlist the local population in clearing and cultivating land he considered part of his "estate." When the workers failed to indulge his zamindari aspirations for the paltry wages he was offering, Finnie interpreted their behavior through a cultural lens that mixed familiar British Orientalist perspectives with a medley of American attitudes toward race and miscegenation, as well as capitalism and coercion.[51]

These sometimes discordant lenses emerge and converge most clearly in a journal that Finnie started writing for his "own amusement and future reference," as he put it. Later, the lieutenant governor, having apparently learned of its existence, requested its formal submission and inclusion in the government's records. The American took the opportunity this presented to counsel his imperial overlords on public policy in frank terms.[52] Finnie's journal entries, organized into units of time and framed by frequent observations on the weather, interspersed extensive commentaries on the land, its people, its colonial masters, and their programs with the author's own dreams of grandeur and evolving sense of identity, from a fortune-seeking settler colonialist to a pro-South American nationalist. His reflections offer glimpses of a mercurial temperament, swinging between wild optimism and portraits of aristocratic splendor that found their way into initial American press reports of his Indian sojourn, as described previously, and growing despair over the elusiveness of American-style settler-colonial fulfillment in British India. An entry on 17 December 1841, for instance, crowed, "To-day 1 had 151 zemindars' ploughs, and about 40 of my own; native and American together making altogether nearly 200 ploughs. Mississippians! well may you fear our enterprise here, when we can muster so formidable a force for cultivating cotton.... I hope to see the day when many officers will follow Captain Bayles's noble example, and throw away the sword for the plough."[53]

But equally often his journal musings brimmed with a sense of loneliness. In sharp contrast with the feudal lifestyle he claimed in press reports back home, an early journal entry bemoaned the desolation of the "single-poled tent" that he called his new home, with "not one European in 10 miles of me." Compared with the "extensive fields" to which he had been accustomed, he regarded his new farm as a collection of "little patches." Outbreaks of diarrhea and dysentery exacerbated the trials of those early days, and occasioned a hasty visit to an English doctor in Kanpur. Still, he dwelled on how "skill and industry" might transform an "uncultivated, poverty-stricken" country into a cotton kingdom, "to the advantage of India and England as well as to our own interests."[54]

The experiences of a brutally dynamic, violently modern Slave South shaped Finnie's racialized vision of settler colonialism, in which Indians would learn the ways of free labor under duress. White "practical planters" would transform India by doing away with the indirect rule over resources favored by the EIC. They would turn the torpid "Hindu" countryside (a formulation that conflated religion with constructs of race and space) into a model of agrarian capitalism, by planting new elites. In addition, they would improve and educate local workers in the virtues of free labor and the Protestant work ethic, both by setting an example and through the coercive ways of slave society.

In this context, Finnie's use of language—his reference to workers as "hands," and "coolies"—encoded the mentality of mastery given to driving enslaved and indentured labor. Caitlin Rosenthal has noted that scientific management and innovative accounting techniques on antebellum plantations adopted the "hand" as a "standardized metric" for measuring and comparing worker productivity.[55] Finnie's commentaries on the colonized started by asserting the "natural" deficiencies of different classes of India's native populations. From his perspective, the landed elites exhibited tyranny, thriftlessness, and a lack of enterprise, while the peasants and farmworkers had poor work habits. The Americans—schooled in the color-coded languages for indentured labor common in the Atlantic world—styled them "coolies." As historians of transnational labor movements have noted, the term *coolie* defined workers of color considered not qualified to assume the privileges or responsibilities of the free white worker. Finnie believed that rural India's weaknesses of nature and culture would not be mitigated through reforms in rent law or land reform as Anglo-Atlantic abolitionists argued. Rather, redress required the steady custodial hand of permanently settled "just, liberal-minded European practical planters throughout the country," each of whom would use his superior management skills and practical knowledge to produce staple crops for export and spend all his profits within the village where he lived to fund its residents' land rents and taxes, "without one rupee leaving the village." Such a planter would dig "gold from the bowels of the earth, thus benefiting himself and the people, developing the resources of the country, by which he springs a mine of inexhaustible wealth."[56] In this context, Finnie portrayed himself as a mentor, civilizer, and advocate for an idle, fatalistic, and oppressed but malleable laboring Indian poor, on the one hand, and a hands-on, enterprising antidote to the bureaucratic "theoretical agriculturists" and scientists belonging to the colonial establishment, on the other.

This vision of transformation embodied an ambitious stranger's frustration at the seemingly ossified and impenetrable worlds of privilege and deference in rural India. Finnie's contempt for the "old zamindars"—a title he had appropriated in his self-representations to Mississippians—betrayed contests over labor control, as much as over what proper landed elites should look like. Describing these "self-styled respectable men" as "conceited, ignorant, superstitious," he noted that they had failed to meet their contractual obligations to meet cotton quotas set by the overseer. They appeared to have no respect for the dignity of labor, having been "taught from infancy that work is degrading. . . ." Moreover, they struck him as improvident, with one mortgaging his land while asking to borrow Finnie's tent "to have a dance and feast under" in celebration of his daughter's wedding, pleading that "he would be ruined, his character would be destroyed, if he did not give a grand feast upon that occasion." As Finnie saw it, such attitudes defined a culture hostile to industry, on par with festivals that interrupted work schedules. One July day, he noted, "The Hindus must have a feast today, consequently there is nothing doing."[57] In fact, as agrarian historians have observed, social rituals like weddings and festivals not only offered relief from the tedium of rural life, but also fashioned the networks of family and patronage that entered into negotiation over resources. The performativity and spectatorship associated with rituals like weddings, moreover, helped cement etiquettes of social status and deference in agrarian society.[58]

It was precisely such structures of patronage and deference, with their implications of competition for and control over labor, that posed some of the gravest challenges to the overseers' command of wage work. It is possible to discern these tensions in Finnie's construction of himself as a champion of the "more worthy lower classes," whose labor he accused the landlords of exacting without payment. This posture, he wrote, had earned him the "unutterable hatred" of the landlords. He mused, "I console myself with the fact that the poor, hard-working people look to me for protection, and their love amply repays me for the hatred of these hardened wretches."⁵⁹ Yet, such "love," if it existed, certainly did not forestall the considerable labor troubles that Finnie and his compatriots confronted—circumstances that the Mississippian attributed to instigation by local elites or "half-caste" (biracial) managers.

The story of the American planter's complicated relationship with his workers unfolds through his frequently conflicting narratives of their character and behavior. For a start, rural Indians' alleged physical fragility—emphasized by the overseers' mention of their vegetarian diet—came to be conflated with their "innate" traits of indolence and inertia. These traits, in turn, ostensibly mirrored the static structures and customs that seemed to limit their mobility and productivity. The Mississippians remarked frequently on African Americans' superior capacity for physical labor over that of the Indians. Finnie observed in his diary one October day, "All hands picking cotton, but they pick so little each, that if we had made a crop we would have to hire hands to pick it. It is strange that people here have only picked from 7 lbs. to 10 lbs., while our negroes will pick from 100 lbs. to 500 lbs. per day."⁶⁰

Fatalism bred lethargy, the Americans assumed, even as meanings got lost in translation. Accustomed to the frenetic pace at which humans cleared land on the banks of the Mississippi, they chafed at the sight of peasants "sitting under the shade of a tree ten hours in the day," after having cleared grass over a portion of the field only as large as a dining table. The locals may have been allowing the field to lie fallow in-between crops, but the Americans interpreted their schedule as the product of "inexcusable laziness." When Finnie lectured such a man about the rewards of hard work, he would "fold his hands, look to heaven, and say, 'Sahib, hum gurreeb hy jo Ram kurreh sohogah.' 'Sir, I am a very poor man; what can I do? if God wills that I should have a good crop, I will have it at any rate'; . . . forgetting the proverb, 'You may as well expect that God will make you rich without industry, as that he will make you . . . happy without your own endeavours.'" The uncertainty of the seasons lent such fatalism some logic, as the planters themselves would discover, but for the moment, Finnie used this example to make his case against land tax relief. In his own peculiar twist of logic, the land tax, he argued, insured against idleness: "The ryot does not calculate how much land he can cultivate by hard work, but how little land with very little work will make him a support and pay the "land-tax." Reduce that land-tax, and instead of benefiting the ryot, you only indulge him in a greater degree of idleness."⁶¹

But the American was determined to bring change by enforcing industrial work discipline and spreading the "Protestant work ethic" among India's agrarian population. He wanted to teach peasants that time was money, and that hard work, thrift, and discipline would lead to prosperity. In practice, that vision blurred the lines between a free market for labor and the violent tactics of slavery. Thus, Finnie refused to let his people off work on July 17, a Sunday. There was too much to be done; "besides," he maintained, "many of my Coolies celebrate it, as they do their own feast-days, by getting drunk... for they are like other low-caste people in other countries, when they get a little money they enjoy the luxury of getting drunk." He recorded that this approach had "greatly improved" a majority of them—that they lived and dressed better than when they first entered his employ. The Mississippian also sought to keep his hired laborers busy in diverse tasks. In January 1842, when there was no plowing, planting, or picking to be done, Finnie set them to sundry tasks. Some lugged wood, worked with masons, repaired old wells, cleaned up the gin, or towed bricks, for their American employer believed it was bad policy to "discharge them after learning them how to work."[62]

Moreover, Finnie experimented with industrial discipline, organizing them into military-style labor battalions. His diary entry for August 11, 1842, noted that they "came up in martial order this evening, as usual, for their pice [one-hundredth of a rupee]; they have formed themselves into a regiment.... Their hoes are their guns, and my assistant their captain, and the peons, according to grade, are lieutenants, Serjeants [sic], &c. They are delighted with this arrangement...."[63] Payday coincided with a local holiday, which he commemorated with a *buksheesh* (tip) for his regular employees. He was tickled when they flattered him by "promoting" him as their "Chowdry," an honor that appeared to signify his acculturation to local structures of deference.

When, however, his workforce proved less tractable, Finnie resorted to measures of coercion shaped not simply by his training as an overseer but also by his imaginings of etiquettes of Indian caste relations. When the "gentlemen drivers," using unfamiliar American plows proved so "careless" and "impudent," as to destroy "much cotton," he threatened to enlist state support to discipline them by dispatching them to the district magistrate. When ostensibly fatalistic workers negotiated for higher wages commensurate with the new American plowing skills he had taught them, Finnie saw them not as rational agents in a free market for labor but rather as creatures driven by blind instinct and impulse: "it is the nature of the animal to grasp, and the more he gets the more he wants." When the workers' claim to mobility and control over their employment terms threatened the stability expected of a standing labor force, Finnie responded by deviating from the contractual obligations of free labor. Finding that his hands were apt to leave for a day or two upon receipt of their wages in full at the end of the month, he started withholding their pay. The workers responded by resorting to informal collective bargaining, arriving at his door en masse on the brink of the rainy season when he needed them most, to press for arrears in their pay plus a bonus. Faced with the prospect of "no hands to work" with "thunder and lightning flashing" above his head, the American tried physical retribution, boxing the ears of their ringleaders. He went to bed that night satisfied that "they have gone off perfectly humbled, with, no doubt, a very exalted opinion of me; for they are so much accustomed to the exercise of arbitrary power among themselves ... that, unless it is exercised occasionally, they begin to think they are forgotten and neglected. They will now go to work with renewed energy...."[64]

Thus, even as Finnie was resorting to physical punishment reminiscent of the workings of a Mississippi slave plantation, he was rationalizing these measures as consistent with the performativity of power relations in caste-ridden India, as a necessary response, even, to subaltern expectations of a display of authority by their superiors. Imagine his surprise, then, when a few days later, his day laborers failed to arrive for work as usual. He sent to the village for them, and learned that "every man, woman and child of the working class had fled to the jungles. I inquired the cause, and was told that it was because I slapped a fellow the day before for cutting up all the cotton." But he suspected that other factors were at play. Given the season, competition from local zamindars, and the urgency of Finnie's labor needs, they were holding out for "very high wages," and he was forced to give in, for "they have me completely in their power.... [T]o wait now, would only sacrifice my whole crop." These circumstances forced his resort to a practice about which he had heard, namely "to go and catch men." Accompanied by a peon, he ventured into the jungles, secured twenty men, and put them to work on his fields, and "they were as gentle in a short time as if they had been brought up pets about one's own door." Finnie was convinced that the men had been driven to rebellion by the village "Chowdree ... who lays up and never works any himself, but makes each man of his clan give him part of their earnings every day." The American considered roughing up this thorn in his side by "letting him feel the weight of my old Egyptian 'Cawbash'... for interfering with my business." But if he did settle the dispute with a physical fight, he kept the altercation out of his record books.[65] What distinguishes this observation is the further evidence it offers of Finnie's clash of interest and authority with entrenched agrarian power structures.

If local authority figures in the village instigated his "coolies," another source of trouble materialized right on his own farm. A "half-caste" overseer colluded with subordinate workers to thwart the work schedule that Finnie had set for them. The Mississippian unleashed a volley of racialized explanations for his employees' untrustworthiness that acknowledged that coercion made the difference to Mississippi planters' control over their workers: "In America we are under the necessity of avoiding exposure, and still our work goes on profitably; but here, if I am away from the field my business stands almost still.... The only difference between a Coolie and a negro is this: [one] we can make work out of our sight by operating upon his fears, [the other] we must persuade and drive together, which answers very well as long as we are present, but has no effect as soon as our backs are turned."[66]

Finnie judged that European planters could rely on neither "half-castes or country born" Europeans to serve as "confidential assistants." The former, he deemed a "miserable race, with all the indolent, luxurious habits and low cunning of the native, and the dissipated habits of low Europeans, without the hardiness of the one, or enterprize [sic] or judgment of the other...." He was equally contemptuous of India's European-born residents, proclaiming them "afraid of dying if they let the sun or wind of heaven shine and blow rudely upon them." The answer to India's workforce and managerial challenges, according to Finnie, lay in "teaching the young men of the public schools how to plant, and as they become competent," to give them custody of villages "that have fallen in balance, and are in the hands of Government, making them responsible for the *Jumma*, [rent] but allow them to cultivate what land they like in cotton." Such trainees would have to be "well managed and mildly controlled," presumably under the direction of a mentor such as Finnie. As an example, he pointed to the promise of a "Hindoo boy" from a public school in the regional city of Allahabad that he had hired and trained. A class of public school–educated, native planters might set an example of enterprise to the "stubborn race" of zamindars he so despised and redeem the work ethic of ordinary workers. For Finnie had found "the common people, that is, the Coolies," to be "usually tractable, good-natured, inoffensive souls." He attributed their tendency to "injure their employers" to habits of ethical bankruptcy forged by the despotism of caste.[67]

Finnie's vision of "the white man's burden" left little room for sympathy with the ends of British abolitionism or radical politics. The Mississippian denounced West Indian emancipation in the same breath as he deprecated Daniel O'Connell's Indian land tax reform proposals. Indian ryots were better off, he insisted, than peasants in Italy and France, or the working classes of Great Britain; it was not India's land tax but the "indolent, licentious and prodigal habits of the people themselves"—given to feasts and dancing—that kept them in poverty. There followed a racist diatribe against emancipation: "Dan! Dan! remember that charity begins at home.... Place all your poor, half-starved brother Irishmen, ay, and Britons too, in good circumstances, and then ... we shall be glad to see you extend your benign wings over the remotest corners of the globe.... Calm your heaving breast and lull your sympathies for the sufferings of them fat, sleek, curly-headed, thick-lipped, flat-nosed beauties on the side of the Atlantic, where labour insures them subsistence and comfort.... Give up your juvenile reformation societies at the Cape of Good Hope ... and above all, do not attempt to legislate for the people of India until you have lived among them as a planter for a few years."[68] Clearly you could take the man out of Mississippi, but not the slaveholders' Mississippi out of the man!

THROUGH THE OVERSEERS' LOOKING GLASS: HOW RACE, TARIFFS, AND SETTLER COLONIALISM PLAYED BACK HOME

Finnie's early ambiguity about his prospects in India, complemented by the sometimes contradictory accounts of compatriots like Terry, registered in diverse ways in various Atlantic circuits of economic exchange and reform. These different registers prompted debate over fundamental points of policy and politics that wove the United States into an Atlantic political economy.

Consider, for instance, the controversy over tariffs, one iteration of which drew varied outlets into a larger discussion about nature, culture, and race in distant India. They included the pragmatic New York *Journal of Commerce* and the compatible *Natchez Free Trader*, published in a major axis of cotton production with a large population of planter-millionaires and close ties to northern business interests.[69] Other voices spoke through the *Independent Democrat* of Carroll, a cotton county sitting astride "the fertile Yazoo-Mississippi River Delta and adjacent hill country in northwest Mississippi,"[70] and the protectionist Whig *Mississippi Creole*, an organ of the rich cotton realm and railroad hub of Canton. One strand of the argument unfolded in the pages of the *Mississippi Creole*, which reproduced a piece published in the *Journal of Commerce* by A. Jones, a North Carolina–born physician and gin wright. Jones had accompanied the overseers as far as England, only to turn his back, he claimed, on a six-thousand-dollar annual salary at the last moment, on the pretext of patriotism.[71] EIC records offer a different version of events, suggesting that it was Jones who was so anxious to join the expedition that Captain Bayles, impressed with his technical skills, paid his passage to England on condition that he would expect no further aid from the government and would share with the EIC his know-how on gin manufacturing.[72]

Jones purported to show why India could never rival the United States in cotton cultivation, advancing an analysis that mixed the weaknesses of state policy with a race-infused perspective on settler colonialism. He argued that the EIC's rent and tax policies inhibited agricultural productivity. The town of Madras, covering 154,000 square miles of territory and home to a population of fifteen million, exported merely 800,000 pounds sterling worth of goods. Yet the Government of India extorted from this "miserable population" 5 million pounds sterling worth of revenue, or 20–25 million dollars, deemed "sufficient to support the entire Government of the United States!" Proslavery free traders also argued for the superior strength and training of enslaved laborers, implicitly or explicitly endorsing the material conditions of African Americans under slavery, as well as the supposedly salutary effects of coercion on productivity. Jones argued that although "Hindoos were said to work for 6.25 cents of our money" per day, they were feeble, subsisting on a scanty diet of rice in debilitating weather: "one able bodied American negro well fed on animal food will do more work than half a dozen Hindoos would, and do it better, so that [India's] cheap labor exists in name." Equally important, every cotton estate could count on the services of its workers all year along. In India, by contrast, the voluntary nature of cotton cultivation left the peasant with the option to "make opium, rice, or cotton." Moreover, that population was "ignorant of and prejudiced against the use of machinery, ploughs, mills, and the use of horses," relying instead on bullocks and primitive hoes. In short, the odds against bringing "free" Indian laborers voluntarily into extensive cotton cultivation seemed formidable.[73]

American free traders noted that the poor state of domestic infrastructure and exorbitant export taxes also militated against competition from Indian cotton. In addition, freight charges from India to Great Britain, with insurance, were higher than that from America to England. While the average expense of shipping cotton from the United States to Britain was estimated not to exceed one cent per pound, and the voyage took no longer than four to six weeks, freight from an Indian port such as Calcutta, Bombay, or Madras was likely to cost two cents per pound and take four months. The average price of *Surats,* or India cotton, was 8 cents per pound in Liverpool; while cotton transported from New Orleans commanded from 10 to 14 cents. Accounting for expenses associated with inland freight, land rent, export duty, warehouse expenses, freight to England, and marine insurance, one writer concluded that the producer of the article in India would be left with only 2.5 cents per pound to cover profit as well as production costs. The American producer by contrast, was likely to make 7 cents per pound after paying for parallel expenses.

American skeptics like Jones also racialized the preconditions of successful cotton production, holding out white settler colonialism as the ideal model for successful plantation agriculture. Yet England maintained her power over India through military means alone. 'We never see English families, men, women, and children, leaving the rural districts of England, to settle in India, as cultivators of the soil, carrying with them, their skill, industry, and enterprise. If the military government of India was favorable to their emigration, the unhealthy nature of the climate would act as a bar to their doing so."[74]

Free traders like Jones were convinced that India's climate did not favor cotton production. The long dry season stunted the growth of the cotton plant, producing "a short and inferior article of cotton; such as that Surat now appears in the Liverpool market." The rainy season destroyed the plant. Nor was irrigation likely to help, for it subjected the roots of the plant to excessive moisture while leaving the branches and leaves un-watered, producing small-sized pods and short, brittle fibers. Skeptics also argued that the culture of other products—rice, indigo, sugar, and opium—was more profitable to both native growers and the EIC. These commentators contended that it was for that reason that the English capitalists, like the "celebrated Mr. Gladstone, M.P., of Liverpool, whose forefathers made their great fortune in the American slave trade," were supposedly about to invest in sugar, rather than cotton cultivation. Jones averred that the recent increase in the supply of Indian cotton in Britain owed much to the closure of Chinese ports to British trade. Moreover, he held that the march of empire and concomitant expansion of trade and "civilization" would foster, among the vast populations in the tropical climatic zones of India and China, a demand for cotton articles greater than their capacity to produce raw cotton could match. "And as far as America is concerned, she must *ceteris paribus*—forever take the lead in its production."⁷⁵

The protectionist *Mississippi Creole*, however, dismissed Jones's argument as "done for political effect, and by a northern free-trade man." It divined a purpose far more sinister in the EIC's Indian ventures than northern free traders appeared willing to acknowledge: nothing less than a scheme to avenge Yorktown. The *Creole* editors contended that the free traders' argument about the deleterious impact of land rent on cultivation was overruled by its own assertion that the EIC "held all land in India in its possession." Moreover, the cheapness of Indian labor neutralized the advantage of the enslaved's productivity. As for India's poor infrastructure, the *Creole* reminded readers that Mississippi too was once poorly endowed in that realm, but that "a spirit of improvement and enterprise" leveled hills, raised valleys, and plowed "impassable streams" by "the mighty steamers so emblematic of American energy, which we must suppose is partially shared, if not by the ignorant and savage Hindoo, by the Hon. East India Company." The recruitment of white settlers such as the Mississippi overseers would surely bring India the necessary capital and skill.⁷⁶

In this context, the overseers' dueling testimonies, conveyed through letters published widely in the southern press, fed both sides of the tariff argument. The *Natchez Free Trader* drew upon "intelligence" from the field to proclaim the cotton experiments an "East India humbug": "the laborers won't do, the seasons won't do."⁷⁷ By 1843, evidence weighed heavily on the skeptics' side, shaping a new discourse of the Indian peasant's degradation and racial inferiority. The Natchez paper was able to quote triumphantly from the letter of another cotton planter, a certain Mr. Hawley, who had relocated from Madras to assume custody of an experimental farm in Broach following the departure of the three Americans at the close of 1841. Hawley had left the British with the impression that he had been "much struck by the native drill husbandry of Broach." Having failed to either wrest lucrative yields from forty acres planted with cottonseeds of New Orleans, Sea Island, and Bourbon strains, or to "improve" the "native way of growing their own cotton," he had concluded that "the crops now standing in the Kukarwára farm will not be better in any respect than some of the cotton on the fields near, which has not cost half the labour."⁷⁸

Yet in his letter sent to Franklin County, Mississippi, from Broach, Hawley attributed the failures of American cotton ventures in India to British Asia's alleged racial handicap. He portrayed Indian workers as an unenterprising "race" of nominally free "negroes" with "straight hair." He assured slaveholders that "With the native cotton, we Americans can make twice as much per acre as the natives can; ... the poor, straight-haired negroes will never adopt our system.... [T]he whole enterprise will turn out nothing more or less than a great expense to the East India Company...." The *Natchez Free Trader* noted that the abolitionists would now have no recourse other than to incite direct insurrection in America, but that their most "formidable obstacle" would be the "faithfulness ... of the slaves [of the South], and their attachment to the institution which feeds and clothes them in health, and nourishes and protects them in sickness and old age."[79]

As these exchanges suggest, when antebellum Americans with a stake in slavery argued about tariffs and trade, race talk could never be far behind—whether in the form of the free trader Jones's reflection on the inevitability of cotton's failure in a society without white settler colonialism, or the protectionist *Mississippi Creole*'s apprehension that southern white enterprise would transform India into a rival of slave-grown cotton. It was, however, Hawley's juxtaposition of a construct of the unchanging "poor, free negroes" of India with the fantasy of the well-cared-for, loyal American slave that would dominate slaveholder discussions about slavery and freedom in Britain's Asian empire.

BACK IN INDIA ... THE EXPERIMENTS WIND DOWN

In India, Finnie and the others feared that they were living out Hawley's prophesy of failure. Two years after their arrival, disheartened by Bundelkhand's dry climate, the planters relocated. Finnie picked lands further north, held by the government on either side of the Jamuna River at Agra near Delhi. There he proceeded to establish a model farm and a cotton gin house in April 1843. Terry moved to the "lower provinces" of Bengal to the east. Mercer was directed to report on the cotton-growing potential of Berar near Bombay to the west.

The Americans grew impatient with the bureaucratic directives that impeded their operations. The government supplied "diminutive and useless" Goruckpore bullocks, and then insisted that the planters wait for official sanction to procure larger breeds of cattle capable of working "the American plough with ease." Moreover, Finnie blamed "armchair agriculturists" within the colonial establishment for misleading him about the vicissitudes of Indian climate. In Bundelkhand he had at first agonized constantly about the lack of rain: "I was led to expect a deluge during the rains, and planted my cotton on high ridges to prevent its being drowned, and now find that if I had followed the course I pursued at home, my cotton would have been 50 per cent, better."[80] When the monsoons finally arrived, they lasted only six weeks and, as Superintendent Bayles noted, they were succeeded by easterly winds, "bringing with them swarms of insects which ... checked the growth of the plant." There were no warehouses in which to store the little cotton that was produced, so that it had to be ginned "in a mud shed with a chopper roof, pervious to winds, dusts and white ants."[81]

Meanwhile, the inaugural failures of the American experiments placed Finnie's dreams of land ownership increasingly in jeopardy. The government instructed the commissioner of the Agra division not to allow the Mississippian to bring large tracts of land under his direct management but rather to "encourage" the local landholders to cultivate cotton on their own property in accordance with his directions, supplemented by the supply of seeds and plows. The zamindars were to supply stated quantities of uncleaned cotton at market price set at a fixed price ceiling, and would receive advances for that purpose for one-third of the purchase price. Finnie would contract to clean and dispatch the cotton directly to London. Local authorities would carve out of lands lapsed to the government a model farm of 538 *bighas* (less than one hundred acres), and valued at Rs. 1,580 of "Government revenue," later reduced to 200 *bighas*. A mechanic was installed in Agra with a view to introducing innovations in cleaning cotton, but his expensive machinery remained underutilized due to the failure to purchase enough cotton early in the season.[82]

The Agra experiment failed. Despite some initial show of enthusiasm, most of the zamindars backed out of the arrangement, thanks to the price ceiling, according to the collector. Finnie blamed soil quality, an erratic rainy season, insects, and "depredations of the natives."[83] Workers charged him more for labor than they did local zamindars and insisted on higher daily rates of pay rather than lower monthly ones. Although Finnie tried to convince them that idle days and bad weather warranted the lower rate, they finally walked off the job when their wages fell into arrears. The cash-strapped American blamed the heavy cost of infrastructure and a superfluous supply of bullocks sent him by the superintendent of cotton plantations. He complained that "Government is not a good manager of a plantation" and that it had refused to defer to the judgment of those with "experience and successful management of estates in other countries."[84]

The Mississippian had even less faith in scientific agriculturists, who asserted the importance of soil—with less than 15% lime—in making a good cotton crop. He advised, "Doctor, lock up your chemical tests, and locate yourself where the climate is favourable, and commence upon any soil you please, and you will make cotton, if you hoe and plough it properly." He scoffed at the suggestion of a secretary of the Allahabad Agricultural Society—whom he described as a "theoretical agriculturist"—that light hoes fitted with short handles suited locals "who did not work in an upright posture."[85] He blamed the government's parsimony, explaining that after accounting for the salaries of the staff on his farm (assistant, accountant, carpenter, smith, cleaners, and revenue collectors), bullock feed, and contingent expenses such as iron, wood for harrows, and yokes, he had only two thousand rupees left to spend on wageworkers. The best he could do with this meager outlay was "employ 48 Coolies, 35 of which ought to be employed constantly at the ploughs, which leaves only 13 to do the hoeing, which will readily be seen is not enough. You are aware that this 2,500 rupees would only buy a negro and a half in the United States."[86] The lack of adequate supplies or infrastructure rendered him dependent on locals for the "loan of even their miserable carts."[87]

Failure prompted Finnie to develop a more sophisticated perspective on the challenges facing rural India in many parts of the country. During his tour of the

Doab, as he gazed upon "vast tracts of land lying waste" due to the emigration of its famine-stricken population, he wondered why the government did not build canals to counteract the irregularity of the seasons. Who, he wondered, "will exert themselves without a ... well-founded hope of a remuneration in proportion to the exertion?" His Agra disaster mortified him, opening up the possibility that he would return to the United States worse off than when he left. He had dreamed of accumulating "enough capital while I served the Honourable Company to engage in agriculture in India on my own account." Finnie's journals were peppered with phrases in a local dialect of Hindi, and more or less correct translations of these, suggesting that he had learned the local language—however imperfectly—in fairly short order. Given his enthusiastic letters home early on, it seemed that he had plans to stay and do business in the country long term. In other words, at the start, he had clearly seen himself as a settler colonialist.[88]

Finnie's sense of frustration with British bureaucratic inertia grew hand in hand with a self-conscious articulation of American nationalism. He noted wistfully that unlike in British India, effort in his native land was sure to bring reward. He began to refer to himself as a "Yankee," even though he would identify as a pro-South defender of slavery upon his return to the United States. He projected a self-image as a practical, egalitarian, industrious, and individualistic man on a mission to improve the fortunes of a country and with it his own fortunes as well. His relational matrix of identity formation incorporated not just Indian ryots and zamindars but also British imperialists as foils.

The government, speaking through Collector C.C. Jackson, offered a different perspective on the failure of free cotton experiments in India's Northwest jurisdiction. Drawing attention to the American's "want of experience," the officer, ironically enough, turned Finnie's arguments about ossified native ways on their head. It was the former overseer who had failed to adapt his methods to a new environment. The Mississippian, having arrived with "a large cargo of American ploughs and hoes, endeavoured to introduce precisely the same kind of cultivation as that pursued in America," with the result that it took additional labor to plow the land. "The cotton was sown in lines for the convenience of cleaning it, which operation, again, was performed in a manner quite novel to the natives, in an erect posture, by means of hoes." Jackson believed the locals pursued a better option. They rotated cotton with other crops on superior lands, already "thoroughly cleaned and ... ready for sowing after two or three ploughings with their wooden ploughs." In the absence of powerful cattle, these primitive implements did as well as the American plow, which went deeper into the soil and "turned it over." The locals sowed much of the crop at the start of the rainy season in order to save expenditures on irrigation. When the seed germinated, it was irrigated and cleansed of weeds every 10 days, a process better "performed ... by the natives in a sitting posture by means of the Koorpa, as, being nearer the plant, they injure it less...."

Although Finnie's model farm had failed, Jackson pointed to the successful cultivation of American cotton by a district revenue collector, "showing that the country is capable of producing cotton fit for the English market." Jackson was equally critical of Finnie's superintendence of the gin, accusing him of demanding expensive and unnecessary alterations of the engineer in charge of the machinery. The collector concluded that the sole advantage conferred by the American experiment consisted in "the cleaning gins," but these posed the danger of injuring the small-seeded domestic cotton crops. The "cultivation I would leave to natives," he concluded.[89]

From Madras in the south came a similar conclusion. There, Superintendent of Cotton Wright in Coimbatore, like Jackson in Agra, was struck by the Americans' inability to innovate and adapt to a new agrarian landscape. He judged the planters an "uneducated" class, ignorant of agricultural principles, who clung to familiar American techniques "whether applicable or not to present circumstances." It was the "negroes" these white men supervised who "understood and did the work" of cotton culture while they watched. Indeed, "Mr. Simpson [one of the recruits outside of the Bundelkhand "four"], the most assuming of the three, was a gin-wright until within two or three years of his coming to India." One bureaucrat explained that the cotton districts of Mississippi were so fertile that "with no other manuring than what it obtains from the ashes of the previous crop, which in spring is burned on the ground, it yields year after year, with only an occasional relief, large crops of cotton." In India by contrast, the locals practiced "a methodical system of rotation" in order to combat soil exhaustion. He concluded that what Indian farmers needed to cultivate cotton was not American instruction, but rather incentives through reforms in credit and infrastructure.[90]

THE OVERSEERS' RETURN: ABOLITIONISTS, IMPERIAL TYRANNY, AND "REPUBLICAN SLAVEHOLDERS"

One Saturday morning in the early fall of 1845, arriving in New York from Calcutta aboard the *Zenobia,* Terry brought tales of a ruthlessly exploitative and wasteful British government. This southerner's account of oppressive imperial structures circulated in the pages of politically diverse news media, where it shaped a common narrative of colonial tyranny in India. Partisans on opposite sides of the slavery debate would draw quite different lessons and agendas of activism from this shared conclusion.

Consumers of varied news outlets learned that the government of British India, ostensibly sunk in debt thanks to the Afghan and other wars, as well as extravagant company salaries, printed and circulated paper money "with little hope of ... future redemption." Terry represented India as a "squeezed orange—little else being left beyond the rind.... When the English first obtained sway over the country they found it full of the accumulated treasures of ages, which they have succeeded in removing from the country, while reducing its owners to a species of bondage worse than that endured by the African race in any part of the world. For be it known, that they deprived the conquered Hindoos of all title to the land on which God had placed them, without treaty, or other means than the sword. They claim one half of all the rice or other produce raised by the natives, as land-tax or rent!" Terry reported that famines—produced periodically by drought, merited no tax relief from India's British rulers, forcing people to meet their "government dues" by selling cattle and other possessions: "They would cut down their tree, strip their houses and themselves of clothing, and even sell their children into bondage, in order to save themselves from destruction."[91]

A few years later, from the opposite side of the political aisle on slavery, Harriet Beecher Stowe took to the pages of the Washington, DC–based abolitionist *National Era*, which would come to be known for the literary bent of its coverage—from the poetry of John Greenleaf Whittier to the serialization of *Uncle Tom's Cabin*. She narrated, in vivid terms, the chicanery and violence with which the East India Company had, in 1839, dispossessed the Raja of Satara, "an illustrious Hindu prince," of his ancestral possessions, on the pretext of a false charge of treason. "The Prince was dragged from his bed at night, torn from the palace of his ancestors, carried nine hundred miles across the country, and imprisoned in Benares." As the company seized his territory and treasures, twelve hundred of his subjects, "with tears and lamentations, followed their Prince into exile." She went on to recount that a couple of years later, "on a murky afternoon, in the dingy hall of the Court of Proprietors, in Leadenhall Street, filled with merchants and speculators in India stocks, eager to pocket the spoils" of India's plunder, there "rose from one of the back benches," the tall figure of George Thompson, with an account of the Raja's case, and a proposal to bring it to court. This preface segued into Stowe's reminder to her readers of the genesis and mission of the British India Society: to publicize the colonized's condition, abolish slavery, cultivate cotton in India, reform the land tax and monopolies, and to "quench the lust of conquest."[92] By the time Stowe wrote, Thompson was in Parliament, arguing for fiscal policy changes to promote cotton cultivation in India. He had participated in the crafting of a parliamentary report on cotton in India that drew upon the overseers' Indian experiences to build a case that Westminster would tap when the crisis of the Union threw the structures of transatlantic trade and tariffs awry.[93]

In the Slave South, however, the failure of free cotton in India, filtered through the plural lenses of its native sons on the ground, buttressed not only the notion of an invincible Cotton Kingdom but also cemented the connection between free trade and southern interests. Moreover, this argument unfolded within a framework that pitted the imagery of a patriarchal paradise of republican slave masters against the "real slavery" of abolitionist imperialism.

In 1854, from the banks of Lake Borgne in southeastern Louisiana, reportedly within sight of the harbor near which the "avenging sword of Andrew Jackson" had, in 1814, sent British forces fleeing "in terror," Samuel Cartwright, a Louisiana physician of Drapetomania notoriety, wielded his pen to warn darkly against "British hirelings and fanatics stealthily introduced into this country" to "subdue" the South and sunder the Union. He had earlier written that the "sophism of racial equality" embraced by Robespierre had torn "the prosperous colony of Hayti [sic]," setting in motion the EIC's designs to "transfer" and monopolize indigo culture in the "East Indies." Thus enriched by the practical operation of the "doctrines of the French revolution," Great Britain proceeded to export them across the Atlantic, "urging us to give the negro liberty—the same thing as to urge us to give up our cotton and sugar culture." For, Cartwright asserted, the British knew that "free negroes will not work ... and that white people cannot endure the hot sun of a cane or cotton field." And so, the EIC, "the lords of the loom, ... have almost out-Yankeyed the Yankees (as they call all Americans), being in a fair way to carry back ... the cotton and sugar culture to its old home in India, by humbugging us with abolition literature, abolition divines, and agents, like George Thompson, to give up our glorious Union for a vain abstraction of Jacobin origin."[94]

Now the returning overseers seemed to offer firsthand confirmation of the ills of British mastery. Cartwright cited vital statistics of birth and death to reiterate the familiar argument that a democratic republic of slaveholders in the American South secured benevolent paternalism and served as a safeguard against the sort of absentee rule that had lent West Indian slave societies notoriety for their indifference to the enslaved's well-being. He claimed that under American patriarchy, each republican master lived among "his negroes" and took care of them, so that a mere three hundred thousand had become four million, while in the British West Indies, "the 2,130,000 originally imported, have under despotism of true slavery, been reduced to 626,777.... The American mistress often sits up all night ... in nursing sick negro children ... a large portion of whom would die if their mistresses lived on the other side of the ocean, or if they had no masters and mistresses to take care of them, as the free negroes of the West Indies and our northern States."[95]

Such "charges," Cartwright maintained, were especially well-off compared with the "150,000,000 ... nominal freemen [in India] ... belonging to the largest slave proprietor in the world [the EIC]....The fish in the waters, the birds of the air, the wild game and fruits of the land, are not more inaccessible to prisoners in jail than they are to the inhabitants of those vast countries in Asia." British masters had changed "the fairest portion of the Oriental continent into a vast prison where one hundred and fifty millions of human beings have the liberty of starving, or working for a pittance of wages insufficient, after all taxes and expenses are paid, to purchase shoes for an equal number of negro slaves."[96]

For defenders of slavery like Cartwright, the failed cotton planters supplied the grist for defining the meaning of "true" slavery within a comparative framework. The Louisianan urged readers to listen to the testimony of "the ten Mississippi overseers," whom the EIC had "enticed" to India, but who "left in disgust, not having the inhumanity to make laborers work whose masters failed to furnish them the necessary food and clothing." It was to the ravages of British "abolitionist" "despotism," that Cartwright attributed the "depopulation" of British Asia—its high mortality rates. He ended ominously with the observation that if New England, New York, and the Ohio Reserve continued "to be the dupes of British policy, and force upon the country a dissolution of the Union," the South "*would be compelled, in self-defence, to revive the African slave trade on a grander . . . scale than the world has ever witnessed.*" Cartwright was under the illusion that the enslaved would side with their masters if war broke out, fulfilling the "decree of God, that Japhet, the white man, shall be enlarged, and Canaan, the negro, shall be his servant."[97]

As the sectional crisis gathered storm in the 1850s, British manufacturers, insecure about the prospects of uninterrupted raw cotton supplies from the United States, renewed their campaign to develop what Finnie called a "vast cotton field" within British Asia. Under these circumstances, in 1857 some "leading merchants" appealed to Finnie to explain why the great cotton experiment in India, "which at one time caused so much anxiety lest our best interests should be subverted by another country superseding us in the production of [our own] great staple product," had failed. He had returned to the United States in 1850 and was working as an attorney-at-law in Memphis, Tennessee.

In a letter to the editor of the Philadelphia daily the *North American and U.S. Gazette,* written from the Girard House, Philadelphia on February 16, 1857—that fateful year of Dred Scott, furor over the Lecompton Constitution, and a financial panic—Finnie once again struck a different chord from Terry, steering clear of blaming state policy or structures of oppression. Instead, he offered an American southern brand of Orientalism to explain his failure to wring cotton from India on competitive terms. He classified the causes into two, physical and moral, both symptomatic of India's supposedly static mores and the insuperable workings of nature. For Finnie, India was a "far distant land, where Brahminee bulls and deified monkeys are objects of profound adoration. . . ." Nonhuman impediments to cotton cultivation consisted in the extremes of humidity and aridness or prolonged drought and heat, the depredations of the boll worm, and the lack of irrigation. But equally, he blamed the "moral defect" of the population, claiming it was "the immobility of the Hindoo character. They . . . will do as their fathers did forever; they will not adopt the means of improvement. . . ."[98] Thus, having conveniently forgotten his own inability to adapt to Indian conditions, Finnie offered an Orientalist analysis of the cultural malaise at the root of failure. Resistance to change made India impervious to government policy or private initiative. That apparently inherent, immutable "moral" deficiency implied that no amount of state action would ever place India in a position to supersede the American South in cotton production. Happily for southern planters, American cotton degenerated in the plains of India to the point where "in a few years it will not germinate, and the staple soon becomes short and weak."

For Finnie, his Indian experiences carried important lessons for the politics of slavery in his own country. The US territories suited to the growth of cotton were located in climatic environments that made it impossible for white people to work "in the open field." The great staple must, therefore, be produced by enslaved workers whose numbers would have to keep pace with the galloping demand for cotton cloth produced by the march of civilization around the world. The Mississippian saw the fortunes of millions resting upon the African-descended shoulders of the South: "*Cotton will be King,* we shall be in the ascendancy, being the sole producers. Our manufactures increasing rapidly, England cannot get a supply of the raw material; her mills stop; millions of her people are thrown out of employment—so many *hungry* Englishmen clamoring for *bread, bread,* will overrun the country—cause revolution in England, what then? Where will it stop? ... Statesmen! Ponder this well. If you abolish slavery in the South today, all these contingencies occur tomorrow."[99]

A different analysis of the failure of "free cotton" in India had thus led Finnie to the same destination of proslavery triumphalism that Terry's or Hawley's critiques of imperial misgovernment had rationalized.

Ironically enough, abolitionists associated with free produce movements had also arrived at an indictment of colonial despotism from a very different angle. For George Thompson, Frederick Douglass, Lydia Maria Child, and the various women's free produce movements, the answer to the failures of free cotton lay in the reform of imperial policies of taxation, trade, and infrastructure. African Americans, meanwhile, turned to strategies for the domestic production of free cotton. Pro-South polemicists, however, selectively appropriated abolitionist denunciations of British imperialism to tarnish the enslaved's cause in North America and freeze the so-called "Hindoo" into a symbol of inertia.

The story of American slaveholders' interaction with empire and abolition did not end there. Britain's discourse of difference between slaveries, East and West, would evoke parallel arguments for slavery as an antidote to poverty—as representing a form of private, familial social insurance within the framework of patriarchal households no different than benign "Oriental" relations of dependence. And at least one plantation mistress—of the class that Cartwright had praised as housewives burning the night oil to minister to enslaved charges—would forcefully articulate her section's commitment to chattel bondage and white supremacy in these terms. So let us turn, in the next chapter, to the transnational resonances of a brand of "proslavery maternalism" that connected South Carolina's Louisa McCord to women depicted as "daughter-purchasing" courtesans in British Asia, while helping to shape a fractured public sphere capable of making war.

4

The Slave Mistress and the Courtesan

Poverty, Patriarchy, and "Proslavery Maternalism"

So far I have lived with my sable subjects, the busy but contented sovereign over a petty realm, believing that I was fulfilling my duty by staying at home, and devoting to their comfort . . . a large portion of my time as well as my moderate income. . . .
—LOUISA MCCORD, CHARLESTON MERCURY, 1853

I, Anghonee Bewah, village Sotahmukhi, at present residing at Chomar Pottee Purgunnah, Hajo, do write this bond of assignment of my daughter in 1771 BS to the effect that on receiving Rupees 20 from Mussamat Sona Nuttee of Nuttallah of the same Purgunnah, I give up my daughter Roho to her, who will remain with her according to her wishes and the custom of the country. . . . Sona Nuttee says that I voluntarily adopt this girl as my daughter.
—TRANSLATION OF A BILL OF SALE, GAUHATI, 1872

In the last half-century, the analytical paradigm of gender has transformed the study of slavery, revising our understanding of demography, work, resistance, reproduction, family, community, culture, property claims, violence, politics, and the law in "unfree" societies. Moreover, scholars have located the intersection of identity formation, gender roles, and power structures not simply in relationships between men and women but rather in the intertwined lives of women themselves. The rich insights of this literature have paved the way for recasting androcentric cross-cultural slavery histories around women's experiences and perspectives.[1] In this context, some scholars have argued that "multicultural" models of female mastery endowed the Atlantic world with unstable gender hierarchies.[2] In this chapter, we broaden the comparative analytical gaze of this discussion to the Indian Ocean world, where women predominated among those populations of "freed, pawned, indentured, junior wife, concubine, maidservant ... and chattel slave" targeted for incorporation into the masters' communities across a spectrum of corresponding statuses and forms of productive and reproductive labor.³ Nineteenth-century debates over dependence cannot be understood apart from a discussion of women's roles in reproducing, engaging, or subverting existing power regimes in different geopolitical locales. Let us follow the circulation of arguments about slavery, poverty, and the kinship trope that could be adapted to rationalize disparate structures of bondage in far corners of the nineteenth-century Anglophone world.

Recall that British colonialists contrasted the Americas' brutal chattel principle with Afro-Asia's ostensibly familial relations of dependence as a form of social insurance. American slaveholders disagreed. Indeed, some of them sought to establish an ideological kinship with long-standing benign British visions of "Oriental" slave systems—whether Arab, Indian, or African—even as they distanced themselves from now discredited (and abolished) Anglophone Caribbean models of bondage. Invoking especially the argument that servitude represented a superior alternative to "poor law," US proslavery theorists fashioned a sophisticated rationale for a system of exploitation very different from the myriad incarnations of bondage in the Indian Ocean. It was a justification that bore echoes of colonial discourses of British Asian servitude, even though savants of a later date would see it as a marker of southern exceptionalism.

This chapter tracks these global connections and comparisons by first considering the braided discussions of slavery and poverty that shaped the worlds of two utterly disparate female "masters" from distant corners of the Anglophone world. It proceeds to illustrate how a common well of trans-Atlantic ideas about servitude and social insurance, as well as framings of race and caste—fashioned into what we call models of "proslavery maternalism"—could be tailored to justify fundamentally different power structures and gender relations across half the world. But first, who were the female "masters" in this narrative, and just how different were they?

INTRODUCING THE FEMALE "MASTERS"
LOUISA MCCORD AND TOFA BAI

Few women in antebellum North America championed the twin pillars of patriarchy and white supremacy that anchored the foundations of privilege in the Old South with more vigor than essayist Louisa S. McCord (fig. 2). Born in 1810 to a planter-politician-banker, she inherited her aristocratic family's Lang Syne cotton plantation in Columbia, South Carolina. McCord countered Anglo-American abolitionist attacks against slavery's moral bankruptcy by substituting familial imagery and charity for the chattel principle. Historians have represented her as a bundle of contradictions—as one who combined a late marriage; a "masculine" taste for Latin, mathematics, and political economy; and a public role as a writer

FIGURE 2 (Left). Louisa McCord (1810–1879), Library Company. Originally from Evert A. and George L. Duyckinck, eds., *Cyclopaedia of American Literature*, 1855, 2:251.

FIGURE 3 (Right). Unidentified painter, miniature portrait of Indian courtesan, c. 1830–50, 4½ x 3 1/16 in. (11.4 x 7.8 cm). Courtesy of the Walters Art Museum, Baltimore, accession no. 38.518.

identified only by her initials with ferocious assaults upon abolitionism and women's rights. Yet extant sources reveal less a fascinating figure of mystery than a transparently self-interested pragmatist with a keen eye for irony and a talent for words. Her writings simultaneously offered an outlet for her intellectual aspirations and a defense of her racialized class prerogatives, especially when the death of her politician husband David James McCord in 1855 left the reins of the family fortune in her hands.[4]

Across two oceans from the Carolina coast and several months' voyage by sea and over land via England, Egypt, and the Red Sea, there lived a woman named Tofa Bai. She belonged to communities in the eastern Indian district of Cuttack whom British officials defined as "slaveholding prostitutes"—a category that conflated distinct groups of courtesans, dancers, temple attendants, and sex workers (fig. 3). The colonial archives recorded these women as the prime practitioners of "slavery" following its delegalization in British Asia. The women paid nominal prices to adopt destitute girls during seasons of want on the plea of saving them and assimilating them into matriarchal familial-professional guilds. The worlds they forged arguably approximated a model of servitude that functioned less as a fixed status than a process by which adoptees were absorbed into the enslavers' communities.[5] These groups often eschewed fixed religious and social identities and defied both Victorian and Indian norms of female respectability. Tofa Bai entered the colonial archives of slavery in the 1860s as a defendant in a case against child-trafficking prostitutes.[6]

Louisa McCord and Tofa Bai lived worlds apart in time, place, culture, and power. Yet each mustered the language of parental care and social insurance to rationalize slavery or "trafficking" in their particular contexts, utterly erasing, in McCord's case, the critical role of Black women in producing and reproducing not simply the plantation household but the larger political economy of which it was a part. McCord and Tofa Bai were enmeshed in profoundly different systems of exploitation against the common backdrop of interlocking Anglo-American debates over varieties of bondage, East and West; over poverty and poor relief; and over the virtues of liberalism versus paternalism in ordering society. Needless to say, the "dependents" over whom female sovereigns claimed custody or outright ownership often offered—through word or action—quite different portraits of slaveholding households (as we narrate in the next section). By placing local defenses of, and resistance to, servitude within transnational frames of reference, we are able evaluate claims of southern proslavery exceptionalism in the context of the larger intellectual currents of McCord's day.[7]

CONTEXTS: FREE LABOR REPUBLICANISM VERSUS PROSLAVERY "EXCEPTIONALISM" IN ANTEBELLUM AMERICA

A good place to begin untangling the international roots of local thinking about race, gender, and dependence, is the United States at mid century, where bitter disputes over slavery and freedom appeared poised to turn McCord's world upside down. An emerging politics of antislavery that articulated the aspirations of an unstable, inchoate middle class—soon to be institutionalized in the Republican party of the 1850s—defined freedom as self-ownership, and people as individuals with the right to sell their labor power in free and competitive markets in the incipient industrial capitalist order. Republicans maintained that such labor—if founded upon the values of hard work, sobriety and thrift, offered the potential for social mobility, and with it, the guarantee of harmony between capital and labor.[8]

Their slaveholding adversaries, however, decried the values of competitive individualism, invoking instead the "innate" unfitness for survival and self-government of particular groups of people, defined principally by race and sex. Familiar antebellum defenders of chattel bondage in the United States, like the Virginian George Fitzhugh, pronounced slavery a humane alternative to profit-driven free markets for labor. He contended that slavery, in effect, guaranteed an ostensibly inferior "race" of people—and the "naturally" dependent female sex—the security of subsistence from the cradle to the grave—a safeguard to which the white "wage slaves" and women workers of northern factories had no access. The failure of "free" society, Fitzhugh claimed, was plain for all to see: "The statistics of France, England and America show that pauperism and crime advance *pari passu* with liberty and equality," bringing in their wake class war and the debilitating specter of public relief.[9]

Voices such as Fitzhugh's persuaded the American historian Eugene Genovese in the 1960s and 1970s that the Old South had developed a unique precapitalist ideology of the master class that distinguished it from other slave societies of the western hemisphere. Flowing more or less organically from the realities of southern social relations, such ideology centered on *paternalism*—a hegemonic paradigm of master-slave relationships sustained as much by a web of reciprocal duties and rights as by the lash. By conceding the humanity of the enslaved, the framework of paternalism left room for negotiation shaped by a dialectic of accommodation and everyday resistance by the enslaved. Southern exceptionalism rested on the development of a sophisticated rationale for slavery as a "positive good" rather than the "necessary evil" of Jefferson's day.[10]

Scholars of slavery, the domestic slave trade, and capitalism have debunked the sincerity of claims to paternalism quite thoroughly. The question that remains is, At what point did slaveholders launch a concerted effort to project and publicize a self-image of benevolent patriarchy that took good care of allegedly inferior dependents? And how do we contextualize the progress of this proslavery rationale within the framework of the international politics of slavery? Lacy Ford argues that following the prohibition of the international slave trade, Christian masters and Protestant ministers in the Lower South sought to align their section's growing dependence on enslaved labor with republican and humanitarian principles by reconfiguring slavery as a "domestic institution." Among other things, this formulation injected a familial idiom into the ideology of master-slave relationships. It envisioned the master of the Big House as the lord and protector of Black as well as white dependents inhabiting his household in return for their "loyalty and obedience." Such emphasis upon reciprocal rights and responsibilities was expected to encourage the native-born enslaved, severed from the African or Caribbean cultural and political influences brought to American shores by fresh "imports" from overseas, to acculturate more readily to the norms and institutions of the South, work harder, reproduce more prolifically, and refrain from mounting insurrections. Propagandists of paternalism held that African American slavery would secure the foundations of republican liberty for white men and harmonize the interests of labor and capital, promoting racial concord and obliterating class conflict.[11]

Edward B. Rugemer has drawn attention to the larger Atlantic context, which in the 1830s influenced a turning point in the development of the Old South's proslavery argument. He has rightly highlighted the critical role of British abolitionism, which culminated in Parliament's enactment of West Indian emancipation in 1833, leaving the Old South as the last stronghold of chattel slavery in the English-speaking Americas. Southerners in general, and South Carolinians in particular, paid rapt attention to the debates over colonial slavery unfolding across the ocean. They watched in alarm as a home-grown crusade materialized, partially inspired by British abolitionist successes, that pronounced chattel bondage a moral outrage. Convinced that slave rebellions had followed on the heels of every step in the path to West Indian emancipation, and that such insurrections were infectious, proslavery advocates in the United States launched an aggressive campaign to portray the South's so-called peculiar institution as a model of civilization superior to its free labor alternatives.[12]

Two key ideas marked this campaign. First was the assertion that slavery in the American South was different—more humane—than that in the Caribbean, a point southerners sought to substantiate by pointing to the higher rates of natural reproduction of the enslaved population in North America than elsewhere in the western hemisphere. Second was the contention that slavery offered a solution to the problems of poverty and poor relief in modern societies by recognizing the naturalness of dependence based on race and gender. These arguments were taking shape not solely in response to organic developments within the American South, however, but rather within larger global contexts of public discourse over connections between slavery and poverty. If we broaden our gaze beyond the North Atlantic, we encounter similar tropes in imperial conversations about destitution and bondage in British Asia. Moreover, we find references to the transoceanic sources of some of these discussions in proslavery treatises produced by southern partisans. Let us work out these associations with a flashback to that momentous year in both Anglo-Atlantic and British Indian history: 1833.

BRAIDED DISCOURSES OF SLAVERY AND POVERTY ACROSS OCEANS: FLASHBACK TO 1833

There transpired that year two events of significance for the intertwined discourses of slavery and poverty. First, the Whig government that presided over the advent of Caribbean emancipation also ordered the printing of a report by a royal commission about Britain's controversial old poor laws. Second, the East India Company sought a renewal of its charter. The company's quest forced the question of Indian slavery into the deliberations of the English Parliament, thanks to British abolitionists and imperial reformers who were beginning to turn their attention to Afro-Asia. The ideas contained in Britain's 1834 Poor Law Report echoed in official evaluations of slavery in India, and may have provided American rhetoricians of proslavery paternalism additional ammunition for ramping up their own brazen defense of slavery.

From Paternalism to Liberalism in British Poor Law Reforms, 1832–34

The 1834 poor law report, and the "reforms" that it inspired on both sides of the North Atlantic, drew heavily on the ideas of the political economist Thomas Robert Malthus, who denounced Britain's old poor laws in his 1798 work, *An Essay on the Principle of Population*. The laws required local parishes to provide relief to working men on the assumption that the resulting growth in population would create a ready pool of soldiers and laborers. They also entitled an unmarried mother to parochial relief in the form of lying-in expenses and child maintenance, while the parish tried (often unsuccessfully) to secure reimbursement from the man she named as the father of her child.[13] Malthus and other later critics believed that these provisions—together with the public welfare institutions they created, such as maternity hospitals and foundling homes—stifled poor people's sense of personal responsibility and encouraged sexual promiscuity and imprudent marriages, fueling a population boom that outstripped the demand for labor, causing poverty.[14] Laissez-faire proponents believed that the answer was to abolish altogether these incentives for the rate-receiving poor's allegedly irresponsible and immoral behavior. Unwed mothers, of course, came in for a particularly large share of the blame. In what may have been an early formulation of the infamous "welfare queen" stereotype of our own day, the 1834 report claimed: "To the woman ... a single illegitimate child is seldom any expense, and two or three a source of positive profit."[15]

The New Poor Law, enacted in 1834, proposed to replace welfare assistance at home with relief in the workhouse, where the poor would receive training in those personal habits of work and life that would supposedly fit them to compete in the marketplace. The most controversial aspect of the poor law reform, however, was the role it envisioned for single mothers: they were no longer to be treated in a gendered way, as mothers who might rely on community support as they nurtured and raised their young. Such a course was thought to encourage "strumpets" to either seduce or otherwise "affiliate" children upon innocent men. Rather, they were now constructed as individuals on par with men, with the agency and responsibility to sell their labor for the support of themselves and their children, failing which, they had the option to enter a workhouse.

These new "bastardy" clauses provoked widespread criticism of liberalism from Tories and Radicals alike: it was said to codify a sexual double standard, punish children, falsely assume that women enjoyed a level playing field in the wage market, and fuel prostitution and infanticide. Moreover, as Lisa Forman Cody has shown, while Radicals held up "women's helplessness" as a symbol of the larger problem of class oppression, Tories used the occasion to argue for the superior virtues of paternalism over liberalism. They asserted that while paternalism "domesticated the poor by guaranteeing docility and gratitude," market society promoted a "language of political rights" and individual freedoms, weakened patriarchal authority, atomized the community, encouraged sexual misbehavior, and increased "illegitimate" births. The "bastardy" clauses were ultimately repealed, but not before they had generated very public protests in many forums—from the pages of newspapers and the halls of Parliament to the streets of London's radical parishes. The point is that these very public showdowns over the problem of "pauperism" and its attendant peril of class conflict would resonate powerfully in justifications of slavery as social insurance in diverse contexts.[16]

Poverty and the Parliamentary Report on Slavery in India

The debate over the relative merits of paternalism versus liberalism that mediated poor law reform seeped into the rhetoric of international struggles over slavery unfolding simultaneously in British India and the American South. British officials who had a stake in Indian forms of servitude defended those systems as bearing greater likeness to Britain's reformed poor laws than to slavery in the Carolinas or Georgia. This perspective dominated the parliamentary report on slavery in India, containing the results of investigations by a body known as the Indian Law Commission, originally dispatched to the subcontinent with the mandate of drafting a uniform penal code for the colony.[17]

The Law Commission report of 1841 reflected official British reluctance to strike firmly against Indian incarnations of chattel bondage, not simply in order to avoid alienating local elites allied to imperial rule or disturbing revenue-generating land tenure arrangements, but also because the imperial state preferred private solutions to statist ones in convulsive moments of destitution, such as during famines. In the 1850s, the American economist Henry Charles Carey, who advised President Lincoln, would echo critiques mounted by Maharashtrian intellectuals a decade earlier, alleging that colonial policy impoverished India by imposing onerous taxes and destroying Indian manufacturing—especially textiles—with tariffs that favored British industry while flooding Indian markets with cheap, machine-made British products. These policies fueled rural poverty among spinners and weavers. Cary also charged that Britain was transferring wealth produced in India to Britain, rather than spending it within the colony, in what he called a "perpetual drain" of no less than "four million pounds sterling" per annum. These arguments anticipated the "drain theory" articulated by Indian Liberal Party Member of Parliament Dadabhai Naoroji in his 1901 classic, *Poverty and Un-British Rule in India*.[18]

The EIC also opposed price controls of grain to prevent hoarding and price gouging during droughts that drove up food prices. Colonial officials' reluctance to involve the state in the dispensation of rural credit empowered moneylenders, upon whom peasants relied for the supply of seeds and grain. Colonial famine relief policies drew inspiration from the 1834 poor law reform. They disdained free kitchens, set low wages for state-funded "famine work" for fear that reliance on public charity would fuel indolence, and turned to private agencies for relief.[19] Morever, as Durba Ghosh has illustrated, such charity as the EIC dispensed for the relief of the widows, wives, and concubines who supplied its soldiers with domestic and sexual labor, and for the aid of the children that resulted from these unions, often discriminated against Indian and mixed race dependents.[20]

It is in the overall context of the EIC's aversion to public relief that we must evaluate Law Commissioner C. H. Cameron's claim that slavery was a function of the endemic nature of poverty in India: "slavery mitigates the evils of poverty . . . in times of dearth. . . . Slavery may be regarded as the Indian Poor Law and preventive of infanticide." The commissioner maintained that even though it bore greater resemblance to "Pauperism (in England) than to the Slavery of the ancients or of the western world," it was less "pernicious" than "Pauperism had become" before the enactment of recent poor law reforms, because while the pauper felt *entitled* to the "good will of the parochial authorities" charged with his upkeep, the Indian slave was motivated to labor by the knowledge that there was no "rate in aid" to supply his master's income, upon which he depended for the support of himself and his family.[21]

The crux of Cameron's argument was that slavery in India functioned not as a mode of extracting surplus labor or turning a commercial profit but rather as a paternalistic institution founded upon an understanding of mutual commitment. It was a *domestic* institution in that it was intricately woven into the traditional fabric of the Indian household: "Slavery in the East is not like slavery in the West, a system of mere violence and oppression," held together by the "dread of the cart whip." Rather, slavery in India was cemented by "the mutual interest of master and slave. . . . The perpetual and hereditary service of their domestics is what the upper classes in India particularly desire, as conducive to that privacy that belongs to their households. On the other hand, the lower classes are glad to bind themselves and their posterity to such perpetual service in order to be secure of subsistence in sickness and in old age," as well as during all too frequent episodes of scarcity.[22]

For evidence that terror did not supply the ties of bondage in India, the British relied on Brahminical interpretations of Hindu law laid down by the ancient Hindu lawgiver Manu. Cameron noted that Manu classified erring slaves with wives—among other dependent kin—as candidates for patriarchal punishment: "A wife, a son, a slave (mistranslated servant by Sir William Jones), a pupil . . . may be corrected when they commit faults, with a rope, or the small shoot of a cane. Manu Chap 8, v. 299." In the case of more severe transgressions, a master might pull his slave's hair and force him to ride a donkey. To Cameron, these provisions smacked of formal laws to regulate family relations, rarely put into practice: "The thin stick reminds one of the *alleged* right of an Englishman to correct his wife with a similar instrument." He then contrasted Manu's prescription with coercive tools to extract labor in the

American South: "If applied with the frequency with which the cart whip is applied in Georgia or Carolina, it would soon cease to be a punishment at all."[23]

The commissioners concluded that since bondage in India functioned as poor relief within the framework of a private, extended family, "slaves" in India assumed the role of "hereditary servants" and favored confidantes who conferred honor rather than profit upon their masters, and showed no "general desire for freedom." As expected, the report invoked Colebrooke's observation that throughout India, the master-slave relationship levied the responsibility of protection and care on the master's part in exchange for loyalty and obedience by the enslaved.[24] Moreover, the commissioners portrayed chattel bondage as *natural* rather than peculiar in the context of Indian society. They saw it as one form of dependence—more benign than most—in an unequal society structured by hierarchies of caste. Thus, British representations of Indian slavery fit into imperial constructs of the colonized Other as inherently averse to Enlightenment notions of liberty and equality, and harmonized with racialization of the "Hindu character" as passive and effeminate.[25] In Colebrooke's words, the supposed "mildness and equanimity" of Indian masters resulted in kind treatment of the slave.

Note that the argument for locating social insurance within private households accorded with the deference that colonial authorities had historically paid to the inner workings of elite Indian domestic establishments, even as they disregarded the claims to political power of "illegitimate" progeny within many royal households. In other words, as long as slavery did not interfere with the expansion and consolidation of imperial power, it assumed a special immunity from regulation when it entered the sanctum of familial relations within the patriarchal household. Such accommodation echoed in antebellum southern rhetoric about slavery as a matter of *domestic* governance, not subject to trespass by outsiders.[26]

INTERNATIONAL CONTEXTS OF MASTERY: ENGLISH POOR LAW, INDIAN SLAVERY, AND SOUTHERN "EXCEPTIONALISM"

British imperial arguments that relations of dependence in Asia departed sharply from slave systems in the New World drew strident dissent from the architects of an emerging American case for slavery as a "positive good." Even as sugar planters and cotton barons used Black bodies as capital and collateral, they mounted a rationale parallel to the colonial discourse of bondage as poor law that was administered privately by a benevolent patriarch. Listen to William Harper, an Antigua-born South Carolina politician, in his *Memoir on Slavery*, published in 1838, the year that brought an end to apprenticeship in the British West Indies: "The tendency of slavery is to humanize rather than to brutalize." He noted that English travelers remarked upon kindly master-slave relations in "Oriental countries," while hastening to protest that they would never endorse slavery "as it exists in America." Harper maintained, however, that despite the "imperfect" civilization of Eastern slaveholders, "human nature" was the same everywhere, so that "if the general tendency of the institution in those counties is to create friendly relations, can it be imagined that it should operate differently in this?"[27]

Nor was Harper the only defender of American slavery to make references to sympathetic portrayals by British observers of human bondage in the East. A leading antebellum legal treatise on institutions of the South bears testimony to the interoceanic circulation of both Orientalist discourses of bondage and abolitionist critiques. Thomas R. R. Cobb, a scion of Georgia's politically connected planter aristocracy and himself a leader of the Georgia bar who went on to serve both as a Confederate brigadier-general and leading architect of the Confederate Constitution, authored in 1858 an influential exposition of slave law titled *An Inquiry into the Law of Negro Slavery*. This landmark work of proslavery propaganda, targeted at northern lawyers and judges, became what the legal historian Paul Finkelman called "an important practical source for attorneys and judges at the time of its publication and a vital tool for scholars of slavery . . . ever since."[28] Cobb prefaced twenty-two chapters on slave law with a 228-page-long interpretation of the comparative world history of slavery under the title *An Historical Sketch of Slavery*. As the Georgian attorney told the story, the South's so-called peculiar institution was not all that peculiar after all, except in terms of its supposedly relatively good treatment of enslaved African Americans, especially compared with the British West Indies. Cobb drew upon research conducted on visits to libraries in New York, Washington, and Philadelphia, as well as information contained in copies of works supplied by Harvard Law Professor Simon Greenleaf, to range widely across other times and places—from the ancient Jews, Egyptians, Indians, Assyrians, Greeks, and Romans, through medieval Europeans to the settler colonists of the Americas. He selected material purporting to show that slavery was pretty nearly universal and in accord with natural law, that his construct of the "African negro" was inherently suited to bondage, and that emancipation wreaked havoc everywhere.[29]

Cobb devoted chapter 3 to India, cherry-picking portions of both Colebrooke's defense of Indian forms of bondage and Adam's critique of Colebrooke's justification, in his quest to buttress his proslavery perspective while undermining the moral authority of British imperial abolition. Thus, he chose quotations on the alleged mildness of Indian slavery from Colebrooke, and the supposedly unlimited powers conferred by Hindu and Muslim lawgivers on slave masters from Adam's book on slavery in India. But he never mentioned that Adam was an abolitionist critic of Colebrooke who was proposing alternative (antislavery) readings of the religious laws of slavery in India. Cobb repeated, more or less correctly, Adam's account of how the British had created new categories of unfreedom by turning the families of criminals into slaves of the state: "Thus, by the Hindoo law, men were enslaved for their own crimes; by the British law, for the crimes of their parents." On the racial dimension of slavery in South Asia, however, he misquoted his abolitionist source outright. Whereas Adam had noted the presence of "negro slaves" in the British colony of Bencoolen along the coast of Sumatra, Cobb cited this reference as the basis of his observation first that "the servile class in India are very nearly the color of the African race," and moreover, that "the negro proper ... has found his way to India, and is there, as he is everywhere, in a state of slavery." In truth, enslaved Africans who arrived in India over the *longue durée* served in all sorts of roles, rising to become kings and kingmakers in some instances. Cobb, on the other hand, conflating centuries of Indian history with nineteenth-century British usages in Southeast (rather than South) Asia, focused on how the "East India Company early discovered [the African's] adaptation to the labor of this hot climate, and worked their extensive plantations of the nutmeg and clove by African labor."[30] The point is that antebellum southerners were keeping up with controversies surrounding British abolition and empire, and appropriating materials from these sources to refine their own rationales of American slavery as a "positive good" within comparative frames of reference.

No wonder then, that one William S. Speer would later experience a sense of déjà vu when he arrived in Zanzibar in October 1862 to assume charge of the US Consulate there. An antislavery Unionist exiled from his native Tennessee and "an affluent fortune" by the ongoing "Rebellion," Speer had traveled reluctantly to the unfamiliar dot off the East African coast that his son had pointed out to him on a school atlas. During an evening stroll through the island's most "animated" spot— its slave market—he was approached by a "coarse man,"—a "merchant's spy," he suspected, who asked, "What do you think of our slavery?" The American demurred: "I am just making up my mind. What do you think?" Speer recounted that the man pointed to a large group of (Black African) slaves crouched on the ground, "not in a very presentable plight," and declared: "We bring slaves here—they looked like that. We buy him. In three days he looks clean and fit. We put cloth on him. We give him muhogo (cassava) to eat. We teach him religion.... Over yonder he had nothing to pray to." Speer reported to the State Department, "[The man's] argument was ingenious. But I had heard it on the other side of the Atlantic."[31]

Sure enough, Speer would have known of antebellum polemicists who similarly represented slavery as paternalistic social insurance. Apologists like Fitzhugh echoed Tory critiques of liberal English poor law reform provisions that treated groups they classified as "naturally" weak—like women and African Americans— as free and equal individuals. Others, like Governor James Henry Hammond of South Carolina, argued that public charity in free societies—"your pauper system"—supported by the community at large and administered by "hired agents," was costly, wasteful, and inefficient. In comparison, Hammond claimed that the "interested care," "economy," and "humanity" that the slaveholder maintained marked the management of privately owned plantations by their own proprietors.[32] Masters of human chattel insisted that such "interested care" stemmed from the familiarity shared by ruler and ruled within the framework of a *domestic* polity, as an alternative to the fantasies of public custody harbored by "radical democrats." The "genius" of domestic slavery, claimed the Presbyterian theologian Robert Lewis Dabney of Virginia, was "to make the family the slave's commonwealth. The family is his State. The master is his magistrate and legislator.... The commonwealth knows him as only a life-long minor under the master's tutelage."[33]

TWO MODELS OF PROSLAVERY MATERNALISM AS SOCIAL INSURANCE

It is within these overlapping transoceanic discursive frameworks of Anglo-Atlantic patriarchy that Louisa McCord and Tofa Bai, a world apart from each other, configured the tropes of poverty, charity, and mastery as parental care, to articulate rationales for slavery or trafficking, respectively.

One of McCord's moments as a ferocious public defender of her class prerogatives as a woman of the ruling race arrived in 1853. That year, the *Charleston Mercury* published a letter by McCord to the Duchess of Sutherland, in response to an appeal issued from the Englishwoman's London residence, known as Stafford House. Titled "The Affectionate and Christian Address of Many Thousands of Women of England to Their Sisters, the Women of the United States of America," the duchess's Stafford House Address had invoked the spirit of female Christian benevolence to urge the abolition of slavery in the United States.[34]

McCord's response to the duchess drew upon intercontinental strands of thinking about poverty and patriarchy taking place within the Anglo-Atlantic world. These she fashioned expediently into a conservative vision of charity, maternal duty, and authority defined by nature. A comparison of her position with the validation of South Asian forms of bondage contained in the *Indian Law Commission Report* issued over a decade earlier suggests striking parallels between the justifications of two very different, hierarchical societies. In a piece heavily laced with derision, McCord presented herself as a Christian sister and South Carolinian householder rather than a beneficiary of racial slavery's capitalism. Repeatedly invoking the superiority of empirical experience over "intuition" in judging the "truths" of slavery, she conjured a portrait of her plantation as a benevolent matriarchy. She was a "busy but contented sovereign" of a "petty realm," staying home to live among and take care of her "sable subjects" on a "modest" income. McCord thus represented her custody of the family business of staple crop production as a domestic obligation discharged for the benefit of her less fortunate wards. Her portrait recalled the theme of mastery as surrogate parenthood, common in British Orientalist defenses of Indian forms of servitude by the destitute.[35]

McCord went on to use the idea of divinely ordained racial and gender roles to justify slave society's power relations. In terms that echoed British descriptions of Hindu caste and class, even as they implicitly critiqued liberal English poor reform, she claimed that immutable differences in intellectual and physical strength between whites and Blacks, as well as women and men, called for an organic society in which each group performed functions suited to their natural ability: "I have believed that God Almighty has seen fit, in his wisdom, to suit his creatures to the positions which they are intended to occupy ... that as he has formed you and me to be daughters, wives and mothers ... unfit and unable to [the duties] of man, that He has equally formed diverse men for divers positions in society, according to their powers of mind and body." She declared that it was God who sealed the "stamp of inferiority" upon the brow of "the negro." But such inferiority supposedly conferred bliss: "many a wooly head lays itself to sleep, while the aching brow of the master is burdened with watchfulness and care."[36] The contrast with nominally free workers teetering on the brink of "pauperism" in Sutherland's England was all too clear.

McCord's kinship trope of mistress-slave relations turned the brutal fact of a self-reproducing forced labor force into comforting images of physical proximity and familial intimacy extending across generations. Her portrait of the plantation household bore a close resemblance to the Indian Law Commission's observations on the hereditary nature of Indian master-slave relationships. She mocked the duchess for presuming to know more about the "negro people," upon whose faces the British peer had never trained her *lorgnette,* than one of McCord's own tribe, who "born and bred among them, have played with them and sorrowed with them and wept with them, even from our babyhood upward." Even as she was beginning to gray, McCord claimed, she was still "cheerfully served by many of the faithful negroes who watched with hope my tottering baby steps; their children labor for me, and their grandchildren are ... reared by me."[37] Just as Sutherland, as a mother, must feel most intensely for the son of her "home and bosom," so, the South Carolinian maintained, slave mistresses were likeliest of all to harbor sentiments "approaching the relation of parent and child" for the dependents who shared their household. It was, moreover, this very maternal concern that McCord advanced as a reason to oppose abolition, for freedom would lead to the extinction of the "helpless creatures" in her protective custody.[38]

McCord's portrait of slaveholding maternalism required an act of utter elision of Black women's complex lives and the productive and reproductive labors that peopled the Slave South and produced its wealth. She also excluded the everyday violence that lurked behind the colonnaded grace of Classical Revival mansions and the sensory charm of magnolias and mint juleps that make up the stuff of Old South nostalgia today. We look in vain within McCord's letter for depictions of enslaved women's sinews and sweat driving the sowing, winnowing, hoeing, weeding, and building of drainage systems that, according to Leslie Schwalm, kept South Carolina's rice and cotton plantations humming. Or for references to the hands that swept, scrubbed, and polished the pillars and porticoes, the hallways and stairways, and the furniture and furnishings that kept white mistresses in comfort. There is little hint in McCord's missive that the comforting image of "Mammy"—a maternal and asexual emblem of loyalty, domestic authority, and racial concord—veiled the harsher reality of the commodified wet nurse, or the victim of a slave master's sexual abuse and his wife's wrath. Not a word about the whipping, maiming, scalding, scolding, and emotional abuse that Thavolia Glymph has found mistresses to have visited upon enslaved women within the privacy of the Big House, nor white women's "quiet, tortured compliance" with the sexual double standards of the slaveholders' patriarchy, which Brenda Stevenson has documented. Nor is there any hint of the resistance of enslaved women who, as Wilma King put it, were "mad enough to kill."[39]

Moreover, McCord's true attitude toward her slaves as more like capital with liquidity than her children is evident from her opposition to an 1848 proposal to amend slave law so as to "annex" the enslaved to their owners' freeholds—a measure that would have safeguarded slave families against separation through sale.[40] A vigorous champion of free markets (for cash crops rather than labor), McCord overcame her opposition to public welfare just enough to send to the Charleston workhouse a slave who dared to remind her dying father of his promise of emancipation. She later sold the person in question. No wonder, then, that her Black "wards" demonstrated their feelings toward her by burning up her plantation records during the Civil War.[41] McCord represented a perfect example of the slave-owning women portrayed by Stephanie Jones-Rogers, members of the ruling race who jealously guarded their property interests in human chattel, profited from the spoils of the slave market, and embraced harsh methods of plantation management to no less a degree than men of their ilk.[42]

In the end, then, this South Carolinian matriarch's defense of slavery as a form of private, familial charity was no more than rhetoric to secure her investment in the political economy of racial slavery and to reinforce the power structures of her society.

ARCHIVING "DANCING GIRLS" AS SLAVEHOLDERS IN BRITISH INDIA

Nearly two decades after Louisa McCord juxtaposed her imaginary of the Slave South's "benevolent matriarchy" against the double standards of British imperial abolition, the colonial state in India archived a document that muddied the boundary between chattel and daughter. The relic in question consists of a translated bill of sale associated with a Hindu temple in the northeastern province of Assam. It represents both parties to the contract as "nottis," meaning dancers. The "seller" gave up her daughter to a fellow performer for the sum of twenty rupees, binding the child to "remain" with her owner "according to her wishes and custom of the country." The buyer declared "I voluntarily adopt this girl as my daughter. I will give her no inconvenience or trouble. She will remain with me and behave according to our profession."[43]

Colonial authorities classified this contract, which materialized in the course of an 1872 investigation into child trafficking by "prostitutes," as part of its official records on "Slavery" in nineteenth-century India. We treat it as a narrative point of entry to a brand of "proslavery maternalism" embedded simultaneously in imperial discourses of bondage as poor law and the redefinition and representation of a category called prostitutes as the principal practitioners of slavery following the Abolition Act of 1843. Recall that Tofa Bai of Cuttack, whom we introduced as McCord's counterpoint in the early pages of this chapter, belonged to one of these communities of female sex traders (conflated in colonial discourse with courtesans and dancers both secular and religious) who defended their "purchases" of impoverished young girls as a mechanism to incorporate kin networks that would perpetuate their profession. The case of South Asia's "dancing girls" offers an interesting opportunity for cross-cultural comparison and contrast with American proslavery within the framework of Anglo-Atlantic formulations of slavery's connections with poverty.

Let us begin with a contemporary historian's visit to the offices of the West Bengal State Archives in Calcutta, where British India was once headquartered. A request for records related to "slavery" yields tomes of musty files on the judicial proceedings of the province of Bengal. A rather curious fact of colonial knowledge production emerges immediately: registers of private deeds of sale from 1864 identify the slaveholder who is designated "purchaser" by her name (*Monjoree, Pearee, Tarukasaree*) followed by her profession, listed invariably as "prostitute." The objects of sale consisted of girls or teenaged women sold for nominal amounts by husbands, parents, or in some cases, by themselves: Bisho, sixteen years, sold by her husband at Narainee, Rs 20; Kanto Bewa, sixteen years, sold herself according to permission of husband, Rs 45; Bootkini, six or seven years, sold by father at Narainee, Rs 6; Sorisa, eight years, sold by mother, Rs 15. British imperial authorities recorded these dealings as market transactions and accorded them a level of official scrutiny not leveled at other circumstances of bondage following Parliament's delegalization of slavery in 1843. For instance, the Indian (acting) sessions judge of the princely territory of Cooch Behar in northern Bengal reported in 1864 that in recent years, the sales or purchases of slaves of the local royal family had not been documented, nor had instances of slave trading across territorial borders, but that only "sales of girls to prostitutes are found registered." Thus, colonial record keepers promoted an epistemology of slavery that married chattel bondage firmly with the practices of some of the most marginalized—and feminized—groups in nineteenth-century India.[44]

Two related questions arise at once before we can proceed to explore how these women fit into Anglophone thinking about slavery and poverty. Why did the state single out what it called prostitutes as the primary offenders against its antislavery initiatives, and who exactly belonged in this colonial category by the early 1860s, when the Cooch Behar sessions judge filed his report? The selective classification of prostitutes as slaveholders represented the convergence of multiple cross-cultural strands of thinking about gender, straddling the Anglo-American sexual politics of abolitionism, imperialism, Victorian morality, and emerging Indian middle-class ideas about domesticity. On the one hand, abolitionists on both sides of the Atlantic had long invoked the imagery of sexual promiscuity to define slavery. For instance, Senator Charles Sumner of Massachusetts literally described the institution as a "harlot."[45] This personification of slavery as a degraded woman (of color), captured its sanction of the rape of African American women, the destruction of white and Black families, and the specter of sexuality—both male and female—run riot. On the other hand, as the historian Philippa Levine has argued, the "woman of the *bazaar*" of the East represented the quintessential colonized Other: the specter of unbridled, purposeless female sexuality at odds with Victorian ideals of domesticity and feminine purity, and with Christian notions of procreative sex. Indrani Chatterjee has written that markets authorized by commanders of regiments and supervised by *kotwals* (law enforcement officers) supplied British officers and soldiers with various forms of labor, including the sexual services of enslaved women available for hire through the medium of matrons and their brokers. According to Erica Wald, in the first decades of the nineteenth century, colonial medical professionals concerned about both miscegenation and the explosion of venereal diseases in European military cantonments joined missionaries in launching initiatives to regulate female sexuality by subjecting sex traders to invasive forms of surveillance and treatment. Such women were subjected to medical examinations, registered, and then housed in tents or other buildings in a designated square.[46]

Meanwhile, an emerging nationalist intelligentsia in India was in the process of crafting a new cultural politics of domesticity that sex workers challenged. Swapna Banerjee has argued that the myriad pressures of colonialism, including racism, western critiques of Indian culture, socioeconomic tensions associated with competitive job markets, famines, disease, and the technologies of modernity prompted educated Indians to reconfigure the home as a laboratory for formulating meanings of "modernity, ... and [a] new nation." Prescriptive (often male-authored) manuals in Bengal and popular literature in Maharashtra drew inspiration from precolonial Indian sources on romantic love and symbols like the Goddess Lakshmi. They also drew from the Anglo-Atlantic cult of domesticity to re-vision an autonomous domestic domain in which the educated, chaste, and industrious mother and devoted wife labored under the supportive glow of a companionate marriage.[47] According to Partha Chatterjee, these genteel guardians of an "authentic Indian spirituality" in the domestic realm were distinguished not just from westernized upstarts, but also represented the reverse mirror image of the "common" woman, portrayed as "vulgar ... quarrelsome ... sexually promiscuous" and epitomized by a variety of "lower class female characters who make their appearance in the social milieu of the new middle-class—maidservants, washerwomen ... and prostitutes."[48] Hindu patriarchy was distinguished by the presence of men and the practice of fatherhood as key attributes of masculinity.[49]

Likewise, Sarah Waheed has shown that Muslim social reformers responding to colonial modernity sought to erase the "rituals of gossip and social visiting" of the *zenana* that formed an inter-class women's space bridging the "domestic quarters and the public *bazaar*." They sought instead to fashion a new cultural identity that held up the "educated housewife" who was also "self-disciplined and properly Muslim" as the epitome of *ashraf* (genteel) morality.[50] Thus, in the course of the nineteenth century, the new politics of respectability located the woman of honor within the private realm of the patriarchal family, defining her in opposition to women who transacted any sort of labor—sexual or otherwise—in the public sphere. The latter were outside the "normative moral order of marriage," whether they were courtly courtesans, divinely sanctioned dancing girls, lowly merchants of sex attached to European military cantonments or, as Samita Sen has shown, widowed mill workers later in the nineteenth century.[51]

Under these circumstances, in the latter half of the nineteenth century, when the Cooch Behar judge commented on the selective nature of "slave trade" registration, the colonial category of "prostitute," with its connotations of moral turpitude, had broadened to cover an array of sexual activities outside marriage. These ranged from the urban sex trade to extramarital sexual relations and "temporary marriages" into which the urban poor in cities like Calcutta entered, in defiance of genteel ideals. They also included practices that had not carried the stigma of depravity in precolonial times, such as stylized secular traditions of courtesanship, as well as their religious counterparts, the temple dancers known as *devdasis* who were dedicated to the gods, performed labor and rituals associated with religious worship, and often combined extensive training in the performing arts with long-term sexual relationships with the sons of temple patrons.[52] Indeed, before the early nineteenth century, "public women" of "art and learning" such as the *tawa'ifs* or courtesans associated with the court and noble families of the princely states of Hyderabad and Lucknow, occasionally managed to parlay their mastery of music, dance, and poetry (and according to one account, archery and horse riding as well) into wealth and political leverage. The declining power of princely states under colonialism robbed these women of their courtly patronage.[53]

As early as 1818, the colonial judge Harington recorded the opinion of Muslim legal experts that it was "customary ... among the zumeni tewaif ..., to [illegally] purchase female children from their parents," for training as dancing girls and prostitutes.[54] Macnaghten's *Precedents* included the case of a six-year-old hired out by her mother to a prostitute for a term of ninety-five years. A colonial court declared the transaction illegal, on the grounds that Muslim law did not empower parents to "dispose of" their children "beyond puberty," and second because prostitution was impermissible.[55]

The 1843 Abolition Act did not explicitly prohibit the sale of people. Still, the acquittal by a divided court of a brothel keeper who had leased two female infants for periods of ninety and ninety-five years prompted such great outrage that it spurred the incorporation of sections 372 and 373 into the new, uniform Indian Penal Code in 1860. These provisions prohibited the selling and buying, respectively, of minors under the age of sixteen years for purposes of prostitution or other "immoral" ends.[56]

Yet the problem of poverty suffused with tension the colonial discourse of sex workers outside established norms of marriage or concubinage. The linked themes of slavery, poverty, and a particular sort of "matriarchy" came into focus in the case of Tofa Bai as a rather different kind of "slaveholding maternalist" than the South Carolinian Louisa McCord. It is to Tofa's world that we next turn.

POVERTY, CHARITY, AND THE DANCING GIRLS OF CUTTACK

Throughout the nineteenth century, women described as "dancing girls" vigorously resisted the criminalization of their trade and their mode of perpetuating it through the purchase of young people. Some British bureaucrats supported these moves for diverse reasons ranging from arguments that these communities represented custom, rested on free will, or most important, offered subsistence to the destitute. Thus, close on the heels of the 1833 slavery debates in Parliament, Resident Henry Pottinger, stationed in the princely state of Kutch on the Arabian seacoast, noted that while itinerant "nautch [dancing] girls" in that part of the country had entered the lives they led through purchase at tender ages from neighboring territories in Gujerat and Marwar, "their life (however immoral) is one of perfect free will" and they belonged to "fraternities" that would reject any state interference as "tyrannical."[57] In 1846, the "entire community of prostitutes and dancing girls" resident in the city of Kota in present-day Rajasthan submitted an appeal through the medium of a *Vakeel* (legal official) in the area. They requested that they be granted an exemption from the prohibition of the purchase of girls "as without this privilege their occupation would be injured," leaving them no choice but to abandon the territory and "seek their fortune in some more accommodating state." Female slaves in nearby provinces like Mewar were said to command the price of 125 rupees. In Rajput states of an earlier era, enslaved performers with artistic skills had symbolized elite status for their owners, and favored concubines had exercised power during eighteenth-century succession struggles. But in the first decades of the nineteenth century, the march of imperialism had reduced these princely chiefdoms to subsidiary powers, and established norms of lineage purity that curbed the rights of enslaved progeny. It was against this backdrop of the declining status of the enslaved in elite families that the "dancing girls" of this part of South Asia entered the colonial archives as perpetrators of "slavery" as a mode of incorporating professional communities.[58]

The Indian Penal Code vested colonial authorities with the legal ammunition to strike decisively against communities like these on the grounds that they purchased children for "immoral purposes." But the outcome of a case in Cuttack, in the eastern province of Orissa, revealed not only the persistence of the construct of slavery as a sort of poor law but also the ways in which Indian women transacting artistic and sexual labors in the public sphere drew upon both their own traditions and imperial representations of Indian slavery to defend their acquisition of girls.

One Friday evening in February 1867, Birjoo, an employee of Reverend W. Miller of Cuttack District, delivered a note from his master together with a young girl named Koondo, to W. C. Lacey, the local district superintendent of police. The reverend's note claimed that Koondo, a seven- or eight-year-old, had fled the quarters of her mistress, a prostitute named Poona Bai, and sought refuge with Birjoo the day before. Poona, aided by two male "paramours," then appeared at Birjoo's home and "endeavored by threats to recover possession of the girl." According to Lacey's official account of the case, Koondo revealed upon questioning that she had been sold in infancy by her destitute mother to Poona Bai. She had run away to Birjoo's in order to escape a beating by her mistress, brought on by the girl's failure to discharge an errand. Koondo was said to have alerted the authorities to the presence of another young captive like herself in Poona's household. Lacey placed Cuttack Sub-Inspector Hari Kisen Dass in charge of the investigations. Dass seized Soondree, the second child in Poona's custody, and traced the child's mother, described as a "pauper," to a red-light district. Soondree's mother testified that her child had "left her" for Poona Bai a few months before, and that she, the mother, had repeatedly attempted to get the child back, to no avail. Poona's neighbors offered a conflicting narrative: Soondree's mother, a disreputable widow, had surrendered the child to Poona five years before, "for a consideration."[59]

These developments transpired amid heightened publicity surrounding the alleged appropriation by "women of the town" of large numbers of female children rendered homeless by the famine of 1866. Moved to act by the clamor of missionaries and the local press, Cuttack authorities arrested Poona Bai and tried her under Section 373 of the 1860 Penal Code, along with two other women charged with identical offenses, one of whom was Tofa Bai.[60] Cuttack's presiding additional sessions judge acquitted all three women on the strength of the testimony of the *defendants themselves*. Tofa Bai's statement became the basis of his opinion that "... a woman, almost dead of starvation, made over her child, four or five months of age, to a woman, *a prostitute by caste and profession,* and this prostitute took charge of the infant from charity, and was bringing her up kindly till interrupted by the Police. It seems to me that it would be very wrong to convict the prisoner [who] ... from motives of charity ... took to herself a female infant, who would, considering the *caste and profession* of her protector, in all probability, be brought up to prostitution, but it would have been a greater sin had the *charitable prostitute* [our italics] refused to receive the infant and allowed her to die on the road as many thousands did at that time."[61]

In her testimony, Tofa Bai apparently successfully invoked her own traditions as well as elements of the colonial establishment's rationale of slavery as a virtual "poor law," and the construction of degradation as an occupational hazard of certain "castes," as the judge's subsequent words made clear: "But the *prisoner in her defense states* that the infant is the child of a woman named Bhaig Bai, *of her own profession and caste,* who owing to want and starvation, left the place last year, leaving with the prisoner this infant to take care of."[62] This outcome provoked vigorous dissent from colonial bureaucrats in Cuttack, who pronounced Section 373 a dead letter, impossible to enforce, for the sessions court had set a precedent to judge child-purchasing cases on the *motive* of a prostitute at the *time* the child was acquired—a circumstance that would invariably allow the plea of charity to intervene.[63]

THE TRADE IN GIRLS: THE INVESTIGATION OF 1872

Still, in the years that followed the cases of the Cuttack sex workers, a steady stream of reports on the traffic in young girls prompted the government of Bengal to initiate an inquiry into the practice of buying and "bringing up very young girls to the profession of prostitution."[64] This 1872 investigation yielded a portrait of sex workers in northeastern India carving out semi-autonomous matriarchal spaces defined by a measure of sexual freedom and legally enforceable property rights based on the "shared degradation" of "debased" women, on the fringes of genteel British Indian society. Through the medium of Indian deputy magistrate interlocutors, these women represented their species of commerce as a mechanism to establish familial-professional guilds from the ranks of the nominally "free": victims of famines or floods, abused wives and widows, and African concubines.[65]

Crown officials described the prevalence everywhere of "adoptions by purchase" that crossed the line between market and family. In Sirajgunj, every "bazar woman" was reported anxious to acquire a "daughter" to keep her in her old age. One reporter claimed that he had heard of a case in which a prostitute exchanged her son for a cultivator's daughter, "on the ground that neither was of any use to its natural parent."66 In other cases, single women or widows cast out by their families surrendered their daughters—usually born out of wedlock. The purchase of an infant entailed the execution of a deed on stamped paper, obliging the adopted mother to feed, clothe, and sometimes marry off her charge. Any such deed, one magistrate reported, could be "kept in terrorem over the victim, her protectress threatening her with legal proceedings in the event of her leaving."67 The magistrate of Dacca (present-day Dhaka in Bangladesh) wrote that he had personally thwarted the quest of several women to register deeds giving their children—mostly "Hindu bastards" he called them—to prostitutes. He went on to raise the question whether this action "would not lead to an increase of child murder...."68

Official reports reflected the growing conflation of the *devdasi* tradition with what the British understood as common prostitution. A district superintendent of police in Assam wrote that the professional prostitutes of Hajo, descended from a tradition of dancing girls attached to the temple of Madhob, purchased girls as literal surrogates of daughters of their clan. The girls were dispatched to Gauhati to make a living as public prostitutes, and were expected to remit their earnings back to the families at Hajo. The dancers in question customarily contracted relationships with men of "any caste" in order to produce female heirs. In the absence of natural heirs, these women purchased stand-in daughters.69 A bill of sale attached to this report conformed to the portrait of a surrogate kin-style network grounded in a common occupation and social status. Along these lines, Babu Taraknath Mullick, Deputy Magistrate of Madaripur noted, "Sometimes ... daughters of one prostitute go to the possession of others by the death of their parents."70

Defined on the one hand by oppressive power relations, these communities could also function as subversive spaces. According to the commissioner of Calcutta, the nearly seven thousand registered prostitutes in the city replenished their ranks not only by rearing young children but also by importing adult women from the interior provinces. These women included those widowed in childhood with no option to remarry, refugees from abusive husbands, and wives of seafaring men who had secured their husbands' consent to "drive a profitable trade by prostituting themselves." The commissioner ventured the opinion that women found "a better means of subsistence than their relatives at home ..." in the brothels of Calcutta, not to mention greater personal freedom than their extended families would allow. This would have been particularly true of another category of women found among sex workers: victims of [Kulin] polygamy, who were sometimes forced to share "a husband with 40 or 50 other women" because as members of groups with the highest ritual status, they were forbidden to marry men of lower castes.71

Samita Sen's work on late nineteenth-century Bengal's jute workers supplies important contextual information to help us make sense of the presence of widows across caste lines in the sex worker cohorts that populate the 1872 investigation reports. Sen argues that a general devaluation of women's labor had prompted a shift in marriage transactions from bride price (paid to the father to compensate for the loss of his daughter's farm and domestic labor) to dowry. This transition made it difficult for widows to remarry in what represented an acculturation of the lower social orders to the usages of the upper castes. As several scholars have noted, marriage became central to upholding ritual status among the Hindus of nineteenth-century Bengal, so that the choice of an appropriate marriage partner was deemed essential for preserving the purity of a family's lineage. Those with the highest ritual status within the three upper castes—Brahmans, Kayasthas, and Vaidyas—were pronounced "kulin." The high demand for "kulin" grooms nurtured the worst excesses of polygamy. Impoverished "kulin" men adopted marriage as a profession, tying the knot with several women at once, visiting them at their respective parents' home at infrequent intervals to collect an allowance. A "kulin" girl was not permitted to marry outside her caste. Lest she remain unmarried, her parents married her off—occasionally in infancy—to much older men. If widowed, she was not allowed to remarry.[72]

Local magistrates repeatedly blamed the presence of "respectable"—even Brahman—widows among sex traders on the one ancient legal tradition that the British had established as an authoritative source of Hindu law: the *Manusmriti*, which prescribed marriage at puberty.[73] The resulting scourge of "Kulinism" meant, according to one Indian official, that "on the death of a single Brahmin, a hundred Brahmin ladies become widows, some in the bloom and some in the prime of their lives."[74]

Child marriages and social sanctions against widow remarriage reflected strict controls on female sexuality designed to maintain genealogical purity. But shifts in legal, economic, and political-cultural landscapes prompted less exalted social orders to adopt some of these upper-caste practices. The Hindu Widow Remarriage Act, passed in 1856 following a campaign by reformers on the conservative grounds that the sexual appetites of widows, if left unfulfilled, would lead to illicit sex, failed to win social acceptance. Moreover, widows of intermediate and lower castes, who had customarily been able to remarry without losing property inherited from their late husbands, lost that privilege under this law. Furthermore, the social capital that widow celibacy carried by virtue of its association with the upper castes facilitated its infiltration among the popular classes aspiring for upward mobility in Bengali society. All in all, waning widow remarriages combined with the marginalization of women's labor to relegate widows to low status, material deprivation, emotional and sexual abuse, and expectations of ascetic living within extended family economies. These developments coincided with declining paid employment opportunities for women in the countryside. The suppression of Bengal's hand loom industry destroyed the widows' customary spinning trade, driving many into low-paid wage labor in urban domestic service. Another alternative was to work in jute and rice factories, which contemporaries held on par with prostitution because these mills paid so badly and presented fertile theaters for sexual transgression.[75]

From such venues of low repute to the establishments of sex workers represented but a short step, especially if a widow or "temporary wife" of the lower social orders had already crossed a well-guarded line of respectability. Bankim Chandra Chatterjee, a novelist who forged a new nationalist model of heroic Indian womanhood and a deputy magistrate of Murshidabad in 1872, noted society's lack of forgiveness of the "fallen"—whatever her marital status: "the life of a Hindu family woman is peculiarly lonely and secluded.... The extreme vigilance with which Hindu society watches female propriety renders indulgence except out of its pale a matter of difficulty." According to the special sub-registrar of Kumillah, a Hindu widow was "no more than a prisoner in her home," forced to rely upon the "uncertain support of her relatives." She was sometimes said to contract a clandestine affair and, with the complicity of her paramour or even family members anxious to avoid scandal, escape to a distant and anonymous realm—such as the booming city of Calcutta. As G. S. Park, an officiating magistrate within the Chittagong jurisdiction, observed, "the independent life of the prostitute must awaken in [widows] feelings of envy—they can only escape and often do by an intrigue, occasionally with a member of the family. If a female child be the result, the mother is but too anxious to get rid of it, and listens only too readily to the offers of the procuress."[76]

Or such a woman might join a prostitute's household herself. The district superintendent of the Hooghly police explained the appeal of prostitution to poor or abused women—whether wives or widows—as follows: "As a prostitute she finds herself better dressed, better fed, better housed, less worked, less beaten, less dependent, vastly more propitiated ... [than] the wife of a working man," adding that he could not remember a single instance in which a prostitute committed suicide. Nineteenth-century Bengali newspapers such as *Vidyadarshan* published letters penned ostensibly by literate prostitutes that tended to confirm these narratives.[77]

Once a young woman entered a prostitute's household, she was said to have joined a proxy family of mother and sisters held together by shared professional rituals rather than affiliations of caste or religion. A dialectic of coercion and affection was reported to structure these relationships. In Chittagong, the household of a prostitute was described as serving as a sort of refuge for destitute girls—transforming virtual orphans from potential financial liabilities into sources of profit.[78] The courtesan-slaveholders adopted their "slaves" as their daughters-cum-apprentices, training them in the tools of their craft, including music and dancing, and "sometimes even reading, writing, sewing, knitting, and other female accomplishments," as Bankim Chandra Chatterjee put it.[79] K. D. Ghosh, the officiating civil surgeon of Rangpur, reported that "these girls are treated as daughters and they generally look up to the woman who brings them up as their own mother. It is often difficult for a stranger to find out that such a relation does not exist."[80]

Yet Deputy Magistrate Bhagwan Chandra Bose emphasized the fact that any indulgence in the treatment of surrogate daughters had the character of capital investment designed to enhance the value of human chattel. He reported that in eastern Bengal, prostitutes preferred to purchase and adopt girls too young to remember their parents—children between the ages of one and five years. The young charges were taught to call their mistresses Grandma and were "brought up with especial regard to personal cleanliness and beauty, butter and cream being generally used for giving smoothness and glossiness to the skin. In fact, they are regarded rather as *miniature property than human beings* and no pains or expense is spared in order to render them acceptable in the market."[81] Others described a routine that recalls the tasks to which enslaved children were put in the antebellum South. The adopted child became a sort of servant in her mistress's household, running errands and amusing visitors. As she approached puberty, she was "decked out" to attract the highest bidder who made application to her mistress. Thereafter, the child assumed the "functions and privileges of a woman of the household, and if in good circumstance, is in turn waited upon by a child younger than herself." Her virtual chattel status remained intact, however: "she belongs still to her old mistress and continues so till she either runs away (carrying with her generally some good portion of her mistress's ornaments), or till her own death or that of the mistress dissolves the contract implied to exist between them."[82]

The "adopted daughters" were expected not only to perpetuate their surrogate-mother-mistress's lineage and profession but to support her in old age.[83] They inherited their adoptive mothers' property, and in due course they became procurers of apprentices themselves, thus repeating the cycle of familial-professional community building. According to Bankim Chandra Chatterjee, "those who became particularly distinguished for their personal gifts or accomplishments acquire(d) respectable fortunes."[84] In the course of the nineteenth century, the courts invented rules to regulate the "devolution of the estate of degraded Hindu women." In 1846, a Bengal court faced with a property dispute among the daughters of a prostitute sought the opinion of a *pundit* on the following question: if a Hindu woman who had lost caste as a result of having practiced prostitution was survived by three daughters, one of whom was a respectable wife and mother and the other two prostitutes, which of the three was entitled to inherit her property? The *pundit* responded that the prostitute daughters, by virtue of their shared degradation with their mother, were the rightful heirs to her property, for the "relationship of the respectable daughter to her mother had been severed." According to the legal historian Kunal Parker, "the view that shared degradation was the basis of preferring the claims of the degraded heirs became law until the end of the 19th century," paving the way for matriarchal succession among prostitutes.[85] The commissioner of Patna relayed the information that in parts of Bihar, Muslim men from respectable families fortified their fortunes by marrying wealthy prostitutes.[86] If the adoptive mother died early, a surrogate sister might take her place in relation to the apprentice-in-waiting.[87] Thus, the shifting statuses of the denizens of sex worker households appeared to preclude the formal social barriers between master and slave familiar in North America.

Still, observers underscored the unequal power relations that underpinned the market transactions in surrogate kin: a girl committed to a prostitute found it very hard to escape from her adopted "mother," who might retaliate against such resistance by bringing a criminal charge of stealing ornaments or other property against her protégé. Such a charge, filed in the local police station, was usually enough to intimidate the fugitive into returning and signing a registered bond "ostensibly for money borrowed, but in fact as security that she will remain with her adopted mother for the future. The bond secures the prostitute a contract over the girl's actions and earnings probably forever."[88]

In terms of the social distinctions striating the larger society, though, Indian bureaucrats painted a collective portrait of these women as unconventional groupings that observed few distinctions of caste, color, or religion. The members of "slaveholding" sex-trading matriarchies reportedly assumed a variety of different religious identities depending upon the preferences of their clients, often worshipping their own pantheon of goddesses. Many eschewed marriage to men, performing symbolic ceremonies in which they contracted unions with nonhuman objects like trees or swords. Once an inmate of a Calcutta brothel, a Brahman woman might disguise her upper-caste origins by changing her name so that she could service lesser-born clients. She might embrace Islam if it offered the opportunity to remarry.[89] The household of which she became a member might be inter-caste, where well-born victims of Kulinism mingled with what Presidency Division Commissioner Mr. H.A. Cockerell described as respectable widows "of low castes," including weavers, gardeners, artisans, dessert chiefs, and barbers.[90]

Accounts of the fluidity with which prostitutes reinvented their caste and religious identities suggest that sexual autonomy went hand in hand with opportunities to subvert social divisions and forge culturally pluralistic, socially heterodox female communities. Enslaved Muslim women in East Bengal, or the second or third wives of Muslim men, saw in prostitution a means of escape from restrictive *zenanas* just as Kulin Brahmins did, or even the chance to contract a *nikah* (marriage) with a different man. Some of these fugitives were of East African descent, incorporated as servants or concubines into the homes of wealthy Muslims. Some adopted Hindu names and affected Hindu manners in order to recruit both Hindu apprentices and clients: "Tajban is soon metamorphosed into Jay Tara."[91] Or they may have sought to elude the opprobrium attached to common prostitution among Muslims. The magistrate of Faridpur noted that even "the poorest" Muslims regarded the sex trade with greater reproach than did Hindus, who had a long tradition of courtesanship.[92] The rich history of *tawa'ifs* in precolonial Islamic courts belied this observation, of course, but as Waheed has noted, colonial-era clerics joined with imperial bureaucrats to write these women out of the codes of respectability. Thus, Deputy Magistrate Taraprasad Chatterjee recounted that in Barisal the daughter of a Muslim vendor adopted the Hindu name Rajkumari upon becoming a prostitute, and conflicted with another woman over the worship of the goddess Mansa.[93]

These reports offered many examples of fraternization among Hindus and Muslims belonging to the lower rungs of society. One woman, originally a Hindu, converted to Islam when she married a Muslim, then left him on the ground of "conjugal infidelity," became a prostitute, and reverted to Hinduism under her old name Uma Tara. Neel Das Money of Kumilah confirmed that Muslims in his district took Hindu names: "Fuljan is nicknamed Kumadini, a Rupjan [becomes] a Mon Mohini," in which role they performed Hindu [religious] ceremonies, such as *Dolpuja* and *Kartik puja*. From Bihar came the report that prostitute "castes" were indeterminate in terms of their religious identities—Ramjanee, Gundhurpin, and Rajputar—ate (animal food), drank, and had "illicit relations" with Muslims,. H.W. Alexander, a magistrate of Shahbad, considered them more "Mahomedan than Hindu in their habits and general mode of living." Another, the Naeks, were reported to often bring up their daughters as Muslims.[94]

Deepening these portraits of counterculture, officials classified another unconventional association of singers and dancers with promiscuous slaveholders: the Vaishnavite mendicants. Consisting of a motley crew of the low-born, the outcaste, and free spirits, these women were reputed to enter into temporary alliances with a succession of male partners through the ritual of *kanthi-badal*—that is, marriage by exchanging beads. They pursued various occupations—as flower sellers, milkmaids, hairdressers, and so on—and performed at weddings and religious festivals like Rasa-Leela, which commemorated the god Krishna's capers with milkmaids. That colonial bureaucrats conflated these women with professional prostitutes suggests how closely they associated indeterminate caste status with transgressive sexuality. O. Nolan, Assistant Magistrate of Sirajgunj, epitomized this mode of thinking when he described *Boistomis* as "Hindu widows who have thrown off the restraints of caste and morality and devoted themselves to a life of prostitution under the cloak of religion.... Their practices are as much censured by ordinary Hindus as those of the free love operatives we hear of under Mr. Owen in America by ordinary Christians...."[95]

Malleable as their caste and religious identities appeared to be, prostitutes were described as adopting, instead, ritual markers of their occupational affiliation. Initiation ceremonies launched the professional lives of young prostitutes like Uma Peshgar at the age of twelve. If the symbolic marriages involved human males, such males were said to be discarded within twenty-four hours.⁹⁶ In Bihar, Krishna Chattopadhyaya, headmaster of the Gaya Zilla School, noted disapprovingly that young women marked their loss of virginity with "ceremonial rejoicings" akin to marriage festivities among other classes. Such rejoicings commemorated *nuthni*— or the formal taking off of the ring worn on the nose as a sign of virginity.⁹⁷

English bureaucrats and their Indian deputies offered a wide range of opinions on the sources of and solutions to the problem of the "slaveholding prostitutes."⁹⁸ Suggestions ran the gamut from educating and finding husbands for the rescued girls and women, to remanding them to the custody of caste-Hindu homes, or existing Magdalene asylums, or government-sponsored orphanages, or to fund their emigration to other colonies for labor. There emerged a consensus, however, that all these proposals for redress entailed the assumption of some official role— with attendant costs—on the colonial state's part. The net result of these exchanges flowing from the 1872 investigation was that the government chose to do little about the traffic in "slavery and sex." Indeed, reporters produced evidence suggesting that colonial policy in previous decades had generated the destitution that stimulated the sex traffic. For instance, an 1864 report from Cooch Behar complained that an ordinary farmer who leased land was forced to mortgage or sell his wife or children to prostitutes in order to defray the crushing burden of rents, taxes, and debts.⁹⁹ These observations may have fortified the government's ambiguity about penalizing "slaveholding" among prostitutes, for such action would have involved not only some acknowledgment of the role of colonialism in breeding the famines and clientele that sustained the sex trade but also the expenditure of resources to rehabilitate its child victims.

The cases of US plantation mistress Louisa McCord and the Indian "slaveholding" prostitute Tofa Bai offer different incarnations of "proslavery maternalism" masquerading as private poor relief. McCord depicted white mistresses fulfilling their ostensibly "natural" role by taking maternal care of their dependents within the framework of organic plantation households. She rationalized the twin pillars of patriarchy and white supremacy upon which racial slavery and capitalism rested in antebellum America by presenting Black bodies as people freed from want rather than as commodities. By contrast, the child-trafficking prostitutes of nineteenth-century India erected matriarchal hierarchies at odds with androcentric power structures. Their worlds, at once exploitative and subversive, complicated Anglo-American constructs of slavery by alienating the experience of female bondage from the function of reproductive labor. Their market transactions served as a tool to propagate heterodox worlds of professional practice and proxy kinship that scrambled the spheres of master and slave, chattel and kin, and market and family. But within formal structures of arbitration, they appeared to justify such traffic by drawing upon not only age-old traditions of courtesanship in India but some of the same imperial rhetoric of slavery-as-poor-law that resonated with American defenders of slavery—including the imagery of poverty, charity, parental care, and the links between work and "caste" or "race." Thus, the transoceanic circulation of a tangled web of highly contested proslavery tropes that rationalized servitude as social insurance woven into the fabric of private households could, in the "bazaars" of Calcutta, be made to support conventions of marriage, family, and inheritance that departed sharply from those governing McCord's world. By following the trail of these historical characters within the surprisingly interconnected world of slavery politics in which they lived, we may appreciate the ways in which migration made meaning—how ideas and identities were forged (or mutated) in transit from one place to another, translating at local levels into lived experiences that carried quite different implications for gender roles and expectations.

PART THREE

How Migrations Made Meaning

Imperial Abolition, Slave Trading, and Subaltern Subjects

5

"Domestic" Slavery and Colonial Belonging

You cannot be a whole African Nation brethren [in Canada], but you can be part of the Colored British nation. This nation knows no one color above another, but being composed of all colors, it is evidently a colored nation.
—PROVINCIAL FREEMAN, ED. MARY ANN SHADD CARY, 1854

The interior of the palace being the only thing which is left to the King, delicacy would make one desirous of not interfering with the zenana *concerns and domestic quarrels of its inmates, while humanity revolts at the idea of surrendering, against her will, an unfortunate female who has succeeded in effecting her escape from thraldom.*
—EDWARD COLEBROOKE, RESIDENT, DELHI, 1828

One Saturday in June 1851, several months after the passage of the notorious Fugitive Slave Act in the United States, transatlantic abolitionists and colonial reformers came together to stage a dramatic intervention at the Great Exhibition in London's Crystal Palace. The British abolitionist William Farmer later explained the germination of the idea for that demonstration in a letter laced with sarcasm and published widely in the US antislavery press. He noted that the international exposition had offered a perfect opportunity for slaveholders to prove the truth of their claims that their human chattel were better off than "the laboring classes" of England by exhibiting "some specimens, not merely of hams, locks, revolvers, and firearms, but of the more peculiar staple produce of America—Slavery." After all, such enslaved "specimens," if they could have been made to provide "verbal testimony" of their "extreme happiness upon the plantation," might have saved the American republic of the taint of "moral leprosy" that afflicted its reputation in the world. Instead, whereas members of the British proletariat were "seen daily, in their common dresses, engaged in their ordinary employments," the American pavilion had erased the figure of the American slave entirely.[1] What was more, that erasure was thrown into sharp relief by the United States' ironic choice of an alabaster *Greek* slave to represent their prowess in sculpture.[2]

Originally conceived in Florence against the backdrop of the Greek War of Independence from the Ottoman Empire, expatriate sculptor Hiram Powell's sensational *The Greek Slave* had entranced transatlantic spectators in the previous decade. It evoked for Victorian consumers the spectacle of a helpless and bashful white woman in the nude, exposed to the "licentious gaze of a wealthy Eastern barbarian," as the Official Catalogue of the 1851 Great Exhibition in London's Crystal Palace put it.³ From New England to New Orleans, the intersectional appeal of this traveling work reflected the success with which the artist had tapped into American solidarity with the Greeks in their struggles against Ottoman rule. That solidarity—manifested across the terrains of politics and the press, diplomacy and charitable giving in the 1820s and 1830s—unfolded within a clash of cultures paradigm that bound the European Mediterranean with the Anglo-Atlantic in a common challenge to "Oriental" imperialism and its alleged cultural barbarism. Following fresh on the heels of philhellenistic movements in the United States, the Greek Slave transfixed transatlantic audiences by presenting a model of a classically beautiful white woman with downcast eyes, shielding her nakedness with chained hands, one of which rested upon a column bearing signs of her Christian faith—a crucifix and a locket.⁴ On one level, she signified democracy's descendants shackled by Eastern autocracy. But she also offered an archetype of the purity, piety, chastity, and deference that defined the racialized middle-class Victorian cult of domesticity.⁵ Her nakedness turned her not into Jezebel but rather a victim of lascivious "Oriental" masters of the harem who appeared to violate every norm of the private, heterosexual nuclear family that had emerged as the anchor of morality and republican civic virtue in an evolving market society.⁶

Black American abolitionists, in particular, were quick to note the denial and deflection signaled by the American choice of Powell's artwork. Yet they turned the occasion into an opportunity to construct a framework of comparative slavery that did not extol the high civilization of slave societies in antiquity but rather brought the Slave South into the orbit of "Oriental" despotism. Accompanied by their British friends, including Farmer and that "friend of India" George Thompson, fugitives from slavery William Wells Brown and William and Ellen Craft strolled through the exhibition in interracial groups of twos and threes. In a moment of high drama marked by the proclamation of his enslaved roots, Brown inserted into the American enclosure an image of "The Virginia Slave," published by the British satirical newspaper *Punch*. Representing what the abolitionist *National Era* called "a sad parody on the Greek slave," it depicted a manacled woman of color "standing on a drum head, leaning against a post covered with the star spangled banner."⁷ In addition, Ellen Craft juxtaposed her real-life physical presence, clothed in respectable Victorian garb, against the Greek woman in stone.⁸

The light-skinned Ellen had escaped slavery in Georgia by pretending to be a white slave master in ill health traveling in the company of his slave, who in real life was her darker-skinned husband William. Together, they traveled by various forms of public transit—stagecoach, boat, and train—to freedom in Philadelphia. Ellen rubbed shoulders with slaveholders in public accommodations and fine hotels en route, listening to them complaining about the perfidy of runaways from slavery! The fugitive slave law drove the Crafts overseas, to the antislavery haven of England. Their story, like other fugitive accounts, highlighted the refrain of miscegenation, which called attention to Black women's rape by white masters, raised the perverse spectacle of master and chattel bound by blood, and challenged the racial logic of slavery grounded in a bipolar construction of society into black and white, slave and free.[9] Ellen's nearly white, formerly enslaved body wove the icon of the Greek victim into an imaginary continuum of oppression extending from the Ottoman Empire to Macon, Georgia. Within this perspective, American "Christian" masters paralleled modern Turkish autocrats rather than ancient Greek democrats.[10] As a pastor reminded his audience at an antislavery convention, the "Greek Slave" recalled America's real-life human chattel like Williams, a coachman to successive presidents, who had watched his family board the auction block for sale in New Orleans.[11]

The interracial, transatlantic performance of abolitionism at the London exposition drew an august international audience of "some 15,000, mostly of the upper classes ... including the Queen, Prince Albert," bishops, members of Parliament, merchants, bankers, and foreign dignitaries. The visitors included the Duchess of Sutherland, whom you may recall the South Carolinian slave mistress Louisa McCord would later treat as a sort of adversarial pen pal in the pages of a Richmond newspaper.[12] The occasion encoded the symbolic promise of imperial abolition, built on decades of Britain's reputation as a friend of Black America. That promise invested the migration of Black Americans to Britain or to territories within its jurisdiction with the hope of freedom.

African American migrations to British dominions in the North Atlantic held special meaning against the backdrop of an ostensibly clear contrast between expansionist movements at opposite ends of the world. By 1850, the "empire of liberty" that Jefferson had once envisioned had overspread the North American continent, stretching the geography of racial slavery and, with it, the reach of the "domestic" slave trade from the Upper South to newly annexed domains in the Southwest wrested from American Indians, French, Spanish, and Mexicans.[13] British dominion in Afro-Asia, on the other hand, aspired ostensibly to delimit slavery's frontiers through diplomacy as well as naval power. In practice, for many architects of the British empire, antislavery activism served at least partly as a tool for consolidating their legal and material power and for assimilating colonial subjects and laborers. Moreover, ambiguity and inconsistency marked colonial policy toward bondspeople within elite households.[14] The next pages follow the disparate interplays of subaltern agency, so-called domestic slavery, and colonial belonging that materialized as imperial abolition migrated from the Atlantic to the Indian Ocean world.

WEST VERSUS WEST: THE MIGRATION OF EMELINE, NANCY, AND MARY ANN SHADD CARY

One Saturday in November 1852, eight African American plaintiffs entered a New York City courtroom through lobbies and passages jammed with onlookers "anxious to know the result" of a hearing on a freedom suit in progress. Two years before, the litigants had been anonymous, signified by mere slashes of a pen on an 1850 slave schedule. Now, a writ of habeas corpus filed in their behalf by a lower Manhattan resident named Louis Napoleon had transformed their civic identities and etched their names into official records as plaintiffs with rights and people with kin in the case of *Lemmon v. The People (of the State of New York)*. They included Emeline, aged twenty-three, and her brothers Lewis, sixteen, and Edward, thirteen; her daughter Amanda, two; Nancy, twenty; her daughter Ann, five; and twin boys Louis and Edward, seven. The plaintiffs' would-be master, forty-year-old Jonathan Lemmon, had been on his way with his family and the African Africans he had "inherited" from his father-in-law from Bath County, Virginia, to the cotton frontier of Texas.[15]

Migration promised to help invent new identities and remake lives, but in October 1852, when the Lemmons set out for the Southwest, it encoded very different meanings for the master and the human chattel he claimed. For nineteenth-century European-descended Americans, mobility was intricately bound with the notion of freedom, perhaps partly because of their foundational experiences with immigration across the Atlantic in flight from persecution or in the quest for opportunity. Once in the New World, the dynamics of settler colonialism fueled a mystique of westward expansion as a liberating experience laden with the promise of social mobility. For the influential late nineteenth-century historian Frederick Jackson Turner, the process of settling what he called successive "frontiers"—the "hither edges of free land"—created a new man. This was the individualistic, pragmatic, democratic, wholly exceptionalist "American." White yeoman strivers yearning to amass land, hold slaves, and get rich from the business of plantation agriculture, or else East Coast farmers, small producers, and laborers seeking economic independence, would certainly have viewed the American West as a land of promise. But African Americans entered this scenario either as chattel or not at all.[16]

The Louisiana Purchase of 1803 had extended American sway over a vast expanse of territory stretching from the Mississippi River in the east to the Rocky Mountains in the west, and bounded by the Gulf of Mexico to the south and Canada to the north. It paved the way for the further expropriation of American Indian lands through war or treaty. Territorial expansion proceeded apace with the War of

1812, the acquisition of Florida, and the annexation of Texas from Mexico. A new South emerged, Thomas Jefferson's vision of an "empire of liberty" inhabited by sturdy republican freeholders transmogrified into a formidable and highly capitalized but volatile empire of slavery. At its throne sat "King Cotton," raised up by the cotton gin, steam-powered riverboats, imported credit, and the power of government at all levels. A major driver of global capitalism, the Slave South cast expansionist eyes west across continental North America, south toward Meso-America, and far out into the Caribbean.[17]

Behind it all lay the grind of backbreaking Black labor. Aspiring planters migrating to the cotton- and sugar-growing realms of Alabama, Mississippi, Louisiana, Arkansas, and Texas transported legions of human chattel in chains.[18] In the last several decades, scholars of the domestic slave trade have shifted our scrutiny from the plantation to the slave market. Notwithstanding the romantic, sentimental image of magnolias and mint juleps, kind masters, and happy slaves that pervades Old South nostalgia, the historian Walter Johnson reminded us that the Louisiana business census of 1854 tells a sobering story. It lists nineteen slave pens located across the French Quarter, better known to modern day revelers for its jazz clubs and Mardi Gras festivities. Memphis and Natchez harbored major slave marts of their own. During the slave trading season from September to May, traders rated and priced slaves, treated them with medicine, adorned them with clothing and jewelry, and exhibited them along the walls in their showrooms or in the streets in front of their markets. In Johnson's words, "the entire economy of the antebellum South was constructed upon the idea that the bodies of enslaved people had a measurable monetary value."[19] Between 1790 and 1860, as many as 1.1 million captives were transported from Virginia and Maryland on foot, tied in coffles, or crammed into railroad cars and ship holds for the devastating odyssey to the South.[20] There the enslaved would hack plantations out of forests and hunting grounds, raise crops and livestock, construct buildings and mend fences, run ferries and transport assortments of cargo, while enduring infectious diseases, hunger, and torturous forms of discipline and punishment. Women suffered sexual abuse and the additional hazards of poor prenatal care and maternal deaths. Poignant traumas entailed the severance of family ties, and the haunting *déjà vu* of natal alienation, signified by descendants' use of the metaphor of "stealing" to capture the essence of forced migration and the chattel principle.[21]

The thing about human chattel was that the enslaved could, and did, thwart slaveholder expectations, as Jonathan Lemmon was about to discover. The group he led traveled to Norfolk. In the absence of a more direct passage to their destination, the Virginians boarded the steamer *City of Richmond* for New York, intending to proceed directly from there to New Orleans. When they arrived in New York at four o'clock in the afternoon, the clerk of the steamer advised Lemmon to purchase tickets for their onward journey to New Orleans from a man in South Street.

Lemmon alleged that the ticket seller tricked his family into boarding two carriages that conveyed them not to the steamship *Memphis* bound for New Orleans but to a boardinghouse in Carlisle Street, dropped them off on the sidewalk, and drove off. By then it was dark, so the Virginians decided to stay the night in New York, only to discover the following day that the *Memphis* had already sailed. The eight people the Lemmons had hoped to transport to America's Cotton Kingdom had migrated instead to New York City's Superior Court, presided over by Judge Elijah Payne. New York had ended slavery in 1827. An exception allowing slaveholders traveling through the state to keep their human chattel as long as they left within nine months had been repealed in 1841. Only fugitives were liable to be returned to slavery.[22]

Louis Napoleon, who applied for a writ of habeas corpus on behalf of the Lemmon "slaves," described himself to census takers in 1850 as a forty-eight-year-old polisher and varnisher who lived with his wife Catherine in the heavily Black Fifth ward of Lower Manhattan.[23] A recent account of the *Lemmon* case by Sarah L. H. Gronningsater suggests that laboring New Yorkers like Napoleon drew upon formal institutions like the law as well as connections with interracial abolitionists to pressure local governments against slavery.[24] Working-poor African Americans also forged informal webs of vigilance that used city institutions like station houses and juvenile reformatories like the New York House of Refuge to harbor children and adults from slave-catching shipowners and masters. Moreover, their social and work connections networked them into the mobile populations of ship labor that may have provided opportunities to keep track of enslaved persons in transit.[25] Thus for instance, a couple of decades after the *Lemmon* case transpired, a Troy newspaper reported the claim of a former steamship steward aboard the *Richmond* of his part in instigating and coordinating the escape of the Virginia slaves and bringing them into Napoleon's orbit.[26] This account accords with the composition of the Napoleon household at the time. According to the 1850 census, the Napoleons shared a household, perhaps in order to pool resources, with twenty-seven-year-old Samuel Livingston, his twenty-five-year-old wife Sarah, and their five-year-old daughter Margaret, all marked "Mulatto." The South Carolina–born Livingston listed his job as steamboat steward, so it does not take a leap of imagination to speculate that he may have had something to do with the events surrounding the Lemmon case.[27]

Napoleon's complaint described Lemmon as a "slave trader." But the defendants had very different delusions about their relationships with the people they claimed as capital, collateral, and labor. The *New York Times* reported that before the judge arrived, the slave mistress Juliet Lemmon "took a seat opposite the alleged slaves, and made a pressing appeal to the feelings of the two women, urging her former kindness, and calling on them as they had a conscience, not to rob her of their labor." Emmeline and Nancy remained unmoved, perhaps thinking, as later testimonies of ex-slaves revealed, that it was the mistress who had for too long gotten away with stealing their persons. They seemed to understand that slavery's essence lay not in Juliet's professions of good feelings but rather in the chattel principle upon which the defense drew: Lemmon's lawyer argued that the plaintiffs were in truth property, with which a citizen of one slaveholding state was entitled to travel to another through a nonslaveholding harbor under the principle of comity of states within the Union.[28] Yet the fact that the former slave mistress was forced to make a personal appeal to memories of "kindness" highlighted a reality that Judge Payne upheld: the move to New York had transformed a species of property into people; it had turned anonymous marks on the federal slave schedules of 1850 into willful owners of their own selves and their labor power, into families and communities with the sanction of the law. When the Lemmons' westward travel itinerary opened a door to this transformation along the fault lines of a Union half slave and half free, the once-enslaved Virginians walked right through the doorway to a different, ostensibly free West under the flag of the British Empire. They left for Ontario, or Canada West as it was known in their time.

The same year that the *Lemmon* case unfolded, a pioneering African American journalist and émigré to Canada named Mary Ann Shadd Cary published a case for a feminist vision of color-blind colonial citizenship under a benevolent female majesty. Her pamphlet, *A Plea for Emigration; or Notes of Canada West, in its Moral, Social, and Political Aspect: with Suggestions Respecting Mexico, West Indies, and Vancouver's Island, for the Information of Colored Emigrants,* touted the locale to which the Lemmon plaintiffs would flee. The freed Virginians' abolitionist friends compensated their former master, even as the case itself wound its way through an appeals process, pitting the claims of New York against those of Virginia in an intensifying crisis of Union.

If working-class Black New Yorkers and their white allies tapped the institutions of a dividing America—institutions of law, state, and benevolent reform—to thwart forced migration to the empire of slavery, African American émigrés of all strata, especially those of education and standing, deployed the tools of diplomacy to engage with a diasporic politics of freedom and empire beyond the boundaries of the nation-state.

Since the birth of the American republic, Canada had established itself as a magnet for refugees from North Atlantic slavery: Revolutionary-era loyalists, Jamaican maroons, Black veterans from the War of 1812 (some of whom had received land grants in south central Ontario for siding with the British), and fugitives who fled to Nova Scotia.[29] African American expatriates engaged in an exercise of what Ikuko Asaka has described as "strategic self-fashioning."[30] Official British avowals of antislavery, however precarious, marked an improvement over federal sanction of African slavery and white terror in the land of their birth. Thus Black refugees in Canada sought to forge bonds of solidarity and a sense of diasporic identity with Britain's emancipated subjects in the West Indies, and to incorporate this Black British diaspora into an imagined imperial nation premised upon British benevolence. They celebrated Caribbean emancipation, emphasized Black British subjects' piety, industry, and capacity for labor, and sought British help to advance Black education. Above all, they actively lobbied metropolitan authorities to protect fugitives from extradition to the United States, harking back to Britain's mantle as Atlantic emancipator. The Black New Yorker Samuel R. Ward played a prominent role in projecting African American Canadians and Afro-Caribbean freed people as members of a common diaspora under Crown protection, cemented by the civic identity of "British Negro." Ward had lived life as a free Black man and Underground Railroad operator before the fear of retaliation for his role in the rescue of a fugitive slave in Syracuse drove him to Canada. The historian Jeffrey Kerr-Ritchie has shown that Ward transformed himself into an imperial subject by sojourning through Canada, the United Kingdom, and Jamaica, arguing for legal equality without regard to race and promoting the vision of a Pan-African evangelical Christianity.[31]

It is within the context of this African diasporic politics of "strategic self-fashioning" that we must evaluate Shadd Cary's vision of colonial citizenship under the protective umbrella of an antislavery Crown. What set her apart from the male champions of these politics was her injection of the discourse of gender into a diasporic conception of imperial belonging.

EMIGRATION AND COLONIAL BELONGING UNDER A FEMALE SOVEREIGN

Mary Ann Shadd Cary came of age in a new republic founded in compromise on racial slavery (fig. 4). There, masters of human chattel constructed a mythology of the Old South as a patriarchal paradise populated by benevolent paternalists and blissful slaves, along with "inhuman bondage" as a species of social insurance. Into this bipolar society divided starkly by law and etiquette into black and white, slave and free, where free Blacks were rendered an anomaly, Mary Ann Shadd Cary was born in 1823 into a free family of color of racially mixed descent in Delaware. The basic outlines of her biography are well known. As the slave state of her birth on the borders of the Mason-Dixon line grew increasingly inhospitable to Black people during the antebellum era, Shadd Cary's father Abraham shifted his family to free Pennsylvania. There, in Westchester, he set himself up as a shoemaker while immersing his family in abolitionist and Underground Railroad activism. His eldest daughter Mary Ann attended a private Quaker boarding school in Westchester and entered the one profession open to African American women in those days, teaching school. Her job took her across the Mid-Atlantic, from Delaware to Pennsylvania and New Jersey.

FIGURE 4. Unidentified artist, portrait of Mary Anne Shadd Cary (1823–1893). Artwork in the public domain, courtesy of National Archives of Canada, C-029977.

Shadd Cary startled contemporaries by publishing controversial critiques of her community on grounds that included charges of conspicuous consumption against the Black bourgeoisie, the alleged perpetuation of "ignorance" and "superstition" by Black churches, and the supposed dearth of action on the part of African American convention organizers. On the heels of the draconian Fugitive Slave Act, which stripped suspected fugitives of their Fourth Amendment rights, subjected them to arrest without a warrant, and offered no recourse to trial by jury, thus endangering entire communities of free Blacks, Shadd Cary joined an exodus of people of color from the United States to Canada. She settled in the intimate farming community of Windsor, a spot that served as the first destination of refugees from slavery south of the border. With funding from the evangelical Christian abolitionist American Missionary Association—associated with the New York merchant Lewis Tappan who had also helped fund William Adam in India—she established an interracial school.[32]

At the same time, she embarked upon tours of her newly adopted home and researched its potential as a haven for Black Americans. Her labors materialized in a forty-page pamphlet, published in 1852 under the title *A Plea for Emigration*. The following year, she launched a newspaper, the *Provincial Freeman*, "devoted to Anti-Slavery, Emigration, Temperance and General Literature" (fig. 5).[33] Although male collaborators fronted as editors of this publication, Shadd Cary was its guiding light and de facto operator, thus blazing a trail for Black women in the field of journalism.

As the full title of the pamphlet *A Plea for Emigration* suggests, Shadd Cary placed her data on Canada's climate, natural resources, and politics of race relations within a comparative framework informed by emigration debates raging within African America: whether to stay and fight for immediate abolition and civil rights within the United States, as Frederick Douglass championed, or to seek equality and opportunity in less formidable realms like Central and South America as Martin Delany argued, or to repatriate to Africa, as the American Colonization Society envisioned. At the same time, however, her emigrationist perspective sought to write women and people of color into a teleological, Hegelian representation of history as a march of freedom unfolding from east to west, and culminating

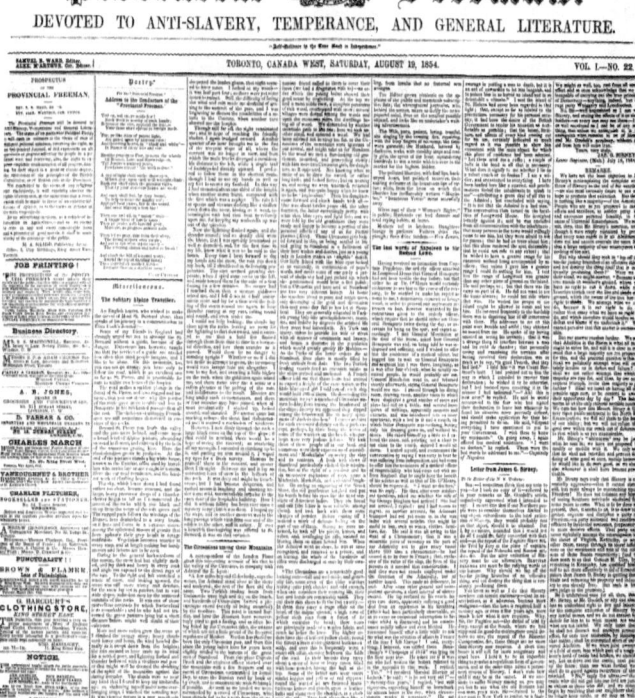

FIGURE 5. *Provincial Freeman,* front page, Toronto, Canada West, 19 August 1854, vol. 1, no. 22, African American Newspapers—Provincial Freeman online database. © Courtesy of Accessible Archives Inc., 5 Great Valley Parkway, Malvern, PA 19355, 866–296–1488, www.accessible-archives.com/.

perhaps, in Vancouver, within the framework of what Shadd Cary depicted strategically as a color-blind, antislavery empire with a woman at its helm. Within this haven, Vancouver would become, Shadd Cary wrote, "the first island in importance on the globe."[34]

This land's destiny lay not in agriculture. Rather, Shadd Cary wrote, "The Western Continent, and particularly the northern part, say 'wise men of the east,' must eventually leave the eastern far in the distance, (a fact that should not be lost sight of by colored men,) and that over the Pacific will the trade with eastern nations be prosecuted." Vancouver refueled whale ships en route to the northern seas and lay directly in the path of trade with Asia, so that "the people there settled, of whatever complexion, will be the 'merchant princes of the world,' under the protection of Great Britain." From this angle, Shadd Cary judged "any eastern move ..., as for instance to Africa," as a "retrograde step." She deemed Africa the colonizationists' "land of promise"—a means of ridding North America of free Blacks. In order to dissuade African Americans from fulfilling racist fantasies of a Black-free America, she painted "Tropical Africa" as an inhospitable destination for repatriation, especially for women of color and poorer Blacks. The continent allegedly raised the specter of "pestilence, a burning sun and fearful maladies," in addition to "big spiders, lizzards, snakes, centipedes, scorpions, and all manner of creeping and biting things." The *Provincial Freeman* warned that complexion offered little guarantee of equal treatment. Gesturing to a derisive label forged in empire, she noted that "colored nabobs" might prove hostile to less well-off newcomers, and "as merciless as other men, when possessed of the same amount of pride, conceit and wickedness, and as much, if not more ignorance." Nor did Mexico and South America offer attractive prospects of refuge, for they were supposedly weak states aligned with the Roman Catholic Church. Only one government, Great Britain, promised to offer within her dependencies "a *secure* home for the American slave, and the disgraced *free* man."[35]

Shadd Cary asserted to her compatriots that while they could not be "a whole African nation" in Canada, they could "be *part* of the Colored British nation. This nation knows no one color above another, but being composed of all colors, it is evidently a *colored* nation." British soil, "under the protection of the Queen" offered African Americans of both sexes their best chance at freedom.[36] This argument added a womanist twist to strategic African American proclamations of Anglophilia. As we have seen, Britain's perceived emancipationist leanings extended from the landmark colonial-era court decision, *Somerset v. Stewart*, through British invitations to the enslaved to join the loyalist cause on the promise of freedom during the American Revolution, the British role in the abolition of the international slave trade and in West Indian emancipation, to the hospitality that greeted notable African American fugitives from slavery in Great Britain. African American celebrations of Britain's ostensible commitment to liberty as a matter of moral principle sought at least partly to cement a strategic political and diplomatic alliance with an officially antislavery imperial state.[37] What Shadd Cary added to this connection was the observation that it was a *female* sovereign that would now steer the imperial project of freedom.

In this context, *A Plea for Emigration* portrayed Ontario as Black people's answer to the liberating mystique of westward expansion, in which geographical mobility offered a path to prosperity and personal reinvention. This land supposedly boasted a temperate climate, rich vegetation, arable land, plentiful timber, beautiful waterways, fine livestock, and affordable rural land prices, so that even men without capital could, "with an axe and a little energy," achieve "an independent position." Yet the values of "personal freedom and political rights" invested this soil with its most priceless quality, rendering it the genuinely liberated—and liberal—reverse mirror image of the US West.[38]

But what, in Shadd Cary's worldview, did freedom really mean? In an age in which proslavery interests defended masters of the lash as benevolent paternalists, and chattel bondage as a form of "poor law" for the inherently dependent, she upheld self-sufficiency, above all, as the hallmark of liberty. She famously clashed with the Refugee Home Society, run by a fellow émigré, the former fugitive slave Henry Bibb, which raised funds to purchase lands for resale to fugitive slaves. Shadd Cary criticized the venture for excluding "nominally free" African Americans, and its leaders for allegedly lining their own pockets at the expense of their ostensible beneficiaries. But most of all, she charged that the Society's reliance on the largesse of white philanthropists reduced freed people to "beggary." Her publications maintained that indiscriminate charity perpetuated stereotypes of the refugees' helpless degradation, playing, she seemed to be saying, into proslavery depictions of free societies as beset with "the perils of pauperism," class conflict, and radical ideologies of all stripes. *A Plea for Emigration* quoted disparagements of such aid at length: "We do not think it right that twenty-seven thousand colored persons, who are supporting themselves by their own industry, should lie under the disgrace of being called public beggars, when they receive nothing, and don't want anything."[39] Her portrait of the settlement of Dawn, "on the Sydenham river," posed the very antithesis of the proslavery prognosis of free societies: "Instead of [registering] an increase of vice, prejudice, improvidence, laziness, or a lack of energy," this settlement was law-abiding and paid "due attention" to "moral and intellectual culture." Moreover, "the former prejudices on the part of the whites, has given place to a perfect reciprocity of religious and social intercommunication. Schools are patronized equally; the gospel is common, and hospitality is shared alike by all."[40]

Shadd Cary, then, embraced an emigrationist vision that engaged transoceanic discourses over slavery, poverty, and patriarchy. Deeply entangled with emerging global systems of capitalism and empire, her perspective melded Whig poor law reformers' disdain for dependence with a Republican free labor vision of social mobility emerging on the US side of the Atlantic. The foregoing pages have recorded that the same Whig government that presided over the advent of Caribbean emancipation also spearheaded a process to reform Britain's poor laws based on the principle that poor relief for the unworthy indigent encouraged laziness and immorality. The *Plea*'s observation that "boxes of clothing and barrels of provisions" dispatched to Canada by misguided US philanthropists had been "employed to support the idle, who are too lazy to work" but made up a minority of Canada's "colored population," smacked of Whiggish indictments of the so-called unworthy poor on both sides of the Atlantic. The quintessentially American answer to proslavery charges of pauperism in free society lay in the ideology of free labor associated with the Republican Party in the 1850s. This emerging politics of antislavery made self-ownership a cardinal feature of freedom, one that conferred upon individuals the ability to sell their labor power in a free market for labor and, by exercising the virtues of the Protestant work ethic, the promise of earning upward mobility.[41]

Of course, as historians have long shown, such thinking failed to account for labor and class conflicts that were always part of the American scene and offered a free market alternative to more progressive Free Soil antislavery approaches that defined freedom not merely as self-ownership but also as access to land. Nevertheless, in light of Shadd Cary's alliance with British antislavery liberalism, it made strategic sense for her to celebrate the dignity of work and equal *opportunity* in Canada in Whiggish terms that were also steeped in Republican free labor thinking. A segment on "Labor-Trades" in the *Plea* highlighted the demand for labor in Canada's thriving villages and its agricultural and timber sectors. Moreover, "complexion" excluded no man from any trade. "If a colored man understands his business, he receives the public patronage the same as a white man. He is not obliged to work a little better, and at a lower rate—there is no degraded class to identify him with, therefore every man's work stands or falls according to merit...." At the same time, Shadd Cary encouraged her compatriots of color to become entrepreneurs and small producers, buying land directly from the Canadian government rather than contracting to labor for planters elsewhere—even under British governance, say in Jamaica.[42]

Shadd Cary's most striking and unique contribution, however, consisted in writing women of color—as wives and mothers, workers and citizens—into these Anglo-American narratives of equal opportunity and sturdy independence. While the *Plea* said little about family or gender, the *Provincial Freeman* wove these themes into a compelling composite picture of the mutual workings of economic oppression, sexual abuse, and family breakdown in US communities riven by slavery and race prejudice. The newspaper highlighted injuries to women and families that commonly featured in abolitionist novels and fugitive slave narratives and were woven into the lived experiences of enslaved Black women: the specter of families separated on the auction block; of Margaret Garner killing her child in a hideout in Cincinnati rather than have it "live as a slave"; a jealous Tennessee mistress scalding and hanging her husband's enslaved mistress; and a runaway ad for a slave mother with a "nearly white" infant—a visible marker all at once of sexual abuse, perverse paternal ties, and the illogic of racial slavery.[43]

In addition, the paper's spotlight on race prejudice north of the Mason-Dixon line illuminated the difficulties of creating and sustaining families even in the free states of the American republic. Black exclusion from all but the most menial of trades and shrinking opportunities for property ownership drove African American youth off to sea, leaving Black women without prospective marriage partners or breadwinners.[44]

Shadd Cary's newspaper juxtaposed these accounts with the economic exploitation of working women in the United States. "Of all the classes of workers in this country," one account began, "the females are the most completely prostrated by underpaid labor. In no department of human industry is so much robbery endured and so much humiliating contempt inflicted, as upon poor, weak, working women." The piece underscored that economic justice for women built both wholesome families and female virtue, for without it, "no woman deprived of a husband or a father can be anything in America but a pauper and a beggar, unless by the sale of HER CHASTITY." It reinforced the argument for emigration by placing ostensibly free northern men on par with the worst despots of their sex in autocracies elsewhere: "What is really the difference between the Russians flogging their women—the Southerners flogging their negro women, and the Northerners starving and cheating theirs?"[45]

This portrait of US working women's degradation contrasted forcefully with strategically placed arguments for women's rights within the British Empire. One article noted that Englishmen in general agreed that women "may be a clerk, a partner, banker, a proprietress, a queen." It went on to challenge the logic of limiting women from the public sphere of politics and the professions within an imperial realm under female suzerainty. "A woman may be a nurse to both sexes. Oh, yes! And as a nurse or "granny" she may administer medicine, at second-hand, but to prescribe! Oh! That would be dreadful! All we have to say about this, is —Pshaw! It certainly but ill becomes us, to say a great deal against a Woman's having to do with politics, when at the head of our Government, the greatest and freest on ... earth, stands a Woman, and she the very best Sovereign that ever swayed the British scepter.... And, by the way, the ruling of Queens will bear the most triumphant comparison with the ruling of Kings, past and present....There now! Can you tell where we stand on Women's Rights?"[46]

It was clear where Shadd Cary stood on women's rights. Defined by the economic and political conditions necessary to sustain individual autonomy, personal integrity, and family life, such rights stood at the center of her conception of freedom. Mobility via emigration comprised a practical, activist mode of realizing such freedom. And British colonial nationalism under the protective eye of a female emperor offered the institutional framework for its accomplishment. At the same time, her idea of freedom as self-sufficiency, shaped by the equal opportunity to work for wages and build private property, drew strategically upon the principles of Whig traditions of antislavery on both sides of the Atlantic. She would later return to the United States, recruit soldiers for the Union during the Civil War, earn a law degree from Howard University, and fight for women's suffrage. For the purposes of our story, however, it was her interface with imperial abolition that makes her an iconic figure in comparative histories of slavery, freedom, and empire.

Shadd Cary's gendered vision of a strategic alliance with the British Empire forms our point of departure for grappling with the question of how her hopeful, arguably idealized perspective on an antislavery Britain measured up to colonial administration in British Asia. In what ways did the relationship among empire, family, work, and freedom mutate as it navigated the complex, confounding skeins of Indian Ocean world slaveries and slave trades? How did the women and children who made up the bulk of the chattel or "clients" within the domestic realms on those trading routes write themselves into the choppy narrative of colonial freedom several seas away from the Atlantic world of Mary Shadd Cary and Ellen Craft?

CONCUBINES OR MERELY SERVANTS?

During the years that Shadd Cary's father Abraham was helping to turn anonymous marks on slave schedules into people through his work with North America's Underground Railroad, a different sort of migration was remaking the identity of a Rajput woman named Radha. In forced transit from the North Indian village of Muthra into the royal household of the emperor of Delhi, this captive assumed a new identity: alleged concubine, and a new name, Gul Bihar.

In his harem paintings, the British painter John Frederick Lewis portrayed western fantasies of the domestic settings that women like Radha/Gul Bihar supposedly entered in Muslim worlds stretching from the Ottoman Empire across the Indian Ocean. A review of one, published in the *Art-Journal* (London and New York), offered a detailed description of the Orientalist gaze in the nineteenth century. It took readers into "... the interior of a harem at Cairo, wherein is seated in luxurious ease a young Turk, attired in the excess of Moslem fashion. Near him, and reclining upon cushions, are two Circassian women, also dressed in the extremity of Oriental taste.... On the right is seen a tall Nubian eunuch, who removes from the shoulders of an Egyptian slave the shawl by which she had been covered, in order to show her to the master of the harem; ... The Circassian women look languidly to the Egyptian with an expression of supreme contempt, which is responded to by a sneer on the face of the Nubian eunuch."[47]

Yet female denizens of the harem could transform themselves from objects of Orientalist fantasies into subjects of colonial history by transgressing the walls of seclusion and stepping into the archives via carefully constructed spaces of imperial munificence. In 1828, Radha/Gul Bihar, accompanied by another alleged royal concubine, scaled the walls that separated her royal *zenana* in Delhi from the world outside and arrived in a colonial police station, asserting the right to leave the extended family she served.

The Delhi zenana women's "freedom flights"—if they qualified as such—coincided with an era in the British Empire's transition from decline in North America to triumph in Asia. It was an era informed by a vision of redemption that imbued the colonial project in Afro-Asia with antislavery purposes. Yet, as we have noted in earlier chapters, professions of good intention collided with the overriding imperial imperatives of political expansion and revenue collection, generating inconsistent and often arbitrary attitudes toward Indian forms of servitude. We have encountered intercontinental abolitionists and social reformers, as well as critics of British imperialism like William Adam and George Thompson, who made a compelling case that the imperial policy of legal pluralism had, in fact, created and codified forms of servitude not recognized by the East India Company's Muslim predecessors.[48] Governor-General Warren Hastings had set the tone of British Indian law in 1772 by declaring that in civil cases involving matters of property, marriage, religious usages, and social relations, Hindus and Muslims would be governed by their respective religious laws. Subsequently, a British Indian court had brought slavery within the purview of these principles, presumably because it involved both marriage and property rights.[49] As long as these arrangements did not hamper their own quest for power and profit, colonial officials preferred not to interfere with them for fear of disrupting their fiscal interests and alliances with local elites. They expediently distinguished Indian forms of servitude from both the international slave trade and Atlantic slavery. They constructed an Orientalist discourse of difference that maintained that slavery in the East was fundamentally different from slavery in the West. Around Indian incarnations of bondage, they crafted a rhetoric of domestic slavery with overlapping meanings. Domestic slavery implied both a man's mastery over his household and imperial deference to local customs, especially those that involved the privileges of the well born.[50]

Nevertheless, debates over slavery within the colonial establishment spurred proposals for amelioration. One judicial authority, J. H. Harington, while suggesting regulations for the guidance of courts on slavery cases, sought to establish legal grounds for Atlantic-style freedom suits by or on behalf of the enslaved. He did so by raising the question of whether people claimed by would-be masters were lawful slaves as interpreted by Muslim and Hindu jurists, and by making maltreatment grounds for dispossessing a master of his servile dependents. Moreover, he sought to bring these cases under the purview of the criminal rather than civil courts; in other words, making them about not property but rather personal freedom.[51] The proposal was never adopted. Nonetheless, a patchwork of discordant colonial practices offered subalterns some maneuvering space. Thus, for instance, a proclamation issued in 1812 against the import of slaves into Delhi "for any purpose whatsoever" by the city's Resident (imperial political agent) Sir Charles Metcalf marked a departure from company policy elsewhere.[52]

The story of the alleged concubines in flight unfolded against the backdrop of these developments. The sort of elite households they belonged to often incorporated enslaved women into lineages they were expected to perpetuate through reproductive labor, earning certain privileges in exchange. For instance, one who bore her master a child whose paternity was acknowledged might earn the right to be freed following her owner's death. Moreover, such a child enjoyed the same rights in matters like inheritance as siblings born of "legitimate" marriages. In later years, the colonial state would chip away the inheritance and succession rights of kin descended from lineages tainted by enslavement, furthering its own interests.[53] Still, domestic slavery was often held to be immune to colonial fiat, and contributed to the perception of slavery in the Indian and Islamic worlds as different, familial, and "mild."

Of course, the oft-repeated defenses of these systems raises the question, mild compared with what? Colonial bureaucrats might reference the Caribbean or the American South, but modern scholarship on places like the Ottoman Empire, Arabia, and India has challenged some of these assumptions. Thus, Madeline Zulfi has shown that while some enslaved women in Istanbul could indeed wield power as mothers of the throne, the vast majority were liable to be torn from their homes at a young age and suffer material, emotional, and sexual abuse or even death on their way to urban slave marts.[54]

The Delhi fugitives, by the very act of fleeing, troubled narratives of contented concubines, if they were indeed concubines. Colonial officials hesitated to free them, for the Mughal Sultan claimed them as his son's mistresses. The women's restoration, then, became a matter of "honour ... of the King himself and of the whole palace...." Edward Colebrooke, then Resident at Delhi, wrote that "the palace is thronged with women of this description, kidnapped by persons employed for the purpose, and bought from those persons.... [O]f the hundreds of brothers and sisters, sons, daughters, and grandchildren of his Majesty, scarcely one ... will be found to have been born from any but such mothers." The King expressed to colonial bureaucrats his apprehension that liberating the two alleged concubines would set a dangerous precedent that might invite other women in the palace under similar circumstances to follow suit. "And he asks," wrote the Resident, "what would be the consequence if one of the Begums (wives) themselves should elope from the palace, and claim the protection of the police?" One of the women in the 1828 "elopement" case, Radha testified that she was the daughter of a Rajput formerly of Jaipur, and that she had moved to the village of Muthra, where she operated a sweet shop. Kidnappers disguised as customers had drugged and forcibly carried her away to a slave trader's safe house, where she was dressed "in the clothes of a (Muslim) woman" and conveyed in a palanquin into the interior of the Prince Mirza Saleem's household. The British assistant Resident at Delhi questioned her about the claims of male relatives or masters to her status: did she have a husband in Muthra? Did she have marital or sexual relations with any man in the zenana? No, Radha swore. Her parents had died before she could be betrothed to any man. At the palace, she was but a common servant mistreated by the Prince's wife, a testimonial she buttressed by presenting evidence of physical abuse. Only then did the colonial government sanction her release.[55]

This case reflected, then, the tensions that beset Britain's approach to "domestic slavery" in India. On the one hand, it illustrated the spirit of the principle upheld since the 1770s, that bondage entered the realm of personal law and assumed (within the limits of expediency) a special immunity from regulation, when it occurred within the sanctum of the patriarchal household. There was, in other words, no refuge from slavery as long as it was judged a matter of *domestic* governance, not subject to trespass by outsiders. Yet, Harington's proposal and Metcalf's regulations, which defined slavery in terms of personal freedom rather than familial relations and judged maltreatment grounds for emancipation, may have offered these women a resource for engaging the formal institutions of colonialism in their quest to escape servitude. Their success, however, was predicated on proof that they had no sexual or conjugal relations with the men who claimed to be their masters.

Cases of "freedom flights" in other parts of British India suggest that Metcalf's policy may have created unique opportunities for Radha/Gul Bihar in Delhi that were not available to women who sought to flee abusive households in other parts of the country. A couple of years before Parliament "delegalized" slavery, which in theory at least bound colonial authorities not to return alleged fugitives to their masters, a young woman in Mysore named Deyavummah paid for her quest to escape from bondage with death. The case underscores both the existence of everyday forms of collective resistance by marginalized women and the limits of British antislavery policy when it brushed up against the prerogatives of posh allies.[56]

MURDER IN MYSORE

In September 1841, H. Montgomery, acting superintendent of Bangalore, wrote the secretary to the commissioner for government of the territories of the Raja (king) of Mysore, a tributary state. His letter discussed a disturbing case of torture and murder of a servant to an aristocratic family by Krishna Urs, a close relative of the monarch. The victim belonged to "the unfortunate class" of people—numbering hundreds he estimated—who served as "domestic drudges" within the palace and the households of the ruler's relatives. They were slaves purchased as children from their parents or young women sold off by husbands or other relatives. But such sales did not always go unchallenged by their victims. Streaks of rebellion among them surfaced in the case of a young woman's murder, and the willingness of a community of her fellow women in bondage to offer damning depositions against their royal masters. Imperial handling of the matter, however, suggested the extreme reluctance of the colonial state to interfere with the private realms of masters of status, even at the risk of condoning domestic violence of the most egregious kind.[57]

The twenty-something Deyavummah fled the home of her abusive master Urs one night in August 1841. While on a public road around a fortress in town, she was seized by soldiers in the private service of the Mysore king, imprisoned in their guardroom, and following orders from the ruler, restored to Urs's custody. Informants of the colonial authorities in the area claimed to have learned about this incident through unofficial reports. Is it possible that some of Urs's servants who helped drag Deyavummah back to captivity served as sources for this report?

Four days later, the local police learned that "a female body was being removed for internment from Krishna Urs's house, together with the report that it belonged to a woman who, four days earlier, had been restored to her master." A judicial official in British employ immediately ordered a halt to the body's last rites, pending an inspection of the corpse and an investigation. Called upon to explain the circumstances surrounding the death of the young woman, Urs deposed that the deceased had died from disease and a fall down a flight of stairs. He claimed that the dead woman was not the one who had attempted a futile escape days before. He allegedly produced another woman before a colonial official to "impersonate" the now dead escapee, according to the official. The investigator's suspicions were confirmed when he questioned the woman out of her master's earshot. The witness offered a powerful testimony that contradicted her master's account of events. She recounted that it was the dead woman who had absconded and had met her fate through "ill-usages." She went on to confess that she herself had contemplated fleeing to escape maltreatment, naming seven female servants who would corroborate her version of the story. She also "exhibited wounds on her wrists and ankles, [around] which some descriptions of ligature had evidently been applied," as well as marks of abuse on her thighs and other parts of her body.[58]

This damning testimony prompted the British Resident to summon other domestic workers in Urs's household for questioning. The women offered, in excruciating detail, eyewitness accounts of Deyavummah's death by torture, implicating their master and mistress directly and personally in the dead woman's ordeal. They reported that following her coerced return to her master's home, the victim had been starved of food for three days, kicked and beaten with her limbs tied, and had hot oil poured over her body: "she was latterly bound naked in the form of a crucifix, her hands and feet being fastened to four different points; that while in this situation, a lighted torch was applied to her thighs and private parts, and hot oil from the torch dropped all over her body. The torch and hot oil were applied on this occasion personally by Urs's wife, but not in his presence—under this treatment, deceased is said to have expired."[59]

Acting Superintendent Montgomery sought "special orders" on how to proceed with his case. He deemed it a delicate one because Urs was said to be the Raja's closest surviving blood relative—although descended from an "illegitimate" branch of the royal family—and mentally unstable. Still, the Mysore ruler had until recently treated this family member with "respect and consideration," although that attitude had reportedly changed thanks to a palace feud. From imperial headquarters in Fort William, Calcutta, came the direction to "pay attention to the peculiar circumstances in this case and the high rank of the person involved," as well as the facts that the master was of "unsound mind," and that the murder had taken place within the sanctum of "female apartments." British authorities also deemed it unlikely that the female servants would testify at a public trial before a colonial court. They recommended, therefore, that Montgomery appoint a commission to conduct a private hearing at Urs's residence "with such observance as due respect for the rank of the accused may properly suggest." The members of the commission would consist of "native gentlemen" nominated by the Raja and the superintendent. Moreover, in the case of a conviction of the high-ranked defendants, Fort William suggested that local colonial officials consult with the Raja on the nature of the punishment to be meted out.[60]

As these prescriptions suggest, Deyavummah became a casualty of a brutal patriarchy in which both colonizers and the colonized participated. She was a victim of its corollary, domestic slavery, justified by colonial apologists as more benign than its Atlantic counterparts and judged to lie outside the purview of British antislavery interventions. Shadd Cary imagined in Canada the promise of color-blind colonial belonging, respect for individual rights, protection against violence, and equal opportunity for women within a benevolent Empire governed by a female potentate. In British India, however, such promise proved chimerical for a woman like Deyavummah. It languished before the dictates of expediency in imperial diplomacy and a lack of political will to interfere with the domestic arrangements of elite patriarchal households, unless such arrangements somehow involved the interests of the colonial state.

The Mysore victim's misfortunes were compounded by the fact that she had entered bondage through local circuits of servitude. Ironically enough, had she been transported by slave traders overseas, she might have qualified as a suitable target of imperial protection, although there was of course never any guarantee that such protection would have led to genuine emancipation. Nor is it clear that all subjects of ostensible British benevolence abroad welcomed the attention they received.

The migrations remaking the lives of a multinational cast of marginalized women and children in western Indian Ocean societies make a complicated story that confounds binary constructs of slavery and freedom. Subaltern paths—varying from the intensely local precincts of zenana walls to intercontinental sea-crossings along age-old trade routes among states—intersected with the intent or institutions of British antislavery under diverse circumstances. Some on the move sought out imperial benefactors, others spurned them, and those in the middle strove to preserve some control over the terms of their engagement with their would-be rescuers. Let us seek archival glimpses of these women and youth captured in moments of their negotiation with the formal infrastructure of imperial abolition against the backdrop of regional slave trading and intercontinental business alliances. Such explorations reveal the points at which the worlds of a once-enslaved Ellen Craft intersected with that of Indian Ocean bondspeople. But they also illustrate the nebulous boundaries among "free will," forced assimilation, and coerced labor that sometimes attended British abolition, as subalterns negotiated variously with that campaign.

6

Rulers, Rebels, and Refugees in Transnational Transit

My attention was first attracted to the subject [of the African slave trade to India] by frequently observing African boys in attendance upon the chiefs of Kattywar.... The suspicion this circumstance originated ... was finally placed beyond doubt, by my discovering that the Custom-house books, at the port of Porebunder, contained entries of slaves, upon whom regular duties had been levied.... African slaves ... are highly prized.... I have heard it surmised that the late Rana of Porebunder was of African origin, and certainly, if physiognomy can be trusted, I should say that the present chief of Limree, a boy of about 14 years of age, is of the same extraction....

—J. P. WILLOUGHBY, BOMBAY POLITICAL CONSULTATIONS, DECEMBER 1835

FROM "DOMESTIC" SLAVERY TO INDIAN OCEAN SLAVE TRADES

On 29 December 1835 a woman of African descent, represented in a colonial police magistrate's register as "Marianah," aged fifteen years, arrived in Bombay on the East India Company's brig *Thetis*. She was among dozens of children discovered concealed in boxes amid consignments of limestone and gum incense aboard three Arab vessels from the port of Al Mukalla on the Gulf of Aden, in the Hadhramaut region of southern Yemen. The ships had docked in the Arabian Sea port of Porbandar in the Kathiawar peninsula on their way to the commercial hub of Bombay several months before. The port's local ruler, the Rana, seized the children under pressure from the British government in Bombay. Following months of controversy over who should provide for their subsistence, during which the "refugees" slept on grass bedding in flimsy tents near a fort in the port town, they were taken to Bombay and placed under the custody of John Warden, the senior magistrate of police. Warden lodged them in a house formerly occupied by a European constable and assumed charge of securing food, clothing, and medical attention for them. He also produced a registry that wrote them into colonial history. Neatly classified by name, age, parentage, and country of origin, this document listed 38 boys ranging in age from four to ten and 27 girls, who were older on average. Marianah, recorded as fifteen years old, and Jafranah, fourteen, may have been destined for domestic service or for sale as brides within provinces in the interior, at lower prices than local women commanded. The children were made to share names, as the same ones recur at regular intervals through the registry, made up perhaps jointly by the recorder, and the lisps of four-, five-, and six-year-olds: Sangolo, Nassib, Mubarak, Jehenjah, Faidah, and Salamah, among less common ones. The children appeared shorn of natal context. For most of them, Warden recorded "Parents: dead or unknown; Country: unknown." Surely Marianah was old enough to remember something? Was she observing a vow of silence, borne of a deliberate decision not to divulge origin stories to parties she could ill afford to trust?[1] There were exceptions to these records of erasure, amnesia, or defiance, however. A few of the boys appeared to remember place names that the Magistrate's office spelled as "Mocondeh" and "Kilvah," suggesting birth or sojourns in the vicinity of present-day Tanzania and Mozambique.[2]

Marianah and her younger co-captives left their mark in British colonial archives as part of what emerged as an early, extensively documented case of rescue of enslaved Africans by British patrollers in nineteenth-century India. The action represented an inaugural phase of strikes against the African slave trade that accompanied the rise of the British Empire in the western Indian Ocean.[3] It belonged in a flurry of anti–slave trade campaigns launched by the Bombay government in 1835–36. It generated enough protests and conundrums around sovereignty, national identity, international law, and transnational trade relations from Arabian Sea shores to the Atlantic Ocean to prompt words of censure from a London-based board of directors and to shape a cautious approach to antislavery activism in the IOW at the time. The Porbandar incident presents an early case study of the colonial establishment's "indirect" approach to slave trade regulation by prevailing upon tributary states to assume the risks and costs of such action. The Rana had difficulty balancing the seemingly irreconcilable imperatives of satisfying an imperial overlord on the one hand and calming local merchants fearful of Arab reprisals on the other. These difficulties were compounded by controversies over who would assume responsibility for the freed children's care and how such care might cohere with imperial understandings of free will. As such, the story of Marianah and her fellow captives anticipates the indistinct lines between emancipation and coercion that dogged British antislavery actions in the IOW throughout the nineteenth century, while illustrating how subalterns used the language and structures of imperial abolition to register a complex range of aspirations to personhood and belonging.

These subplots unfolded within an increasingly integrated international framework of trade and population dispersal, anchored in age-old commercial webs shifting and expanding to accommodate new interoceanic relations. These networks forged what Abdul Sheriff has characterized as the "dhow cultures" of the IOW. Commerce and Islam strung port city-states from East Africa through the Middle East to South and Southeast Asia into exchange webs of culture and commodities, propelled from shore to shore by the ubiquitous silhouette of the dhow.[4] Defined by their physical features such as "lateen sails, raked masts, teak hulls, and nail-less construction," dhows, according to Johan Mathew, derived their particular meaning by reference to the contexts in which they sailed: captained by *nakhudas* who also referred to their vessels as *baghlas,* a type of precarious-looking dhow "with a tall slanting mast and lateen sail." The *nakhudas* traded on their own account, tapping the advantages conferred by their mobility to "exploit information asymmetries, market imperfections, and arbitrage opportunities." The crews they commanded "loaded and unloaded their ships and were paid as a share of the journey's profits," giving them few incentives to "leak information" about contraband goods aboard. Operating as feeders to steamships, they wove nimbly in and out of the legal boundaries and red tape established by the colonial order. Collaborators on land might send out signals of danger through "flashing lamps and bonfires." The merchant capitalists supporting dhow trade spread their investments over varied cargoes, mixing enslaved captives with other commodities.[5]

Against this background, the passage from Africa to India of the tender captives whose saga opened this chapter offers at once a window to the multinational, multidirectional slaving paths that traversed the western Indian Ocean and a narrative link to British antislave trade measures that brought North American merchants into controversies over slavery and national identity in the IOW. Motivated by both economic and political concerns, colonial bureaucrats distinguished supposedly age-old indigenous forms of servitude in British India from both slavery in the Americas and the international slave trade in the Atlantic and Indian Oceans. An 1822 treaty contracted between the Mauritius-based Captain Fairfax Moresby and the Imam of Muscat, Sayyid Saʿīd ibn Sulṭān, had prohibited the export of slaves south of Cape Delgado in Mozambique, to India, or to the Mascarene Islands.[6] Over two decades later, between 1845 and 1847, the pioneering British consul in Zanzibar, Atkins Hamerton, steered agreements that sought to limit human trafficking on the Swahili coast between Kilwa in present-day Tanzania to the south and Lamu, lying a few hundred miles north of what we know as Kenya in the north. These compacts gave the British navy the right to search and seize dhows beyond these boundaries.[7]

On the level of practical policy however, the distinction between trafficking and "domestic" incarnations of bondage proved hard to maintain. British South Asia encompassed both areas under direct colonial control and semi-independent "native states" subject to indirect rule under the stewardship of imperial "Residents" and bound with the larger IOW by intricate, centuries-old ties of commerce and population exchanges. Under the circumstances, colonial directors, administrators, and lawyers squabbled over precisely where slave trading ended and "local" practices of "domestic" slavery began. Not only was bondage embedded in resilient precolonial webs of trade and travel that extended overseas—beyond British spheres of influence in the early nineteenth century—it occurred in varieties that blurred the lines between family and property, with women and children dominating captive cohorts. While the bipolar construction of race and freedom in North America denied the blood relations that all too often bound a slaveholder to his human chattel, the IOW laws and practices of bondage formally imbricated some categories of slavery in local structures of kinship, patronage, and dependence. In the process, they confounded the jurisdictional and legal boundaries of imperial regulatory regimes.

Indeed, the discourse of domestic slavery supplied slavers across the political map of the IOW with multiple tools—of argument, clothing, physical space, and religious symbols—to evade British anti–slave trade monitors, even as it gave some women and children on the margins a limited space to express different aspirations—from personal autonomy to communal belonging. Regarding the slavers' tactics, for instance, a colonial official expressed concern for Ethiopian Christian women transported by Arab vessels from Mocha (al Makha in Yemen) on commission from affluent "Persian citizens" of Bombay. Their captors were said to elude British proscriptions against the slave trade by claiming that the victims were their wives or concubines. Africans of all sexes and genders who arrived in Bombay on Arab ships were often dressed in women's clothes and conveyed in palanquins into the hinterlands for sale.[8] If curtained palanquins afforded mobile spaces to cross-dress and transgender the enslaved into pretended kin, then women's quarters in elite homes offered walls of seclusion to perpetuate the same subterfuge. In the princely state of Gwalior, for instance, female members of the royal family were said to own slave markets in the early 1830s. They collected a commission on the sale of slaves in their bazaars and warehoused children traded at these markets in "female apartments," which men (and the colonial state) were prohibited from entering.[9]

Traffickers of less exalted rank, on the other hand, deprived of the class privilege of privacy, tapped the protections of domestic slavery by assuming the role of adoptive parents. Such was the modus operandi of traders in the north central city of Agra, according to its commissioner of circuit. The independent states that surrounded the city to the south and west supplied a steady stream of captives kidnapped by traffickers claiming sanction in the practice of the sale of children by parents reduced to desperation by crop failure. Noble families purchased the children for purposes of adoption and education, the commissioner reported in 1830. Or because "the ready sale of a young girl or woman for a sum equivalent to the hire of a laborer for a year" was "too great a temptation to pass up." A kidnapper might entice or steal a girl from her home, secrete her across the Chambal River into Gwalior, and sell her to a local *dalal* or broker for thirty or forty rupees, "or more according to her caste and personal charms." The broker would register the sale with a *kotwal* or law enforcement officer, representing himself or the original seller as the captive's parent or other kin. The *kotwal* would then write up a deed of sale, deducting a fee from the purchase price. The local police in Gwalior apparently tolerated this practice.[10]

When claims to the safeguards of domestic slavery intersected with the intricate skein of slave trading networks in the Indian Ocean, there emerged difficult, sometimes inconvenient questions about distinctions between the "local" and the "international," and between "slavery" and the slave trade. These concerns challenged the limits of imperial abolition from both jurisdictional and legal perspectives. In the western Indian Ocean, centuries-old commercial webs bound population centers governed directly by the East India Company with tributary states throughout South Asia—from the Arabian Sea ports of Kutch and Kathiawar to the west, and the Makran coast of present-day Pakistan further north, to Awadh ("Oudh" in colonial records), in the heart of the Gangetic plains of north central India, and Hyderabad, further south in the region of the Deccan. These pathways extended beyond the landmass of the Indian subcontinent through the Red Sea and the Gulf to the coasts of North and East Africa. Coerced migrations followed these intercontinental trails in multiple directions. As in the Atlantic world, they were propelled by trading collaborations that crossed identities of region, nationality, race, or religion—and, in the age of empires, colonial "belonging." Political jurisdictions—the "state" if you like, played a somewhat different role than in the western hemisphere. In the case of the United States, for instance, the nation-state invoked national sovereignty to protect slavers operating under its colors even while passing stringent measures against the international slave trade at home.[11] In contrast, in the absence of strong centralized states in the IOW, the logic of the market had historically dictated trade flows in human trafficking with the acquiescence or active participation of dues-receiving or commercially oriented local political authorities. That logic, grounded variously in demands for status, labor, or the incorporation of dependent circles of kin, workers, and soldiers, transplanted Africans (among others) in the Middle East and South Asia while dispersing the subcontinent's children all over the Indian Ocean world.

The high profile of African slavery in Atlantic debates over freedom in the 1830s drew the attention of abolitionists and colonial bureaucrats to this particular species of human trafficking in South Asia. Writing two years after the abolition of chattel slavery in the British Caribbean, J. P. Willoughby, the political secretary to the Bombay government who had formerly served as Resident at the princely state of Kathiawar on the Arabian Sea coast, recorded his wonder at the African boys who attended chiefs of Kathiawar on their visits to the city of Rajkot. The Rana of Porbandar was himself reported to be of African descent.[12] Willoughby's curiosity about Africa's stamp on Gujarat would help launch sustained inquiries into British

India's connections with the African slave trade—inquiries that spun off policies with implications for American businesses on the Swahili coast of East Africa.

CONTEXTS: AFRICANS, ARABS, AMERICANS, GUJARATIS

Africa's presence in Kathiawar may have surprised Willoughby, but there was nothing new about it. The compact but growing and influential body of twenty-first-century scholarship on Africans in Asia has illustrated that documentary evidence of contact among various civilizations around the rim of the Arabian Sea occurred as early as the *Periplus of the Erythraen Sea,* dating back to the first century. As Edward Alpers has written, however, it was the ascendancy of Islam and its corollary of broader trade and cultural interaction in the northwest Indian Ocean that fueled the most "meaningful" migrations of Africans to South Asia.[13]

By Willoughby's time, African Indians had emerged as legatees of many pasts, fragmented by time and place, and roots and routes, by work and status, and gender and culture. The fourteenth-century Moroccan traveler Ibn Batuta remarked upon the presence of enslaved soldiers and sailors of Ethiopian descent ("Habshi" to contemporary Arabs, after "Habash," the Arabic label for Ethiopia) throughout the Indian subcontinent and all the way to Sri Lanka.[14] East Africa contributed to multiracial cohorts of military slaves (including Turks, Persians, Afghans, and Mongols) who arrived from the tenth century onwards, often via commercial centers in the vicinity of the Red Sea and the Gulf. In milieus of fragile state institutions and fratricidal political rivalries, an enslaved soldier alienated from all social ties or paths to power save those through the master might prove a more reliable dependent than any other. A favored few might even ascend to positions of great influence, like the celebrated sixteenth-century soldier-turned-kingmaker in the Deccan, Malik Ambar (fig. 6). Ambar, as Richard Eaton has written, belonged in the population streams of captives bartered along with gold and ivory by Christian elites of the Ethiopian highlands, transshipped to the Deccan from the Red Sea port of Mocha and commercial bustle of Baghdad.[15]

In medieval South Asia, military slaves of Ethiopian descent also rose to power in Bengal to the east and forged ethnically based noble factions within the cavalry of the Sultan of Gujarat to the west. At Hyderabad's eighteenth-century *Asafiya* court, enslaved Africans doubled as entertainers and members of a royal guard. Meanwhile, from the sixteenth to the early nineteenth centuries, Africans established naval supremacy on the fortified island of Janjira in the Arabian Sea off the Konkan coast, switching their allegiances at various times from the Deccan's Bijapur Sultanate through the Mughals to the British until the British defaulted on promised payments to Janjira's rulers from Surat's customs receipts.[16] These African Indian masters of the sea are known to us as the "Sidis" of Janjira, evoking a term

FIGURE 6. Unidentified artist, portrait of Malik Ambar, c. 1605–10. National Museum, New Delhi, *https:// artsandculture.google.com/asset /portrait-of-malik-ambar-unknown /dAEtBfx6C17b7w*, available under the Creative Commons CC0 1.0 Universal Public Domain Dedication.

used widely in colonial India to signify both generic African descent and enslaved status. In the 1840s, the ruler of Awadh maintained a regiment of five hundred Africans, who fought on their master's side during the Indian revolt of 1857.[17]

Like enslaved soldiers, eunuchs (castrated males) attained great power in fractious royal houses. The loyalty of these dependents was presumed upon both their natal alienation and their inability to form new ties of loyalty through procreation. In other times and places—such as medieval Byzantium—their peculiar gender construct conferred upon them a preternatural mystique. They were empowered to enter intimate imperial spaces that no mere mortal dared tread, attending to the emperor's dining table, bath and bed chambers, and guarding access to his harem.[18] Europeans and Americans encountered them across the western Indian Ocean during the nineteenth century—from the courts of Murshidabad in Bengal to the palace of Mtoni in the Sultanate of Zanzibar. By the colonial era, Africans had also joined a multinational cast of young chattels incorporated by Arab and South Asian masters into hierarchical communities as artisans, domestics, concubines, and secondary wives.

It was however, changes wrought by the quickening pace of global economic integration and western imperialism in the late eighteenth and nineteenth centuries that most directly influenced the experiences of Marianah's cohort of captives in motion and likely produced the communities whose "Sidi" descendants now live in modern-day Indian locales in Gujarat, Hyderabad, and Uttar Kannada. The development of port cities in the Arabian peninsula, together with the spread of date plantations and the pearl economy in the Persian Gulf and Red Sea, generated a rising demand for servile dockworkers, porters, ship crew, agricultural laborers, and deep sea divers. During the same period, plantation agriculture spanning the Indian and Atlantic Oceans—sugar in the French colonies of Mauritius and Réunion, sugar and coffee in Brazil and Cuba, and clove in Zanzibar called for labor battalions.[19]

East Africa figured prominently in supplying these needs with servile labor. Up and down its coast, Gujarati-speaking merchants from present-day India's Arabian Sea coast sites like Kutch and Kathiawar collaborated with Arab and African traders and consumers in creating and consolidating the chains of market research, credit, shipping, and trade that dispersed commodified humans together with other goods far and wide across the western Indian Ocean.

The registry of slave origins for Marianah's cohort compiled by the Bombay police magistrate—featuring references to "Mocondeh" and "Kilvah"—reflected East African slaving paths that bore the stamps of Kathiawar and Kutch. In the south, these paths ran through the Indian Ocean portion of Portugal's interoceanic empire extending from Delgoa Bay to Cape Delgado.[20] Within this framework, Pedro Machado has shown that a Vaniya merchant (or "Baniyan" as Americans knew them, a term signifying a mercantile caste), such as Laxmichand Motichand, hailing from the "island entrepôt of Diu located at the southern end of the Kathiawar peninsula of present-day Gujerat,"[21] could establish a business empire in Mozambique that linked the South Atlantic with the Indian Ocean through exchanges of South Asian textiles, New World silver, and African ivory and slaves, underwritten by Gujarati credit and shipping. This *Vaniya*'s agents tracked seasonal changes in southeastern African consumer tastes in Gujarati textiles and relayed this information to weavers in South Asia. The highly coveted cloths these artisans wove bought African ivory that Indian craftspeople fashioned into bangles and knife handles for markets in Kutch and Kathiawar, as well as in the western Indian seaports of Bhavnagar on the Gulf of Khambhat (Cambay) and Surat on the Arabian Sea. But equally important, Gujarati merchants exchanged Indian textiles for New World silver with slave traders from Bahia, Rio de Janeiro, Montevideo, and the Río de la Plata, who were drawn to southeastern Africa by cheaper prices and the region's exemption from slave trade abolition under treaties signed between Britain and Portugal in the early nineteenth century. According to Patrick Harries, Brazilian traders marshaled their superior command of capital and skills to dominate the transoceanic slave trade via Cape Town from Mozambique, to which they had been admitted by the Portuguese Crown in 1811. Jane Hooper and David Eltis have estimated that in the nineteenth century, 40 percent of the captives departing southeastern Africa shipped to the Americas—to Brazil, Río de la Plata, Cuba, and US ports like early republican Charleston, with the active complicity of American shippers, investors, and proslavery politicians. Moreover, the American flag provided slavers of other nationalities protection from British surveillance—protection guarded jealously by a sovereignty-conscious United States until 1862. Meanwhile, South American silver filled the coffers of Gujarati bankers and helped fund the slave trades that extended from Mozambique to the South Atlantic and Caribbean, to the plantations of the French Mascarene Islands, to the Merina-ruled highlands of Madagascar, and to slavers who transshipped captives to the Middle East and India.[22]

If Kathiawar figured prominently in the expansion of the slave trade in southeastern Africa until the first half of the nineteenth century, then it was Kutch to its north on the Arabian Sea coast that shaped the commerce of Swahili city-states north of Cape Delgado. In the seventeenth century, Bhatia merchants from the Kacchi port of Mandvi forged commercial and political alliances with the Āl Bū Saʿīd dynasty of Oman, which ejected the Portuguese from Muscat in the Arabian Peninsula and Mombasa in East Africa by the end of that century. By the 1840s, the Omanis under Sayyid Saʿīd, who bore the title "Imam" signifying descent from elected religious leaders who had become merchant princes,[23] came to claim the allegiance of chiefs who governed the African coast from Cape Delgado to Cape Guardafui. The Omanis moved the seat of their government to the verdant, breezy entrepôt of Zanzibar with the support of Bhatia merchant capital.[24]

That locale emerged as a significant node in the structural framework of global exchanges and imperial aspirations that linked the Atlantic and Indian Ocean worlds. The Omani capture of the mainland harbor of Kilwa, south of Zanzibar, had fueled the island entrepôt's emergence as a major center of the East African slave trade. The fall of the French Mascarenes into British hands during the Napoleonic Wars had helped drive down slave prices in the region by the early 1820s. It may have helped redirect some Omani capital investments into a clove plantation complex in Zanzibar and Pemba based on slave labor imported from east central Africa and the Swahili coast. But Zanzibar was also a site for commercial congregations of American cotton merchants, Arab and African ivory and slave traders, Gujarati bankers and brokers, and multinational dealers of Indian rice and Persian pearls and drugs. Business-minded American consuls, European slavers, and British imperial antislavers negotiated with the sultan, local merchants, and mainland consumers on terms that shaped multilayered coalitions and competition. It was also in Zanzibar that mercantile sojourners from Salem would displace Indian textiles with slave-grown American cotton through the medium of their Gujarati business partners.[25]

Along this Swahili coast, the world that Ellen Craft had fled would intersect with the markets that merchandized Marianah further east. Thus, the next step in untangling interoceanic threads of slavery and abolition histories takes us to the vicinity of Zanzibar Island, located twenty-five miles from the mainland. In this region, plantation slavery—whether producing cloves in the first half of the nineteenth century or sugar in the decades that followed—took root amid regional traditions of patron-client relationships. Jonathan Glassman has argued that in northern Tanzania, until the emergence of a more coherent cohort of Arab sugar planters committed to profit making through commodity production in the late nineteenth century, *mtumwa* (the local word for "slave") signified status rather than a class engaged in irreconcilable conflict with the master's world.

Descended from kinless foreigners who were violently uprooted, transported, and transplanted into the dominant society, the enslaved were often distinguished by occupation, which in turn was shaped by their level of assimilation to Swahili culture. Among those who did not enter private households as secondary wives or concubines, recently arrived outsiders (denigrated as "barbarian") might be put to work on the master's *shamba* (farm) cultivating commercial crops like cloves or coconut for a certain number of days per week, while practicing subsistence agriculture on their own on less fertile land allocated to them by the community. By contrast, their native-born descendants, assimilated to Swahili culture, might secure the right to farm on their own, on condition of making tribute payments to their masters. Glassman notes that both categories of agricultural slaves enjoyed a certain degree of autonomy, with the right to live in villages with their own governance structures, sell their labor when not working for the master, raise livestock, practice crafts, and sell their surplus produce in internal markets. Other acculturated slaves might hire out their time as urban wage workers or contract to serve as porters on the caravan trade into the interior, sharing a portion of their earnings with their masters. Coastal-born men sought to overcome their social marginalization and natal alienation not simply by pursuing a semblance of economic independence as cultivators, traders, artisans, and porters, but also by establishing patriarchal families, embracing Islam, and asserting their claims to Swahili cultural markers of language and dress, to commerce and urban life. They conducted these activities often in tension with the authority of their masters, but within a framework of patronage by powerful overlords that conferred legitimacy on subaltern quests for social belonging.[26]

Whatever the distinctions between IOW and Atlantic slaveries, British naval commanders committed to imperial abolition dwelled on the Indian Ocean slave trade in terms that evoked horrors of the Atlantic world's own Middle Passage. With the focus of our own story trained on subalterns in transit, let us follow such a British commentator on a sojourn from Muscat to Zanzibar, weaving the insights of his antislavery gaze together with other accounts into a reflection on the paths that Marianah and her fellow captives may have trod on their way to Porbandar.

IMAGINING MARIANAH'S PASSAGE TO INDIA: THE GAZE OF IMPERIAL ABOLITION

During 1842–43, Lieutenant W. Christopher, Commander of the HC Brig of War *Tigris,* was on a mission to accompany His Excellency Ally Bin Naseer (as his name is spelled in British colonial archives), envoy extraordinary for the Imam of Muscat to her Britannic majesty, from the Persian Gulf back to East Africa. The report Christopher wrote of his travels established a direct connection between slave-grown American cotton and Indian Ocean slavery on many levels. The first was through the workings of international trade. The Americans, he wrote, traded "with our Indian subjects nearly always, and their clothes return with the slave dealer into the heart of Africa." Second, he remarked upon proslavery defenses among Arab slaveholding "paternalists" that appeared to bear an uncanny resemblance to the rationales of American slaveholders. Finally, he portrayed the Zanzibar slave market as a mirror image of Atlantic auction blocks.[27]

En route from Muscat to Zanzibar, Christopher sought to engage Naseer in a conversation about the merits of free versus slave labor. The Omani, who claimed to own sixty to seventy slaves to perform the work of his Zanzibar household, warned that "should [the Imam] put a stop to buying and selling servants, [he] would ... infuriate his people." He defended slavery with the argument that "We find them naked, hungry ... We save their children, and bring them up as our children and true believers." Christopher concluded that "These are the usual arguments used by Mahomedans, the great traffickers in human bodies to dispel their own scruples."[28]

Upon reaching their destination, Christopher found the island to be "beautifully fertile," especially compared with "sterile" Oman, suffering only from the drawback of harboring a one- to two-mile band of swamplands that surrounded the "filthy town of Zanzibar" on three sides and bred frightful fevers. Its ruler, the Imam, commanded twelve hundred slaves. Upon invitation, the British lieutenant visited the monarch's clove plantations as well as his two palaces, which boasted "loop holed upper stories." He wandered through halls paved with marble flags and passed niches ornamented with porcelain or glassware. Large mirrors hung in the rooms. The British officer's tour guide was the twenty-two-year-old "very communicative" son of a "high functionary," who was "dressed in rich Arab costume, and rode a bay palfrey of the 1st blood." His late mother was a French woman who had spent her youth in the zenana of a "rich Mussalman" in Muscat. Christopher noted that "the plantations have a most pleasing appearance." The Imam had constructed an aqueduct extending two thousand yards into the woods to convey water "as pure as crystal" through the palace to the beach. The clove trees, he reported, were planted "on the oldest soil or higher grounds of the island at about 14 feet apart, the intervals being kept well weeded . . ., the dead branches being cut off." The oldest trees, "bushy and of circular form" grew as tall as forty feet. He estimated the output at one thousand frazillas per three thousand trees, which fetched from 1,000 to 5,000 dollars at Zanzibar per year. The buds were dried in the sun for three days in preparation for sale. The Imam's plantations provisioned his household, with enslaved workers performing a diverse range of outdoor labor. They received two days off to work for themselves, producing "more for the market than the other five days, so that on a slaves' holiday, the market is abundantly supplied with mats, fruits, vegetables, and coconut oil."[29]

Yet Christopher presented a damning portrait of Zanzibar that paralleled abolitionist denunciations of Atlantic slave societies. Defying the familial imagery associated with defenses of Indian Ocean slavery, he focused his report on the brutal workings of the market in human chattel. Zanzibar's position as the "great source of slaves for Arabia, Persia, and northern India," drew the lieutenant to the slave marts that convened every afternoon for two hours before sunset to sell and ship "human cargo." He was astounded that "our 'fellow British Indian subjects' (as they are lovingly styled in England)," both the "mild and harmless [Hindu] Banians" and the Muslim Bohras had for centuries served as the "great slave purchasers in the first instance." While Indian merchants were not themselves to be seen at these venues, their brokers—as many as a thousand "depraved characters"—carried on a brisk business on their behalf. They trafficked their human wares within the precincts of Zanzibar, but many of the victims—often children—ended up far from home, brought there by *nakhudas*. The sales were announced "by outcry," and privately circulated among the wealthy inhabitants of the island, who then sent brokers to bid on human chattel. It is possible that the children seized at Porbandar constituted part of a consignment transacted privately with purchasers with ties to India. Christopher's testimony agrees with Mathew's evidence for a later period of fluid slave markets dispersed through chains of brokers serving prearranged customers.[30]

The colonial archives offer no clues as to what sense the children themselves made of the ordeals they had suffered in the course of their forced passages. But let us draw upon secondary sources and eyewitness accounts such as those of Christopher to imagine these horrors. Scholars in our own time have located the origins of captives like the children rescued in Porbandar in "southeastern Africa, the region bounded today by Mozambique, Malawi, and southern Tanzania."[31] According to the registry of Porbandar detainees, many had passed through Kilwa, the mainland harbor south of Zanzibar, which was exporting twenty-two thousand slaves by 1865. This port was close to the "Chibinga slave depot" where Christopher had run into "scores" of Baniyans. Other children mentioned Makonde, suggesting that they may have hailed from the plateau abutting the southern coast of Tanzania where warring groups of "Makua, Makonde, Ndonde and Yao" sold captives into slavery. Did some of the children join the forced exodus from Mozambique Island—the "gate of no return" on the southeast African coast—which swelled to an annual figure of seventeen thousand by 1837?[32] According to Machado, captives in coastal Mozambique arrived by way of the Yao and Makua lands extending to southern Lunda and Tanzania or via Quelimane with hinterlands that extended to present-day Zimbabwe. They belonged principally to the "Nsenga, Manganja and . . . southern Chewa chieftaincies in the highlands north of the Zambesi."[33]

Americans who traded along the coast of East Africa saw slaves everywhere. The Salem merchant Ephraim A. Emerton recalled a visit to Quillimane aboard the brig *Richmond* in 1843. The captain had rented a house on shore and set up a retail store there, selling unbleached cottons, powder, muskets, furniture, provisions, boots, and shoes taken from Atlantic cargoes. The sixteen-year-old Emerton helped out in the store and took walks with the captain among coconut trees afterward. As they did, they came upon "gangs of Slaves just as they came in from the interior of Africa, thin almost as Skeletons." The captives marched in lines, connected by a chain threaded through iron rings around their necks. When night fell, they were loaded on boats and warehoused in "barracoons erected at the mouth" of the river. "When the coast was clear of cruisers they were hurried off on board a vessel kept in waiting for them and taken to Rio de Janeiro for sale."[34]

Marianah's cohort, of course, embarked upon multiple intermediate passages in the other direction. The Mahra identity of their alleged slavers that would later emerge prompts the question whether they may have been traded by Arab mariners from Hadhramaut or Oman. Or were they perhaps kidnapped by northern Arabs from Sur, Batinah, and the Trucial Coast who visited Zanzibar annually, kept houses, and kidnapped and exported children?[35] The Bombay Registry gave the children names that bore a striking resemblance to ones that would appear on manumission lists in Zanzibar created later in the century by the British consul Christopher Rigby. Names like "Nasib," "Faida," and "Salamah," which show up in the Rigby records analyzed by Hideaki Suzuki, had appeared in Warden's account of the Porbandar captives nearly three decades earlier.[36] Of naming conventions in East Africa, Frederick Cooper has observed that masters and slaves were subject to the same "normative and symbolic system" but not on equal terms, so that "Islamic names, such as Mohammed or Ali or Aesha, were reserved for the free, while slaves were often named after a day of the week (Juma) or . . . what they brought him (Faida—profit)."[37] "Mubarak" and "Faida" were both common names attached to Africans brought to India.

But so many other questions remain about the Porbandar children that we can only begin to consider within the contexts of their time and place. Were they war captives, or victims of kidnapping or want, sold with criminals or defaulting debtors by slave dealers to some commercial group with connections to settlements that sprang up in the area of Lake Nyasa as caravans penetrated the interior of the mainland? How much (or little) cloth, ivory, beads, and gunpowder did it take to buy one child? What did they think of their purchasers, whom Lloyd described as "white-clad Arabs marching under the red flag of the Sultan of Zanzibar . . . armed with a long musket and a curved sword," who occasionally traveled on horseback? Did they traverse "narrow forest paths" in single file, strung together by a rope? Did they witness adults whose necks had been "wedged into forked sticks" with their arms tied behind their backs? Did those that arrived in Kilwa change hands or find themselves tightly packed into noisome dhows for the twenty-four-hour passage to Zanzibar, for transshipment to Arabia?[38]

One eyewitness account by a former slave from 1865, reported crowded spaces that made it hard to breathe or sleep, and disease, heat, hunger, and thirst that were barely assuaged by a little water and small portions of manioc roots during the passage from Mozambique to Zanzibar.[39] These were horrors that read like Olaudah Equiano's famous description of the Atlantic "Middle Passage" to potential abolitionist audiences in the late eighteenth century. Over two decades earlier, closer to the time of the Porbandar affair, the American merchant Michael Shepard had offered a similar representation of overcrowding, disease, and starvation: "Often 1000 slaves are stowed into a space hardly capable of receiving as many bags of rice." Shepard likened the fate of captives landed in Zanzibar to sheep, with "the dead ones thrown overboard to drift down with the tide and if in their course they strike the beach . . . the natives come with a pole and push them (away). . . ."[40]

Shepard had watched those captives who survived clamber over the dhow in neck-deep water and wade ashore to the customhouse. There they sat in a circle and were "served with parched corn and water to their fill." They were then carried to their respective owners' homes, where they spent a few days before being sent to the market for sale. Hours before the bidding began, they were "greased with a large profusion of cocoanut oil from head to foot and covered with a very showy robe." At the slave market over a mile "back of the town," the captives were lined up before the gaze of potential buyers. "The purchaser walks up to one he likes the looks of and throws a stick at some distance and tells the slave to pick it up. . . . He is then taken apart from the rest of the group and examined from head to foot. . . . If the slave is purchased the dress is taken from them." The following day, you could expect to see these objects of sale "walking the streets with nothing but a small piece of cloth around their loins. . . ."[41]

But the New England gaze upon the East African slave trade—unlike that of British naval commanders like Christopher—often paired scenes of brutal Atlantic-style slave voyages and auction blocks with observations about the supposed compassion of Arab slave masters. Thus, Shepard noted that Arabs sent their slaves to school, offering them the opportunity to acquire an education on par with "the head arabs [sic] of the place." Likewise, Putnam observed that while enslaved captives were treated like "cattle" during sale, they were treated well afterward: "Strictly speaking they are not slaves, but are almost as much masters as [their] owners are. They have three [days] of the week to work for themselves." Moreover, some slaves owned as many as "three or four" slaves of their own. The American had gained the impression that slaveholders in Zanzibar owned bondspeople because "it is fashionable ... not because it is profitable." Slave prices were low compared with the United States: "The best of men generally bring fifteen to twenty dollars, and ... [women of mixed blood] bought for concubines, often twenty five dollars, which is a high price...."[42]

The British Lieutenant Christopher offered a more macabre portrait of a makeshift Zanzibar auction block. One slave market that he visited was held in a "filthy yard" four hundred feet square, filled with garbage. "The slaves stand in rows of 6 or 8 generally, the males and females usually separate, but sometimes placed indiscriminately." Afterward, the officer was haunted by the gesticulations and "incessant rattle of the auctioneers' tongues," with the broker for each group of captives "calling out the biddings made for each individual, chucking the women under the chin to make them look sprightly and occasionally expending his vocabulary in their praises." The Englishman agreed with Shepard that the humans on sale appeared well clothed, with "even children" granted new clothes for the occasion, which struck the British observer as unusual, because the offspring of more fortunate "respectable parents" customarily went naked until the ages of "8 or 10." The buyers in these areas were not confined to the well-to-do. Christopher observed that the "poor sort of inhabitants examine their intended purchase a few paces away" in the most "indelicate" and "offensive" fashion. He witnessed the "hand of the merchant passing over every muscle of the body; sometimes two or three men join in an inspection, the clothes of the subject of it being put aside; the mouth is opened, the ears and eyelids all pulled about, the proportion in eight and roundness of the body ascertained by spanning, and finally a stick is thrown to some 40 paces distance, and the human victim urged to run and fetch it, to prove the limbs sound."[43]

For Christopher, these daily public exhibitions of dehumanization damaged "the rising generation," breeding an immoral society that valued neither human life nor such ostensible bedrocks of civilization as monogamous marriages. Indeed, the Imam, he wrote, offered concubines from his own harem to his younger male relatives, including sons, "before he thinks it prudent or necessary for their respectability to marry." Moreover, the diseased enslaved, far from being treated as family members, were "thrown out on the beach ... and became food for dogs." Christopher sketched a horrific spectacle that had once assaulted the eyes of the British consul, Captain Atkins Hamerton: "four dogs were devouring a young female who had died in childbirth, parturition not having been effected, the dogs were completing it, two wallowing in the womb, and two tearing the breasts away: the Mahomedans look on with perfect indifference at such a scene. She is only a slave," they say. Apparently, the envoy protested to the Imam, forcing him to issue a mandate that dead slaves receive burial.[44]

Whether Marianah's cohort experienced the sights and slights of Zanzibar slave "markets" that Shepard and Christopher portrayed, we shall never know. What seems more certain is that they ended up in the port of Al Mukalla alongside the Gulf of Aden. The slaving paths that these children—silenced in the archives—may have traveled are more traceable through the narrative of the loquacious Christopher. So let us sail with the lieutenant northward along the East African coast in the early 1840s. This sojourner recorded that when he put down anchor in Mombasa (present-day Kenya), he encountered a fort garrisoned by South Asian Baluchis (from the northwestern part of the Indian subcontinent), who supplied their own arms. The town of Uzi, about 20 miles to the south of Lamu, appeared to be the major commercial center in the area, where Arab merchants purchased slaves belonging to tribes from the interior. Christopher wrote that slavers in these parts did not "know the use of money," so that "they are dealt with in barter very much to the advantage of our Indian subjects." On the Somali coast, he passed Arab merchant boats known as "bedus" carrying cargoes of slaves to Oman. These boats arrived from southern Arabia in October carrying dates and cloth. They were hired out "to carry slaves to Zanzibar, to bring wood for housebuilding, and in fishing, and return to Arabia early in the south-west monsoon." He described the "Somali spearman" as a central figure in the Indian Ocean trade. He was equipped with one "cloth of cotton, six yards long and two wide; sandals of camel-leopard's hide, which is found to be light and very durable; a calabash of water; a neck crutch, a quantity of tobacco, a pair of tweezers, and a tooth brush, carried in a leather bag, slung by a becket close under the left arm; two spears, a shield, and sometimes a knife. . . ." Men like this trader bought raw cotton from India, and coffee and dates from Arabia, in exchange for "grain, gums, hides, ivory, rhinoceros' horns, hippopotamus' teeth . . ."[45]

On the southern coast of the Gulf of Aden, in the Somalian city of Bandar Qasim (present-day Bosaso), Christopher encountered an informative witness to the dynamics of the slave trade in this part of the world. This intelligent young man" had combined a pilgrimage with a business tour. In the month of Ramazan (October) of that year, he had set off on an Arab *baghla* for Jeddah in present-day Saudi Arabia, laden with gum Arabic and jars of ghee (clarified butter). In Jeddah, he sold his wares, bought Indian cloth from Kutch, and completed his pilgrimage. He then returned to the coast of northeast Africa by sea, making his way for seven days by land on camel back to the commercial hub of Adhari or Harrar, a fortified settlement in eastern Ethiopia. According to Christopher's informant, Harrar was "the name of the country which extends within two days of Habesh"—the

Ethiopian highlands that sent forth generations of slaves who had become military generals, king-makers, and kings—to South Asia's Deccan region. The source described Harrar as "twice as large as Jidda" but less densely settled. It grew coffee and counted among its items of export "habush (captives of war)," in addition to frankincense, saffron, ghee, hides, ostrich feathers, gum Arabic, and millets. Its ruler, a "just man" named "Imir Mahomed" existed under constant threat of attacks from the neighboring Galla people. It was here that our pilgrim-trader acquired slaves—"Christian Habushi" (Ethiopians)- for "to buy and sell a Mussulman is haram (forbidden)." Christopher's informant then embarked with his human chattel together with a cargo of coffee and hides for the twelve-day sojourn to the Somalian entrepôt of Barbara (Barbaria) and from thence by sea to the port of Bandar Qasim. His father "gave [the Ethiopians] as an honour to the Nakib of Maculla who returned 105 German crowns."[46]

It was, of course, from this same South Arabian port that appeared in Christopher's journal—Al Mukalla—that Marianah and her fellow captives had set sail for India following their passages through East Africa.

Christopher's cruise followed, and contributed to, an acceleration of debate among various parties within the British imperial establishment over what to do about Indian Ocean slave trading that followed multiple routes through nodes in British Asia. It was precipitated by the Bombay Government's attention to this issue—attention that triggered the rescue of Marianah's group while bringing to light the cases of Indian women and children on the move in the other direction—to the dominions of the Imam of Muscat and Zanzibar.

So let us follow Marianah's trail into the heart of India by turning to narratives of imperial campaigns against IOW slave trades that were unfolding in 1830s Bombay. These offer clues to the places and lives to which the children at Porbandar may have been headed before the colonial state intervened. But such narratives also evoke the transnational reach and multidirectional flows of mobile enslavers and enslaved, offering glimpses of subaltern stories that began in British India but stretched across its borders to distant lands bordering the Arabian Sea. An account of these transnational crossings will circle back to the Porbandar affair, tracing the reverberations of slave trade politics from ocean to ocean.

SUBALTERN CROSSINGS: AFRICANS IN INDIA AND INDIANS IN ARABIA

Marianah's case signaled that as the enslaved's cause was gaining momentum in the 1830s Atlantic, the official archives of a rising British empire in Asia chronicled stories of African slavery in the Indian Ocean world through the "moral capital"-laden prism of colonial abolition. Willoughby's investigations into the custom-house books at Porbandar had revealed entries on enslaved Africans subject to regular levies, but the records of the East India Company's Kathiawar agency contained no references to slavery before Willoughby's time, suggesting that his predecessors had perhaps turned a blind eye to this trade. His own investigations revealed the extent of its decentralized and multinational character. Africans like those belonging to Marianah's cohort arrived in Kathiawar via the dominions of the Imam of Muscat, other Arabian ports, Kutch, or Sind. Assistant Resident at Kutch A. Burnes had witnessed forty slaves sold publicly at a bazaar in Muscat in 1833—a "daily" occurrence, he reported.[47] Two years earlier, the British Resident in the Gulf had estimated that the Swahili coast sent three-quarters of the 1,400 to 1,700 slaves who entered Muscat, as well as a sizeable number to the Red Sea region for transshipment to India and beyond. Ethiopians accounted for the rest.[48]

British reports also designated Portuguese strongholds in Kathiawar as key hubs of the African slave trade to South Asia. Captives from southeastern Africa arrived on ships designed to carry ivory. Machado has estimated that enslaved exports from Mozambique to the Portuguese colonies of Goa, Diu, and Daman between 1770 and 1834 numbered a total of 8,534, with a mortality rate of 18 percent. In the first half of the nineteenth century, some years saw annual imports of 350–500 slaves into Portuguese India from Mozambique; Karachi (in present-day Pakistan) received 150 annually, and Mandvi in Kathiawar, 400–500. Based on these figures, Machado estimates that the number of Africans imported into India annually in the first half of the nineteenth century hovered in the region of one thousand.[49]

Colonial officials identified the "Budalla and Carwa castes" as the chief operators of this trade. These groups contracted with owners of ships trading with the Middle East and Africa to conduct voyages at fixed rates but were assigned a portion of tonnage to trade on their own account, which they expended in part on the slave trade. Slaves brought from Zanzibar to western India, for instance, were not part of the regular cargo, but rather represented the private ventures of *nakhudas* and *lascars* (sailors), who might pass them off as servants, wives, or concubines to avoid detection.[50] At least one leading merchant of Mandvi, who worked as an agent for the Muscat government, received consignments of African slaves from the Imam and his relatives, and he brought them to South Asia under the charge of Turkish middlemen.[51]

The high demand for children stemmed from their potential for acculturation to the relations of dependence. Many a Mubarak in the Porbandar group might have been intended for apprenticeship as sailors on mercantile vessels, as attendants to wealthy personages, or as the operators of various "mechanical arts." Mandvi merchants who commuted to Zanzibar brought back slaves who took care of their shops in Africa or gifted them to others without heirs. The chiefs of Rajkot and affluent Muslim households were said to be avid consumers of these human wares. The average price of young boys at Rajkot was about 60 rupees. At Porbander, a "stout healthy boy" aged eight or nine years commanded Rs. 40, "the value increasing up to a certain age.... A youth of 20 is not readily disposed of from his not being likely to bear easily the yoke of slavery." These sums—under 20 dollars—represented a pittance compared with prices that human chattel commanded in the North American South. Girls fetched more, owing to their demand as brides among various communities. Faidah, Marianah, and Jaffranah might have been intended for transport north to the province of Sindh (in present-day Pakistan), where "the poorer class of Sindhis and other Muslims ... paid less for [African brides] than they did in bride prices within their own communities."[52] African women who remained in Kutch might have been married off to members of the area's African-descended Sidi community, which Burnes described romantically as "numerous" and "happy."[53] The Rao of Kutch concurred, noting to the British Resident at Bhuj that the "limited number" of African boys imported into his territories were treated kindly as family members rather than "menials," and some rose to command the vessels "in which they are educated."[54]

It is also possible that the cohort seized at Porbandar would have ended up in colonial cities right under the noses of British overlords. Bombay, Calcutta, and Madras were all distribution points for supplies of African children to the households of India's princes. The vice consul of Basra (Iraq), on a mission to Bombay, noted the presence of "one or two cafries" and an "Abyssinian" approximately ten years old in a neighbor's household. On a Basra-bound ship from Bombay in 1835, this official encountered "a rich Mogul merchant" accompanied by "ten Abyssinians" who came aboard to see off a departing family member. This merchant reportedly had two eunuchs "to guard his seraglio in Bombay."[55] Ethiopian women consigned to the marriage market in that city were said to fetch 100–150 rupees each. Captives arrived on Arab vessels, manned in part by enslaved crews. Whatever their genders, they were disembarked in women's clothes and whisked away on palanquins under the noses of customs officials who looked the other way. The Basra-based vice consul had seen such "*buglas* [from Africa] ... navigating the whole coast of the Red Sea with slaves on board." The captives were made to disembark at Jeddah and Mocha, among other points, from which slave dealers purchased them for the Bombay market. Moreover, Basra and Bushire (or Bushehr, in present-day Iran) each received nearly four hundred slaves annually, with the acquiescence of English agents, the vice consul suspected. The captives arrived around September during an unhealthy season, which led to high mortality rates, with one-third losing their lives.[56]

Enslaved Africans who entered the Bombay market where the Porbandar captives were headed might also be dispatched to tributary states governed by "native" princes far from the Arabian Sea coast. In July 1833, for instance, two Arab slave dealers sold eighteen Africans, ten of whom were women, to the household of the king of Awadh in north India. Having arrived in Bombay from Mocha, the slave traders, who knew little about the geography of the land, hired locals to pilot them through independent territories free of imperial surveillance. In covered hackneys, they wound their way east to Awadh across Rajasthan, from Jodhpur through the towns of Jaipur, Ajmer, and Agra, without interference from customs officials.[57] Awadh already boasted enslaved Ethiopian jockeys, imported in the late eighteenth century. They had been trained by a Frenchman who served the royal stables of Versailles until the French Revolution forced him to leave. In the 1840s, the Nawab's African regiment of five hundred soldiers testified that they had been brought from Africa. These men would side with their master during the 1857 rebellion against colonial rule.[58]

Further south, the princely state of Hyderabad in the Deccan served as another hub of the slave trade linking the Indian mainland with Africa and the Middle East. About the same time that British authorities were igniting a furor over their seizure of Arab ships carrying African children at Porbandar in the west, there arrived in the Nizam's dominions to the south an Ethiopian named Yacoub. He came from Jeddah as the slave of one Syed Abdullah Sukkat and reportedly stayed a short while before returning to Muscat. Colonial records referred to him as the "Habshee of Jidda." A year later he was back in Hyderabad, this time in the role of a slave dealer and accompanied by an Afghan collaborator identified as Sheikh Mahmoud Ameen. Ameen was a mufti (interpreter of religious law) based in the holy Arabian city of Medina, or so he claimed on visits to Hyderabad—a representation that earned him "considerable distinction" and valuable gifts from influential residents. He was married to an Ethiopian, while Yacoub took as his wife a local woman. All of them shared a home in Hyderabad's Char Minar neighborhood. The slave dealers had brought with them several Ethiopians. The sale of these captives generated enough profits to fund the purchase of Indian children in Hyderabad's vicinity for both the domestic and international markets. Indeed, Yacoub and Ameen's customers extended from local communities of "dancing girls" who purchased apprentices to perpetuate their occupation, to transnational merchants, ship captains, and elite households. Yacoub had purchased one woman from an Arab master through a broker for 72 rupees, which included the agent's fee of 2 rupees. Since brides and concubines sold in Bombay for as much as 150 rupees, it is possible that she would have netted her purchaser a 100 percent rate of return within India.[59]

British regulators wondered "by what means" these slave dealers smuggled "their purchases through the Company's territories." The testimonies of rescued children suggested that the traffickers used private households and mosques as warehouses safe from law enforcement authorities, claiming familial connections to mask their transactions.[60]

Although British observers identified Arab sojourners as the primary slavers in South Asia, merchants from India's Arabian Sea ports also played important roles in transporting bondspeople across international borders. Enslaved sailors piloted

Gujarati ships in the Mozambique Channel, serving as cooks on board. They labored as dockworkers and porters unloading cargo and transporting them to warehouses, bore palanquins, and worked garden plots. Masters hired out skilled artisans like caulkers on a wage-sharing basis. Slaves served as collateral and as payment for trade goods and debts.[61] On occasion, Indian merchants in the Middle East used their slaves to capture and guard business associates to settle disputes. Such slaves might be Hindu, like the boy brought to Muscat by Baluchi traders whom the EIC's Muscat agent, Reuben Aslan, intercepted while the child was stealing dates from the customhouse.[62] H.D. Robertson, Resident in the Persian Gulf, thus recommended that colonial officials search houses, temples, and small boats along slave trails from Hyderabad to Bombay, to interrogate "Patels [Gujarati merchants] traveling with children." He suggested instituting generous rewards for informers willing to help the police identify culprits. Muster crews of "country crafts" plying between Bombay and West Asia, he urged. And let police boats commanded by Europeans search them.[63]

What paths led to enslavement? Kidnapping or poverty ensnared some Indian children in Yacoub's inventory of human chattel. One girl, seven or eight years of age, left her drought-stricken home in Kanpur for Calcutta in the company of her parents. As she narrated her life story at the age of twelve in 1841 to Aslan in Muscat, she had been enticed away on the streets of that metropolis "by an Arab" with the offer of sweets, carried to Hyderabad, and sold to Yacoub. The child was stowed away in a safe house along with several young captives belonging to the traffickers. They included seven girls belonging to Yacoub and two boys and a girl belonging to Ameen. Days later, the traders and their victims set out for Aurangabad (in the present-day western Indian state of Maharashtra). There, Yacoub and his wife sold two of the girls to courtesans before traveling to Bombay, spending the night in a mosque in Panvel along the way. They transported the children in batches, apparently using the mosque as a warehouse. In Bombay, they passed off the enslaved girls as their daughters, claiming that they maintained quarters in the market. Following the sale of three girls in Bombay, the entire crew sailed for Muscat. Along the way, the girls were distributed among various parties located in different Arab towns, among them the Imam of Zanzibar and a Hindu barber in Basra. The girl from Kanpur, "deposited" in the home of a "Habshee" in Basra, spared herself a forced passage to Baghdad by crying incessantly. She changed hands a few times before being sold to Umber, the servant of one of her masters. Umber, whose name suggests that he may have hailed from India, disposed of her for 37 dollars to a Muscat shopkeeper.[64]

Aslan learned of the sale in an open bazaar and demanded that the girl be delivered to him. Her master claimed that he planned to free and marry her, but a disbelieving Aslan assumed custody of the captive. The British agent reported that the girl, frightened and weeping, "entreated to be returned to her master." But lodged in Aslan's home, she confirmed upon further questioning the agent's suspicion that "she had been terrified" into declaring loyalty to her master, when in fact, she harbored "no regard whatever" for the man.⁶⁵

If drought and kidnapping landed one child in the IOW slave markets, domestic intrigue spurred the disposition of another. Aslan discovered another Hindu girl, from the South Indian city of Mangalore, who ended up in Muscat through the connivance of her stepmother. According to the child's narrative, her father worked as a butler in the home of a "Muslim gentleman," who entered into an affair with her stepmother. With this deadly guardian's help, the lover apparently tricked the girl into following a pair of slave dealers—one of them Yacoub—from her family quarters in a local bazaar through a fish stall to the coast, and thence to Muscat. Sold to a dealer for $42, she was merchandized to a pastry cook for $78.

Yacoub happened to be visiting Muscat as the girl told her story. The British agent found and placed him under arrest just as he was about to sail back to Bombay. But Yacoub's forced "confession" differed from his victim's recollections. His version held that three years before, a *baghla* belonging to him, named *Mahmoodee,* had set out for Mangalore when it encountered a fishing boat, "in which was a little girl of nine or ten years of age" whom the boatman sold for 60 rupees. The captive had remained with Yacoub until the year before, when he took her to Zanzibar for sale. He could find no buyer there so he sold her in Muscat instead for $42 to a buyer, who used a broker to transfer her to the pastry cook, Mahmood Mebranee, for $78. Thus, between India and the Arabian peninsula, the girl's market value had more than doubled. According to Aslan, "Yacoob begged strenuously that this affair might not be represented to Government (of India) so he left [$42] on deposit," before leaving for Bombay. Aslan summoned the various parties through whose hands the girls had passed, "a great discussion ensued," compensation exchanged hands, and Aslan achieved her release by involving the Imam of Muscat in his negotiations.⁶⁶

SLAVE TRADE REGULATION THROUGH INDIRECT RULE

British rescue of enslaved African and Indian children usually transpired in realms not under direct British governance but rather ruled by semiautonomous princes whom colonial authorities had contracted to defend under treaties of alliance, in exchange for steep tribute payments. Willoughby, who from his perch in the Bombay government emerged as a key figure in the drive against the trafficking of Africans to India in the 1830s, recommended against direct intervention by the British government in slave trade–related prosecutions, opting instead for the strategy of persuading the tributary chiefs in western India to assume the risks and costs associated with enforcing "the cause of humanity." To lend such exhortations the teeth of power, the Bombay government sought to place Kutch and Kathiawar under surveillance by the British commodore at Surat, empowering him to detain ships suspected of trading in slaves.[67]

But even as local rulers pledged to punish the perpetrators of the slave trade and liberate its victims, they hastened to distance IOW slavery from its Atlantic counterparts. The British Resident at Bhuj wrote that His Majesty the Rao of Kutch had emphasized that the only "slaves" brought into his kingdom were "negroes from Zanzibar," and that "in our sense of the term, as applied to West India slaves (these are His Highness's own words), the situation of these people is quite different," as their masters treated them as members of the family, "with great kindness, some of the females being even married." Evidently, more than commerce linked the Indian chiefs and their mercantile subjects with Arab-governed societies in the IOW. The Rao's embrace of a narrative of benevolent slavery in the East brought him firmly within the orbit of a shared discourse of dependence with Muscat and Zanzibar. But there were other concerns at stake. The Kacchi ruler expressed apprehension about the impact of slave trade prohibition on his subjects' mercantile relations with Arab worlds. In late 1835, he urged imperial authorities to suspend the order to detain slavers until the close of the current slaving season, for fear that it might ensnare the many Kutch trading vessels "now absent on the east coast of Africa" without a fair warning.[68]

The Rao's apprehensions coincided with a mighty tempest brewing on the coast of Porbandar. It grew out of the rescue of Marianah and her fellow African captives at Willoughby's instance. Representing what Captain A. T. Reid of the Commanding Detachment at Porbandar called "the first occasion in which the authorities here have aided in the suppression of this inhuman traffic," the Porbandar affair would reverberate across multiple international channels of the politics and diplomacy of slave trade abolition.[69] The ruling Rana's conduct in dealing with the several dozen African children landed in his port illuminated local chiefs' ambiguous attitudes toward the slave trade. It was difficult for them to reconcile conflicting imperatives: pressure from the British government, local merchants fearful of inflaming the ire of their Arab trading partners, and contradictory understandings about financial responsibility for the rescued captives. As such, the Porbandar affair would raise thorny issues that illuminate the transregional reach of the IOW slave trade and related conundrums around sovereignty, nationalism, imperial politics, international law, and transnational trade relations, not to mention relief expenditures for the rescued captives. Before the controversy died down, it would trigger both retaliatory strikes against Indian merchant vessels along the Arabian coast and disagreements among diverse entities within the colonial establishment (from London through Calcutta to Bombay) about the limits of antislave trade policy. The disagreements anticipated the campaign's future course of relative ineffectiveness in the IOW through much of the nineteenth century.

THE TEMPEST AT PORBANDAR

As winter approached in 1835, the Rana of Porbandar reported to Reid, commander of a British detachment at this port city, that three Arab dhows from Al Mukalla had stopped in his port for water and provisions. They carried limestone and loban (a gum resin used for incense and thought to be associated with spiritual qualities) consigned to Bombay. Much to Reid's chagrin, the Rana waited several days before notifying the captain that he suspected the presence of slaves aboard the vessels. With great reluctance, he dispatched men to help British soldiers search the boats. Concealed in boxes "and other private places in the hold," they discovered several dozen "totally naked" children.[70] When the captives disembarked, they numbered eight to ten fewer than the 79 the Rana had originally reported to his British overlords. The ruler would later try to explain away the missing children by claiming that they were the *nakhuda*'s progeny. Given Indian Ocean practices of adoption through the purchase of children for nominal amounts, it is impossible to tell whether the Rana was in fact telling the truth. In any case, Reid, accustomed to thinking of parental relations in strictly biological terms, and to conflating enslaved with Black African identities, was incredulous. He doubted the story for "the nakhodas are evidently Arabs, and the children Africans, a totally distinct race, and their appearance certainly is against the supposition...."[71]

Reid arranged temporary accommodations for the children in a tent belonging to his detachment, but wondered how these "poor creatures" were to be "subsisted, accommodated, and clothed, they being totally naked."[72] The search and seizure operation immediately triggered anxieties among local merchants concerned that British antislavery pressures would hurt their trade interests in the Gulf. The Rana, conveying these sentiments to the colonial authorities, adopted a tone distinctly conciliatory to the Arab slave traders, even as he downplayed his relations with them and appealed to the Government's powers of protection. He pleaded that the alleged Arab slavers had accepted the captives as "mere passengers," without knowledge of British proscriptions against the slave trade, and asked that the sailors be allowed to depart because they were "poor people" who operated the vessels on hire, and promised to never again transport slaves to the Indian coast.[73]

The Rana went on to underscore the uniqueness of the current situation. "These people seldom visit my port," he claimed. A famine in southern Arabia had propelled the traffic in human flesh to his shores. He played on the prejudices of his imperial supervisors, describing the particular Arabs in question as "an ignorant race," whose dealings with his regime were limited to refueling stops. They paid him no duties, but vessels from his port traded with the Arabian coast, "where the sovereign authority is exercised by the Mussalman powers." He petitioned the British to ensure that his port "not be destroyed" by Arab reprisals. Claiming his right to colonial protection in exchange for his cooperation with British antislave trade regulations, he wrote, "I have nothing to fear here, having Government on my side; but I beg you to consider that my vessels and people on the coasts of Arabia will be subjected to annoyance and ill-usage." Along this vein, he lamented that if the British failed to pay compensation for the liberated slaves, he would have to pick up that expense, for fear that otherwise the Arabs would exact that payment from his subjects when they visited the Gulf. In other words, his kingdom would have to bear the pecuniary brunt of British humanitarianism.[74]

Another sort of financial consideration reared its head early in the proceedings. The issue of the rescued children's subsistence prompted disagreement even among the relevant British officials. Captain Lang, the district's assistant political agent, called upon Porbandar authorities to provide "wholesome food" and clothing for the captives, arguing that forcing them to bear this expense would "make it the more their interest to discourage this inhuman traffic."[75] Willoughby, by contrast, felt that such a financial burden would bring the opposite result, prompting local chiefs to turn a blind eye to human trafficking for fear of being forced to assume responsibility for the subsistence of freed people.

Lang directed that the children be housed in more "comfortable quarters this cold season" than tents pitched under the fort walls afforded. The Rana protested that the group—seventy-five children, tended by ten caretakers—was too large for other accommodations. Betraying his own prejudices of race, caste, and culture, he complained: "These slaves are scarcely human beings; they eat, sleep, do everything on one spot, and wear no covering . . .; they are eaters of fish, which they consume half-cooked." Their tent quarters emanated an "offensive" odor that spread too far to remove them to more crowded sections of the city. The city of Porbandar suffered from want of room; its (presumably mostly vegetarian) Brahman and Baniyan residents were prohibited by their religion from "intercourse with . . . people" such as the Africans and coastal Arabs who lived "solely on fish." Whether or not this was an excuse to make the British back their antislavery professions with funding, Reid was soon forced to deputize Muslim sepoys in his detachment to supply the children with food.[76]

The parsimony of Reid's superiors in the colonial establishment exacerbated the situation. For about five weeks following their rescue, the children had subsisted at the rate of "five Porebunder pice per diem"—the minimum necessary to provide them with the simplest of food. But this expense increased with the appointment of a cook and the procurement of a small quantity of grass for their bedding. Moreover, they had survived without a stitch of clothing, "literally without a rag," as Reid put it, even as winter arrived. Lang ordered Captain Reid to procure coarse cotton to clothe the rescued, keeping costs as low as possible.[77]

As days turned into weeks and the children remained in the Rana's territory, the ruler's deferential, supplicatory tone gave way to explicit protest against the empire's practice of righteousness at his expense. He made it clear that he would deduct any expenses incurred for the upkeep of the freed children from the customs revenues he owed the British. He noted that other ports dotting the west coast of India continued to do business with visiting Arab vessels bearing slaves; why should Porbandar alone bear the costs of a feud with the Arabs that might result from cooperation with the British? He complained that the 26,000 rupees he owed the government in tribute swallowed up his share of the customs revenue. Even as he was "ordered" to support the slaves and crews of the three offending vessels "amounting in all to about 200 persons," he was losing 500 rupees in unlevied duties. Moreover, the dhow Arabs were becoming quarrelsome, for their vessels had goods on board for Bombay, so he begged the government's permission to let them depart for that mega port.[78]

Thus, when Reid discovered shortly afterward that the three detained vessels had escaped to Bombay with their commanders and crews intact, he suspected connivance by the Rana.[79] The children, having been made by their imperial benefactors to overstay their forced "welcome" in Porbandar, were finally placed on the Company's brig *Thetis* on December 29 and brought to Bombay. Meanwhile, British benevolence was reverberating in the Arabian peninsula in ways that fulfilled the Rana's worst fears of reprisal against Porbandar merchants.

REVERBERATIONS IN THE ARABIAN PENINSULA: SLAVERY, "PIRACY," AND COLONIAL BELONGING

In April 1836, Jivan Udhoji [spelled Oodhowjee in the documents], agent of a Bombay-based firm with a branch in Kathiawar identified in the colonial archives as "Dhurumay Lukmedass," petitioned the Bombay government for help to resolve a crisis that had befallen his company's property on the coast of Al Mukalla. On February 5, their ship named *Bhowany Prasad* made its maiden voyage under British colors from Porbandar to the southern coast of Arabia. The vessel was laden with cotton, grain, and piece goods, with an estimated value of 13,500 rupees. Commanded by a boatswain named Arjun, it carried nineteen people including the crew, two Baniyan supercargoes, and a couple of passengers.[80]

About 3 o'clock in the afternoon of February 29, a sharp gale forced the *Bhowany Prasad* to drop anchor about one hundred miles north of Al Mukalla, in what appears to have been the coastal town of Qishn in southern Yemen. The petition recounting these events emphasized that lying alongside the ship from Porbandar were a vessel from Kutch and an Arab *baghla* captained by an inhabitant of "Wadee" (or Wadi) belonging to what appears to have been the Al Mahra tribe inhabiting southern Arabia and the island of Socotra. The Indians spent the night in the harbor, but as day broke, the Arab vessel "broke anchor and made sail" toward them, captured the *Bhowany Prasad* with arms, and sailed with it to Wadi, with the Indian crew on board. After landing the captives ashore in Wadi, the perpetrators allegedly robbed and imprisoned them for four days.[81]

In his petition claiming colonial protection, the company agent Udhoji invoked the specter of slavery and the language of piracy embedded in a discourse of imperial abolition shaped by the British themselves. Udhoji asserted that at Wadi, the captured vessel's entire crew and passengers had been slated "for sale as slaves," and that a local Baniyan had helped them to escape on a boat to Al Mukalla. From there, six sailors secured passage on an Indian vessel to Bombay, where they informed the company of the fate that had befallen its property on the Arabian coast. Meanwhile, their compatriots back in Al Mukalla had appealed to the local ruler, the Hakim, to help restore their lost property, worth in the aggregate 17,500 rupees, later raised to 18,920. But the Hakim, claiming that he had no power over the Al Mahra Arabs who had attacked the Indian vessel, referred them to the British government. Invoking the language of colonial nationalism and imperial honor, the firm's Bombay-based agent urged that the British government demand "full reparation for the injury done to their subjects, and insult offered to their flag."[82]

Udhoji also made an explicit connection between British antislavery measures at Porbandar and the act of "piracy"—as slavery was defined in colonial antitrafficking parlance—perpetrated in Arabia. The Wadi chief Syed, he wrote, had "committed the act of piracy ... in retaliation for the seizure a few months ago of a number of African children which were brought to [Porbandar] in ... Arab vessels, to be sold as slaves." Udhoji warned that Indian merchants who traded extensively in the Middle East could not bypass the coastal strongholds of the Al Mahra, and that therefore, unless the colonial government took "prompt and decisive measures," its subjects would continue to suffer the pillage of their property by "a barbarous tribe, and, what is far worse, they will be exposed to all the horrors of slavery." He recommended an embargo against Al Mahra vessels in the ports of Bombay and Porbandar as a strategy to secure indemnities for the company against its losses on the Arabian coast.[83]

Depositions given by some members of the plundered vessel's crew upon their return to India diverged in some respects from the agent's account. The pilot, for instance, added the detail that his fellow crew members had sought to deflect the attack at Qishn by pretending to be from Mangalore in South India rather than Porbandar, but that Syed's men had evidently visited the west coast of India often enough to have recognized them, so that the lie did not work.[84] The supercargo credited a "respectable Arab" rather than a Baniyan with their escape to Al Mukalla.[85] Moreover, the commander, when asked whether the Arabs intended to sell the Indian crew as slaves, clarified that their captors were interested only in children, in this case three boys about ten years of age on board the Indian ship, but finding no buyers, had released them.[86] Notwithstanding the Bombay merchants' denunciation of Arab "savagery," the slippage in the crew's depositions between the identities of Baniyan and Arab saviors from slavery, and the familiarity of the deponents with the Wadi chief Syed's men that identified their vessel as having sailed from Porbandar, spoke to the intimacy and intricacy of coastal Indo-Arab trading relations. Meanwhile, the Baniyan merchant community in southern Arabia joined in the campaign to secure restitution for the lost property.[87] Back in India, the Rana of Porbandar warned that the attack on the Indian ship had brought mercantile activities in his realm to a halt, making it difficult for him to meet his tribute obligations.[88]

Faced with these pressures to act against the "piratical" assault on their subjects' business operations, the Bombay government considered dispatching cruisers to embargo offending ports in southern Arabia.[89] But colonial authorities found it difficult to pinpoint responsibility or negotiating partners.[90] Historically, the diversity of Yemeni terrain had prevented the emergence of centralized powers and promoted the isolation of regional ruling groups and local communities from one another.[91] The British Lieutenant Welstead, who had earlier unsuccessfully sought to negotiate the purchase of the island of Socotra in that region,[92] shared his impression that the Bedouins who inhabited the Mahara district in the vicinity of Qishn were among the "wildest" people in southern Arabia, and fractured into "various hordes under separate sheikhs."[93] But in Bombay, Captain Charles Malcolm, superintendent of the Indian Navy, was convinced, based on Acting Commander S. B. Haines' journal, that a brother of Qishn's deceased sultan was the only one with trading vessels plying the Indian Ocean and was therefore likely to be behind both the Porbandar trafficking vessels and the piracy against the Indians on the Arabian coast. He recommended that if negotiations failed, the British should seize Socotra, which "belongs to the tribe," and destroy their fishing enterprises.[94]

The following month, in August 1836, word of a resolution arrived from Haines in Mocha. He confirmed that the Mahra Arabs owned the vessel intercepted at Porbandar and that on its return to Arabia, "she was despatched to cruise off Ras Furtuk, for the purpose of intercepting the first vessel under British colors that should make her appearance," in the hope of exacting compensation for the seized slaves. But the British officer had been assured that the ruling sheikh and his council of tribal elders had rescinded this course of retaliation and agreed to restore the Indian vessel and its cargo to their owners.[95] Baniyan merchants in southern Arabia, however, disputed the truth of this settlement.[96] In the end, the Bombay government determined to dispatch a sloop of war *Coote* to the Red Sea, with instructions to offer the Wadi chief compensation for the slaves seized at Porbandar "on the lowest scale possible," as well as to recover the Bombay firm's vessel and cargo.[97]

FALLOUT IN THE NORTH ATLANTIC: FROM BOMBAY THROUGH CALCUTTA TO LONDON

The East India Company's London-based court of directors was not pleased. Events at Porbandar and the Arabian coast had convinced them that Kathiawar's Political Agent Willoughby had allowed "his zeal to put down the traffic in slaves" to get the better of "his judgment" when he ordered the seizure of the enslaved children at Porbandar without compensating their owners. His actions had proved "embarrassing and costly" to the British government, who would now have to support the children and pay reparations.[98]

The directors' cautious approach echoed the counsel of British India's Advocate General, offered in January 1836 as thorny questions about subsistence, compensation, and reprisals surrounding the Porbandar rescue bedeviled the Bombay government. His office essentially advised that a double firewall of sovereignty protected the alleged perpetrators in this case. While treaties with certain Atlantic nations allowed the British to search vessels sailing under such nations' flags, no such treaty with an Arab state covered the Red Sea parties apparently involved in the Porbandar case. Moreover, the offending vessels had been seized in Porbandar, which while a tributary state, was a foreign port, not subject to "ordinary rules and regulations in force" within Bombay Presidency.[99] But since British laws did not apply to the rescued captives, neither the government nor the Rana could pay for them, the Advocate General opined. Rather, he recommended that in the absence of any treaty with the [Mahra] Arabs, the government should return the "slaves" to the governments to which their owners belonged, together with "a strong remonstrance against this traffic." He deemed it neither "practicable" nor "safe" to interfere with slavery in west Asia, "considering the wild and lawless character of the Arab."[100]

Such sentiments may have anticipated the lack of resources and will that marked British campaigns against slave trade abolition in the Indian Ocean later in the nineteenth century, as documented by scholars of that part of the world. What is equally instructive, however, is that in the 1830s the rationale against antislavery zeal on the high seas of Afro-Asia drew on both developments in the Atlantic and colonial acquiescence in slavery within EIC's own territories in India. The Advocate General reminded the Bombay government that even in "civilized" Britain, the African slave trade was abolished only as recently as 1807, following a twenty-year struggle. It took another twenty-seven years to "obtain a limited and local abolition of slavery itself in the British colonies...." As for the international slave trade, the British had had to induce cooperation from Spain and Portugal through the payment of compensation. Most important of all, despite its best efforts, the Atlantic slave trade was still in full swing, aided and abetted by "America," among other states, illustrating the trade's tenacious hold on these nations' commercial success. In the British lawyer's interpretation, the Indian Ocean slave trade was more alike than different from the Atlantic, because it was entwined with "the commercial prosperity" of nations in both locales, as the Porbandar Rana's troubles with the Arabs demonstrated.[101]

Finally, erasing the distinctions drawn by the colonial state between domestic slavery and the international slave trade, the Advocate General pointed out that on the very Malabar coast where the drama of the African children unfolded, slavery was "recognised and sanctioned by law." Its existence was institutionalized by a Charter Act providing for measures to ameliorate and eventually extinguish slavery, but only when it was "safe" and "practicable" and by paying "due regard" to the "laws of marriage, and the rights and authorities of fathers and heads of families...."[102] The upshot of this legal advice was that even as the furor over events at Porbandar consumed Indian merchants, their Arab partners, and colonial bureaucrats and military officers on the ground, the Bombay government suspended orders for the commodore at Surat to detain ships carrying slaves.[103] The government also abandoned plans to prosecute their owners.[104] We do not know for sure whether the Indian firm managed to recoup the full extent of its losses. What is well known, of course, is that the British bombarded and occupied Aden on other pretexts just a couple of years later, in 1839. Meanwhile, the court of directors issued orders—conveyed to the Political Resident at Bushire—to negotiate with the Imam of Muscat for the extension of the existing antitrafficking treaty of 1822 to the subcontinent's "native states" of Kutch and Kathiawar.[105] But it would not be until 1856 that the Government of India ruled that subjects of native states like Kutch, which had ceded control over foreign policy to the British, were "morally" entitled to the same protection as British subjects in foreign lands, compelling them, according to one colonial interpretation, to uphold British laws against slavery.

Regimes of regulation, structures of law, and debates over diplomacy among transnational rulers have, in this chapter, offered us glimpses of multinational, multidirectional subaltern crossings. Against the backdrop of this discussion, let us proceed to recenter our vantage point on Indian Ocean slavery histories from the bottom up, by scouring the colonial archives for evidence of subaltern pressures on imperial abolition.

7

Subaltern Prisms and Meanings of Freedom

I was taken from Calcutta by the Nacodah of the ship Hoomayun Shah, and there made over to ... the mother of the Sultan of Muscat with whom I remained about 3 years and a half, as a slave. About 4 months ago, I was given over to one Hillal, the brother of my mistress. He matched me with his slave Abdool Khair Nubie, my marriage was not celebrated according to the law of the Muhamedans, but I considered him my husband and he considered me his wife. I was afterwards sent to the house of the English agent, who sent me to Bombay. I do not wish to be sent to my country. I was formerly a Hindu, but I am now [a Muslim]. I wish to be sent back to Muscat, to join my said husband.

—STATEMENT OF "LIBERATED SLAVE" FATIMA, 1844

As the halls of power from London to Bombay rang with debates over the legality and prudence of antislave trade campaigns on the high seas bordering Afro-Asia, the ostensible beneficiaries of these measures were waging their own negotiations with the structures of colonial abolition on land under British jurisdiction. Let us begin our reflections on imperial infrastructures' interplay with subaltern actions in mid-1830s Bombay, where the African children rescued in Porbandar had been transported for rehabilitation. From the archival traces that survive, we can arrive at some arguments about the shape of subjectivity and claims to belonging that the children fashioned amid extreme adversity once they reached Indian shores. The Bombay Senior Police Magistrate John Warden's reports bring to light the contours of a makeshift community, forged in very recent trauma and woven on paper with the names of involuntary refugees so very young. Their ordeal had taken a toll. At least five died while still in Porbandar.[1] Sickness dogged them in Bombay, with four ill enough to be committed to Native General Hospital shortly after their arrival and thirteen following suit. Meanwhile, two of the girls succumbed to a sudden and mysterious illness following dinner. Alarmed, Marianah then joined fourteen-year-old Jafranah in leading a hunger strike. Their custodian described the communal solidarity they appear to have developed: "The two elder girls have set this example of abstinence which the rest have followed. They say, if they eat, they will become sick, be carried away, and die."[2] The elder girls informed the police magistrate that they had stopped eating because "they wanted to know their fates."[3]

Meanwhile, both the casualties and the hunger strike prompted the government to pay closer attention to the children's material conditions. The political secretary directed Warden to ensure that the children got plenty of exercise under the guard of police peons to prevent anyone from stealing them. Warden speculated that the children may have abandoned the mats and blankets he had given them, sleeping on a cold cement floor. This, in turn, led him on a quest for an "upper-roomed house, with boarded floors, for their accommodation," which a constable was able to locate in Military Square, in the Fort area of present-day downtown Bombay. M.T. Kays, surgeon to the police, who visited the children daily, testified that "they are kept clean, well clothed, and well fed. All of them appear cheerful and fill of spirits...."[4]

But what did freedom mean in this context, especially when the rescued captives were children in need of guardianship? As imperial officials grappled with the problem of what to do with their young "beneficiaries" in order to prevent them from becoming public charges, they came perilously close to erasing the boundaries between coercion and free will. Willoughby's first thoughts on the subject drifted toward agreements of indenture or apprenticeship with private families. Under this proposal, the government might enter into agreements with custodians who would "feed, clothe and protect them, and ultimately ... assign wages to them in return for their services," even though such wages would "for some time to come ... be of little value."[5] Later in the century, the British would construct mission schools for freed children in Ahmednagar, Nashik, and Shirur within commuting distance of Bombay.[6] Like such US juvenile asylums as the New York House of Refuge, these institutions sought to train domestic workers and tradesmen, but these options did not exist in the 1830s.

Several would-be guardians materialized, but Warden "anticipated the wishes of Government in recording the requests of Christians alone." The most enthusiastic on this list was the Army's agent for clothing, a Captain Henderson, who applied to "procure" three of the boys as "laborers" for his estate in the Cape of Good Hope, where labor was "high and abundant." He seemed in a hurry to seal the deal, securing passage for the boys on board ships sailing for South Africa within less than two weeks after filing his request. Other applicants included army officials and colonial bureaucrats—a brigadier-major of King's troops, a member of the Native Infantry, clerks in the Secretary's office and warehouse, a treasury accountant, a retired commissariat clerk, a vicar-general of the Apostolic mission, a constable, a court keeper, and persons described as "respectable Portuguese."[7]

Acting Advocate General H. Roper, however, raised some concerns about the need to maintain an appearance of commitment to freedom, defined by the British as contracting for labor by free will. Roper counseled that the government did not have "legal title ... to place itself *in loco parentis*" over the children. The rescued were "entitled to be considered as freemen," with control over proposals for their disposition. This raised a related legal question. If a private family were willing to assume charge of the children, contracting to provide subsistence and ultimately wages in return for their services, then how to characterize the relationship that would arise between the two parties? Would it be defined as that existing between master and servant, or master and apprentice? The officer offered an expedient path out of the legal conundrum created by a set of tricky circumstances: the desirability of private subsistence, the rescued children's tender age, and an abstract commitment to free will. He advised that an infant could, under common law, "bind himself an apprentice," even without the consent of a parent, but apprenticeship contracts as they operated in England were not applicable in India. Thus, he advised written contracts—although not under seal—establishing the relationship of master and servant between the children and families willing to receive them. Such contracts would "contain promises" by the servant to "faithfully" render service for a fixed term, while the master would undertake to provide "good treatment, feeding, clothing, and instruction of the servant, and also to pay wages to the servant," with amount and time specified in the agreement.[8]

Nevertheless, given the tender age of the children, the government decided to stand *in loco parentis* as to the children. While they were "too young to be treated as freemen," they were not to be forced to join the Indian navy or any service "any more than a child would be forced by a parent of proper feeling." Willoughby authorized Warden to place them out in service, under the terms of a master-servant relationship recommended by Roper, "but with the obligation to be brought up Christians,"—and equally important, Protestants. They were to be produced at the nearest police or magistrate's office twice a year until they reached eighteen years of age.[9]

The children, however, proved less tractable than their benefactors had imagined. Their actions bespoke an assertion of personhood that encompassed not simply opinions about what kind of work they were willing to perform but also the sort of culture and community to which they preferred to belong. Only eight of the boys proved willing to serve in the Indian navy. Moreover, seventeen boys and eleven girls firmly rejected the predicate of cultural assimilation to Christian colonial subjecthood that underlay the promise of "free labor" under imperial auspices by "positively" refusing "to serve Christians, or at all events to be Christians. They wish to follow the Mahomedan faith," Warden reported. Thus, he was forced to omit from the agreements they signed with their prospective "masters" the provision that required that they be raised as Christians. Once again, the two eldest young women led the revolt, as they had done the hunger strike. The only people with whom they had been able to have a conversation were "their countrymen" in Bombay, and these African compatriots practiced Islam. Much to Warden's chagrin, some of these "wayward" children balked at accompanying those he regarded as the worthiest of applicants such as a "respectable Portuguese" gentleman named Roger de Faria. By contrast, little Tummasa was pleased to follow Mary, an "aya" (domestic worker/nanny) in Captain Sinclair's employment. Mary was herself African, and wished to "adopt the child as her own." Thus, the final roster of "masters" turned out to be rather different from the original list of applicants. These included fewer military men and a larger number of custodians in more modest circumstances: pensioners, clerks in civil service, and constables.[10]

Warden continued to hope that the younger children might yet be proselytized. To that end, he recommended remanding them to the custody of a Mr. Townsend, acting secretary to government, without a formal agreement.[11] Townsend promised to say nothing about religion to them, nor to interfere with "their manner of food and clothing." Rather, he would admit them to schools where they would be "well taught and kindly treated, and instructed in a manner which might eventually lead to their embracing Christianity. The object would be to enlighten their minds, to make them acquainted with our sacred books, and to give them such a course of education as would enable them hereafter to earn their bread."[12] On that basis, he secured a temporary grant for the support of twenty-four of the children from the Bombay government.[13]

Meanwhile, the government reversed its earlier decision to reject the clothing agent Henderson's proposal to put some of the boys to work on his Cape Town estate. The agent made a convincing case for raising the children with kindness, as productive Christians. He had arranged their passage with attention to the minutest details. The four boys he sought would have their own custodians, as he had arranged for a carpenter, a boatswain, a butcher, and a cook to assume charge of one child each. A wagon would take the boys from Cape Town to Henderson's farm, "far removed from any town ... where, from bad company, their morals are likely to be corrupted." Moreover, the overseer and his wife, expected to take over the children's care at the farm, were "strictly religious and kind people," who were expected to treat the boys as members of their own family and pay particular attention to their religious instruction. The government was persuaded, and Songon, Nusseeb, Nusseband, and Mahaboob were assigned to travel with Henderson, provided that they did so "with their own free consent." Ironically, when these "freed" people returned to Africa, it was as laborers far away from their places of birth—to a white-owned farm in Cape Town, South Africa. If they really did go of their own accord, it is not clear what other options they could have exercised.[14]

How do we wrestle with the related problems of agency, identity, and freedom in the case of the African children rescued at Porbandar? It is clear that the will they asserted—on clear display in colonial officials' chronicles of their actions—registered in the archives in the context of imperial abolition. The public relations and policies, the rhetoric and legal advice, the guns and boats, afforded at least in theory an infrastructure for reinventing the captives as British constructs of "freemen." The children, however, seized the opportunities afforded by those institutions to define the meaning of freedom rather differently than their colonial custodians would have it. Against the British formulation of a *future* promise to the right to contract for free labor (in this case presumably because the "freemen" were children), and a concomitant acculturation to Christianity, the children asserted a claim to community, based on religious and linguistic affinities forged perhaps in transit and transplantation within the larger Afro-Asian Indian Ocean world. On that principle, they upheld their own *present* predilection for (or their *right* to choose?) certain custodians or employers—identified in the archives as African and Muslim—over Europeans and Christians deemed more appropriate by the colonial establishment.

It is tempting to argue that they exhibited a diasporic consciousness distinct from, and in tension with, colonial nationalism. Such a consciousness may have been anchored in what the cultural studies scholar Shaden M. Tageldin has described, in a different context, as a "convergence of 'Arab' north and 'Black' south," shaped by the historical experiences of what Abdul Sheriff calls the "dhow cultures of the Indian Ocean World." These cultures centered around cosmopolitan, multilingual port cities extending from East Africa through the Middle East to Southeast Asia, woven into exchange webs of peoples and commodities by free trade and Islam. Here, violence, coercion, and exploitation coexisted with patronage structures that offered paths to social inclusion, if not equality, because masters derived status and influence from their command over sizeable circles of dependent "clients."[15]

These dialectics assume special importance given the limits of the colonial campaign for freedom. Consider how the Porbandar case exposed the cramped choices available to rescued captives who were more or less theoretical "freemen." Join the navy. Or become an indentured servant. Or else travel to South Africa to labor on a farm. Given these options, and the variety of master-slave relationships that structured patron-client interactions in the IOW, it is no wonder that these beneficiaries of imperial abolition did not always seem grateful for their deliverance. Nor did the vision of "freedom" as the performance of autonomous liberal individualism play out in quite the way that Anglo-American abolitionists imagined.

Depositions by other rescued captives reflect similar tensions between subaltern priorities and imperial meanings of freedom that often shaded into coercion. At the same time, however, the depositions themselves constitute tangible instruments of negotiation generated by the rhetoric of imperial abolition that afforded the most marginalized members of circulating populations—women and children—room to record their voices. And those voices hint at a sense of identity rooted—like those of the Porbandar children—in the peripatetic cosmopolitanism and patronage structures of "dhow cultures."[16]

Take the case of three African boys whose paths converged in a sojourn to Bombay amid the Porbandar controversy in 1837. That shared experience began as the three lay concealed in two different ships flying British colors while anchored in the Red Sea harbor of Jeddah. Commander Rogers of the East India Company's Brig of War *Eupharates,* acting on intelligence suggesting their presence in the vicinity, discovered one, identified in the archives as "Comineree" or "Cominee" crouched in the galley of a ship, the *Frances Warden*. Upon interrogation, the boy told two different stories. At first, he admitted that he was a slave, but later, in the presence of his master, the *nakhuda* Sheikh Hameed, he changed his story, claiming that his earlier account was a coerced confession made under "restraint." Rogers, however, preferred to privilege the first version of the boy's tale and transferred him to the *Euphrates*. There he was joined by two other boys, Salim and Sugur, "rescued" from yet another vessel, the *Fatteh Karim*.[17]

The depositions recorded in the three boys' names, peppered with references to the ideas and languages of "consent," "wages," and absence of natal family, fleshed out British meanings of slavery and freedom. Their statements were organized around leading questions designed to distinguish the status of slave from free framed by a binary Atlantic perspective. Were they slaves? Had they enjoyed leave to "quit the ship" or received wages? Had they consented to come to Jeddah? It transpired that all three had traversed islands and ports like Java, Penang, and Lanour in the South Pacific. They were never allowed to disembark nor received wages, and each was forced to "go with my master" rather than accompany him of their own free will. The depositions suggested natal alienation. Sugur explained, "I was originally from another country. People came and spread dates and fat. I was hungry and took some to eat. Then they carried me away. I have neither father nor mother. I was sold for 5 dollars." Comineree, who had arrived in the Red Sea via Bengal and Bombay, had no known parents either.[18]

Weeks later, the boys had touched Bombay's shores in the heat of May. But there soon erupted a controversy over exactly what happened next. Rear Admiral Charles Malcolm of the Indian Navy informed Willoughby that on their arrival from the Red Sea, the boys had "requested to remain on board," and that "in the hurry of dispatching the vessel to the Persian Gulf [their] removal was forgotten." Willoughby then directed the navy superintendent to enter the boys as "volunteers" on board the *Hugh Lindsay,* the ship that had taken them away. The reclassification of the three rescued captives from "slave" to "volunteer," ostensibly at their own request, sustained the illusion that they had joined the British navy of their own free will. Later events, however, suggested that the boys perceived this distinction in status to be more rhetorical than real. Upon their return to Bombay, the police magistrate who met and questioned them came away with an alternative reading of their status aboard the British vessel. They had, he reported, "been *detained* on board the *Hugh Lindsay* to form part of her crew." On orders from the Bombay government, Malcolm then sought the boys' "opinion on the matter." This chink in the dialectic of imperial coercion and benevolence gave the boys the opportunity to refuse to stay on board. They disembarked in Bombay. There they reentered the colonial archives with new names, ages, and identities that placed their origins in Zanzibar: Sangar (ten), Salman (thirteen), and Kanap (twelve). Like their Porbandar compatriots, they "objected strongly to go to Christian families," forcing the magistrate to place them with "respectable Mussalmans" under covenants pledging the new custodians to "protect, feed and clothe" their charges and to "employ them as domestic servants, and ... to assign them suitable wages for their trouble and labor."[19]

It may be that in the end, for the boys taken at Jeddah, "emancipation" occasioned the exchange of one form of domination for another. Yet given an opportunity to negotiate, thanks to intraimperial consultations premised upon the need to at least pay lip service to British understandings of freedom, the boys, like the Porbandar children, chose to remain within the folds of the Muslim community. That was the community they were presumably more familiar with and that resonated with more familiar patronage-oriented structures of subordination.

In no case do these dynamics emerge more clearly than in the experiences of a young Ethiopian named Yacoob, for whom "manumission" under British auspices threatened not only his claims of belonging within his master's community but also his aspirations to upward mobility.

SLAVES WITH "FREE WILL" AND SLAVES IN THE FAMILY

Yacoob was an enslaved Ethiopian youth who boarded a ship bound for the Kutch port of Mandvi from the Arabian peninsula in the waning months of 1836. He had secured the permission of his master—related to a local sultan—to make the trip, intending to learn the carpenter's trade in South Asia. He reportedly hoped to "take service, earn something, and return in a fitting condition to my master."[20] Much to his consternation, the vessel on which he was sailing came to halt near the salt marshes of the Gulf of Kutch instead of proceeding to the city of Mandvi. On board were at least eleven other enslaved "Abyssinians," some as young as six or seven years old. All passengers received orders to disembark. Three of their number—a family consisting of a father and two sons—were then released, but the remaining Africans found themselves on a forced trip to Porbandar. Before long, Yacoob learned the identity of his new custodians. These were not Indian or Arab slave traders but rather would-be emancipators—a British detachment acting on orders from James Erskine, the political agent stationed in Kathiawar. Erskine had learned that a Mandvi moneylender had borrowed and dispatched a boat to

Arabia that had returned ten months later bearing "Abyssinian slaves." With Bombay-based Willoughby's blessings, colonial authorities stepped in to intercept the captives' onward journey.[21] They brought the children to Porbandar and lodged them in the Residency's military quarters. But as with the larger contingent to which Marianah belonged, the rescued faced appalling living conditions. Bereft of sufficient resources for food, clothing, or bedding, one succumbed to smallpox, four others were hospitalized, and the rest remained in danger of infection with the same "loathsome disease," as British Commander A. P. Reid put it.[22]

Among the survivors was Yacoob, sufficiently annoyed to file an official complaint about his "rescue" with his ostensible "benefactors." Not only had British action foiled his professional plans to learn the trade of carpentry in Kutch, earn money, and return to his master, his new guardians had divested him of his *property*. On the way to Porbandar, "the authorities took from him" among other things, a sword, a matchlock, and a knife. "I wish my property to be restored," the complainant demanded. Evidently his story had some effect, because the Bombay government directed its agent in Kathiawar to help Yacoob recover his property and to inform him that he was "entirely free."[23]

It is not at all clear that the "entirely free" status that the British conferred upon Yacoob, represented for this "slave" a material difference from the condition that he had envisioned for himself when he set out for Kutch. His testimony trained a sharp light on the complexities involved in defining the boundaries of slavery and freedom on an IOW ship carrying "slaves." Yacoob had secured his master's permission to seek his fortunes abroad, was armed, and deemed himself the owner of that "property" of weaponry. Moreover, he intended to return to his master after he had made good—an aspiration that spoke directly to the tradition of patron-client relationships that influenced various forms of slavery in the western Indian Ocean region. Glassman, for instance, notes that the Swahili word for slave, *mtumwa*, "could be used to denote a 'delegate', a 'person who is sent on an errand, and who does not act in his own name.'" Such a slave belonged in the master's household, "or as part of a personal following which endowed the master with power and prestige."[24] Usually assimilated to Swahili culture, if such a slave learned a craft, becoming a *fundi* (possessed of "specialized knowledge"), he might achieve some amount of "respect and domestic autonomy" as did "caravan leaders, fishermen and sea captains." He expected to establish a household of his own without the threat of sale. His master, in turn, expected a share of his earnings, and might even take some pride in his enslaved dependent's success.[25] In short, Yacoob had traveled to India to climb the ladder of success with his patron's stamp of approval within the community to which they both belonged, a mission that rendered British promises of "freedom" less meaningful.

Colonial emancipation might spell cultural assimilation—as in the case of Mozambican, Ethiopian, and Somali children sent to a missionary-run asylum set up in Bombay a couple of decades later. There the girls, instructed in the medium of English, were trained as seamstresses, domestic workers, and wives, or teachers, while the boys learned cricket and were channeled into clerical positions or apprenticeships in various trades. For others, however, British "freedom" might well have meant starvation. Take the case of hundreds of African slave soldiers and dependents who had served the Nawab of Awadh. They lost their means of subsistence when the East India Company conquered that kingdom following the 1857 revolt. But, as Rosie Llewellyn-Jones has reported, when these penniless retainers petitioned the British government for aid, they were turned down on the grounds that "freedom" had brought with it the responsibility of self-support. The Lieutenant Governor of the North-West Provinces adopted a racist prism through which to weigh their supplications for relief: "Their own African laziness seems to be the chief bar to their prosperity." At the annexation of Awadh, "the Africans obtained their liberty and then found as free men they must support themselves. This they do not like, but that seems to be no reason why they should be kept by the Government in idleness."[26] That these enslaved dependents had sided with their former master, the Nawab, during his war with the British, suggests that from their perspective, the choice between colonial "liberty" inflected with racism and Awadhi "slavery" was clear.

The archives of the British Indian Empire's foreign department are littered with similar instances of ambiguous or reluctant beneficiaries, overwhelmingly women or children. Consider, for instance, the reactions two women and three children had to British intervention. All were associated in some way with the circles in which the Imam of Muscat and Zanzibar moved. These cases unfolded in 1844, the year an enslaved Circassian woman bore Sultan Sayyid Saʿīd of Zanzibar a daughter. This child grew up to write her memoirs over four decades later—a work worth considering in some detail because it contextualizes the intimate worlds that shaped our subjects of imperial abolition from the 1840s. Styling herself a "Princess of Oman and Zanzibar," named at birth Salamah bint Saïd, Sayyida Salme,[27] she took curious western readers from Zanzibar's plantations into the elusive inner recesses of the women's quarters where she had grown up. Her pen-and-ink sketches belong in what Billie Melman has identified as "the vast body of ethnographic literature on domestic life in the harem," which achieved great popularity with the ascendency of western imperialism during the nineteenth century (fig. 7).[28] But typical contributions to this "feminine literary genre" were filtered through the gaze of European women visitors—"travelers, missionaries, and colonists"—who were invited into elite Muslim households within the Ottoman Empire and the western Indian Ocean. By contrast, Salme's observations crossed the inner/outer divide that the word "haram" evoked. Born in Zanzibar's royal zenana, she left it to elope with an itinerant merchant from Hamburg, married him, converted to Christianity, assumed the name "Emily Ruete," and following her hus-

FIGURE 7. John Frederick Lewis, *The Harem*, 1876. Photo by Birmingham Museums Trust, licensed under CC0.

band's early death, settled into "a life of genteel poverty in bourgeois, parochial, Wilhelmine Hanseatic Germany, in a society that regarded her as an exotic stranger" (fig. 8). Written ostensibly to leave her children a record of the palace life she had abandoned, her text sought to demystify stereotypes of Arab-Muslim women in Europe, even as it adopted "Orientalist conventions of representation"—invoking colonialist imagery of the Other—to bring the world of her childhood to life.[29]

For scholars of comparative slavery, the value of Salme's vivid, often controversial account lies in its potential as a window to the varieties and hierarchies of bondage in the western Indian Ocean. The author was the daughter of an enslaved woman who was ascribed the status of a "secondary wife" in the Arab-Swahili society into which she had been sold. As such, the remembrances of the "Arabian princess" offer us (a) a basis for placing the women "rescued" by British functionaries in 1843–44 in the context of zenanas associated with the sultan's extended family and (b) insights into the dynamics of "assimilation" and diasporic subaltern identity formation within comparative frames of reference. The *Memoirs* also signal another sort of acculturation—to privileges of race, class, and imperial power. The

FIGURE 8. Heinrich Friedrich Plate, photograph of Emily Ruete (Sayyida Salme), princess of Oman and Zanzibar, c. 1856–80. Artwork in the public domain.

work's composition in the late nineteenth century coincided with what scholars of East Africa have identified as an era marked by the dissemination and intensification of commodity production of grain and sugar in places like Malindi and Pangani, along with the rise of cohesive Arab planter classes bound by culture, economic interest, and connections with the state of Zanzibar. Unlike Swahili-speaking mercantile elites, these migrants from Oman were inclined to turn the enslaved from "personal clients" into an exploited workforce producing cash crops.[30]

In this milieu, Salme's defense of "Negro" slavery in East Africa would echo the racist caricatures of the North American Slave South. The *Memoirs*' section on "Slavery" focused its commentary on Black African enslaved labor alone, excluding the complex multiracial variants and functions of bondage that the reader glimpses throughout the rest of the princess's account. The "Slavery" chapter of her work was firmly embedded in the white supremacist discourses and proslavery nostalgia common in Europe and North America during the time period when the *Memoirs* were published, one distinguished by the highwater mark of imperialism in Afro-Asia and the emergence of the legend of the "lost cause" in North America's vanquished former Confederacy. Salme's blind spot about her own place within this order as the daughter of an enslaved mother reveals much about the varieties of enslaved statuses and levels of assimilation within elite slaveholding households in the western Indian Ocean world.

Salme was born in Zanzibar's oldest palace, Bet il Mtoni, and lived there until she reached the age of seven. From the outside, the American seaman Horace Putnam saw this royal residence as a "large and ... quite a respectable Arab Palace," surrounded by a profusion of fruit trees: orange, pineapple, and coconut. Macadamized walkways paved with sea shells wound around it. The plaza in front boasted mounted brass cannons pointing toward the sea, where the sultan's navy lay anchored. Putnam had heard that forty concubines lived in a "harem" housed in one part of Mtoni. He claimed to have seen them when they roamed the grounds of the palace, attended by two eunuchs on the two days when they were rumored to enjoy "liberty." He imagined that these women, "from Persia and Caucasia mostly" were "the most beautiful girls" he had seen. "Their dresses are of the most gorgeous colours trimed [sic] with silver and gold tinsel and embroidered with fine laces.... Most of them have a profusion of ornament about their person, which is more pleasing to the savage than the civilized man. They are very young, 16 to 25...."[31]

One of the Circassian "concubines" that Putnam claimed to have spied may have actually been a secondary wife, Salme's mother. Judging by what we know about the history of enslaved Circassian women, she may have been the daughter of a farmer, captured in war—possibly with the Russians—and whisked away by horsemen who murdered her parents, separated her from her siblings, and admitted her to slave markets, possibly within the Ottoman Empire, that eventually brought her into the Zanzibar sultan's household. So young was she that "she lost her first tooth" there, according to her daughter. In due course, she joined a multinational cohort of some seventy-five "secondary wives" whom Said had purchased "from time to time," most of them when they were over the age of sixteen to eighteen years. Salme drew finely grained portraits of the spectrum of skin colors these women represented and the babble of tongues they spoke: "A painter would have found rich material for his brush on the veranda at Bet il Sahel [another palace on the island]." She counted "eight or nine different facial hues" and garments that offered many contrasting colors amid the "bustle and stir" of life: "Children of all ages tore about, squabbled ... shouting and clapping of hands taking the place of the Western bell-ringing" for servants. Women clattered about in wooden sandals "inlaid with silver or gold." Arabic, the official language of the household, was spoken in the presence of the sultan. His daughter recalled, however, that "no sooner was his back turned than a sort of Babel would break loose, Persian, Turkish, Circassian, Suahili, Nubian, Abyssinian, to say nothing of dialects."[32]

Besides language, other signifiers of cultural identity and status assimilated newly purchased "secondary wives" into palace life and its hierarchies. While Arabic, Persian, and Turkish cuisine dominated the kitchens of Bet il Mtoni and Bet il Sahel, Arabic clothing superseded all others. The rules required a Circassian to abandon her "flapping garments" and an Abyssinian her "fantastic draperies" for the robes of the Arabian peninsula within three days of her arrival. Moreover, she received jewelry and was assigned domestic attendants by the head eunuch in accordance with her rank.[33]

The organization of space structured both status and the rituals of daily life, encoding distinctions of gender, marital status, color, and age. Thus, the sultan's principal wife, Azze bint Sef, a member of the royal family of Oman, enjoyed her own quarters and rarely rose to greet visitors. At dinner, Said took his position at the head of the table, with his "senior children" seated closest to him, and the others taking their place at distances proportional to their age.[34]

Salme observed that "secondary wives" had borne every one of the sultan's thirty-six children at his death so that "we were all equals, and no questions as to the colour of our blood needed to be raised." Indeed, she inherited her share of the king's fortune at the age of twelve, which rendered her an "emancipated citizen." Decades later, she would press claims to this inheritance against a brother, then the reigning ruler of Zanzibar. Moreover, her mother had her master's ear, for the sultan was said to have granted nearly all her wishes and proffered her the "signal distinction" of rising and stepping toward her when she visited him.[35]

Yet the princess's account also bristles with color prejudice, especially against darker-skinned populations of African descent within the palace walls, on the plantations, and in the public sphere, suggesting that the practices of everyday social interaction may have diverged from law and custom. Within the community of enslaved concubines and secondary wives belonging to the royal household, fault lines between Circassian and Ethiopian mothers appear to have arisen from, among other things, the different prices they commanded in the slave market. These fueled mutual suspicions among their children and encouraged segregated seating at mealtimes. Salme noted without a hint of irony that the "handsome and *expensive* [our italics] Circassians, fully conscious of their superior merits and value, refused to sit at a table with the brown Abyssinian women." In one breath she asserted that the sultan's Circassian wives were "much finer in appearance than the Abyssinians," and blessed with such "natural advantages" as a "noble bearing." In the next, she attributed the "ridiculous race hatreds ... among the children," to the Abyssinian women's "envy" and "spiteful, revengeful disposition.... We daughters of Circassian mothers were called "cats" by our [Abyssinian sisters], because some of us had the misfortune to possess blue eyes." Her report that those with "white skin" were sarcastically styled "your Highness" and included two of the king's favorite children, suggests that light-skinned offspring may have been marked out for special privileges among the sultan's brood.[36]

To some extent, regional origins and race constructs appear to have shaped distinctions of function and power among the bondspeople who inhabited Salme's childhood world in Zanzibar. The princess noted that in the noisy courtyard of Bet il Sahel, where butchers slaughtered cattle for the household's meat supply, "Negroes" sat in one corner, "having their heads shaved" next to languid water carriers. These darker-skinned enslaved workers were ubiquitous, an integral part of every scene, from intimate spaces like the bedroom, the bathhouses, the nursery, the schoolroom, and the dining room, to the more public domains of the guardroom, the river, the streets, the marketplace, and the plantations. They put children to bed, bathed their mistresses' feet in *eau de cologne* at the end of the day, and fanned them as they slept. They nursed infants and accompanied children to the schoolhouse, sitting behind young charges scattered around mats as they absorbed the lessons of the day. Salme contrasted such nurses with what she alleged as the "neglect and heartlessness" of German caregivers, asserting that they frequently secured freedom as a reward for their devotion, and did not have to separate from their own children, who enjoyed "the same brew of milk, the same chicken," the same baths, and the cast-off clothes of their more "exalted comrades," including the children of mistresses who had themselves been purchased as "secondary wives."[37]

Artisans trained in carpentry and saddlery, needlework and millinery brought their owners profit. Africans dispatched to Oman to learn these crafts "went up considerably in price." Enslaved messengers ran between elite residences, and to letter writers, delivering confidential verbal missives—a task conferring leverage that could be parlayed into especially good treatment. Others carted fruit and other food supplies back to the palaces from rowboats supplying the plantations, landing their heavy baskets on the veranda floor with a thud.[38] Amateur musicians entertained the family by playing the *sese* (zeze, a stick zither). The most reliable— like a "cantankerous ... Nubian slave" who had once restrained her father from striking a man with a sword, served as doorkeepers. It also fell to the door attendants to arrange the slippers of visitors in a semi-circle according to the owners' ranks, with those belonging to the "noblest" placed in the center.[39]

Trusted eunuchs performed the most sensitive of tasks, laden with status and responsibility. They served as bulwarks against unauthorized access to the women's quarters, shaved the heads of infants in a customary ceremony on the fortieth day after birth, and accompanied women on ferry rides between palaces. They stood in attendance at dinner, "smart" and "well-armed," and afterwards passed around "genuine Mocha in tiny cups resting on gold or silver saucers." They took their place in the advance guard that led the sultan into an audience hall for his daily interface with the public. Their less ceremonious duties involved giving the children riding lessons in the courtyard and yelling at "lazy water-carriers" in the veranda to answer "urgent calls for water" among the residents.[40]

Black African women served both as attendants assigned to secondary wives and as subsistence farmers or agricultural laborers on the island. Thus Salme recalled that on a visit to a plantation as a little girl, a "little old Negro woman" had tugged at her sleeve and given her a gift wrapped in banana leaf, of a "freshly picked head of maize" raised on the woman's plot. The princess had later learned that the woman "was a long-standing favourite" of her mother. Women like these taught their mistresses the art of chewing the betel leaf, at which Salme's Arab relatives apparently scoffed, and which the sultan had forbidden in his homes. Notwithstanding these strictures, this "Suahili habit" remained a "favourite pastime," the author observed, for "those of us born on the east coast of Africa, and brought up among Negroes and mulattoes."[41]

Overall, Salme portrayed a layered slave society that hewed closely to idealized Orientalist depictions of "slavery in the East" as a familial affair, except when it came to Black Africans. She defended "Slavery"—under which system she seemed to classify those she described as "Negroes" alone—in virulently racist language recalling American slaveholders. Writing at the height of European imperialism in Africa, white supremacy in North America, and the rise of sugar plantation agriculture in the IOW, she assumed a scathingly antiabolitionist stance. Parroting familiar proslavery cant, she argued that "anybody who has visited Africa, Brazil, North America, or any country where Negroes live, must be aware of their antipathy against work," and suggested that the only answer to idleness was the lash.[42]

Still, her own evidence in the rest of her *Memoirs* told a different story. Enslaved women of all races—whether Circassian and Ethiopian secondary wives or the devoted nurses she characterized as "Negro"—lay at the heart of processes of social and biological reproduction that shaped elite status. Such status was wrapped up in the concept of *heshima*—which the historian Frederick Cooper has defined as respect derived from the command of large dependent circles in addition to wealth, genteel Omani communal ties, and Islamic piety.[43] Salme recalled that a child who reached the age of three or four months received "a couple of slaves" in addition to her nurses, "who remain [the recipient's] property from that date." Age brought an entitlement to additional slaves, and "if one dies the father bestows another or a corresponding sum of money." Dominion over large circles of clients played out visually in the exhibition of entourages in public spaces. Salme sketched the spectacle of a "lady" setting forth with an armed escort of "a dozen or more . . . slaves, by twos preceding her and her lantern bearers, a number of highly bedizened waiting women bringing up the rear. If a pedestrian were met, whatever his rank, the slaves motioned him out of the road . . . until the procession had gone by." An even more performative display of patronage attended the sultan's daily audiences with courtiers and the public in a grand, sea-facing hall or *barza,* on the ground floor of his palace: "When the *barza* is full the Sultan starts. In my father's lifetime the procession would move as follows: First a company of Negro guards, then the junior eunuchs, the senior eunuchs, the Sultan, the Sultan's elder sons, and finally his younger sons. At the door of the hall guards and eunuchs formed a lane, through which my father and brothers entered the *barza*. All present rose to greet [Saïd], his departure taking place in the same order again."[44]

The *Memoirs* of the Princess of Oman and Zanzibar bear out interpretations of slavery's value to Arab slaveholders that scholars of East Africa have offered. Slave ownership carried social value apart from the income it generated through coerced labor in staple crop production. Profits from the clove plantation economy certainly supplemented earnings from commerce and customs duties and underwrote the purchase of imported consumer goods that conferred status. But the pecuniary gains of investment in land and slaves formed merely one element in the cultural dividend of *heshima*. Ample circles of dependents and personal retinues carried implications for political power and social status that tied Zanzibar's dominant culture to its forebears in Oman.

This context of the social significance of dependent relations might offer a meaningful framework for thinking through the saga of some women and children in 1843–44 who spurned British imperial offers of rescue from Arab zenanas. The colonial archives launch this story with a scene in a Muscat public square. There, a broker was leading an enslaved eleven-year-old Indian girl from one Arab shopkeeper to another, "crying" her for sale. In the quarters above the square these cries caught the ear of none other than Khojah Reuben, the East India Company's Muscat Agent. Reuben had received intelligence that the Sultan of Zanzibar's sister had arrived in Muscat and settled into a neighboring house previously inhabited by Captain Atkins Hamerton, the British consul in the dominions of the Imam of Muscat, who had recently moved to Zanzibar. She had reportedly brought with her an enslaved Indian girl. Reuben debated what to do with the information he had received. Ought he to demand that the little girl's owners give her up? He decided in the end that "if she herself came to me," then he would plead the cause of her freedom, but if not, then "I should appear not to see it." But then the die was cast when the girl materialized in a public space—a street below Reuben's premises, the object of a transaction in the open market within Britain's official field of vision. Reuben accosted the broker, warning him that the sale of the girl would represent a flagrant violation of the terms of a treaty that Saïd had signed with the British government, prohibiting trade in Indian girls.[45]

As Reuben recounted the exchange, the broker countered, "This is a woman, and the sea is ignorant. What can I do?" Reuben offered to take charge of the girl in return for compensation, but to no avail. He was told that he could purchase her from a third party, to whom the child had already been sold. But the new owner pleaded religious integrity as grounds for his refusal to transfer his new "property" into non-Muslim hands: "we have taught her the prayers ... of the Mahomedan religion, and will not allow of her returning to heathens." British authorities then proceeded to address a volley of messages that escalated in tone from requests to commands to the sultan and his sons in Muscat, including an injunction against allowing any master to cohabit with a child who had not yet reached puberty. Eventually, Reuben extricated her from a chain of commercial transactions through the intervention of Sayyid Thuwaynī bin Sa'īd Āl Bū Sa'īd, the Muscat governor and a son of the sultan, at her purchase price of 65.5 reals.[46]

Once ensconced securely in Reuben's home, the girl proved eager to talk. Yet this was clearly not an easy choice for the young informant, for she begged the British agent not to tell on her, sensing "at present much ill feeling against her." She divulged that other Indian women and children were secreted away in Muscat sites belonging to powerful men: for instance, the Angreezah, a building belonging to the Imam himself. Or the home of Ali Durmukhee, the Vazir of Muscat. British entreaties, backed by the barely subtle threat of naval force, then began to land at the doors of Thuwaynī in Muscat and his father Saïd in Zanzibar. The imam was forced to send "peremptory orders" to Muscat for the release of the Indian women and children from the homes of the Vazir and the royal family. Thuwaynī expressed pique: "The letters have caused me much grief, for I always punish those who bring slaves [who are British subjects] to this country." He accused British officers like Hamerton of "making misrepresentations to Government regarding me." Hamerton, now based in Zanzibar, urged Bombay not to take the prince's displeasure too seriously: "His Highness always is distressed, feels hurt whenever I have anything relative to slavery to communicate to him."[47]

Meanwhile, it soon became clear why the other Indian women and children may not have welcomed their liberation at British hands with the same degree of enthusiasm as the eleven-year-old girl rescued by Reuben. Through the grapevine of official communications emerged the narrative that one of them may have contracted a "legal" marriage with Ali Durmukhee. Colonel Samuel Hennel, the British Indian Army officer who was serving as Political Resident in the Gulf, then conferred upon this woman the decisive voice in resolving the case. It was left to her to satisfy the commander of the cruiser consigned to bring the Indians "home" to Bombay, that she was "legally married" to Ali Doormukhi and that "she really prefers remaining with him to returning to her native land."[48] She may have been a "secondary" wife, and other records suggest that the Vazir himself may have died about the time of her "emancipation." Whatever her status, however, she preferred not to leave Oman or her master's home.

As it turned out, given a chance, the others in this group would have made the same choice. By the end of the monsoon season in 1844, the company brig *John Adam* had brought four of those "freed" from Muscat to Bombay, where they entered the custody of P.W. LeGeyt, senior magistrate of police. Before long, LeGeyt discovered that the two young women, Halima and Fatima, and two boys, Sadulla and Ghulam, seemed anxious to return to "captivity" in Muscat. He concluded that they all appeared "from long absence at the tender age from their native countries to have adopted the habits of the persons with whom they have off late associated."[49] The petitions they submitted expressing their wishes for their own futures stand as records of their role as mediators between Arab masters and British "liberators." Such roles, while enabled by the mission of imperial abolition, generated outcomes that questioned key assumptions about the benevolence of colonial emancipation.

Fatima's statement, sealed by a mark—presumably from her thumb, and accompanied by a bangle that belonged to her, was rendered in deferential language, addressing the magistrate who signed it as "Worshipful," identifying the petitioners as "emancipated slave girls," and describing the actions of the English "sirkar"(authorities) as "benevolent" and the petition itself as "humble." She and the other petitioners acknowledged that the government's agent had supplied them with "provision and clothing" during their stay in India, but pleaded that they "[found India] no comfortable place to live in for they do not speak the native language." They "earnestly pray[ed]" to be sent back to Muscat "where they will pass their lives freely and comfortably...." The colonial archives record actions by the young women that seem far less deferential than the language of their petitions suggested. LeGeyt noted that Halima, aged sixteen or seventeen years, "*obstinately* [our italics] refuses to enter the family of any stranger [in India] and implores that she may be sent back to Muscat." Halima said she hailed not from India at all, but from Turkish Arabia—a claim the police magistrate corroborated on the basis of her appearance. She had no recollection of her parents. As she told the story, when she was four, she was begging in the streets of her native town, when a man carried her away to Baghdad where he sold her to a Hindu merchant. Her owner brought her to Bombay "in a ship." Seven months later, an Arab belonging to the house of the Vazir of Muscat purchased her and brought her to Muscat, where she entered the Vazir's zenana. Two or three months before the British "rescued" her, the Vazir died, and she was transferred to the household of the son of the Sultan of Muscat. "From that house," her statement continued, "I was taken to that of the English agent, who wrote something, and put me on board a ship." She stated categorically that she did not wish to return to her country of birth: "My parents are dead and I know of no one there that would receive me." Back in Muscat, she had testified to a "native agent" retained by the British authorities that she had never been married, and that her master had "kept me in his harem with his other concubines," suggesting that her status was lower than that of a secondary wife. Nevertheless, she maintained, "I do not wish to remain in Bombay, I wish to be sent back to Muscat, where I could go to the house of Shaikh Saif, the brother of my late master; he would support me for the remainder of my life...."[50]

Like Halima, Fatima belonged to a household associated with the family of the Sultan of Zanzibar. Born to Hindu parents in the Indian countryside, she had been kidnapped and sold to a European clerk in Calcutta, "seduced" (read: raped) by the master, and resold by her enraged mistress to a slaver bound for Oman. The *nakhuda* of that vessel had in turn sold her to the mother of the Sultan of Muscat. Following three years of service in this royal household, Fatima was transferred to the custody of her mistress's brother. She testified that her new master "matched me with his slave Abdool Khair Nubie," whom she regarded as her husband. She also firmly rejected the option of repatriation to Calcutta, preferring to join her partner in Muscat instead, for "I was formerly a Hindoo, but am now a [Muslim]."[51]

The boys who had accompanied Halima and Fatima to Bombay recorded similar reactions to the option to embrace a version of "liberty" attached to colonial "belonging," namely rejection. Fourteen-year-old Sadulla recounted that he was a native of Hyderabad but could recall nothing of his parents. The name he did remember belonged to his kidnapper, Shaik Ali, who brought him to Bombay, instructing the boy that if asked, he must say that he was the kidnapper's son. Sadulla changed hands at least four times, the last of which led to his forced migration to Muscat. There he was sold to Amber Sultan, a servant in the household of the Imam of Muscat. It was Amber who in turn transferred him to the Vazir's household. When the Vazir died, the English agent had him moved from the home of his last master and sent him "on board a ship which conveyed me to Bombay." Sadulla too wished to return to Muscat. The other boy, Golam Hussein, only eleven years old, remembered that he had been born in Lucknow. While he had no recollection of his father, he remembered that his mother had died six years before. About the same time, a "Habshee" kidnapped him, carried him to Hyderabdad and thence to Bombay. He then placed the boy on a *baghla* and sailed to Muscat, where further transactions placed him in the Vazir's household. Following his master's death, an English agent sent him to Bombay. Like the other children, this boy preferred to return to Muscat.[52]

These women and children thus used the context that the colonial establishment's rhetoric of free will established, to negotiate the terms of their future in ways that defied imperial assumptions about the interconnectedness of liberty, Christianity, and western dominion.

ENSLAVED FUGITIVES

Colonial records also illuminate the ways in which structures of "benevolence" sometimes left room for figures on the margins to exercise different choices from those made by Fatima. Subalterns emerge as rebels and resisters, when they chafed at captivity and ill-treatment, were alienated from the dominant society, or when masters acted in ways that frayed the promise of patronage. Under such circumstances, those held in bondage registered their voices as arbitrators among the claims of figures more powerful than they—sultans, high officials, brokers, and imperial Residents and commanders.

A few years before Halima and Fatima petitioned against separation from their Omani masters, Moobarak (Mubarak), a seventeen-year-old African boy living in a Kutch town, decided to end his relationship with his owner's household. He walked out of its premises and into the Rajkot office of the British Political Agent of Kathiawar, James Erskine. Dressed in rags and bruised all over, he reported having been severely beaten by his Sindhi owner, who had bought the boy in Mandvi four years before. Mubarak used his deposition to indict rather than exonerate his master. He declared that he was originally an inhabitant of Africa, belonging to the "Mukwana" (possibly Makua) "caste," as the records classified his identity. He had been taken from his native land to Muscat, where he remained for a few years before traveling to Mandvi in the company of six other African males and three females under the custody of an Arab trader. The children were separated and sold to different parties in Mandvi. Mubarak changed hands a couple of times before he was sold to the Sindhi, apparently in exchange for a buffalo and dairy cow valued at 65 company rupees—estimated to be a low price for a slave compared with the average price of 100 rupees that an adult African in Kutch reportedly commanded. Mubarak testified that his master considered him neither a prized family member nor a particularly valuable investment: "I served my late master with fidelity but was ill-treated, starved, and severely beaten; and therefore being unable to suffer such bad treatment, I effected my escape and came to Rajcote." An Indian clerk in Erskine's office provided Mubarak with clothing, food, and ointment for his wounds and "assured him that he was entirely at liberty."[53]

Unfortunately, higher authorities in the colonial government were not so sure. They maintained that their laws did not outlaw slavery within the dominions of British India, much less autonomous princely states such as Kutch and Kathiawar. Fortunately for Mubarak, James Farish, who became governor of Bombay, countered that he was not aware of any regulation under which a magistrate within the jurisdiction of British courts could "interfere to punish a runaway slave or to compel him to return to his Master." Eventually, the Bombay government secured approval to authorize Erskine to buy Mubarak's freedom by paying his master the price he had paid for the boy, describing this resolution as a "special case."[54]

Mubarak had resorted to the most common form of resistance among slaves in India: running away, and he appeared to have counted on the colonial promise of freedom to effect it. The very presence of a colonial office in the region together with the dissemination of information through subaltern grapevines may have armed him with word of that promise. The formal institutions of colonial governance—a Political Residency office, a deposition—became tools to persuade the British to act on their professions of antislavery. The testimonies of captives assumed special importance, of course, when they were deemed victims of slave traders across international borders, within spaces of contention with the British Empire. In these instances, rescued children, by the very act of narrating their life stories as they remembered them, could become central figures in imperial prosecution cases against powerful local figures—including chiefs and wealthy merchants. For such cases turned on the identity of the captives. Were they slaves divorced from familial connections to their masters? Where were they sold? How many times were they sold? Were they "Negroes," "Abyssinians," "Somalis," or "Indians"? Such questions helped colonial authorities to determine whether the purchases of these witnesses violated the terms of existing treaties by transgressing proscribed boundaries of political jurisdictions, geographical limits, and nationalities or ethnicities.

Thus, in December 1841, African children aboard Arab vessels helped convict three men, among them Mirza Goolam Kuza, an agent of His Highness Meer Nasir Khan of Sind, in a trial before the Supreme Court of Judicature in Bombay, on a charge of slave trading. Four of the girls had emerged from hiding places in the hold of an Arab ship off the mouth of Bombay harbor. The vessel was on its way to Karachi when the British navy seized it. The captives rescued in this operation joined children seized from other Arab vessels and sailed to Bombay, where their temporary guardian Police Magistrate LeGeyt classified them as follows: "six of the girls are Abyssinians, a boy and a girl negroes, and one is a Hindoostani Mussalman [Indian Muslim] girl." The testimonies they bore against their captors dispatched Mirza to the house of corrections for three years and other defendants to Singapore for five years.[55]

In the long run, freedom flights of the sort effected by Mubarak and the Delhi refugees may have helped to shape Parliament's rather peculiar view of abolition in British India. As we have noted in this book's foregoing pages, instead of outlawing slavery outright, the ambiguity of servile statuses and conflicting claims to family and freedom may have served as a rationale for the imperial state's decision to merely "delegalize" slavery in India in 1843. This meant, among other things, that colonial bureaucrats reserved the right not to return fugitives from servitude to their masters.

Subaltern prisms unveil a complex mix of responses to imperial abolition. Such prisms are as multifarious as the Indian Ocean spaces within which they materialized. From the archives of colonial antitrafficking crusades—the patrols and police courts, and market squares and depositions by the "rescued"—to the palaces and memoirs stamped by the perspectives of more privileged "slaves," these spaces commemorate the diversity of slavery and the disparate status of "dependents" within IOW societies. To Atlantic correlations of freedom with liberal individualism (under colonial auspices, for empire builders), heterogeneous subaltern voices from the IOW added alternative visions of security, community, and hierarchy.

In the meantime, British action against Indian Ocean slave trading was about to draw American operators in that part of the world into a larger diplomatic controversy over abolition, imperialism, nationalism, and sovereignty. The clashes that ensued pitted New England merchants of slave-grown American cotton in East Africa against transatlantic abolitionists aligned with the goals of colonial antislavery. These transnational arguments over slavery, overlaying skeins of global capitalism that knit the Americas with the Indian Ocean world in the nineteenth century, would occasionally offer refugees additional contexts to negotiate the terms of their lives and work by mediating between warring powers from the North Atlantic. And so, our narrative now broadens beyond the courts, bazaars, and zenanas near the western Indian Ocean to take in the counting houses and consulates of American operatives in the region.

PART FOUR

Americans in Sultanates

8

Business, Sovereignty, and Fugitive Slaves

> *I am the slave of Captain __, of American bark* Laconia. *I was bought by him some six months ago from an American merchant in Johanna, who I used to work for at the sugar-mills. I did not wish to leave him, but was placed by force on board the* Laconia *by Captain __, where I was made to work against my will. I have worked in the ship for six months, and have not received any pay.*
> —M'CASSI, 1878

In the winter of 1851, Commodore John Aulick of the USS *Susquehanna* guided his steam-powered warship into Zanzibar harbor with guns blazing, at least metaphorically. Aulick was on a mission to uphold the twin causes of slavery and American nationalism on behalf of Millard Fillmore's State Department. New England merchants who supplied slave-grown American cotton to African consumers on the Swahili coast had complained about Sayyid Saʿīd ibn Sulṭān's deference to British measures against slave trading in the region. These regulations targeted predominantly Kutch-based Gujarati-speaking merchants, brokers, and creditors who served as the principal agents through whom the Americans conducted their business in East Africa, threatening American loans that remained to be repaid and contracts that were yet to be fulfilled. The slavery controversy drew the Salem sojourners into contests over the question of the nationality of so-called Indian merchants in Zanzibar and elsewhere in the western Indian Ocean. Secretary of State Daniel Webster agreed with his fellow New Englanders that the Baniyans were subjects of Zanzibar rather than the British Empire, and hence immune to the dictates of imperial abolition. The sultan's failure to endorse this position may have had something to do with pugnacious US Consul Charles Ward's umbrage over the ruler's failure to pay public tribute to the American flag flying over the consulate on July 4, 1850. The *Susquehanna* sailed to demonstrate American power and material prowess in the face of these slights to national honor and the corporate purse.[1]

Fortunately, no hostilities followed. But the issues at the heart of the warship's East African cruise pointed up complex clashes of interest that placed Indian merchants, an Arab sultan, and enslaved Africans at the center of Anglo-American clashes over slavery, imperialism, and nationalism in the western Indian Ocean. These issues intersected with the larger controversy over imperial abolition in the nineteenth century. That debate would pit some New England merchants purveying slave-grown American cotton in East Africa through the medium of slave-trading Gujarati-speaking business partners, against transatlantic abolitionists aligned with the goals of colonial antislavery, and later with an officially antislavery post–Civil War Washington.

INTEROCEANIC INTERWEAVINGS

New England's commercial interests in Zanzibar blossomed in the 1820s, spinning off of early trade contacts with Madagascar and later with the Indian Ocean islands of Mauritius and Réunion. North Americans had, of course, interfaced with the western Indian Ocean world for centuries through the medium of the transoceanic slave trade, transporting captives to the Americas during the seventeenth and eighteenth centuries from locales like Madagascar.

Let us digress for a moment to take a brief measure of this US-borne commerce in East African chattel. When our story opens in the early nineteenth century, we behold American investors and shippers shifting the principal sources of their East African captive supplies to Mozambique and Quelimane south of the equator, where an 1810 Anglo-Portuguese treaty preserved the legality of this traffic in human chattel. Following the abolition of the Atlantic slave trade effective January 1808, a sovereignty-conscious United States protected ships flying under its flag from British surveillance. During the nineteenth century's first decade, at least thirty voyages undertaken to the western IOW under US colors transported captives to places as disparate as Charleston, Louisiana, Montevideo, Havana, Buenos Aires, and the Cape of Good Hope. The vast majority of these (twenty-four of the voyages) purchased their human chattel at Mozambique (table 1). The largest number (eleven) disembarked those who survived in Montevideo, which emerged as the major slave entrepôt of the Río de la Plata Viceroyalty when Bourbon Spain opened the port to traders of all nationalities in an attempt to shore up colonial prosperity (table 2). Until the abolition of the slave trade in the province in 1812, Montevideo merchants in trans-imperial networks with Luso-Brazilian, Portuguese, and North American operators exchanged Potosí silver for Gujarati hand looms—a common medium of exchange that could be used to buy ivory and slaves inland from Mozambique. These transactions wove three continents into a web of complicity in the transoceanic slave trade.[2]

TABLE 1 Transoceanic Slave Trade to the Americas: Principal Places of Purchase by Slaving Ships Sailing under the US Flag in the Western Indian Ocean, 1800–1869

Voyage Year	Place of Purchase		
	Mozambique	Quelimane	Zanzibar/Kilwa
1800–1808	24	4	2
1809–1819			
1820–1829			
1830–1839			
1840–1849		1	
1850–1859	3	2	
1860–1869			

Patrick Harries tells the story of the Irishman Michael Hogan, who, following careers in the Royal Navy and the East India Company, joined hands with the Mozambique-based trader Joaquium do Rosario Monteiro of Goa (India). When Europeans resumed war in 1803, these men—both married to women from India's west coast—traded slaves from Mozambique to the neutral port of Charleston, South Carolina, via the reprovisioning station of Cape Town.[3] Other IOW-bound slave ships were registered in and/or sailed from US ports across free and slave states in the first decade of the nineteenth century. For instance, *Oneida*, registered at Newport, sailed from Rhode Island in June 1804, picked up 286 slaves in Mozambique, landing the 239 who survived in Havana following a voyage lasting 221 days. Two years later, a vessel named *Active* traveled from Philadelphia to Zanzibar and sold 83 captives in Montevideo after sixty-five days and eight captive deaths at sea. The same year, *Juliana*, registered in New York, sailed from Boston and picked up 146 slaves in Mozambique for sale in Montevideo. The same year that the US Congress abolished the foreign slave trade, the Charleston-registered *Agent* disembarked 135 of the 180 chattel who had survived the eighty-five-day Middle Passage from Mozambique in Louisiana. US-owned ships sailed from Europe as well—as in the case of the brig *Minerva*, which set forth in July 1803 from Bristol, picked up captives at Cape Coast Castle, and proceeded via the Cape of Good Hope to Quelimane, where it made the bulk of its purchase of human chattel. Of the 205 enslaved who embarked on this voyage, 160 made it to the Americas, where they were sold principally in Havana in February 1804. A few ships were waylaid by privateers, such as the *Horizon* of Charleston, which hired Hogan as an agent during a Cape Town stopover. This vessel apparently managed to land in South Carolina only 243 of the 543 captives it had picked up, principally in Mozambique. Others disposed of their human chattel at numerous stops. The *Almanac*, which began

TABLE 2 Transoceanic Slave Trade to the Americas: Principal Places of Disembarkation of Western Indian Ocean Captives Traveling on US ships, 1800–1869

Voyage Year	Principal Place of Disembarkation							
	Montevideo	Havana/Elsewhere in Cuba	Charleston	Buenos Aires	Rio de Janeiro	Louisiana	Cárdenas	Cabo Frio	Cape of Good Hope/Other
1800–1808	11	6	4	3		1		1	4
1809–1819									
1820–1829									
1830–1839								1	
1840–1849									
1850–1859		2			2		1		
1860–1869									

its voyage in Rhode Island in April 1800, sold 25 of the 368 enslaved it had purchased at Quelimane, at the Cape of Good Hope, disposing of the remaining 320 survivors at Montevideo.[4]

When Brazil shuttered its market to the international slave trade in the 1850s, Portuguese smugglers and their US accomplices set up shop in Lower Manhattan's mercantile, shipping, and financial districts, breathing new life into the business, according to John Harris. New York and New Orleans emerged as "key nodes in a new slaving nexus that stretched from Ouidah and Cabinda in Africa to Havana and Matanzas in Cuba."[5] East Africa registered a minor presence in this momentum. The 1850s traffic was distinguished from that of earlier eras by the ships' departure points (often Cuba), the much larger size of human cargoes (no doubt to offset the risks of this illegal trade), the greater probability of thwarted slaver plans, and higher mortality rates compared with the 18.4 percent estimated on routes from East Africa to the Americas for 1800–75 overall. One American ship that sailed from Marseille in 1859, for instance, is recorded as having managed to land in Cárdenas, Cuba, only 70 of the 1068 captives it had purchased in Mozambique. Another brig, *Camargo,* which made a round trip from Rio de Janeiro to Quelimane in 1852, was shipwrecked after disembarkation. The bark *Minnetonka,* which began its voyage in Havana, lost 37 percent of the 970 enslaved it purchased in Mozambique. The *Lady Eclipse,* which left Bahia Honda, Cuba, for Mozambique in 1852, did manage to transport 1283 out of the 1487 captives it had acquired. Some American sailors who joined the large multinational crews on these slavers had started their careers as whalers in the Indian Ocean. Nor were their captives limited to the western IOW. One destitute seaman named Jack, who had deserted from an "English Merchantman," was recruited on a Bombay beach by a shipping agent to participate in a venture—without his foreknowledge—to smuggle "contraband coolies" from the Straits of Malacca to Jamaica.[6]

All in all, only about 7 percent of human chattel transported from Africa on ships flying under the US flag in our sample originated in the western IOW during the period 1800–75. They voyaged for two months on average, and their demographic profile differed from those bound for the Middle East and South Asia by the predominance of adult men within their ranks (73%). Leaving other chroniclers to flesh out this chapter of the international slave trade in greater detail, let us return to the lands from which our captives were torn, to the IOW, which American merchants and slaveholders were endeavoring to make the theater of their operations.

* * *

Following the 1812 War, competition from New York merchants in commercial hot spots across Asia and Europe drove Salemites to seek opportunities outside established trade routes.[7] A New Hampshire merchant named Edmund Roberts, who had gleaned word of Zanzibar's business potential during a trip to Bombay, secured the support of his state senator, Levi Woodbury, to negotiate a treaty with the Sultan of Muscat and Zanzibar in 1833. The agreement conferred "most favored nation" status upon the United States, granting its nationals the right of free trade in all the ports under the sultan's jurisdiction, subject only to the requirement that they pay a 5 percent import duty on all goods brought into his dominions. There followed, in 1837, the establishment of a consulate presided over for much of the nineteenth century by agents of New England mercantile houses, with a few exceptions—notably during the US Civil War. Persuaded that Americans did not harbor the imperialistic designs of European nations in the neighborhood, Saʿīd shared warm relations with these predominantly business figures, who received a token salary, earning their real remuneration through trade.[8]

The first consul, Richard P. Waters, selected by Salem merchants to represent their interests, quickly figured out upon his arrival where the real power in Zanzibar lay. As Lieutenant W. Christopher of the British Brig of War *Tigris* observed on a visit to Zanzibar a few years later, the most significant bureaucrat in the Imam's employ was Jairam Shivji, "a Banian [sic]" who had inherited his position at the helm of the sultanate's customs establishment from his father. The sultan farmed out that sinecure to Shivji for an annual fee of 150,000 dollars on a three-year contract. Shivji was said to maintain a coast guard backed by 150 paid "matchlock Arabs" and to exercise "more authority in many places than the Imam himself."[9] The Baniyan supplied the Imam with cash and goods, which the ruler balanced against the annual rent every three or four years. The cash-strapped sultan relied on the customs master to fund his military expeditions against rivals and rebels in Arabia and East Africa. No wonder, then, that Waters found the sultan distinctly reluctant to intervene on his behalf when he ran into difficulties with Shivji during his early days in Zanzibar.

Those troubles, however, soon gave way to a long and lucrative phase of *rapprochement* between the American and the Kacchi. The Salem-based firms that Waters represented merchandized unbleached calicos made from slave-grown cotton (known as *merekani* in Swahili) to East Africans. With India's textile industry under siege from cheaper British machine-made manufactures, *merekani*—whether embellished for African elites or made into burial or sail cloths—had become all the rage in the East African interior by the early 1840s. On the other hand, coastal customers, according to Jeremy Prestholdt, coveted "furniture, clocks and agricultural goods."[10] In exchange, Africans exported hides and gum copal (a resin used on varnishes) to furnish New England's leather and furniture industries. As per Abdul Sheriff, from the 1820s western consumers had developed a preference for East African "soft" ivory over the hard variety that West Africa produced. Such ivory, more readily turned into "combs, piano keys and billard balls" initially traveled to the North Atlantic via Bombay. But then Salem merchants, who had been trading hides at Madagascar to furnish Salem's tanning industry, established a direct line to the ivory trade through their collaboration with Indian merchants in Zanzibar. Katherine Frederick has noted that by the early 1840s, American merchants bartered munitions that were exchanged in Kilwa for slaves to work Zanzibar's plantations. Africans, as Prestholdt has illustrated, were discerning consumers, with varying tastes in the tint and texture of cloth, gauges of beads, and types of musket.[11]

The Bhatia customs master Shivji mediated these exchanges. Americans frequently lacked the language skills to do business in East Africa. The captain of one ship that stopped in Portuguese territories to the south, for instance, had to rely on two intermediaries to communicate with the local customs collector, Miguel C. Pinto. Pinto relayed a message intended for the American in Portuguese to a clerk in his office, who translated it into Swahili for the captain's American supercargo, Ephraim A. Emerton. Emerton, who had learned that language in Zanzibar, then rendered the missive in English for the captain.[12] Besides, the Americans' perception of the dangers on the East African mainland—of a formidable climate and "treacherous" natives—drew Waters into a close alliance with the customs master.[13] The two established what critics charged was a monopoly to funnel Zanzibar's trade through their hands. Waters consulted Shivji on the composition of inbound and outbound cargoes, and arranged through the customs czar to present samples to local merchants and fix their prices. He had the captains of the ships with which he had contracted to do business deliver their wares to Shivji's offices, whence they were distributed to middlemen on credit. Indian brokers put together cargoes that combined Lowell cottons together with "Muskets, Powder, Brass Wire and piece India goods." Caravans laden with these cargoes headed for the mainland, where traders used porters—including enslaved ones—to transport ivory to the coast, selling these captives together with their valuable burdens. Lieutenant Christopher reported that the "very ivory is carried down on the shoulder of a naked slave who is frequently sold with his burthurn [sic] to Banians residing permanently on the coast immediately opposite [the island of Zanzibar]."[14] In 1847, US Consul Charles Ward estimated that as many as ten to fifteen thousand slaves entered Zanzibar annually. Credit networks—inextricably linking American cottons with African ivory and slaves—bound Kacchi fortunes with those of the Americans.[15]

By the 1840s, New England merchants had emerged as the dominant Atlantic trading interests in Zanzibar. Ships from Salem and Boston made several stops along the way. In the late spring and early summer of 1843, the *Richmond,* for instance, sailed for ninety-five days before reaching the Portuguese port of Delgoa Bay, "a few hundred miles to the northward of Port Natal"; spent several days exchanging cottons and weapons at Quelimane for "ivory, sea horse tusk and tortoise shell"; and headed to Majunga on the coast of Madagascar. But failing to secure permission to trade there, the brig crossed the Mozambique channel to Mozambique, landed some cargo there, picked up more ivory, and sailed to the Querimba Islands north of

Mozambique to load up on gum copal. Then began the voyage to Zanzibar. During the approximately seven months the crew spent there, the captain rented a house on the shore and had his ship's steward cook for him while he transacted business with local merchants.[16] At mid century, one US consul estimated American trade to Zanzibar to be worth approximately one million dollars, with Africans consuming an annual average of six hundred bales of cotton textiles, brought to the island aboard ten to twelve ships of 250 tons each, on voyages that usually lasted a year and included stops at ports on the Red Sea and the Gulf.[17]

The Americans' business alliances with their Baniyan partners drew them into controversies over the politics of slavery in East Africa—controversies that intersected with questions of the nationality of so-called Indian merchants in the western Indian Ocean. For British bureaucrats in the early 1840s, antislavery measures targeting South Asian merchants whom they claimed as subjects presented a way of killing a few birds with one stone: shore up the moral capital of imperialism, uphold free trade on their own terms, and safeguard the interests of British merchants. From the American mercantile perspective, the suppression of the Indian Ocean slave trade smacked of imperial overreach, attended by fraud and abuse that threatened their own business interests.

AMERICANS AND THE CONTROVERSY OVER SLAVERY, SOVEREIGNTY, AND NATIONALITY

In the early months of 1842, Atkins Hamerton, the British agent in Muscat who also shuttled to Zanzibar as Her Majesty's first consul there, poured out his frustrations with Richard Waters, the American consul-cum–ship broker operating in that thriving entrepôt of trade off Africa's east coast. In a report to his government, Hamerton charged that Waters had instigated the sultan to summon to his court "principal native merchants" who were of Indian descent, and "required them to sign a declaration [apparently crafted by Shivji] to the effect that they no longer considered themselves British subjects, but of their own free will [had become] citizens of the city of Zanzibar." Hamerton claimed that a majority of those in attendance refused because of their family and property ties in British India.[18]

Waters initially represented the two firms of Bertram-Shepard and Pingree-West, as well as all American ships visiting Zanzibar. After 1840, he accepted a partnership in the Pingree-West interest and broadened his transactions with Indian and Arab merchants and plantation owners beyond Shivji, amassing a tidy sum of 80,000 to 100,000 dollars before he returned to Salem over seven years later. After the mid 1840s, merchants from Boston, New York, and Providence joined the commercial scene in Zanzibar, maintaining a cozy relationship with Shivji and even naming a ship after him. Indian merchant capital financed loans to American groups that by the 1860s had reached 600,000 dollars.[19]

This capital was, of course, intricately bound with Kacchi investments in slavery, whether directly or indirectly. The omnipotent Shivji reportedly owned two hundred slaves who labored on plantations, raised fruits and vegetables, and served as porters. Hideaki Suzuki has concluded, on the basis of an analysis of the British Consul Christopher Rigby's records of 5221 Kacchi-held slaves compiled in 1860–61, that the size of slaveholding among Indians varied considerably. The then customs master Ladha Damji held 455, but 96 percent of this slaveholding population owned fewer than twenty-five, and over 31 percent could claim just one bondsperson each. Over one-third of the people that Ribgy freed apparently worked in domestic service in town, while the rest labored on plantations.[20] When Horace Putnam, a shipmaster and future mayor of Manchester, New Hampshire, visited Zanzibar in 1847, he saw slaves working amid a few dozen overseers and soldiers around the thatch-covered shed which passed for "Custom House," carrying massive burdens: "A bale of cotton weighing two hundred and over is no task for them."[21]

Americans in Zanzibar hired slaves to perform domestic labor in their households. American Consul Daniel H. Mansfield reported in 1856 that "negro Slaves are almost the only common laborers." American businesses employed them on hire "to clean gum copal or orchilla weed and prepare copra." These bondspeople, like enslaved professional porters and artisans, earned 12.5 cents per day or $2.50 to $3 per month, while the "higher order of Servants" overseeing the preparation and shipping of cargoes received monthly wages of $7.50 to $10. Slaves who hired out their time shared their earnings with their masters.[22] During Waters's time in Zanzibar, Shivji frequently shared with him intelligence on slave market trends. In October 1842, for instance, the Kacchi informed the American that slaves were plentiful and cheap, going for $7 each. In Zanzibar, each would fetch between $14 and $25, with women selling for more that year because fewer had been brought to the coast. Shivji estimated that every day a hundred slaves changed hands at the Zanzibar market. Waters noted that within the past few weeks, "His Highness has [about] seven hundred slaves ... put on a sugar plantation which he is preparing."[23]

American narratives of nineteenth-century Zanzibar departed from the reports of British naval officers, bureaucrats, and missionaries in their attitudes toward slavery. While not openly critical of abolition as some of his successors would turn out to be, Waters's journals focused on the beauty of Zanzibar's clove plantations, redolent of "spicy breezes" rather than on the misery of the labor system that produced them. One Tuesday in August 1837, the consul accompanied one of the princes on a visit to the sultan's plantations "about six miles out in the country." Following breakfast, during which the American drank fine coffee in gold cups, the men mounted their "first rate Arabian" horses at 7 am, before the heat set in, and set out for Saʿīd's country seat. A guard of sixteen soldiers clad in "red coats and white pantaloons" led the way. Ninety minutes later, they had reached what Waters described as a "most delightful place." The one-storied stone house, plastered and white-washed, stood atop a tall hill overlooking the surrounding country. Whereas British naval officers tended to focus on the horrors of the slave market in Zanzibar, Waters gushed over the spectacle of the staple crop plantations it generated: "One of the most beautiful sights I ever beheld was the extended plantation of Clove trees. His Highness has *two hundred thousand* on this plantation. They are set out in rows of a mile or more, in length, and about 20 feet apart. The tree grows to about 20 feet in [height] and it is of a most beautiful green." He also saw coffee and nutmeg trees and large quantities of cloves drying in the sun before they were packed into bags for the market.[24]

British bureaucrats and commanders felt differently. When Hamerton arrived in Zanzibar in 1841, he found not only that Waters's firm enjoyed special favors through the slaveholding Shivji's offices, but also that Salem's privilege had translated into American political influence in the sultan's court. Hamerton complained that local merchants were "detained at the customs house, and had to sell to those the monopolists dictated.... American vessels in want of cargo were supplied in preference to others."[25] The British consul also discovered with consternation that two paintings hanging in the Imam's Zanzibar *darbar* (audience hall) depicted American defeat of British naval forces, with the "English Ensign ... being hauled down and the American hoisted...."[26] There followed negotiations aimed at persuading the sultan to uphold both the trade rights of British subjects and the cause of slave trade abolition in exchange for British help in securing to him the island of Bahrain. Higher authorities in the imperial establishment did not, however, go along with this bargain, suggesting fault lines in colonial strategies of engagement.[27]

For British bureaucrats and naval commanders, the path to the dual goals of safeguarding British business interests and achieving slavery's abolition in the western Indian Ocean lay through imperial regulation of transnational mercantile populations they deemed their "Indian" subjects. Sketching racialized portraits that vested Gujaratis with commercial virtues that Arabs supposedly lacked, Lieutenant Christopher argued, "The Indian merchants are the capitalists of Zanzibar; if they were bona fide to withdraw from the slave market, the number purchased would be lessened one half in a few years." He maintained that "Arabs of the present day," allegedly deficient in the "enterprise, the painstaking and plodding habits and intelligence of the Indians," as well as the "integrity which the Banians from their ... unwarlike disposition ... have been obliged of old to evince in their commercial dealings," would not be able to sustain the traffic in humans on their own.[28]

Accordingly, the British passed a series of laws targeting slave ownership and trading by South Asians, fueling controversies over these merchants' nationality. While the British claimed them as subjects on account of their cultural and historical affiliations with regions within British spheres of influence on the Indian subcontinent, Americans preferred to deal with them as nationals of Zanzibar. The sultan found himself in a delicate position, caught between the practical need to supplicate the British while defending the jealously guarded claims to slaveholding of mercantile communities within his realm. Hamerton's correspondence to his superiors in Bombay hinted at these tensions. In April 1851, he commended Saʿīd for taking pains to prevent the export of slaves from Zanzibar by shutting down the slave market until "the northern Arabs have left Zanzibar" but noted that such measures had elicited stringent opposition from the sultan's slaveholding subjects.[29] Meanwhile, this British agent's antislavery measures on the ground blurred distinctions between colonial subjects under direct British rule and citizens of "protected (or tributary) states" in South Asia, threatening American business interests directly. When Hamerton persuaded Saʿīd to forbid Zanzibar nationals from buying or selling slaves to Indian-descended operatives who held mortgages of slave-worked plantations, Americans prophesied a wave of bankruptcies on the island.[30]

US Consul Ward wrote the merchant Michael Shepard back in New England that the sultan's [British-instigated] edict forbidding the "Banyans ... from trading in slaves at Kilwa" raised the specter of mayhem in Zanzibar's business world. Those merchants who had already dispatched trade goods to Kilwa for exchange begged for a lag in enforcement so as to give them an opportunity to "dispose of their Goods on the coast, & to close up their business.... They told the Sultan that they were largely [indebted] to the Americans for Goods &c...."[31] Ward explained to another business associate that "The people from the interior of Africa use Slaves to bring ivory to the coast, and will not sell one without the other. And as soon as they hear that Slaves cannot be sold it is the custom of the first comers to return and report to the other caravans on the road and they generally bury the Ivory in the ground, and return to their own country...."[32] In 1850, the British navy razed to the ground alleged "barracoons" owned by Gujaratis around Cape Delgado, which turned out to warehouse "legitimate" commodities rather than slaves. Powerful members of that community went to jail. Shivji's anti-British brother Ebji reportedly suffered losses amounting to no less than MT$50,000.[33] Reporting on the incident, Ward complained that the English ship of war *Castor* had arrested Baniyans in Portuguese territories and burned down $7000 worth of good belonging to a Zanzibar-based merchant, imprisoning him "without examination." He wrote that agents of Indian descent, no matter what their business, now hesitated to trade at Kilwa for fear that the same British commodore would falsely implicate them in slave dealing through the medium of lying interpreters.[34] These predominantly Kacchi merchants had long grown accustomed to the same protections and privileges as the "Sultan's own subjects," and their sudden loss of "security for trade and property in Zanzibar" would force them to close their businesses there, jeopardizing the $120,000 worth of American cargoes they held in trust. He claimed that these merchants, having "the highest confidence in the Americans" had pleaded with him to intercede with the sultan on their behalf.[35]

Ward maintained that so-called British Indian nationals in Zanzibar were in fact "subjects of the [Kutch] Sovereign" and carried papers from the Rao's realm. "The King of Cutch" was under "the protection of the East India Company & not of the British Government." The American reported that the Kacchi ruler had merely undertaken to pay the British company a portion of his revenues in exchange for defense against potential invaders like the Afghans, and that he was in all other respects an independent sovereign. If his merchants who did "nearly all the business of Zanzibar and on all the coast" were to "fall into the hands of the British Consul," that bureaucrat would be "possessed of more power than the Sultan himself." He suspected that the sultan owed his deference to the British position on the Kacchis' nationality to his fear of "Britain's grasping policy in India" and its "designs upon his continental possessions." Ward's apprehensions about this state of affairs stemmed not only from the difficulties that British antislave trade measures would pose for the disposal of American goods in the African mainland but also from his lack of confidence in the aptitude of the British consul ("not a businessman") to arbitrate in commercial disputes with the Baniyans, who were known to "keep their books" in opaque fashion.[36]

It was in this context of a crisis of business confidence that jeopardized the flow of American exports to African consumers and threatened default on American loans that Secretary of State Daniel Webster sent the *Susquehanna* to the Indian Ocean. Ward, who betrayed more race prejudice than some other New Englanders in East Africa, wrote that there was "nothing so convincing to Mohamedans and Asiatics as a display of physical force."[37] The dust settled with the arrival of a new consul, John F. Webb, who renounced any claim to interfere with the Sa'īd's antislave trade edict. He banded with other mercantile interests in Zanzibar to assure Commodore Aulick that Ward's belligerence toward the sultan was rooted in a communication gap, and that American interests remained unharmed.[38]

Meanwhile, Consul Hamerton urged his own government to bring the "protected states" in India explicitly under the purview of antislavery legislation.[39] Not until the Civil War would Washington's policy on slavery in East Africa align with the intent and purposes of British imperial abolition. But such alignment would occasionally pit the interests of American merchants and consuls against the mandates of their own government.

DURING THE US CIVIL WAR AND RECONSTRUCTION: SLAVEHOLDING IN THE IOW

As Americans went to war over the Union and slavery in the months following South Carolina's secession, William Webb, now US consul in Zanzibar, adopted an attitude of studied neutrality on the British campaign against the slave trade.[40] But when the question of imperial abolition and Kacchi nationality flared again, it presaged a parting of ways between the US government and New Englanders in Zanzibar. Christopher Rigby, who had arrived in Zanzibar as consul in 1858 following stints in the Indian army, took radical steps to manumit the slaves of masters he deemed subjects of British India. He issued a notice giving British subjects a month to emancipate their slaves, and he prevailed upon Sultan Majid, who had succeeded his father Sa'īd, to prohibit his subjects from trading in slaves with Indians.[41] Webb disapproved. A month after the firing on Fort Sumter, he wrote Washington, "The strong measures taken by the English government to suppress the slave trade are very injurious to business, and as slavery among the Arabs is merely a name, their slaves being treated like members of their family, these proceedings seem unnecessary."[42] The American representative had earlier sought instructions on how to deal with British seizures of slavers operating in the Indian Ocean under American colors, one of which was found to carry 846 captives. What sort of proof might serve as grounds for condemning vessels seized by British cruisers? Which party had the right to claim such ships as a prize since there were "no American vessels of war on this coast"?[43]

In the early days of the Civil War, Sultan Majid addressed pleas to a sympathetic US Consulate that British actions against the slave trade were both illegal and provided cover for indiscriminate plunder. Webb contended that strong evidence pointed to such abuse, throwing in racist observations about why Africans were unequal to the task of resisting unlawful incursions against their legitimate trade. "His Highness" had complained to him that two English armored boats had entered the port of Tanga, which lay within Zanzibar's jurisdiction, "fired upon two dhows at anchor there and loaded ready for sea and bound [to Zanzibar]—their cargo consisting of orchilla weed, cocoa nut, etc. The captain and crew being ignorant blacks were alarmed and jumped on shore (the dhows in that port anchor close to the bank). The crews from the boats got on board, cut the cables, took the larger one a short distance outside and set her on fire; from the smaller one they threw out the orchilla weed into the sea and took her to sea with them." The cargoes belonged to a French citizen. The aggressors furnished no reason for their action, nor could it be justified in terms of "the English treaty with His Highness for the suppression of the slave trade" because that trade was permitted within the limits of the area in which the dhows were seized. Webb believed that such "outrages" threatened mercantile interests in Zanzibar, which its ruler was too weak to protect.[44]

Official US policy during and after the Civil War, however, came to be aligned with the stated mission of British imperial abolition, opening up a chasm between Washington and its citizens and consuls over slavery in the Indian Ocean. The Lincoln administration replaced Consul Webb with the Tennessee antislavery Whig William S. Speer. All consular officials now had to take an oath of allegiance to the Union.[45] Moreover, anxious to establish its moral authority in relation to the

Confederacy in the British public sphere, the Lincoln administration authorized Secretary of State William Seward to conclude a treaty for the suppression of the African slave trade with the British envoy to the United States, Lord Lyons, in April 1862. The agreement conferred the reciprocal right to search and detain merchant cruisers suspected of engaging in trafficking slaves due to tell-tale signs: hatches with open gratings, a suspiciously large number of bulkheads in the hold or on deck, spare plank fitted for laying down as a second or slave deck, shackles, bolts, or handcuffs, great quantities of water in casks, large boilers for cooking, an "extraordinary quantity of rice, of the flour of Brazil, of maniac ... commonly called farinha, of maize ... beyond the probable wants of the crew;" and more matting than a merchant vessel crew was likely to need for its own use. The compact established mixed commission courts in Sierra Leone, Cape Town, and New York to adjudicate cases. The original terms of the Lyons-Seward treaty, as it became known, targeted the slave trade to Cuba, limiting searches to the vicinity of that Caribbean island and within two hundred miles of the coast of Africa.[46]

Henry Brougham, the only veteran of the 1807 campaign against the international slave trade still alive during the Civil War, hailed the treaty in the House of Lords as the most important landmark in "his 60 years of warfare against the African Slave Trade" and suggested that the field of search be extended to other parts of the world. An additional article to the treaty, signed and sealed in April 1863, did just that, bringing the waters of the Indian Ocean around Madagascar—in addition to Puerto Rico—within the orbit of these regulations.[47]

A few months after the conclusion of the Lyons-Seward treaty, William Speer arrived in Zanzibar on the bark *Sea Ranger* via Mozambique, where Governor General Joao Tavares de Almeida had received him graciously, professing support for the Union cause.[48] Speer visualized his role differently from his mercantile predecessors, drawing a distinction between diplomacy and commerce. He claimed that the sultan had described previous US representatives in his kingdom dismissively, as "half trader, half consul." In order to redress the lack of information about Zanzibar in the United States, the Tennessee native compiled a detailed "Report on Zanzibar," which included a section on slavery. Speer touched on the customs duties the enslaved commanded ("$2 per head without regard to age, sex, or value"); the extent of the trade ("about 500 slaves per week" entered the Zanzibar market); and the work they did (carrying stones from quarries for building purposes, farming, domestic work, concubinage). There were differences with American slavery: "slaves frequently own slaves." Moreover, slaves could work for themselves two days of the week, Thursday and Friday, and if their master were a Baniyan, they had four days to themselves: "that is a sort of English nominal slavery." Like many antislavery Unionists, Speer combined anti-Black racism with his distaste for slavery, peppering his missives with the N-word: he had observed "slave girls" fanning their "beautiful young Arab mistresses," but "I saw no one fan the n———r."[49]

Whatever Speer's personal opinions of New England merchant-consuls who had gone before him, he shared with many of them a warm regard for the sultan and deep suspicion of the British campaign against the slave trade. From his perspective of exile from a war-torn nation, Zanzibar was "a city of peace" troubled only by British "plunderers of the East" and their monopolistic subjects, the Baniyans. English cruisers demanded that Arab dhows carry European-style papers, and they intercepted legitimate traders indiscriminately, motivated by greed for bonuses amounting to "five pounds sterling per head for all recaptured slaves." Speer doubted the sincerity of British benevolence: "Last year [the British] captured nearly 1000, some of them they took to the Cape, some to Seychelles, but in every case the n__r is apprenticed for a term of years sufficient to repay for British beneficence, which is equivalent to an *indefinite hopeless servitude in exile* [his emphasis]." He urged the United States to protest against the "high handed outrages" perpetrated against the sultan's subjects by English cruisers and mariners.[50]

As for the sultan's "thousands of slaves," Speer described them as a "comparatively free ... sort of tenants." He reported that "His Majesty [had] remarked bitterly" to the American "upon [British abolitionist] proceedings." When the consul ventured, "we have trouble in the States on account of the slaves," Majid "replied quickly, 'Slaves in a State are like rats in a house—very troublesome and ... hard to be got rid of.'"[51] Still, the sultan was said to harbor strong sympathies for the Union, and marked President Lincoln's assassination by ordering the firing of guns, "one for each year of his age." Flags in Zanzibar flew at half mast for three days.[52]

Even as the United States entered its own era of Radical Reconstruction to experiment briefly with racial democracy, a Conservative interregnum in London that punctuated the reign of the antislavery Liberal Party put IOW slave trade regulation in retreat. In 1867–68, slaveholding was about to emerge as a litmus test for nationality rather than the other way around. In December 1867, the political agent and her majesty's consul in Zanzibar wrote the Bombay government that following Colonel Rigby's liberation of a large number of slaves held by "British Indian subjects"—with the approval of the Government of India—such subjects continued to hold more than twelve hundred slaves under the protection of "His Highness, Syed Majid." Moreover, Baniyans under British protection were reported to circumvent laws against domestic slavery in their native land by claiming that their slaves belonged to a brother or uncle under the sultan's protection. Rigby's successors had apparently facilitated these subterfuges by requiring subjects of protected Indian states to register for British protection in foreign territory, presumably giving those who did not apply for such protection the "freedom" to hold slaves.

This path contradicted a ruling issued in 1856 by the Government of India that conferred upon subjects of native states like Kutch, which had surrendered charge of diplomacy to the British, a "moral" right to the same protection abroad that other British subjects enjoyed. Were such subjects then not bound to respect British antislavery laws? The Agent believed so, and protested the slaveholding practices of Kacchis to the sultan.[53]

Sultan Majid, less accommodating of British antislavery pressures than his father, disagreed. He maintained that Rigby's successors had deemed Kacchis who declined British protection the same as "His Highness's Arab subjects. His Highness had allowed them to purchase slaves, and ... it was not fair now to punish them for what they had done innocently...."[54] The Zanzibar ruler recalled that his father Saʿīd had secured from Colonel Hamerton a two-year delay in the implementation of an order requiring all natives of India in his dominions to free their slaves. Before the two years elapsed, both Saʿīd and Hamerton died, leaving Rigby to execute the understanding the two men had reached. But Rigby's successors had respected the British Crown's jurisdictional limitations, calling upon subjects of protected Indian states to register for British protection. The sultan understood them to have established the principle that Indians who did not register for such protection had "assimilated" to the status of Arabs, subject to the sultan's jurisdiction, and armed with the "liberty" to buy slaves. Moreover, there were "many natives of India in our service.... Many of these, although of Indian parentage, are born in the country, some of them as far back as fifty years ago, and we look upon them and their children as our subjects, the Arabs."[55]

The sultan's appeal to historical ties of culture and economic engagement, grounded organically in the arrangements of a precolonial IOW that transcended the intricacies of imperial law, dovetailed with the Government of India's cautious approach to slave trade abolition in the 1860s. Questions of sovereignty and nationality in the larger IOW resuscitated distinctions between "trafficking" and domestic servants. Colonial legal authorities asked not only whether the natives of Kutch who trafficked in slaves at Zanzibar were subject to British laws but also whether the terms "purchasing or selling or trafficking in slaves" meant that "no Kutchee should be allowed to purchase a slave for his own household service."[56] In March 1868 the Bombay government dissented from the position of the political agent at Zanzibar on the right of the British government to interfere with those subjects of the Rao of Kutch who had not registered for British protection: "The British Government have practically said to certain Kutchees—You are not our subjects, and are not entitled to our protection, because you have not been registered by our Consul." If they were not British subjects by birth or registration, how could they be held liable for actions not considered crimes in either their native country or country of origin? The government suggested instead that the British enter into an understanding with the Rao of Kutch to assume responsibility for his subjects' protection and, in return, secure their liability to British jurisdiction. But the British government would then need to pay compensation for the liberated slaves held by Kacchis.[57] The Government of India followed up this discussion with an opinion in December 1868 that it was not "necessary" to "interfere" with existing arrangements of household slavery, but that it would be appropriate to prohibit the purchase of slaves for all purposes—whether domestic labor or traffic—in the future.[58] Accordingly, they pressured Kutch's ruler to proclaim the British the ultimate arbiter of claims and disputes involving those of his subjects who lived in Africa, Arabia, and the Persian Gulf. Sheriff has argued that British policy toward these operators of Indian descent transformed "an indigenized merchant class" into an "an entrenched alien body" that the British colonial state could use to consolidate its political control over the Swahili coast.[59]

Americans in Zanzibar agreed with this assessment, critiquing the British both for their imperial designs and for the implementation of their campaign against the slave trade. Even as the United States entered its brief but hopeful era of racial democracy during Congressional Reconstruction, Vice Consul Francis R. Webb evoked an alarming specter of economic ruin, anarchy, and insurrection in the event that slavery met immediate death in Zanzibar—which prospect was looming large with the arrival of new British Consul Henry A. Churchill. A former consul general at Algiers who spoke Arabic and was said to "understand fully the Arab character," this official was reportedly attempting to broker "a total abolition of slavery" in exchange for transferring to Bombay a previously concluded commitment by Zanzibar to pay a subsidy to Muscat. Webb preferred a more gradual approach to abolition, on the grounds that Arab property in Zanzibar "consists largely in slaves who work on the clove and cocoa nut plantations ... and who with their owners and his children form a happy family." Resorting to cultural stereotypes of the Arab character, he expressed the apprehension that "being ignorant of the world and its institutions except that ... of their own," the masters would be unprepared to make a transition to a free society. Webb advised the US government to dispatch a man of war to protect American interests and lives in the event of slavery's abolition in Zanzibar.[60]

Moreover, Webb lamented that, blinded by the lust for prize money, English marauders on the coast had torched fifty dhows within the past year and destroyed many innocent traders: "a man's dhow is boarded, his papers when produced torn up, his valuable cargo taken out, his vessel then burned and with his crew he is landed destitute at the first port his captor enters." The alleged slave trader would have to make his way back to Zanzibar and prove his case in an Admiralty Court inclined to privilege the word of British officers over those of lowly Arab or Indian traders.[61] Indeed, the Lyons-Seward treaty had established Atlantic standards of incriminating evidence that proved misleading in the IOW.[62] Accustomed to "bulky, square-rigged" European ships built for slave trading, and bearing tell-tale signs like shackles and spacious decks, the antiquated naval patrollers could not keep up with the lighter lateen-rigged dhows that traveled swiftly against the wind and could take cover within the creeks, reefs, and thickly forested areas hugging the coast, operating a covert warning system based on flag signals. Perversely, the abolition of the slave trade drove a surge in kidnapping, which flourished along alternative land routes or under the flags of European or Middle Eastern countries immune to British regulation, notably the French. Modern scholars have also noted that British antislave trade activities suffered from inadequate supplies of money and ships, racist officers, high death rates from smallpox and other diseases, and the problem of what to do with the captives. The fact that imperial Britain's Slave Trade Department did not always see eye to eye with the Foreign Office, which in turn was not always on the same page as the Colonial Office, militated against a coherent antitrafficking strategy.[63]

The reservations of Americans in Zanzibar against British antislavery measures may have stemmed from these missteps but also from the fact that American business interests and alliances there were deeply implicated in enslaved labor. After the Civil War, Americans from all walks of life set out to seek their fortunes in Afro-Asia, a few rising to great wealth and power on the far side of the world. American ships bound for Zanzibar traded coffee and gums in Aden, dates and hides in Muscat, and ivory in Mozambique. Several maintained close relations with Indian firms such as that of Tharia Topan, selling kerosene for lighting in East Africa, even as the trade in American cottons bounced back somewhat.[64] No wonder transplanted American slaveholders, merchants, and diplomats, in business with local lords of human chattel, often combined denunciations of what they described as British abolitionist excesses with observations about the gentleness of India Ocean slavery.

A startling divergence between official US policy and American consuls on the ground in the IOW occurred in the context of Britain's decisive strike against the slave trade in 1873. When Sir Edward Thornton, the British representative in Washington, solicited American support of its antislavery initiative, Secretary of State Hamilton Fish obliged, dispatching the USS *Yantic* helmed by Captain Byron Wilson with orders that the American Consulate cooperate with the British mission in Zanzibar. Wilson addressed a letter to Sultan Barghash (who had succeeded Majid), drawing upon his own nation's experience with chattel bondage and disunion in urging slavery's abolition in Africa: "My people were the last among the civilized nations of the globe to completely abolish slavery" through a "bloody war in which the lives of many of our best citizens of the North and South were lost. The decision of this conflict was in favor of freedom for all men." Wilson recalled "the celebrated traveler" [David] Livingstone's observation that "some of your districts are valueless and almost depopulated by wholesale trade in slaves," and held out the prospect of peace and prosperity as dividends of freedom.[65]

US envoy John Webb, however, never transmitted an authentic Arabic translation of this missive to the sultan, instead endorsing Barghash's offer of a watered-down plan for gradual emancipation. Sir Bartle Frere, a former governor of Bombay who had arrived in Zanzibar in charge of Britain's antislave trade mission, complained to Washington, prompting the Grant administration to successfully pressure John Webb's successor Francis Webb to fall in line with the British position. Under threat of a naval blockade, Zanzibar concluded a treaty that abolished the slave trade, closed all slave markets, and forbade Indians from owning slaves.[66]

But meanwhile, new rigor in British naval operations against the slave trade and American ambivalence on Indian Ocean slavery opened cracks for the mediating voices of marginalized subjects caught in the cross-currents of great power rivalries, empire building, and labor conflicts. The testimonies of "rescued" Africans assumed special significance in a milieu in which vessels carrying enslaved captives exhibited few of the material markers of slavers in the Atlantic. So, we ask, how did the marginalized engage with these Anglo-American discourses of slavery? For clues, we turn to the saga of three Africans aboard an American vessel, the *Laconia*, which set sail from the Comoros as Reconstruction drew to a close in the United States.

AFRICANS ABOARD THE LACONIA

The paths of three alleged East African slaves from the Comorian island of Ndzwani in the Mozambique Channel crossed the feuding worlds of British imperial abolition, US diplomacy, and American planters and merchants in the IOW one December evening in 1878. The 1862 Lyons-Seward treaty contained instructions that could potentially pit the claims of national sovereignty against the erection of a unified Anglo-American bulwark against slave trafficking. These tensions came to a head aboard the American bark *Laconia* as it lay anchored in the port of Zanzibar. They produced dueling narratives mediated by the varied stories that three Africans aboard the whaler apparently told before different audiences. The resolution of the case turned on the pivot of these testimonies. It placed the narrators, whoever they were—whether captives, as the British maintained, or fugitives, as the Americans told the tale—on a passage to Massachusetts, far away from the Indian Ocean slave societies where they began their sojourn to visibility in the archives of two nations.[67]

The Anglo-American rupture struck when an armed and uniformed British naval officer, Lieutenant Johnson, burst in on Rufus W. Gifford, the captain of the *Laconia*, as he rested in Zanzibar's Victoria Hotel. Johnson read to him an order from Captain Hamilton Earle of the HMS *London*. The *London* had arrived in Zanzibar in 1875 in response to the British Consul John Kirk's efforts to strengthen antislave patrols in the Indian Ocean. It served as a "depot ship"—a launching pad for smaller patrol vessels.[68] Earle, acting on information from a *Laconia* crew member, had authorized a search of the American vessel for slaves under the terms of the Lyons-Seward treaty. Two investigators repaired to the whaler, where over Gifford's protests, a British officer picked out and carted off the three Africans from Ndzwani to the *London* for questioning by two Swahili interpreters.[69]

The testimonies that resulted were intended to play a key role in the settlement of the case. The absence of institutional signifiers of slaving on ships and people plying the Indian Ocean had prompted the British to devise a system that required each legitimate slaver to carry passes and African passengers to carry manumission certificates, wear linen cloths around their wrists and have their names and legal statuses recorded in the ship's manifests.[70] The absence of these markers lent the depositions of the *Laconia* Africans special importance in determining the question of their status and the meaning of the voyage upon which they had embarked. These testimonies designated each witness a slave. The first was recorded as saying that he was a slave of the captain of the American bark *Laconia*, bought against his will from an American merchant who employed him in a Ndzwani sugar mill, and made to work on the *Laconia* for six months without pay. The other two witnesses swore that they had been fishing on the beach by the home of their masters when the American captain came ashore on a whaling boat, offered them work in exchange for cash and clothes, and upon their refusal to accept, forced them into his ship and covered them with a sail in the bottom of the boat. After the bark set sail, the Africans were brought on deck and set to work without wages.[71]

Despite these claims of forced migration and wage deprivation, the alleged captives were returned to the *Laconia* at noon the following day. They then sailed for New England with the promise of wages. What happened?

British action had triggered vigorous protest from the US Consul W.H. Hathorne. There existed much bad blood between the American and his British counterpart John Kirk. Some of the enmity may be traced to Hathorne's friendship with the American explorer Henry Morgan Stanley, notorious for his warfare with Africans in his path to the Congo and much disliked by the British. *Laconia* unfolded against the backdrop of Kirk's allegation of Hathorne's participation in an 1878 scheme to perpetuate the slave trade. The American consul had joined other Zanzibar merchants faced with a labor shortage in a petition asking the sultan to prevent slaves from hiring out their services on the caravan trade into the mainland. The ivory trade had opened up opportunities for enslaved men on the Swahili coast to engage as porters. While many shared their profits with their masters, others ran off to become trader-porters or initiated these ventures by taking loans from Indian lenders without first seeking their masters' permission. When local masters protested, Hathorne registered his support of their grievances, prompting Kirk to dispatch a complaint to Washington. That move elicited a reprimand against the Hathorne by his own government. The chastened US consul admitted to a conflict of interest between the different hats he wore: "... being the representative of a free government, as well as a merchant ... my act was a thoughtless and wrong one." He assured the US State Department that he had at once visited the Sultan of Zanzibar and "asked him not to allow my signature to have any influence on him. ..."[72]

The case of the *Laconia*, however, raised questions of sovereignty that Hathorne could deploy against the British envoy. Complaining that Kirk's intervention had trampled upon his own jurisdiction over American merchant ships that lay in Zanzibar harbor, the US consul seized the right to conduct an investigation of his own. That exercise yielded testimonies at variance with key British claims. Captain Gifford set the template for the American narrative by referring to the Africans as "negroes" rather than "slaves," who left lives of bondage to join his ship of their own volition. On a visit in July to the Ndzwani sugar plantation of the former Union surgeon Benjamin F. Wilson, formerly of New Bedford, the shorthanded *Laconia* captain claimed to have agreed to take away a troublesome slave identified variously in unpublished and printed sources as Feregie or Fereggie, who lay restrained with chains around his feet. Fereggie reportedly had his irons struck off at a blacksmith's shop and was escorted to the beach, whence he waded far into the shallow waters to board the American whaler without coercion. Meanwhile, the other alleged captives, Similla and M'cassa whom Gifford encountered on the beach, were said to have freely accepted his offer to join his ship for a payment of cash and clothes. Second Officer Edward S. Ripley and boatman George Antonio corroborated Gifford's story that the two Africans had relieved the captain of the valise that he had been carrying and eagerly clambered into the bottom of the boat, leaving the impression that they were runaways. That night, as the waters surged and the *Laconia* sailed, even Fereggie "attempted of his own accord to pull one of the oars going off." The Americans maintained that they did not know whether the Africans had been slaves, only that once they entered the *Laconia*'s world, they became men, on par with other members of the crew: 'I did not consider or treat them as [slaves]," Ripley testified. "[They] were men, and have been treated exactly the same as the rest of the sailors." The day after they sailed, the newcomers were said to have received clothing and tobacco, and told that they would be shipped at the first port serviced by a US consul, at which "they seemed much pleased."[73]

The testimonies of Similla and M'cassa before the US consul appeared to sustain the American narrative of their transition from enslaved fugitives to free sailors: they were quoted as saying that they had entered the ship's service freely on promise of clothes and pay, had consented to lay down under the thwarts shrouded by a sail to hide from locals in Ndzwani, and had received soap, clothes, as well as "liberty" or time off in Zanzibar together with allowances that ranged from 3 to 5 rupees. Similla admitted that although "the 1st officer has sometimes slapped me in the face with the flat of this hand," he treated other crew members similarly.[74]

Fereggie was more ambiguous. He testified that he had boarded the *Laconia* because "the Captain bought me, and I had to go with him." Asked whether he saw any money exchange hands with his former master, he admitted that he had not, but since he had been in chains when the *Laconia* captain visited, and was ordered to proceed to the ship following an exchange between Gifford and his master in a language that he did not understand, he had assumed that he had been sold. Thus, while Gifford rested his defense against the charge of slave trafficking on the fact that he had neither bought the man from Wilson nor physically coerced the youth into entering his ship, the African apparently saw his lack of control over the decision to remove him from Ndzwani as signifying the continuity of his slave status from the plantation to the whaler. Still, upon cross-examination by Hathorne, Fereggie appeared to agree with the other alleged fugitives that he had been well treated and enjoyed time off on two occasions with an allowance of 5 rupees.[75]

The US consul explained the discrepancies between the Africans' sworn statements before the British, on the one hand, and the Americans, on the other, by arguing that these witnesses were not natives of Ndzwani and understood little of Swahili, the language in which they were interrogated aboard the *London*. The US Consulate asserted that the Makua interpreter it hired faced no communication gap with the African witnesses and therefore produced more authoritative interviews.[76]

Yet to what extent did meanings really get lost in translation from disparate African languages into the common medium of English, refracted through competing Anglo-American claims to national sovereignty and imperial abolition? Between the lines of the different questions and assumptions that framed the ostensibly clashing accounts documented by the United States and Britain, and within the words, the silences, and the omissions they held, it is possible to sense a continuity of the Africans' aspirations from the HMS *London* to the US Consulate. Before British interrogators, the Africans seemed to agree that regular wage payments were a litmus test of freedom—a test that the *Laconia*'s captain had failed. The Americans avoided the subject of wages in their own investigation, emphasizing instead in-kind payments like provisions and free time received by the Africans. On the other hand, US Consul Hathorne broached another criterion of free will on which the British remained silent, namely mobility, the option of migration to a destination of the witnesses' own choosing. The American account maintained consistently that all three fugitives dreaded returning "to Johanna" (Ndzwani), preferring instead to be shipped to New Bedford or St. Helena. In this context, Hathorne recorded Similla as saying: [the British] "asked me whether I would like to remain on the *London* or go on to the beach, to which I made no reply."[77]

It is plausible that neither impressment in the British navy nor transport to Ndzwani's slave society appealed to the Africans. Historians have pointed out that liberated slaves sometimes suffered ill-treatment at missions such as the one at Frere Town, or were drafted into forced labor on plantations at mission stations, where they earned the moniker "slaves of the British." In Seychelles they produced export staples like vanilla, cocoa, coffee, and cloves. Bombay-bound "freed" people worked on railroads, docks, or model farms in Khandesh and Badgaon. Cape Town and Natal coveted "prize negroes" to work in cities and plantations.[78] Indeed, Salme's racist perspectives on the indiscipline and indolence of "Negroes" mirrored the attitudes of colonial bureaucrats charged with the management of abolition. If the African men on the *Laconia* had received any inkling of the fates of those liberated at British hands, whether through grapevines in their own communities or via the stories of American sailors, it is no wonder that they chose to forgo the option of becoming colonial subjects. On the other hand, the Africans' emphasis on wages in accounts tendered aboard the *London* did figure in the resolution that transpired. That outcome arguably appropriated gauges of freedom—wages and mobility—from both sets of testimonials, British and American. As the US consul informed his British counterpart, the "negroes have been shipped of their own free will, according to law, in the *Laconia* for New Bedford, their wages or 'lay' dating back to the night of July 10 when they ran away from Johanna to join the vessel."[79]

We will never know for sure the exact measure of persuasion or coercion that lay behind the Africans' presence on the whaling bark, or what happened to them afterward. What we do know is that the *Laconia* never returned home. It sailed from Zanzibar laden with sperm oil and ship's stores, bound for New Bedford, on 1 January 1879. A month later, it ran into a deadly gale, sustained heavy damage to its masts and bowsprit, and leaking heavily limped to the nearest port, Mahé in the Seychelles. There, it was pronounced unseaworthy. Were the three Africans who had boarded from the Comoros present when the local US consul boarded the bark with surveyors, summoned all its officers and seamen, and asked whether they were willing to sail on the injured vessel to Mauritius for repairs? Were they among the majority who declined to proceed any further on what promised to be a perilous journey? Did they receive any of the proceeds from the sale of this ship by public auction "for the interest and benefit of all concerned"? Although we know that Captain Gifford made it by steamer to London via Marseille, we have no record of the presence or fate of the Africans beyond the consular offices at Zanzibar.[80]

At the point at which we lose track of them in the archives, however, the Africans who embarked at Ndzwani appeared to be leveraging their value as witnesses, mediating the jurisdictional boundaries that traversed Anglo-American consensus against the slave trade. Within the paradigms set by dueling interrogations, they weighed in on what it meant to be slave and free with strategic expressions of their aspirations for pay and the right to migrate. These aspirations may have conformed neither to the assimilationist purposes of British imperial abolition nor to the possibly exploitative ends of American mercantile commerce. Whether fugitives or rescued captives, the Ndzwani Africans in Zanzibar, like the South Asian women and children in Oman, rejected the protective custody of colonial subjecthood upon which the British officially predicated their regulation of the slave trade. Still, the imperial politics of abolition and the diplomatic schisms with the United States that transpired afforded these figures the opportunity of mediation and transit, and with it, the prospect of transformation from formless statistics in customs ledgers into visible historical actors.

This chapter has portrayed American businesses in alliance with IOW slavery interests irrespective of sectional divides on "domestic slavery" before the Civil War. Such alliances guided US mercantile diplomats' takes on contentious questions of nationalism and sovereignty involving British imperialists, Indian merchants, and local potentates from Kutch to Zanzibar. Transitioning to cagey acquiescence in official US opposition to slavery in the postbellum era, these operatives nevertheless upheld the right of their compatriots across the seas to hold slaves where local laws allowed that sort of property. These compatriots included a New England sugar baron who built a fortune on the very same Indian Ocean island the three *Laconia* Africans had escaped from. It is to his story that we turn next.

9

A Yankee Slaveholder, "Black Sultan," and European Imperialists in the Indian Ocean, 1870–1906

Dr. Wilson has always maintained that an American residing in a country where slavery is allowed has a right to own slaves if he wishes.
—F. W. CHENEY, US CONSUL IN ZANZIBAR, 1884

One afternoon in March 1891, a "tall broad-shouldered" American expatriate, graced with a "frank, handsome face" arrived in New York's Grand Central Station to take a train to New Bedford, Massachusetts. This traveler, Dr. Benjamin Wilson, had reportedly risen to command "the power of a king and a home in the Indian Ocean." He had returned to the land of his birth on a two-year leave of absence just as his adopted home entered an era of political turbulence, transitioning from sultanate to French protectorate amid a slave rebellion. A former Union surgeon and Freemason reborn as a so-called "island autocrat" abroad, Wilson had set sail for South Africa as supercargo aboard a "little trader" in the aftermath of the US Civil War. That trip yielded a fateful encounter. The young doctor was said to have so impressed a "black sultan" reigning over the island known to Anglo-Atlantic travelers as Johanna (present-day Ndzwani or Anjouan) in the Mozambique Channel that "his Indian Ocean highness" had begged "his white friend" not to return home. Instead, the king had offered the physician "5000 acres of the richest land and 600 slaves" to launch the large-scale production of sugar within his domain for export.[1]

In due course, Wilson had moved from a "rude cabin" to what US naval officers visiting the Comoro archipelago to which Ndzwani belongs described as a "magnificent modern mansion on the top of a rugged mountain." The doctor-turned-planter's home was said to overlook "groves of stately palms, golden stretches of sugar cane and a pretty inland lake" that nestled "along the edge of a dark forest [stretching] down to the white sea beach." Visitors noted that this transplanted

Yankee enjoyed the distinction of commanding the sole stable of horses—English racers—on the island. One report asserted that Wilson "owned" a "plantation two miles square, his own gas and water system, all the luxuries of civilization and something peculiar to barbarism—the favor of the sultan and the power of life and death over his dependents." The portrait that emerged of this former Union surgeon was that of a home-grown Horatio Alger who brought modernity to his "primitive" Indian Ocean surroundings even as he assimilated at least partially to their native "savagery."[2]

Newspaper reports in the early 1890s do hint at stains in Wilson's business dealings, notably allegations that he had purchased a New Bedford whaler accused of trading in slaves. But these accounts offered few hints of the ways in which slave-trading charges against the doctor connected with webs of political intrigue and international power rivalries that had frayed his personal relationship with the Ndzwani sultan and threatened his control over land and labor in the Indian Ocean. The same month that the New Englander was spotted in New York boarding a train to visit his home in Massachusetts, there appeared in the American press cursory mentions of "a revolution" of armed "natives" on the island the French called "Anjouan," which French warships in the Indian Ocean were preparing to quell.[3] Wilson's exalted reputation at home obscured his loss of the surefootedness with which he had hitherto navigated plural national identities. What his American neighbors perhaps did not know was that it was only when his political fortunes began to shift in the 1880s that this "Johannaman" of New England descent had rediscovered his claims to American nationalism. Soon he was straining to save his Indian Ocean investments from sultanic and subsequently French threats with an appeal to US naval power. He would find it difficult, however, to persuade an officially antislavery US government uninvested in the western Indian Ocean to sink money or lives to secure the assets of an American—however wealthy or influential—embroiled in controversies over slavery and imperial abolition.

Wilson's career as a sugar baron in the Comoros opens up interesting possibilities for comparing the experiences of slaveholding settler colonialism in the Indian Ocean with the fortunes of planters who had enlisted state cooperation to transform North America into an empire of slavery earlier in the same century. What follows is a story of precarious mastery, featuring a Yankee planter seeking to adapt an agro-business empire to norms of personal patronage, unwritten contracts, corporate land ownership, and elite and enslaved groups fractured horizontally along lines of status and ethnicity, as well as regional, national, and religious identity. On the cusp of the Comoros' transition from sultanate to protectorate, Wilson's entrepreneurial endeavor threatened to falter in the cross fire of local wars of succession, enslaved resistance, and imperial power plays enmeshed in the international politics of slavery.

FROM NEW BEDFORD SURGEON TO "ISLAND AUTOCRAT" IN THE INDIAN OCEAN

Benjamin F. Wilson entered his part of the world just as slavery seemed poised to strain the ties that held it together. The year was 1838. His father was a well-to-do farmer in Bristol County, Massachusetts, home to the whaling town of New Bedford, which featured prominently in the migration routes of traders and commodities to the Indian Ocean.[4] A couple of years earlier, pro-South Congressmen in the United States had voted to table all petitions from abolitionists, even as the American Antislavery Society gained a quarter of a million members. Former slaves ended their terms as apprentices in the British West Indies, and many decamped to independent farms, triggering lamentations from American slaveholders about the ostensibly catastrophic impact of emancipation on staple crop production.

Most ordinary white Americans went about their business as usual, among them Wilson's father David, who, following Benjamin's seventeenth birthday, moved the family from Dartmouth to New Bedford. Wilson studied medicine, graduating from the College of Physicians and Surgery in New York City just as his nation went to war in 1861. Like many young men of his generation, Wilson enlisted in the US Navy, serving as an assistant acting surgeon on the US gunboat *Fearnot*. He was reportedly "with Farragut at New Orleans and Porter at Fort Fisher, and in other hot fights between Southern forts and Northern gunboats." He sustained serious injuries while dressing the wounds of a gunner at Fort Fisher and nearly drowned when a storm buffeted a small boat that he was riding off Beaufort on the coast of North Carolina. Four years later, Wilson resigned from his Union service on grounds of ill health.

While many former Union soldiers were heading South to establish plantations and to facilitate the freed people's transition to wage labor, Wilson sought his fortunes on more distant shores. Seeking, he maintained, a moderate climate to alleviate his bronchial troubles, he sailed for South Africa in the position of supercargo aboard a merchant vessel trading in the Indian Ocean. That parts of South Africa should also be on the cusp of a gold rush may or may not have been a happy coincidence. The American merchants stopped at various points along the African coast before rounding the Cape of Good Hope on their way to the Comoros, a cluster of four islands located in the Mozambique Channel. This archipelago had long served as a conduit of peoples, commodities, and cultures between Madagascar to the east and Mozambique on Africa's southeastern coast to the west. Maritime commerce with Arabia, India, and Portuguese Africa, and an amalgam of cultures—Shirazi, northern coastal Swahili, Arab, and African—molded its cosmopolitan towns. It was one of these islands—Ndzwani—that would become the "remote" locale of Wilson's plantation empire. The British called it "Johanna." To the French, it was "Anjouan."[5]

Since the sixteenth century, Ndzwani, together with Mwali (Mohéli) its neighbor to the west, had offered European ships trading in the Indian Ocean a convenient way station supplied with fresh water, abundant fruits, a safe harbor, and a business-friendly population. By contrast, a barrier of coral reefs rendered low-lying Mayotte to the southeast less accessible. Ngazidja (or Grand Comore), the largest island of the group, lacked fresh water and arable land, making it less attractive to visitors from the Atlantic.[6] Eighteenth-century sources noted that Ndzwani had emerged as a dominant economic power among the Comoro Islands. Its residents procured weapons and cotton from ships arriving from Bombay, and gold and other currency from European players in the region. They exchanged these commodities for ivory and cotton in the Mozambique market, selling them in turn to neighboring islands. Moreover, Ndzwani residents had famously developed an affinity for the English language and culture. That affinity dated at least partly from the support of British squadrons against Madagascar-based Sakalava raids targeting the island in the late eighteenth century, and may have been the reason that local nobles assumed British titles like "Marquis Cornwallis" and "Lord Fitzroy."[7]

American whalers too had been visiting the island for decades. Seamen remarked upon the abundance and variety of the fruits it boasted, as well as its loquacious population, which appeared anxious to engage in trade and cultural exchanges with strangers from the Americas. One visitor from Salem who arrived aboard the bark *Palestine* in the summer of 1840 was convinced that the locals were "fast losing their original customs.... Time has been when it was next to impossible to see any of their *wives* or *daughters*. But I have had the pleasure today myself of not only seeing one of the daughters, but also of shaking hands with the young Lady." He went on to describe the inhabitants as having complexions and clothing similar to the Malay, and wearing many ornaments.[8]

What were the people of the local society like, the upper reaches of which a son of New England was about to embrace as his own, for a little while at least? In the early nineteenth century, Ndzwani's inhabitants struck one European visitor as being divided broadly into "two distinct races": Arab settler colonialists and the "original natives" who had been pushed "to the hills" and who warred with the Arabs.[9] A few decades later, the Zanzibar-based British Consul Holmwood, on a visit to negotiate antislavery treaties with Comorian sultanates, portrayed a cosmopolitan and unequal society. Elites of Shirazi descent, who had arrived centuries before, were known as "Johannamen." They numbered about one thousand out of a population of "15,000 to 16,000," spread over an "an island of singular beauty and fertility" one-third the size of Zanzibar. Betraying his own religious prejudices, the consul described them as "bigoted Mahommedans" but conceded their remarkable multilingual skills: "nearly everyone speaks English, many fluently, without the slightest foreign accent," without ever having left the island. They could also boast command of local and regional languages like Makua, Malagasy, and Arabic in addition to their own tongue, a hybrid of Swahili and Madagascar dialects.[10]

Sultan Abdullah, who was to become Wilson's patron, was drawn from this ruling class. Arab culture and identity defined its status and may even have inspired invented genealogies in some cases.[11] David Livingstone, on a visit to the Comoros, described the king as an "intelligent" man, a devout Muslim well versed in the English language. Only twenty-three when he met the famous explorer, the sultan played a mean game of chess and struck Livingstone as a handsome man of medium height, olive-complexioned, dark-eyed, somewhat reserved, but courteous and "refined." On his head perched a "military cap with a large silver band round it and a badge inscribed with Arabic characters." Other members of the elite wore a "loose light sort of cloak . . . ornamented with silk and silver lace, which they say come from Mecca," and slung swords inlaid with precious metals over their left shoulders.[12] According to Holmwood, they presided over a free aboriginal population of "bushmen" numbering between eight and ten thousand, segregated in "a separate suburb adjoining every town," in addition to villages nestled in the hills. Unlike "Johannamen" who paid no taxes, these "nominally free" subjects suffered the burden of "irregular imposts" levied according to the sultan's caprices, as well as forced personal service to the state. The remaining inhabitants consisted of five thousand mostly enslaved Makua people of whom 70 percent labored on plantations, with the rest serving as domestic workers.[13] Other snapshots of the Comoro islands' bonded population from the 1860s suggest that they included masons and carpenters apprenticed to artisans who built "fine stone houses with carved doors."[14]

By July 1871, when Wilson arrived in Ndzwani as a passenger and "companion" of the owner of the *E. S. Twisden,* Captain E.W. Holmes of the firm of G. S. Holmes & Co. of Cape Town, Sultan Abdullah had developed a keen interest in the sugar agro-business.[15] Indeed, by the mid 1860s, US consuls in the western Indian Ocean were reporting on a "new branch of industry" on the rise in the region, namely sugar. From Zanzibar came the news that a moneyed English company had established joint ownership of two large plantations "with His Highness" who "furnished land, labor of negroes . . . The English Company the capital and necessary machinery. Profits to be shared."[16] In Ndzwani, a former British consul known as William Sunley had emerged as the largest sugar planter in the neighborhood until the American arrived. Drawing upon British experience with staple crop production in Mauritius, Sunley established a vast estate on a lush elevated plain on the island's southwestern coast, fifty miles from the capital city of Mutsamudu. He had secured from Sultan Selim, Abdullah's father, a forty-year lease on at least three hundred acres of land near the village of Pomoni at the mouth of a deep-sea harbor surrounded by coral reefs, in the shadow of lofty mountains covered with vegetation and supplied with a fresh water stream. By 1861, he commanded a labor force of five hundred, consisting principally of enslaved workers hired out by local owners, according to Charles Livingstone, the brother of the explorer David.

Reports of the enslaved's conditions varied, with Sunley's defenders then and now describing bondspeople as the only option for laborers available to planters, and claiming that they were well treated, with access to the opportunity to purchase their freedom for fifty dollars, payable in installments. The Islamic law of freeing an enslaved woman and her child if sired by her master found its way into these justifications of the consul's departure from British avocations of antislavery. These defenses echoed impressions of the "domestic" quality of slavery on the British master's estate that were common in Orientalist discourses of slavery in India and Arabia. But eyewitness reports of the enslaved at work illuminate the vast variety of their tasks and the hard labor that underlay them. One ship captain noted admiringly "how ably and intelligently" they went about their assignments: "They drive the engine, make the wagons, break in cattle for draught and drive them and conduct all the different operations without any white overlooker besides Mr. Sunley."[17]

Slave-grown and processed sugar in Ndzwani fit the pattern of a spike in demand for labor in the nineteenth century that turned the Comoros into an important node in the Indian Ocean world's expanding networks of commerce in human chattel.[18] Following their losses of territory during the Napoleonic wars, the French established themselves in the strategically situated island of Nosy Bé off the northwest coast of Madagascar, taking over Mahoré (Mayotte) in the early 1840s. The slave trade, officially proscribed by the French since 1848, nevertheless continued under the guise of the so-called Free Emigration Scheme. Arab and Swahili traders along the African coast "emancipated" the captives they purchased and indentured them for long terms to coffee and sugar planters in French colonies and protectorates, notably Réunion. William Stamps Cherry was a Missouri-born explorer and big game hunter who claimed to have lived in a house built by the Zanzibari slave trader Tippu Tipp while at Stanley (now Boyoma) Falls. He wrote that in "Congo Francaise," Arab traders deputized local chiefs to undertake raids for slaves, and that to celebrate one such expedition, an overlord named Rashid had held a magnificent banquet outfitted with "material ... carried from Zanzibar on the heads of men for six weary months," even as smallpox and crop failures had reduced the camps housing skeletal captives to something worse than the notorious Confederate prison of Andersonville. Cherry had encountered "a caravan of Arabs" carrying "native women" purchased at the rate of "one tusk for two ... [nubile] girls." Since "one gun of the old muzzle loading musket order" fetched "three or four tusks of ivory, this made some six or eight women for 15 francs, the value of a gun here. . . ."[19]

Ships flying the French flag were exempted from searches by British anti–slave trade patrols, incentivizing multinational slave traders to establish toeholds in French-held territories like Madagascar, Réunion, and Mayotte for the privilege of buying into the protection of the French banner. Comorians, whether elites or artisans, were avid slave traders. In the 1850s, they could sell *engagés* secured in Portuguese Africa two hundred miles away for 8 to 10 dollars each for as much as 30 to 40 dollars to French planters operating on Indian Ocean islands. In the Comoros, indentured workers who were officially contracted to labor for eight hours a day with breaks on Sundays and public holidays were in practice reported to have been forced to put in thirteen hours a day, after which they had to husk, winnow, and cook their own ration of rice. The *engagé* system, in other words, did not amount to much freedom.[20]

Meanwhile, when civil war ruptured the United States, it tested the principles of British abolitionism across the oceans. In 1863, months after Lincoln issued his emancipation proclamation, a pair of Sultan Abdullah's political rivals arrived in London with disturbing allegations of Sunley's mistreatment of slaves in Ndzwani in cahoots with its ruler. The British consul was said to have reneged on his contract to pay the masters of hired slaves $1.50 per slave, and the slaves half a dollar each per month; he coerced his slaves to work twelve hours a day, six days a week rather than six hours per day, four days a week as he had originally agreed; he used British warships to capture fugitives; and he tarred, feathered, and drove a nail through the ears of an alleged enslaved thief who then committed suicide by jumping off a cliff, among other outrages. The British government felt compelled to give Sunley an ultimatum: give up slaveholding or resign as consul. Sunley chose the latter option, claiming that he was "civilizing" the "slaves and their progeny," who were fast replacing the "Arab element" as the dominant population group on the island.[21]

Freed from diplomatic obligations to pay lip service to antislavery, Sunley continued to prosper, acquiring a plantation in Mwali from its queen, who had sought to introduce the plantation system on her island. By the early 1870s, the British planter commanded seven hundred acres worked by four European managers, and a mostly enslaved labor force of eight hundred, with the owners of those hired out pocketing three-fifths of their earnings. A member of the delegation led by Sir Bartle Frere who forced Sultan Barghash of Zanzibar to prohibit the slave trade in 1873 commented that thanks to Sunley's success, sugar agri-business had become "quite the rage among the fashionables of Johanna." The island's planter class now included the sultan and his brothers, with the ruler producing two hundred tons of sugar in 1872.[22]

In this context, it appears likely that the business-minded Abdullah saw in Wilson a potential agent for advancing the commercial prosperity of his dominions. The New Englander entered the sultan's service as physician and, by his own accounts, served him so well that the monarch persuaded him to settle on the island, with "promises and written agreements" of assistance.[23] Attracted by the agreeable climate and the king's generosity, he agreed, contracting to take out a loan jointly with his patron from Mauritius-based creditors to fund the enterprise.[24] The terms of an agreement dated 28 October 1871, a copy of which was recorded with the US Consulate in Zanzibar in 1887, suggest that the sultan may have been anxious to promote the settlement and cultivation of "unoccupied" land on the island for a profit. To that end, he authorized the American to settle on one thousand acres of such land anywhere on the island for growing sugar, coffee, and cotton. The king also agreed to furnish labor at the rate of $1.50 per month for each male and $1 for each female, together with funds for operating the plantation, repayable once the project became self-sustaining. The deal exempted all commodities produced by the plantation from duties and taxes.[25]

A subsequent agreement in May 1872 established a thirty-year lease and set the boundaries of "Patsy," as Wilson's estate came to be known. By now, the property may have extended over 1,500 acres of land to the east of Mutsamudu. The compact authorized the American to introduce machinery and build roads and other infrastructure in the property around his plantation. It gave him full control of water "flowing into or bordering upon" his land and to fell all the timber he needed. Wilson received "all of the rights and privileges" of a "Johannaman," signifying his "naturalization" as a national of Ndzwani and his induction into its governing class. In exchange, the sultan retained the right of possession to all buildings erected upon Patsy at the expiration of the lease, although "the present" residents of the estate were given the right to remain on the property if they chose. Moreover, Wilson contracted to pay the Sultan a rent of $200 per annum. Six years later, Wilson claimed to have "bought" additional land adjoining his estate for $325.[26]

AMERICAN SETTLER COLONIALISM IN THE COMOROS: PERSONAL PATRONAGE, UNWRITTEN CONTRACTS, AND "CORPORATE" LAND TENURE

Fast forward to 1882, a little over a decade after the visitor from New Bedford set foot on the verdant ground of Ndzwani. Benjamin Wilson's domain included six hundred acres of land under sugarcane cultivation. Holmwood described Patsy as a "fine estate at an elevation of 1,000 feet above the sea," equipped with a "powerful steam-plant of the best construction...."[27] A labor force of six hundred men and women worked in gangs of eighty under the supervision of overseers, often free "Johannamen." Half of these workers were enslaved hands, hired from the king and other members of the island's ruling classes. The rest included 150 free men and 150 slaves. Wilson later claimed in statements to the US government that he had bought the slaves and given them free papers, but they were obliged to work for him for a term of years. Wilson estimated that he had invested $150,000 in machinery and buildings, as well as paving the property with roads.[28] The American commanded a multinational staff drawn from all over Europe and the Indian Ocean: General Manager Jules Magny was French; George Euan, who served as engineer in charge of all machinery at the estate, hailed from Scotland; a Portuguese clerk, S. C. DeSouza, managed the time books and payroll; Drayman Jaba—overseer, marker, interpreter—was a "Johannaman"; and head mason Pearce Edwards, an Englishman.[29] When Wilson visited the United States in 1891, newspapers noted that he inhabited a mansion fitted with electric bells and marble baths, along with a library containing five thousand books. He dispatched his steam launch to meet a French mail steamer sixty miles into the ocean in order to secure supplies of English and American newspapers and magazines. A plant on his estate manufactured ice. He was said to house his enslaved workers in "villages of modern cabins, ... surrounded with every comfort." The sugar they produced traveled by a chartered vessel to Mauritius for sale.[30]

Based on early 1860s accounts of the operation of a sugar mill on Sunley's estate—"a long stone building covered with cocoa nut matting"—we can visualize enslaved workers on Wilson's plantation engaged similarly in the myriad stages involved in processing cane into sugar. They would have cut and heaped the cane in the morning; when rollers crushed the juice out of the cane, the laborers would have carried away the remains, spread them out, and burned them. They would have overseen the running of the juice into boilers for cooking before cooling, removing scum from the sugar, and placing it in vessels "to settle for the night" before treating it with lime and cooling it, ladling it "into flat wooden boxes" to crystallize. Finally they would feed it into a turbine, packing the finished sugar into bags.[31] Wilson, who earned a reputation as a gracious host to visiting diplomats, naval officers, and adventurers from the Atlantic, no doubt relied heavily on enslaved labor to turn out delectable dishes from the local cuisine. These involved painstaking tasks like "grat[ing] coconuts, grind[ing] rice flour on millstones, knead[ing] dough ... and pound[ing]" ingredients in "pestles in addition to gathering foodstuffs, firewood and water."[32]

The island boasted other thriving sugar plantations. Those belonging to the sultan occupied the most coveted sites and were appointed with sugar manufactories that used "powerful steam machinery" equipped with "vacuum-pans" to produce an output of "500 tons of fine sugar." The king's labor force included one thousand slaves and six British factory workers. The other prominent estate on the island belonged, of course, to Sunley. Consul Holmwood noted admiringly that through his "energy and talent for organization" he had built up a powerhouse that "yielded as much as 1,000 tons of sugar in one year." "Johannamen" produced smaller quantities of sugar using bullock-powered mills. They also traded actively in slaves, hiring out their bondspeople to European and American planters on the island. Reports on the conditions of the enslaved varied, but Holmwood portrayed a generally harsh system of slavery that ill-treated and underfed its victims. He maintained, however, that those on estates under European or American control were better off, and supplied with adequate subsistence, even though they worked hard and faced the threat of separation from their families through sale. As a result, he noted that "their women do not bear children." Enslaved adults on hire earned—besides food, clothing, and housing—twenty-four dollars per annum, of which masters kept eighteen.[33]

Ndzwani's multiracial planter class and its enslaved communities alike were splintered along lines of cultural identity and closeness to the sultan. In general, Comorian bondspeople varied not simply by age and gender, but also according to religious affiliation, regional origins, and acculturation, function, and status. As Gil Shepherd has written, the French observer Alfred Gevrey, imperial judge at Mayotte from 1866 to 1868, found that locally born, Islamized *wazalia* enjoyed higher status than the alien *wamakwa,* who had been imported more recently from Portuguese Africa and were labeled *warumwa,* meaning "used" people. Native-born slaves and their children reserved the right not to be sold; yet in the 1880s, amid war and political instability, even free locals found themselves vulnerable to captivity and enslavement. Concubines were valued objects of conspicuous consumption as well as progenitors of children that masters within matrilineal clans could incorporate into their own matrilineages. The Makua no doubt dominated the ranks of plantation labor on estates operated by Atlantic settlers in the 1870s and 1880s. They were also said to engage in lowly work such as fishing, cattle herding, and leather tanning.[34]

The enslaved people's worlds in Ndzwani intersected with that of their masters in ways that the antebellum South's self-conscious planter class would have found confounding. When a Comorian master acquired and integrated slaves into his circle of dependents after the fashion of many Arab and African patrons, master and slave might well be vertically integrated against rival political groupings of other masters and slaves. Under these circumstances, it was perfectly natural to arm loyal, acculturated slaves.[35] Circles of enslaved dependents assumed special importance in light of schisms within a planter cohort of diverse ethnicities and national origins, religious identities, political affiliations and influence, and relationships with the sultan/state. The king himself reportedly relied on a massive army of enslaved soldiers to put his enemies—whether political rivals, plantation lords, or both—in their place.

These conditions of Ndzwani's slave society rendered Wilson's hold on power and property far more precarious than that enjoyed by the pre–Civil War South's master class, or for that matter, than New York press accounts of his autocratic and grandiose lifestyle suggested. The shaky foundations of Wilson's fortunes in the Indian Ocean rested on bonds of personal friendship with a monarch vulnerable not simply to the machinations of local pretenders to his throne but increasingly to those of foreign powers. Such political instability was compounded by norms of Comorian land tenure and labor arrangements. In the United States, planter-dominated local and state governments and federal policy buttressed the scaffolding of what Beckert calls "war capitalism."[36] American Indian removal from fertile lands through war or treaty, the protection of private property contracts in land, and constitutional protections for human chattel, for instance, lent slaveholding interests a degree of security for decades before the emergence of antislavery politics shifted the ground under their feet. By contrast, Wilson's arrangements with the sultan were neither immediately codified in written contracts subject to the arbitration of western-style law courts nor secured through ownership rights in the land upon which he had built much of his estate. The advent of French imperialism, and with it a regime of documentation in the French language, would in the future raise questions about the legitimacy of Wilson's rights to the plantation empire he called his own.

Written records of Wilson's understandings with Sultan Abdullah materialize in the US State Department's archives in moments of crisis with the island's political authorities, when Wilson was forced to defend his claims to his investments with documentation. Thus, in 1887, a year after the French had established a protectorate in Ndzwani, the American planter filed a copy of the 1871 agreement with the sultan with the US Consulate in Zanzibar. It was handwritten, with a makeshift quality about it, and without official certification by the sultan's seal.[37] As Patsy flowered and flourished, its American operator had sought repeatedly to secure title to the estate in perpetuity, but Abdullah refused, apparently on the ground that "it was an old and sacred law of the Arabs not to grant any land to Europeans on these conditions." Rather, in the interests of retaining Wilson's "goodwill," in 1879 the Sultan gave him a promise of a sixty-year renewal of his lease at its expiration in 1892 on the same terms as before, plus the right to another one thousand acres of "unoccupied land." But since the aboriginal land was considered "unoccupied," the agreement threatened to expand settler colonialism at the expense of smaller, less powerful residents of the land.[38] A report filed by the British emissary Holmwood in the early 1880s attributed to the king "ownership" of all land on the island, and noted his steadfast resistance to "sell or even grant long leases to white men, many of whom have tried to purchase freeholds in the island." From the sultan's perspective, relatively short-term leases to Atlantic sojourners safeguarded the land from "idle" squatters while bringing the benefits of European capital. In theory at least, the so-called bushmen were entitled to as much land as they needed to subsist, but such rights carried burdensome responsibilities of taxes, imposts, and forced labor, prompting the British consul to muse that they may have been worse off than the slaves on the island.[39]

As these conditions suggest, the American slaveholder in the IOW, unlike his counterparts in the Atlantic world, controlled the land and labor upon which his business enterprises relied only at the pleasure of the reigning political authority. The importance of *personal relationships* with power, and the ability to navigate local culture and political sensibilities that shaped entrepreneurial successes in pre-French Ndzwani, emerges in the story of Wilson's clash with a rival American planter during the happy first phase of his Comorian career in the 1870s. Initially,

Wilson enjoyed Abdullah's unreserved confidence, serving multiple roles close to the throne: personal physician, "foreign advisor," and a business broker of sorts. It is possible that as British interest in the island faded—Ndzwani offered no striking economic or strategic advantages in the late nineteenth century—the sultan may have sought to forge an alliance with the United States through Wilson as a buffer against his domestic and foreign rivals. Indeed, in the course of the 1870s, the American appears to have supplanted the former British consul Sunley as the Sultan's chief consultant on diplomatic affairs. In that role, he negotiated a treaty with Commodore Robert Wilson Shufeldt of the US flagship *Ticonderoga* on a visit to the Comoros en route to Zanzibar from the Cape of Good Hope. The compact proposed to confer on Americans the right to residency and property ownership on the island, among other things, but was never ratified by the US Senate.[40]

As long as Wilson enjoyed the sultan's confidence, he could expect to seize the upper hand in disputes with business rivals. Consider, for instance, his feud with fellow New Englander F. P. Robinson—one grounded either in intrigues involving money and sex, or illegal land grabs, depending on who told the tale. This particular vignette begins in Mauritius, where the paths of Wilson and Sultan Abdullah crossed that of the Massachusetts-born Robinson, who was at the time a partner of the Port Louis–based mercantile/banking/maritime agency firm of Houdlette and Company.[41] Robinson later claimed that the king had lured him to his island with the promise of land, inducing him to give up a lucrative business in the process. The sultan, on the other hand, maintained that Wilson had been in Mauritius to procure machinery for his plantation and Robinson, confronted with a failing operation, approached him about the possibility of securing a land lease for plantation agriculture from the sultan.[42] Whatever the truth of the matter, Robinson moved with his wife to Ndzwani, and Houdlette agreed in June 1878 to loan their former partner two hundred dollars per month through the year 1879, secured by the coffee crop that the American intended to raise on that island.[43]

Robinson's plans fell through almost immediately, apparently languishing in the face of wildly misplaced expectations of American-style settler colonialism on land with preexisting inhabitants. Robinson was soon complaining that the sultan had allowed "others to occupy land promised to him,"[44] failed to pay him a commission on cargo consigned to Ndzwani by Houdlette,[45] and appointed as government agent in this dispute none other than Benjamin Wilson, with whom Robinson had fallen out soon after his arrival on the island. Robinson attributed the conflict partly to Wilson's failure to repay a loan advanced him by Houdlette, whose interests Robinson claimed to represent.[46] Yet what really sealed the enmity between the two men, Robinson insisted, was his own intervention to protect female servants and slaves from sexual abuse by Wilson.[47]

Robinson attempted to enlist the US government's mediation to resolve his difficulties with the sultan and his "agent," Wilson, bringing financial claims against

Abdullah to the US consul in Zanzibar, W.H. Hathorne. The appeal prompted the State Department to authorize an investigation by Commodore Shufeldt of the USS *Ticonderoga*.[48] But Robinson was out of luck. Both the commodore and Sunley, to whom Shufeldt referred the matter for arbitration, rejected his complaints against the sultan.[49] Shufeldt was in the neighborhood in the wake of the economic downturn of 1873, on a larger mission to expand US commercial relations with "unfrequented ports of Africa, Asia, the islands of the Persian Ocean, and the adjacent seas."[50] Thus, it is possible that he was disinclined to act against the sultan's refusal to back Robinson's "rights" to evacuate locals from land they were farming.[51] Moreover, regarding labor problems that Robinson had attributed to the intimidation of workers by the king and his American agent Wilson, the sultan responded that "he will have no trouble [with labor] ... if he paid for it like others."[52]

Shufeldt, while sympathetic to the sultan's perspective, managed to negotiate a promise for Abdullah to give Robinson some of the land he claimed.[53] No sooner had the *Ticonderoga* departed, however, than the sultan unleashed a campaign of persecution against the New Englander. The king's handlers allegedly tampered with his mail, set fire to his house, ordered his workers—enslaved and free—to depart "under pain of death," locked up his foremen, and pulled down the workers' quarters on his plantation. Robinson's money accounts were refused, he was himself denied an audience with the king, and neighboring villages were instructed not to sell him provisions. His temporary shelter leaked from the rains, and the withdrawal of labor kept him from completing a more permanent residence. He portrayed a state of dire distress, in which his troubles with the Ndzwani state were interfering with his ability to provide for his daughter. Robinson lamented that he would have made a sound return on his investments in capital and labor if he had workers to gather his crop: "I see it dropping on the ground, for want of men to pick it up.... A large part of the coffee trees are so choked with grass and weed that many are dead, and more dying."[54]

Although Robinson's case was eventually referred to the US consul in Mauritius, it was clear that this American traveler's aspirations to reinvent himself as a landed coffee entrepreneur had gone up in smoke. As the 1880s dawned, Benjamin Wilson stood as the undisputed master of Ndzwani's Atlantic planter "class," assimilating to its culture and politics. Rumors flew back in the United States that he had embraced Islam and traded in slaves. Postbellum American governments may officially have endorsed IOW antislavery. But Frederick Cheney of the Zanzibar Consulate, a Boston merchant who had visited Wilson several times in the early 1880s, noted his pragmatic accommodation to local usages: "Dr. Wilson has always maintained that an American residing in a country where slavery is allowed has a right to own slaves if he wishes."[55]

Crucially, the immigrant from Massachusetts intervened in local political intrigues in ways calculated to secure his economic future in the region. But the shifting sands of power in that part of the world, on scales that were at once intranational, transnational, and imperial, boded ill. Against the backdrop of Comorian coups entangled with the international politics of slavery and empire, Wilson fell out with his royal patron. Starting in 1882, bad blood with the sultan would fuel a cycle of alleged official persecution that recalled the experiences of fellow New Englander Robinson.

FROM THE SULTAN'S FRIEND TO FOE: COMORIAN COUPS, EMPIRE, AND THE INTERNATIONAL POLITICS OF SLAVERY

As the year 1883 wound down, a disturbing report arrived on the desk of the Third Assistant Secretary of State in Washington, DC. It consisted of a deposition from Sultan Abdullah of Ndzwani, leveling allegations of slaveholding by an American citizen who three decades earlier had fought on the Union's side to make the republic of his birth a free one. Dr. Benjamin Wilson's infractions against free labor supposedly violated key provisions of the antislavery treaty that the sultan had lately concluded with the British Foreign Office. The State Department directed inquiries about the truth of these complaints to Consul Cheney in Zanzibar. The consul, who had enjoyed Wilson's hospitality on his island estate a few times, testified in his response to the presence of "about five hundred black people engaged on [the American's] estate," who were either "slaves of his, or hired." The Boston merchant hastened to offer a rationale for this departure from US policy: "Anyone living at Johanna was allowed to own slaves," unlike Zanzibar and its dependencies, where "no white man is allowed to own slaves." Since the only slave laws "are those included in the treaties with the different nations," and "I cannot find that the United States has a treaty of any kind with the king of Johanna," Wilson was not violating the laws of any land, Cheney concluded.[56]

Abdullah's complaint against Wilson represented but one maneuver in a complex power play underlying a great rupture between the two. The men would advance competing narratives of what fueled the break. Wilson swore that the sultan's real object was to appropriate the valuable estate developed over many years and with much capital, for the benefit of his own son, Prince Salim. Abdullah, for his part, would accuse his former physician and friend of complicity in an antigovernment coup mounted by the ruler's own brother, as part of a deal with the rebel prince for Wilson to purchase all rights to Patsy. The conflict between Abdullah and Wilson unfolded in 1882 within a framework of archipelago-wide wars of succession, entwined with great power rivalries and slavery politics.

Let us begin to untangle the strands of this conflict by following leads in British colonial records that take us to London in January 1882. Troubling reports had begun to filter into the Foreign Office about a friendly state's role as a linchpin in the southwestern Indian Ocean region's slave dealing networks. In this context, the antitrafficking naval commander Lieutenant-Colonel S. B. Miles had reported that the Ndzwani sultan had dispatched mercenaries to help install a notorious, slave-trading, French-schooled usurper named Said Ali in a position of paramountcy in Ngazidja, and collaborated with him in securing captives on the African coast. The deposed king, named Msafumu, from a rival Hadrami-descended matrilineal ruling house in Ngazidja, was aligned with a British client, Sultan Barghash of Zanzibar. Barghash, we should note, was seeking to consolidate his political power and economic influence on the Swahili coast. The succession struggle that followed pitted Enfield-rifle-equipped (possibly mainland) African "Nyamwezi" soldiers dispatched by the British-affiliated Barghash to fight on Msafumu's side against Said Ali, an ally of the French at Mayotte. Abdullah, together with Ndzwani's slave traders, had reportedly joined the fray on Said Ali's side, supplying him with mercenaries and arms.[57] British intelligence suggested that Said Ali had imposed heavy taxes on residents of lands under his control in order to raise the resources to compensate Abdullah for his troubles. He was said to have seized the domestic slaves of masters who defaulted on their tax payments and shipped them to Ndzwani.[58]

This state of affairs piqued the interest of the British Foreign Office, which had turned renewed attention to the scourge of trafficking in the Mozambique Channel.[59] That Abdullah appeared to be reneging on earlier antislaving promises to British emissaries like John Kirk was particularly galling. Accordingly, in September 1882, the Zanzibar-based British Consul Holmwood sailed in the Zanzibar imam's steamer *Sultani*, accompanied by an honor guard of forty-eight men, to investigate Comorian affairs. He arrived in Mutsamudu on the night of 4 October. Local elites, having received word from disaffected Zanzibar residents that the British were at war with their fellow Muslims in Turkey, received the envoy with distrust. The sultan himself was ensconced in his sugar plantation at Bambao on the island's east side.[60] The one slaveholder in the Ndzwani capital who appeared anxious to curry Holmwood's favor was Wilson, who wrote to say that he would have visited him aboard his ship but was forced to stay away because the king had placed his estate—where an epidemic raged—under quarantine.[61]

What does not appear in Holmwood's records is the fact that there was more to the quarantine than a mere attempt by the Ndzwani government to protect public health. It represented one act in a saga of conflict between Wilson and Abdullah that was playing out even as Holmwood was conducting his antislavery diplomatic mission. Two months earlier, the mail steamer *Argo* from Mauritius had docked in the waters lapping the Patsy estate, during an outbreak of "quanga" described as a "native skin disease" among several of the workers. When the plantation's engineer George Euan went aboard to procure supplies and load it with sugar for the Mauritian market, he learned that the sultan's crew had preceded him, bearing the news that the estate had suffered an outbreak of smallpox. The captain refused to transact any business with Patsy under these circumstances. Wilson interpreted the incident as a deliberate act of sabotage on the part of the king, designed to starve his business of its channels of trade and exchange. The American threatened to sue his royal patron for damages.[62]

Holmwood learned of Wilson's threat of a suit when he proceeded to the sultan's sugar estate in Bambao for negotiations. But he was preoccupied with his government's mandate to extract an antislavery agreement from Comorian authorities. In Bambao, the British consul stayed not in Abdullah's palace but rather in a luxurious suite of rooms in the residence of his eldest son, Prince Salim. The prince's home was also designated the venue of their conference. Holmwood was convinced that "this arrangement" was designed to keep him from bearing witness to the fresh influx into the king's harem of enslaved concubines, many of them "Comoro girls" gifted by Said Ali. Abdullah arrived for the talks accompanied by handsomely attired gentlemen, apparently representing the leading slaveholders of the island. Holmwood offered a detailed account—from his vantage point—of the tortured exchanges that followed, punctuated at different times by prayers, consultations with a religious judge, and a lavish dinner attended by over a dozen "richly-dressed women" who entered the salon holding aloft metal dishes. The "Johannamen" led by the sultan and his religious authorities claimed ignorance of the terms of previous antislave trade agreements concluded with the British, invoked the danger of instigating popular revolt against antislavery mandates, and raised religious objections, especially to the implications of abolition for domestic arrangements involving enslaved concubines. Holmwood countered by holding up the example of British India, where "the Mahommedan population was greater than the whole population of Great Britain, and no real inconvenience had arisen from [abolition]."[63]

Eventually, Holmwood induced Abdullah to ratify and promise to publicly promulgate an emancipation agreement in exchange for British recognition of his son Salim as his successor to the throne of Ndzwani. The treaty provided for the immediate suppression of traffic in slaves on land and at sea, as well as the official registration and consular protection of all slaves within the sultan's dominions, to culminate seven years later in the total abolition of slavery, which the British consul estimated would emancipate twenty-seven thousand slaves. Holmwood believed that abolition would both solve the problem of a shortage of free labor that perennially plagued western planters and unleash British capital into various sectors of agro-business on the islands.[64]

Proceeding to Ngazidja, Holmwood discovered that the usurper Said Ali had secured food and ammunition for his rebellion through the sale of slaves and free Comoro children to Sultan Abdullah.[65] The envoy found this French-speaking "youth" surrounded by a retinue of well-dressed and armed attendants, several of whom he recognized from their complicity in slave-trading cases that he or Kirk had arbitrated in Zanzibar.[66] But the Consul pinned his hope for staunching the flow of slave trafficking in the neighborhood on British pressure on the Sultan of Ndzwani. He returned from Ngazidja to accommodations within the Mutsamudu home of Abdullah's brother-in-law, lavishly furnished with items that included gifts sent over the years by Queen Victoria. The following afternoon, Holmwood presided over a reception to publicly seal his transaction with Abdullah. As the British emissary entered the palace, the Zanzibari steamer *Sultani*, which had brought the consul to Ndzwani, saluted the sultan's flag with twenty-one guns. Holmwood congratulated Abdullah and his newly anointed successor Prince Salim on their antislavery proclamation, issuing a public warning that rebellion against the new treaty would provoke "exemplary punishment."[67]

Rumblings of popular discontent surfaced immediately. An "aged priest" framed British antislavery as a Christian crusade against Muslims everywhere in the world and threatened to appeal to the Ottoman empire for protection. Holmwood recounted that Abdullah berated the *kazi* (religious judge) for his ignorance: "Did he not know that the English were the one Christian nation who had constantly supported weak Mahommedan countries. Johanna had been virtually under British protection for more than a century, and he wished it always to remain so." The same night, Abdullah led Holmwood to a palace library filled with English-language books, which he declared he was about to "transfer to his son." The consul seized that opportunity to counsel him to bring all his subjects—including the island's enslaved and aboriginal populations—under the protection of equal laws. He held out the prospect of English capital investment as an incentive for carrying out such reforms.[68]

Upon his return to Zanzibar in early November, Holmwood submitted to Foreign Secretary Earl Granville a report on the antislavery treaties he had negotiated with Comorian powers, via a dispatch by naval officer Lieutenant-Colonel Miles.[69] Almost immediately, however, the HMS *Harrier* brought news of fresh ferment from Ndzwani. The vessel had departed that island in order to bring before the Admiralty Court at Zanzibar the case of a Creole defendant from Seychelles alleged to be engaged in running slaves between Ndzwani and the French island of Glorioso. But when the *Harrier* touched Ndzwani's shores, it had discovered that two of Abdullah's brothers had risen in revolt against him and, taking advantage of popular sentiments against the promulgation of the antislavery treaty with the British, seized the capital city of Mutsamudu. The king appealed to the *Harrier*'s Captain Wilcox for help, noting that his own acquiescence in the demands of imperial abolition had "menaced" his rule. Wilcox, however, judged his authority to extend merely to the ability to offer asylum aboard his ship.[70]

It soon became clear that the British Foreign Office had little interest in enforcing Holmwood's antislavery treaties with blood or treasure, or in securing Abdullah's power against the threat of coups. Among other things, the inauguration of the Suez Canal had diminished Ndzwani's importance as a way station along the passage to India. The Foreign Office asserted: "The political and commercial interest of this country in the Comoro Group are not sufficient to call for any active interference except in regard to the suppression of the Slave Trade. Nor does his Lordship consider that the past conduct of the Sultan of Johanna has been such as to entitle him to any special consideration from Her Majesty's Government...."[71]

Thus, when Abdullah eventually managed to quell the rebellion against him at home, it was without British support. What did not surface in British diplomatic exchanges was the fact that a certain New Englander appears to have played a role in the uprising against the sultan. Wilson was about to pay dearly for this betrayal of his royal patron.

FREE ENTERPRISE, "FREE" LABOR, AND AMERICAN HONOR

Towards the close of 1884, the US Consulate in Zanzibar received an Indian trader bearing a charge sheet from Benjamin Wilson alleging that Sultan Abdullah was scheming to drive him "off the land and give my plantation to his son Salim."[72] The king had failed to raise the $300,000 he had earlier offered in payment for Patsy.[73] Encumbered by a vast circle of dependents and a luxurious lifestyle to support, he had also defaulted on his share of a loan contracted jointly with Wilson from Mauritius-based creditors.[74]

Wilson's complaint belonged in a litany of charges and countercharges exchanged with his former patron in the months that followed the abortive rebellion of 1883. Fierce competition for labor surfaced in these allegations. When Abdullah accused the American of slaveholding in a deposition dispatched to the State Department, Wilson countered that the sultan was intimidating Patsy's labor force into staying away from the estate. Thus it was the king who was interfering with the free will of employees to work for whomever they wished. Wilson's managers and staff corroborated these reports of escalating harassment. The estate's engineer Euan swore that in September 1884, the king's soldiers (a large proportion of them enslaved) passed along the sugar fields during the workday, firing shots into the air. Frightened laborers moved away from the plantation, forcing Euan to suspend factory operations at the height of the sugar season.[75] Several overseers had departed but were afraid to say openly that the sultan "told them to go."[76] An interpreter was imprisoned "for saying he would work for [Wilson] and that he was not a slave." The sultan had also prohibited other masters in town from hiring their slaves out to Wilson, and had one worker who remained captured and chained in the stocks.[77] Wilson's work force of six hundred had shrunk by half, depriving him of "at least two half crops of sugar."[78]

The American complained that the sultan had further impeded the operation of free enterprise in his domain by ordering Arab and Indian traders not to transact any business with Patsy on pain of a penalty of two hundred dollars for violations, along with veiled threats to their lives.[79] The monarch's men were said to have boarded an Indian dhow in Patsy's harbor, dislodged the workers bagging a cargo of paddy (unmilled rice) aboard, and tried to force the captain to sail to town against his own wishes and sell his supplies to the sultan instead. Neighboring planters had thus joined the American in securing weapons in self-defense.[80] Wilson feared that his life itself was in danger. The clerk DeSouza testified that sixteen of the sultan's men had camped out in a spot that fell within the doctor's morning beat and had even disclosed the disquieting intelligence that they had orders from the sultan to kill the doctor if they saw him: "they said they would drive out the white man and give the place to Prince Salim."[81] Then one Tuesday night in October 1884 the American's steam launch was sunk as it lay anchored; the following Thursday, a mysterious fire destroyed the home of an employee after suspicious men dressed in women clothing were seen lurking in the neighborhood.[82]

These offenses amounted to a breach of contract, Wilson maintained. The sultan had failed to fulfill the terms of his agreements of October 1871 and May 1872 "in regard to the supply of labor, cash, and machinery, causing me great loss of time and capital." For these and other assorted grievances, Wilson sought the assistance of the US government in securing an indemnity of $600,000. In his charges, Wilson described himself conspicuously as an "American citizen." Even though he had long maintained that he was bound by the slavery laws of his country of residence rather than those of the land of his birth, he now invoked his claims to American national belonging and consular protection of his business interests. For good measure, the doctor alleged that Abdullah's men had fired upon an American flag flying over the Patsy estate.[83] Wilson urged Washington to send a US man-of-war to the Indian Ocean to defend American interests.[84] But no warship was available for dispatch to the vicinity at the time. Afraid that procrastination would leave his fellow New Englander "financially ruined," the Zanzibar Consul Cheney sent US Vice Consul Edward Ropes, a Salem merchant, on the SS *Akola,* provided by the Sultan of Zanzibar in a gesture of goodwill.[85]

The Ropes investigation would yield allegations by Abdullah of Wilson's complicity in the attempted coup mounted by the rebel princes of Ndzwani. Upon his arrival, Ropes first visited Patsy, leaving with the conviction that Wilson was telling the truth. A ride across the estate with the planter in what represented Wilson's first appearance for months was met by cheering workers. Ropes noted as well that bullet holes pierced the road near the American planter's house. A few days later, he rode a donkey over a mountain to King Abdullah's sugar estate at Bambao, where the king received him "with all civility." The sultan returned Wilson's charge of a breach of contract, alleging that the doctor had fomented a rebellion against him, supplying its chief leader, the sultan's brother Muhamed, with 280 guns and ammunition. A series of witnesses, including Prince Muhamed himself, corroborated

Abdullah's version, implicating both Wilson and, indirectly at least, the Sultan of Zanzibar—who we may recall had supplied military aid against Abdullah's ally in Ngazidja, Said Ali. Now the defeated rebel Prince Muhamed swore that he had signed an agreement with Wilson in English for the disposal of the sugar estates on the island: "the Doctor agreeing to back me up . . . and I agreeing to let him retain Patsy." He went on to disclose that the weapons of war had been transhipped on the steamship *Akola* from Zanzibar to Patsy via Mayotte, and that Wilson himself had brought the prince fifteen hundred cartridges in a bag tied around his waist.[86]

Yet another former rebel claimed that Wilson had offered to install him on the throne of Mwali in return for raising a rebel fighting force at the rate of $50 for free men and $10 for slaves.[87] But having supposedly received advance notice from one witness that he was going to swear a false oath against Wilson for fear of retaliation if he acted otherwise, the US envoy rejected all testimonials in favor of the sultan as false and coerced. Ropes demanded as well that, pending the outcome of his investigation, the king send a public crier into the capital to permit all laborers to return to work at Patsy and announce an end to all restrictions on commerce with the American planter. The vice consul demanded to know what size of indemnity the Sultan was going to pay Wilson and what he would "say to our government for the way he had used an American citizen?" Pragmatism apparently prompted a cautious Abdullah to effect mock deference before American might. He lamented that he was too poor a man to pay what Wilson was asking.[88]

Meanwhile the witnesses for Wilson—the engineer, bookkeeper, general manager, an Indian trader, and a recently hired overseer—corroborated the American's various charges of persecution. The overseer, Syed Abdallah, who had served for just a week at the time of his testimony, claimed that royal soldiers, with their guns drawn, had driven him off the estate on the pain of death, broken into his home, and stolen his property, leaving him with the threat of unemployment.[89] An interpreter, Mohammed Salim, nursing a head wound, swore that the king's soldiers had driven him to the stocks handcuffed, left him without food and water for two days, and "asked me if I would work (with Wilson)." He also testified that the king's crier roved the streets, ordering all masters who hired their slaves out to Wilson to withdraw them.[90] An Indian merchant who conducted Ndzwani's export-import trade with Zanzibar and Mauritius confirmed that the king had read the island's Hindu merchants a proclamation, establishing a fine of two hundred dollars for trading with Patsy estate.[91]

As for the crux of the sultan's charge that the American had instigated war, Ropes's open-ended questions left room to absolve Wilson of direct involvement in Muhamed's rebellion. The vice consul asked employees what they knew about guns on the property. Engineer Euan steered the discussion to one about the estate's security arrangements (twenty policemen carried arms, but there were never more than one hundred pounds of powder or fifty pounds of dynamite on the premises). Were employees allowed to fire "promiscuously" around the estate? The response was, not surprisingly, a strong denial. Yet bookkeeper DeSouza's testimony hinted that Wilson had played a larger role in the recent turmoil than he was willing to acknowledge. He confirmed that Prince Muhamed had received a supply of arms from Zanzibar that arrived at Patsy with a cargo of paddy. Ropes asked whether the transaction involved any invoice made out in Wilson's name, but the response was no. DeSouza and his brother had advanced the funds for the purchase with the expectation that they would get paid, which had not happened.[92]

Based on his examination of the witnesses that Wilson produced Ropes concluded that the doctor had merely sympathized with Muhamed and served as a peace broker, but played no role in supplying arms to the rebels. By contrast, his indictment of Abdullah was scathing. He judged "King Abdullah and his crowd... unscrupulous liars who have spared no means, fair or foul, to drive Dr. Wilson away or make it so hard for him that he will be glad to sell out at half price." Ropes urged the United States to back the American planter's rights with a man-of-war, for the sultan would not relent "except in the presence of a stronger force than this fort and thousand armed slaves."[93] When Ropes returned to Zanzibar, he brought a gift of sugar from Wilson for Syed Barghash in appreciation of the loan of the *Akola*, which had ferried the investigator to Ndzwani.[94]

Abdullah protested Ropes's verdict, invoking the sanctity of the Quran to assert the truth of the testimonials he had arranged.[95] Wilson countered by producing further anecdotes about witness tampering by the sultan.[96] Yet the administration of President Chester Arthur, once an abolitionist associated with the *Lemmon* fugitive slave case we encountered in chapter 5, proved reluctant to defend the rights of slaveholding Americans in the IOW with military might. Moreover, the doctor's champion Ropes resigned his post in March 1885.[97] The State Department placed Wilson on the defensive by questioning his relationship with slavery and the slave trade. Had he imported slaves into Ndzwani from Africa? Did he have difficulties with his employees and workers? The doctor hotly denied these charges, acknowledging instead that he did buy slaves on the island, only to free and register them as required by the terms of the antislavery treaty concluded by Abdullah with the British.[98] When the sultan suggested that Wilson had created his own labor problem by exploiting workers, the American responded that his employees were "most... contented with me if left alone by the Sultan's soldiers." He went on to allege that Abdullah was deceiving the British into thinking that he was complying with the terms of the anti–slave trade treaty that he had signed with them, when in fact he frequently imported slaves from Africa into his territories, selling them in Mayotte, and showed no signs of freeing all the slaves by 1 August 1889 as the British demanded. He wrote that the sultan "has said that he does not care for the English government as they would take no more notice of the treaty than they have of any former treaties."[99]

Enslaved testimonies stored in the British colonial archives support Wilson's allegations about Abdullah's two-faced stance on slavery, while presenting a more complicated picture of the American planter's own relationship with Ndzwani's slave economy than his dispatches to the State Department acknowledged. For instance, a deposition by twenty-year-old free-born Mlamali of Ngazidja, taken by Consul Holmwood during his visit to the Comoros and reproduced by Edward Alpers in 2015, implicates the American planter in the purchase of slaves. At the same time, it notes Wilson's good treatment of his "workers," his willingness to inform them of the antislavery agreement with the British, and his employment of so-called bushmen fleeing the sultan's net of virtual enslavement. Mlamali, a Moroni native liberated by the British, testified that in Said Ali's Ngazidja, a local chief had expanded the target list of trafficked humans from Makuas to "Comoro people both free and slaves."

The witness Mlamali had been kidnapped and sold together with four others as *engagés* to a Frenchman, ending up in the hands of Abdullah's sister Bueni Jumbe via Mwali and Mayotte. The royal sibling emerges in this testimonial as an avid consumer of slaves, buying several young Comorian women to serve as concubines for her son and selling four recently arrived captives to Wilson. Mlamali himself was either hired out or sold to the American. He reported that he had been so well treated at Patsy that he wished to return there as a free worker. He also corroborated Wilson's version of the sultan's duplicity, stating that while the American had explained the implications of British regulations to his workers, Abdullah had continued to capture and dispatch free bushmen to Mayotte as *engagés*. And when members of these communities descended from their hillside homes to seek refuge with Wilson, the doctor hired them to work for him, only to have Abdullah resort to police interventions to drive them away. But Consul Holmwood's records also suggest that during the political strife of 1883 the sultan, in deference to British will, seized a consignment of Makua slaves shipped from the Mozambique coast south of Angoche. The master and owner of the dhow that transported them claimed that they were bound for Patsy.[100]

The muddy tenor of Wilson's reputation on the question of slave trading would have made unequivocal intervention by post–Civil War US administrations rather awkward. Nevertheless, the American planter rued his government's lack of support, reflecting that British and French subjects were better off in this regard.[101] His business partners who were subjects of the sultan were reportedly as anxious to see a US man-of-war in Ndzwani as he was, for the sultan was supposedly unpopular, propped up solely by his mastery over a large gang of armed slaves.[102] Wilson's exchanges, with their emphasis on the role of enslaved soldiers in buttressing a corrupt and confiscatory monarchy, may have had some effect, especially as the Arthur presidency yielded to the more sympathetic Democratic administration of Grover Cleveland. Under Arthur, the United States had moved toward the development of a modern navy with steam-powered steel cruisers. Cleveland's Secretary of State Thomas F. Bayard, inclined to defend the lives and property of American citizens abroad with the use of force if necessary, dispatched to Ndzwani a man-of-war, the USS *Juniata* under the command of P. F. Harrington, in September 1885.[103] Harrington, however, found it very difficult to persuade witnesses to board the vessel to testify against the king.[104]

The following year, in April 1886, Captain Potters of the flagship USS *Lancaster* of the South Atlantic Squadron arrived in the island to follow up on investigations into the Wilson case. Now the doctor all but conceded his role in the uprising against Abdullah, explaining his stance in terms of his commitment to the rule of law and tradition rather than his own economic interests. He maintained that he had opposed the sultan out of respect for the island's political tradition of term limits amounting to thirty years per ruler. The current sultan had failed to relinquish the crown to his brother, the defeated rebel prince, who the American insisted was the more popular choice for sovereign on the island.[105]

Unfortunately for Wilson, the *Lancaster*'s arrival coincided with the appearance of the French gunboat *Chacal*, bearing the Mayotte Commandant with instructions to assume control over the "Protectorate" of Anjouan. The Third Republic of France was about to extend the colonial overlordship it had established in Madagascar to Ndzwani, Ngazidja, and Mwali. Wilson and the Zanzibar Consul Pratt maintained that the presence of an American warship drove Sultan Abdullah to accept the French arrangement against his will. The *Lancaster* retreated from the Comoros, firing "a national salute" as it sailed away. Clearly, the Cleveland administration was not about to tangle with French imperialists in a part of the Indian Ocean that European states meeting recently in Berlin had decided lay within the French sphere of influence. And US interests in the area were relatively undeveloped in any case. The departing American investigators reflected wishfully on the probability that the French government would settle Dr. Wilson's claims against the sultan.[106] Unfortunately for the doctor, French rule was about to inaugurate a desperate new phase of conflict with the colonial authorities over labor, language, and the authenticity of the American's property rights.[107]

LAND, LABOR, AND LANGUAGE:
FRENCH IMPERIALISM

The French protectorate phase of Benjamin Wilson's Ndzwani career began with rumors back home that the doctor had engaged in slave trading. American newspapers reported that the schooner *Emma Jane* of Edgartown had been fitted as a whaler on US shores, but her master, in violation of the owner's wishes, sailed her to Ndzwani and sold her to Wilson, who then used her to transport sugar but also, it was suspected, to perpetuate human trafficking. The man-of-war USS *Alliance* sailed from Gibraltar in December 1886 to investigate these charges. It cruised through the Mediterranean, Suez Canal, and Red Sea, arriving in Aden on 26 January 1887. From there the vessel continued to Zanzibar and reached the island of Ndzwani in early March.[108]

Wilson was at hand to greet the captain. He plied the crew with fine food and wine, offering them grand tours of his estate with its bathhouses and stables full of fine horses. The planter explained to his guests that he had repaired *Emma Jane* at an expense of eight thousand dollars in order to ship sugar, but that she was condemned in Mauritius as unseaworthy and sold by a representative of the American Lloyds company. He denied having had anything to do with the slave trade. Proceeding to Mauritius, the *Alliance* seized a "part of the outfit of the *Emma Jane*" (which later turned out to be kettles used to make whale oil), but found the vessel in too poor a condition to confiscate.[109]

While the *Alliance* was anchored in Ndzwani, three French warships appeared on the horizon. Some news outlets reported that by this time the doctor had raised his own army, consisting of "a major general, a couple of colonels and a small company of privates. This army threatened to wipe out the Sultan and his forces, and it was when civil war was imminent that the French cruisers appeared." Wilson's army lined up on the beach, "ready to receive the invaders in the surf," but retreated into a trench upon sighting the glisten of a gun mounted on the French man-of-war.[110] Under duress, Abdullah concluded a treaty with the commander of Mayotte, Gerville-Réache, in April 1886. A new French protectorate was born, now known officially as Anjouan. The sultan soon clashed with his French "protectors" over the terms of his surrender, interpreting them to limit French rule to foreign affairs, and objecting to the installation of a Resident in Mutsamudu.[111]

But Abdullah's problems were not confined to the French. Internal dissension materialized, and Wilson seems to have been right in the middle of it. The doctor, together with Beresford d'Esté, the Mauritian manager of the Pomoni estate belonging to the late William Sunley, who had been succeeded by his nephew Robert, incited the sultan's brothers Said Ali and Muhamed to challenge the sultan. Charging that Abdullah had sold his nation to the colonists from Europe, the rebel princes proceeded to build up a following. But when in 1887 the French sent a naval expedition to force the king to accept a Resident in his capital, Wilson bowed to the dictates of expediency and greeted the invaders cordially, probably hoping that a French state would honor the sultan's debts to various parties, including, of course, himself. Later, at a difficult moment in his relations with the colonial regime, the American would remind the inspector of colonies in France that his "boats, men and magazines [were] placed at their disposition and all assistance accorded to them" in support of the French bid to force the sultan to accept a Resident in Mutsamudu. A new Tribunal Mixt (a hybrid court consisting of a French bureaucrat, a planter, and a local) was established to govern internal matters. The fate of slavery's abolition, scheduled take effect in 1889, was thrown into uncertainty. But any hopes that Wilson may have had of the French guaranteeing Abdullah's debts and enforcing his other claims were about to be dashed.[112]

In January 1888, Secretary of State Bayard requested from the French Foreign Office information about "the rights reserved ... to American citizens residing in the Comoro Islands" under the arrangements the French had entered into with Comorian rulers. The French government forwarded two conventions signed between the "Sultan of Anjouan" and the French Republic on 21 April 1886 and 15 October 1887, pledging the Ndzwani sultan "to take the necessary steps for the abolition of slavery in his States." They also absolved French colonial authorities of all responsibilities for the execution of "previous deeds and conventions" concluded by foreigners with Abdullah, but did reserve for France a mediating role in any disputes that might arise from such preprotectorate agreements.[113]

Bayard drew upon this arbitration provision to instruct the US Ambassador to France to raise Benjamin F. Wilson's damages claim of alleged contractual violations "verbally" with Paris. Over the past couple of years Wilson had assembled letters of support from business partners in Mauritius attesting to his integrity,[114] offered testimonies by experts including an "agricultural chemist" and independent plantation managers on the extent of his business losses,[115] and secured retractions of earlier testimonies implicating him in the coup against the sultan.[116] Impressed by this evidence, Bayard wrote that Wilson had endured "the Sultan *taking away his slaves* [our italics], terrorizing the freedmen so that they refused to work, sending soldiers to kill Dr. Wilson, firing into his house, and destroying a small vessel owned by him." Bayard also asserted that recent testimony had exonerated the American of charges of sedition against the sultan.[117]

From the perspective of the international politics of slavery, what is striking is the nonchalant reference to Wilson's slaveholding by the Cleveland administration. The complaint that Sultan Abdullah was "taking away" Wilson's slaves (among other "injuries") marked a sharp departure from previous admonitions by the Republican Grant and Arthur administrations against American operators' accommodation of slavery in different Indian Ocean settings, whether Zanzibar or the Comoros. Later, France's colonial establishment would level allegations of the American's violation of its free labor measures as an excuse to attack his business interests in Anjouan, even as French planters' labor demands made a mockery of imperial pretensions to abolition. Unfortunately for Wilson, however, Bayard was on his way out, to be replaced in 1889 by the Republican regime of Benjamin Harrison, who proved less inclined to defend the claims of slaveholding American citizens around the world.

All in all, then, for the moment at least, the appearance of French guns augured badly for the doctor from New Bedford. The feud between the sojourner and the sultan gathered steam within the framework of new, colonial configurations of power after 1886. Perhaps emboldened by apparent US indifference to the Wilson case signaled first by the departure of the *Lancaster* and subsequently by Secretary of State Bayard, the king mounted a campaign of what the American insisted was calumny against his character and professional reputation. Abdullah continued to thwart Wilson's access to labor, fomented worker unrest on that estate, and plotted with the French to dispossess him of his properties.

The first crippling blow to the planter's enterprise within the structure of French protectionism materialized in the form of a tax imposed by the protectorate on the right to work on the island's leading American and British estates. In May 1888, Wilson returned from a trip to French offices in Mayotte, where he had sought to press his claims against the sultan, to find that a large proportion of the free laborers on his estate had failed to show up for work. It transpired that the sultan had decreed that Patsy and Pomoni employees must pay a "poll tax" of $5.50, whereas all other workers were charged a lower fee of $1.50.[118] Moreover, the sultanate deployed armed policemen on the plantations and in a neighboring village to enforce payment, frightening free men into staying away from Patsy.[119] Wilson called upon the acting French Resident in Anjouan to warn the sultan against trespass, to "inform him that this estate is private and he has no right to make disturbances here by sending armed men upon the estate."[120]

Other news of labor unrest filtered in. The sultan's decrees offered disaffected workers latitude to resist the Anglo-Atlantic planters or demand better terms of employment in a context in which plantation agriculture had debased labor since the mid nineteenth century. The workers on the British-operated estate in Pomoni went on strike, and in the absence of any action by the French Resident, the plantation's custodian Robert Sunley was "obliged to submit to them or lose his crop."[121] Rebels, one of them an *engagé* of Wilson, started a fire, not just burning down some young trees but also depriving the estate of fuel for the factory and wood for construction. Wilson managed to have the suspect imprisoned.[122]

Yet while the French authorities were willing to act against some recalcitrant *engagés,* no doubt in order to protect the stability of their own regimes of indentured servitude, they proved distinctly reluctant to entertain Wilson's claims of indemnity against their client, the sultan. The doctor bemoaned the fact that whenever he complained to the French government against the king, they referred him to the US government. Meanwhile, the sultan argued that Wilson had forfeited his right to American citizenship—a case he had made to the *Juniata* investigator and continued to press in Washington. Wilson protested vigorously, peppering his correspondence to the US State Department with references to his patriotism and his "unimpeachable character." The American flag, he insisted earnestly, flew over "all of my boats and over my magazine at the beach and over my residence, and at the time that the Sultan's soldiers were firing upon my house daily, for two months I had the U.S. ensign flying night and day until it was blown away.... Still I cannot have the aid and protection of my government?" He pleaded that the United States salvage its reputation as a defender of its overseas citizens: "I am becoming the laughing stock of all French officials out here behind my back for the reason that I rely upon my government for protection and they ignore me!"[123]

When direct appeals to national honor failed to move the State Department, the American planter proceeded to marshal his multinational creditors based in Zanzibar and Mauritius to lobby the US government to support his indemnity claims.[124] An indenture dated 16 February 1894 between Wilson and receivers of the estate of the late Zanzibar-based Indian entrepreneur, Sir Tharia Topan, gave the Topan estate first charge on Wilson's claim against the sultan toward the settlement of his $12,385.76 debt to Topan. The agreement set a deadline of 1 September 1895 for the repayment of this sum. When that deadline passed, the Topan estate pressed the US consul in Zanzibar for information about whether the US ambassador in Paris had reached an accord with France on Wilson's claims.[125]

By this time, however, the death of Sultan Abdullah and a war of succession among rival contenders within the sultanate's royal family, intertwined with a slave insurrection in 1891, had ushered in a consolidation of imperial power and an ominous new phase in Wilson's fortunes.

The immediate phase of the trouble began when Sultan Abdullah, on the advice of the French Resident, issued a decree in 1889, effectively postponing emancipation by requiring freed people to serve their masters as hired workers for two terms of five years each at nominal pay. The move was intended to win over Arab slaveholders and Atlantic planters on the island. Moreover, by 1887 the sultan had signed a contract with the Oriental Bank of Port Louis that allowed them to exploit his Bambao estate until his large debt to them had been paid. The bank expected to draw upon the labor of six hundred workers, including the sultan's slaves. But large portions of the enslaved population, especially those identified as Makua, were in no mood to comply. By the end of 1890, workers deserted the estates at Bambao, Patsy, and Pomoni, and bands of bondspeople wandered through the interior of the island. Soon after Resident Ormières retreated to Mayotte, the ailing Abdullah died in Bambao in early February 1891, precipitating a crisis of succession entwined with a populist uprising of peasants and slaves.[126]

The sultan's heir apparent, the twenty-five-year-old Mauritius-educated Prince Salim, well versed in French and English, was as leery of the French as his father had been. Committed to plantation agriculture and hostile to immediate abolition, he did not enjoy the confidence of Anjouan's rural and underprivileged populations. These groups rallied to the standard of the prince's uncle Saïd Athman, who promised emancipation and land redistribution among the freed people. Salim endeavored to raise an army by equipping three hundred Makua in the area of Bambao with rifles, only to see them join Athman's supporters. The rebels took over the town of Mutsamudu and celebrated the liberation of the enslaved with rice alcohol, torching homes belonging to Arab elites, storming rice granaries, and killing adversaries. Salim, who had taken refuge in the village of Bambao, relented, conceding Ndzwani's throne to Athman, whom a majority of the island's residents recognized as their new ruler. During these days of unrest, Wilson's estate was said to have sheltered more than five hundred refugees—mostly women and children—from the violence. But its business operations all but came to a halt, with 190 workers staying away. Patsy's manager, initially supportive of Athman and his enslaved constituency, seems to have disagreed with the new sultan's insistence that even those absent from work be paid wages. The pro-British, Anglo-Atlantic interests centered in Pomoni and Patsy generally grew disenchanted with the new order's prospects for leading Anjouan to economic recovery.[127]

French warships eventually reconquered Mutsamudu in the face of peasants and slaves who greeted them on the beach shouting pro-British slogans. Anxious to rid Anjouan of both the Anglophilic Salim and the Makua-supported Athman, Governor Papinaud at Mayotte declared that the dynasty of the late Sultan Abdullah III had forfeited its rights to succession, installing instead a pro-French octogenarian prince named Saïd Omar. Athman took to the hills, from where he carried on guerrilla warfare until he was deported, together with most of his followers, to Obock, Djibouti. Planters—whether British, French, American, or Arab—appear to have acquiesced in these arrangements for fear of where Athman's populist leadership and the empowerment of former slaves might lead. Wilson remained in the United States for two years during these events, among other activities renewing his membership in the Eureka Masonic lodge of Massachusetts. But he later noted that "at the time of the revolution of 1891 during my absence at home my [representative] gave [the French] much valuable assistance...."[128] However, the Patsy's manager had apparently earned the distrust of the French by allowing Makua women sheltering on the estate during the insurrection to supply their rebel husbands in the hills with millet from the plantation. He avoided deportation on the plea that the charges against him were unproven. But the French may have held these allegations against Wilson in the years to come.[129]

One significant outcome of the slave insurrection of 1891 was that the French reversed the gradual emancipation policy promulgated by Abdullah III, directing Omar to issue a new decree enacting the unconditional abolition of slavery in Anjouan in May 1891. With the European and American planters and Arab landlords anxious for the resumption of normal economic activity, and the workers in need of employment, relative calm returned to the island. The following year, the French tightened their control over the protectorate, assuming control of its budget and vesting the Resident and his agents with the power to appoint village chiefs. Meanwhile, rumors flew that a large French corporation open only to French investors was about to drive all "strangers" off the land. Two Parisians—Bouin and Alfred Regoin—obtained leases of the estate at Bambao for 10,000 francs.[130]

Wilson's troubles with Sultan Abdullah paled in comparison with those about to follow from the ruthlessness of Ndzwani's new colonial overlords, especially after the French brought the entire Comorian archipelago under the unified control of the governor of Mayotte in 1899. According to the narrative of the French chapter of Wilson's career crafted in 1902 by the US Consul in Zanzibar Charles Mason Mitchell, a former Rough Rider, the administration treated "Dr. Wilson" as "persona non grata" from the start.[131]

Ongoing disputes over land tenure, labor, and debt claims on the outgoing sultanate were compounded by new requirements of documentation in the medium of the French language. Accustomed to dealing with Ndzwani elites who spoke English fluently, Wilson lamented the inauguration of a new regime of record keeping in a land that had traditionally relied upon oral compacts, communal understandings, and personal patronage to authenticate claims to property. That such record keeping had to occur in French, and French alone, added a double challenge to his quest to secure the legal foundations of his holdings. Moreover, bureaucratic etiquette complicated the arbitration of his outstanding issues with the fading sultanate. When Wilson notified one French official of the sultan's ostensibly unpaid debt to his estate, that functionary "said he would not accept a letter written to him in English...." Asserting that the work of translating Wilson's documents in support of his claims would take time, the colonial bureaucracy forced the doctor to make repeated trips to their Mayotte offices over his protest that travel from Patsy was not easy. They treated him dismissively when he kept appointments.[132]

Before long, the challenges posed by language and documentation generated a more menacing threat. The colonial establishment launched a campaign to dispossess Wilson of his estates by questioning the authenticity of his claims to those properties. In the face of imperial encroachment, Wilson had taken advantage of factionalism within the Ndzwani royal family to expand his landholdings. In 1899, a wife and sister of the deceased sultan, together with another female donor, apparently transferred certain properties described in agreements they signed with Wilson as "inherent and unencumbered," covering two thousand acres of land, upon which stood "several native villages, gardens, and cocoanut groves which yield a profitable return...." When the French governor sought an explanation, the royal women responded that the land would serve as payment for the doctor's professional services to their families but also for "clothing, sustenance, etc. he had furnished them for years."[133]

The colonial establishment required that all properties be registered and registration papers be authenticated by the French Resident. Wilson claimed to have paid cash in September 1878 for tracts of land adjoining his original grant, and he retained documents constituting "receipts and transfers of land." But the land titles he presented to the French did not pass the test of validity.[134] The American protested that all his "titles and papers were made in good faith and honestly and not by a lawyer."[135] He went to great pains to explain that Arab African practices did not seal land transfers through formal, written documents validated by lawyers. Rather, communal sanction and the witnesses of neighbors and residents sufficed as proof of an owner's claims to their property: "Scarcely any Anjouans have any titles in writing of their properties. They buy and sell without written documents as a rule." Rather, Wilson's titles were "witnessed by a large number of persons."[136]

But did the parties who sold or gifted Wilson land and gardens during the 1890s have a legal right to the properties they had bestowed? No, argued the French Resident and the tribunal. For these lands had belonged to the sultanate. They "were governmental lands and the givers or sellers of the properties had no right to dispose of them." Perhaps colonial officials were harking back to the sultan's position that the state owned all land on the island. The identity of the state had of course changed—it was now a French colonial entity. From Wilson's vantage point, his bureaucratic adversaries were using an argument about local traditions of corporate land ownership in order to further the ends of French settler colonialism.[137] The colonial police assumed custody of properties that Wilson claimed to have purchased or received as gifts and placed them under the charge of the assessor of the French tribunal. The imperial authorities allegedly divested native residents on those lands of the coconuts that they had cultivated as part of their subsistence arrangements with the American.[138]

Wilson judged these actions "tyrannical" and designed to "rob" Anjouan inhabitants of their property.[139] He maintained that such residents did indeed possess something akin to private property rights: "The fact that the former owners have been in peaceable possession for a long term of years (more than forty) would give them undisputed ownership." The American argued that the fact that no one had challenged their property rights proved the existence of communal consensus on the legitimacy of such rights. Wilson offered to produce an army of witnesses for "interrogation" by the French in support of his claims. Ironically enough, his assimilation to local norms of property ownership had now run afoul of western European constructs of contract law.[140]

Moreover, when Wilson provided written versions of what he maintained were long-term agreements to support his claims of communal sanction of his property rights, the French authorities refused to accept them because they were written in English and Arabic. When Wilson supplied translations of these documents in French, they claimed that he had missed his deadline for registration.[141] Wilson's subsequent appeal that the land's new custodians help him to recover the purchase price of the lands he had acquired fell upon deaf ears.[142]

Before long, local agents of the imperial state targeted Patsy itself. Two years before the estate's original lease was due to expire in May 1902, Wilson notified a visiting inspector of colonies that the late Sultan Abdullah had agreed to extend it for sixty years more on the same terms, sharing with the French official what he maintained were certified copies of the agreement.[143] A few months later, a new secretary general arrived, with his eye on Wilson's estate, and he reportedly discouraged local residents from selling their lands to Wilson on the grounds that he was a "foreigner." Wilson was outraged: "I have been on this island now 29 years." But from the French perspective, the American's acculturation to Ndzwani culture did not matter. He was an imposter with a valuable estate that they themselves coveted. The secretary general proceeded to impose taxes and duties from which the Sultan had exempted him.[144] Oral agreements relieving Patsy's produce from such excises did not impress Anjouan's new customs house, which refused to release Wilson's merchandize until he had paid customs fees.[145]

Wilson then appealed to Governor Pierre Pascal at Mayotte to certify the lease extension agreement ostensibly signed by Sultan Abdullah in December 1879.[146] The governor deferred to the minister of colonies in France on the matter, informing Wilson at the same time that French planters on the island had made bids to buy parts of the estate. What did the American propose to offer in support of his application to retain possession of Patsy? Wilson suspected that Pascal was in fact in the pockets of Regoin, a Frenchman with designs on the estate. The dispute got personal before long, with the governor informing the American that he had established a reputation as a Francophobe who "hated Frenchmen and ignored French authority in the island." The doctor denied this charge strenuously, seeing it as an excuse to rid the island of his presence, so that the colonial government could usurp his property and cancel the sultanate's debts to his estate.[147]

Wilson's struggles with the French over land tenure unfolded in tandem with competition with French planters for labor—a contest that inevitably assumed the garb of slavery politics and the color of national identity. These clashes turned on the legal status of workers—whether free or indentured, on rivalrous claims to their labor and the obligation of employers to pay wages on time. In this context, the American planter and French officials accused each other of instituting slavery under different guises—whether by failing to pay wages required by indenture contracts, by coercing free workers into *engagé* arrangements against their will, or by infringing on the rights of free laborers to work for whomever they wanted.

The Mitchell Report on Wilson's claims asserted that following emancipation, the Resident of Anjouan issued an order requiring employers of workforces numbering greater than 150 to pay their workers twice a year, in the presence of a colonial official such as a commissary of police. Wilson claimed to have complied with this directive until imperial monitors stopped coming, apparently on the assumption that such compliance would continue.[148]

The imperial requirement of wage payment gave those on the margins new resources with which to resist exploitation by their employers, while providing the imperial order with a tool to siphon Wilson's workers off to favored French employers in a tight labor market. In December 1901, the Mayotte-based French governor notified Wilson that two of his workers had complained against him for defaulting on their wage payments.[149] The American version of what happened next diverged from the French position. According to Mitchell, in a hearing on the subject, the two workers in question denied having filed a complaint against Wilson, for they had been paid in full. Yet, subsequent events revealed that Wilson was not in fact a consistently reliable paymaster. In response to a French query about his schedule of wage payments, he responded that "more than half of his men, about 275 had overdrawn their pay and were indebted to him, but he would pay the balance, almost 4500 Rupees, on February 2, 1902." When payday arrived, however, Wilson defaulted. In his letters to Zanzibar, he blamed bad weather for stalling the shipment of specie from Mayotte. Yet as Mitchell's investigation later revealed, the American's London- and Madagascar-based banker had suspended payments to his account, presumably because of his business difficulties.[150]

A police brigadier next arrived in Patsy and released Wilson's *engagés* from their indenture agreements, informing them that they were now "at liberty to seek work wherever they chose."[151] The workers were now invited to go to "Hombo (seat of government) and thank the administration." The American planter reported that almost none of his workers took the French up on this offer, for fear of being impressed into engagements with other employers against their will. Still, out of demoralization or fear of retaliation, Wilson surmised, many of his "people" had chosen to either stay home or take to the mountains. In fact, the French administrator's "release" may have afforded these workers a welcome respite from coercion by both the French and the American.[152]

Two weeks later, eight men who had labored for Wilson were found working on the rival estate of a Frenchman. Mitchell's report charged the French police with having removed these men from their village homes on Wilson's properties and carried them off by night, against their will, to work for a new imperial employer. But the French Resident countered Wilson's protests with the rejoinder that the men were no longer his *engagés*.[153] French operatives for their part complained that it was the American who enticed indentured workers away from competitors to his own estates. These allegations instigated police raids on Patsy to round up "deserters." As early as 1898, a large number of what Wilson asserted were "his" free laborers had been carted off to prison apparently against their will, on the word of a Frenchman who claimed them as his *engagés*. Wilson asserted that some of these men sent him word through their wives that they wished to work for the American, so it was the French who were actively thwarting Anjouan's transition to a free market for labor.[154]

In a complaint addressed to the inspector of colonies in France, with a copy to Washington, the American planter recounted a vicious cycle of virtual enslavement perpetrated by colonial bureaucrats in Anjouan. He charged that these officials forced local residents into labor engagements against their knowledge or will. Some of the so-called "indentured workers" deserted their employers and hid out in the mountains, foraging for food in nightly raids on privately owned gardens until they were caught and imprisoned. As evidence, Wilson cited the case of a porter from Pomoni who arrived at his estate looking for work. Wilson asked him if he was an *engagé*. No, the job applicant replied. But had anyone measured his height, Wilson asked. The man answered in the affirmative, leading the American to conclude that the worker had in fact been drafted as an indentured worker but without his consent or understanding. According to Wilson, when he asked the apparent victim to return to Pomoni, "he said that no one ... asked him to engage and he nor anyone else understood that they were engaged when they were measured and description taken."[155]

Months later, the colonial police clashed with the American planter's own security staff over the status of a "free laborer" who Wilson claimed had worked for him since he was a boy. Over Wilson's protests, the French Resident dragged the man away in captivity on the grounds that the man was an *engagé* on a Pomoni estate. Wilson's complaint to France bristled with instances of labor abuse by the Anjouan's imperial establishment: indiscriminate shootings, floggings, and imprisonment without trial; sexual abuse of women; and retaliation against family members seeking to protect workers against forced labor or abuse. A number of women had left Pomoni, he charged, to escape the estate manager's maltreatment. Some sought employment at Patsy, while others fled to villages on the island. The French manager then had the women followed to Wilson's estate and arrested for allegedly deserting their husbands. "These were free women and not [*engagés*] but had been forced to work as well as their husbands...."[156]

In short, Wilson's allegations of worker exploitation by French planters and officials in Anjouan assumed the cast of nothing less than a scathing critique of colonialism. In his letters to the minister of colonies in Paris, the planter represented himself as a champion of not simply his own interests but of colonized locals as well. He sketched a dismal picture of imperial oppression: unauthorized and unreasonable decrees and circulars, a rapidly depleting population, especially of males, and unattended complaints from locals to the governor at Mayotte.[157]

The American framed his ceaseless pleas to his own government in the language of American national honor, equal "rights," "liberties," and the sanctity of private property. He claimed that the French were trampling upon these cardinal principles of free society for the main purpose of transferring his assets to "French subjects."[158] For Wilson, French imperial taxes represented a contractual violation of his arrangements with the late sultan, and his deprivation of the "common rights and liberties granted to other citizens." The planter wove appeals to American nationalism into narratives of French attacks against free labor and the sanctity of private property in Anjouan. Local administrators "will take by force all (the labor) that is wanted by Frenchmen first. All of this on account of my nationality, and unless I am assisted by my government I and my possessions are doomed," Wilson wrote.[159] He beseeched the US government to dispatch a man-of-war in order to uphold the security of US citizenship and national honor in the face of European imperial aggression.[160] In August 1902, the urgency of his pleas escalated, for not only were the French imprisoning his workers, they had seized his cattle to sell at auction. His crime? He had refused to pay a fine that "they condemned me to pay because I cannot speak French!" By this time, all he wanted was for the US government to arbitrate a settlement of his claims (including unpaid debts from the sultan's estate that allegedly totaled over $50,000) so that he could "sell out and leave these ... frenchmen [sic] forever."[161]

It was these entreaties that eventually prompted a four-month investigation of Wilson's claims by the Zanzibar-based US Consul Mason Mitchell in 1902.[162] Mitchell's report recommended that the State Department lodge a formal protest against Wilson's eviction and other aspects of his treatment by the French government. The consul believed that it was the New Englander's "genial and easygoing nature" that had rendered him a ready target of persecution by an avaricious imperial state with an eye on his valuable property, estimated to be worth $200,000. Wilson was said to have invested over $125,000 in his sugar mill alone.[163] Mitchell urged the State Department to dispel the widely held view that "Dr. Wilson is a man forsaken by his country."[164]

The governor at Mayotte responded that the minister of colonies had raised questions about the authenticity of the American's lease extension agreement. The Frenchman held out the prospect of a resolution: an appeal to the High Court at Réunion.[165] Alas for Wilson, the State Department agreed. Priorities other than a lone American's business empire on an Indian Ocean island dominated US foreign relations with France. In 1898, the two nations had, "in the spirit of conciliation," concluded a reciprocal tariff reduction compact covering a wide range of goods—from American canned meats, fruits, cider, common woods, logs, and hops to French crude tartars, wine lees, brandies and spirits, and paintings.[166] And in May 1902, President Theodore Roosevelt invited French luminaries to a special dedication ceremony designed to mark France's foundational role in bringing the American republic to life: the unveiling in Washington, DC, of the monument of Marshal de Rochambeau, celebrated for helping the patriots to bring Cornwallis to his knees at Yorktown.[167]

Besides the historical ties of "lasting gratitude" that bound descendants of the American Revolution to France, Roosevelt's project to realize a long-standing mission of great powers to build a transisthmian commercial corridor across Panama involved a French role. In 1902, even as Mitchell was conducting his investigation of Wilson's troubles with the French in the Comoros, the Roosevelt administration purchased the title and rights to a canal enterprise from the French Panama Canal Corporation for $40 million, in what Maurice L. Muhleman described in 1904 as "the largest single international payment in the nation's history."[168] Sadly for Wilson, the western Indian Ocean was unlikely to have ranked high on the Roosevelt administration's diplomatic agenda with the French. The United States had few trade interests in the region anymore and was on the verge of closing down its consulate in Zanzibar. As the Panama Canal project roared along—albeit in fits and starts—the French Tribunal Mixt in Anjouan summoned "experts" who testified that the lease extension agreement that Wilson had supplied, dating back to 1879, was an inauthentic document. Wilson's foreboding that he would not receive a fair trial at the hands of a body headed by Regoin, a French planter who coveted Patsy, proved to have foundation. The tribunal denied his right to appeal its decision to the superior court in Réunion.[169] The terms of its judgment were harsh: Wilson was required to vacate Patsy and pay a fine of 20,000 francs, as well as a fine of 100 francs for each day that he remained on his beloved estate after fifteen days following the receipt of this judgment.[170]

But even as French plantation companies went on to appropriate much of the arable land on the Comorian archipelago during the remainder of the colonial period, Wilson managed to negotiate a settlement to retain Patsy until his death in 1920.[171] Two years before he passed away, he filed an application with the US Consulate in Madagascar to register as an American citizen, describing himself as a resident of Anjouan, engaged in the business of "supervising landed estates" on his own behalf.[172] Soon after his death, a French concern, the Société Coloniale de Bambao, acquired the estate.[173]

French colonialism would go on to leave an enduring legacy of neglect and dispossession in the Comoros. But meanwhile, it was the American that posterity would continue to associate with the piece of Ndzwani land known as "Patsi." A historical dictionary from the 1990s described Patsi as the area "east of the community of Mutsamudu ... named after the plantation founded and operated in the late nineteenth century by the American physician Benjamin F. Wilson."[174] Oral histories of this corner of Africa commemorate the exploits of the New Englander without going into the subplots that unfolded in the foregoing pages: the irony of a Union surgeon who reinvented himself as a slaveholder overseas; the limits of a mastery susceptible to political instability and imperial chicanery, as well as subject to shifting norms of corporate landownership and labor control; the illusory boundary between slavery and freedom that entrapped workers and became a tool of navigation among warring powers seeking leverage. Rulers wielded this leverage not simply against rebels but against each other as well—the sultan and his brothers, the American planter, the US government, and British and French colonialists. Meanwhile, the enslaved who helped build Wilson's fortune over the decades emerge mostly as fragments in these tales of adventure.

Epilogue

Crossing Slavery's Interoceanic Boundaries: Reflections

By the time Benjamin Wilson formally registered as an American citizen in Madagascar, the United States was in full sectional reconciliation mode. Tired of war and struggles for racial justice, the increasingly conservative party of Lincoln had long abandoned southern Blacks to the tender mercies of white supremacist Bourbon "redeemers," who turned the clock back on Reconstruction's experiment with racial democracy. Amid the enactment of brutal measures of race control—of segregation, disenfranchisement, and anti-Black violence—the so-called legend of the South's lost cause waxed strong. History and political propaganda, as well as popular culture and performative media, invoked a nostalgic vision of an antebellum slave society of mammies, magnolias, and mint juleps, marked by the values of chivalry, order, paternalism, and racial concord. White Americans embraced the "romance of reunion," reframing Memorial Day, for instance, as an occasion to honor *all* soldiers who had perished in the Civil War, rather than simply those who had fought for abolition and the Union.[1]

In this era of white fraternal reconciliation, as schisms between North and South receded in public memory, it seemed only fitting that American newspapers across sectional divides should resurrect the curious tale of the Union soldier from New England who fought against slaveholders at home only to build an enormous fortune on the backs of human chattel abroad. Under the lead "Kept Slaves after 1875—Former Surgeon of Navy Lived like a King on Tropic Isle," the *Watchman and Southron* of Sumter, South Carolina, heir to a history of anti-Reconstruction politics, revisited the incident of the contraband schooner *Emma Jane*, rumored to have been pressed into slave trading by Wilson. The piece it published in 1914 combined Slave South nostalgia with Orientalist imagery as it recounted the reminiscences of naval officers who had been dispatched to the Comoros in 1886 to investigate the charge. It noted that the reconnaissance party saw "naught of the missing vessel." Instead, it had discovered a "tropical paradise" covering "thousands of acres, many slaves … and the luxuries of all climes." The Yankee master of this realm was said to exercise "pretty near absolute sway" under the protection of his patron, "the dark sultan of Comoro." The report portrayed a cosmopolitan life of privilege underwritten by slavery. American and English magazines graced Wilson's table, as did fine food and wines. A steam launch went out to sea to fetch his mail once a week. Horses and dogs had the run of his extensive grounds. "Scores of slaves worked the plantation, while others, in scant costume, served the master in the great … house," fitted with "baths and pleasure houses" and even an ice machine, which helped dispense "juleps and cocktails" (after the fashion of the still-present plantation South). Although the *Emma Jane* had left the island, as we know, Wilson admitted that he had retained the whaler's "trying out kettles" (used to boil whale blubber into oil) and turned them into vats for boiling sugarcane. The US warship's landing party then "loosened" the kettles "from their seats" and confiscated them with no objections from their owner, "leaving the former surgeon still lord of the plantation and his slaves." The column speculated that on a visit back to the United States, Wilson had perhaps run into the officers whom he had entertained so graciously. It concluded that "naturally, nobody asked how he reconciled it with his conscience to own slaves in Africa twenty years after Lincoln's emancipation proclamation."[2]

As the world prepared for war, the *Watchman and Southron* offered a timely reminder that slavery had long crossed the borders of the American South, perpetrated on a global scale by unlikely standard-bearers. It was here to stay, resilient and unrepentant, leaving generations of human rights activists to grapple with its protean character and combat its legacies. The foregoing pages have sought to capture some of that protean shape, some of those border crossings, by following the trails of people, politics, and ideas from Anglo-Atlantic societies into the Indian Ocean world. The age of Atlantic revolutions bequeathed a common framework of understanding about what slavery and freedom were supposed to look like but generated fierce debate over the merits of each. Operating within that frame of reference, our globe-trotters—depending on their positioning within the international politics of slavery—set out to square imperial ambition with antislavery professions in Afro-Asia, marry the causes of marginalized populations at opposite ends of the world, grow "free cotton" in India, merchandize slave-grown American cotton to consumers in East Africa, and build sugar plantations in the Comoros. They found that oceanic worlds integrated by capitalism, empire, and technologies of travel and communication harbored local societies textured by systems of hierarchy, patronage, and dependence; of land tenure and labor control; of forms of family and norms of community different from familiar usages in the Anglo-Atlantic world.

On one level, the encounters that transpired highlighted the regional distinctiveness of IOW slave trading and slaveries. We need to understand these on their own terms, even as we deepen our knowledge of US links in exchange webs of people and commodities that integrated the western Indian Ocean with the Americas in the nineteenth century. Intra-IOW slave trades, older than their Atlantic counterparts, were multidirectional. They combined trafficked humans with other items of exchange within the body of the nimble dhow, and involved multiracial, intercontinental slavers and captives. Bondage varied in nature, function, demography, and season over time and place, defined by power relations ranging from patron-client relationships and kin incorporation to Atlantic-style chattel labor. Women and children loomed large among enslaved cohorts. Nonbinary conceptions of slavery and freedom, and of family and the market, lent some forms of servitude in the IOW a particular aura of difference from the Atlantic world. Such difference carries implications for thinking comparatively about subaltern agency and diaspora in ways that we will suggest a bit later.

Turning a lens onto regional distinctiveness also reveals unique configurations of circumstances that hampered the transplantation of American-style settler colonialism in diverse Indian Ocean locales caught up in slavery politics. Absent the infrastructure of what Sven Beckert calls "war capitalism"—consistently supportive states vested with the political, legal, judicial, and military power to enforce land expropriations and coerce labor for private enterprise—individual Atlantic fortune hunters faced precarious prospects in the IOW. A would-be "free cotton" zamindar in British India, such as Finnie, suffered chronic shortages of resources. He failed both in mastering the social and governance structures that mediated control over land and labor, and adapting his cultivation strategies to the culture, climate, and technologies of his new field of operations. A New England–born Comorian slaveholder, on the other hand, floundered between conflicting norms of land ownership and labor regulation as his island home passed from the patronage regime of a sultanate to French imperialism amid the international politics of abolition, domestic wars of succession, and a slave insurrection. Alas for Benjamin Wilson, a post–Civil War US government proved insufficiently invested in the region to commit blood or resources to defend this native son's claims to private property and American patriotism.

Notwithstanding the IOW's regional particularities, Atlantic interactions with/in Afro-Asia also accentuated interoceanic "hemorrhages." They helped shape polarizing narratives of comparative slavery that drew the Indian Ocean world into transatlantic arguments over the virtues of free societies, and scrambled bipolar notions of a British empire of abolition versus an American republic of slavery.

"Slavery in the East" assumed multifarious incarnations and served conflicting political purposes in the telling of Atlantic interlocuters. For East India Company officials who selectively accommodated South Asian forms of servitude for reasons of profit, politics, or aversion to public welfare, "Oriental" slavery was a reciprocal system of social insurance, timelessly anchored in religious law and custom, distinguished by its ostensibly familial character from the cruelty of New World chattel bondage. Anglo-Atlantic legacies of legal pluralism buttressed colonial knowledge production about "domestic slavery" in Indian Ocean societies, a central plank of which was constructed to consist in the right to self-sale during hard times. Imperial bureaucrats sought to codify informal arrangements of dependence into the poor's contractual "rights" to mortgage their labor for subsistence.

To transnational colonial reformers and abolitionists, on the other hand, such perspectives distorted local religious laws to perpetuate slavery by so-called free will, occluded the brutality of "agrestic slavery" in the East, and masked the exploitative authoritarianism of imperialism. Indicting slavery and colonialism as twin evils in the language of humanitarian reform, liberal individualism, and a free market for labor, they envisioned a universal dawn of "freedom" from the parched pockets of poverty in rural India to the auction blocks of the American South.

Ironically, such liberal reformist critiques joined eyewitness accounts of disappointed entrepreneurs like the Mississippi overseers in British India to supply "republican slaveholders" of the American South ammunition for decrying the hypocrisy of imperial abolition and crafting an alternative version of comparative slavery. On the one hand, imperial knowledge production about humane forms of "domestic slavery" in the East echoed in the rhetoric of paternalism in the Slave South and fueled assertions of slavery's humanity and universality. Idioms of family and tropes of slavery as "poor law" could be adapted to defend vastly different manifestations of subordination in disparate parts of the world, as Louisa McCord and the Tofa Bai illustrated. From the perspective of American proslavery polemicists, however, the *real* victims of a distinctive slavery in the East consisted of colonized populations starving on the imperial watch of antislavery autocrats, even as North America's human chattel flourished under the benign gaze of slaveholding democrats. Meanwhile, certain New England businessmen, who defended the claims to sovereignty of their slaveholding Gujarati-speaking business partners in East Africa and denounced the indiscriminate plunder of British antitrafficking patrols in the Indian Ocean, maintained that the true goal of abolition was imperialism.

These warring accounts revealed that the fault lines in contests over slavery in the nineteenth-century Anglophone world transcended—rather than followed—the boundaries of nation-states and empires, pitting intercontinental coalitions of reformers against multinational slavers and defenders of servitude in diverse guises from Charleston to Calcutta, and Salem through Kutch to Zanzibar.

But what of the legions of slaves and second-class citizens whose blood and toil and reproductive labor helped build the landscapes that our more privileged protagonists traversed? What meanings did migrations make from vantage points located at the bottom of power structures? The international politics of slavery supply structural and discursive frameworks for reflecting on concepts that scholars of African America have long pondered: "agency," "diaspora," and subaltern identity formation. Subaltern actions as they enter the historian's field of vision within the British colonial archives are inscribed in the edifice of Britain's antislavery diplomacy. Such actions appear in the language and records of imperial pronouncements and policies, police stations and law courts, bazaar raids and depositions, and naval cruisers and foreign relations. Imperial abolition thus emerges as what the Latin Americanist William Roseberry might have described as a hegemonic field of struggle. Subaltern subjects, positioned at the intersection of different discourses of power, seized the material and symbolic resources that the professed "ethics" of empire offered to register voices of dissent or assert claims to community. Such voices and claims, emanating from the margins of societies on an interwoven global stage, added up to a notion of agency that meant more than a liberal, individualistic impulse for autonomy under the aegis of an antislavery empire.

Framed by the international politics of slavery, moreover, agency materialized in tandem with diverse configurations of what we might think of as diasporic consciousness and subaltern identity formation. For Mary Ann Shadd Cary, collective memories and contemporary traumas shaped by the sordid histories of capture, enslavement, and racial terror provided the foundational ingredients for forging an African diaspora out of the disparate groups that slave ships had forcibly transported to the New World. Paul T. Zeleza envisions such a diaspora as embracing both a sense of community created by "real or imagined genealogies and geographies" and a space for negotiating multiple belongings.[3] Diasporic identities exist in tension with nation-states, visualizing "transnational imaginaries with which displaced people plant new roots along fresh routes."[4] Moreover, as James Sweet has noted in the context of mobile Africans like Olaudah Equiano, "the savviest and most well-traveled Africans took careful measure of their environments, adroitly crafting group identities that allowed them to survive, resist, and in some instances thrive in the Atlantic World."[5]

This discussion is particularly meaningful as a prism through which to understand Shadd Cary's strategic vision of diaspora and colonial belonging. From her vantage point at the intersection of race, gender, class, and US birth, she rejected an American nationality that denied her people basic human dignity. But she did not seek a return to "roots" in Africa either—a position that many abolitionists charged would merely play into proslavery hands by emptying North America of free Blacks. A person of color born free in North America, she appropriated her birth land's mystique of westward migration as spelling freedom and opportunity, but transposed it to a *different* West, a Canadian West, that ostensibly promised to live up to its liberating potential under the guardianship of an antislavery empire. She forged a vision of diaspora in solidarity with the Black Caribbean, based both on the common history of racial slavery and on solidarity with British antislavery. At the same time, her gendered perspective turned Black women into emancipated subjects: subjects at once of migration narratives—as mothers, workers, professionals, and seekers of opportunity—and of a female emperor presiding over a global campaign against slavery. She strategically seized the Whiggish discourse of that campaign—of freedom defined as equal opportunity, self-sufficiency, and a free market for labor—to challenge proslavery allegations of free society's devolution into "pauperism" and revolution.

By comparison, Indian Ocean world subalterns profiled in this book staged complicated, often contradictory relationships with British imperial abolition. The sheer variety of subordinate statuses in their diverse historical contexts emerges in interactions between marginalized figures and colonial power, while exposing the limits of antislavery imperialism. At the same time, these encounters prompt new ways of thinking about connections between slavery and diaspora. This work's scope does not, of course, extend to extrapolating conclusions about African diasporic consciousness in present-day South Asia and the Middle East from evidence of these nineteenth-century interactions. Nevertheless, it does become possible to reflect on the ways in which people on the margins defined or sought community beyond the boundaries of nations and imperial states on terms that invite comparison with contemporaneous Afro-Atlantic articulations of diaspora.

We might begin such comparative diasporic analysis by asking why enslaved secondary wives or concubines like the Indian-born Fatima and Turkish-Arabian-born Halima chose their Arab enslavers over British "emancipators," why the Ethiopian Yacoob hoped to impress his master by traveling to India to learn a trade, or why the rescued Black African children like Marianah preferred Black or Indian Muslim custodians over European Christian guardians upon their arrival in Bombay. As scholars of Africa have noted, group affiliation conferred empowerment.[6] But for our marginalized protagonists, who or what constituted the "group" or the communities with which they identified?

In this context, why not reframe an old debate over diaspora by moving away from the traditional question of whether there is or was such a thing as an Afro-Asian or Afro-Arab diaspora with a consciousness of African roots along the lines of the Atlantic world? Obviously, Africans traveled to the Middle East, South Asia, and beyond over centuries and in various capacities. For the limited purposes of our story, and from the perspective of our nineteenth-century subjects, it may be more relevant to consider how we define Africanness itself. A postcolonial theorist of Africa such as Shaden M. Tageldin has argued that twentieth-century intellectual and political figures like Léopold Sédar Senghor and Gamal Abdel Nasser offered a "'diasporic' defiance" of "imperial taxonomies" by "redefining Africanness as a symbiosis of Arabness and Négritude," whether based on "racial or cultural hybridity" or "historico-political and geographic contiguity."[7] We might read this analysis back to the age of abolition, in Afro-Asian settings where slavery assumed the incarnation of patron-client relationships, especially before the full-blown emergence of plantation slavery. There, within a framework of exploitation, the dynamics of "dhow culture" may nevertheless have promoted a comparative sense of belonging woven by mobility and multilingualism, by trade and Islam across port city-states from Kilwa to Kutch.[8] Before the late nineteenth-century emergence of plantation slavery on the Swahili coast, attended by gang labor and the "coalescence of planter classes," slaves were designated by labels akin to the language used for other subordinate groups, such as women.[9] Enslaved peoples in the IOW—often women and children—not only entered their masters' societies at tender ages but many of them would already have been displaced and caught in a vortex of "environmental, social, and political" turmoil before that. Sweet makes this point in a different context for the Atlantic slave trade, but the argument about the captives' subjection to upheavals applies to the IOW as well.[10] As Jonathan Glassman has noted, we must complicate functionalist perspectives on slavery as a mode of incorporating outsiders into the masters' world by acknowledging that the process of incorporation was attended by coercion and conflict, with subalterns mounting struggles for "fuller rights of social inclusion."[11]

Nevertheless, as the case of the Ethiopian Yacoob revealed, slavery-as-clientship offered a paradigm for belonging as junior members in the masters' world of community and kinship. It may be why Marianah and other African children rescued by the British seemed to prefer Muslim guardians. Their Islamic affiliations may have recalled religious community and held the promise of social reproduction that "freedom" in the custody of culturally alien Protestant Christians (whom their liberators preferred as guardians) could not. Princess Salme, a vastly more privileged product of the system of slavery–as-kinship, firmly foregrounded her Arab identity in her *Memoirs* but acknowledged the different valences it assumed in Africa. She expressed color prejudice and anti-Black racism as she ranted against abolitionists, but her symbiotic Arab-African sense of self came through in her comments on the snobbery of her Omani relatives and references to her Circassian mother's assimilation—and her own—to elements of East African culture: the Swahili language, the musical sound of *sese,* and the practice of chewing betel leaf. Raised by African nurses and protected by African eunuchs, Salme conveyed an Arab-African vision of diaspora—at once plural and syncretic, hierarchical and oppressive—within which other, far less fortunate captives who materialize as emancipated subjects in Britain's colonial archives also seem to have been embedded. And it may be that sense of diasporic belonging that prompted some of them to choose the worlds of their Arab masters over "free" labor and colonial belonging in the British Empire.

The practical workings of imperial abolition also reveal its limits: the deference to elite patriarchies and reluctance to undertake public assistance of rescued captives, the nebulous lines between slave trade on the high seas and domestic slavery on land, reliance on tributary states to assume the risks and costs of abolition, linguistic sleights of hand to accommodate coercion couched in the language of "free labor" and "free" will to make contracts, and the use of antislavery discourse to advance the ends of empire—materially, territorially, jurisdictionally. For the slavery scholar however, imperial abolition also yields rich archival dividends in the form of subaltern testimonies inscribed within imperial discourses. From the African children rescued at Porbandar in the 1830s through the conduct of the East Africans leaving the Comoros on an American merchant vessel over four decades later, they show how "refugees" in the Indian Ocean jumbled imperial narratives that meshed British abolition with notions of freedom, Christianity, and colonial assimilation. In the Black Atlantic, many abolitionists placed the American slaveholder in the same (im)moral universe as his ostensibly barbarian "Eastern" counterpart, while strategically fashioning the refugees from slavery in the Americas as the natural allies, subjects, and citizens of an antislavery British Empire. Freed persons in the Indian Ocean turned out to be more complicated symbols of imperial benevolence, challenging neat polarities of "Oriental" slavery and English freedom. So let us invoke their elusive lives as the last word in the case we have tried to make for crossing slavery's interoceanic boundaries on a granular level.

NOTES

INTRODUCTION

1. *Christian Recorder,* July 1, 1865, www.accessible.com.ezproxy.gc.cuny.edu/accessible/print. On Black soldiers of the time, see Deborah Willis, *The Black Civil War Soldier: A Visual History of Conflict and Citizenship* (New York: New York University Press, 2021).

2. The catalog entry is available at www.britishmuseum.org/collection/object/C_M-4994.

3. Sean Willcock, "A Neutered Beast? Representations of the Sons of Tipu Sultan—'The Tiger of Mysore'—as Hostages in the 1790s," *Journal for Eighteenth-Century Studies* 36 (March 2013): 121.

4. Zoë Laidlaw, "'Justice to India—Prosperity to England—Freedom to the Slave!': Humanitarian and Moral Reform Campaigns on India, Aborigines and American Slavery," *Journal of the Royal Asiatic Society* 22 (April 2012): 313.

5. On Roy and constitutional liberalism, see Christopher A. Bayly, "Rammohan Roy and the Advent of Constitutional Liberalism in India, 1800–30," *Modern Intellectual History* 4 (April 2007): 25. On the Unitarian connection between Roy and Adam, see Clare Midgley, "Cosmotopia Delineated: Rammohun Roy, William Adam, and the Calcutta Unitarian Committee," *Itinerario* 44, no. 2 (2020): 446–70, published by Cambridge University Press on behalf of the Research Institute for History, Leiden University.

6. We define *subaltern* as a relational subordinate identity. We discuss our use of this term more fully later in this introduction in connection with our discussion of related terms in African American history, such as *agency* and *diaspora.*

7. We have borrowed the expression "material and meaningful framework" from William Roseberry, "Hegemony and the Language of Contention," in *Everyday Forms of State Formation: Revolution and the Negotiation of Rule in Modern Mexico,* ed. Gilbert M. Joseph and Daniel Nugent (Durham, NC: Duke University Press, 1994), 360–61, and the term

cross-fertilization from David Rainbow, organizer of the *Russia's Races* conference at New York University, February 26–27, 2015.

For overviews of transnational history, see C.A. Bayly, Sven Beckert, Matthew Connelly, Isabel Hofmeyr, Wendy Kozol, and Patricia Seed, "AHR Conversation: On Transnational History," *American Historical Review* 111 (December 2006): 1440–64; and the essays by Nancy F. Cott, Stephen Tuck, Jean Allman, and Matthew Pratt Guterl in "AHR Forum: Transnational Lives in the Twentieth Century," *American Historical Review* 118 (February 2013): 45–139. See also Thomas Bender, *Rethinking American History in a Global Age* (Berkeley: University of California Press, 2002), and for the Indian Ocean world (IOW), Sugata Bose, *A Hundred Horizons: The Indian Ocean in the Age of Global Empire* (Cambridge, MA: Harvard University Press, 2006).

On global/comparative approaches to slavery histories, see Joseph C. Miller, *The Problem of Slavery as History* (New Haven, CT: Yale University Press, 2012); and the earlier classic, Orlando Patterson, *Slavery and Social Death: A Comparative Study* (Cambridge, MA: Harvard University Press, 1982); Richard A. Posner and David Brion Davis, *Challenging the Boundaries of Slavery* (Cambridge, MA: Harvard University Press, 2009); David Eltis, Stanley L. Engerman, Seymour Drescher, and David Richardson, eds., *The Cambridge World History of Slavery* (Cambridge: Cambridge University Press, 2017). On Africa, see Paul E. Lovejoy, *Slavery in the Global Diaspora of Africa* (New York: Routledge, 2019); and on capitalism, Sven Beckert, *Empire of Cotton: A Global History* (New York: Vintage Books, 2014).

An essential digital archive and essays on international slave trades involving Africa are accessible at www.slavevoyages.org. A recent example of comparative overviews of Atlantic slavery is Daina Ramey Berry and Leslie M. Harris, eds., *Sexuality and Slavery: Reclaiming Intimate Histories in the Americas* (Athens: University of Georgia Press, 2018). For approaches that focus on the Anglo-Atlantic, see note 16.

An authoritative synthesis of abolition in the North Atlantic is Manisha Sinha, *The Slave's Cause: A History of Abolition* (New Haven: Yale University Press, 2016). On Britain, see Christopher Leslie Brown, *Moral Capital: Foundations of British Abolitionism* (Chapel Hill: University of North Carolina Press, 2006), and Richard Huzzey, *Freedom Burning: Anti-slavery and Empire in Victorian Britain* (Ithaca, NY: Cornell University Press, 2012).

Overviews of slavery in the western IOW include Indrani Chatterjee and Richard M. Eaton, eds., *Slavery and South Asian History* (Bloomington: Indiana University Press, 2006); Robert Harms, Bernard K. Freamon, and David W. Blight, eds., *Indian Ocean Slavery in the Age of Abolition* (New Haven: Yale University Press, 2013); Edward Alpers, *The Indian Ocean in World History* (New York: Oxford University Press, 2014); Gwynn Campbell and Elizabeth Elbourne, *Sex, Power, and Slavery* (Athens: Ohio University Press, 2014); Gwynn Campbell, ed., *Abolition and Its Aftermath in Indian Ocean African and Asia* (London: Routledge, 2005); Gwynn Campbell, *The Structure of Slavery in Indian Ocean Africa and Asia* (Portland: Frank Cass, 2004); Gwynn Campbell, Suzanne Miers, and Joseph C. Miller eds., *Women and Slavery: Africa, the Indian Ocean World, and the Medieval North Atlantic* (Athens: Ohio University Press, 2007); Richard B. Allen, *European Slave Trading in the Indian Ocean, 1500–1850* (Athens: Ohio University Press, 2014); Hideaki Suzuki, *Slave Trade Profiteers in the Western Indian Ocean* (London: Palgrave Macmillan, 2017). See also note 17.

A foundational work for South Asia is Indrani Chatterjee, *Gender, Slavery and Law in Colonial India* (New Delhi: Oxford University Press, 1999). See also Gyan Prakash, *Bonded*

Histories (Cambridge: Cambridge University Press, 1990); Dharma Kumar, "Colonialism, Bondage, and Caste in British India," in *Breaking the Chains: Slavery, Bondage and Emancipation in Modern South Africa and Asia*, ed. Martin A. Klein (Madison: University of Wisconsin Press, 1993), 112–30. On abolition and empire in India, see Andrea Major, *Slavery, Abolitionism, and Empire in India* (Liverpool: Liverpool University Press, 2012). On IOW "subalterns," see Clare Anderson, *Subaltern Lives: Biographies of Colonialism in the Indian Ocean World, 1790–1920* (Cambridge: Cambridge University Press, 2012).

8. The term *hemorrhaged* is borrowed from Peter Coclanis, "Atlantic World or Atlantic/World?" *William and Mary Quarterly* 63 (October 2006): 727–28.

9. Dorothy Ross, "Lincoln and the Ethics of Emancipation: Universalism, Nationalism, Exceptionalism, *Journal of American History* 96 (September 2009): 380. For a debate over whether the campaign against the international slave trade specifically anticipated modern human rights law, see Philip Alston, review of Jenny S. Martinez, *The Slave Trade and the Origins of International Human Rights Law* (New York: Oxford University Press. 2012), and the works of Samuel Moyn in "Does the Past Matter? On the Origins of Human Rights: An Analysis of Competing Histories of the Origins of International Human Rights Law," *Harvard Law Review* 126, no. 7, May 20, 2013, https://harvardlawreview.org/2013/05/does-the-past-matter-on-the-origins-of-human-rights/. Ross, drawing upon the work of David Brion Davis, explains nineteenth-century Anglo-Atlantic perspectives on this question as involving a moral argument against slavery rooted in Protestant and Enlightenment notions of humanism. David Brion Davis, *The Problem of Slavery in the Age of Revolution, 1770–1823* (Ithaca: Cornell University Press, 1975), is a classic on antislavery in Anglo-America. See also Robin Blackburn, *The American Crucible: Slavery, Emancipation and Human Rights* (2011; repr., London: Verso, 2013). Many Indian Ocean slaveries were of course not based on the chattel principle in the Atlantic sense. Nevertheless, many Atlantic abolitionists explained them through human rights prisms honed in their part of the world, fueled in the case of missionaries by strong proselytizing impulses.

10. The Indian parts of this discussion build on existing literature on slavery in colonial India listed especially in notes 7 and 17. On legal pluralism in colonial North America, see Jonathan A. Bush, "Free to Enslave: The Foundations of Colonial American Slave Law," *Yale Journal of Law and the Humanities*, 5, no. 2 (May 2013), https://digitalcommons.law.yale.edu/yjlh/vol5/iss2/7. For a classic account of colonial knowledge production about the "Orient," especially Arabs, see Edward Said, *Orientalism* (New York: Pantheon Books, 1978).

11. Christopher Florio, "From Poverty to Slavery: Abolitionists, Overseers, and the Global Struggle for Labor in India," *Journal of American History* 102 (March 2016): 1005–24, discusses how the overseers resorted to coercive labor practices in India—a perspective that Alan L. Olmstead disputes in "Antebellum U.S. Cotton Production and Slavery in the Indian Mirror," *Agricultural History* 91 (Winter 2017): 5–38. In this work, we fold discussions of labor struggles into broader themes of settler colonialism in India and sectional politics in the United States within intersecting Indian and US historical frames of reference.

12. Simone M. Müller, "From Cabling the Atlantic to Wiring the World: A Review Essay on the 150th Anniversary of the Atlantic Telegraph Cable of 1866," *Technology and Culture* 57 (July 2016): 507–26, quotation on p. 518. For developments in the late nineteenth century, see Glen O'Hara, "New Histories of British Imperial Communication and the 'Networked World' of the 19th and Early 20th Centuries," *History Compass* 8 (July 2010): 609–25.

13. On this point, see Seymour Drescher, "The Fragmentation of Atlantic Slavery and British Intercolonial Slave Trade," in *The Chattel Principle: Internal Slave Trades in the Americas*, ed. Walter Johnson (New Haven: Yale University Press, 2005), 234–55.

14. Alison Games, "Atlantic History: Definitions, Challenges, and Opportunities," *American Historical Review* 111(June 2006): 741–57, and "Beyond the Atlantic: English Globetrotters and Transoceanic Connections," *The William and Mary Quarterly* 63 (October 2006): 675–92; James Sidbury, "Globalization, Creolization, and the Not-So-Peculiar Institution," *Journal of Southern History* 73 (August 2007): 618; Frank Tannenbaum, *Slave and Citizen: The Negro in the Americas* (New York: Knopf, 1946). On some of the historiography Tannenbaum's book inspired, see Peter J. Parish, *Slavery: History and Historians* (New York: Harper and Row, 1989).

15. Paul Gilroy, *The Black Atlantic: Modernity and Double Consciousness* (Cambridge, MA: Harvard University Press, 1993). On the politics of Black Atlantic scholarship, see Robert Stam and Ella Shohat, *Race in Translation: Culture Wars around the Postcolonial Atlantic* (New York: New York University Press, 2012). Gilroy has been criticized for neglecting the roles of both Africa and gender in shaping modernity, privileging the racialized "minority" paradigm of the African American experience when the Caribbean is predominantly Black, and decrying essentialism while constructing the Atlantic world as "Black." See Paul Tyambe Zeleza, "Rewriting the African Diaspora: Beyond the Black Atlantic," *African Affairs* 104 (January 2005): 37.

16. A tiny sample of these transnational/comparative approaches focused on or incorporating North America includes Craig Steven Wilder, *Ebony and Ivory: Race, Slavery, and the Troubled History of America's Universities* (New York: Bloomsbury, 2013); Jennifer Morgan, *Reckoning with Slavery: Gender, Kinship and Capitalism in the Early Black Atlantic* (Durham: Duke University Press, 2020), and *Laboring Women: Gender and Reproduction in New World Slavery* (Philadelphia: University of Pennsylvania Press, 2004); Edward B. Rugemer, *Slave Law and the Politics of Resistance in the Early Atlantic World* (Cambridge, MA: Harvard University Press, 2018); John Harris, *The Last Slave Ships: New York and the End of the Middle Passage* (New Haven: Yale University Press, 2020); Rebecca J. Scott and Jean M. Hebrard, *Freedom Papers: An Atlantic Odyssey in the Age of Emancipation* (Cambridge, MA: Harvard University Press, 2012); Dylan C. Penningroth, "The Claims of Slaves and Ex-Slaves to Family and Property: A Transatlantic Comparison," *American Historical Review* 112 (October 2007): 1039–69; Vincent Brown, *The Reaper's Garden; Death and Power in the World of Atlantic Slavery* (Cambridge, MA: Harvard University Press, 2008); Saidiya Hartman, *Lose Your Mother: A Journey along the Atlantic Slave Route* (New York: Farrar, Straus and Giroux, 2007); Marcus Rediker, *The Amistad Rebellion: An Atlantic Odyssey* (New York: Penguin Books, 2012); Gerald Horne, *The Deepest South: The United States, Brazil, and the African Slave Trade* (New York: New York University Press, 2007); Stephanie Smallwood, *Saltwater Slavery: A Middle Passage from Africa to American Diaspora* (Cambridge, MA: Harvard University Press, 2007); Gwendolyn Midlo Hall, *Slavery and African Ethnicities in the Americas: Restoring the Links* (Chapel Hill: University of North Carolina Press, 2005); Judith A. Carney, *Black Rice: The African Origins of Rice Cultivation in the Americas* (Cambridge, MA: Harvard University Press, 2009); Bayo Holsey, *Routes of Remembrance: Refashioning the Slave Trade in Ghana* (Chicago: University of Chicago Press, 2007); Ira Berlin, *Many Thousands Gone: The First Two Centuries of Slavery in North America* (Cambridge,

MA: Harvard University Press, 1998); Michael A. Gomez, *Exchanging Our Country Marks: The Transformation of African Identities in the Colonial and Antebellum South* (Chapel Hill: University of North Carolina Press, 1998); Joseph Inikori, *Africans and the Industrial Revolution in England* (New York: Cambridge University Press, 2000); Sylvia R. Frey and Betty Wood, *Come Shouting to Zion: African American Protestantism in the American South and the British Caribbean to 1830* (Chapel Hill: University of North Carolina Press, 1998); W. Jeffrey Bolster, *Back Jacks: African American Seamen in the Age of Sail* (Cambridge, MA: Harvard University Press, 1997); John K. Thornton, *Africa and Africans in the Making of the Atlantic World, 1480–1800* (New York: Cambridge University Press, 1992); Eliga H. Gould, "Entangled Histories, Entangled Worlds: The English-Speaking Atlantic as a Spanish Periphery," *American Historical Review* 112 (June 2007): 764–86.

A few examples of comparative emancipation studies in the Atlantic world include Frederick Cooper, Thomas C. Holt, and Rebecca J. Scott, *Beyond Slavery: Explorations of Race, Labor, and Citizenship in Postemancipation Societies* (Chapel Hill: University of North Carolina Press, 2000); Seymour Drescher, *From Slavery to Freedom: Comparative Studies in the Rise and Fall of Atlantic Slavery* (New York: New York University Press, 1998); Pamela Scully and Diana Paton, eds., *Gender and Slave Emancipation in the Atlantic World* (Durham: Duke University Press, 2005); Eric Foner, *Nothing but Freedom: Emancipation and Its Legacy* (Baton Rouge: Louisiana State University Press, 1983); Stanley L. Engerman, *Slavery, Emancipation, and Freedom: Comparative Perspectives* (Baton Rouge: Louisiana State University Press, 2007); Jeffrey R. Kerr-Ritchie, *Freedom's Seekers: Essays in Comparative Emancipation* (Baton Rouge: Louisiana State University Press, 2014).

On transnational approaches to "slavery's capitalism," see Sven Beckert and Seth Rockman, eds., *Slavery's Capitalism: A New History of American Economic Development* (Philadelphia: University of Pennsylvania Press, 2016); Dale W. Tomich, "The Second Slavery: Mass Slavery, World-Economy, and Comparative Microhistories, Parts I and II," special issues of *Review* (Fernand Braudel Center) 31 (2008); Daniel Rood, *The Reinvention of Atlantic Slavery: Race, Technology, Labor, and Capitalism in the Greater Caribbean* (New York: Oxford University Press, 2017); Johnson, *Chattel Principle*. On US slavery and capitalism, see Walter Johnson, *Soul by Soul: Life Inside the Antebellum Slave Market* (Cambridge, MA: Harvard University Press, 1999); Edward E. Baptist, *The Half Has Never Been Told: Slavery and the Making of American Capitalism* (New York: Basic Books, 2014).

For enslaved women in the United States, see chapter 4, note 1.

17. Isabel Hofmeyr, "Universalizing the Indian Ocean," *PMLA* 125 (May 2010): 721–29, quotation on p. 723. For general histories of the IOW, see Alpers, *Indian Ocean in World History*; Bose, *Hundred Horizons*; Abdul Sheriff, *Dhow Cultures of the Indian Ocean: Cosmopolitanism, Commerce, and Islam* (New York: Oxford University Press, 2014); Johan Mathew, *Margins of the Market: Trafficking and Capitalism across the Arabian Sea* (Oakland: University of California Press, 2016); Pedro Machado, *Ocean of Trade: South Asian Merchants, Africa and the Indian Ocean, c. 1750–1850* (Cambridge: Cambridge University Press, 2014). Anderson, *Subaltern Lives*, while not focused on slavery per se, uses "biographical fragments" to very productive effect.

For overviews of western IOW slaveries and slave trades, see the works listed in notes 7 and 17 by Allen, Alpers, Campbell, Chatterjee and Eaton, Elbourne, Harms et al., and Suzuki. See also Patrick Harries, "Middle Passages of the Southwest Indian Ocean: A Century of

Forced Immigration From Africa to the Cape of Good Hope," *Journal of African History* 55 (2014): 173–90; Janet J. Ewald, "Bondsmen, Freedmen, and Maritime Industrial Transportation, c. 1840–1900," *Slavery and Abolition* 31 (September 2010): 451–66; John C. Hawley, ed., *India in Africa, Africa in India: Indian Ocean Cosmopolitanisms* (Bloomington: Indiana University Press, 2008); Patrick Manning, *Slavery and African Life: Occidental, Oriental, and African Slave Trades* (Cambridge: Cambridge University Press, 1990); James L. Watson, ed., *Asian and African Systems of Slavery* (Berkeley: University of California Press, 1980); Bernard Moitt, ed., *Sugar, Slavery and Society: Perspectives on the Caribbean, India, the Mascarenes, and the United States* (Gainesville: University of Florida Press, 2004).

Works focused on East Africa and/or Arabia include Frederick Cooper, *Plantation Slavery on the East Coast of Africa* (New Haven: Yale University Press, 1977); Elisabeth McMahon, *Slavery and Emancipation in Islamic East Africa: From Honor to Respectability* (New York: Cambridge University Press, 2013); Matthew S. Hopper, *Slaves of One Master: Globalization and Slavery in Arabia in the Age of Empire* (New Haven: Yale University Press, 2015); Joseph E. Harris, *The African Presence in Asia* (Evanston, IL: Northwestern University Press, 1977); Jonathan Glassman, *Feasts and Riot: Revelry, Rebellion, and Popular Consciousness on the Swahili Coast* (Portsmouth, NH: Heinemann, 1995); Laura Fair, *Pastimes and Politics: Culture, Community, and Identity in Post-Abolition Urban Zanzibar* (Athens: Ohio University Press, 2001).

Works focused on India include Chatterjee, *Gender, Slavery and Law*; Prakash, *Bonded Histories*; Dharma Kumar, *Land and Caste in South India* (Cambridge: Cambridge University Press, 1965); Utsa Patnaik and Manjari Dingwaney, eds., *Chains of Servitude: Bondage and Slavery in India* (Hyderabad: Sangam Books, 1985); Benedicte Hjejle, *Slavery and Agricultural Bondage in South India* (Copenhagen: Scandinavian Institute of Asian Studies, 1967); Dev Raj Chanana, *Slavery in Ancient India, as Depicted in Pali and Sanskrit Texts* (New Delhi: People's Publishing House, 1960). On abolition/"delegalization" in India, see Major, *Slavery, Abolitionism*; Campbell, *Abolition and Its Aftermath*; Howard Temperley, ed., *After Slavery: Emancipation and Its Discontents* (London: Routledge, 2000). For a synthesis of some of this literature, see Alessandro Stanziani, "Slavery in India," in Eltis et al., *Cambridge World History of Slavery*, 246–71.

18. Michael E. Woods, "What Twenty-First Century Historians Have Said about the Causes of Disunion: A Civil War Sesquicentennial Review of the Recent Literature," *Journal of American History* 99 (September 2012): 420. On the Slave South and/or the Civil War in Pan-American/Caribbean perspective, see Edward B. Rugemer, *The Problem of Emancipation: The Caribbean Roots of the American Civil War* (Baton Rouge: Louisiana State University Press, 2008); Matthew Pratt Guterl, *American Mediterranean: Southern Slaveholders in the Age of Emancipation* (Cambridge, MA: Harvard University Press, 2008); Brian Schoen, *The Fragile Fabric of Union: Cotton Federal Politics and the Global Origins of the Civil War* (Baltimore: Johns Hopkins University Press, 2009); Laura Jarnagin, *A Confluence of Transatlantic Networks: Elites, Capitalism, and Confederate Migration to Brazil* (Tuscaloosa: University of Alabama Press, 2008); Matthew J. Clavin, *Toussaint Louverture and the American Civil War: The Promise and Peril of a Second Haitian Revolution* (Philadelphia: University of Pennsylvania Press, 2010); Matthew Karp, *This Vast Southern Empire: Slaveholders at the Helm of American Foreign Policy* (Cambridge, MA: Harvard University Press, 2016); Matthew Mason, "A World Safe for Modernity: Antebellum Southern Proslavery Intellectuals

Confront Great Britain," in *The Old South's Modern Worlds: Slavery, Region, and Nation in the Age of Progress*, ed. L. Diane Barnes, Brian Schoen, and Frank Towers (New York: Oxford University Press, 2011), 47.

19. Our nineteenth-century Anglo-American protagonists in the western IOW used the term *Oriental* to include Arabs and Indians.

20. William Adam, *The Law and Custom of Slavery in British India: In a Series of Letters to Thomas Fowell Buxton, Esq.* (London: Smith, Elder, 1840); Thomas R. R. Cobb, *An Inquiry into the Law of Negro Slavery in the United States of America. To Which Is Prefixed, an Historical Sketch of Slavery*, vol. 1 (Philadelphia: T. & J.W. Johnson & Co; Savannah, GA: W. Thorne Williams, 1858).

21. On these topics, see, for instance, Michel Gobat, *Empire by Invitation: William Walker and Manifest Destiny in Central America* (Cambridge, MA: Harvard University Press, 2018); Guterl, *American Mediterranean*; Jarnagin, *Confluence of Transatlantic Networks*.

22. Jane Hooper and David Eltis, "The Indian Ocean in Transatlantic Slavery," *Slavery and Abolition* 34, no. 3 (2013): 353–75; Allen, *European Slave Trading*; Patrick Harries, "Mozambique Island, Cape Town and the Organisation of the Slave Trade in the South-West Indian Ocean, c. 1797–1807," *Journal of Southern African Studies* 42, no.3 (2016): 409–27; Machado, *Ocean of Trade*; Harris, *Last Slave Ships*.

23. Jeremy Prestholdt, *Domesticating the World: African Consumerism and the Genealogies of Globalization* (Berkeley: University of California Press, 2008); Anna Arabindan-Kesson, "From Salem to Zanzibar: Cotton and Cultures of Commerce, 1820–1861," in *Global Trade and Visual Arts in Federal New England*, ed. Patricia Johnston and Caroline Frank (Lebanon: University of New Hampshire Press, 2014); Katharine Frederick, *Twilight of an Industry in East Africa, 1830–1940* (London: Palgrave Macmillan, 2020); Alexandra Celia Kelly, *Consuming Ivory: Mercantile Legacies of East Africa and New England* (Seattle: University of Washington Press, 2021); Jane Hooper, "Yankees in Indian Ocean Africa: Madagascar and Nineteenth-Century American Commerce," *African Economic History* 46, no. 2 (2018): 30–62.

24. On multipositionality, see Earl Lewis, "To Turn as on a Pivot: Writing African Americans into a History of Overlapping Diasporas," *American Historical Review* 100 (June 1995): 783; Gunja SenGupta, "Elites, Subalterns, and American Identities: A Case Study of African-American Benevolence," *American Historical Review* 109 (October 2004): 1104–39; Florencia E. Mallon, "The Promise and Dilemma of Subaltern Studies: Perspectives from Latin American History," *AHR Forum, American Historical Review* 99 (December 1994): 1511; Gyan Prakash, "Subaltern Studies as Postcolonial Criticism," *AHR* 99 (December 1994): 1475–90, and Frederick Cooper, "Conflict and Connection: Rethinking Colonial African History," *AHR* 99 (December 1994): 1516–45. On mobile IOW subalterns, see Anderson, *Subaltern Lives*.

25. Rosalind C. Morris, ed., *Can the Subaltern Speak?: Reflections on the History of an Idea* (New York: Columbia University Press, 2010); Saidiya Hartman, *Scenes of Subjection: Terror, Slavery, and Self-Making in Nineteenth-Century America* (New York: Oxford University Press, 1997); Marisa J. Fuentes, *Dispossessed Lives: Enslaved Women, Violence, and the Archive* (Philadelphia: University of Pennsylvania Press, 2016).

26. Clare Anderson, "Subaltern Lives: History, Identity and Memory in the Indian Ocean World," *History Compass* 11 (July 2013): 503–7.

27. Walter Johnson, "On Agency," *Journal of Social History* 37 (Fall 2003): 113–24, quotations on pp. 113 and 118.

28. Penningroth, "Claims of Slaves."

29. Richard Eaton, introduction to Chatterjee and Eaton, eds., *Slavery and South Asian History*, 2, 6–9; Jonathan Glassman, "The Bondsman's New Clothes: The Contradictory Consciousness of Slave Resistance on the Swahili Coast," *Journal of African History* 32 (1991): 277–312; Chatterjee, *Gender, Slavery and Law*. See also the references listed in notes 7 and 17.

30. On Islam, slavery, and gender in the western IOW, see the essays in Campbell and Elbourne, *Sex, Power*; Cooper, *Plantation Slavery*; Hopper, *Slaves of One Master*; Emily Ruete (Salamah bint Saïd; Sayyida Salme, Princess of Zanzibar and Oman, 1844–1924), *Memoirs of an Arabian Princess*, trans. Lionel Strachey (New York: Doubleday, Page, 1907), http://digital.library.upenn.edu/women/ruete/arabian/arabian.html. One example of military slavery occurs in Richard Eaton, "The Rise and Fall of Military Slavery in the Deccan, 1450–1650," in Chatterjee and Eaton, eds., *Slavery and South Asian History*, 115–35.

31. Zeleza, "Rewriting the African Diaspora," 37, 41–42; Awam Amkpa and Gunja SenGupta, "Picturing Homes and Border Crossings: The Slavery Trope in Films of the Black Atlantic," in *Paths of the Atlantic Slave Trade: Interactions, Identities, and Images*, ed. Ana Lucia Araujo (Amherst, NY: Cambria Press, 2011), 359–87.

32. Pier M. Larson, "Reconsidering Trauma, Identity, and the African Diaspora: Enslavement and Historical Memory in Nineteenth-Century Highland Madagascar," *The William and Mary Quarterly* 56 (April 1999): 335–62; Lovejoy, *Slavery in the Global Diaspora*; Joseph E. Harris, "Expanding the Scope of African Diaspora Studies: The Middle East and India, a Research Agenda," *Radical History Review* 87 (Fall 2003): 157–68; Patrick Manning, "Africa and the African Diaspora: New Directions of Study," *Journal of African History* 44 (2003):487–506; Gwyn Campbell, "The African-Asian Diaspora: Myth or Reality?" *African and Asian Studies* 5 (2006): 305–24; Chatterjee, *Gender, Slavery and Law*.

33. See, for instance, Sheriff, *Dhow Cultures*, as well as references in note 17.

34. Brown, *Moral Capital*; James Walvin, introduction to *Parliamentary History Supplement* 26 (June 2007): 2–3; Seymour Drescher, "Public Opinion and Parliament in the Abolition of the British Slave Trade," *Parliamentary History Supplement* 26 (June 2007): 42–65.

35. Essays in Beckert and Rockman, eds., *Slavery's Capitalism*; Tomich, "Second Slavery."

36. Van Gosse, "'As a Nation, the English Are Our Friends': The Emergence of African American Politics in the British Atlantic World, 1772–1861," *American Historical Review* 113 (October 2008): 1003–28.

37. See note 11 for an explanation of how our approach to this topic compares with articles authored by Florio and Olmstead.

38. Bhavani Raman, "The Familial World of the Company's Kacceri in Early Colonial Madras," *Journalism of Colonialism and Colonial History* 9 (Fall 2008), doi: 10.1353/cch.0.0011.

39. Memorandum by the political secretary, dated 1 December 1835, Extract Bombay Political Consultations, 23 December 1835, Slave Trade (East India).—Slavery in Ceylon. Return to an Order of the Honourable The House of Commons, dated 1 March 1838;—*for,* COPIES or ABSTRACTS of all Correspondence between the Directors of the East India Company and the Company's Government in India, since the 1st day of June 1827, on the

subject of Slavery in the Territories under the Company's Rule; also respecting any Slave Trade therein; also of all Orders and Regulations issued, or any Proceedings taken, by Order or under the Authority of the Company, with a view to the Abolition of Slavery and the Slave Trade, since the above Date; also of any Correspondence between the Board of Control and the Court of Directors on the said subjects. Also,—Return to an Address of the Honorable The House of Commons, dated 1 March 1838;—for, COPIES or EXTRACTS of all Communications relating to the subject of SLAVERY in the Island of Ceylon, and to the Measures there taken for its Abolition. Ordered, by The House of Commons, to be Printed, 31 July 1838. Accounts and Papers, 17 vols., Slavery, Session 15, November 1837–16 August 1838, 108. Digitized by Google Books. Hereafter known as *Slave Trade (East India)*.

40. Drescher makes the point that the enslaved enter our field of vision in moments and spaces of conflict in "Fragmentation of Atlantic Slavery," 234–55.

41. The authors are grateful to Edward Alpers for drawing our attention to the following piece focused on translation and based on British sources in Zanzibar, which mentions the *Laconia* captives: Edward Alpers and Mathew S. Hopper, "Parler en son nom? Comprendre les témoignages d'esclaves africains originaires de l'océan Indien (1850–1930)," *Annales: Histoire, Sciences Sociales* 63, no. 4 (2008): 799–828. Our interpretation, based on US State Department documents, reads the evidence for the insights it generates about subaltern subjectivity.

CHAPTER 1. EMPIRE, RELIGIOUS LAW, AND SLAVERY BY "FREE WILL"

1. Magistrates of Calcutta to Bayley Esq., Secretary to the Government in the Judicial Department, November 1823, included in extract of Bengal Criminal Judicial Consultations, 25 March 1824, Board's Collections, vol. 1234, part of IOR/F Records of the Board of Commissioners for the Affairs of India, 1620–1859, indexed under the title: "Question of the extent to which slavery is permitted in India under Hindu and Muhammadan Law—relevance of the Act of 51 George III c. 23 to India—Importation to India of slaves on Arab ships," March 1817–August 1827, India office records and private papers, Archives and Manuscripts, British Library. Hereafter, Board's Collections.

2. Walvin, introduction, 2–3; Seymour Drescher, "Public Opinion and Parliament," *PHS* 26 (June 2007): 43.

3. Sinha, *Slave's Cause*, 9, 24–33; Walvin, introduction, 6. See also Ira Berlin, *The Long Emancipation: The Demise of Slavery in the United States* (Cambridge, MA: Harvard University Press, 2015), and Patrick Rael, *Eighty-Eight Years: The Long Death of Slavery in the United States, 1777–1865* (Athens: University of Georgia Press, 2015).

4. See, for example, Davis, *Slavery in the Age of Revolution;* Dorothy Ross, "Lincoln and the Ethics."

5. Brown, *Moral Capital,* 2, 159, 388.

6. Gosse, "'As a Nation,'" 1007.

7. Rugemer, *Slave Law,* 172; Michael H. Fisher, "Bound for Britain: Changing Conditions of Servitude, 1600–1857," in Chatterjee and Eaton, eds., *Slavery and South Asian History,* 191–99; Walvin, introduction, 3.

8. Rugemer, *Slave Law,* 180–81; Bush, "Free to Enslave," 431; Sinha, *Slave's Cause,* 22–23.

9. Gosse, "'As a Nation,'" 1008.

10. Gosse, 1008–10; Sinha, *Slave's Cause*, 48, 49, 51.

11. Gary B. Nash, "Forging Freedom: The Emancipation Experience in Northern Seaport Cities," in *Race, Class, and Politics: Essays in American Colonial and Revolutionary Society*, ed. Gary B. Nash (Urbana: University of Illinois Press, 1986), 283–321; Sinha, *Slave's Cause*, 47–51; Gunja SenGupta, *From Slavery to Poverty: The Racial Origins of Welfare in New York, 1840–1918* (New York: New York University Press), 34.

12. Gosse, "'As a Nation,'" 1008–10; Sinha, *Slave's Cause*, 48, 49, 50–53. On loyalists more broadly, see Maya Jasanoff, *Liberty's Exiles: American Loyalists in the Revolutionary World* (New York: Vintage Books, 2011).

13. Deirdre Coleman, *Romantic Colonization and British Anti-Slavery* (Cambridge: Cambridge University Press, 2005). For an excellent historiographical essay on some of these themes, see John W. Sweet, "The Subject of the Slave Trade: Recent Currents in the Histories of the Atlantic, Great Britain, and Western Africa," *Early American Studies* 7 (Spring 2009), 1–45.

14. Drescher, "Public Opinion and Parliament," 43.

15. Eric Williams, *Capitalism and Slavery* (Chapel Hill: University of North Carolina Press, 1944, repr., 1994); Robin Blackburn, *The Overthrow of Colonial Slavery, 1776–1848* (New York: Verso, 1988): David Brion Davis, *The Problem of Slavery in Western Culture* (Ithaca, NY: Cornell University Press, 1966); Davis, *Problem of Slavery in the Age of Revolution*. See also the discussions among Davis, Thomas L. Haskell, and John Ashworth in Thomas Bender ed., *The Antislavery Debate; Capitalism and Abolitionism as a Problem in Historical Interpretation* (Berkeley: University of California Press, 1992).

16. Brown, *Moral Capital*; Sweet, "Subject of the Slave Trade," 19, 20, 21.

17. Drescher, "Public Opinion and Parliament," 47.

18. Slaveryimages.org, a digital archive originally hosted by VA Foundation for the Humanities and UVA; relauched by Jerome S. Handler and currently hosted by the University of Colorado Boulder with many contributors and supporters; Drescher, "Public Opinion and Parliament," 47–51, 55.

19. Sinha, *Slave's Cause*, 34.

20. Tara Helfman, "The Court of Vice Admiralty at Sierra Leone and the Abolition of the West African Slave Trade," *Yale Law Journal* 115 (March 2006): 1130.

21. Stephen Farrell, "Contrary to the Principles of Justice, Humanity and Sound Policy': The Slave Trade, Parliamentary Politics and the Abolition Act, 1807," *Parliamentary History Supplement* 26 (June 2007): 141–71; Helfman, "Court of Vice Admiralty," 1131.

22. Randy J. Sparks, "Blind Justice: The United States's Failure to Curb the Illegal Slave Trade," *Law and History Review* 35 (February 2017): 53–79; Harris, *Last Slave Ships*.

23. Graham Russell Hodges, *Root and Branch: African Americans in New York and East Jersey, 1613–1863* (Chapel Hill: University of North Carolina Press, 1999), 170; Shane White, *Somewhat More Independent: The End of Slavery in New York City, 1770–1810* (Athens: University of Georgia Press, 1991), 31, 43.

24. Baptist, *Half Has Never Been Told*; Beckert and Rockman, introduction to *Slavery's Capitalism*, 11–22, 26–27; Anthony Kaye, "The Second Slavery: Modernity in the Nineteenth-Century South and the Atlantic World," *Journal of Southern History* 75 (August 2009): 627–28, 633–34, 640; Tomich, "Second Slavery." The quotation on experts is from Rood, *Reinvention of Atlantic Slavery*, 2.

25. Edward A. Alpers, "On Becoming a British Lake: Piracy, Slaving, and British Imperialism in the Indian Ocean during the First Half of the Nineteenth Century," in *Indian Ocean Slavery in the Age of Abolition,* ed. Robert Harms, Bernard K. Freamon, and David W. Blight (New Haven: Yale University Press, 2013), 46.

26. Minute of the Chief Judge of the Sudder Dewanny [sic] and Nizamut Adawlut, Mr. J. H. Harington 21 November 1818, *Slave Trade (East India),* 316–17. See this book's introduction, note 39, for the full title of this archive.

27. Bush, "Free to Enslave," 420.

28. Carney, *Black Rice;* essays by S. Max Edelson, Gwendolyn Midlo Hall, Walter Hawthorne, David Eltis, Philip Morgan, and David Richardson in "AHR Exchange: The Question of Black Rice," *American Historical Review* 115 (February 2010): 123–71; Lorena S. Walsh, "The Transatlantic Slave Trade and Colonial Chesapeake Slavery," *OAH Magazine of History* 17 (April 2003): 11–15; April Lee Hatfield, *Atlantic Virginia: Intercolonial Relations in the Seventeenth Century* (Philadelphia: University of Pennsylvania Press, 2004); John C. Coombs, "Beyond the Origins Debate: Rethinking the Rise of Virginia Slavery," in *Early Modern Virginia: Reconsidering the Old Dominion,* ed. Douglas Bradburn and John C. Coombs (Charlottesville: University of Virginia Press, 2011), 239–78; Edmund S. Morgan, *American Slavery, American Freedom: The Ordeal of Colonial Virginia* (New York: Norton, 1975).

29. Bush, "Free to Enslave," 421; William Waller Hening, *Statutes at Large: Being a Collection of all the Laws of Virginia from the First Session of Legislature in the Year 1619,* vol. 11 (Richmond, VA: Printed by and for Samuel Pleasants, Junior, printer to the Commonwealth, 1809–23), 170, 260, 266, 270.

30. Rugemer, *Slave Law,* 111–16.

31. Bush, "Free to Enslave," 425, 426. 428.

32. Bush, 458–60.

33. Bush, 463–69.

34. Stephanie McCurry, *Confederate Reckoning: Power and Politics in the Civil War South* (Cambridge, MA: Harvard University Press, 2010), 219.

35. Lauren Benton, "A Place for the State: Legal Pluralism as a Colonial Project in Bengal and West Africa," in *Law and Colonial Cultures: Legal Regimes in World History, 1400–1900,* Studies in Comparative World History (Cambridge: Cambridge University Press, 2001), 127. On India, see Chatterjee, *Gender, Slavery and Law.*

36. Benton, "Place for the State," 128.

37. Benton, 129.

38. Major, *Slavery, Abolitionism,* 139–40; Chatterjee, *Gender, Slavery and Law;* Eric Lewis Beverley, "Property, Authority, and Personal Law: Waqf in Colonial South Asia," *South Asia Research* 31 (2011): 155–82, quotation on 158; Benton, "Place for the State," 134.

39. Benton, "Place for the State," 134; Chatterjee, *Gender, Slavery and Law;* Major, *Slavery, Abolitionism,* 141. The abolitionist William Adam drew attention to some of these points in *The Law and Custom of Slavery in British India: In a Series of Letters to Thomas Fowell Buxton, Esq.* (London: Smith, Elder, 1840).

40. Chatterjee, *Gender, Slavery and Law;* Major, *Slavery, Abolitionism,* 45–46, 131–32. Adam, *Law and Custom.*

41. Sumit Guha, "Slavery, Society, and the State in Western India, 1700–1800," in Chatterjee and Easton, *Slavery and South Asian History,* 163, 166, 168; Stanziani, "Slavery in India," 250.

42. Richard B. Allen, "A Traffic Repugnant to Humanity: Children, the Mascarene Slave Trade and British Abolitionism," *Slavery and Abolition* 27 (August 2006): 219–36.

43. A useful compendium of these parliamentary acts is available online at www.pdavis.nl/Legis_26.htm.

44. *Reports of the Indian Law Commission Upon Slavery in India*, January 15, 1841, with appendices, 2 vols., India Office Records, British Library, 1:311. Hereafter, *Indian Law Commission Report* I.

45. On some of these issues and a Bengal Regulation (X) that followed, see Chatterjee, *Gender, Slavery and Law*, 195; Major, *Slavery, Abolitionism*, 170–75; *Indian Law Commission Report* I, 310; *Slave Trade (East India)*, 340–41.

46. Extract of a Judicial Letter from Bengal, 29 October 1817, Board's Collections. Abstracts of some of these records (but not all) are published in *Slave Trade (East India)*.

47. On this transmission of Sanskrit texts to the United States, see, for instance, Russell B. Goodman, "East-West Philosophy in Nineteenth-Century America: Emerson and Hinduism," *Journal of the History of Ideas* 51 (October 1990): 625–45. A classic argument about the configuration of power and knowledge in representations of the East occurs in Said, *Orientalism*.

48. Sir T. E. Colebrooke, *Miscellaneous Essays, by H. T. Colebrooke, with Life of the Author, by His Son, Sir T. E. Colebrooke*, 3 vols. (London: Trübner and Co., 1873), 1:76–77.

49. Rosane Rocher and Ludo Rocher, preface to *The Making of Western Indology: Henry Thomas Colebrooke and the East India Company* (London: Routledge, 2012); Herman Tull, Review of Rosane Rocher and Ludo Rocher, *Founders of Western Indology: August Wilhelm von Schlegel and Henry Thomas Colebrooke in Correspondence 1820–1837* (Wiesbaden: Abhandlungen für die Kunde des Morgenlandes, Harrassowitz, 2013), in *Religious Studies Review* 40 (June 2014): 119; Thomas R. Trautmann, review of Rocher and Rocher, *Founders of Western Indology*, in *Journal of the American Oriental Society* 136 (2016): 658.

50. Rocher and Rocher, *Making of Western Indology*, 89–90; Colebrooke, *Miscellaneous Essays*, 74–75.

51. J. H. Harington, *Elementary Analysis of the Laws and Regulations Enacted by the Governor General in Council, at Fort William in Bengal, for the Civil Government of the British Territories under that Presidency*, 3 vols. (Calcutta: Honorable Company's Press, 1805–17); Rocher and Rocher, *Making of Western Indology*, 96; Extract of Judicial Consultations, 29 December 1826, Board's Collections. Abstracts of some of these records are published in *Slave Trade (East India)*, 310–19.

52. Adam, *Law and Custom*.

53. Handwritten minute by Mr. Colebrooke, Extract of Bengal Judicial Consultations, 29 December 1826, Board's Collections; *Slave Trade (East India)*, 311.

54. *Slave Trade (East India)*, 311.

55. *Slave Trade (East India)*, 311–12.

56. *Slave Trade (East India)*, 312–13.

57. *Slave Trade (East India)*, 313–14.

58. *Indian Law Commission Report* I, 311, 313.

59. Minute of the Chief Judge of the Sudder Dewanny and Nizamut Adawlut, Mr. J. H. Harington, November 21, 1818, in *Slave Trade (East India)*, 316. Hereafter, Harington's Minute.

60. Orby Mootham, *The East India Company's Sadar Courts, 1801–1834* (Bombay: N.M. Tripathi, 1983), Silver Jubilee of the Indian Law Institute, publication no. 6, 63; Harington's Minute, 315–19.
61. Harington's Minute, 317.
62. Extract of Judicial Letter from Bengal, 1 March 1817, Board's Collections.
63. Harington's Minute, 318.
64. Harington's Minute, 318.
65. "A Regulation for the Guidance of the Courts of Judicature in Cases of Slavery," signed by W. H. Macnaghten, Register, Board's Collections, published in *Slave Trade (East India)*, 320.
66. Board's Collection; *Slave Trade (East India)*, 321.
67. *Slave Trade (East India)*, 321.
68. *Slave Trade (East India)*, 321–22.
69. *Slave Trade (East India)*, 324–25.
70. Minute of Chief Judge Mr. Leycester, 28 May 1823, Board's Collections; *Slave Trade (East India)*, 315.
71. Minute by the Governor General, 3 May 1826, signed by Amherst in Board's Collections; *Slave Trade (East India)*, 329.
72. Howard Temperley, "The Delegalization of Slavery in British India," *Slavery and Abolition* 21 (August 2000): 169–71. On Macaulay, see Robert E. Sullivan, *Macaulay: The Tragedy of Power* (Cambridge, MA: Harvard University Press, 2009).

CHAPTER 2. HUMAN RIGHTS FROM CALCUTTA THROUGH LONDON TO BOSTON

1. Indrani Chatterjee, "Abolition by Denial: The South Asian Example," in *Abolition and Its Aftermath in Indian Ocean African and Asia*, ed. Gwynn Campbell (London: Routledge, 2005), 150–68.
2. "Letters from the Editor, no. II," *Liberator*, 18 August 1843.
3. "The Standard. British West India Emancipation. An Address, delivered at Northampton, on the 1st day of August, 1843," *National Anti-Slavery Standard*, 7 December 1843.
4. Andrew Sartori, *Bengal in Global Concept History: Culturalism in the Age of Capital* (Chicago: University of Chicago Press, 2008), 77, 82.
5. *Liberator*, 27 December 1844. On May's receipt of Roy's locks, see Clare Midgley, "Transoceanic Commemoration and Connections between Bengali Brahmos and British and American Unitarians," *Historical Journal* 54 (September 2011): 787–88.
6. *Liberator*, 16 October 1840.
7. Lynn Zastoupil, "Defining Christians, Making Britons: Rammohun Roy and the Unitarians," *Victorian Studies* 44 (Winter 2002): 219–20; Lynn Zastoupil, *Rammohun Roy and the Making of Victorian Britain* (Palgrave Macmillan, 2010).
8. Bayly, "Rammohun Roy," 25; Midgley, "Cosmotopia Delineated," 446–70.
9. Huzzey, *Freedom Burning*, 7.
10. Sartori, *Bengal*, 82.
11. Bayly, "Rammohun Roy," 26–27.

12. Adam Hill, "William Adam," *Dictionary of Unitarian and Universalist Biography*, Unitarian Universalist History and Heritage Society, 1999–2018, http://uudb.org/articles/williamadam.html.

13. Zastoupil, "Defining Christians," 226.

14. *The Life and Letters of Raja Rammohun Roy, Compiled and Edited by the Late Sophia Dobson Collet, and Completed by a Friend*, 2nd ed., ed. Hem Chandra Sarkar (Calcutta, 1914), 60. Hereafter, Collet, *Life and Letters*.

15. Bayly, "Rammohun Roy," 29; Zastoupil, "Defining Christians," 222–23.

16. Collet, *Life and Letters*, 61, 58, 68–69.

17. Collet, 70–71, 75; Zastoupil, "Defining Christians," 234.

18. Spencer Lavan, *Unitarians and India: A Study in Encounter and Response* (Boston: Beacon Press, 1977), 63–64.

19. On some of these themes, see Midgley, "Cosmotopia Delineated."

20. On Reed's views on antislavery, see Denis Brennan, *The Making of an Abolitionist: William Lloyd Garrison's Path to Publishing* The Liberator (Jefferson, NC: MacFarland, 2014), 119.

21. Zastoupil, *Rammohun Roy*, 7–8; Alan D. Hodder, "Emerson, Rammohan Roy, and the Unitarians," *Studies in the American Renaissance*, 1988, 133–48; Richard H. Davis, "Henry David Thoreau, Yogi." *Common Knowledge* 24, no. 1 (2018): 56–89, www.muse.jhu.edu/article/686197.

22. Lata Mani, *Contentious Traditions: The Debate on Sati in Colonial India* (Berkeley: University of California Press, 1998); Zastoupil, *Rammohun Roy*, 84, 78–87.

23. Sinha, *Slave's Cause*, 195–214. David W. Blight, *Frederick Douglass: Prophet of Freedom* (New York: Simon & Schuster, 2018).

24. The scholarship on movements against slavery in North America is so voluminous that no list could do it justice. Sinha's *Slave's Cause* offers the most recent, comprehensive synthesis of this work. On the generational factor shaping hostility to slavery, see James L. Huston, "The Experiential Basis of the Northern Antislavery Impulse," *Journal of Southern History* 56 (November 1990): 609–40. Classic works on free labor include Eric Foner, *Free Soil, Free Labor, Free Men: The Ideology of the Republican Party before the Civil War* (New York: Oxford University Press, 1970), and Jonathan Glickstein, *Concepts of Free Labor in Antebellum America* (New Haven: Yale University Press, 1991). On Jacksonian Free Soil politics, see Jonathan H. Earle, *Jacksonian Antislavery and the Politics of Free Soil, 1824–1854* (Chapel Hill: University of North Carolina Press, 2004).

25. Joanne B. Freeman, *The Field of Blood: Violence in Congress and the Road to Civil War* (New York: Farrar, Straus, and Giroux, 2018).

26. William J. Novak, *The People's Welfare: Law and Regulation in Nineteenth-Century America* (Chapel Hill: University of North Carolina Press, 1996); Richard B. Kielbowicz, "The Law and Mob Law in Attacks on Antislavery Newspapers, 1833–1860," *Law and History Review*, 24 (Fall 2006): 559–600.

27. Leonard L. Richards, *"Gentlemen of Property and Standing": Anti-Abolition Mobs in Jacksonian America* (New York: Oxford University Press, 1970).

28. Michael Kent Curtis, *Free Speech, The People's Darling Privilege: Struggles for Freedom of Expression in American History* (Durham, NC: Duke University Press, 2000).

29. Bayly, "Rammohun Roy," 36.

30. Ralph Edmund Turner, *James Silk Buckingham, 1786-1855: A Social Biography* (London: Whittlesey House, 1934), 65, 76, 111-12.

31. Turner, *James Silk Buckingham*, 128, 136; Bayly, "Rammohun Roy," 36-37.

32. Magistrates of Calcutta to Bayley Esq., Secretary to Government in the Judicial Department, November 1823, included in Extract Bengal Criminal Judicial Consultations, 25 March 1824, Board's Collections.

33. Bayly,"Rammohun Roy,"37-38.

34. Turner, *James Silk Buckingham*, 275, 280-81.

35. On Buckingham introducing Rammohun to British reformers, see Zastoupil, *Rammohun Roy*, 6.

36. Zastoupil, *Rammohun Roy*, 1-2.

37. Frances Anne Kemble, *Journal of a Residence on a Georgian Plantation in 1838-1839* (New York: Harper & Bros, 1863); Collet, *Life and Letters*, 199-200.

38. Zastoupil, *Rammohun Roy*, 1-3; Michael J. Altman, *Heathen, Hindoo, Hindu: American Representations of India, 1721-1893* (New York: Oxford University Press, 2017), 45.

39. *Liberator*, 7 January 1832.

40. *Liberator*, 26 November 1831.

41. *Liberator*, 10 and 17 March 1832. On the Virginia slavery debates, see Eva Sheppard Wolf, *Race and Liberty in the New Nation: Emancipation in Virginia from the Revolution to Nat Turner's Rebellion* (Baton Rouge: Louisiana State University Press, 2006); Erik S. Root, ed., *Sons of the Fathers: The Virginia Slavery Debates of 1831-1832* (Lanham, MD: Lexington Books, 2010).

42. "The Mentor," *Godey's Lady's Book*, February 1837. On rereadings of Barbara Welter's classic interpretation of "true womanhood," see Mary Louise Roberts, "True Womanhood Revisited," and Nancy A. Hewitt, "Taking the True Woman Hostage," both in *Journal of Women's History*, 14 (Spring 2002): 150-55 and 156-62, respectively. A classic interpretation of republican motherhood is Linda K. Kerber, *Women of the Republic: Intellect and Ideology in Revolutionary America* (Chapel Hill: University of North Carolina Press, 1980).

43. On Garrison's visit to England, see Sinha, *Slave's Cause*, 221.

44. John Hyslop Bell, *British Folks and British India Fifty Years Ago: Joseph Pease and His Contemporaries, Containing letters by Thomas Clarkson, Daniel O'Connell, Wendell Phillips, William Lloyd Garrison, Joseph Pease, Richard Cobden, Francis Carnac Brown, George Thompson, James Cosmo Melville, and others* (London: John Heywood, 1891), 72.

45. Bell, *British Folks*, 69, 71, 72, 73.

46. Bell, 69; Laidlaw, "'Justice to India,'" 304. For a biography of Joseph Pease, see Bell, 4.

47. Laidlaw, "'Justice to India,'" 306.

48. Anna M. Stoddart, *Elizabeth Pease Nichol, with Portraits and Other Illustrations* (London: J.M. Dent and Company, 1899), digitized by Google, 72-74; Bell, *British Folks*, 14-15.

49. Bell, *British Folks*, 6; Stoddart, *Elizabeth Pease Nichol*, 74.

50. Stoddart, 75; Bell, 12.

51. Cited in Stoddart, 76.

52. Laidlaw, "'Justice to India,'" 309-10; Stoddart, 78.

53. For a recent biography of Adam, see Julie L. Holcomb, "'The Second Fallen Adam': William Adam and Nineteenth-Century Transatlantic Reform," in *Currents in Transatlantic History: Encounters, Commodities, Identities*, ed. Steven G. Reinhardt (College Station: Texas A & M University Press, 2017), 77-98.

54. Lavan, *Unitarians and India*, 47–50.

55. *Boston Daily Advertiser*, cited in M. F. Hubbard, ed., *American Annals of Education, for the year 1839*, vol. 9 (Boston: Otis, Broaders, and Company, 1839), 519; Josiah Quincy, LLD, president of Harvard University, *The History of Harvard University*, vol. 2 (Cambridge, MA: John Owen, 1840).

56. Bell, *British Folks*, 42; Stoddart, *Elizabeth Pease Nichol*, 85–86.

57. Stoddart, 92; Bell, 26.

58. Pease to Thompson, February 25, 1839, reproduced in Bell, 50–51.

59. Bell, 51.

60. *Liberator*, 9 May 1845. On the BIS, see also Florio, "From Poverty to Slavery."

61. Bell, *British Folks*, 67.

62. "Biographical Sketch of George Thompson," *Liberator*, 9 May 1845; "Sketches of Modern Reforms and Reformers, in Great Britain and Ireland," *National Era*, 10 May 1849.

63. Sartori, *Bengal*, 90–91.

64. Bell, *British Folks*, 142.

65. Sartori, *Bengal*, 91–92.

66. The passages that follow draw from William Adam, *The Law and Custom of Slavery in British India: In a Series of Letters to Thomas Fowell Buxton, Esq.* published in London by Smith, Elder and Co., and in Boston by Weeks, Jordan and Co., in 1840.

67. Adam, *Law and Custom*, 8, 9, 10.

68. *Principles of Hindu and Mohammadan Law Republished from the Principles and Precedents of the Same by Sir William Hay Macnaghten*, ed. the Late H. H. Wilson Boden Professor of Sanskrit in the University of Oxford, 4th ed. (London: William and Norgate, 1868), 128.

69. Adam, *Law and Custom*, 16–17.

70. Adam, 18–19.

71. Adam, 20.

72. Adam, 25, 26–27, 33.

73. Adam, 27.

74. Adam, 31, 44–45.

75. Adam, 54–55, 56–57.

76. Adam, 38, 40.

77. Adam, 138–40, 158–60.

78. Adam' reference to both Colebrooke and Harington's *Analysis of the Laws and Regulations*, 3:743, occurs on page 138 of *Law and Custom* (Boston edition).

79. Adam, 174–75, 176.

80. Adam, 169, 176, 170, 173.

81. Adam, 178–79, 180.

82. Adam, 174. The British inherited the practices of slaves being sold to recover tax arrears of masters, as well as the state's use of forced labor for public works, from precolonial regimes, according to Kumar, "Colonialism, Bondage, and Caste," 117–18.

83. Adam, *Law and Custom*, 183, 185.

84. Adam, 235–36.

85. Adam, 225, 232–33.

86. Cited in *Liberator*, 16 October 1840.

87. *Liberator,* 7 August 1840; *National Anti-Slavery Standard,* 16 July 1840.
88. James Silk Buckingham, *The Slave States of America.* 2 vols. (London: Fisher, 1842).
89. Bell, *British Folks,* 50, 143.
90. Turner, *James Silk Buckingham,* 348, 350, 352.
91. Turner, 354.
92. Buckingham, *Slave States,* 2:2, 2:6, 2:7.
93. Buckingham, 2:2, 2:7, 2:8.
94. Buckingham, 2:429, 2:430–31.
95. Buckingham, 2:485, 2:486, 2:487.
96. Buckingham, 2:30.
97. Buckingham, 2:29–30, 2:31.
98. Buckingham, 2:31–32.
99. Buckingham, 2:561–62.
100. Buckingham, 2:537.
101. See for instance, the essays in Barnes, Schoen, and Towers, eds., *The Old South's Modern Worlds,* and Beckert and Rockman, eds., *Slavery's Capitalism.*
102. Buckingham, *Slave States,* 1:4.
103. *Indian Law Commission Report,* 15 January 1841; Temperley, "Delegalization of Slavery," 171–73, 181–83; Nancy Gardner Cassels, "Social Legislation under the Company Raj: The Abolition of Slavery Act V 1843," *South Asia* 11(1988): 59–87; Kumar, "Colonialism, Bondage, and Caste," 121; Major, *Slavery, Abolitionism.*
104. Chatterjee, "Abolition by Denial"; Gyan Prakash, *Bonded Histories*; Kumar, "Colonialism, Bondage, and Caste," 122; Stanziani, "Slavery in India," 264; Huzzey, *Freedom Burning,* 179–80.

CHAPTER 3. REVERBERATIONS

1. "From the *Mobile Journal*," *Edgefield Advertiser,* 21 October 1841. In general, we identify places by their familiar twentieth-century or present-day names but retain the spelling of the names of people as they appear in the colonial records, while contextualizing these figures with reference to geographies and contemporary designations whenever possible. We also quote offensive terms and racial labels from the original texts when they are relevant to the argument.

2. *Edgefield Advertiser,* 21 October 1841. Aspects of the "free cotton" experiments in India—different in emphasis from our account—occur in Beckert, *Empire of Cotton*; Sandip Hazareesingh, "Cotton, Climate and Colonialism in Dharwar, Western India, 1840–1880," *Journal of Historical Geography* 38 (2012): 1–17; Florio, "From Poverty to Slavery"; and Olmstead, "Antebellum U.S. Cotton Production." We contextualize free cotton experiments in India within Indian historical frames of reference, while seeking to illustrate how these experiments played out in debates over settler colonialism, slavery, tariffs, abolition, and empire in the American South.

For nineteenth-century reports on these experiments, see J. Forbes Royle, *Review of the Measures which Have Been Adopted in India for the Improved Culture of Cotton* (London: Smith, Elder, 1857), and J. Talboys Wheeler, *Madras versus America: A Handbook to Cotton Cultivation, Exhibiting Contents of Public Records in a Condensed Form, in Accordance with the Resolution of the Government of India* (New York, 1866); Walter R. Cassells, *Cotton: An Account of its Culture in the Bombay Presidency, Prepared from Government Records and Other Authentic Sources, in Accordance with a Resolution of the Government of India* (Bombay: Smith, Elder, 1861).

3. For an application of Jürgen Habermas's notion of the "commercial origins of the public sphere"; that is, news as both driven by the needs of commerce and a profit-generating commodity itself, see Leonard von Morze, introduction to *Urban Identity and the Atlantic World*, ed. Elizabeth Fay and Leonard von Morze (New York: Palgrave Macmillan, 2013), 9–11.

4. Müller, "From Cabling the Atlantic; O'Hara, "New Histories of British Imperial Communication."

5. For an overview, see Beckert and Rockman, *Slavery's Capitalism*.

6. For a synthesis of Anglo-Atlantic abolitionism, see Sinha, *Slave's Cause*.

7. Jerome I. Hodos, *Second Cities: Globalization and Local Politics in Manchester and Philadelphia* (Philadelphia: Temple University Press, 2011), 20–28, 100–102; quotation on 101.

8. On colonial famine policy in early nineteenth-century India, see Sanjay Sharma, *Famine, Philanthropy and the Colonial State: North India in the Early Nineteenth Century* (Delhi: Oxford University Press, 2001).

9. Accounts and Papers: 37 vols. Contents of the ninth volume. *Cotton (India).* (439). Return to an Order of the Honourable The House of Commons, 15 February 1847; for a Return of "Papers in the Possession of the East India Company, Showing what Measures Have Been Taken since 1836 to Promote the Cultivation of Cotton in India, with the Particulars and Result of Any Experiments which Have Been Made by Said Company, with a View to Introduce the Growth of AMERICAN COTTON, or to Encourage the Production of Native Cotton in India." By James C. Melville, East India House, 5 May 1847; ordered by the House of Commons to be printed, 21 May 1847, vol. 42, Session 19 January – 23 July 1847, 2, 26 (Hereafter, *Cotton [India]*).

10. "Biographical Sketch of George Thompson," *Liberator*, 9 May 1845; "Sketches of Modern Reforms and Reformers, in Great Britain and Ireland," *National Era*, 10 May 1849.

11. *Liberator*, 16 October 1840.

12. *Liberator*, 4 September 1840.

13. *Liberator*, 7 January 1842.

14. *Liberator*, 31 July 1839.

15. Minute by the Right Honorable Governor-General, memorandum by the political secretary, 1 December 1835, Extract Bombay Political Consultations, 23 December 1835.

16. Robert Wright, Esq., Surgeon, Madras, to the Chief Secretary to Government, Fort St. George, 21 February 1840, *Cotton (India)*, 40.

17. J. Vibart, Esq., Revenue Commissioner, Bombay, to L.R. Reid, Esq., chief secretary, Bombay, 15 February 1840, *Cotton (India)*, 59.

18. E.A. Webster, Vice Consul, Bombay, to Daniel Webster, 1 July 1841, in Despatches from United States Consuls in Bombay, 1838–1906, Register, 1838–1906, and vol. 1, 12 October 1838 – 16 November 1857, microfilm edition, National Archives, Washington, DC, 1950. Hereafter, Despatches from Bombay Consul.

19. Thomas Bayles to James Cosmo Melville, Esq., Secretary, East India House, *Cotton (India)*, 25.

20. *Cotton (India)*, 25–26.
21. Captain T. Bayles' memorandum, with a statement, 24 January 1842, *Cotton (India)*, 115.
22. Brian Schoen, *The Fragile Fabric of Union*, 157–59; Florio, "From Poverty to Slavery," 1050. On overseers, see William Kauffman Scarborough, *The Overseer: Plantation Management in the Old South* (Baton Rouge: Louisiana State University Press, 1966); William E. Wiethoff, *Crafting the Overseer's Image* (Columbia: University of South Carolina Press, 2006).
23. Bayles to Melville, *Cotton (India)*, 26–28.
24. *Liberator*, 2 October 1840.
25. Schoen, *Fragile Fabric*, 143.
26. Chronicling America, https://chroniclingamerica.loc.gov/lccn/sn9205323.
27. *Liberty Advocate*, 16 July 1840; *Illinois Free Trader*, 26 June 1840.
28. *Liberty Advocate*, 16 July 1840.
29. Speech of Hon. Oliver H. Smith of Indiana, on the Resolutions of Mr. Clay, and in reply to Mr. Wright, of New York, Delivered in the Senate of the United States, 3 March 1842, *National Intelligencer* (Washington, DC), in *Speeches in Congress Delivered by Henry Clay and Others, 1833–1842*, Ohio State University Libraries, https://catalog.hathitrust.org/Record/100216628/Home, 14–15.
30. Smith, speech, 3 March 1842, 16–17.
31. Smith, 18–19.
32. Smith, 21.
33. Beckert, *Empire of Cotton*, 98–135.
34. David Ludden, *An Agrarian History of South Asia*, the New Cambridge History of India, vol. 4 (Cambridge: Cambridge University Press, 1999), 6, 169.
35. Ludden, *Agrarian History*, 127–28.
36. Ludden, 23, 25, 141, 143, 159, 161; Najmul Abedin, "The Impact of Whig and Utilitarian Philosophies on the Formative Phase of Local Administration in British India," *Journal of Third World Studies* 30, no. 2 (2013): 193.
37. Ludden, *Agrarian History*, 29.
38. Abstract Proceedings of the Honorable the Lieutenant-Governor of the North-Western Provinces, in reference to the Experimental Cotton Cultivation, *Cotton (India)*, 89–90.
39. Ludden, *Agrarian History*, 142.
40. J.G. Bruce, Esquire, Humeerpore, to H. Torrens, Esq., secretary to the Asiatic Society, Calcutta, 18 October 1841, *Cotton (India)*, 103.
41. *Mississippi Creole*, 28 May 1842.
42. *Mississippi Creole*, 28 May 1842.
43. For a background on this newspaper, see Chronicling America, www.accessible-archives.com/collections/national-anti-slavery-standard/.
44. *National Anti-Slavery Standard*, 13 January 1842.
45. *National Anti-Slavery Standard*, 4 November 1841.
46. Clippings from *Bombay Times*, appended to letter, E.A. Webster to Daniel Webster, 1 October 1841, in Despatches from Bombay Consul.
47. E.A. Webster to Daniel Webster, 1 July 1841, Despatches from Bombay Consul.

48. E.A. Webster to Daniel Webster, 1 October 1841.

49. J.M. Campbell, *Gazetteer of the Bombay Presidency Prepared under the Orders of Government. Gujarat Surat and Broach*, vol. 2 (Bombay: Government Central Press, 1877), 397. Hereafter, *Bombay Gazetteer* II.

50. E.A. Webster to Daniel Webster, 1 October 1841.

51. Extracts from T.J. Finnie's private journal, *Cotton (India)*, 107.

52. Finnie's journal, *Cotton (India)*, 151.

53. Finnie, 129.

54. Finnie, 107, 109.

55. Caitlin Rosenthal, "Slavery's Scientific Management: Masters and Managers," in Beckert and Rothman, *Slavery's Capitalism*, 75–77.

56. Finnie's journal, *Cotton (India)*, 162.

57. Finnie, 161, 158, 108.

58. Ludden, *Agrarian History*, 30.

59. Finnie's journal, *Cotton (India)*, 161.

60. Finnie, 111.

61. Finnie, 162.

62. Finnie, 173, 152.

63. Finnie, 179.

64. Finnie, 109, 168.

65. Finnie, 176.

66. Finnie, 155.

67. Finnie, 154, 154–55, 156.

68. Finnie, 161–62.

69. On Natchez, see Mary Jane Brazy, *An American Planter: Steven Duncan of Antebellum Natchez and New York* (Baton Rouge: Louisiana State University Press, 2006).

70. "About Independent Democrat (Canton, Miss.), 1842-1844," Chronicling America, https://chroniclingamerica.loc.gov/lccn/sn83016863/.

71. Joan J. Hall, "Jones, Alexander," in *Dictionary of North Carolina Biography*, ed. William S. Powell, 6 vols. (Chapel Hill: University of North Carolina Press, 1979–96), republished on NCpedia.org, North Carolina Government & Heritage Library, https://www.ncpedia.org/biography/jones-alexander.

72. *Cotton (India)*, 27.

73. A. Jones, "On the Cultivation of Cotton in India," *Journal of Commerce*, reprinted in the *Mississippi Creole*, 7 May 1842.

74. Jones, "On the Cultivation."

75. Jones.

76. Jones.

77. Cited in *Mississippi Creole*, 14 May 1842.

78. *Bombay Gazetteer* II, 398.

79. Cited in *Independent Democrat*, 19 August 1843.

80. Finnie's journal, *Cotton (India)*, 108–9, 110.

81. Thomas Bayles to R.N.C. Hamilton, Esq., Secretary to Government, North-Western Provinces, Agra, 14 March 1842, *Cotton (India)*, 117.

82. Abstract Proceedings of the Honorable the Lieutenant-Governor of the North-Western Provinces, in reference to the Experimental Cotton Plantation, *Cotton (India)*, 93, 99.
83. Lieutenant-Governor, *Cotton (India)*, 94–95.
84. Finnie's journal, *Cotton (India)*, 229.
85. Finnie, 162, 161.
86. "Mr. Finnie's Answer," *Cotton (India)*, 142.
87. Finnie's journal, *Cotton (India)*, 154.
88. Finnie, 195, 223.
89. C. C. Jackson, Esq., Collector of Agra, to J. Thornton, Esq., Secretary to Government, North-Western Province, 24 May 1845, *Cotton (India)*, 255.
90. To Chief Secretary to Government, Fort St. George, Revenue Department, Coimbatore, 14 March 1842 from (signed) R. Wright, Sup' of Cotton Farms, *Cotton(India)*, 334.
91. *Mississippi Democrat*, 15 October 1845.
92. "Sketches of the Moral Reforms," *National Era*, 10 May 1849.
93. Florio, "From Poverty to Slavery," 1024.
94. Samuel Cartwright, "The Slave Trade and the Union," *New Orleans Delta*, reprinted from *The Washington Union*, in the *North Carolina Standard*, 16 and 20 September 1854.
95. Cartwright, "Slave Trade."
96. Cartwright.
97. Cartwright.
98. *Wilmington Journal*, 12 June 1857.
99. *Wilmington Journal*, 12 June 1857.

CHAPTER 4. THE SLAVE MISTRESS AND THE COURTESAN

1. Recent works on comparative slavery and gender in the Atlantic world include Daina Ramey Berry and Leslie M. Harris, eds., *Sexuality and Slavery: Reclaiming Intimate Histories in the Americas* (Athens: University of Georgia Press, 2018); Gwyn Campbell, Suzanne Miers, and Joseph C. Miller, eds., *Women and Slavery*, vol. 2: *The Modern Atlantic* (Athens: Ohio University Press, 2008); Brenda E. Stevenson, "Introduction: Women, Slavery, and the Atlantic World," *Journal of African American History* 98, no. 1 (Winter 2013); 1–6, together with the issue's other essays by Stevenson, Jane Landers, Jessica Millward, Margaret Washington, and Andrew Apter. Examples for the IOW include Gwynn Campbell and Elizabeth Elbourne, *Sex, Power, and Slavery* (Athens: Ohio University Press, 2014); and for South Asia in particular, Chatterjee, *Gender, Slavery, and Law*.

On enslaved women in the US South through the Civil War era., see the introduction by Jennifer L. Morgan and the essays by Daina Ramey Berry, Stephanie M. H. Camp, Leslie M. Harris, Barbara Krauthamer, and Jessica Millward, as well as the afterword by Deborah G. White, in the Roundtable, "The History of Women and Slavery: Considering the Impact of *Ar'n't I a Woman? Female Slaves in the Plantation South*," *Journal of Women's History* 19, no. 2 (Summer 2007): 138–69. A tiny sample of works on women, slavery, and race in the United States also includes Deborah Willis and Barbara Krauthamer, *Envisioning Emancipation: Black Americans and the End of Slavery* (Philadelphia: Temple University Press, 2012); Morgan, *Laboring Women*; Thavolia Glymph, *Out of the House of Bondage: The Transformation of the Plantation Household* (Cambridge: Cambridge University Press, 2008); Sophie White, *Voices of the Enslaved: Love, Labor, and Longing in French Louisiana* (Chapel Hill: University of North Carolina Press, 2019); Daina Ramey Berry, *"Swing the Sickle for the Harvest is Ripe": Gender and Slavery in Antebellum Georgia* (Urbana: University of Illinois Press, 2007); Wilma King, *The Essence of Liberty: Free Black Women during the Slave Era* (Columbia: University of Missouri Press, 2006); Tiya Miles, *Ties That Bind: The Story of an Afro-Cherokee Family in Slavery and Freedom* (Berkeley: University of California Press, 2005); Stephanie Camp, *Closer to Freedom: Enslaved Women and Resistance in the Plantation South* (Chapel Hill: University of North Carolina Press, 2004); Brenda Stevenson, *Life in Black and White: Family and Community in the Slave South* (New York: Oxford University Press, 1996); Emily West, *Chains of Love: Slave Couples in Antebellum South Carolina* (Urbana: University of Illinois Press, 2004); Betty Wood, *Women's Work, Men's Work: The Informal Slave Economies of Low Country Georgia, 1750–1830* (Athens: University of Georgia Press, 1995); Tera Hunter, *To 'Joy My Freedom* (Cambridge, MA: Harvard University Press, 1997); Amrita Chakrabarti Myers, *Forging Freedom: Black Women and the Pursuit of Liberty in Antebellum Charleston* (Chapel Hill: University of North Carolina Press, 2011); Rebecca J. Fraser, *Courtship and Love among the Enslaved in North Carolina* (Jackson: University of Mississippi Press, 2007); Nell Irvin Painter, *Southern History across the Color Line* (Chapel Hill: University of North Carolina Press, 2002); Dylan C. Peningroth, *The Claims of Kinfolk: African American Property and Community in the Nineteenth-Century South* (Chapel Hill: University of North Carolina Press, 2003); Cynthia M. Kennedy, *Braided Relations, Entwined Lives; The Women of Charleston's Urban Slave Society* (Bloomington: Indiana University Press, 2005); Leslie A. Schwalm, *A Hard Fight for We: Women's Transition from Slavery to Freedom in South Carolina* (Urbana: University of Illinois Press, 1997).

Insights into the lives of white women in slave society occur in Stephanie E. Jones-Rogers, *They Were Her Property: White Women as Slave Owners in the American South* (New Haven, CT: Yale University Press, 2019); Drew Gilpin Faust, *Mothers of Invention: Women of the Slaveholding South in the American Civil War* (Chapel Hill: University of North Carolina Press, 1996); Elizabeth Fox-Genovese, *Within the Plantation Household: Black and White Women of the Old South* (Chapel Hill: University of North Carolina Press, 1988); Stephanie McCurry, *Masters of Small Worlds: Yeomen Households, Gender Relations, and the Political Culture of the Antebellum South Carolina Low Country* (New York: Oxford University Press, 1995); Kirsten E. Wood, *Masterful Women: Slaveholding Widows From the Revolution to the Civil War* (Chapel Hill: University of North Carolina Press, 2004). Micki McElya, in *Clinging to Mammy: The Faithful Slave in Twentieth-Century America* (Cambridge, MA: Harvard University Press, 2007) explored the persistence of a mythology of women in slavery.

On women's freedom flights during the Civil War, see Amy Murrell Taylor, *Embattled Freedom: Journeys through the Civil War's Slave Refugee Camps* (Chapel Hill: University of North Carolina Press, 2018) and Thavolia Glymph, *The Women's Fight: The Civil War's Battles for Home, Freedom, and Nation* (Chapel Hill: University of North Carolina Press, 2020).

2. See for instance, William H. Foster, "Women Slave Owners Face Their Historians: Versions of Maternalism in Atlantic World Slavery," *Patterns of Prejudice* 41(2007), 303–21.

3. Quotation from Claire Robertson and Marsha Robinson, "Re-modeling Slavery as if Women Mattered," in Campbell et al., *Women and Slavery*, 2:261.

4. For a full-length biography of McCord, see Leigh Fought, *Southern Womanhood and Slavery: A Biography of Louisa S. McCord, 1810–1876* (Columbia: University of Missouri Press, 2003).

5. Eaton, introduction to Chatterjee and Eaton, *Slavery and South Asian History*, 2, 6–9. On slavery in the IOW, see also note 17 to this book's introduction.

6. Extract from the Abstract Statement of Prisoners Acquitted by the Additional Sessions Judge of Cuttack, March 1867, Bengal Judicial Proceedings, during June 1867, nos. 208–10, West Bengal State Archives, Kolkata, India. Hereafter, BJP. See also Bengal Police, no. 14, First Report, Special Report of Crime, Cuttack District, dated 25 February 1867, BJP, during November 1867, nos. 85–86.

7. Thomas Bender, *Rethinking American History in a Global Age* (Berkeley: University of California Press, 2002).

8. For a classic exposition on Free Labor Republicanism, see Foner, *Free Soil, Free Labor*.

9. For George Fitzhugh's proslavery ideas, see *Sociology for the South, or, The Failure of Free Society* (Richmond: A. Morris, 1854) and *Slavery Justified/by a Southerner* (Fredericksburg, VA: Recorder Printing Office, 1850).

10. Eugene D. Genovese, *Roll Jordan Roll: The World the Slaves Made* (New York: Pantheon, 1974).

11. Lacy Ford, "Reconfiguring the Old South: "Solving" the Problem of Slavery, 1787–1838," *The Journal of American History* 95 (June 2008), 109–12. Some recent works on slavery and capitalism in the US South include Beckert, *Empire of Cotton*, 98–135; Walter Johnson, *River of Dark Dreams: Slavery and Empire in the Cotton Kingdom* (Cambridge, MA: Belknap Press of Harvard University Press, 2013); Johnson, *Soul by Soul*; Baptist, *Half Has Never Been Told*.

12. Edward B. Rugemer, "The Southern Response to British Abolitionism: The Maturation of Proslavery Apologetics," *Journal of Southern History* 70 (May 2004): 221–48. See also Ford, "Reconfiguring the Old South," 118, and Larry A. Tise, *Proslavery: A History of the Defense of Slavery in America, 1701–1840* (Athens: University of Georgia Press, 1987).

13. James P. Huzel, "Malthus, the Poor Law, and Population in Early Nineteenth-Century England," *Economic History Review* 22 (December 1969): 430; Anna Clark, "The New Poor Law and the Breadwinner Wage: Contrasting Assumptions," *Journal of Social History* 34 (Winter 2000): 262; Lisa Forman Cody, "The Politics of Illegitimacy in an Age of Reform: Women, Reproduction, and Political Economy in England's New Poor Law of 1834," *Journal of Women's History* 11, no. 4 (Winter 2000): 134–35.

14. Huzel, "Malthus," 432.

15. Quotation from Thomas Nutt, "Illegitimacy, Paternal Financial Responsibility, and the 1834 Poor Law Commission Report: The Myth of the Old Poor Law and the Making of the New," *Economic History Review* 63 (May 2010): 338; Cody, "Politics of Illegitimacy," 263–64.

16. Cody, "Politics of Illegitimacy," 146–48.

17. Indian Law Commission Report, 15 January 1841.

18. For Carey's critique of British India, see the chapter "How Slavery Grows in India," in Charles H. Carey, *The Slave Trade, Domestic and Foreign: Why It Exists and How It May Be Extinguished* (Philadelphia: A. Hart, Late Carey and Hart, 1853), 130–73; on "perpetual drain" see p. 138. A classic statement of the "drain theory" is in Dadabhai Naoroji, *Poverty and Un-British Rule in India* (London: Swan Sonnenschein, 1901). On Maharashtrian critics of

colonial economic policies in the 1840s, see J.V. Naik, "Forerunners of Dadabhai Naoroji's Drain Theory," *Economic and Political Weekly* (November 2001): 4428–32.

19. On colonial famine policy see Sharma, *Famine, Philanthropy*.

20. Durba Ghosh, *Sex and the Family in Colonial India: The Making of Empire* (New York: Cambridge University Press, 2006), 206–45.

21. "Mr. Cameron's Minute," *Indian Law Commission Report*, 1:13; "Observations," *Indian Law Commission Report*, 1:320–21.

22. "Mr. Cameron's Minute," 13.

23. "Mr. Cameron's Minute," 14.

24. "Observations," 1:326. See also Adam's critique in *Law and Custom of Slavery*, 225.

25. On feminizing the Other, see for instance, Mrinalini Sinha, *Colonial Masculinity: the 'Manly Englishman' and the 'Effeminate Bengali' in the Late Nineteenth Century* (Manchester, UK: Manchester University Press, 1995).

26. Edward Colebrooke to Chief Secretary Swinton, 4 August 1828; T.T. Metcalf, Esq., judge and magistrate, Delhi, to J.E. Colebrooke, 2 August 1828; Deputy Secretary Stirling to Colebrooke, 29 August 1828, all in *Slave Trade (East India)*, 37–39; Chatterjee, *Gender, Slavery and Law*; Major, *Slavery, Abolitionism*.

27. "Harper's Memoir on Slavery," in *The Proslavery Argument, as Maintained by the Most Distinguished Writers of the Southern States: Containing the Several Essays on the Subject, of Chancellor Harper, Governor Hammond, Dr. Simms, and Professor Dew* (Philadephia: Lippincott, Grambo, 1853), 33.

28. Paul Finkelman, "Thomas R.R. Cobb and the Law of Negro Slavery," *Roger Williams University Law Review* 5 (Fall 1999): 75–115, quotation on p. 85.

29. Finkelman, "Thomas R.R. Cobb," 85–86, 92–93; Thomas R.R. Cobb, *An Inquiry into the Law of Negro Slavery*, preface and table of contents pages.

30. Cobb, "Slavery in India," in *Inquiry into the Law*, lii, liii, liv, lv.

31. William S. Speer to William H. Seward, 17, 24, and 25 November and 6 December 1861; 10 and 13 October 1862; Speer, "Report on Zanzibar, 26 November 1862," all in US State Department, Dispatches from US Consuls in Zanzibar, 1836–1906, National Archives, microfilm edition. Hereafter, DCZ.

32. "Hammonds' Letters on Slavery," in *Proslavery Argument*, 122.

33. Robert Lewis Dabney, *A Defense of Virginia (and Through Her, of the South) in Recent and Pending Contests against the Sectional Party* (New York: E.J. Hale and Son, 1867), 229.

34. Louisa McCord, "A Letter to the Duchess of Sutherland from a Lady of South Carolina," in *Political and Social Essays by Louisa Susanna Cheves McCord*, ed. Richard Cecil Lounsbury (1853; repr., Charlottesville: University of Virginia Press, 1995), 351–59.

35. McCord, "Letter to the Duchess," 354; *Indian Law Commission Report*, 1:320–21.

36. McCord, "Letter to the Duchess," 354.

37. McCord, 356, 358. The *Indian Law Commission Report* defended Indian forms of servitude in similar terms on pages 13 and 317–26.

38. McCord, "Letter to the Duchess," 356, 358.

39. On Black women's lives, labors, and relations with white mistresses, see the references cited in note 1. On enslaved women's work in South Carolina, see particularly Schwalm, *Hard Fight for We*; on violence within the plantation household, see Glymph, *Out of the House of Bondage*; on "compliance" by slaveholding women, see Brenda Stevenson,

"What's Love Got to Do With it? Concubinage and Enslaved Women and Girls in the Antebellum South," *The Journal of African American History* 98, no. 1 (Winter 2013): 112; on enslaved wet nurses, see Emily West with R. J. Knight, "Mothers' Milk: Slavery, Wet-Nursing, and Black and White Women in the Antebellum South," *Journal of Southern History* 83 (February 2017): 37–68; on enslaved women charged with killing masters or their own children, see Wilma King, "'Mad' Enough to Kill: Enslaved Women, Murder, and Southern Courts," *Journal of African American History* 92 (Winter 2007): 37–56.

40. Thomas Morris, *Southern Slavery and the Law, 1619–1860* (Chapel Hill: University of North Carolina Press, 2004), 65.

41. Fought, *Southern Womanhood and Slavery*, 114.

42. Jones-Rogers, *They Were Her Property*.

43. Account of A. Auby, District Superintendent of Police, Kamroop, in Memorandum by officers consulted on the subject of forbidding the possession of girls under ten years of age by prostitutes, attached to report by Colonel Henry Hopkinson, Agent, Governor-General of Northeast Frontier and Commissioner of Assam, to the Secretary to Government of Bengal, Judicial Department, 11 August 1872, BJP, during October 1872, 252–335.

44. Report of Baboo Anund Chunder Ghose, acting Sessions Judge and Sheritadar of the Raj Subha of Cooch Behar, Appendix A, in BJP, during June 1864, nos. 139–41; List of persons sold till Falgoon 1270 BS, in Hat Bowaneegunge, Nij Behar, in BJP.

45. James Corbett David, "The Politics of Emasculation: The Caning of Charles Sumner and Elite Ideologies of Manhood in the Mid-Nineteenth-Century United States," *Gender and History* 19, no. 2 (August 2007): 328.

46. Philippa Levine, *Prostitution, Race, and Politics: Policing Venereal Disease in the British Empire* (New York: Routledge, 2003); Indrani Chatterjee, "Coloring Subalternity: Slaves, Concubines and Social Orphans in Early Colonial India," in *Subaltern Studies X: Writings on South Asian History and Society*, ed. Gautam Bhadra, Gyan Prakash and Susie Tharu (New Delhi: Oxford University Press, 1999), 64–68; Erica Wald, "From Begums and Bibis to Abandoned Females and Idle Women: Sexual Relationships, Venereal Disease and the Redefinition of Prostitution in Early Nineteenth-Century India," *Indian Economic and Social History Review* 46 (2009), 5–25; Erica Wald, "Defining Prostitution and Redefining Women's Roles: The Colonial State and Society in Early 19th Century India," *History Compass* 7 (November 2009): 1470–83. On Bengal, see Sumanta Banerjee, *Dangerous Outcast: The Prostitute in Nineteenth-Century Bengal* (Calcutta: Seagull Books, 1998).

47. Swapna M. Banerjee, "Debates on Domesticity and the Position of Women in Late Colonial India," *History Compass* 8 (June 2010): 455–73, esp. 460; Swapna M. Banerjee, *Men, Women and Domestics: Articulating Middle-Class Identity in Colonial India* (Delhi: Oxford University Press, 2004).

48. Partha Chatterjee, "The Nationalist Resolution of the Women's Question," in *Recasting Women: Essays in Indian Colonial History*, ed. Kumkum Sangari and Sudesh Vaid (New Brunswick, NJ: Rutgers University Press, 1990), 244–45.

49. Swapna Banerjee, "Blurring Boundaries, Distant Companions: Non-Kin Female Caregivers for Children in Colonial India (Nineteenth and Twentieth Centuries)," *Paedagogica Historica* 46 (December 2010): 775–88.

50. Sarah Waheed, "Women of 'Ill Repute': Ethics and Urdu Literature in Colonial India," *Modern Asian Studies* 48 (July 2014): 986–1023.

51. On mill workers, see Samita Sen, *Women and Labor in Late Colonial India: The Bengal Jute Industry* (Cambridge: Cambridge University Press, 1999), 177–86; Ratnabali Chatterjee, "The Queens' Daughters: Prostitutes as an Outcast Group in Colonial India," report, Chr. Michelsen Institute, Department of Social Science and Development, Bergen, Norway, December 1992, 1–2.

52. On "temporary marriages" see Sen, *Women and Labor,* 179. On the broadening conception of the colonial category of "prostitute," see Kunal M. Parker, "'A Corporation of Superior Prostitutes': Anglo-Indian Legal Conceptions of Temple Dancing Girls, 1800–1914," *Modern Asian Studies* 32 (July 1998): 559–633, and Wald, "Defining Prostitution."

53. Karen Leonard, "Political Players: Courtesans of Hyderabad," *Indian Economic and Social History Review,* 50 (2013): 423–48.

54. W. H. Macnaghten signed, "A Regulation for the Guidance of the Courts of Judicature in Cases of Slavery," in *Slave Trade (East India),* 320–21, and in Board's Collections.

55. *Principles and Precedents of Moohummudan Law, Being a Compilation of Primary Rules Relative to Inheritance, Contracts and Miscellaneous Subjects, and a Selection of Legal Opinions Invoving Those Points, Delivered in the Several Courts of Judicature Subordinate to the Presidency of Fort William: Together with Notes Illustrative and Explanatory, and Preliminary Remarks, by W. H. Macnaghten, Esq., of the Bengal Civil Service With Additional Notes, Questions for Students, and a Digest of Principles of Decisions on the Law and Customs, relating to Moohummudans from 1793 to 1859 by William Sloan, of Lincoln's Inn, Barrister-at-Law,* 5th ed. (Calcutta, 1825; Madras: Higginbotham, 1882), 321.

56. Parker, "'Corporation of Superior Prostitutes,'" 585–87, 561–62.

57. Henry Pottinger, Resident in Cutch, to John Bax, Chief Secretary to Government, 13 October 1834, in *Slave Trade (East India),* 107.

58. Enclosure from the Kotah Vakeel in, and Appendix to No. 90 of 1846, Capt. C. E. Burton, Political Agent in Harowtee to Lt. Col. Sutherland, Agent, Governor General for States of Rajpootana, 18 March 1846, PC # 132–36, 18 July 1846, in National Archives of India (hereafter NAI). Ramya Sreenivasan, "Drudges, Dancing Girls, Concubines: Female Slaves in Rajput Polity, 1500–1850," in Chatterjee and Eaton *Slavery and South Asian History,* 136–61.

59. Bengal Police, no. 14, First Report, Special Report of Crime, Cuttack District, dated 25 February 1867, BJP, during November 1867, nos. 85–86.

60. Lacey to W. MacPherson, Magistrate of Cuttack, 26 July 1867; MacPherson to the Commissioners of the Cuttack Division, 29 August 1867, in BJP.

61. Extract from the Abstract Statement of Prisoners Acquitted by the Additional Sessions Judge of Cuttack, March 1867, BJP, during June 1867, nos. 208–10.

62. Abstract Statement of Prisoners, BJP.

63. Lt. Colonel J. R. Pughe, Inspector General of Police, Lower Provinces, to the Secretary to the Government of Bengal, 9 September 1867, and W. MacPherson to the Commissioner of the Cuttack Division, 29 August 1867, and enclosures, all in BJP, during November 1867, nos. 122–26; Memorandum from W. C. Lacey, district superintendent of police, to the Deputy Inspector General of Police, First Circle, 26 July 1867, BJP, during November 1867, nos. 85–86.

64. E. C. Bayley, C.S.I., Secretary to the Government of India, Home Department, to the Officiating Secretary to Government of Bengal, Judicial Department, 9 April 1872; C. Bernard, officiating Secretary to Government of Bengal in the Judicial Department, to All

Divisional Commissioners, and to the Officiating Commissioner of Police, Calcutta, 19 April 1872, all in BJP, during April 1872, nos. 68–69.

65. On the Bengal government's inquiry into alleged violations of Section 373 of the Indian Penal Code, see Circular No. 89, 16 July 1873, from A. Mackenzie, Junior Secretary to the Government of Bengal, to all commissioners, BJP, during September 1873, nos. 68–70.

66. Response of P. Nolan, Assistant Magistrate of Serajgunge, in Abstract of the Replies of the Divisional Commissioners consulted on the proposal of the Government of India to register all girls now in the possession of professional prostitutes, and in future to make such possession penal, BJP during October 1872, nos. 76–77 (hereafter, Abstracts).

67. Response of E.E. Lowis, Magistrate of Dinajpore, in Abstracts.

68. Response of Mr. D.R. Lyall, Magistrate of Dacca, in Abstracts.

69. Account of A. Auby, District Superintendent of Police, Kamroop, in *Memorandum by Officers Consulted on the Subject of Forbidding the Possession of Girls under Ten Years of Age by Prostitutes,* attached to report by Colonel Henry Hopkinson, agent, Governor-General of Northeast Frontier and Commissioner of Assam, to the Secretary to Government of Bengal, Judicial Department, 11 August 1872, BJP, during October 1872, 252–335.

70. Response of Mullick, Deputy Magistrate of Madaripore to the Magistrate of Backergunge, 24 May 1872, BJP, October 1872, nos. 252–335.

71. Report of Calcutta Commissioner of Police, in BJP.

72. Sen, *Women and Labor,* 181–85; Tapan Raychaudhuri, "Love in a Colonial Climate: Marriage, Sex and Romance in Nineteenth-Century Bengal," *Modern Asian Studies* 34 (2000): 353–54; Sekhar Bandyopadhyay, "Caste, Widow Remarriage and the Reform of Popular Culture in Colonial Bengal," in *Women and Social Reform in Modern India: A Reader,* ed. Sumit Sarkar and Tanika Sarkar (Bloomington: Indiana University Press, 2008), 100–17.

73. Account of A. Acercrombie, officiating Commissioner of Dacca, to Secretary to Government of Bengal, BJP, October 1872, nos. 252–335.

74. Neel Dass Money, special sub-registrar, to Magistrate of Tipperah, 11 May 1872, in BJP.

75. Sen, *Women and Labor,* 181–85; Raychaudhuri, "Love in a Colonial Climate:," 353–54; Bandyopadhyay, "Caste, Widow Remarriage," 21–23.

76. Baboo Bankim Chandra Chatterjee to W. Wavell, officiating Magistrate of Moorshidabad, 31 May 1872, in BJP, during October 1872, nos. 252–335; Money to Magistrate of Tipperah, in BJP; G.S. Park, officiating Magistrate of Tipperah to the Commissioner of Chittagong, Coumillah, 5 June 1872, in BJP.

77. Larrymore, District Superintendent of Police, Hooghly, to Magistrate of Hooghly, 5 August 1872, in BJP; Banerjee, *Dangerous Outcast,* 117.

78. Account of H. Hankey of Chittagong, in Abstracts.

79. Chatterjee to Wavell, in BJP.

80. K.D. Ghose (Ghosh) to Commissioner of the Rajshahye Division, 27 May 1872, in BJP.

81. Baboo Bhagwan Chander Bose, Deputy Magistrate of Brahmenbareah to the Magistrate of Tipperah, 25 May 1872, in BJP.

82. Larrymore to the Magistrate of Hooghly, 5 August 1872, in BJP.

83. Krishna Chattopadhyaya, headmaster, Gya Zilla School, to Magistrate of Gya, 9 June 1872, in BJP.

84. Chatterjee to Wavell, in BJP.

85. Parker, "'Corporation of Superior Prostitutes,'" 567, 580.

86. C. Hayley, officiating Commissioner of Patna to the Secretary to the Government of Bengal, Judicial Department, 30 July 1872, in BJP, October 1872, nos. 252–335.

87. Memorandum from H. Bell, legal remembrancer, to the Officiating Secretary to the Government of Bengal, Judicial Department, 11 August 1876, and attachments, in BJP, during November 1876, nos. 14–16.

88. Response of Nolan, in Abstracts.

89. Baboo Taraprasad Chatterjee, Deputy Magistrate of Jungipore, to Commissioner of Rajshahye Division, 22 May 1872, in BJP, October 1872, nos. 252–335.

90. Report of Presidency Division Commissioner H.A. Cockerell, in Abstracts.

91. Bose to Magistrate of Tipperah, 25 May 1872, during October 1872, nos. 252-335, in BJP.

92. W.S. Wells, Magistrate of Furreedpore, to Commissioner of Dacca, 23 May 1872, in BJP.

93. Taraprasad Chatterjee to Commissioner to Rajshahye, 22 May 1872, in BJP.

94. Money to Magistrate of Tipperah; H.W. Alexander, Magistrate of Shahbad to Commissioner of Patna, 29 June 1872, in BJP.

95. Nolan to Commissioner of Rajshahye, 7 May 1872, in BJP; Banerjee, *Dangerous Outcast*, 26–27.

96. E.V. Werhuacott, officiating Magistrate of Dinjapore, to the Commissioner of Circuit, Rajshahye District, 15 May 1872, BJP, during October 1872, nos. 252–335.

97. Chattopadhyaya to Magistrate of Gya, 9 June 1872, in BJP.

98. Accounts of W. MacPherson, W.H. D'Oyly, and S.C. Bayley, in Abstracts.

99. Extract of a letter from Norman MacLeod, Commissioner of Cooch Behar, to George Dowdswell, Chief Secretary to Government, 31 January 1814, Appendix B, BJP, during June 1864, nos. 139–41.

CHAPTER 5. "DOMESTIC" SLAVERY AND COLONIAL BELONGING

1. Letter of William Farmer, London, 26 June 1851, published in *National AntiSlavery Standard*, 24 July 1851.

2. On *The Greek Slave*, see Charmaine Nelson, *Color of Stone: Sculpting the Black Female Subject in Nineteenth-Century America* (Minneapolis: University of Minnesota Press, 2007), 75–140; Lisa Merrill, "Exhibiting Race 'under the World's Huge Glass Case': William and Ellen Craft and William Wells Brown at the Great Exhibition in Crystal Palace, London, 1851," *Slavery & Abolition* 33 (June 2012): 321–36.

3. *Official Catalogue of the Great Exhibition of the Works of Industry of All Nations, 1851*, 2nd ed., (London: Spicer, 1851); J.R. Piggott, *Palace of the People: The Crystal Palace at Sydenham, 1854–1936* (Madison: University of Wisconsin Press, 2004), 27.

4. On philhellenistic movements, see Maureen Santelli, "'Depart from That Retired Circle': Women's Support of the Greek War for Independence and Antebellum Reform," *Early American Studies* 15 (Winter 2017): 194–233.

5. Roberts, "True Womanhood Revisited"; Hewitt, "Taking the True Woman Hostage."

6. A classic analysis of the Jezebel mythology of women in American slavery occurs in Deborah Gray White, *Ar'n't I a Woman?*

7. *The National Era*, 17 June 1851; *Frederick Douglass' Paper*, 26 June 1851. On Afro-Atlantic activists in inspiring and organizing movements against slavery, see Sinha, *Slave's Cause*; Blight, *Frederick Douglass*.

8. Merrill, "Exhibiting Race."

9. William and Ellen Craft, "Running a Thousand Miles for Freedom, Or, the Escape of William and Ellen Craft from Slavery" (1860), in Sterling LeCarter Bland, *African American Slave Narratives: Anthology*, vol. 3 (Westport, CT: Greenwood Press, 2001), 891–946.

On enslaved women in the US South, see note 16 in the introduction and note 1 in chapter 4 of this book.

10. For comparisons of Greeks under Ottoman rule with enslaved Americans, see, for instance, "People of Color," *Freedom's Journal*, 6 April 1827.

11. "British and Foreign Anti-Slavery Society," *Frederick Douglass' Paper*, 21 August 1851.

12. Letter of J. McBride, *National Anti-Slavery Standard*, 24 July 1851.

13. See, for example, Walter Johnson, *Soul by Soul* and *River of Dark Dreams*.

14. See the essays in Harms et al., eds., *Indian Ocean Slavery*; Chatterjee, "Abolition by Denial"; Major, *Slavery, Abolitionism*; Huzzey, *Freedom Burning*.

15. Schedule 2—Slave Inhabitants in District No. 8, in the County of Bath, State of Virginia, Slave Schedule, 1850 US Federal Census, Ancestry.com; *Report of the Lemmon Slave Case: Containing Points and Arguments of Counsel on Both Sides, and Opinions of All the Judges* (New York: H. Greeley, 1860).

16. On Turner's so-called "frontier thesis," see Frederick Jackson Turner, "The Significance of the Frontier in American History," *Proceedings of the Forty-First Annual Meeting* (Madison: State Historical Society of Wisconsin, 1894), 79–112. A classic refutation occurs in Patricia Nelson Limerick, *The Legacy of Conquest: The Unbroken Past of the American West* (New York: Norton, 1987).

17. Johnson, *River of Dark Dreams*, 34; essays in Beckert and Rockman, *Slavery's Capitalism*.

18. For a review of this literature, see Calvin Schermerhorn, "The Everyday Life of Enslaved People in the Antebellum South," *OAH Magazine of History* 23, no. 2 (April 2009): 31, 31–36.

19. Johnson, *Soul by Soul*, 25.

20. Schermerhorn, "Everyday Life," 31.

21. For overviews of this literature, see Schermerhorn's synthesis, examples cited in note 9, and the essays in Edward E. Baptist and Stephanie M.H. Camp, eds., *New Studies in the History of American Slavery* (Athens: University of Georgia Press, 2006). The metaphor of stealing occurs in Baptist, "'Stol' and Fetched Here": Enslaved Migration, Ex-slave Narratives, and Vernacular History," in Baptist and Camp, *New Studies*, 243–74.

22. *Report of the Lemmon Slave Case*.

23. Schedule 1—Free inhabitants in the Fifth Ward of the County of New York in State of New York, 16 August 1850, 1850 US Federal Census, Ancestry.com.

24. Sarah L.H. Gronningsater, "'On Behalf of His Race and the Lemmon Slaves': Louis Napoleon, Northern Black Legal Culture, and the Politics of Sectional Crisis," *Journal of the Civil War Era* 7 (June 2017): 206–41.

25. See for instance, SenGupta, *From Slavery to Poverty*, 140–50.

26. Gronningsater, "'On Behalf of His Race,'" 216–17.

27. Schedule 1—Free inhabitants in the Fifth Ward, 16 August 1850, Ancestry.com.

28. *New York Times*, 9 November 1852. On comity, see Paul Finkelman, *An Imperfect Union: Slavery, Federalism, and Comity* (Chapel Hill: University of North Carolina Press, 1981).

29. Karolyn S. Frost, *I've Got a Home in Glory Land: A Lost Tale of the Underground Railroad* (New York: Farrar, Straus, and Giroux, 2007); Robin Winks, *The Blacks in Canada: A History*, Carleton Library Series (Montreal: McGill–Queen's University Press, 1997).

30. Ikuko Asaka, "'Our Brethren in the West Indies': Self-Emancipated People in Canada and the Antebellum Politics of Diaspora and Empire," *Journal of African American History* 97 (Summer 2012): 219–39, quotation on 220.

31. Asaka, "'Our Brethen,'" 228–30; Jeffrey R. Kerr-Ritchie, "Samuel Ward and the Making of an Imperial Subject," *Slavery and Abolition* 33 (June 2012): 205–19.

32. For a full-length biography of Shadd Cary, see Jane Rhodes, *Mary Ann Shadd Cary: The Black Press and Protest in the Nineteenth Century* (Bloomington: Indiana University Press, 1999); Erica Armstrong Dunbar, "Writing for True Womanhood: African-American Women's Writings and the Antislavery Struggle," in *Women's Rights and Trans-Atlantic Antislavery in the Era of Emancipation*, ed. Kathryn Kish Sklar and James Stewart (New Haven, CT: Yale University Press, 2007), 304–10.

33. *A Plea for Emigration; or Notes of Canada West, in its Moral, Social, and Political Aspect: with Suggestions Respecting Mexico, West Indies, and Vancouver's Island, for the Information of Colored Emigrants* (Detroit: John W. Pattison, 1852). Hereafter, *A Plea*. Prospectus of the *Provincial Freeman and Weekly Advertiser*, African American Newspapers Collections, Accessible Archives, www.accessible-archives.com/collections/african-american-newspapers/provincial-freeman/. Hereafter, the *Provincial Freeman*.

34. *A Plea*, 43.

35. *A Plea*, 40.

36. *Provincial Freeman*, 15 April and 1 July 1854.

37. On these points, see Gosse, "'As a Nation.'"

38. *A Plea*, 10, 8.

39. *A Plea*, 31–32.

40. *A Plea*, 22.

41. Foner, *Free Soil, Free Labor*.

42. *A Plea*, 18.

43. *Provincial Freeman*, 25 March 1854, 3 November 1855, 22 March 1856, 2 February 1856.

44. *Provincial Freeman*, 27 January 1855.

45. *Provincial Freeman*, 15 August 1857.

46. *Provincial Freeman*, 12 August 1854.

47. *The Art-Journal*, vol. 12 (1850): 179.

48. Adam, *Law and Custom*, 26–27.

49. Beverley, "Property, Authority and Personal Law," 158.

50. On these points, see Chatterjee, *Gender, Slavery, and Law*; Chatterjee and Eaton, *Slavery and South Asian History*; Campbell, *Abolition and Its Aftermath*; Campbell, *Structure of Slavery*; Major, *Slavery, Abolitionism*.

51. *Slave Trade (East India)*, 322.

52. *Indian Law Commission Report* I, 313.

53. See, for instance, Sreenivasan, "Drudges, Dancing Girls, Concubines."

54. Madeline Zulfi, *Women and Slavery in the Late Ottoman Empire: The Design of Difference* (New York: Cambridge University Press, 2010).

55. Edward Colebrooke to Chief Secretary Swinton, 4 August 1828; T.T. Metcalf, Esq., judge and magistrate, Delhi, to J.E. Colebrooke, 2 August 1828; Deputy Secretary Stirling to Colebrooke, 29 August 1828, all in *Slave Trade (East India)*, 37–39.

56. The South Indian kingdom of Mysore had entered into a "subsidiary alliance" with the East India Company, which stripped it of military and diplomatic powers and placed it under the protective custody of the company's forces, for which it paid a tribute.

57. H. Montgomery to the Secretary to the Commissioner for the Government of the Territories of the Rajah of Mysore, 28 September 1841, in Political Consultations nos. 32–38, Political Dispatches to and from Court of Directors, Foreign Department, National Archives of India (NAI), New Delhi. Hereafter, Political Dispatches, NAI. Sylvia Vatuk has written about the death of a domestic slave in a different context in "Bharattee's Death: Domestic Slave-Women in Nineteenth-Century Madras," in Chatterjee and Eaton, *Slavery and South Asian History*, 210–33.

58. Montgomery to the Mysore Secretary to the Commissioner, Political Dispatches, NAI; Lt. Col. J.D. Stokes to J.H. Maddock, Secretary to Government of India, Fort William, 26 October 1841, Political Department dispatch, 22 November 1841, Political Consultations Nos. 41-42, Political Dispatches, NAI.

59. Montgomery to the Mysore Secretary to the Commissioner, Political Consultations, NAI.

60. Stokes to Maddock, 26 October, 1841, Political Department dispatch, 22 November, 1841.

CHAPTER 6. RULERS, REBELS, AND REFUGEES IN TRANSNATIONAL TRANSIT

1. In a different context, Darlene Clark Hine offered a Black feminist paradigm, "the culture of dissemblance," to think through Black women's public silence on their inner lives. See Hine, "Rape and the Inner Lives of Black Women in the Middle West: Preliminary Thoughts on the Culture of Dissemblance," *Signs: Journal of Women in Culture and Society* 14 (1989): 912–20.

2. F. Apthorp, commanding Detachment at Porebunder [commonly spelled Porbandar today] to the Acting Political Agent, Rajcote, 12 December 1835, and J.P. Willoughby, Secretary to Government to the Acting Political Agent, Rajcote, 14 January 1836, Extract Bombay Political Consultations, 20 January 1836, in *Slave Trade (East India)*, 126–27; Charles Malcolm, Superintendent Indian Navy to the Right Honourable the Governor in Council, 1 January 1836, Register of Children received from Porebunder, accompanying letter of John Warden, Senior Magistrate of Police, Bombay Police Office to the Political Secretary to Government, 11 January 1836, in Extract Bombay Political Consultations, 27 January 1836, in *Slave Trade (East India)*, 127–28.

3. For example, see Alpers, "On Becoming a British Lake," 45–60.

4. Sherrif, *Dhow Cultures*.

5. Mathew, *Margins of the Market*, 21, 22, 24, 30, 31.

6. Abdul Sheriff, *Slaves, Spices and Ivory in Zanzibar: Integration of an East African Commercial Empire into the World Economy, 1770–1873* (Athens: Ohio University Press, 1987), 223; Hopper, *Slaves of One Master*, 148–49; Matthew, *Margins of the Market*, 54.

7. Sheriff, *Slaves, Spices and Ivory*, 223; Hopper, *Slaves of One Master*, 150.

8. Summary of Bombay Government's Measures to Suppress the Slave Trade by Willoughby, 31 December 1838, handwritten manuscript, Political Consultations (PC) no. 30, 13 February 1839, in Foreign Department, NAI.

9. R. Cavendish, Resident, Gwalior Residency to W.H. Macnaghten, Esq., Secretary to Governor General, Shimla, 8 June 1832, PC nos. 55–57, Foreign Department, NAI.

10. C. Harding, Magistrate, to C. Macsween, Commissioner of Circuit, Agra, 9 December 1830, PC no. 65, Foreign Department, NAI.

11. See, for instance, Sparks, "Blind Justice," 53–79; Harris, *Last Slave Ships*.

12. Memorandum by the Political Secretary, dated 1 December 1835, Extract Bombay Political Consultations, 23 December 1835, *Slave Trade (East India)*, 107.

13. Edward A. Alpers, "Africans in India and the Wider Context of the Indian Ocean," in *Sidis and Scholars: Essays on African Indians*, ed. Amy Catlin-Jairazbhoy and Edward A. Alpers (Noida, U.P, India: Rainbow Publishers and Trenton, NJ: Red Sea Press, 2004), 27–28.

14. Alpers, "Africans in India," 31; Helene Basu, "Slave, Soldier, Trader, Faqir: Fragments of African Histories in Western India (Gujarat)," in *The African Diaspora in the Indian Ocean*, ed. Shihan De Silva Jayasuriya and Richard Pankhurst (Trenton, NJ: Africa World Press, 2003), 223; essays in Hawley, *India in Africa*.

15. Richard Eaton, "The Rise and Fall of Military Slavery in the Deccan, 1450–1650," in Chatterjee and Eaton, *Slavery and South Asian History*, 115, 117–20, 124–26.

16. Basu, "Slave, Soldier, Trader, Faqir," 231–33, Alpers, "Africans in India," 33–34.

17. Rosie Llewellyn-Jones, "The Colonial Response to African Slaves in British India—Two Contrasting Cases," *African and Asian Studies* 10 (2011): 61.

18. Kathryn M. Ringrose, *The Perfect Servant: Eunuchs and the Social Construction of Gender in Byzantium* (Chicago: University of Chicago Press, 2003), 83.

19. Cooper, *Plantation Slavery*; Sheriff, *Slaves, Spices and Ivory*; Hopper, *Slaves of One Master*.

20. Christopher Lloyd, *The Navy and the Slave Trade: The Suppression of the African Slave Trade in the Nineteenth Century* (1949; repr., London: Routledge, 2012), 208.

21. Machado, *Ocean of Trade*, 1.

22. Machado, *Ocean of Trade*, 1–17, 208; Hooper and Eltis, "The Indian Ocean," 367; Harries, "Mozambique Island," 423, 419, quotation on 420.

23. Sheriff, *Slaves, Spices and Ivory*, 18–19.

24. Machado, *Ocean of Trade*, 12; Lloyd, *Navy and the Slave Trade*, 192.

25. On some of these themes, see Cooper, *Plantation Slavery*; Sheriff, *Slaves, Spices and Ivory*; Hopper, *Slaves of One Master*, 34; Lloyd, *Navy and the Slave Trade*, 193; Suzuki, *Slave Trade Profiteers*.

26. Glassman, "Bondsman's New Clothes," 277–312, esp. pp. 289–91 and 297–98.

27. Extract of a journal kept during a partial enquiry into the present resources and state of Northeastern Africa with memoranda, by Lieutenant W. Christopher, Indian Navy, commanding Hon. Company's Brig of War *Tigris*, 5 January 1843, handwritten manuscript, in

Foreign SC no. 9, 4 November 1843, NAI. Hereafter, Christopher's journal. Much correspondence regarding western IOW slave trades passed through the Secret Committee of the East India Company (SC) and the Secret Department of the government of Bombay.

28. Christopher's journal.
29. Christopher's journal.
30. Christopher's journal; Mathew, *Margins of the Market*, 58–59.
31. Hopper, *Slaves of One Master*, 43.
32. Hopper, 35; Lloyd, *Navy and the Slave Trade*, 193, Sheriff, *Slaves, Spices, and Ivory*, 42.
33. Machado, *Ocean of Trade*, 228; Lloyd, *Navy and the Slave Trade*, 192, identified the mouth of the Zambesi River as the chief center of the slave trade.
34. "Ephraim A. Emerton's Sketch of His Life," in *New England Merchants in Africa; A History through Documents, 1802 to 1865*, ed. Norman R. Bennett and George E. Brooks (Brookline, MA: Boston University Press, 1965), 258, digitized by Boston Library Consortium Member Libraries.
35. On the slave trade on the Arabian peninsula, see Hopper, *Slaves of One Master*, 33, 47–49.
36. Hideaki Suzuki, "Enslaved Population and Indian Owners along the East African Coast: Exploring the Rigby Manumission List, 1860–1861," *History in Africa* 39 (2012): 209–39, esp. 232.
37. Cooper, *Plantation Slavery*, 217; cited also in Suzuki, "Enslaved Population," 230–31.
38. This discussion is based on contexts described in Hopper, *Slaves of One Master*, 40, and Lloyd, *Navy and the Slave Trade*, 193, 194–95.
39. Hopper, *Slaves of One Master*, 45.
40. "Michael W. Shepard's Account," in Bennett and Brooks, *New England Merchants*, 261.
41. "Michael W. Shepard's Account," 262.
42. "A Visit to Eastern Africa, 1849," in Bennett and Brooks, *New England Merchants*, 427–28.
43. Christopher's journal.
44. Christopher's journal.
45. These portions of Christopher's journal, copies of the handwritten manuscript version of which are lodged in NAI, were published under "Account signed by W. Christopher, Lieut., commanding on Secret Service. H.C. Brig of War Tigris, at Sea, 8 May 1843. True Copy signed by S.B. Haines, Captain, I.N., Political Agent, Aden," in *Transactions of the Bombay Geographical Society*, vol. 5 (September 1841–May 1844): 389–90, 394–95.
46. "Account signed by W. Christopher, Lieut., commanding on Secret Service. H.C. Brig of War Tigris, at Sea," 8 May 1843, 401–402.
47. A. Burnes to Secretary to Government, 29 December 1835, *Slave Trade (East India)*, 106.
48. Sheriff, *Slaves, Spices and Ivory*, 38–39.
49. Machado, *Ocean of Trade*, 249, 250–51, 254–55; Senior naval officer at Surat to the Superintendent of the Indian Navy, 20 January 1836, Foreign Department, NAI; Mr. Secretary Willoughby to A. Burnes, Assistant Resident in Charge, 23 January 1836, *Slave Trade (East India)*, 106; Henry Pottinger, Esq., Resident in Cutch, to John Bax, Esq., Chief Secretary to Government, 13 October 1834, *Slave Trade (East India)*, 107.
50. Memorandum by the Political Secretary, 1 December 1835, *Slave Trade (East India)*, 107; Senior naval officer at Surat to the Superintendent of the Indian Navy, 20 January 1836,

Foreign Department, NAI. See also Willoughby, Summary of Bombay Government's Measures to Suppress the Slave Trade, 31 December 1838, Foreign Department, NAI.

51. Political Agent in Katteewar, at Rajcote, to the Secretary to Government, Bombay, 15 August 1836, *Slave Trade (East India)*, 164; Resident in Cutch to the Political Agent, Rajcote, 4 July 1836, *Slave Trade (East India)*, 169.

52. Memorandum by the Political Secretary (J.P. Willoughby), 1 December 1835, in Extract from the Proceedings of Government in the Political Department, 23 December 1835 in NAI, published in part as Memorandum by the Political Secretary, dated 1 December 1835, Extract Bombay Political Consultations, 23 December 1835, in *Slave Trade (East India)*, 107–8.

53. A. Burnes to Secretary to Government, 29 December 1835, *Slave Trade (East India)*, 106.

54. Henry Pottinger, Esq., Resident in Cutch, to John Bax, Esq., Chief Secretary to Government, 13 October 1834, in *Slave Trade (East India)*, 107.

55. Willoughby, Summary of Bombay Government's Measures.

56. Willoughby.

57. Deposition of slave dealers before I. Low, Resident, Lucknow, 4 July 1833; I. Low to W.H. Macnaghten, Secretary to Government in Political Department, Fort William, 5 July, 1833 in PC no. 41, 18 July 1833; Low to Macnaghten, in PC no. 42, 18 July 1833, NAI.

58. Llewellyn-Jones, "Colonial Response," 61–63.

59. Memorandum prepared by Captain Malcolm, Assistant Resident, relative to the traffick [*sic*] in slaves at Hyderabad, 25 June 1842, PC no. 336, 3 August 1842, NAI (hereafter, Malcolm memorandum). Translation of a letter from Reuben Aslan, Agent at Muscat to Captain Hennel, dated 27 Ramzan/12 November 1841, PC no. 335, 3 August 1842, NAI (hereafter, Translation of Aslan).

60. Malcolm memorandum.

61. Machado, *Ocean of Trade*, 220–24.

62. Extract of two letters from Khojah Reuben, Agent at Muscat, to Lieutenant A.B. Kemball, Assistant Resident in the Persian Gulf in Charge, 30 August and 16 October 1843, enclosed with letter by Kemball to J.P. Willoughby, Secretary to the Government, Bombay, 14 November 1843, in PC no. 6, 1 June 1844, Foreign Department, NAI.

63. Lieutenant Colonel H.D. Robertson, Resident in the Persian Gulf to J.P. Willoughby, 31 March 1842, PC no. 335, 3 August 1842, Foreign Department, NAI.

64. Translation of Aslan.

65. Translation of Aslan.

66. Translation of Aslan.

67. Political Secretary to Government to the Resident in Cutch, 19 December 1835; J.P. Willoughby, Esq., Secretary to Government, to the Political Commissioner for Guzerat [*sic*], 19 December 1835; Political Secretary to Government to the Superintendent of the Indian Navy, dated 19 December 1835, all in *Slave Trade (East India)*, 120.

68. A. Burnes to Secretary to Government, 29 December 1835, *Slave Trade (East India)*, 106.

69. Officer commanding Detachment, Porebunder, to the Political Agent, Rajcote, 5 November 1835, *Slave Trade (East India)*, 113.

70. Quotations from *Slave Trade (East India)*, 113; Captain A.T. Reid, commanding Detachment, Porebunder, to the Political Agent, Rajcote, dated 6 November 1835, in *Slave*

Trade (East India), 115; Rana of Porebunder to Captain Lang, Assistant Political Agent in Charge, dated Kartik Vud, 1 Sumvut 1802, 6 November 1835, translation into English, *Slave Trade (East India)*, 113–14; W. Lang, Esq., acting Political Agent in charge, Kattywar, to Captain Reid, commanding Detachment at Porebunder, 10 November 1835, *Slave Trade (East India)*, 114; W. Lang, Esq., acting Political Agent in charge, Katteewar [sic], to J. P. Willoughby, Esq., Political Agent in Kattywar, Bombay, *Slave Trade (East India)*, 115.

71. Officer commanding Detachment, Porebunder, to the Political Agent, Rajcote, 16 November 1835, *Slave Trade (East India)*, 124.

72. Officer commanding Detachment, Porebunder, to the Political Agent, Rajcote, 5 November 1835, *Slave Trade (East India)*, 113.

73. Rana of Porebunder to Captain Lang, *Slave Trade (East India)*, 114.

74. *Slave Trade (East India)*, 114.

75. Lang to Reid, 10 November 1835, *Slave Trade (East India)*, 114.

76. Rana Wikmathjee of Porebunder to Captain Lang, dated 13 Kartig Vud, 18 November 1835, signed by W. Lang, acting Political Agent, *Slave Trade (East India)*, 122; Captain A. T. Reid, 12th Regiment N. I., to Captain Lang, acting Political Agent, Rajcote, 12 December 1835, *Slave Trade (East India)*, 126.

77. Officer commanding Detachment at Porebunder, to the Acting Political Agent, Rajcote, 12 December 1835, *Slave Trade (East India)*, 126; Reid to Lang, 12 December 1835, *Slave Trade (East India)*, 126; W. Lang, Esq. to Captain Apthorp, commanding Detachment Porebunder, 20 December 1835, *Slave Trade (East India)*, 126.

78. Rana Wikmathjee to Lang, 18 November 1835, translation signed by Lang, *Slave Trade (East India)*, 123.

79. Commander of the Detachment, Porebunder, to the Political Agent, Rajcote, 18 November 1835, *Slave Trade (East India)*, 123.

80. Petition from Jeevun Oodhowjee, Gomasta or manager of the firm of Dhurumsy Lukmedass, to the Right Honourable Sir Robert Grant, G.C.H., Governor and President in Council, Bombay, 30 April 1836, *Slave Trade (East India)*, 143–45 (hereafter, Oodhowjee Petition). The Examination of Dewa Govind, taken, upon Oath, before me, John Warden, Esq., one of His Majesty's Justices of the Peace for the Town and Island of Bombay, on Monday the 16th day of May 1836; the Examination of Dhurumsee Geerdhurdass, taken upon Oath, before me, John Warden, Esq., one of His Majesty's Justices of the Peace for the Town and Island of Bombay, on Monday the 16th day of May 1836, both *Slave Trade (East India)*, 157–58; and Petition from (Jeevun) Oodhowjee, Goomashta to the Right Honourable Sir Robert Grant, G.C.H., Governor and President in Council, 29 August 1836, *Slave Trade (East India)*, 162.

81. Oodhowjee Petition, 30 April 1836.

82. Oodhowjee Petition, 30 April 1836, 145; C.W. Whitehead, Lieutenant 12th Reg. commanding at Porebunder, to James Erskine, Esq., Political Agent, Kattywar, Rajcote, *Slave Trade (East India)*, 152.

83. Oodhowjee Petition, 30 April 1836, 144–45.

84. Deposition by Maalum Jadow Govund, translated and enclosed with Memorandum by the Chief Secretary, 21 May 1836, *Slave Trade (East India)*, 146–47.

85. Examination of Dhurumsee Geerdhurdass, taken upon Oath, before me, John Warden, Esq., one of His Majesty's Justices of the Peace for the Town and Island of Bombay, on Monday the 16th day of May 1836, *Slave Trade (East India)*, 158.

86. Deposition taken before J. Erskine, Esq., Political Agent in Kattywar, of Urzen Heera Karwa of Porebunder, aged 30 years, taken … [in Porebunder], translation, 14 April 1836, *Slave Trade (East India)*, 154.

87. J.H. Rowland, Commander, *Slave Trade (East India)*, 149.

88. Rana Veekmatjee of Porebunder to James Erskine, Esq., Political Agent in Kattywar, translation, *Slave Trade (East India)*, 152–53.

89. Petition from Jewun Oodhowjee to the Right Honourable Sir Robert Grant, G.C.H., Governor and President in Council, 20 December 1836, *Slave Trade (East India)*, 178. On British orders to investigate the Wadi, see Extract of Paragraphs 4 to 8 from a Minute by the Right Honourable the Governor, 5 July 1836, *Slave Trade (East India)*, 154.

90. Memorandum by the Chief Secretary, 14 May 1836, *Slave Trade (East India)*, 156.

91. Stephen W. Day, *Regionalism and Rebellion in Yemen: A Troubled Union* (New York: Cambridge University Press, 2012), 25.

92. Serge D. Elie, "State-Community Relations in Yemen: Soqotra's Historical Formation as a Sub-National Polity," *History and Anthropology* 20 (December 2009): 363–93, esp. 367–68.

93. Minute by the Right Honourable the Governor, 9 May 1836, signed R. Grant, *Slave Trade (East India)*, 145; Memorandum by the Chief Secretary, 21 May 1836, *Slave Trade (East India)*, 146; Memorandum by the Chief Secretary (W.H. Wathen), 14 May 1836, *Slave Trade (East India)*, 156.

94. Charles Malcolm, Esq., Superintendent of the Indian Navy, to the Right Honourable Sir R. Grant, G.C.H., President and Governor in Council, 28 July 1836, *Slave Trade (East India)*, 163.

95. Extract of a Letter from Acting Commander S.B. Haines to the Superintendent of the Indian Navy, Mocha, 24 August 1836, *Slave Trade (East India)*, 166; From J.P. Willoughby, Esq., Secretary to Government, to the Superintendent India Navy dated 20 November 1836, [enclosing] Copy of a Letter from the Right Honourable the Governor to Sheikh Eesa bin Moobaruk, of the Tribe of Mehera Sheikh, of Wadee, 26 November 1836, *Slave Trade (East India)*, 172.

96. Petitions from Jewun Oodhowjee to the Right Honourable Sir R. Grant, G.C.H., Governor and President in Council, 11 October, 17 November, and 20 December 1836, *Slave Trade (East India)*, 168, 174–75, 178.

97. Malcolm to Grant, 27 January 1837, *Slave Trade (East India)*, 82–83; Willoughby, Esq., Secretary to Government, Bombay, to Malcolm, Esq., Superintendent of the Indian Navy, 22 March 1837, *Slave Trade (East India)*, 186.

98. W.H. MacNaghten, Secretary, Government of India, Fort William, to Secretary to Government of Bombay, 19 September 1836, PC no. 16, 9 September 1836, Foreign Department, NAI.

99. Political Secretary to Government [of Bombay] to the Advocate-General, 19 December 1835, NAI.

100. Advocate General (A. Le Messurier) to the Political Secretary to Government, 4 January 1836, in *Slave Trade (East India)*, 132–33.

101. Advocate General to Political Secretary, 4 January 1836, *Slave Trade (East India)*, 132–33.

102. *Slave Trade (East India)*, 132.

103. Minute by the Right Honourable the Governor, subscribed to by Mr. Sutherland, 13 January 1836, *Slave Trade (East India)*, 125; Political Secretary to Government to the Acting Political Agent in Kattywar, 20 February 1836, *Slave Trade (East India)*, 137.

104. Further Minute by the Right Honourable the Governor, subscribed to by Mr. Ironside, 12 July 1836, *Slave Trade (East India)*, 159; Further Minute by Mr. Farish, subscribed to by the Right Honourable the Governor, *Slave Trade (East India)*, 160; Secretary to Government of Bombay to Secretary to the Government of India, *Slave Trade (East India)*, 160.

105. Minute by the Right Honourable the Governor, subscribed to by Mr. Ironside, 5 July 1836, *Slave Trade (East India)*, 158–59.

CHAPTER 7. SUBALTERN PRISMS AND MEANINGS OF FREEDOM

1. Acting Political Agent in Katteewar [sic] to the Political Secretary to Government, 20 December 1835, in *Slave Trade (East India)*, 125.

2. Senior Magistrate of Police to the Political Secretary to Government, 16 January 1836, *Slave Trade (East India)*, 129.

3. Senior Magistrate of Police to the Political Secretary to Government, 18 January 1836, *Slave Trade (East India)*, 130.

4. M.T. Kays, Esq., M.D., surgeon to the police, to John Warden, Esq., Senior Magistrate of Police, 18 January 1836, *Slave Trade (East India)*, 130.

5. Political Secretary to Government to the Senior Magistrate of Police, 22 January 1836, *Slave Trade (East India)*, 128–29.

6. Mathew, *Margins of the Market*, 77.

7. Senior Magistrate of Police to the Political Secretary to Government, 25 January 1836; Statement of Applications from Christian Families for the African Children, in *Slave Trade (East India)*, 131–32.

8. Acting Advocate-General to the Political Secretary to Government, 25 January 1836, *Slave Trade (East India)*, 133–34.

9. Political Secretary to Government to the Senior Magistrate of Police, 13 February 1836, *Slave Trade (East India)*, 134; Minute of the Right Honourable the Governor, subscribed to by Mr. Sutherland and Mr. Ironside, 20 February 1836; Political Secretary to Government to the Senior Magistrate of Police, 4 March 1836, *Slave Trade (East India)*, 140.

10. Senior Magistrate of Police to the Political Secretary to Government, 23 February 1836, *Slave Trade (East India)*, 137; Register of African Children who have been Disposed of [by Warden], *Slave Trade (East India)*, 138.

11. Secretary to Government of Bombay to the Secretary to the Government of India, 22 August 1836, *Slave Trade (East India)*, 161.

12. Senior Magistrate of Police to the Political Secretary to Government, 23 February 1836, *Slave Trade (East India)*, 137.

13. Chief Secretary [W.H. Wathen] to Government to the Acting General Paymaster, 6 May 1836, *Slave Trade (East India)*, 143.

14. Captain Henderson to the Private Secretary to the Right Honourable the Governor, 16 February 1836, *Slave Trade (East India)*, 139; Political Secretary to Government to the Senior Magistrate of Police, 29 February 1836, *Slave Trade (East India)*, 139.

15. Shaden M. Tageldin, "The Place of Africa, in Theory: Pan-Africanism, Postcolonialism, Beyond," *Journal of Historical Sociology* 27 (September 2014): 304; Sheriff, *Dhow Cultures;* IOW scholarship listed in the introduction, note 17.

16. See also Edward A. Alpers and Matthew S. Hopper, "Speaking for Themselves? Understanding African Freed Slave Testimonies from the Western Indian Ocean, 1850s-1930s," *Journal of Indian Ocean World Studies* 1 (2017): 60-88.

17. Acting Commander of the *Euphrates* to Captain Charles Malcolm, Superintendent of Indian Navy, March 10, 1837, PC nos. 10-12, Foreign Department, NAI.

18. Statements in PC nos. 10-12, Foreign Department, NAI.

19. Malcolm to Willoughby, 9 May 1837; Willoughby to Malcolm, 22 May 1837; E. E. Elliot [Acting senior Magistrate of Police] to Secretary to Government, 27 May 1837; Malcolm to Chief Secretary to Government, 16 June 1837; W.A. Walthen to Superintendent of Navy, 17 June 1837; Elliot to Walthen, 2 July 1837, PC nos. 10-12, 24 January 1838; Covenant signed by Hyderally Cussumjee, Bombay, 8 July 1837, PC no. 18. 28 March 1838, all in Foreign Department, NAI.

20. Statement by Yacoob signed by William Foquett, captain commanding Detachment at Porebunder, 10 December 1836, enclosed with letter from Captain Lang, acting Political Agent in Katteewar, to Willoughby, 23 January 1837, *Slave Trade (East India)*, 185. Hereafter, Yacoob's Statement.

21. James Erskine, Esq., Political Agent in Katteewar, to Willoughby, 2 December 1836; Willoughby to Erskine, 12 January 1837, *Slave Trade (East India)*, 180.

22. A.P. Reid, captain commanding Detachment at Porebunder, to Captain Jacob, Assistant Political Agent, 2 February 1837, *Slave Trade (East India)*, 183; William Lang, Esq., acting Political Agent in Katteewar, to Willoughby, 8 February 1837, *Slave Trade (East India)*, 184.

23. Yacoob's Statement.

24. Glassman, "Bondsman's New Clothes," 288-89.

25. Glassman, 291-92.

26. Llewellyn-Rose, "Colonial Response," 66-68.

27. Saayyida Salme, *Memoirs of an Arabian Princess*, 6.

28. Melman, Review of E. van Donzel, ed., *Sayyida Salme/Emily Ruete: An Arabian Princess between Two Worlds: Memoirs, Letters Home, Sequels to the Memoirs, Syrian Customs and Usages* (London: E. J. Brill, 1993), in *International Journal of Middle East Studies* 26, no. 3 (1994): 525-27, quotation on 526.

29. Melman, 526, 527. See also Abdul Sheriff, "*Suria:* Concubine or Secondary Slave Wife?: The Case of Zanzibar in the Nineteenth-Century," in Campbell and Elbourne, *Sex, Power, and Slavery,* 99-120.

30. Glassman, "Bondsman's New Clothes," 289, 298-99; Cooper, *Plantation Slavery,* 98-99.

31. Horace Putnam, "ZanGuebar or More Properly Zanzibar," in Bennett and Brooks, *New England Merchants,* 402.

32. Saayyida Salme, *Memoirs,* 9-10, 24.

33. Salme, 12.

34. Salme, 10, 15, 31.

35. Salme, 10, 48.

36. Salme, 24, 25.

37. Salme, 22, 30-31, 37, 35.

38. Salme, 40, 19, 22–23.
39. Salme, 20, 55.
40. Salme, 34, 15–16, 28, 32, 56, 7, 22.
41. Salme, 15, 29.
42. Salme, 56.
43. Cooper, *Plantation Slavery,* 78. See also McMahon, *Slavery and Emancipation.*
44. Salme, *Memoirs,* 35, 53, 56.
45. Khojah Reuben, Agent at Muscat (also known as Reuben Aslan), to Lt. Colonel H. D. Robertson, officiating Resident, Persian Gulf, translation, 4 Mohurrum 1259/4 February 1843 and 18 Mohurrum 1259, PC nos. 4–12, 19 August 1843, Foreign Department, NAI.
46. Reuben to Robertson.
47. Reuben to Robertson; Chief Secretary to the Government of Bombay to Captain A. Hamerton, 11 May 1844, PC no. 9, 1 June 1844; Captain S. Hennell, resident in the Persian Gulf, to Willoughby, 27 February 1844, PC no. 8, 1 June 1844; Robertson to W. Lowe, Commodore in the Persian Gulf (not delivered), Foreign Department, NAI; Syed Saeed Imam of Muscat to the Hon. the Gov., 29 March 1844, received 13 May 1844, PC no. 9, 6 July 1844, Foreign Department, NAI.
48. Hennell to Willoughby, 12 September 1844, PC no. 32, 5 October 1844, Foreign Department, NAI.
49. P. W. LeGeyt, Senior Magistrate of Police to Secretary to Government, 21 August 1844, PC no. 33, Foreign Department, NAI.
50. Statement of Huleemah, 20 August 1844, in LeGeyt to Secretary to Government, 21 August 1844.
51. Hennell to Willoughby, 12 September 1844; Huskall, Acting Agent at Muscat, to Hennell, 8 June 1844, translated abstract; Statement of Fatimah, 20 August 1844, in LeGeyt to Secretary to Government, 21 August 1844, Foreign Department, NAI.
52. Statements of Sadulla and Golam Hussein, 20 August 1844, in LeGeyt to Secretary to Government, Foreign Department, NAI.
53. Deposition of Seedee Moobarik, Rajcote, 15 September 1837, enclosed with letter from Erskine to Willoughby, 31 December 1837; Erskine to Willoughby, 24 March 1838, PC no. 20, 12 September 1838, Foreign Department, NAI.
54. Minute by the Hon. Mr. Farish, 3 February 1838; Willoughby to the Assistant Political Agent in Charge, Katteewar, 10 February, 1838, Foreign Department, NAI.
55. LeGeyt to the Officiating Secretary to Government, 15 December 1841; Willoughby, officiating Chief Secretary, to Major James Outram, Political Agent in Sinde and Belochistan, 20 December 1841, PC nos. 52–54, 3 January 1842, Foreign Department, NAI.

CHAPTER 8. BUSINESS, SOVEREIGNTY, AND FUGITIVE SLAVES

1. Norman Robert Bennett, "Americans in Zanzibar: 1845–1865," *Essex Institute Historical Collections* 97 (January 1961): 47–50.
2. Alex Borucki, "The Slave Trade to Rio de la Plata, 1777–1812: Trans-Imperial Networks and Atlantic Warfare," *Colonial Latin American Review* 20 (April 2011), 81–107; Harries, "Mozambique Island," 412; Machado, *Ocean of Trade.* Data on voyages are taken from Voyages: The Trans-Atlantic Slave Trade Database, www.slavevoyages.org.

3. Harries, "Mozambique Island"; Machado, *Ocean of Trade*, 1–17, 208; Hooper and Eltis, "Indian Ocean," 367.

4. Harries, "Mozambique Island," 419–23; Voyages database ID nos. 36809, 25535, 37115, 36782, 25415, and 37041.

5. Harris, *Last Slave Ships*, 3.

6. Voyages database ID nos. 4313, 4154, 4266, 4154, 4266, 4166; Spun Yarn Series, n.d., Charles Walter Agard Collection, New Bedford Whaling Museum, Massachusetts; "Jack" [Slave Trade], n.d., Box 2, Charles Water Agard Collection.

7. Norman Robert Bennett, "Americans in Zanzibar: 1825–1845," *Essex Institute Historical Collections* 95 (July 1959): 239, 241; Hooper, "Yankees"; Prestholdt, *Domesticating the World*, 72.

8. Bennett, "Americans in Zanzibar, 1825–1845," 246–47, 250.

9. Christopher's journal, NAI; Charles Ward to State Department, 21 February 1846, 357; Richard P. Waters to John Forsyth, 6 May 1837, 216; Richard P. Waters to William C. Waters, 17 December 1839, 222; the latter three cited in Bennett and Brooks, *New England Merchants*.

10. Prestholdt, *Domesticating the World*, 74; Bennett and Brooks, *New England Merchants*, 265n5.

11. Sheriff, *Slaves, Spices and Ivory*, 87, 90, 92, 95; Frederick, *Twilight*, 83; Prestholdt, *Domesticating the World*, 63–66.

12. "A Visit to Eastern Africa, 1848. Ephraim A. Emmerton's Journal," in Bennett and Brooks, *New England Merchants*, 406.

13. Charles Ward to George Abbot, Kennebunkport, 13 March 1851, in Bennett and Brooks, *New England Merchants*, 477.

14. Christopher's journal.

15. Charles Ward to James Buchanan, 7 March 1847, 375; Richard P. Waters, Notes, 16 November 1842, 254. Ward to Abbot, 13 March 1851, 480. The major currency consisted of the German crown. One American reported, "The German Crown, and Pice & pie from the Hon. E. India Company's possessions are the only Currency. The number of pice to a German Crown . . . varies according to supply, from 116 to 128." Daniel H. Mansfield to William L. Marcy, 31 January 1856, 499. All four letters are cited in Bennett and Brooks, *New England Merchants*.

16. "Ephraim A. Emerton's Sketch of his Life," in Bennett and Brooks, 258–59.

17. John F. Webb, William H. Jelly, and Samuel R. Masury to John Aulick, 5 December 1851, in Bennett and Brooks, 489.

18. Captain F. A. Hamerton to Hon. Court of Directors of the East India Company, 9 February 1842 and R. Cogan to Hamerton, 30 December 1841, SC nos. 74–79, June 1842, Foreign Department, NAI.

19. Sheriff, *Slaves, Spices and Ivory*, 97, 99, 107.

20. Suzuki, "Enslaved Population," 233, 237.

21. "A Visit to Zanzibar, 1847. Horace B. Putnam's Notes of a Cruise to the Indies or a Life in the Forecastle," in Bennett and Brooks, *New England Merchants*, 399, quotation on 401.

22. Mansfield to Marcy, 31 January 1856, 500; Sheriff, *Slaves, Spices and Ivory*, 149–50.

23. Waters, Notes, 1842, 1843, 1844, in Bennett and Brooks, *New England Merchants*, 253.

24. Bennett and Brooks, 200, 201.

25. Hamerton to Court of Directors, 9 February 1842.

26. Bennett, "Americans in Zanzibar, 1825–1845," 254.

27. Hamerton to Court of Directors, 9 February 1842; Cogan to Hamerton, 30 December 1841.

28. Christopher's journal.

29. Major Atkins Hamerton, Her Majesty's Consul and Hon. Company's Agent in the Dominions of His Highness the Imam of Muscat to A. Malet, Chief Secretary to Bombay Government, 9 April 1851, PC no. 51, 10 October 1851, Foreign Department, NAI.

30. Sheriff, *Slaves, Spices and Ivory,* 203, 204.

31. Charles Ward to Michael Shepard, Zanzibar, 16 July 1850, in Bennett and Brooks, *New England Merchants,* 462–63, quotation on 463.

32. Charles Ward to John M. Clayton, July 20, 1850, in Bennett and Brooks, 466.

33. Sheriff, *Slaves, Spices and Ivory,* 205. $MT refers to Maria Theresa dollars, one of the principal currencies in circulation in nineteenth-century Zanzibar.

34. Ward to Shepard, Bennett and Brooks, *New England Merchants,* 463, 464.

35. Ward to Clayton, 466; Ward to George Abbot, 13 March 1851, in Bennett and Brooks, 481.

36. Ward to Clayton, 467–68; Ward to Abbot, 481–82.

37. Ward to Abbot, 478.

38. John F. Webb, William H. Jelly, and Samuel R. Masury to John Aulick, 5 December 1851, 488–90.

39. Hamerton to Malet, Chief Secretary to Government of Bombay, 14 May 1853, PC nos. 98–100, 2 December 1853, Foreign Department, NAI.

40. William G. Webb to Lewis Cass, 1 September and 31 December 1860, in Bennett and Brooks, *New England Merchants,* 513, 517.

41. Suzuki, "Enslaved Population," 212–14, 216.

42. Webb to Seceretary of State, 11 May 1861, US State Department, Dispatches from US Consuls in Zanzibar, 1836–1906, National Archives, microfilm edition. Hereafter, DCZ.

43. Webb to State Department, 1 September 1860, DCZ.

44. Webb to W. H. Seward, 19 September 1861, DCZ.

45. William Speer to Seward, US military telegraph, 17 November 1861; Speer to Seward, 1 November 1861, DCZ.

46. *Treaty between United States and Great Britain for the Suppression of the Slave Trade. Concluded at Washington, April 7, 1862. Ratifications exchanged at London, May 25, 1862. Proclaimed by the President of the United States June 7, 1862,* Avalon Project, Documents in Law, History, Diplomacy, Yale Law School, Lillian Goldman Law Library, https://avalon.law.yale.edu/19th_century/br1862.asp. See also Matthew Mason, "Keeping Up Appearances: The International Politics of Slave Trade Abolition in the Nineteenth-Century Atlantic World," *William and Mary Quarterly* 66 (October 2009): 830.

47. *Additional Article to the Treaty for the Suppression of the African Slave Trade, between the United States of America and her Britannic Majesty, of the 7th of April, 1862; concluded February 17, 1863; ratified by the United States March 5, 1863; ratifications exchanged, April 1, 1863; and proclaimed by the President of the United States, April 22, 1863,* Avalon Project, https://avalon.law.yale.edu/19th_century/br1863.asp.

48. Speer to Seward, 13 October 1862, DCZ.

49. Speer, "Report on Zanzibar," received in State Department, Washington, DC, 26 November 1862, DCZ.

50. Speer, "Report on Zanzibar."

51. Speer.

52. Edward D. Ropes to Seward, 1 and 2 July 1865, DCZ.

53. Political Agent and Her Majesty's Consul, Zanzibar, to Secretary to Government, Bombay, dated 22 December 1867, PC nos. 144–49, in printed document titled "British Interference with Subjects of Kutch at Zanzibar Engaged in Slave Trade," 2, Foreign Department, NAI.

54. "British Interference," 2–3.

55. His Highness Syed Majid, Sultan of Zanzibar, to Political Agent, Her Majesty's Consul, 23 Shaaban 1284/21 December 1867, "British Interference," 4–5.

56. C. Gonne, Esq., Acting Chief Secretary to Government, Bombay to W.S. Seton-Karr, Esq., Secretary to Government of India, Foreign Department, 7 December 1868, Pol A nos. 294–97, January 1869, NAI.

57. Secretary to Government, Bombay, to Foreign Secretary, India, 31 March 1868, "British Interference," NAI.

58. Seton-Karr to Gonne, 31 December 1868, Pol A nos. 294–97, NAI.

59. Sheriff, *Slaves, Spices and Ivory*, 207.

60. Francis R. Webb to US Secretary of State, Zanzibar, 20 August 1868, DCZ.

61. Webb to Secretary of State, 10 March 1869, DCZ.

62. Bennett, "Americans in Zanzibar: 1865–1915," *Essex Institute Historical Collections* 98 (January 1962): 38–39.

63. Mathew, *Margins of the Market*, 62, 64–67; Hopper, *Slaves of One Master*, 150–54, 162–75; Huzzey, *Freedom Burning*, 158.

64. Bennett, "Americans in Zanzibar, 1845–1865," 51, 53, 46, 47.

65. Wilson to [Barghash], 11 December 1872, true copy attested by Francis R. Webb, Acting Consul, 25 August 1873, DCZ.

66. Francis Webb to Second Assistant Secretary of State, 16 April 1873, DCZ; Bennett, "Americans in Zanzibar, 1865–1915," 40–44; Sheriff, *Slaves, Spices and Ivory*, 238.

67. On the *Laconia* affair, see W.H. Hathorne, US consul, to John Kirk, H.B.M. agent and Consul General, Zanzibar, 26, 27, and 31 December 1878; Kirk to Hathorne, 27 and 28 December 1878; Hamilton Earle, Captain and Senior Officer, East Coast of Africa, to Kirk, 27 December 1878; "Statement of 3 Slaves," given to Lt. H.E. O'Neill and Lt. H. Mc A. Cutfield, HMS *London*, Zanzibar, 27 December 1878; "Sworn Statement of Capt. R.W. Gifford of the American barque *Laconia* of New Bedford, Massachusetts, regarding three Negroes on board the said barque claimed to be slaves by the British senior naval officer on this East Coast of African station," US Consulate, Zanzibar, 28 December 1878; "Edward S. Ripley's sworn statement"; "Sworn statement of three negroes unlawfully taken by the officers of HMS *London* from the American barque *Laconia* for examination, said negroes claimed to be slaves by the Captain and Senior officers of H.B.M. East Coast of African fleet"; all in DCZ.

68. The *London* achieved some notable successes, so much so that the historian Christopher Lloyd proclaimed the death of the "Arab slave trade" in 1883. More recently, Mathew Hopper has argued that in fact such trade resumed later in the century—often under the French flag—and eventually declined only in response to trends in world demand for the products of slave labor in the Gulf. See Hopper, *Slaves of One Master*, 156–62.

69. Earle to Kirk, 27 December 1878; Statement of Gifford, 28 December 1878, DCZ.

70. Mathew, *Margins of the Market,* 62.
71. "Statement of 3 Slaves," December 27, 1878, in DCZ.
72. Hathorne to F. W. Seward, Acting Secretary of State, 16 October 1878, DCZ; Bennett, "Americans in Zanzibar, 1865–1915," 49–52. On enslaved porters in the ivory trade, see Glassman, "Bondsman's New Clothes," 291–92.
73. Hathorne to Kirk, 31 December 1878, DCZ; Statements of Gifford; Ripley; George Antonio, boatman; Squeer S. Cornell, first officer, and Frank B. Webster, steward, 28 December 1878, DCZ.
74. "Sworn statement of three negroes," 28 December 1878, DCZ.
75. "Sworn statement of three negroes."
76. Hathorne to Kirk, 31 December 1878.
77. "Sworn statement of three negroes."
78. Hopper, *Slaves of One Master,* 175–76; Mathew, *Margins of the Market,* 75–76.
79. "Statement of 3 slaves"; "Sworn statement of three negroes"; Hathorne to Kirk, 31 December 1878.
80. Folder 1, "General Average and Salvage Loss for the Whaling Bark *Laconia*," New Bedford Whaling Museum; Log of voyage of 1876–1879, kept 30 May 1876–22 February 1879, Rufus W. Gifford, Master, Dukes County Historical Society, Edgartown, MA.

CHAPTER 9. A YANKEE SLAVEHOLDER, "BLACK SULTAN," AND EUROPEAN IMPERIALISTS IN THE INDIAN OCEAN, 1870-1906

1. Quotations taken from news clippings: "Dr. Ben Wilson," "Schooner Wainwright," "Johanna," n.d., 1886, 1891, Charles Walter Agard Collection, New Bedford Whaling Museum (hereafter, Wilson, Agard Collection). "Application for Registration-Native Citizen," 1 September 1918, filed in Ajouan, Comoros, and certified by the US Consulate in Tananarive (Antananarivo), Madagascar, on 11 October 1918; Benjamin F. Wilson, Mason membership card, Massachusetts, "Mason Membership Cards, 1733–1990," Ancestry.com. On the 1891 Anjouan insurrection, see Jean Martin, "Les Débuts du Protectorat et La Révolte Servile de 1891 dans l'île d'Anjouan" *Revue Francaise d'Histoire d'Outre-Mer* 60 (1973): 45–85. For a recent survey of the Comoros, see Iain Walker, *Islands in a Cosmopolitan Sea: A History of the Comoros* (New York: Oxford University Press, 2019).
2. Wilson, Agard Collection.
3. *Record-Union* (Sacramento), 31 March 1891.
4. The Massachusetts State Census for Dartmouth, Bristol County, lists Benjamin F. Wilson as a seventeen-year-old mariner in 1855. The Federal Census of 1860, Schedule 1, Free Inhabitants in First Ward, New Bedford, taken in August 1860, enumerates Wilson as a twenty-one-year-old medical student and his farming family as owning real estate worth six thousand dollars. In the document "Application for Registration-Native Citizen," 1 September 1918, Wilson listed his date and place of birth as 20 May 1838 in Dartmouth, Massachusetts. These documents are available on Ancestry.com.
5. This account is based on newspaper clippings in Wilson, Agard Collection; Report of Investigation of the Claims of Dr. B. F. Wilson, enclosed with letter from Mason Mitchell, US consul in Zanzibar, to H. D. D. Pierce, 29 October 1902, DCZ (hereafter, Mitchell Report); and *Cruise of the United States Flagship Lancaster, Cruise of 1884–87, Including a Few Words on Her*

First Cruise in European Waters, written, printed, and published on board by William J. McCarthy, Ships' Printers, and Lorenzo Hoag, USMC (United States Flagship, Lancaster, 1887), Harvard College Library, the Bequest of Evert Jansen Wendell Class of 1882 of New York, 1918, 101, digitized by Google (hereafter, *Cruise of the Lancaster*); Gary W. Clendennen and Peter M. Nottingham, *William Sunley and David Livingstone: A Tale of Two Consuls* (Madison: African Studies Program, University of Wisconsin-Madison, 2000), xix.

6. Malyn Newitt, "The Comoro Islands in Indian Ocean Trade before the 19th Century," *Cahiers d'études africaines* 23, nos. 89–90 (1983): 139–41, 144–49, www.persee.fr/doc/cea_0008-0055_1983_num_23_89_2260; Newitt, "Comoros: Before 1800," in *Encyclopedia of African History*, 1st ed., ed. Kevin Shillington (New York: Routledge, 2004), *Credo Reference*.

7. Clendennen and Nottingham, *William Sunley*, 5. On Comorian affinity for the English, see also Jeremy Prestholdt, "Similitude and Empire: On Comorian Strategies of Englishness," *Journal of World History* 18 (June 2007): 113–38.

8. "The Log of the Bark Palestine, 1830–1840," in "Two Whaling Voyages in East African Waters, 1838–1840," Bennett and Brooks, *New England Merchants*, 187.

9. Newitt, "Comoro Islands," 155.

10. "Johanna," Report by Consul Holmwood, Inclosure [sic] 4 in no. 187, Consul Holmwood to Earl Granville, 29 October 1882; *Slave Trade. No. 1 (1883)*. Correspondence with British Representatives and Agents Abroad, and Reports from Naval Officers and the Treasury, Relative to the Slave Trade: 1882–83, presented to both Houses of Parliament by Command of Her Majesty (London: Harrison and Sons, 1883), in Accounts and Papers, 48 vols., vol. 29, *Trade, &c. -continued. Life Assurance Companies: Slave Trade*, Session 15 February–25 August 1883, Harvard College Library, 165, digitized by Google; hereafter, *Slave Trade (1883)*.

11. Gill Shepherd, "The Comorians and the East African Slave Trade," in Watson, *Asian and African Systems*, 88–89.

12. Clendennen and Nottingham, *William Sunley*, 32.

13. "Johanna," *Slave Trade (1883)*, 165.

14. Shepherd, "Comorians," 80.

15. Wilson to A. E. B. Govea (acting US consul), 26 December 1888, DCZ.

16. W. E. Hines to Seward, Zanzibar, 31 March 1864, DCZ.

17. Clendennen and Nottingham, *William Sunley*, 10–13, 22; quotation on 33.

18. Shepherd, "Comorians," 73.

19. William Stamps Cherry, "Congo Slave Traders," *San Francisco Call*, 10 January 1904, typewritten copy in Agard Collection.

20. Clendennen and Nottingham, *William Sunley*, 6–8; Shepherd, "Comorians," 78–80, 76, 82.

21. Clendennen and Nottingham, 44–54.

22. Clendennen and Nottingham, 70.

23. Wilson to Govea, 26 December 1888.

24. *Cruise of the Lancaster*, 103; F. P. Robinson to W. H. Hathorne, 29 November 1878, DCZ; Hathorne to Second Assistant Secretary of State, 9 December 1878, DCZ; Wilson, Agard Collection.

25. Copy no. 1, accompanying Mitchell Report.

26. Copy no. 2, Mitchell Report; Clendennen and Nottingham, *William Sunley*, 71.

27. "Johanna," *Slave Trade (1883)*, 165–66.
28. B. F. Wilson, sworn statement before E. D. Ropes, 8 December 1884, DCZ.
29. Sworn statements enclosed with letter, Ropes to Cheney, 12 December 1884, DCZ.
30. Wilson, Agard Collection.
31. Clendennen and Nottingham, *William Sunley*, 35–36.
32. Shepherd, "Comorians," 86.
33. "Johanna," *Slave Trade (1883)*, 165–66.
34. Shepherd, "Comorians," 81, 86, 90–92. On changes in the 1880s, see the depositions by Comoran captives reproduced in Edward A. Alpers, "Slavery, antislavery, political rivalry and regional networks in East African waters, 1877–1883," *Afriques* 6, uploaded 21 December 2015, https://doi.org/10.4000/afriques.1744, paragraphs 35–44.
35. Shepherd, "Comorians," 89.
36. Beckert, *Empire of Cotton*.
37. Copy no. 1, Mitchell Report.
38. Mitchell Report, 2, and enclosure copy no. 4.
39. *Slave Trade (1883)*, 165.
40. On the Shufeldt voyage, see *Commodore Robert W. Shufeldt's Voyage to Africa, the Middle East, and Asia, 1878–1880*, Milestones: 1866–1898, Office of the Historian, US Department of State, https://history.state.gov/milestones/1866-1898/commodore-shufeldt (hereafter, *Shufeldt's Voyage*).
41. On Houdlette, see James P. Espinall, ed., *Reports of Cases Relating to Maritime Law; Containing all the Decisions of the Courts of Law and Equity in the United Kingdom, and Selections from the More Important Decisions in the Colonies and the United States*, vol. 1, New Series, from 1870–1873 (London: Horace Cox, 1873), 541–45.
42. Abdullah to Hathorne, 9 September 1879, DCZ.
43. Copy enclosed with letter, Abdullah to Hathorne, 5 October 1878, DCZ. On Robinson and the sultan's trade dealings with Houdlette, see also Abdullah to Hathorne, 9 and 10 September 1879, and Sultan to Commodore Robert. W. Shufeldt, 5 October 1879, DCZ.
44. Shufeldt to Hathorne, 14 October 1879, DCZ.
45. Abdullah to Hathorne, 9 and 10 September 1879; Abdullah to Shufeldt, 5 October 1879.
46. Robinson to Hathorne, 29 November 1878, DCZ.
47. Hathorne to Second Assistant Secretary of State, 9 December 1878; Robinson to Hathorne, 29 November 1878.
48. Shufeldt to Hathorne, 14 October 1879.
49. Hathorne to Second Assistant Secretary of State, 12 February 1880, DCZ.
50. *Shufeldt's Voyage*.
51. Abdullah to Hathorne, 9 September 1879.
52. Abdullah to Hathorne, 9 September and 14 August 1879.
53. Shufeldt to Hathorne, 14 October 1879.
54. Robinson to Secretary of State, 21, 25, 26 March 1880, enclosed with letters by Leonard A. Bachelder to Second Assistant Secretary of State, 1 July 1880, DCZ.
55. F. W. Cheney to Third Assistant Secretary of State, 10 March 1884, DCZ.
56. Cheney to Third Assistant Secretary of State, 10 March 1884, in response to dispatch dated 26 December 1883, with deposition from the sultan.

57. We have reconstructed this background based on Alpers, "Slavery, antislavery," para. 5–9; Extracts from Journal, etc., Inclosure 4 in no. 187, Lieutenant-Colonel Miles to Earl Granville, 18 November 1882, *Slave Trade (1883)*, 166 (hereafter, Extracts).

58. Miles to Granville, 7 January 1882, *Slave Trade (1883)*, 9.

59. Alpers, "Slavery, antislavery," para. 10–14.

60. Miles to Granville, 28 September 1882, *Slave Trade (1883)*, 144; Consul Holmwood to Earl Granville, 29 October 1882, *Slave Trade (1883)*, 158; Extracts, 167.

61. Extracts, 166.

62. Sworn statement of George Euan before E. D. Ropes, 9 December 1884, DCZ (hereafter Euan's Statement); Extracts, 170.

63. Extracts, 167–69, quotation on 169.

64. Extracts, 169–70; Miles to Granville, 2 November 1882, *Slave Trade (1883)*, 145, 166.

65. "Ngazidja (Grand Comoro Island)," in Extracts, 173.

66. "Ngazidja," 173–74.

67. Extracts, 170.

68. Extracts, 171.

69. Miles to Granville, 2 November 1882, 145.

70. Miles to Granville, 15 December 1882, 180.

71. Mr. Lister to Miles, 27 January 1883, *Slave Trade (1883)*, 181.

72. "Charges brought against His Highness Sultan Abdullah, King of Johanna by B. F. Wilson, an American citizen and now residing at Johanna, enclosed with letter, Wilson to Cheney, 10 November 1884, DCZ (hereafter, Wilson's Charges); Wilson to Cheney, 26 September and 12 December 1884, DCZ.

73. Wilson to Cheney, 12 December 1884.

74. *Cruise of the Lancaster*, 103; Martin, "Les Débuts," 55.

75. Euan's Statement, 9 December 1884.

76. Wilson to Cheney, 26 September 1884.

77. Wilson's Charges.

78. Wilson's Sworn Statement.

79. Wilson to Cheney, 15 November 1884, DCZ.

80. Wilson's Charges; Wilson to Cheney, 10 November 1884, DCZ.

81. Sworn statement of S. C. DeSouza, 11 December 1884, DCZ.

82. Wilson to Cheney, 19 October 1884.

83. Wilson's Charges.

84. Wilson to Cheney, 26 September 1884; Cheney to Third Assistant Secretary of State, 8 November 1884.

85. Cheney to Third Assistant Secretary of State, 8 December 1884.

86. Charges made by H.H. Sultan Abdallah King of Johanna against B.F. Wilson, Johanna, 10 December 1884, sworn before E.D. Ropes, US Vice Consul, Zanzibar, DCZ (hereafter, Abdullah's Charges).

87. Abdullah's Charges.

88. Wilson's Sworn Statement.

89. Sworn statement of Syed Abdallah, 9 December 1884, DCZ.

90. Sworn statement of Mohammed Salim, 8 December 1884, DCZ.

91. Sworn statement of Adamjee Musajee, 9 December 1884, DCZ.

92. Sworn statement of DeSouza, 11 December 1884.
93. Ropes to Cheney, 12 December 1884.
94. Ropes to Cheney.
95. S. Abdalla [sic], King of Johanna to Cheney, 11 December 1884, DCZ.
96. Wilson to Cheney, 12 December 1884.
97. Ropes to Third Assistant Secretary of State, 1 March 1885, DCZ.
98. Wilson to Cheney, 1 April 1885, letter enclosed with Cheney to Third Assistant Secretary of State, 15 April 1885, DCZ.
99. Wilson to Cheney.
100. Deposition reproduced in Alpers, "Slavery, Antislavery," para. 36, para. 44.
101. Wilson to Cheney, 1 April 1885; Wilson to Cheney, 7 May 1885, DCZ.
102. Wilson to Cheney, 13 June 1885, DCZ.
103. Cheney to Third Assistant Secretary of State, 31 August 1885, DCZ; Daniel H. Wicks, "Dress Rehearsal: United States Intervention in the Isthmus of Panama, 1885" *Pacific Historical Review* 49 (November 1980): 582, 585, 589–605. On the presidential foreign policies, see also Justus Doenecke, "Chester A. Arthur: Foreign Affairs," Miller Center, University of Virginia, https://millercenter.org/president/arthur/foreign-affairs; Henry F. Graff, "Grover Cleveland: Foreign Policy," Miller Center, University of Virginia, https://millercenter.org/president/cleveland/foreign-affairs.
104. Seth A. Pratt to James D. Porter, Assistant Secretary of State, 10 November 1887, DCZ.
105. *Cruise of the Lancaster,* 104.
106. *Cruise of the Lancaster,* 104.
107. Pratt to Porter, 10 November 1887.
108. Appendix no. 4—Movements of Vessels, Report of the Secretary of the Navy, Being Part of the Message and Documents Communicated to the Two Houses of Congress at the Beginning of the First Session of the Fiftieth Congress (Washington, DC: Government Printing Office, 1887), 19 (hereafter, Report of Navy Secretary); Wilson, Agard Collection.
109. Report of Navy Secretary, 10; Wilson, Agard Collection; "Kept Slaves after 1875," *Watchman and Southron,* 8 August 1914, Chronicling America, https://chroniclingamerica.loc.gov/.
110. Wilson, Agard Collection.
111. Martin, "Les Débuts," 51.
112. On the expedition, see Martin,"Les Débuts," 52–54. On Wilson's role, see Wilson to Inspector of Colonies, France, 18 May 1899, copy enclosed with Harris R. Childs, acting US consul, Zanzibar, to Honorable Thomas W. Cridler, Assistant Secretary of State, Washington, DC, 30 September 1899, DCZ.
113. McLane to Bayard, 2 February 1888, with Inclosure 1 in no. 554, consisting of letter by Flourens to McLane, February 21, 1888, Inclosure 2 in no. 554, consisting of copy and translation of *Convention of April 21, 1886, between the Sultan of Anjouan and the French Republic,* and Inclosure 3 in no. 554, consisting of copy and translation of *Convention of October 15, 1887, between the Sultan of Anjouan and the French Republic,* in Papers Relating to the Foreign Relations of the United States, Transmitted to Congress, with the Annual Message of the President, 3 December 1888, part 1, digitized by Office of the Historian, US Department of State, https://history.state.gov/historicaldocuments/frus1888p1/d369 (Hereafter, Foreign Relations Papers).

114. Houdlette to Wilson, Mauritius, 12 July 1886, certified by Pratt, US Consulate, Zanzibar, 10 November 1887, DCZ.

115. I.A. Ferguson, attorneys for official signator of Oriental Bank Corporation, Mauritius, to Wilson, 13 July 1886, certified by Pratt, 10 November 1889; A.B. d'Este, Manager of Pomony Estate to Wilson, May 1887; Statement of L. Ehrmann, Fellow, Chemical Society, London, Johanna, 25 April 1886, all in DCZ.

116. Pratt's enclosures, November 10, 1887, including Statement of Ehrmann, Johanna, 25 April 1886; Statement of L. Werber, Mauritius, 1 August 1886, subscribed and affirmed 9 August 1886, by Thomas Prentis, US consul, Port Louis, Mauritius; Statement of Omer bin Said Alloni, 29 August 1886, signature witnessed by William Hill; Statement of Combo Mohamed Zubair, September1886, certified by French Resident Trompel, copy certified by Pratt; Statement of Abas, certified by French Resident at Anjouan, certified by Pratt, 10 November 1887, DCZ.

117. Bayard to McLane, 6 April 1888, in Foreign Relations Papers, https://history.state.gov/historicaldocuments/frus1888p1/d377.

118. Wilson to Governor of Mayotte, 29 May and 13 June 1888, copies in DCZ.

119. Wilson to Govea, 24 July 1888, DCZ.

120. Wilson to C. Cornet, acting French Resident of Johanna, 27 June 1888, DCZ.

121. Wilson to Govea, 27 January 1889.

122. Wilson to Cornet, 31 December 1888, DCZ.

123. Wilson to Govea, 24 July and 26 December 1888.

124. Pratt to William F. Wharton, Assistant Secretary of State, 16 December 1889, DCZ.

125. Messrs. Smith Mackenzie & Co. to R. Dorsee Mohun, 6 and 7 May 1896; copy of indenture between Wilson and Smith Mackenzie, signed in presence of J.H. Allen, acting US Consul, 17 February 1894, DCZ.

126. Martin, "Les Débuts," 54–57.

127. Martin, 58–64.

128. Wilson to Inspector of Colonies, 18 May 1899, copy enclosed with H.R. Childs, acting US consul, Zanzibar, to Honorable Thomas W. Cridler, Assistant Secretary of State, Washington, DC, 30 September 1899, DCZ.

129. Martin,"Les Débuts," 66–75.

130. Martin,"Les Débuts,",73–75; Wilson to Govea, 24 July 1888, 27 January 1889; Pratt to Wharton, 4 April 1890; translated statement of Said Ali bin Sultan Salim, 14 October 1888, enclosed with letter of Wilson to Govea, 26 December 1888, all in DCZ.

131. Mitchell Report, 3.

132. Wilson to Inspector of Colonies at Mayotte, 1 June 1899, copy enclosed with Childs to Cridler, 30 September 1899.

133. Mitchell Report, 3–4, with copy nos. 5–9.

134. Mitchell Report, 2.

135. Wilson to Minister of Colonies, Anjouan, 20 October 1899, copy in DCZ.

136. Wilson to Monsieur Marchal, Secretary General of Mayotte, Anjouan, 16 May and 11 June 1900, copy in DCZ.

137. Mitchell Report, 8.

138. Wilson to Inspector of Colonies, Anjouan, 29 September 1899; Mitchell Report, 8.

139. Wilson to Minister of Colonies, 20 October 1899.

140. Wilson to Marchal, 16 May and 11 June 1900.
141. Wilson to Marchal, c. 14 June 1900 (day hard to decipher), DCZ.
142. Mitchell Report, 8.
143. Wilson to Childs, 22 January 1902, DCZ.
144. Wilson to Childs, 21 July 1900, DCZ.
145. Wilson to Marchal, 9 June 1900, DCZ.
146. Mitchell Report, 6 and copy no. 4.
147. Mitchell Report, 6–8; press copy no. 13, 18, DCZ; Wilson to Childs, 22 January 1902.
148. Mitchell Report, 4–5 and copy no. 10.
149. Mitchell Report, 5.
150. Wilson to Childs, 20 February 1902, DCZ.
151. Mitchell Report, 5–6, copy no. 11.
152. Wilson to Childs, 20 February 1902.
153. Mitchell Report, 6.
154. Wilson to Inspector of Colonies, 18 May 1899, copy enclosed with Childs to Cridler, September 30, 1899, DCZ.
155. Wilson to Inspector of Colonies, 18 May and 18 June 1899.
156. Wilson to Minister of Colonies, 20 October 1899.
157. Wilson to Minister of Colonies, 29 September 1899, copy enclosed with Childs to Cridler, 30 September 1899.
158. Wilson to Childs, 21 July 1900, DCZ.
159. Wilson to Childs, 22 January 1902.
160. Wilson to US Consul in Zanzibar, 24 June 1901, DCZ; Wilson to Childs, 20 February 1902.
161. Wilson to Childs, August 1902 (day hard to decipher), DCZ.
162. Childs to Herbert H.D. Pierce [Assistant Secretary of State], 14 July 1902, DCZ; Mitchell to Pierce, 29 October 1902, DCZ.
163. Mitchell Report, 10.
164. Telegram from Mitchell to State Department, 29 December 1902, confirmed 3 January 1903, DCZ.
165. Mitchell Report, 9–10; Mitchell to Pierce, 1 December 1903, DCZ.
166. Reciprocal commercial agreement between the United States and France, concluded 28 May 1898, proclaimed 30 May 1898, in effect 1 June 1898, in Papers Relating to the Foreign Relations of the United States, with the Annual Message of the President, transmitted to Congress 5 December 1898, Office of the Historian, US Department of State, https://history.state.gov/historicaldocuments/frus1898/message-of-the-president.
167. Inclosure 1: "The President of the United States to the President of France," accompanying letter by John Hay to Porter, 27 March 1902, Papers Relating to the Foreign Relations of the United States, with the Annual Message of the President, transmitted to Congress, 2 December 1902, Office of the Historian, US Department of State, https://history.state.gov/historialdocuments/frus1902/D374.
168. Maurice L. Muhleman, "The Panama Canal Payment," *Journal of Political Economy* 12 (September 1904): 473.
169. Mitchell to Pierce, 5 November and 1 December 1903; Wilson to Mitchell, 12 September and 19 August 1903, DCZ.

170. Mitchell to Pierce, 1 December 1903, DCZ; Wilson to Mitchell, 23 November and 14 October 1903, DCZ.

171. Iain Walker, "The Comoros: Strategies of Islandness in the Indian Ocean," in *African Islands: Leading Edges of Empire and Globalization,* Rochester Studies in African History and Diaspora, 83, ed. Toyin Falola, R. Joseph Parrott and Danielle Porter Sanchez (Rochester, NY: University of Rochester Press, 2019), 382.

172. "Application for Registration-Native Citizen"; Wilson's Massachusetts Mason membership card, Ancestry.com.

173. Walker, *Islands in a Cosmopolitan Sea,* 123.

174. Martin Ottenheimer and Harriet Ottenheimer, *Historical Dictionary of the Comoro Islands* (Metuchen, NJ: Scarecrow Press, 1994), 68, 87.

EPILOGUE. CROSSING SLAVERY'S INTEROCEANIC BOUNDARIES: REFLECTIONS

1. David W. Blight, *Race and Reunion: The Civil War in American Memory* (Cambridge, MA: Harvard University Press, 2001); Nina Silber, *The Romance of Reunion: Northerners and the South, 1865–1900* (Chapel Hill: University of North Carolina Press, 1993).

2. "Kept Slaves after 1875," *Watchman and Southron,* 8 August 1914.

3. Paul Tyambe Zeleza, "Rewriting the African Diaspora Beyond the Black Atlantic," *African Affairs* 104 (January 2005): 41–42. On IOW Africans, see also works by Alpers, Campbell, Harris, Hopper, Larson, Lovejoy, and Manning referenced in the introduction, esp. notes 17 and 32.

4. Awam Amkpa and Gunja SenGupta, "Picturing Homes and Border Crossings," 361.

5. James H. Sweet, "Mistaken Identities? Olaudah Equiano, Domingos Álvares, and the Methodological Challenges of Studying the African Diaspora," *American Historical Review* 114 (April 2009): 284.

6. Sweet, "Mistaken Identities?" 285; Joseph C. Miller, "Retention, Reinvention, and Remembering: Restoring Identities through Enslavement in Africa and under Slavery in Brazil," in *Enslaving Connections: Changing Cultures of Africa and Brazil during the Era of Slavery,* ed. José C. Curto and Paul E. Lovejoy (Amherst, NY: Humanity Books, 2004), 81–121.

7. Tageldin, "Place of Africa," 304.

8. Sheriff, *Dhow Cultures.*

9. Glassman, "Bondsman's New Clothes," 286.

10. Sweet, "Mistaken Identities?" 299.

11. Glassman, "Bondsman's New Clothes," 284.

INDEX

"abandonment law," 33
Abdullah III, Sultan, 22; and American planters, 251, 255, 257–58, 261–266, 268–273; and British antislavery diplomacy, 265–268; Comorian elites, 255; death of, 277; enslaved testimony against, 272; and Ngazidja coup, 265; and personal patronage, unwritten contracts, "corporate" land ownership, 258–264; relationship with Wilson, 22, 257, 261–262, 264, 274–275; and Robinson, 263; and slave trading, 265; and sugar agri-business, 255, 257–262; uprisings against, 267, 269–271, 273; in US newspapers, 251, 252
abolition: of Atlantic slave trade, 29–33; impact in British Asia, 39–51. *See also* abolitionists, delegalization, emancipation, imperial abolition
abolitionists, 2, 3, 4; as critics of colonialism, 61, 64–76, 82; and of colonial slaveries, 10–1, 52–83, 290; and "delegalization" in India, 82–83; reviled by US slavery interests, 6, 114–119; transatlantic, 35, 38, 67, 73, 90, 151; transnational causes, 6, 16–17, 52–83; and US proslavery, 125. *See also* abolition, imperial abolition, freedom
Aborigines Protection Society, 65
Abyssinians. *See* Ethiopians
Active (slaver), 229
Adams, John Quincy, 77
Adam, William, 2, 11, 17, 42, 166; and British India Society, 64–68; and liberal challenge to colonial proslavery, 68–76; Northampton speech, 52–54; and Roy, 56–57; as source for American proslavery, 130–31; and World Antislavery Convention, 69
Aden, 93, 201, 244
Adhari, 187
Afghanistan, 93
Africa/Africans, 5, 8, 92; aboard *Laconia*, 22, 245–250; as consumers, 12, 179, 233, 234, 288; diaspora, 15, 292–295; illegal trafficking in US, 80; in India, 66, 172–182, 188–197, 202–210; as merchants, 12, 179, 242, 280; and military slavery, 177–178; mobile, 291; as patrons, 260; repatriation, 159; in royal household of Zanzibar, 211–217; slavery, 172–223. *See also* Black Atlantic, Comoros, East Africa, imperial abolition, slavery, slaves, subaltern, Swahili, Zanzibar
African American, 5; and civil rights, 19; enslaved women, 123, 133–134; migrations and emigration, 19–20, 151–165; relations with British, 16, 28–33, 151–154, 157–165. *See also* Africa/Africans, agency, Black, Black Atlantic, diaspora, gender, race, slavery, slaves, slave trades
agency, 3, 5; and Atlantic world migrations, 153–165; IOW subalterns and imperial abolition, 5, 7–8, 202–223, 291–294. *See also Laconia* affair

Agra, 45; and "free cotton" experiments, 111–113
agrarian: relations in India, 98–99. *See also* Adam, Colebrooke, Comoros, Finnie, free cotton, slavery
Ahmednagar, 203
Ajmer, 191
Alabama, 77, 79, 88
Albert, Prince, 82
Alger, Horatio, 252
Algiers, 243
Ali, Said, 265–266, 270, 274
Ali, Shaik, 220
Allahabad, 107
Allen, Richard B., 39
Al Mahra, 197–199
Almanac (slaver), 229
Almeida, General Joao Tavares de, 240
Al Mukalla, 172, 188, 197
Alpers, Edward, 177
Alton (Illinois), 59
Ambar, Malik, 177
Ameen, Mahmoud, 191, 192
American Antislavery Society, 53, 59
American Colonization Society, 65, 159
American Revolution, 16, 28–31, 161
Americans in IOW: clashes with British anti-trafficking, 21–22, 227–228, 234–250; cotton planters in India, 17–18, 87–119; and Indian nationality and sovereignty, 234–238, 241–245; merchants, 11, 21–23, 227–250; as slaveholders, 11, 251–285; in transoceanic slave trade, 12, 21–22, 228–31, 289
American (US) South, 9–11, 16, 20; and abolitionists, 53–83; colonial tyrants versus "republican slaveholders,", 114–119; and defense of slavery, 120–125, 129–134; and "free cotton" experiments in India, 87–119; and international politics of slavery, 17–18, 107–111, 114–119, 244–250, 290; "lost cause" legend, 287; on reopening Atlantic Slave Trade, 117. *See also* poverty, proslavery maternalism, public relief
Amherst, William, 50
Amistad, 93
Analysis of the Laws and Regulations of the Fort William Government of Bengal, 42, 51, 73
Anderson, Clare, 13
Andersonville, 256
Anglo-Mysore War, 2
An Inquiry into the Law of Negro Slavery, 130
Anjouan. *See* Ndzwani

antislavery, 2; in British Asia, 4; British image, 5; free soil, 163. *See also* abolition, anti-slave trade, imperial abolition
anti-slave trade: alleged abuses, 237, 239, 243–44; Atlantic World, 31–33; British campaigns, 5, 290; Comoros, 264–268; controversies over nationality and sovereignty, 21–22, 234–50; regulation through indirect rule, 15–16, 20–21, 173, 193–201; treaties, 11, 174, 180, 228, 239, 264, 267, 271. *See also Laconia* affair, Lyons-Seward treaty
Antonio, George, 247
A Plea for Emigration, 159–165
Appeal to the Colored Citizens of the World, 58
apprenticeship, 58, 129
Arabian Sea, 20, 172, 176, 179
Arabs/Arabia, 8, 12, 27, 187, 191, 194, 253, 260, 268, 277, 280; and African diaspora, 292–294; and Americans in Zanzibar, 227–245; and British antislavery, 174, 195–201, 234–245; and the Comoros, 253–285; and Indian merchants, 195–199, 228, 232–45; and IOW slave trades, 20–21, 172–223, 243, 252; and Zanzibar royal household, 210–217
Arkansas, 79, 155
Arthur, Chester, 271, 272, 275
Ashworth, Henry, 68
Assam, 141
Athman, Saïd, 277–278
Atlantic (world), 2, 3, 4, 5, 11; historiography, 2, 8–9, 296–299; and IOW, 9–23, 287–294. *See also* abolition, abolitionists, African American, Americans in IOW, American South, anti-slave trade, Black, British Empire, diaspora, free cotton, migration, slavery, slaves, slave trades
Attucks, Crispus, 30
Augusta, 77, 94
Aulick, John, 227
Aurangabad, 192
Australia, 31
Awadh (Lucknow/Oudh), 15, 73, 176, 190, 191; Africans in, 178; and British India Society, 67

Badgaon, 248
Baghdad, 177, 192
Bahia, 179
Bahia Honda, 231
Bai, Poona, 139–140
Bai, Tofa, 122, 123; and "proslavery maternalism," 132–148

Baltimore, 77, 94
Baluchis, 187, 192
Bambao, 277–278
Bandar Qasim (Bosaso), 187
Banerjee, Swapna, 136
Baniyan/s, 184, 198, 234, 237, 240, 241
Baptist/s, 17
Barbaria, 188
Barghash, Sultan, 244, 257, 265, 271
Barisal, 146
Basra, 190, 192
Bath County, 154
Bayard, Thomas F., 273, 275, 276
Bayles, Thomas, 93–95, 99, 108. *See also* free cotton
Bayly, Christopher A., 54, 56
Beckert, Sven, 33, 98
Bedouins, 199
Beecher Stowe, Harriet, on imperial tyranny, 115
Benares, 44, 115
Bencoolen, 38, 72, 131
Bengal/Bengali, 2, 37, 65, 66; and reformers, 68; and "slaveholding" courtesans, 134–148; slavery, 178. *See also* Adam, Calcutta, courtesans, IOW, Roy, slavery, slaves, slave trades
Bengal British India Society, 68
Bentinck, William, 66
Benton, Lauren, 37
Berar, 111
Bertram-Shepard, 234
Bet il Mtoni, 179, 213
Bet il Sahel, 213, 215
Bhavnagar, 179
Bhuj, 190, 194
Bibb, Henry, 162
Bihar, 37, 44, 82, 145, 146–147
Bijapur, Sultanate, 177
Birmingham, 65, 66
Black Atlantic, 3, 31, 291–292, 294; protest, 58–59. *See also* Atlantic (world), diaspora, Shadd Cary, slavery, slaves, slave trades, subaltern
Blacks: and American Revolution, 30–33; and violence, 287. *See also* Africa/Africans, African American, Black Atlantic, IOW
Bombay (Mumbai), 2, 15, 97, 232, 242, 243, 292; and British India Society, 67; and "free cotton" experiments, 99–100; and IOW slave trades, 172–73, 190–93, 197–201, 231; and slavery, 38, 40, 65
Bombay Times, 100
Bose, Bhagwan Chandra, 144

Boston, 2, 53, 62, 69, 73, 89, 95, 233, 234
Boston Daily Advertiser, 66
Bourbons, 54
Brahmo Samaj, 58, 68. *See also* Roy
Brazil, 9, 11–12, 16, 53, 67, 179–180, 216, 231. *See also* Portugal/Portuguese; Rio de Janeiro
Bristol, 53, 93, 94
British and Foreign Antislavery Society, 66
British antislavery, 4–5, 16–17, 29–30, 153, 170, 291. *See also* abolition; abolitionists; anti-slave trade; imperial abolition
British Empire, 1; and African Americans, 5, 151–165; and Indian slaveries, 4, 16–17, 37–51; intra-imperial critiques, 50; and IOW slave trades, 172–210, 217–223; and US South, 6, 10–11, 17–18, 114–119, 290. *See also* abolition, abolitionists, anti-slave trade, East India Company, free cotton, imperial abolition, slavery, slaves, slave trades, sovereignty
British Guiana, 65
British India Society (BIS), 2, 17, 28, 52, 64–68, 115; and "free cotton" experiments in India, 90–91, 95, 100. *See also* abolitionists; Adam; Buckingham
British Museum, 1
British Parliament, 4
Broach, "free cotton" in, 100–101, 110
Brooks (slave ship), 32
Brougham, Henry, 61, 67–68, 240
Brown, Christopher, 29
Brown, William Wells, 152
Buckingham, James Silk, 28; critiques British imperialism, 60–61; on the Slave South, 76–82
Bueni Jumbe, 272
Buenos Aires, 228
Bundelkhand, 45, 111, 114; and "free cotton" experiments, 88, 98–107
Burnes, A., 189–190
Bushire (Bushehr), 190, 201
Buxton, Thomas Fowell, 69
Byzantium, 178

Cabinda, 231
Calcutta Journal, 27, 60
Calcutta (Kolkata), 2, 20, 38, 41–42, 54, 100, 290; and Buckingham, 76; and IOW slave trades, 20, 190, 192, 194, 220; "slaveholding courtesans," in, 135–136, 137, 141, 142–143; and slavery, 27, 38, 50; and transnational reform, 54–58, 60–64, 67. *See also* Bengal/Bengali
Calcutta Unitarian committee, 57

348   INDEX

Calicut, 75
Cameron, C. H., 128
Canada, 5, 20, 31, 151, 161, 162, 163; and Black migrations, 157–165. *See also* Shadd Cary
Canara, 73, 74
Cape Delgado, 174, 179, 180, 237
Cape Guardafui, 180
Cape of Good Hope, 11, 107, 203, 252, 253, 262. *See also* interoceanic slave trade
Cape Town, 34, 180, 205, 229, 240, 248, 255
capitalism, 3; and Atlantic slavery, 16, 33–34; Buckingham on American South, 81–82; "internationalist," 67, 90; "meliorist," 90; racial, in American South, 132, 133–134, 147; and South Asian slavery, 44, 45–51; "war capitalism," 98, 260, 289; and westward expansion, 154–155. *See also* abolitionists; Americans in IOW; free cotton; free labor; imperial abolition; slavery; slave trades
Cárdenas, 231
Carey, Henry Charles, 127
Caribbean, 53, 65, 77, 155, 167, 176, 291; emancipation, 58, 66. *See also* Black Atlantic
Carleton, Guy, 30
Carolina, 2
Cartwright, Samuel, 116–117, 118
caste constructs, 98, 133; and American cotton planters, 106; and antislavery, 70–71, 74; fluidity among courtesans, 141–148; and gender, 142–143; and IOW slave trades, 189
Catholic emancipation, 54
Ceylon, 34
Channing, William Ellery, 57
Charles, II, 38
Charleston, 2, 77, 80, 93, 94, 180, 290. *See also* interoceanic slave trade
Charleston Courier, 78
Charleston Mercury, 120, 132
Chatterjee, Bankim Chandra, 143, 144
Chatterjee, Indrani, 14, 15, 48, 52, 82, 136
Chatterjee, Partha, 137
Chatterjee, Taraprasad, 146
Chattopadhyaya, Krishna, 147
Cheney, F .W., 264
Cherry, William Stamps, 256
Child, Lydia Maria, 100, 118
children: agency of, 202–210; and courtesans, dancing girls, sex workers in India, 18–19, 120–21, 134–148; in household of Sultan of Imam and Zanzibar, 210–217; and imperial abolition, 5, 293–294; and IOW slave trades, 172–197, 249; in the Middle East, 217–220; runaways, 220–222; sold into slavery, 4. *See also* imperial abolition, slaves
China, 109
Chittagong, 72, 143
Christian Recorder, 1
Christian Register, 57
Christopher, W., 182–184, 185–188, 232, 233, 236
Churchill, Henry A., 243
Circassia/Circassian, 7, 165, 213–216, 293
Civil War (U.S), 5, 6, 7, 9, 21; Benjamin Wilson's service, 253; IOW slavery policy during, 238–41; sectional reconciliation, 287
Clarkson, Thomas, 68
Clay, Henry, 64, 77, 96
Cleveland, Grover, 272, 273, 275
cloves/plantations, 180–181, 182, 183, 217, 235–36, 248
Cobb, Thomas R. R., 11, 130–131
Cockerell, H. A., 145
coconut, 181, 185, 280
Cody, Lisa Forman, 126
coffee, 92, 244, 248, 258
Colebrooke, Edward, 151, 167
Colebrooke, Henry Thomas, 11, 27; biography, 40–42; on South Asian slavery, 40–45; challenges to, 45–47; as source for American proslavery, 130–31
colonialism, 4; law, 37; reformers on, 2, 5, 16–17, 61, 64–76, 82. *See also* abolition, abolitionists, British Empire, capitalism, French Empire, legal pluralism, slavery, settler colonialism
Columbia, 121
communication: and "free cotton," 17–18, 89–119; networks, 6–7, 10–11; reformers, 17, 52–83; technologies of, 2, 56, –57, 59–61, 89
Comoro Islands, 254
Comoros, 7, 12, 252, 253–254, 262, 272, 285; emancipation in, 277–278; *engagés*, 256–257, 272, 276; French Empire in, 273–285; and international politics of slavery, 264–285; and IOW slave trade, 256–257; popular revolt in, 277–278; slavery in, 255–257, 258–260, 272; social structure, 254; sugar plantations in, 255–256, 259. *See also* Abdullah III, Wilson
concubines, 3, 19, 20–21, 181, 186; Colebrooke on, 43; Comoros, 260; and freedom flights of, 165–68; and public relief, 128. *See also* courtesans, dancing girls, slavery in IOW, slaves, *Zenanas*, Zanzibar
Confederacy, 213

Confederate, 11, 256
Congo, 256
Constitution, US, 33
Cooch Behar, 135–136, 137, 147
Cooper, Frederick, 216
Coorg, 74
Cornwallis, Charles, 1–2, 284
cotton, 6; and Comoros, 258; and reformers, 64–83; and Zanzibar, 180–81, 182, 232, 233, 234, 235. *See also* American South, free cotton, India, slavery
courtesans, 3, 6; freedom flights of, 20; and slavery in India, 18–19, 120–21, 134–148; and slave trade regulation, 20–21. *See also* dancing girls, slaves in IOW
Craft, Ellen, 152–153, 165, 171, 181
Craft, William, 152–153
Cuba, 9, 11–12, 16, 53, 67, 80, 179–180, 231, 240. *See also* Havana
Cuffe, Paul, 64
Cugoano, Ottobah, 32
Cuttack, sex trafficking case, 135, 139–140

Dabney, Robert Lewis, 132
Dacca (Dhaka), 141
Daman, 189
Damji Ladha, 235
dancing girls: in India, 18–19, 120–21, 134–148; and IOW slave trades, 191
Darlington, 65, 66, 67
Dass, Hari Kisen, 139
dates/plantations, 179, 187, 244
de Almeida, Joao Tavares, 240
Deccan, 176, 177, 188, 191
Delany, Martin, 159
delegalization, of slavery in India, 52, 82–83, 122, 222
Delgoa Bay, 179, 233
Delhi, 111, 165, 166, 167, 222
DeSouza, S. C., 259
Deyavummah, 168–70
Dharmashastras, 38
Dhow/Dhow Cultures, 15, 174, 207, 289, 293
diaspora, 3; in the Black Atlantic, 20, 157–168, 291–292; and comparative slavery, 15, 291–294; and IOW, 292–294
Diu, 189
domestic slavery, 4, 166–168, 256, 290; and colonial belonging, 157–165; distinguished from trafficking, 16, 20, 39–40, 170–71; and public relief, 128–138; subterfuges involving, 175–176; and the (US) Slave South, 132–134; and violence, 134, 168–170. *See also* slavery, slaves, slave trades
Doormukhi (Durmukhee) Ali, 218
do Rosario Monteiro, Joaquium, 229
Douglass, Frederick, 118, 159
Drescher, Seymour, 31
Dublin Weekly Herald, 76
DuBois, W. E. B., 8
Duchess of Sutherland, and Louisa McCord, 132–134
Dunmore, Lord, 30

Earle, Hamilton, 245
East Africa, 3, 5, 15, 34–35, 44, 60; in IOW slave trades, 20–22, 172–223. *See also* Africa/Africans, Comoros, slavery, slaves, Zanzibar
East India Company, 4, 17, 20; and South Asian slavery, 37–51, 289–290; reformist critiques of, 54, 64–83; and "free cotton" experiments in India, 87–119; and public relief, 127–128; and IOW slave trades, 172–210, 217–223; and Indians in Zanzibar, 234–238
Eaton, Richard, 14, 177
Edgartown, 273
Edgefield Advertiser, 87, 88
Egypt/Egyptian, 61, 77–78, 130
Eltis, David, 180
emancipation: Caribbean, 58; Comoros, 266; US North, 32–22; US proclamation, 288. *See also* freedom, Haitian revolution
Emancipation Day, 52
Emancipation Proclamation, 257
Emerson, Ralph Waldo, 41, 57
Emerton, Ephraim A., 184, 233
Emma Jane, 273, 274, 287, 288
engagé/s/system, 256–257, 272, 276, 281, 282–283. *See also* Free Emigration system
England, 109
Enlightenment, 4
Equiano, Olaudah, 29, 31, 32, 185, 291
Erskine, James, 208, 221
Estlin, John Bishop, 53
Ethiopia/Ethiopian, 7, 177, 187–88, 189, 209; in Zanzibar royal household, 214–15
Euan, George, 259, 265, 268, 270
eunuchs, 178, 215–217
Europe, 6
evangelical: abolitionists, 59. *See also* Adam, Baptists, Missionaries, Unitarians

famines, 4, 65, 127–128. *See also* British India Society (BIS), poverty, slavery
Faridpur, 145
Farish, James, 221
Farmer, William, 151, 152
Fatima, 202, 219–20, 292
Feregie, 247–50
Fillmore, Millard, 227
Finnie, Thomas J.: failure, 111–114; fantasies of feudalism in India, 99–100, 289; impatience with bureaucrats and scientists, 111–113; journal compared with Terry's, 98; prisms of race, caste, coercion, 103–106, 117–18; recruited as cotton planter, 93–95; screed against reformers, 107; on slave South invincibility, 117–118; struggles over land and labor, 101–107
Fish, Hamilton, 244
Fitzhugh, George, 123–124, 131
Florida, 155
Forbes, Charles, 65
Ford, Lacy, 124
Foreign Office (British), 244, 265, 267–268
Fort William, 170
France, 284. *See also* French Empire
Frederick, Katherine, 233
free cotton: and debates over race, tariffs, and settler colonialism, 96–97;107–111; experiments in India, 87–119, 289; imperial tyranny versus "republican slaveholders," 114–119, 290; manufacturers and bureaucrats, 91–93; overseer motivations, 93–95; reactions in the Slave South, 95–97; and reformers, 90–91; and struggles over land, labor and resources in India, 97–107, 111–114. *See also* Bayles, Finnie, overseers, Terry
freedom: Black Atlantic diasporic politics of, 5, 162–165; British imperial definitions of, 292; defined by Shadd Cary, 20, 162–165; and the Enlightenment, 14, 129; flights in India, 20, 165–170; and labor, 2, 3, 292; and *Laconia* Africans, 246–50; as liberal individualism, 3; migration as, 152–165; and poverty, 40, 45–51; religion and slavery, 4; of self-sale, 40, 45–51; subaltern prisms, 5, 12–16, 202–223, 292, 293–294. *See also* abolition, abolitionists, Adam, Black Atlantic, emancipation, human rights, imperial abolition, *Lemmon* slave case
Freedom's Journal, 58
Free Emigration system, 256. *See also* engagés
free labor, 3, 4, 204; in British India, 17–18, 105–110; slippage into slavery, 53; in the US, 59, 162. *See also* abolitionists, free cotton, imperial abolition
Freeman, Joanne, 59
Freemason's Hall (London), 2, 67
free produce, 6, 17–18, 91. *See also* British India Society (BIS), free cotton
Free-Soilers, 59, 163
free trade, and cotton experiments in India, 95–97, 107–111, 288
French Empire: in the Comoros, 22–23, 265–66, 273–285, 289; Revolution, 191; slave trade, 256–257
Frere, Bartle, 244, 257
Fuentes, Marisa, 13
fugitives, 3, 5; East African, 8. *See also* imperial abolition, *Laconia* affair, slavery, slave trades
Fugitive Slave Act, 151

Garner, Margaret, 163
Garrison, William Lloyd, 53, 54, 59, 61, 91. *See also* abolitionists
Gauhati, 141
Gazetteer of the Bombay Presidency, 101
gender, 123–125, 133, 136, 148, 158, 291; as a cover for trafficking, 175–176, 190; and "cult of domesticity," 152; and India, 136–148; and "jezebel" construct, 152–53; roles and expectations in US South, 133–135; and slavery, 120–148. *See also* domestic slavery, eunuchs, slaves, slave trades, women
General Colored Association, 58
Genovese, Eugene, 124
The Georgian, 78
Georgia (US), 77, 79, 93, 100, 129, 130, 152–153
Gevrey, Alfred, 260
Ghana, 14
Ghosh, Durba, 128
Ghosh, K. D., 143
Gibraltar, 274
Gifford, Rufus W., 245, 247–248, 249
Gilroy, Paul, 8
Glasgow, 67, 68, 91
Glasgow Emancipation Society, 64
Glassman, Jonathan, 14, 181, 209, 293
Glorioso, 267
Glymph, Thavolia, 134
Goa, 189, 229
Godey's Lady's Book, on Roy, 63
Gold Coast, 14
Gosse, Van, 29
grain, 212

Grand Gulf, 94
Granville, Earl, 267
Great Britain, 161, 180
Greek/s, 54; and support in US, 152
The Greek Slave, 151–152
Greenleaf, Simon, 130
Grimke, Angelina, 59
Gronningsater, Sarah L. H., 156
Gujarat/Gujarati, 138, 176, 179; and American business interests, 227–245; and cotton experiments, 92; financiers and merchants, 12, 21, 237; and IOW slave trades/slavery, 138, 172–180, 187–192–201, 203, 208–09, 221; and slave trade regulation, 20–21. *See also* Broach, Kutch, Kathiawar
Gulf Coast (US), 77
Gulf of Aden, 172, 187
Gulf of Khambhat (Cambay), 179
Gulf (Persian/Arabic), 3, 8, 177, 179, 207, 218, 234, 243; and IOW slave trades, 20, 172–223
Gwalior, 175–176

Hadhramaut, 172, 184
Hadrami, 265
Haines, S. B., 199
Haiti, 33
Haitian Revolution, 28, 32, 58
Hajo, 141
Halima, 219–220
Hamerton, Atkins, 174, 186, 217, 218, 234, 236–238, 242
Hammond, James Henry, 131–132
"harem," 210, 213. *See also* concubines, Salme, secondary wives, slaves, women, Zenana
Harington, John H., 42, 46–51, 69, 73, 138, 166
Harper, William, 129–130
Harrar, 187
Harries, Patrick, 180, 229
Harrington, P. F., 273
Harris, John, 231
Harrison, Benjamin, 275
Harvard University, 2, 17, 66, 130
Hastings, Warren, 37, 166; Adam on, 72
Hathorne, W. H., 246–247, 248
Havana, and interoceanic slave trade, 228–231
Hennel, Samuel, 218
Herskovits, Melville J., 8
Heshima, 216–217
Hindu College, 68
Hindu/s, 6, 133; Adam on, 68–73; and colonial discourse of law, 17, 37–51, 128, 129, 130, 166;

courtesans in India, 136–148; Finnie on, 103–107, 117–118. *See also* caste, gender, IOW, slavery, slaves
historiography, 2–3, 295–344; on US and IOW slaveries, 8–16; US Slave South, 120–121, 124–125. *See also* Atlantic (world), IOW
HMS *Harrier*, 267
HMS *London*, 245, 248, 249. *See also* Laconia affair
Hodos, Jerome I., 90
Hofmeyr, Isabel, 9
Hogan, Michael, 229
Holmes, E. W., 255
Holmwood, Frederick, 254, 255, 259; and antislavery mission in Comoros, 265–268, 272
Holy Land, 77
Hooghly, 143
Hooper, Jane, 180
Horizon (slaver), 229
Houdlette and Company, 262
human rights: campaigns, 3, 5, 6, 10, 52–83; definition, 4. *See also* abolitionists
Hume, Joseph, 93
Hussein, Golam, 220
Huzzey, Richard, 54, 83
Hyderabad, 15, 137, 176, 177, 179, 191–192, 220

Ibn Batuta, 177
Imam, of Zanzibar/Muscat: and Americans, 232, 234–38; and Anglo-American tensions, 236–38; household of, 210–217; and IOW slave trades, 217–220; of Muscat, 210; of Muscat and Zanzibar, 180, 182–83, 186–188, 201. *See also* Sayyid Sa'īd ibn Sultān, Zanzibar
imperial abolition, 4, 34–35; and American business, 227–228, 234–245; delegalization in India, 52, 82–83; and Indian nationality and sovereignty, 234–245; and IOW slave trades, 172–177, 181–201; subaltern engagement with, 5, 7–8, 202–223, 291–294. *See also* Laconia affair
imperialism, British. *See* anti-slave campaigns, British Empire, domestic slavery, imperial abolition, slavery
imperialism, French. *See* French Empire
India Gazette, 38
India/Indians, 8, 253, 277; Arab reprisals against shipping, 16, 20–21, 195–20; and British antislavery in Zanzibar, 234–245; and colonial reform, 52–83; in Comoros, 268, 270; compared by British with Arabs, 236; and

India/Indians *(continued)*
imperial indirect slave trade regulation, 16; and IOW slave trades, 5, 172–223; nationality and sovereignty in Zanzibar, 234–38, 241–45; traders, 12. *See also* Africans, courtesans, Gujaratis, servants in Britain, slavery, slaves, slave trades, South Asia/Asians

Indian Law Commission Report, 82, 132

Indian Ocean World (IOW), 2, 3; Atlantic interactions and comparisons, 9–23, 289–291; distinctiveness, 289; historiography, 9, 296–297, 299–300, 301–303. *See also* abolition, abolitionists, Africa/Africans, anti-slave trade, Arabs, British Empire, Comoros, diaspora, East India Company, free cotton, imperial abolition, India/Indians, migration, slavery, slaves, slave trades, South Asia/Asians

Indian Penal Code (1860), 138, 139

Indian Slavery Act, 1843, 52, 82–83

Indologists/Indology, 40–41. *See also* Orientalism

Indus River, 93

interoceanic slave trade, 228–231, 262

Ireland, 37

Islam/Islamic, 177, 181; and acculturation, 216, 260, 293; and laws of slavery, 15, 256. *See also* Arabs, Muslim/s, slavery, slaves, slave trades

Istanbul, 167

ivory, 179, 180, 185, 189, 228, 232, 233, 244, 246

Jackson, CC, 113–114
Jafranah, 173
Jaipur, 167, 191
Jamaica, 37, 53, 231
James, C. L. R., 8
Janjira, 177
Java, 34, 207
Jeddah (Jiddah), 27, 187, 190, 191, 207–208
Jefferson, Thomas, 32, 155
Jerusalem, 78
Jodhpur, 191
Johanna (Comoros). *See* Ndzwani
Johnson, Walter, 13, 155
Jones, A., on cotton prospects in India, 108–110
Jones-Rogers, Stephanie, 134
Jones, William, 41
Journal of a Residence on a Georgia Plantation, 61
Journal of the Asiatic Society of Bengal, 73
Juliana (slaver), 229
Jumbe, Bueni, 272

Kacceri, 20
Kalpi, 88

Kanpur, 99, 102
Karachi, 189, 222
Kathiawar, 172; and IOW slave trade/slaveries, 172–201, 207. *See also* Gujarat/Gujaratis
Kays, M. T., 203
Kemble, Fanny, 61
Kentucky, 64
Kenya, 187
Kerr-Ritchie, Jeffrey, 158
Khandesh, 248
Khan, Meer Nasir, 222
Kilwa, 174, 180, 183, 185, 233, 237
King, Wilma, 134
kinship: in South Asia, 120–148; trope of, in servitude, 3, 18–19. *See also* Colebrooke, Orientalism, proslavery maternalism, slavery, slaves, slave trades
Kirk, John, 246–247, 265. *See also Laconia* affair
Knickerbocker Magazine, 77
Kota, 138
Kotra Muckrundpoor [*sic*], 99
Kumilah, 146
Kumillah, 143
Kutch/Kacchi, 15, 138,176,179, 180, 187, 189–190, 194, 235, 238, 242; controversies over nationality, 227, 234–238, 241–245; and IOW slave trade/slaveries, 179–180, 187–190, 194, 208–209, 221, 227–245; and sovereignty, 234–238, 241–245; and US business interests, 227–245. *See also* Gujarat/Gujaratis
Kuza, Mirza Goolam, 222

labor: free, 2, 89, 123–124; and "free cotton experiments," 98–119; and Mary Ann Shadd Cary, 163; slippage between free will and coercion, 82–83. *See also* Republican Party, slavery, slaves, slave trades
Lacey, W.C., 139
Laconia affair, 22, 245–250
Lake Nyasa, 185
Lamu, 174
Lanour, 207
Latimer, George, 53
The Law and Custom of Slavery in India, 11, 52, 69–76
Laxmichand Motichand, 179
legal pluralism: Anglo-Atlantic traditions, 4, 6; challenged, 68–76, 290; comparative colonialism and slavery, 16–17, 35–40, 56, 166, 290
LeGeyt, P.W., 219, 222
Leicester, 67
Lemmon, Jonathan, 154, 155–157

Lemmon, Juliet, 156
Lemmon slave case, 19, 154–157, 271
Levine, Philippa, 136
Lewis, John Frederick, 165
Leycester, William, 50
The Liberator, 52, 54, 62, 65, 76, 91, 95
Liberty Advocate, 95, 96
Lincoln, Abraham, 127, 240, 287, 288. See also Lyons-Seward treaty
Liverpool, 61, 64, 66, 67, 95, 97, 109
Livingstone, Charles, 256
Livingstone, David, 255
Livingston, Samuel, 156
London, 2, 73, 83; and British India Society, 66–68; and "free cotton" experiments, 89, 90–91, 95; and Great Exhibition, 151–153; and IOW slave trade regulation, 20
London Atlas, 100
Louisiana, 2, 116, 155, 228. *See also* interoceanic slave trade
Louisiana Purchase, 154–155
Lovejoy, Elijah, 59, 60, 66
Lowell, 233
Lucknow, 137, 220. *See also* Awadh
Ludden, David, 98
Lunda, 184
Lushington, Charles, 65
Lushington, Stephen, 65
Lyons-Seward treaty, 240, 243, 245

Macaulay, Thomas Babington, 51
M'Cassi, 227. *See also Laconia* affair
McCord, Louisa S., 18, 119, 147–148; erases enslaved labor, 133–134; and proslavery maternalism, 120–125, 134. *See also* slaves, in the American South, slavery, slaveholders
McCurry, Stephanie, 37
Machado, Pedro, 179, 184, 189
Macnaghten, William Hay, 70, 71, 138
Macon, 77, 153
Madagascar, 12, 180, 228, 233, 240, 255–256, 273, 285, 287
Madras, and "free cotton" experiments in, 87, 110, 114; and slavery, 38, 73–75
Magny, Jules, 258
Mahé, 249
Mahra, 184
Majid, Sultan, 239, 242–43
Majunga, 233
Makonde, 184
Makran, 176
Makua, 184, 221, 248, 255, 260, 272, 277–278

Malabar, slavery in, 73–75
Malacca, 34
Malagasy, 11, 255
Malawi, 183
Malay, 254
Malcolm, Charles, 199, 207
Malthus, Thomas Robert, 126
Manchester, 67, 73, 83, 97; and "free cotton" experiments, 89, 90–91, 95
Manchester Times, 91
Mandvi, 180, 189, 208, 221
Mangalore, 193, 198
Mani, Lata, 57
Mansfield, Daniel H., 235
Mansfield, Earl of, 30
Manu, 128
Marianah, 181, 194; and diaspora, 292–294; in India, 195–97; paths traveled, 182–188; resistance by, 202–205; trafficked, 195, 172–173
Marseille, 231, 249
Martin, Montgomery, 65
Martin, Robert Montgomery, 96
Marwar, 138
Maryland, 79, 155
Mascarene Islands, 11, 34, 39, 174, 180
Mason Mitchell, Charles, 279, 284
Massachusetts, 7, 11, 22, 52, 53
Matanzas, 231
maternalism. *See* proslavery maternalism
Mathew, Johan, 174
Mauritius, 65, 83, 92, 179, 228, 249, 255, 257, 259, 262, 265, 268, 274
Mayotte, 254, 256, 265, 270, 271, 272, 274, 277, 279, 281, 283, 284
May, Samuel, 53
Mebranee, Mahmood, 193
Medina, 191
Melman, Billie, 210
Memoir on Slavery, 129–130
Memphis, 117, 155
Metcalf, Charles, 166, 168
Mewar, 139
Mexico, 155, 161
Middle East/Eastern, 12, 15. *See also* Africa/Africans, Arabs, Dhows/Dhow cultures, slavery, slaves, slave trades
Midgley, Clare, 54
migrations, 23; Black, 19–20; to British Empire, 153–154, 157–165; and IOW slave trades, 20–22; subaltern, 290. *See also* Canada, freedom, *Laconia* affair, *Lemmon* slave case, Shadd Cary, slave trades

Miles, S. B., 265
Miller, W., 139
Mill, John Stuart, 61
Minerva (slaver), 229
Minnetonka, 231
missionaries, 7, 17, 68; Baptists in Calcutta, 56; and *sati*, 57. *See also* Unitarians
Mississippi, 6, 73, 77, 83; and "free cotton" experiments, 89, 90, 93–119; and reformers, 67, 79; and slavery expansion, 155
Mississippi Creole, 99, 100; on "free cotton" in India, 108–111
Mitchell, Charles Mason, 279; report by, 281–285
Mlamali, 272
Mobile, 77, 88, 93
Mocha (al Makha), 175, 177, 190, 199, 215
Mohammedan/s. *See* Muslim
Mombasa, 180, 187
Money, Neel Das, 146
Montagu, Basil, 61
Monteiro, Joaquium do Rosario, 229
Montevideo, 179, 228–229
Montgomery, 77
Montgomery, H., 168, 169
Monticello, 79
Moresby, Fairfax, 174
Morgan, Edmund, 36
Moroni, 272
Motichand, Laxmichand, 179
Mozambique, 11, 173–174, 179, 180, 184–185, 189, 228–231, 240, 244, 253, 272
Mozambique Channel, 192, 245, 251, 253
Msafumu, 265
Mughal/s, 37, 177; and colonial reformers, 68
Muhamed, Prince, 269–271
Muhleman, Maurice L., 284
Müller, Simone M., 7
Mullick, Babu Taraknath, 141
Murray, William, 30
Murshidabad, 143, 178
Muscat, 174, 180, 182, 188–189, 191–192, 201, 218–220, 232, 234, 243, 244
Muslim/s, 6; Adam on, 68–73; and courtesans in India, 137–138, 145–148; empire, laws and practice of slavery, 15, 17, 38–51, 130, 166; IOW polities, 15. *See also* Africa/Africans, Arabs, Comoros, Dhows/Dhow cultures, slavery, slaves, slave trades
Muthra, 167
Mutsamudu, 255, 265, 267, 274, 277, 278, 285

Mwali (Mohéli), 254, 257, 270, 272, 273
Mysore, 1; and British India Society, 67; and slavery, 74–75, 168–170

Nakhudas, 174, 183, 195, 207, 220
Naoroji, Dadabhai, 127
Napoleon, Louis, 154, 156
Napoleonic Wars, 32, 256
Narada, 48
Nashik, 203
Nasser, Gamal Abdel, 292
Natal, 233, 248
Natchez, 93, 155
Natchez Courier, 99
Natchez Free Trader, 108, 110
National AntiSlavery Standard, 76, 100
National Era, 115, 152
nationality, and IOW slavery controversies, 5, 21, 173, 234–45
Ndzwani, 22, 245, 246, 247, 248, 249, 254–257, 265, 267; coup, 267, 269–271; emancipation in, 277, 278; French imperialism in, 252, 273–285; peasant and slave revolt in, 252, 277–278; slavery in, 255–261, 264–268, 272–274; war of succession, 277–278; and Wilson, Benjamin, 251–285. *See also* Abdullah III
New Bedford, 7, 22, 247, 248, 249, 251–252, 253, 275
New England, 11, 22, 185, 223, 228, 232, 233, 237, 246, 252, 290
New Hampshire, 231, 235
New Orleans, 77, 93, 94, 101, 109–110, 153, 155
New York, 19, 33, 53, 89, 93, 100; and *Lemmon* slave case, 155–157. *See also* slave trades
New York House of Refuge, 156, 203
New York *Journal of Commerce*, 95, 108
Ngazidja (Grand Comore), 254, 265, 266, 267, 270, 272, 273
Nicaragua, 11
Nizamat Adalat, 45
Nolan, O., 146
Norfolk, 77, 79, 155
North America, 4, 6. *See also* Americans, United States
Northampton, 52, 53
Northampton Association, 52
Northwest Provinces (India), and free cotton experiments, 97–114
Nosy Bé, 256
Nottingham, 67
Nova Scotia, 157
Nubie, Abdool Khair, 220

O'Connell, Daniel, and British India Society, 64–68; Finnie's rantings against, 107
Oman, 180, 184, 220. *See also* IOW, Muscat, slavery, Zanzibar
Omar, Saïd, 278
Ontario, 20, 157, 161. *See also* Canada, Shadd Cary
"Oriental"/ "Orientalist"/ "Orientalism": constructs, of slavery, 4, 10–11, 17, 40–51, 89, 130, 216, 256, 287; and cotton planters, 117–118; of despotism, 8, 152; gaze on harem, 165, 210–211. *See also* Salme
Orissa, 37
Ottoman (empire), 54, 152, 153, 167, 267
Ouidah, 231
Owen, Robert, 61

Pakistan, 176. *See also* anti-slave trade, Baluchi, imperial abolition, slavery, slaves in IOW, slave trades, South Asia/South Asians
Palestine, 78
Panama Canal, 284
Paris, 283
Parker, Kunal, 144
Park, G. S., 143
Parliament (British), 18, 58, 60, 67, 69; and "delegalization" of South Asian slavery, 82; and poor laws, 125–127; and report on slavery in India, 127–129
Pascal, Pierre, 281
paternalism, 290; and British Empire, 1; and colonial slavery discourses, 43–45, 128–129; IOW slave trades, 182; and slavery and poor relief, 6, 10–11; Slave South claims to, 32, 78, 114–117, 120–125, 129–134. *See also* patriarchy, proslavery maternalism
Patna, 2
patriarchy, 6, 20, 132, 137, 147, 162; and constructs of South Asian slavery, 40–51, 168. *See also* paternalism, proslavery maternalism
Patsy estate, 258–259, 261, 265–266, 269, 270, 272, 273, 277, 278. *See also* Comoros, Wilson
Paul, Nathaniel, 64
Payne, Elijah, 156
Peale, Rembrandt, 55*fig.*, 62
Pearl/s/economy, 179, 180
Pease, Elizabeth, 65–68
Pease, Joseph, 65–68
Pemba, 180
Penang, 207
Penningroth, Dylan C., 13–14
Pennsylvania Hall, 59

Periplus of the Erythraen Sea, 177
Persia/Persian, 180, 183. *See also* Bushire, Gulf
Persian Gulf. *See* Gulf
Peshgar, Uma, 146
Petty Gulf, 94
Philadelphia, 1, 59, 61, 77, 117, 229
Phillips, Wendell, 54, 91; and British India Society, 64–68
Pingree-West, 234
Pinto, Miguel C., 233
Pomoni, 255, 274, 276, 277, 278, 283
Poor Law Report (1834), 125–127
Porbandar: Arab reprisals against, 195–201; Rana of, 20; and slavery, 172–174, 176–184, 188–193–201, 202, 209
Port Louis, 262
Portugal/Portuguese, 11, 180, 189, 203, 205, 228, 233, 237, 259; and interoceanic slave trade, 228–231
Potosi, 228
Pottinger, Henry, 138
poverty, 3; British Poor Laws, 125–127; and dancing girls and sex workers in India, 134–148; and Parliamentary Report on Slavery in India, 127–129; and slavery, 4, 6, 10–11, 45–51, 162, 290; in the Slave South, 120–125, 129–134. *See also* proslavery maternalism, public relief
Poverty and Un-British Rule in India, 127
Powell, Hiram, 152
Prakash, Gyan, 82
Prestholdt, Jeremy, 232
Prince, Lucy Terry, 29
proslavery, local and global contexts of, 6, 10, 120–148
proslavery maternalism, 6, 18–19; in the American South, 120–125, 129–134; in India, 134–148. *See also* paternalism, patriarchy
prostitutes/prostitution, and the colonial archives of slavery, 120–23, 134–148
Providence, 234
Provincial Freeman, 151, 159–161
public relief: in Britain, 125–127; defense of slavery in Slave South as, 129–134; and famines, 127–128; imperial aversion to, 4, 127–129; in India, 44, 128, 134–148; and US northern emancipation, 33
Putnam, Horace B., 186, 213, 235

Qishn, 197, 198
Quakers, 29, 65. *See also* British India Society (BIS)

Quelimane, 184, 228–231, 233. *See also* interoceanic slave trade
Querimba Islands, 233
Quran, 15, 271

race: and IOW slavery, 4, 6; and US, 36, 124, 129–134, 131, 148, 287, 291; and Zanzibar royal household, 210–217
Radha/Gulbihar, 165–168. *See also* freedom, women
Raja of Satara, 115
Rajasthan, and slavery, 138
Rajkot, 176, 189, 221
Rajput, 139, 167
Rangpur, 143
Rath, 99
Reconstruction (US), 7, 287; IOW slavery policy during, 241–245
Redmond, Charles, 91
Red Sea, 3, 176, 177, 179, 190, 199–200, 234, 274
Reed, David, 57
Reid, A. P., 209
Reid, A. T., 194–195, 196–197
Republican Party (US), 59; and free labor, 123, 162, 163
Reuben, Aslan (Khojah), 192–193, 217–218
Réunion, 11, 179, 228, 256, 284, 285
Revolt of 1857 (India), 178, 191, 210
Rhode Island, 229, 231
Richmond, 77, 79
Rigby, Christopher, 184, 235, 239, 242
Rio de Janeiro, 179, 184; and interoceanic slave trade, 230–231
Río de la Plata, 179–180; and interoceanic slave trade, 228–229
Ripley, Edward S., 247
Roberts, Edmund, 231
Robinson, F. P., 262–263
Rocher, Ludo, 41
Rocher, Rosane, 41
Roosevelt, Theodore, 284–285
Roper, H., 204
Ropes, Edward, 269–271
Roseberry, William, 291
Rosenthal, Caitlin, 102
Roy, Raja Rammohun, 2, 17, 28; and Adam, 56–57; as American abolitionist pseudonym, 62–63; and Buckingham, 61–62; and Massachusetts antislavery fair, 54; portrait of, 55; and transnational reform, 54–64; and US women, 63–64

Ruete, Emily (Sayyida Salme), 210–213, 214–217, 293
Rugemer, Edward B., 124
Ruggles, David, 52, 53
Rush, Stephen, 53
Ryots, 92, 98, 99, 107. *See also* free cotton

Sadr Diwani Adalat, 38, 42
Sadr Nizamat Adalat, 38, 45, 46
Said Ali, 265, 266, 270, 272
Saint Domingue, 11
St. Helena, 248
Saleem, Mirza, 167
Salem, 227, 233, 234, 269, 290; and East Africa, 231–245
Salim, Mohammed, 270
Salim, Prince, 264, 268, 269, 277–78
Salme, Sayyida. *See* Ruete, Emily
Sancho, Ignatius, 29
Sartori, Andrew, 54, 56
Sati, 6, 17, 57
Saudi Arabia, 27, 187
Savannah, 77
Sayyid Saʿīd ibn Sultān, 174, 180, 210, 227, 235, 242. *See also* Imam, of Zanzibar/Muscat
Sayyid Thuwaynī bin Saʿīd Āl Bū Saʿīd, 218
Schoen, Brian, 94
Schwalm, Leslie, 134
Scotland/Scottish, 2, 64
secondary wives, 181. *See also* concubines, slaves, slave trades, women
Senghor, Léopold Sédar, 292
Sen, Samita, 137, 142
settler colonialism/colonialists, 6, 11, 289; and American slaveholders in IOW, 251–285; American-style, 6, 18, 89, 262, 289; dynamics of, 154; expanding, 261; and free cotton in India, 87–119; French, 280; racialized vision of, 102; US, 11; white, 108–111; Wilson's lifestyle, 22. *See also* British Empire, Comoros, French Empire, Oman, Salme, Zanzibar
Seward, William, 240
sex. *See* gender, women
Seychelles, 248, 249, 267
Shadd Cary, Mary Ann, 5, 19–20; advocates emigration, 159–163; biography, 158–159; on Black Canadians, 161, 163, 170; and colonial belonging, 157–58, 161, 170, 291–292; defines freedom, 162–163; diasporic vision of, 158, 159–161, 291; *Lemmon* case, 19–20, 157; publications, 159–161, 159; and women's rights, 163–165, 170

Sharp, Granville, 30, 31
Sharpe, Samuel, 58
Shastras. See Hindu
Shepard, Michael, 185, 186, 237
Sheriff, Abdul, 174, 232
Shirazi, 252, 253
Shirur, 203
Shivji, Jairam, 232, 234, 235, 237. *See also* Kutch/Kacchis
Shufeldt, Robert Wilson, 262–263
Sidis, of Janjira, 177–79
Sierra Leone, 31, 32, 240
Similla, 247–250
Sind/Sindhi, 189, 221, 222
Sinha, Manisha, 29, 32
Sirajgunj, 146
slaveholders, 6, 29–32. *See also* paternalism, proslavery maternalism, slavery, slaves, slave trades
slavery, 3; in Afro-Asian societies, 4, 5, 14–15; ameliorative proposals in South Asia, 49–50; and the American South, 5, 9–11, 78–81, 114–119; Atlantic and IOW compared, 6, 42–46, 50, 120–148, 183, 212–213, 289–294; British colonial discourses and American proslavery, 10–11, 120–148; and colonial knowledge, practice in British Asia, 4, 16–17, 40–51, 118, 135, 289–290; in the Comoros, 22–23; defense of, 6, 120–148; and diaspora, 15; by "free will," 17; global, 287–294; international politics of, in Comoros, 264–268, 272, 275–285; "in the East," 3, 42, 69, 128–129, 216; and kinship, 18–19; North American origins of, 35–37; and Parliamentary Report on Slavery in India, 127–129; patron-client relationships, 177, 181, 216–217, 289; and Roman law, 36; of self-sale, 40, 45–51; slippage into, of freedom in imperial policy, 47, 82–83; as social insurance, 4, 6, 18–19, 120–148; and US Supreme Court, 59. *See also* abolition, abolitionists, anti-slave trade, delegalization, emancipation, *Laconia* affair, legal pluralism, slaves, slave trades
slaves, in the American South: Buckingham on, 78–81; and fugitives, 152–157; insurrections, 5; and labor, 133–134, 155; mythologies of female slavery, 152; and westward expansion, 154–155; women, 120–21, 123, 133–134. *See also* abolition, abolitionists, anti-slave trade, emancipation, imperial abolition, legal pluralism, *Lemmon* slave case, slave trades

slaves, in IOW: and agency, 202–223; and caravan trade, 181; in Comoros, 245–250, 256–62, 272; courtesans and sex workers in South Asia, 18–19, 122–123, 134–148; concubines and secondary wives in India, 165–168; and in Comoros, 245–250, 256–62, 272; and in Muscat, 182–183, 218–220; and in Zanzibar, 210–217, 233, 235, 237, 239, 241; domestic workers in India, 169–170; eunuchs, 27, 178–179, 293; as fugitives, 165–170, 220–222; labor, 179–181; military, 177–179, 191, 210, 276; multiracial, 172–197, 202–222; patron-client relationships, 179, 209, 181, 292–294; as porters, 233, 235, 246; prices of, 189–90, 191, 193, 218, 221; solidarities among, 168–169; in South Asia (per Adam), 70–76; in South Asia (per Colebrooke), 42–45; violence against, 167–170; in Zanzibar, 210–217, 233, 235, 237, 239, 241. *See also* abolition, abolitionists, anti-slave trade, delegalization, emancipation, imperial abolition, legal pluralism, slavery, slave trades
Slave Trade Department (British), 244
slave trades: Atlantic, abolition of, 4; Buckingham on, 79–80; and Comoros, 256–257, 265–268; and courtesans in India, 134–148; distinguished from domestic slavery and servants, 16, 20, 45, 242, 293–294; interoceanic, 228–231; IOW slave trades, 20–21, 27, 172–223, 289; and subterfuges, 175–176; US domestic, 155. *See also* anti-slave trades
Smith, Oliver, 96
Smritis, 38. *See also* legal pluralism
Société Coloniale de Bambao, 285
Society for the Promotion of Christianity in India, 57
Socotra, 197, 199
Somali, 187–188, 209, 222
Somerset, James, 29, 30
Somerset v. Stewart, 29, 53, 161
Soomairpoor Khas [*sic*], 99
South Africa, 205, 253. *See also* Cape of Good Hope, Cape Town, Natal
South America, 161
South Asia/Asians: subaltern, 5, 11, 15, 236, 249, 289, 292. *See also* Baluchi, Chittagong, Dhaka, Gujarat/Gujaratis, India/Indians, Kathiawar, Kutch, Pakistan, slavery, slaves in IOW, slave trades, sovereignty, subaltern
South Carolina, 6, 18, 36, 78, 83, 88, 95, 119, 121–122, 125, 131, 287. *See also* Charleston, interoceanic slave trade, McCord

South Pacific, 207
sovereignty, and slavery controversies, 5, 21, 173, 199–201, 234–250
Speer, William S., 131, 240–241
Spivak, Gayatri, 12
Spurzheim, J.G., 61
Sri Lanka, 177
Stanley, Henry Morgan, 246
Stanton, Elizabeth Cady, 69
State Department, 246, 271–272, 276, 284. *See also* Americans, Lyons-Seward treaty, Wilson
Stevenson, Brenda, 134
Stewart, Charles, 29
Stono Rebellion, 36
Straits of Malacca, 231
Sturge, Joseph, 66
subaltern/s: agency, 12–16, 291; defined, 12; and diaspora, 12, 290–294; and imperial abolition, 5, 7–8, 12–16, 202–223, 290–294; as mediators in slave trades, 20–22. *See also* diaspora, *Laconia* affair, Marianah, slavery, slaves, women
subcontinent, 2. *See also* South Asia
Suez Canal, 267, 274
sugar: and the Comoros, 256–261; in IOW, 212, 216, 235; and reformers, 66–83
Sukkat, Syed Abdullah, 191
Sultan of Zanzibar, 7, 185, 232. *See also* Barghash, Imam, Majid
Sumner, Charles, 136
Sunley, Robert, 276
Sunley, William, 255–257, 259, 262–263, 274
Surat, 179
Sur Batinah, 184
Suzuki, Hideaki, 184, 235
Swahili, 3, 12, 174, 177, 180, 181, 189, 209, 212, 232, 233, 243, 245, 253, 255, 293
Sweet, James, 291
Syed Abdallah, 270

Tageldin, Shaden M., 206, 292
Tagore, Dwarkanath, 68
"Tamil Country," and slavery, 73–75
Tannenbaum, Frank, 8
Tanzania, 173, 174, 181, 183, 184
Tappan, Arthur, 95
Tappan, Lewis, 57
Tara, Uma, 146
Tennessee, 117, 239
Terry, T.J., 87, 98, 107, 114
Texas, 2, 9, 19, 79
Thompson, George, 2, 54, 77, 91, 115, 118; and British India Society, 64–68

Thoreau, Henry David, 57
Thornton, Edward, 244
Ticonderoga, 262–263
Tigris, 232
Tipp, Tippu, 256
Tipu Sultan, 1, 2
Tomich, Dale, 33
Topan, Tharia, 244, 277
Trautmann, Thomas R., 41
Trucial Coast, 184
Turkey, 265
Turkish, 177, 214, 219
Turner, Nat, 58, 62; and Roy, 62–63
Tyre, 78

Udhoji, Jivan, 197–198
Underground Railroad, 53, 165. *See also* Lemmon slave case, freedom
Unitarian/s, 2, 17, 54, 57. *See also* abolitionists, Adam, Roy
United States, 3, 5, 6, 22–23; State Department, 11, 23. *See also* abolitionists, Americans in IOW, American South, slavery, slaves, slave trades, Wilson
Urs, Krishna, 168, 169
USS *Alliance,* 273–274
USS *Juniata,* 273, 276
USS *Lancaster,* 273, 276
USS *Susquehanna,* 227
USS Yantic, 244
Uttar Kannada, 179
Uzi, 187

Vancouver, 160
Vermont, 32
Versailles, 191
Vicksburg, 94
Victoria, Queen, 82, 267
Virginia, 36, 79, 132; and *Lemmon* slave case, 155–157
"The Virginia Slave," 152

Wadi, 197–199
Waheed, Sarah, 137
Wald, Erica, 136
Walker, Quok, 33
Walker, William, 11
Wamakwa, 260
Ward, Charles, 227, 233, 237–238
Ward, Samuel R., 158, 237
Warden, John, 172–173, 202
Ware, Henry, 57

Washington, DC, 77, 115, 264
Watchman and Southron, 287–288
Waters, Richard P., 232, 233, 234, 235–236
Wazalia, 260
Webb, Francis R., 243, 245
Webb, John F., 238, 244–245
Webb, William, 238–239
Webster, Daniel, 92, 227, 238
Webster, E. A., 92
Wedgwood, Josiah, 32
West Africa, 31
Wheatley, Phyllis, 29
Whittier, John Greenleaf, 115
widows, and slavery, 128, 141–143, 146
Wilberforce, William, 32, 61, 69
Wilcock, Sean, 1
Williams, Eric, 8
Willoughby, J. P., 172, 176, 177, 189, 193–194, 199–200, 203, 209
Wilson, Benjamin F., 22–23, 247, 287; appeals to US patriotism, 276–277, 283–284; arrival in IOW, 251, 253, 255; arrival in Ndzwani, 255; charges against, 270; and Comorian coups, 263–64, 269–271; enslaved testimonies about, 272; father David, 253; Mitchell Report, 281; Patsy estate, 251–53, 257–59; plantations, 247, 251–252, 253, 263; relationship with Sultan Abdullah, III, 251, 255, 257–258, 261–262, 264–266, 268–273; relationship with French imperialists, 273–285; Ropes investigation, 269–271; settler colonialism, 22–23; slave trading charges, 264, 271–275; struggles over labor control, 268–69, 271–73, 276–83; struggles over land control, 260–62, 279–81, 284–85; Union service, 252, 253
Wilson, Byron, 244

women: antislavery feminists, 17; Atlantic migrations of, 152–165; and Comorian uprising, 278; in Comoros, 254, 256; conscripted as *engagés*, 83; "cotton queen," 3; courtesans, dancing girls, sex workers in India, 18–19, 120–21, 134–148, 191; and freedom flights in India, 165–170; IOW slave trades, 20–21, 172–197, 202–220, 249, 293–294; royal households of Oman and Zanzibar, 210–220; slaveholding, 120–148; women's rights, 56, 57, 63–64, 158, 163–165. *See also* concubines, courtesans, gender, imperial abolition, secondary wives, Shadd Cary, slavery, slaves, slave trades, subaltern/s, *Zenanas*
Woodbury, Levi, 232
Woods, Michael, 9
Workmen's Breach of Contract Act, 83
World Antislavery Convention, 69, 91
Wright, R., 87, 114

Yacoob (enslaved), 208–09, 293
Yacoub (slaveholder), 191–193
Yao, 184
Yemen, 172, 197, 199
"Young Bengal," 68

Zamindar, 98, 112; Finnie's contempt for, 103–107; Finnie's fantasies about, 99–100
Zanzibar, 7, 21, 267, 268; and Comorian coups, 265–267; and slave trades/slavery, 179–223; Sultan of, 60, 131
Zastoupil, Lynn, 54, 57, 61
Zeleza, Paul T., 15, 291
Zenana, 8, 21, 137, 165, 183, 211
Zimbabwe, 184
Zulfi, Madeline, 167

Founded in 1893,
UNIVERSITY OF CALIFORNIA PRESS
publishes bold, progressive books and journals
on topics in the arts, humanities, social sciences,
and natural sciences—with a focus on social
justice issues—that inspire thought and action
among readers worldwide.

The UC PRESS FOUNDATION
raises funds to uphold the press's vital role
as an independent, nonprofit publisher, and
receives philanthropic support from a wide
range of individuals and institutions—and from
committed readers like you. To learn more, visit
ucpress.edu/supportus.

www.ingramcontent.com/pod-product-compliance
Lightning Source LLC
Chambersburg PA
CBHW021334230426
43666CB00006B/290